D0151451

ETHNIC THEATRE
IN THE
UNITED STATES

ETHNIC THEATRE IN THE UNITED STATES

Edited by
MAXINE SCHWARTZ SELLER

Greenwood Press
Westport, Connecticut • London, England

Library of Congress Cataloging in Publication Data

Main entry under title:

Ethnic theatre in the United States.

  Bibliography: p.
  Includes index.
  1. Ethnic theater—United States—Addresses, essays,
lectures. I. Seller, Maxine, 1935–
PN2226.E85   792'.0973   81-13494
ISBN 0-313-21230-9 (lib. bdg.)   AACR2

Library of Congress Catalog Card Number: 81-13494
ISBN: 0-313-21230-9

First published in 1983

Greenwood Press
A division of Congressional Information Service, Inc.
88 Post Road West
Westport, Connecticut 06881

Printed in the United States of America

P

Contents

Illustrations

ETHNIC THEATRE IN THE UNITED STATES

Introduction

MAXINE SCHWARTZ SELLER

Despite acculturation and assimilation, identifiable ethnic communities have been and continue to be important features of the American social landscape. This work documents the role of theatre in many of these communities—black, Native American, Hispanic, and European American.

Traditionally much of the scholarship about ethnic communities in the United States has focused on real or imagined social problems within the communities, on difficulties in adjusting to mainstream American life, on economic hardships, and on the impact of ethnic prejudice and racism. In the 1960s and 1970s, however, the scholarship of the "new ethnicity" began to highlight strengths as well as problems. The new scholarship called attention to the rich internal life of ethnic communities and to the institutions that expressed and sustained that life. Ethnic theatre was one of the most important of these institutions.

Although books have appeared on the dramatic traditions of Native Americans and of Jewish and Swedish immigrants, there is surprisingly little literature about most ethnic theatres, and the primary and secondary sources that do exist are often scattered and inaccessible to the nonspecialist. The purpose of this volume is to summarize the results of current research in a form that is useful to the scholar and the general reader. Twenty original chapters, each written by a specialist in his or her field, introduce the reader to the origins and history of representative ethnic theatres. The chapters stress the social, political, cultural, and educational importance of ethnic theatre as a community institution and direct the reader to sources for further research.

ORIGINS OF ETHNIC THEATRE

Ethnic theatres in the United States have sprung from a variety of historical and cultural traditions. Native American drama is rooted in centuries-old religious rituals and communal celebrations. Black theatre came to America on European slave ships, where Africans were forced to sing and dance for exercise

3

and for the amusement of their captors. A well-established French theatre in New Orleans entered the United States through the Louisiana Purchase of 1803, and Spanish-language theatre was acquired with the conquest of the Southwest from Mexico a few decades later. As identifiable European and Asian immigrant communities arrived in the nineteenth century, their theatres arrived too. German theatres performed in New Orleans and New York City before 1840 and in the towns and villages of the rural Midwest soon after. Norwegian and Swedish theatres opened in Chicago in the 1860s. Chinese theatre flourished in San Francisco in the early 1870s. Although large-scale Polish immigration did not begin until the closing decades of the century, by 1890 Polish theatres were performing in urban centers such as New York, Detroit, Chicago, and Buffalo and in smaller communities such as Winona, Minnesota, and Arcadia, New York.

In the nineteenth and early twentieth centuries, ethnic theatre took many forms. In some communities "clubs" met to read, discuss, perform, and sometimes write plays. Amateur theatres were sponsored by lodges and mutual benefit associations, cultural societies, athletic clubs, women's clubs, labor unions, settlement houses, churches, socialist and nationalist societies, temperance leagues, youth groups, universities, and public and parochial schools. In large communities the Chinese, French, Germans, Jews, blacks, and other groups supported commercial theatres with professional or semiprofessional actors and directors.

Amateur or professional, early ethnic theatres had many problems. Serving poor communities, they were chronically short of money. As in other theatres, actors, directors, and playwrights sometimes quarreled among themselves. Often there was opposition within the community. The Augustana Synod of the Lutheran Church condemned Swedish theatre as worldly and sinful, objecting not only to the performances but also, perhaps more, to the parties that followed.[1] A committee of assimilated German Jews tried to block the opening of Yiddish theatre among newly immigrated East European Jews in New York in 1882 because they were afraid of anti-Semitism. "Go out into the country and become peddlars," the committee advised. "Find decent work and don't bring shame upon your people with this foolery you call theatre."[2]

There was outside opposition as well. Defending their lands from white encroachment, Indians burned a German theatre during an attack on New Ulm, Minnesota, in 1862;[3] more lasting damage to German-language theatre nationwide came from the anti-German hysteria and boycotts of World War I. Many ethnic theatres were harassed by local authorities for violating "blue laws" by holding performances on Sunday. Ignorant and disdainful of Chinese immigrant life, white journalists misrepresented and ridiculed Chinaman (Chinese-American) theatre. Influenced perhaps by stereotypes of foreign radicals, police closed a Polish play about the assassination of Alexander II of Russia because of a rumor that a "live dynamite bomb" would be exploded.[4]

IMMIGRANT THEATRES AT THEIR PEAK: 1900–1930

Despite their problems, ethnic theatres flourished. Most of the European and Asian immigrant theatres, including most of the theatres represented in this volume, reached their peak in the opening decades of the twentieth century. During these years of heavy immigration, immigrant theatres provided inexpensive, convenient entertainment in the ethnic languages to hundreds of thousands of new Americans.

During these peak years for immigrant theatre, countless amateur groups played in church basements, barns, social halls, school auditoriums, cafes, and living quarters. Professional and semiprofessional companies performed weekly, daily, sometimes as much as twice a day in handsome, well-equipped structures such as the Astoria Socialist Theatre (Finnish), in Astoria, Oregon, which seated eight hundred, and the Washington Square Theatre (Italian) in San Francisco, which seated a thousand. Swedish theatre in Chicago attracted as many as four thousand to a single performance.[5] Individuals who could afford to do so traveled many miles to see special productions,[6] and road companies brought theatre to communities too small or isolated to support theatres of their own. A San Francisco-based Italian company toured as far east as St. Louis; Chicago-based Swedish companies covered the prairie states; and Chinese and Finnish companies performed in mining camps throughout the West. Large numbers were involved, not only as audiences but also as actors and playwrights. The Yiddish-speaking Workmen's Circle, for example, which encouraged its members to write as well as to produce plays, had 250 lodges in New York City alone.[7]

Early twentieth-century journalists noted that among many immigrant groups ethnic theatre was more important in the United States than it had been in the homeland.[8] Certainly for many immigrants at the turn of the century, theatre was more than an occasional indulgence; it was a necessity. Many people who worked fourteen or more hours a day in mills, mines, or sweatshops spent their few precious hours of leisure attending ethnic theatre, acting in it, or writing for it. Jewish garment workers on New York's Lower East Side went without meals to buy tickets to the theatres on Second Avenue, the "Yiddish Broadway."

Some immigrant groups had acquired their love of theatre in the old country. Many Finns, for example, had seen productions of the National Theatre of Finland before emigration, and they were able to staff their American theatres with professional actors and directors trained in the homeland. Many from southern Italy came with a thorough and deep-rooted knowledge of opera and regional folk comedy, the *commedia dell'arte*. For most Eastern European Jews, on the other hand, formal theatre was a new experience. Yiddish theatre made its first formal appearance in eastern Europe in 1873, only six years before its introduction into New York; yet no immigrant community was more ardent in its support of theatre than the Eastern European Jews.

The importance of theatre among immigrant communities may be at least partly attributed to the impact of immigration. The immigrants had left behind many of the institutions, traditions, and companions that had met their intellectual, emotional, and social needs in their former homelands. Shut out of mainstream American life by cultural and (usually) language differences and by poverty, ghettoization, and discrimination, they developed new ways to meet these needs. One of these ways was ethnic theatre, which provided education, entertainment, and a focus for social and community life.

EDUCATION

Although immigrants often had more education than their counterparts who stayed at home, large numbers were illiterate, not only in English but also in their native languages. Deprived of opportunities to learn about their own culture through poverty, isolation, or political oppression, many arrived in the United States hungry for exposure to their native languages, histories, and literature. Ethnic theatre provided this exposure.

Ethnic theatre made the history, literature, and folklore of the homelands accessible to literate and illiterate alike and gave the new American-born generations at least some understanding of the cultures of their immigrant parents. Based on the complex historical novel *Romance of the Three Kingdoms*, Chinese opera transmitted and reinforced the traditional Cantonese values of loyalty, self-reliance, and personal integrity. Swedish theatre told of peasant uprisings against Danish rule and of the Thirty Years' War. German theatre dramatized the exploits of Frederick the Great. Polish theatres presented so many plays on historical and national themes that a Polish journalist praised them as "the schools of patriotism."[9]

During their peak years, many immigrant theatres presented the classics of theatrical traditions other than their own, as well as the best of contemporary theatre from all over the world in translation or in special adaptations. Shakespeare was performed in Yiddish, German, Swedish, and Italian. German theatres presented a variety of classics as well as the works of modern German dramatists such as Gerhart Hauptmann and Frank Wedekind. Yiddish theatre introduced its audiences to Molière, Schiller, Goethe, Tolstoy, Gorki, Sudermann, Hauptmann, Ibsen, Strindberg, Molnár, and Shaw, as well as to Yiddish playwrights such as Jacob Gordin, Leon Kobrin, and Sholem Asch.

Ethnic theatre was also an important agent of Americanization. Plays adopted and translated from the American stage introduced immigrants to many aspects of mainstream culture. The Finnish theatre of Astoria plunged its socialist audiences into the Anglo-Saxon version of "how the West was won" by presenting Finnish-language cowboy-and-Indian productions.[10] American movies became part of the regular offerings at many theatres, including the Italian "nickelodeons" of San Francisco. Ethnic theatre introduced immigrants who spoke regional dialects to the "standard" vocabulary and pronunciation of their native languages, and it also introduced English in a visual context that promoted understanding. Skits or special productions were occasionally performed in English. English expressions, including contemporary slang and "street talk," slipped into the ethnic-language plays, reflecting the changing speech of immigrants who were becoming Americanized and stimulating such change among the more recent arrivals.

Finally, the educational role of ethnic theatre in the early twentieth century included exposing audiences to sophisticated examinations of social problems. Here immigrant theatres were sometimes ahead of Broadway. For example, in 1896 the Irving Place Theatre presented to its German-American audience Hauptmann's *The Weavers*, a graphic portrayal of a labor uprising in Silesia and its brutal suppression; the play was not presented to the English-speaking public until almost two decades later. Immigrant Germans, Jews, Swedes, Finns, Hungarians, and others formed special theatre groups in which they used the works of Shaw, Ibsen, Strindberg, and others, as well as original plays, to explore temperance, pacifism, the problems of the aged, the class struggle, and the status of women. Radical Finns deliberately, extensively, and effectively used theatre for political education, making theatrical performances a central forum for their critique of capitalist society. Proletarian plays for children and adults indicted capitalism for denying the workers culture and education as well as bread.[11] Like the class struggle, the "woman question" was explored in ethnic theatre. Ibsen's controversial drama *A Doll's House* played in many ethnic languages. The first Polish play in Chicago (produced in 1873) was *The Emancipation of Women*, by feminist actress, author, and community activist Theofilia Samolinska. Samolinska dedicated the play to the Polish Commune.[12]

ENTERTAINMENT

Despite the importance of educational and ideological plays, most immigrant theatregoers, like most other theatregoers, came to the theatre for diversion, excitement, and glamor. A Jewish immigrant who called himself "the average theatre goer" described this.

I do not go to the theatre to think, but to forget. . . . I seek there to forget my wife, the children, the crowded tenement, the littered wash, the bad ventilation. . . . I want to see men dressed in armor or in the costumes of wealthy shepherds who wear silk chemises. . . . On the women I love to see as much exposed as possible because you see I have already been married many years to my own wife. . . . When I am in Thomashevsky's theater and I see on the stage a beautiful room with expensive furniture and chandeliers . . . I pretend that the well-to-do Thomashevsky has invited me to his house and is showing off his wealth to me. . . . I am just a poor fellow . . . and all this costs me but half a dollar. Isn't it worth it?[13]

Some theatres featured elaborate costumes or scenery. Horses pranced across the early Yiddish stage. Swedish companies treated audiences to elaborate folk tableaux with dancing, singing, and realistic representations of battles, sieges, and processions. Pageantry filled a need for the immigrant actors as well as for their audiences. "He who but yesterday earned his bread with a shovel today dons a royal robe and crown, if at least for a moment, to become great before the prompter's dugout," wrote an observer of Polish amateur theatre.[14]

On many European immigrant stages, vaudeville-type entertainment—song, dance, short skits, farce, and satire—was popular. Popular too were "formula" plays about everyday life in the new country or the old. Because their own lives were often marred by problems they could not solve and injustices they could not correct, audiences were delighted when the rapacious landlord was outwitted by the wily peasant, when true love triumphed over all obstacles, and when the hero was victorious and the scoundrel defeated. As the "average theatre goer" put it, "When I see how the villian is finally punished in the fourth act and the hero is rewarded, I am touched to the heart because . . . I am a very honest man, but my neighbor there is a . . . good-for-nothing."[15]

One of the most popular subjects for comedy on European immigrant stages was the new arrival, the "green one," who made ridiculous mistakes and was victimized by his own countrymen as well as by native-born Americans. These comedies allowed immigrants to measure themselves against the "green one" on the stage and to rejoice in how far they had come. These and other comedies also provided opportunities to satirize the ethnic community—the boarding-house proprietor, the saloonkeeper, the clergyman, the self-serving politician, the social climber—and to criticize the hypocrisy and corruption in mainstream American life.

Tragedy as well as comedy was important. Plays filled with anger, violence, revenge, suicide, and murder were often well received, whether they were classical tragedies or original melodramas. Many of these plays dealt with familiar problems in exaggerated but recognizable form. For example, Jacob Gordin's drama *The Jewish King Lear* showed a pious Jewish father abused and neglected by heartless daughters, a theme close enough to reality to bring tears to the eyes of foreign-born parents less than satisfied with the behavior of their Americanized children.

Tragedy as well as comedy could be comforting to audiences. At least their spouses were not so cruel, their children so heartless, their poverty so hopeless as those on stage. Tears, like laughter, provided emotional release. Tragedy allowed immigrants to express the grief they felt at leaving friends and family behind, perhaps forever, and facing the frustrations and disappointments of American life:

I go to a heart-rending drama because my boss has deducted a cent-and-a-half a dozen sleeves and my heart is heavy—and I am ashamed to cry. Therefore when I see . . . how Hamlet holds in his hands the skull of his friend Yorick and speaks of life and death, I suddenly recall that they have deducted a cent-and-a-half a dozen sleeves and I cry real tears.[16]

A FOCUS FOR SOCIAL LIFE

At their peak, many early-twentieth-century immigrant theatres provided a social world for actors and audiences and helped sustain the communities of which they were important parts. Theatre provided a close-knit circle within which actors and other "theatre people" developed rewarding relationships. Many marriages took place within this circle. The children of theatre marriages sometimes made their debuts on stage almost as soon as they could walk and talk.

The social world of ethnic theatre was particularly important for many foreign-born intellectuals, whose lack of fluency in English cut them off from professions they had pursued in the homeland and who had little in common with the majority of their working-class countrymen. Such people often found rewarding careers in the ethnic theatre or press or both, as the two areas were frequently closely connected.

The ethnic theatre also provided a uniquely supportive environment for women, who were shut out of many activities in the ethnic and mainstream communities by narrow stereotypes of "women's place." Energetic, talented, and independent women found the theatre one of the few places where they could escape traditional domestic roles, earn money, acquire power and prestige, travel, and adopt unconventional life styles with relative impunity. Women like Samolinska, Clara Lemberg, Sarah Adler, and Antonietta Pisanelli Alessandro won fame as successful actresses, directors, producers, and owners and managers of theatres.

Theatre also played an important social role for audiences. Like the lodge, the saloon, the church, or the union hall, the ethnic theatre provided a place for individuals and entire families to meet and enjoy being together. In many Scandinavian communities, performances were followed by parties with music, dancing, food, and drink. In Yiddish and Italian theatres, the entire evening took on a festive atmosphere; the theatre was a place for dressing in one's best, courting, gossiping, quarreling, eating, joking, nurturing friendships. In communities such as San Francisco's North Beach area (Italian) and the Lower East Side of New York City (Jewish), the theatre was more effective than any other single institution in bringing together people of widely divergent backgrounds. Here a common experience was shared by the rich and the poor, the young and the old, the educated and the uneducated, the newcomer and the old-timer, the radical and the conservative.[17]

The theatre could be a personal refuge as well as a social center:

What is important is that I, who own nothing that is my own, have here a seat which is reserved especially for me and upon which no one else dare sit—It is mine. Just let any one else try and sit upon it. . . . I would not take another seat were the whole theater empty, oh no.[18]

Important community institutions themselves, ethnic theatres also helped support other institutions within immigrant communities. Swedish theatre groups in Chicago entertained at picnics and other outings sponsored by social and cultural associations and raised money to support employment agencies, legal aid, and other services for the Swedish colony. Japanese theatres in Seattle supported community charities. Italian theatre clubs in St. Louis helped build parochial schools. Polish theatre raised money to build churches and schools and to send to Poland in times of need. Yiddish theatres routinely sublet their entire "houses" for benefit performances sponsored by lodges and other organizations.

In addition to strengthening the internal lives of local immigrant communities, ethnic theatres helped forge links between those communities and the outside world. Traveling companies helped keep local communities in touch with one another and with the mother countries. Sometimes theatres of different groups launched cooperative ventures: Swedish and Norwegian theatre groups gave joint performances in Chicago, and Italians and Jews shared theatres in New York.

Foreign-born actors from the ethnic stage made occasional appearances on the American stage. Jacob P. Adler, for example, gave a highly praised performance of Shylock in Yiddish in an otherwise all-English Broadway production of *The Merchant of Venice* in 1903.[19] Observers from mainstream American life came to the ethnic theatre. Sometimes their reactions were unfavorable; journalist Frederick O. Bushel thought a professional Italian marionette theatre in Boston in 1897 "too dull to be popular, even for an Italian who has little else to do."[20] Observers who approached the ethnic theatre free of negative stereotypes, however, such as journalist Hutchins Hapgood, often came away with admiration for the quality of the performances and increased understanding of the ethnic community.

On at least one occasion, an ethnic community used theatre in a deliberate attempt to improve its public image. In 1908 the Sicilians of Rochester, New York, hoping to combat Mafia gangster stereotypes by convincing the non-Italian community that they had "a great reverence and respect for holy things," staged an elaborate drama about the life of Jesus Christ. Author Jerre Mangione described the venture.

Milkmen, shoemakers, bakers, tailors, factory hands, and ditchdiggers became the actors of the drama. After their day's work and on Sundays these men and women met for . . . months. The undertaking grew. Hundreds of other Italians in the city pitched in to make the sets and costumes and contributed toward the expenses of the production. . . .

October 12, the day celebrating Columbus' discovery of America, was the date chosen for the production, perhaps in the hope that on that day the Americans would "discover" the good qualities of the Italians in their midst.[21]

Although the Italian community came and applauded wildly, no "Americans" were in the audience. A repeat performance drew a large audience from both communities and some favorable comment in the American press, but the impact was short lived. Within a year the press was once again giving disproportionate attention to crime stories involving Italians.

THE DECLINE OF THE IMMIGRANT THEATRES: 1925–1950

The theatres of most of the Asian and European immigrant communities described in this anthology began to decline after 1925 or 1930. The companies became fewer in number and gave fewer and, in the opinion of some critics, poorer performances. Although the audiences had included some who were American born, most of these theatres had catered to the foreign born. Therefore the cessation of large-scale immigration with the new quota laws of 1924, as well as the increasing affluence, Americanization, and geographic dispersion of many of the original patrons and their children, undermined these theatres, shrinking their audiences and their influence. Movies, radio, and, later, television replaced theatre as the favored entertainment of ethnic as well as mainstream Americans.

The immigrant theatres of the nineteenth and early twentieth centuries did not vanish completely, however. Many of their actors, directors, and writers passed into mainstream American entertainment, bringing elements of their tradition with them. Some companies received financial assistance from President Roosevelt's WPA in the 1930s and remained active, though on a limited scale, into midcentury and beyond. Companies with an interest in artistic experimentation, in promoting social change through theatre, or both—the Artef Theatre (Yiddish) in New York City, for example, and the Swedish folk theatre of Chicago—were influential in the 1930s. Between the two world wars, Yiddish theatre served as a bridge over which innovative theatre ideas were transmitted from the old world to the new.[22]

RESURGENCE OF ETHNIC THEATRE: MIDCENTURY AND BEYOND

In the decades following World War II, the black civil rights movement stimulated interest in black history, culture, and identity and served as a catalyst for increased political activism and ethnic awareness among Hispanics, Native Americans, and Asian Americans. Ethnic consciousness was also aroused among Asian Americans by U.S. participation in a war against Asians in Vietnam. The heightened political and cultural ferment among "third-world" ethnic communities in the 1960s and 1970s was reflected in an upsurge of theatrical activity. Blacks, Hispanics, Native Americans, and Asian Americans used drama to explore the past and present realities of ethnic life in America and to protest the injustices their communities had encountered and were still encountering in American society.

The activities of the expanding third-world theatres were conspicuous from coast to coast. In the late 1960s the Puerto Rican Traveling Theatre brought bilingual productions to the Spanish-speaking neighborhoods of New York City and by the early 1970s it provided the Puerto Rican community with a laboratory theatre and an actors' training program as well. Long active, black theatre rose to new prominence on Broadway as well as in communities throughout the nation. The old Chinese operas of San Francisco were gone, but by 1977 there were four Asian-American companies in New York City. On the West Coast the East-West players were presenting original Asian-American plays and training actors of Chinese, Japanese, Filipino, Korean, and Pacific Island ethnic backgrounds.

The post-World War II decades also saw renewed theatre activity in many ethnic communities of European origin. Touring performers and companies from the homelands were hosted and applauded by the children and grandchildren of immigrants. Productions of classic Armenian, Baltic, Polish, and Yiddish plays were mounted by ethnic churches, community centers, cultural societies, universities, and professional companies, sometimes in the ethnic language, sometimes in translation. Original plays were produced dealing with contemporary ethnic life. A good example of the new activity was the Jewish theatre festival in New York City in June 1980, sponsored by the newly organized national Jewish Theatre Association and attended by hundreds of actors, directors, and other amateur and professional theatre people from the United States and Canada. Though a few of the productions were in Yiddish, most were in English. Mime, masks, puppets, and other innovative techniques were explored, and the widely varying productions dealt with Biblical themes, East European Jewish life, the Holocaust, and the experiences of the acculturated current generation.[23]

The increased theatre activity was at least in part a response to new immigration—to the arrival of refugees from Communist-controlled nations in Eastern Europe, to the mass movement from Puerto Rico to the mainland in the 1950s, and to the increase in immigration from Asia and Latin America that followed the liberalization of the immigration laws in 1965. It also reflected the nostalgia of aging immigrants and the desire of the American born to explore their ethnic heritage and their current status as ethnic Americans. This desire was legitimized by the "new ethnicity" of the 1960s and 1970s, which encouraged cultural pluralism rather than the "melting pot" as the model for American society. The national climate of opinion in the 1960s was favorable to the expansion of the arts, including theatre. Finally, at least some members of ethnic communities now had material resources to support theatre, and beginning during the administration of President John Kennedy, the federal government provided encouragement and financial support.

Overshadowed by the mass media (now including radio and television shows in Spanish and other ethnic languages), theatre in the 1960s and 1970s was not as central to ethnic community life as it had been half a century earlier. Nevertheless, it continued to perform some of the same functions. It educated and informed. Hanay Geiogamah's Native American dramas, produced by the Native American Theater Ensemble in the 1970s, used "Western" (Euro-American) style drama to transmit Indian traditions, values, and aesthetics.[24] Classic and contemporary plays from the homelands, in translation, gave the acculturated American born new insights into their backgrounds. Byelorussians, Hungarians, Latvians, Ukrainians, Jews, and others used theatre in ethnic schools, summer camps, and youth groups to teach ethnic language and history.

Like their predecessors, the ethnic theatres of the 1960s and 1970s informed their communities about social issues, but they were far more active than their predecessors in reaching out to inform the mainstream community as well. Dramas from the Baltic nations dealt with issues of political oppression and resistance to tyranny in Eastern Europe and, by implication, everywhere.[25] The Theater for Asian American Performing Artists in New York City performed a series of skits about anti-Asian discrimination for the United States Commission on Civil Rights. The skits became the basis for a satirical review, *Asian American Blues*, presented at the outdoor plaza of Lincoln Center during the July 4 Bicentennial celebration.[26]

"Our drama has a political root and spiritual goal," stated the creed of El Teatro Campesino (The Farm Workers' Theatre), which was born in Delano, California, in 1965 on the picket line of the United Farm Workers. "We developed a broad, fast-paced, slapstick form of comedy using the stock characters of farm labor: the patron, the contractor, the scabs," wrote Luis Valdez, the founder of the theatre. "We . . . developed our own short dramatic form, the *acto*, which can be described as somewhere between Brecht and Cantinflas." Teatre Campesino performed nightly at street rallies during the three-hundred-mile march of farmworkers to Sacramento in 1966 and made a nationwide tour to gather support and funds for the farm workers' union. The company moved from improvisations to full-length plays and films and performed at the World Theater Festival in France in 1969.[27]

SELF-EXPRESSION AND SELF-DEFINITION

In the 1960s and 1970s, as in earlier periods, many ethnic Americans—people whose families had been in the United States for many generations as well as immigrants—were excluded from many areas of mainstream American life by culture and language differences and by isolation, poverty, and discrimination. Bilingual neighborhood and traveling ethnic companies provided entertainment for non-English-speaking Americans. Ethnic theatre gave the actors, playwrights, and audiences of many ethnic groups opportunities for self-expression and self-definition not available in a mainstream society that stereotyped or ignored them.

Like many other ethnic actors, Japanese-American Marc Hayashi turned to ethnic theatre because of the discrimination he encountered in the world of mainstream entertainment. He explained his reasons for joining San Francisco's Asian American Theater Workshop as follows:

Until I joined the Workshop three years ago (1974), I had this longtime secret wish to be on the big screen. But the only yellows in the movies were either foreign Asians or white versions of us. In both cases, there wasn't anything I could take seriously. To Hollywood moviemakers, Asian Americans and Asians were either Charlie Chan's clown-act sons, bad Jap torturers of white women, or ah-so lemme-get-your-noodles-boss houseboys. All sexless jerkoffs, fools, bumbling villains. . . . I couldn't see a future in any of that.[28]

Ethnic theatre allowed Asian-American, black, Native American, Chicano, and other actors to move beyond the stereotypical roles usually assigned them in mainstream entertainment, to define themselves rather than accept others' definitions, and to play the full range of human emotion and human behavior.

Playwrights as well as actors found ethnic theatre the best, sometimes the only, outlet for their talent. "America is illiterate in, hostile to, deadset against the Asian American sensibility," explained Frank Chin, a leading Chinese-American playwright. Chin, a fifth-generation American whose family had immigrated to California in the nineteenth century, wrote Chinaman (Chinese-American) plays because that was the tradition in which his creativity was rooted. "My plays are about my own experiences. They're not about China or white America because I'm a Chinaman. . . . I've always written about Chinese American subjects. It's what I know. My San Francisco ancestry goes way back."[29] Ethnic theatre continued to give people insight into their own experiences. René Remarqués's celebrated play La carreta (The Oxcart), which chronicles a family's disintegration as it moves from rural Puerto Rico to San Juan to New York, helped recent Puerto Rican migrants to the mainland evaluate their gains and losses. Ethnic theatre explored traditional stereotypes—the American Indian alcoholic in Geiogamah's Body Indian and the strong black mother in Lorraine Hansberry's Raisin in the Sun, for example—from inside rather than outside of the ethnic culture, giving them new, multidimensional meaning. Finally, although there was some increase in ethnic materials in mainstream theatre, ethnic theatre remained the main place where ethnic audiences could see plays reflecting their special concerns. The impact of the Vietnam War on the Asian-American soldier; the battle against the destruction of ethnic neighborhoods through "urban renewal"; the impact of the Holocaust on Jewish survivors; the realities of growing up, or getting old, or being a woman in ethnic America—these and similar themes were explored in ethnic theatre.

THE FUTURE OF ETHNIC THEATRE

As the 1980s began, ethnic theatre continued to face problems. Political and ideological cleavages within and between ethnic communities and between those communities and mainstream America were reflected in the theatre. In an inflationary economy, funding continued to be difficult. During the 1960s and 1970s, some funds were provided by public and private foundations, including the Rockefeller Foundation, the National Endowment for the Arts, and state agencies, but as the 1980s opened, budgetary cutbacks and changing political priorities seemed likely to diminish this support.

Nevertheless, reasons remained for optimism. Ethnic theatre was gaining increased recognition among ethnic and mainstream audiences, as well as in university theatre programs, national theatre associations, and academic journals. Collections of ethnic plays were being published, as were scholarly works about ethnic theatre. Actors, playwrights, and directors were experimenting with new forms, materials, and themes and were seeking new outlets for their work through the media. These factors were grounds for hope that ethnic theatre could survive, not just as a curiosity or an exercise in nostalgia, but as a living force in American culture.

ETHNIC THEATRE IN THE UNITED STATES

The purpose of this volume is to introduce the general reader and the specialist in theatre, ethnic studies, and American studies to information about twenty representative ethnic theatres in the United States—their origins and history; their literature; their personnel; their relationship to the theatres of the homelands and of mainstream America; their social, cultural, and political roles in American ethnic communities; and the status of current research about them.

Because scholarly treatment of ethnic theatre requires specialized knowledge of archival sources, ethnic history and culture, and usually ethnic languages, each chapter has been written by an expert in his or her respective field. The authors come from widely varying backgrounds. Some are foreign born; others are from families in the United States many generations, even centuries. Some are conservative in political and social orientation; some are radical. Most, but not all, are members of the ethnic groups about which they write. Some have been actors, playwrights, or directors in the ethnic theatres about which they write. Many are professional researchers or academics in fields such as theatre, foreign languages and literature, and history. Information about each author is provided in a biographical sketch. (See "About the Contributors.")

Because each theatre is unique, and because each author comes to his or her material with a unique perspective and set of experiences, the chapters vary in length, content, and style. They also vary in tone. For example, the chapter on theatre in the German-American community, a well-assimilated, white, Western European community, is presented with relative detachment. Essays on nonwhite communities that continue to face discrimination, on the other hand, reflect their authors' concern about racism in American society. Despite resulting inconsistencies in form and unevenness in tone, I have tried, within necessary editorial guidelines, to let each author present the material in his or her own way.

Neither the individual chapters nor the volume is offered as definitive. Many of the materials needed for a definitive work have been lost. Others remain untapped in attics, basements, and archives or in the memories of actors, directors, playwrights, and audiences. While the theatres of most ethnic groups were geographically scattered and operated under many different sponsorships, individual chapter authors often concentrate on particular locations or companies, choices dictated by the authors' access to information and by their experience. Different authors would, in many cases, have produced entirely different essays. Many important theatres, such as the Chinese, Czech, Japanese, Norwegian, and Russian, are not represented because it was not possible to locate appropriate authors or to obtain satisfactory manuscripts within the designated time. Despite these limitations, I hope this work will be a useful first step in bringing together information about ethnic theatre and that it will stimulate further research, including a second volume with chapters on the theatres not covered here.

In conclusion, I would like to thank Marilyn Brownstein, Cynthia Harris, and Arlene Belzer of Greenwood Press for their support of this project and their skillful help in its realization. Most of all, I would like to thank the authors for their patience with what must have seemed endless editorial details, their enthusiasm for the project, and their diligence in tracking down information and committing it to paper so that others could profit from their expertise.

NOTES

1. Henrietta C. Koren Naeseth, *The Swedish Theater of Chicago 1868–1950* (Rock Island, Ill.: Augustana Historical Society, 1951), pp. 5–6.

2. Lulla Rosenfeld, *Bright Star of Exile: Jacob Adler and the Yiddish Theater* (New York: Thomas Y. Crowell Co., 1977), pp. 217–18.

3. Hermann E. Rothfuss, "The Early German Theater in Minnesota," *Minnesota History* 32 (June 1951); 100–25.

4. Mathew J. Strumski, "The Beginnings of Polish American Theater," *Polish American Studies* 4 (1947): 34. This article is mainly a translation of an essay by Karol Estreicher, "The Polish Theater beyond the Ocean," which appeared in the Polish-American newspaper *Zboda*, June 18, 1890, p. 6.

5. Naeseth, *The Swedish Theater*, pp. 4, 19.

6. Strumski, "The Beginnings of Polish American Theater," p. 32.

7. John Daniels, *America via the Neighborhood* (New York: Harper and Brothers, 1920), pp. 140–41.

8. Robert Park, *The Immigrant Press and Its Control* (New York: Harper and Brothers, 1922), pp. 7–8. Park cites a survey by journalist Mark Villchur demonstrating that many immigrants who had never attended a theatre in their native villages in Russia became regular theatregoers in the United States. Strumski ("The Beginnings of Polish American Theater," p. 36) notes that Polish immigrants in the United States took theatre much more seriously than their counterparts in Poland.

9. Strumski, "The Beginnings of Polish American Theater," p. 36.

10. Walter Mattila, ed., *The Theater Finns* (Portland, Oreg.: Finnish American Historical Society of the West, July 1972), p. 53.

11. Michael G. Karni, *"Yhteishyra"—or For the Common Good: Finnish Radicalism in the Western Great Lakes Region 1900–1940* (Ph.D. diss., University of Minnesota, 1975), pp. 115–95.

12. Joseph Wytrwal, *America's Polish Heritage* (Detroit: Endurance Press, 1969), pp. 240–41.

13. Moishe Nadir, "I, the Theater Goer," reprinted in Etta Black, ed., *One Act Plays from the Yiddish*, 2nd series (New York: Bloch Publishing Co., 1929), pp. vii–viii, by permission of *The Big Stick*, March 1918.

14. Strumski, "The Beginnings of Polish American Theater," p. 32.

15. Nadir, "I, the Theater Goer," p. x.

16. Ibid., p. ix.

17. For vivid eyewitness descriptions of the social world of ethnic theatre, see Hutchins Hapgood, *Spirit of the Ghetto: Studies of the Jewish Quarter of New York* (New York: Schocken, 1966, originally published 1902), pp. 118–20, and J. M. Scanland, "An Italian Quarter Mosaic," *Overland Monthly*, April 1906.

18. Nadir, "I, the Theater Goer," p. ix.

19. Rosenfeld, *Bright Star of Exile*, pp. 305–6.

20. Frederick O. Bushel, *Arena*, April 1897, as cited in Wayne Mocquin, ed., *A Documentary History of the Italian American* (New York: Praeger Publishing 1974), p. 53.

21. Jerre Mangione, *America Is Also Italian* (New York: Putnam), pp. 45–47.

22. David S. Lifson, remarks made as commentator at a panel, "The Role of Ethnic Theater," at the annual meeting of the Organization of American Historians, New York, N.Y., April 14, 1978.

23. Tina Margolis, Susan Weinacht, and John Frick, "The Jewish Theatre Festival, 1980: Introduction and Documentations," *Drama Review* 24, no. 3 (September 1980): 93–116.

24. Hanay Geiogamah, *New Native American Drama: Three Plays*, introduction by Jeffrey F. Huntsman (Norman, Okla.: University of Oklahoma Press, 1980), pp. ix–xxiv.

25. Alfreds Straumanis, ed., *Confrontations with Tyranny: Six Baltic Plays* (Prospect Heights, Ill.: Waveland Press), 1977.

26. David Ozama, "The New York Scene—Varied but Clear," *Bridge: An Asian American Perspective*, Summer 1977, p. 13.

27. *Interracial Books for Children Bulletin*, special issue on Chicano materials, 5, nos. 7 and 8 (1975): 20.

28. Ben Tong, "Asian American Theater Workshop—Alive and Well in San Francisco!" *Bridge: An Asian American Perspective*, Summer 1977, p. 7.

29. Ibid., p. 8.

1

Armenian-American Theatre

NISHAN PARLAKIAN

Armenian theatrical groups appeared in the United States as early as the turn of this century. Raffi, for example, was founded in New York 1903 and Adamian in New York in 1908. During this period Armenian drama groups were also organized in Fresno, Hartford, Chicago, Los Angeles, and Boston. These organizations came into being, were active for several years each, and then ceased to exist.

The earliest performance of an Armenian play about which I could find a reference took place in New York City in 1899. That production was of the historical drama *Arshak II* given by the Armenian Union in Carnegie Hall.[1] Despite this highly auspicious early event and other activities of various amateur dramatic groups in less grand surroundings in New York, Armenian theatre did not show its strongest presence there until after the First World War. It was during that conflict that the purge of Armenians from their historic homeland in the Anatolian peninsula led to the formation of the Armenian diaspora, with several cities in this country becoming important Armenian population centers.

Like so many other ethnic groups in the United States, Armenians first concentrated on making a living in their new homeland, where they found security in the modest homogeneity that a small minority could command. The more they achieved economic security, the more they were able to turn to artistic pursuits. In New York City and other Armenian centers, ethnic theatre was carried on with a great deal of effort by amateurs and semiprofessionals. Writing on the difficulties of these immigrant theatre artists, Charles A. Vertanes, a noted editor, author, and critic, observed:

Even artists with professional backgrounds had to reconcile themselves to the lowly circumstances of immigrant communities and to carrying on their work on the crumbs of time left over from the main occupations imposed upon them by a cruel fate of earning a bare livelihood in most humble and arduous pursuits.[2]

The plays presented were often concerned with the struggles and hopes of the new immigrants. As the communities took deeper roots, the plays of the best

Armenian playwrights became part of the repertoire, as did other dramas of non-Armenian origin.

MUGERDICH NOORIAN

Of all the artistic activities in the various Armenian communities, the ethnic theatre movement in New York City from 1920 on was most noteworthy. For an outline of the history of that movement, I am indebted to Mugerdich Noorian, an Armenian actor of considerable repute in the first half of this century. A summary of Noorian's artistic life, which I obtained in interviews with him, is in itself a kind of overview of the early Armenian ethnic theatre of the city.[3] Noorian's story began far from New York City, however, and elements of it parallel the experiences of many Armenian immigrants. Born in 1895 in a suburb of Sivas, Turkey, Noorian lost his parents in the massacres of that year and was cared for by his grandmother until the age of five. Then he was placed in an orphanage, where at the age of thirteen he acted for the first time in *Arshak II.*

In 1912 an uncle in Providence, Rhode Island, brought Noorian to the United States to settle with him. As a youth of sixteen or seventeen, while still looking for work, he joined that city's amateur Lernayin Taderakhoump (Mountainous Theatre Group) as an actor and took roles in various plays including Shakespearean ones. While in the group he met and worked with Elia Kimatian, then in the paper and twine business, with whom he was later to spend many years in the theatre in New York. In 1913 he went to New York briefly to act in and direct the play *Black Earth* for Ike (Morning), a group of young dramatists from his native city of Sivas. Always with the thought that he would return to his homeland as an actor, Noorian continued to work at his craft. In 1916, for example, he formed and acted with the Paros Taderakhoump (Lighthouse Theatre Group), which operated in Hartford and New Britain, Connecticut. During the 1917 season in Providence, he performed in Schiller's *The Robbers*, Hagop Baronian's *Gentlemen Beggars*, and Alexandre Shirvanzade's *For the Sake of Honor*, in the last playing the key part of Sakhatel with Kimatian in the leading role of Antreas.

In 1920 Noorian moved to New York, where he held various jobs while acting in K'nar (Lyre), a group he had formed with Kimatian, who had transferred his business to New York. Still intent on returning to the homeland as an actor, Noorian wrote for advice to a government authority in Constantinople. He was advised to remain in the United States and to work with Hovhannes Zarifian, the noted actor and director, who was about to arrive to serve the ethnic theatre in New York. Zarifian did arrive in May of 1921, and K'nar and the Armenian Drama Group of New York, an older amateur company, began working under his leadership. This situation lasted a year only, because some members of the Armenian Drama Group of New York, which had not dissolved, objected to Zarifian's taking 10 percent of the group's income as a salary. When that faction pulled out as a result of the dispute, Noorian and Kimatian stayed with Zarifian, who then formed the Hai Arvest Taderakhoump, the Armenian Art Theater. This organization brought about what might be called a renaissance in Armenian drama in New York City during the 1920s and 1930s.

THE ARMENIAN ART THEATER

The Armenian Art Theater had a wide repertoire. In the earliest months of the group's existence, Noorian played Iago to Zarifian's Othello in a 1921–1922 production of one performance at New York's Golden Theater. He played Claudius to Zarifian's Hamlet in the same season. In two other successful non-Armenian presentations, he played Moriarty in *Sherlock Holmes* and Pasha in *Secrets of the Harem*. Of the Armenian plays in that first season, Levon Shant's *Pagan Gods* was very popular. The Armenian Art Theater's repertoire contained numerous other Armenian and non-Armenian works in its earliest seasons, including *The Robbers, The Devil, Trilby, Bride and Mother-in-Law, Madam X, The Vartanantz War, The Madman,* and *Typhoon.*

Three years after Zarifian's arrival, Hohanness Apelian, another great actor, arrived in New York from Armenia to join the group. Vivid in Noorian's mind is the production of *Quo Vadis,* in which Noorian played Nero and Apelian and Zarifian played Petronius and Markos, respectively. Apelian stayed in America for two years, one with the Art Theater. Noorian remembers a great performance of Shirvanzade's *Evil Spirit,* with Apelian as Kijh-Taniel, the half-mad poetic wanderer and Zarifian as Vosgan, the earthy drunkard father. Before leaving for Armenia, along with Shirvanzade, who had been visiting the United States at about the same time, Apelian worked with the group in Avedis Aharonian's popular *Golden Fables.*

Zarifian and the group left New York on theatrical ventures from time to time. There were six out-of-town performances of *Secrets of the Harem,* for example, in nearby cities in the Northeast. Zarifian himself, however, spent considerable time in more distant places. In Fresno, California, and Detroit, Michigan, where there are numerous Armenians, he used local talent for supporting roles in his stage productions because the cost of taking along his whole group would have been prohibitive. When he performed far from New York, he was accompanied at most by Sylvia Kalustian, who played the female lead in all productions. Kalustian was an extraordinarily gifted actress excelling especially in portrayals of Ophelia and Desdemona. During the 1929–1930 season Zarifian went to France (Paris and Marseille) and Egypt, and on two other occasions (1932–1933 and 1936–1937) he visited Armenian communities in South America. Since his absences were not brief, the group at home carried on as best it could. In 1933, for example, a fine production of Shirvanzade's *Honor* was given while Zarifian was in California. In the 1929–1930 season the Art Theater did not function, and Noorian came into his own when he directed and starred in an independent production of Levon Shant's *Caesar.* He rehearsed for six months before presenting it at Hampden's Theater on Broadway for one performance.

Zarifian seems to have done well in life, although he was a displaced, or uprooted, theatre spirit. Despite his fine reputation in Armenia, where he could have earned a good living among professional equals, he chose to base himself in New York, working with nonprofessionals and limited in the range of his repertoire. He complained often that America was the place for comedy, not for deep drama. But he made a living at what he did and was the only regularly paid theatre practitioner in Armenian ethnic drama. His compensation came from the sale of tickets, which in the twenties and thirties ranged from one to three dollars. As many as one thousand persons could see a performance, given only once on a Sunday afternoon at a Broadway house that otherwise would have been dark. Sometimes the Yiddish Art Theater at 27th Street and Madison Avenue, under the old Madison Square Garden, was rented. At other times Hampden's Theater, the John Golden Theater, and the Longacre Theater were used. For one presentation, such theatres could be rented for approximately three hundred dollars. If the curtain did not rise, however, for lack of spectators, a group lost only its fifty-dollar deposit. But even with bad luck and a small audience, it would pay often enough to perform as long as ticket sales covered the rent.

Despite the precarious living the theatre afforded, Zarifian managed to buy a home in Massachusetts, before his death at fifty-eight in 1937. Zarifian was skillful and well organized, both artistically and financially. For the 1930–1931 theatre season, he had contracted to rent the John Golden Theater, at 202 West 58th Street near Seventh Avenue, for one Sunday each month from September to May. His repertoire was remarkably varied. In September he presented *The Princess of the Fallen Castle*, by Levon Shant; in October, *Adventure*, by J. Begian; in November, *The Whole Town's Talking*, by Anita Loos; in December, *Durtad* (the first Christian king of Armenia), by Yeghia Kasparian; in January, *The Taming of the Shrew*; in February, *The Trial of Mary Dugan*, by B. Vieller; in March, *Kean*, by Alexandre Dumas (Dumas fils); in April, *Topaz*, by Bagnol; and in May, *Othello*. Zarifian's offerings were for an Armenian-language audience with an insecure grasp of English; thus he gave them works from the Armenian repertoire as well as plays of current and world interest. Unlike Armenians today, who are completely fluent in English and go to the American theatre and movies, Armenians then needed to experience not only their own but also world drama in their native language.

The advertisement for the 1930–1931 season included ticket prices of two dollars, one dollar and fifty cents, and one dollar, with a 20 percent discount for a season's subscription. Zarifian obviously worked very hard for the money he earned; he had to learn his own part each month and also direct a supporting cast of semiprofessionals and amateurs, who must have come to evening rehearsals tired from a day's work.

Zarifian gave the audience not only the plays it wanted but also productions with a high degree of theatrical competence. Some measure of that competence is attested to by a review in a local newspaper (circa 1924) of a play given in Hoboken, New Jersey, by the Art Theater. The play was *Korrado*, "the master-piece of Jarolamo Jacometti, the famous Italian play writer." The critic reports that Noorian "as the Monsignor was great. . . . His natural actions were very realistic and supported the play to the end to such a satisfactory point that he had to make several curtain calls." "H. Zarifian in the role of Korrado," the reviewer stated, "displayed remarkable talent. His expression and quick change of temperament were very natural and impressive, and he actually lived his part while playing it."

To centralize Armenian theatre in an area where a great number of Arme-nians lived, Zarifian based his group in New York City, touring from this point whenever he could. His dream of buying a theatre to house a permanent and paid company was never realized. Nevertheless, before World War II, with Zarifian giving his undivided attention to his art, there was a level and intensity of theatrical activity that has never been equaled in the Armenian ethnic community.[4]

THE KIMATIAN THEATER LOVERS: 1942–1961

The focus thus far has been on the work of the Armenian Art Theater, based in New York City. However, Armenian theatrical activities also took place outside of New York, often on a casual basis, in places like Fresno, Boston, and Detroit. Some of this activity dates as far back as the turn of the century. A musical theatre group led by Guregh Surabian was based in New York City during and after the Zarifian period. This group was not a resident company with a repertoire of musical plays constantly in performance in New York; its func-tion, rather, was to tour almost constantly with such favorite ethnic musicals as *Arshin Malalan* and *Anoush.*

After Zarifian's death in 1937, there seems to have been no theatre company that functioned on a regular basis in New York City. Zarifian's apparent theatri-cal heirs, Noorian and Kimatian, did not carry on the work of the Armenian Art Theater. Each kept his finger in theatricals, but not with the concentration of old. However, Kimatian organized a group under his own name (The Kimatian Theater Lovers Group) in 1942. I discussed the history of that organization with Mary Derderian Azarian, who was a member from beginning to end.[5]

The Kimatian group was composed of young American-born Armenians, whose grasp of the Armenian language could not compare with that of the immigrant players of the Zarifian era. Kimatian was a strict taskmaster who called rehearsals two or three times a week, always insisting that cast members come to practice with lines fully memorized. Full memorization compensated for the lack of perfect reading ability and saved time during rehearsals. Scenery and costumes were rented. No one in the group was paid. Admission money went to defray production costs and stage rental at such places as the high schools of

Fashion Industries and Central Needle Trades, Hunter and Baruch Colleges, the Central Opera House, the Barbizon Plaza, the Hecksher Theater, and Webster Hall. Kimatian's group was never ultimately responsible for financing productions, since various churches and social and philanthropic organizations acted as producers and sponsors for the individual shows. The group toured often, usually in the Northeast, with host communities paying all costs.

By the 1940s and 1950s the cultural needs of the community had changed. In the 1920s and 1930s when Zarifian had made a living at ethnic theatre, he often produced ten plays a year, original Armenian ones and English and world drama in translation. Kimatian's group produced one play a year, or occasionally two. Thoroughly familiar with the English language and grown in sophistication about the American theatre and movies available to them, immigrant and American-born Armenians no longer needed to see Armenian-language productions of Shakespeare and other foreign dramatists, which were available to them in English on a professional level. The repertoire of the Kimatian group over its nineteen-year history shows only two non-Armenian plays. In 1945 there was a production of *Punchinello*, a comedy based on the Pagliacci story, which was adapted by Mugerdich Noorian and staged by him as guest director. And in 1947, for the first time in the new world, Kimatian staged *The Merchant of Venice*, perhaps in the translation of the famous Houhanues Mahseyan.

During the Kimatian company's ascendancy, the remaining Armenian plays that were produced seem to have fallen into two categories. In the first of these are popular plays from the modern classic repertoire. In 1942 the offering was called *Ascension Day* and consisted of condensed excerpts from the famous Armenian opera *Anoush*, mainly spoken and not sung. In 1946 it was Vahan Krikor's *Swan Song*, with a plot depicting the love affair of a man with a woman much younger than himself. In 1948 the group performed the popular modern classic *For the Sake of Honor*, by Shirvanzade, which I have mentioned earlier. In 1949 Shant's *The Princess of the Fallen Castle* and in 1952 his *Pagan Gods*, perennial favorites I have also already mentioned, were staged. In 1960 and 1961 Kimatian closed his career with two operettas, *The Wandering Minstrel* and *Arshin Malalan*.

In the second category of Armenian plays produced by the Kimatian group were those written or adapted by Kimatian himself. All were on Armenian themes. In 1946 he wrote and produced *Victims of War*, a drama about an Armenian girl who married an American during World War II, when men eligible for marriage became scarce. The play's theme reflected the tendency toward dilution of the ethnic Armenian ranks when many Armenian Americans born in this country married non-Armenians. In 1947 Kimatian transformed Raffi's *Samuel*, about the conflict between Christianity and Zoroastrianism in Armenian history, into a play and staged it. In 1948 Kimatian produced his adaptation of Franz Werfel's novel, *Forty Days of Musa Dagh*, dealing with the heroism of a group of Armenians surrounded in battle by the Turks during the First World War. In 1953 he wrote and produced two short plays, one about a happy religious holiday, the Feast of the Transfiguration, and so titled, and another on ethnic mores called *Armenian Gypsies*. In 1954 he produced his version of the life of the famed clergyman-composer Gomidas Vartabed and, in addition, a comedy of his entitled *Living Ghost*. In a more serious vein in 1957 and 1958, he produced his *Innocent Sinner* and *The Fired Upon*. The latter dealt with the exodus of Armenians from Turkey, who upon entering the presumed sanctuary of Russian soil during the 1917 Revolution, were fired upon and pushed back into Turkey. He wrote on Armenian family life in *Siranoush* (a woman's name), a play he produced in 1959. As a playwright Kimatian never established a lasting reputation, but people today still remember him as a fine actor-director who served ethnic theatre well.[6]

In remembering the Kimatian era, Mary Azarian referred constantly to programs, reviews, and pictures in her scrapbook. A singer and actress with great love for theatre, she continued free-lance performing after the passing of Kimatian. For instance, in 1963 she joined forces with Mugerdich Noorian, who directed a highly praised production of Hampartzouon Gelemian's *The Flutist of the Armenian Mountains*, with music by the noted Alan Hovhaness.

THE 1960s AND 1970s

A few years after the demise of the Kimatian organization, the Sevan Theatrical Group was formed by Angel Havagimian in 1964, "devoted solely to the propagation and glorification of Armenian art and culture through theatrical presentations by non-professionals."[7] Noorian joined the group in 1965 and performed in and directed Shirvanzade's *Honor*, referred to above. In the following year he directed Dumas's *La Dame aux camélias* and Baronian's *Gentlemen Beggars*, both of which toured successfully. In 1967 Noorian acted in and directed *A Golden Tale*, with which he had been associated in his Zarifian days, in a production commemorating "the 100th anniversary of the birth of the author, a great writer, great patriot, great man."[8] In 1968 and 1969, he directed *Swan Song* and *Wheel of Fortune* by Krikor Vahan. In 1970 Sevan produced its last play, an adaptation of Yervunt Odian's *Merchant Artin Agha* with Setrak Terpanjian directing. By the end of that year former Sevan members began a workshop at the diocese of the Armenian Church of America. In that year also, Siranoush Katchouny, at one time briefly with the Zarifian company, assisted by Noorian, directed an independent production of *The Virgin Santoukht* in which Mary Azarian appeared. Since the 1930s Katchouny had produced musicals independently from time to time.

The formation of a new musical theatre company under the direction of Haig Ohanian, former producer of the Armenian Radio Hour, also occurred in 1970. A musician himself who had worked with the Surabian musical group in the twenties and thirties, Ohanian produced the ever-popular operetta *Arshin Malalan* in 1970 and repeated the success in 1974. Azarian took part in both productions. Ohanian directed and produced another operetta called *Let It Be*

Late, but Sweet in 1971 and, two years later, *If Not This One, That One.* All of these musicals were performed in the Kavookjian Auditorium of the Diocese of the Armenian Church of America, which was built in 1968 and became a major Armenian cultural center in New York City.

While Sevan was operating in the 1960s, the Masis Theatrical Group of the Armenian Cultural Association was formed in 1967 by Herand Markarian. In 1979 Masis was one of the two chief theatre companies in New York City. The other was the Diocesan Drama Group, which several actors from the defunct Sevan had formed in 1971. I was invited to become artistic director of the diocesan group in 1972. When I joined, I took over the staging of Shirvanzade's *For the Sake of Honor.* A teacher of drama and a director and playwright with more than twenty-five years in the theatre, I tried to give the group a direction discussed in an article in 1978.

In the years that I have been artistic director of the Diocesan Drama Group, it has stuck pretty much to a classical repertory of some of the best Armenian dramas. . . . It has given Armenians pride in their literary heritage reinforcing the knowledge of the older generation and inspiring youth in the investigation of their cultural background. It has helped, in its own way, to keep the Armenian language alive in America where the forces of assimilation are constantly at work to homogenize ethnic groups in the English speaking melting pot.[9]

The choice of *For the Sake of Honor* as the first offering was auspicious. The tragedy had often been staged successfully in the present Armenian homeland in the USSR and in the diaspora. Shirvanzade, its author—People's Writer of Armenia in 1934—gave the modern realistic drama a westward thrust with plays that examine the social fabric of Armenian life, much as Ibsen's realistic plays examine Norwegian mores. The play is about the unhappy effects of the acquisitiveness and greed of an industrialist, whose daughter commits suicide in order to redeem the family honor.[10] In the usual tradition of Armenian ethnic theater, *For the Sake of Honor* was performed once on its home stage and then toured to other Armenian communities, giving one performance each in Philadelphia, Albany, Hartford, Providence, and Toronto.

By 1979 the Diocesan Players had performed two other Shirvanzade dramas. In 1978 I staged *Did She Have the Right?*, a drama highly reminiscent of Ibsen's *A Doll's House.* Its plot concerns a woman who leaves her husband and children in order to realize her own potential. In the discussion that followed the presentation, one or another older member of the audience noted that Shirvanzade probably had read Russian or French translations of Ibsen's play before creating this play. Some thought that the influence of *A Doll's House* was very direct, noting that Shirvanzade could not possibly have modeled his drama on a real happening because at the turn of the century Armenian women never left their husbands. Throughout the performance, however, members of the audience had given every evidence of taking sides by applauding lines favorable to their viewpoints. Armenian communities in the United States continue to be somewhat socially conservative because of the great number of new immigrants entering their ranks from the patriarchical Near East, especially war-torn Lebanon.

The third Shirvanzade offering by the group was *Evil Spirit*, a drama quite markedly different from its predecessors. The chief difference, as Edward Allworth has noted, is its distinctly eastern view of Armenian life.[11] Setting his tragedy among peasants, Shirvanzade shows how pagan belief in evil spirits and exorcism lead to the murder of an innocent girl. The tragedy contains realistic scenes of Armenian village life and illuminates Armenian folk customs at the turn of the century.

A problem that often arises in the production of Armenian plays is the dialect of the playwright. Shirvanzade wrote in the eastern dialect of Armenian used in present Caucasian Armenia. The members of the Diocesan Drama Group employ—as for the most part does the audience—the western dialect of Armenia, as it was spoken in Anatolia. However, the speakers of one dialect are understood without much difficulty by speakers of the other. The group performed *For the Sake of Honor* in the original dialect. On the other hand, *Evil Spirit* and *Did She Have the Right?* were translated into the Western dialect before rehearsals began.

In presenting the plays of the greatest Armenian dramatist, Gabriel Sundukian, there was no question that translations had to be made. Sundukian wrote in the Tiflis (Georgia) Armenian dialect, which is almost incomprehensible to speakers of Western Armenian. Despite the loss of a great deal of the charm inherent in the originals, Sundukian's plays, it was felt, were too important to leave out of the group's repertoire. Writing on the importance of Sundukian, Vertanes informs us that the dramatist "stands out in the history of the modern Armenian theater as the founder of the realistic school."[12] Creating portraits of humankind drawn from the Tiflis locale, Sundukian transformed the Armenian stage and brought to life "the breathless, bloodless mannequins" of a stale tradition who had "recited like gramaphones."[13]

It was with *Bebo*, Sundukian's unquestioned masterpiece and perhaps the greatest Armenian play, that the Diocesan Drama Group began its Sundukian cycle in the fall of 1975. The fame of the play itself, the fact that it had been made into a musical film, the good reputation of the group, and the interesting plot concerning a poor fisherman cheated by a dishonest merchant helped draw a "standing room only" audience to the Kavookjian Auditorium. Armine Dikijian, noted critic, writing on the event observed:

Five hundred seats had been set out; additional chairs just cleared the 665 person fire rule. Children, teen-agers, young adults, middle-agers and senior citizens, they all came, even by chartered busses. And they all enjoyed the production which had many high points of comedy to relieve the dramatic tension, even a few unaccompanied songs.[14]

Helen Baronian, writing for the *Armenian Reporter*, addressing herself to the timeliness of the drama, noted that the economic and class conflicts depicted hold "as true today as they did when it was first written."[15]

Bebo was presented as part of the year's activities commemorating the 150th anniversary of Sundukian's birth. In the next two years (1976 and 1977), the group presented Sundukian's *The Ruined Family* and *Khatabala* (Personal Calamity) to packed houses. Both plays are not unlike Moliere comedies, but with serious endings. *The Ruined Family* deals with economic ruin brought on a merchant by his spendthrift wife and daughter; *Khatabala* is about a father's attempt to hoodwink a prospective suitor into marrying his ugly daughter by luring him with the view of a beautiful substitute placed at a distant window. The situations are all too human, depicting overreaching people who are made to appear ridiculous. Yet there is something almost pathetic, if not tragic, about these plays—perhaps a mixture of emotions that is strangely Armenian—that is reminiscent of Molière's most serious comedy, *The Misanthrope*. The final outcry of the ruined merchant in the one play is not funny; nor is the insult felt by the ugly and rejected daughter in the other.

Unlike the seriocomic Sundukian plays, those of Hagop Baronian (the plays created from his humorous stories) are purely comic. As a change of pace after Shirvanzade's highly serious *For the Sake of Honor* of 1972, the group decided to produce Baronian's *The Eastern Dentist*. A fast-moving farce short on theme but full of zany events, this play depicts the ridiculous actions of an incompetent and philandering dentist. His wife suspects that he is having an adulterous affair with a woman who is in turn cuckolding her old husband. One evening, while allegedly on a house call, he meets his mistress. His suspicious wife, who has followed him, then chases him into a masquerade ball, where the various characters disguised in costumes and masks conduct a comedy of errors. In this second production of the company, under my direction, the costumes were rendered for the organization—for the first of many times—by Ruth Thomason, who subsequently made herself a reputation by assembling a museum of period Armenian clothing and a collection of photographs of Armenians in clothing worn in Anatolia and the Caucasus.

The Diocesan Drama Group has produced only plays by and about Armenians in the national language. In the late 1970s a group called the Ardashad Theatre Company, sponsored by the New York chapter of the Armenian General Benevolent Union and the Masis Theatrical Group of the Armenian Cultural Association, staged dramas by and about non-Armenians. Under the direction of Krikor Satamian, who trained at the London School of Film and the Bristol Old Vic, the Ardashad Company produced Goldoni's *The Liar* and Chekhov's *The Bear* in Armenian and a short Feydeau farce in English by the end of 1979. As an ethnic theatre group, its chief aim seemed to be to serve youth with theatrical activity. The group played before various church parishes in and around New York City to relatively small audiences, finding its largest following at the Kavookjian Auditorium at diocesan headquarters.

The Masis Theatrical Group, headed by Herand Markarian, a chemist with an interest in theatre dating back to his youth in Baghdad, has also presented non-Armenian plays, but only in the Armenian language. Trained at the Circle-in-the-Square Theater School under Yale University professor Nikos Psacharapolous, Markarian has directed such plays as Anouilh's *Antigone*, Labiche's *The Italian Straw Hat*, and Chekhov's *The Anniversary*. Markarian, however, has produced plays from the Armenian repertoire also. In 1968, for example, he staged the aforementioned *Pagan Gods* by Shant, a dramatist considered by Markarian himself to be the best of those in the modern period. The drama contrasts the lives of a young priest and an older high priest. The former, torn between the desires of the flesh and his faith, turns away from service to God to pursue a woman he loves. The older priest had done exactly the opposite in his youth. A note in the play program indicates that one theme of *Pagan Gods* is "the purification and sanctification of the human soul in defeating the lusts of the flesh and passions of the intellect." But perhaps the most interesting aspects of the play are symbolistic or even expressionistic, dealing with dream visitations; the call of mermaids; the ghost of a dead hermit; and the temple of the pagan gods, who encourage the pursuit of earthly pleasure, which the Christian God does not. This last aspect is of special interest to Armenians, whose existence has depended so much on their Christian faith.

Markarian observed that drama "is the weakest branch of Armenian literature" and that "it is for this reason that Masis has presented foreign works translated into Armenian."[16] Realizing, however, that his cultural concern was the fear of "losing the continuation of 'Armenianism',"[17] Markarian came to believe that "one solution to the problem" of the lack of Armenian plays "would be to adapt Armenian novels to the stage."[18] With the help of his wife, he did just that by transforming Shant's novel, *The Actress*, into a play and staging it in 1969.

But soon thereafter, Markarian turned from deriving dramas to writing original plays. *The Cycle*, the first of these, appearing in 1971, examined in serious fashion the idea that guilt of one sort or another lies behind every person's mask of innocence. Directed by the writer himself, the piece was valid as Armenian theatre although it did not speak to the issue of "losing the continuation of 'Armenianism'."

It was not long before Markarian, one of the few dramatists writing in Armenian in America, found a fittingly ethnic subject. He wrote about genocide carried out against the Armenians by the Turks in 1915 in his *Solomon Teliherian*, a play about the Armenian hero who shot Talat Pasha in Berlin in 1919. The German courts absolved Teliherian of guilt in the death of Talat, who might be thought of as the Turkish Himmler of his time. In referring to the timeliness of the play, Markarian observed, "I wrote the play for the occasion of the commemoration of the 60th anniversary of the Genocide. It is the life history of the man who took it upon himself to avenge the martyred Armenians of 1915."[19]

From a view of the recent past, Markarian looked to the world about him and wrote and staged *Polarization* in 1977. The play was an exposé of present-day Armenian-American community life that, according to one critic, was "his most mature and well-balanced production." Dwelling on the ethnic theme, the critic went on to say:

The playwright had developed two major topics. One was the evolution of an Armenian family in New York, and their struggle to preserve their identity and still adapt to the American life style. . . . The other was the dichotomy of the Armenian community in its political and church affiliations.[20]

In discussing the second topic referred to above, Markarian dealt with the weakening of the contemporary Armenian-American ethnic community by a political split that in turn has created a schismatic church. Critics of Armenians have noted that a small minority cannot effectively get politicians to act in their behalf if they are divided. Markarian hoped for reconciliation of the factions in the interest of a more politically powerful community.

The critic who discussed *Polarization* remarked: "The grandmas and grandpas, young American borns, married couples with American-born children, newcomers from the Middle East . . . everybody felt a strong identification with at least one character."[21] The problems of ethnicity discussed in the play are common to all ethnic groups in America. Two of the sons depicted in the middle-class Armenian family, for example, typify the melting pot dilemma so many ethnic groups face. One son "goes along with his parents' teaching in everything Armenian, yet, deep-down has problems identifying with Armenian groups."[22] The other "changes his name to Jack Adams, to the distress of his family."[23] Markarian has touched on problems that were current from the time of the first heavy migrations to the United States early in this century, and many in his audience have seen reflected on the stage what they have done and become. Other Armenians, who are relative newcomers in the United States, like the playwright himself, have seen the stage representation of the process of assimilation in their own lives.

In his latest dramatic offering in 1979, Markarian drew again on Armenian history, this time the distant past, with the subject of Vartanantz. Other than Christmas and Easter, which Armenians celebrate with all Christians, Vartan's day, or Vartanantz, is the most important holiday in the Armenian religious calendar. For Armenians the day commemorates not the military defeat of General Vartan Mamigonian's army in the Battle of Avrayr with Persia in 451, but the courage of the Armenians to fight against heavy odds and their resolve to die if necessary for their Christian faith. Impressed with the passion of the Armenian devotion to their faith, the Persian enemy relented in its efforts to convert Armenians to Zoroastrianism. Markarian could not have chosen a more powerful theme. In an interview he revealed his motivation:

Historically, Vartanantz has had a tremendous impact on our people, affecting our mental attitudes, the manner of our survival, and the preservation of our heritage. This event is celebrated in all our churches and in public gatherings praising the spirit of Vartan and his compatriots. I felt it would be even more enlightening to see and experience on the stage a portrayal of the actual event. This would also give the younger generation an intimate view of our history.[24]

To balance its theatrical offerings the Masis Theatrical Group produced Armenian comedies, variety shows, and commemorative theater events. In 1970, for instance, it staged Simon Ekmekjian's *Bride and Mother-in-law*, referred to earlier, a farce-comedy that according to a note in the playbill deals with "the ever-lasting misunderstanding between mother-in-law and daughter-in-law." In 1976 M. Ishkhan's fantastic *It's So Hard to Die* was produced. It told of the effects of a transplant of an Armenian's brain into the head of an American. In 1972 Markarian presented a novel offering called *Love in Armenian Culture*, a revue with which the group toured to other cities in the Northeast.

Armenian ethnic theatre groups of New York City often present plays in other northeastern cities. They are in demand outside of New York because they maintain reasonably high artistic standards. Despite limitations of time and energy, members of these groups at their best have reached semiprofessional levels of performance on a par with the off-Broadway theatre in New York. Performance quality varies from year to year, with the highest artistic levels reached by veterans such as Garbis Pokradjian, Setrak Terpanjian, Hrant Gulian, Maral Achian, Seta Bezirdjian Willson, and Lucy Jamgotchian of the Diocesan Drama Group; Hovhannes and Sonia Bezdikian and Herand Markarian of the Masis Theatrical Group; and Krikor Satamian of the Ardashad Theatre Company. The three stage directors, Markarian, Satamian, and myself—try to emulate the standards set by the American theatre, with which they are very familiar. Except for Satamian, who has many cultural responsibilities at the New York chapter of the Armenian General Benevolent Union, people are never paid for their work. As it has always been, most who work in the Armenian ethnic theatre do so as a labor of love.

CULTURAL RENAISSANCE

The 1960s, 1970s, and 1980 saw a renaissance in Armenian culture in New York and other cities in the United States. One reason for this renewed interest in Armenian culture was the focus on ethnicity given to the nation by the black civil rights movement begun in the 1960s. The effect was a diminishing of the melting-pot concept of Americanism and an effort on the part of the government to foster ethnic programs with federal funds. Being American did not mean a dissolution of ethnic background anymore.[25]

For Armenians, especially in the New York port of entry, ethnic awareness was strengthened even more by the immigration of Armenians from the Near East, including Egypt, Jordan, Turkey and especially Lebanon. In the wake of the war conditions at the end of the 1970s, the Armenian sector of Beirut, Lebanon, was almost totally destroyed and Armenians were again pushed into the diaspora, with many being welcomed in New York. In general Middle East unrest has always caused Armenian migration to these friendly shores. In addition, some immigrants who had previously gone to the Soviet Armenian homeland as a haven now joined relatives who had settled in the United States earlier.

The renaissance in Armenian culture had the support of those Armenians who had come to these shores in the 1920s and 1930s and earlier. Many of them, like Alex Manoogian, Haik Kavookjian, and Edward Mardigian, became independently wealthy and supported Armenian cultural programs liberally. With other established Armenian Americans, they created, for example, the marvelous St. Vartan Armenian Cathedral complex and strengthened the Armenian General Benevolent Union. These organizations in turn created educational institutions, dance ensembles, pro-musica programs, literary magazines, cultural endowment funds, college scholarship agencies, and of course theatre groups.

Although many cities have seen the rebirth of interest in ethnic Armenian culture, it is very marked in New York City, where the new immigrants combine with the established Armenian Americans to create a vast cultural interest group. New York supports three organized theatre groups of considerable artistic merit. The interest of the new immigrants in theatre seems to have rekindled the established Armenian American's interest in the Armenian theatre repertoire and in newly written drama.

Will the two forces, America's new interest in ethnicity and new immigration, be sufficient to keep Armenian-language theatre alive? One cannot say for certain, because in time both forces will diminish. New immigration will level out, and despite this nation's professed interest in ethnicity, forces of assimilation go on continually. People make their way in this country by being American.

The history of the Armenian ethnic theatre in New York gives us some idea of what its future content may be. I have noted in this chapter, for example, that plays created by Armenian-American writers interest audiences but tend not to have repertory permanence. The works of established Armenian playwrights who wrote before 1920 and the formation of the diaspora—Sundukian, Shant, Shirvanzade, and Baronian—were all represented on the New York stage, but strangely enough that body of work represents only about a dozen or so plays, giving apparent credence to Markarian's observation that drama is the weakest branch of Armenian literature. But is that statement true for Armenian literature since 1920? Although it might seem so, since contemporaneous plays written in the Near East and staged here are of negligible number, it is not. Though few original Armenian plays have been created in centers such as Beirut and Istanbul since the 1920s, there has been great playwriting activity in Soviet Armenia. The problem in the past has been the lack of cultural contact between the theatre of Yerevan, Armenia's capital, and the theatre of New York. Noorian attributed the lack of contact to the restrictive nature of the Stalin regime, but theatrical interchange did not appreciably increase after Stalin's death.

In an effort to understand Armenian theatre better and to help bring new life to Armenian ethnic theatre in New York City, in May and June of 1979, as director of the Diocesan Players, with an invitation from the Soviet Armenian Committee on Cultural Relations with Armenians Abroad and a grant from the Armenian General Benevolent Union's Alex Manoogian Cultural Fund, I traveled to Armenia to study the theatre of Yerevan. I found a beehive of theatrical activity, centered around the famed Sundukian Theater and the smaller Dramatic Theater. The range of subject matter and themes was not as broad as in this country, but much appeared exportable because of its universal appeal.

One such play was *Go Die, Come I Love You*, by Aram-Ashot Babayan. The plot deals with the pathetic tricks that an old man plays in order to have his sons and daughters-in-law take him to live in their homes. The old man feigns illness and is forced into a hospital. He "escapes," as he puts it. Then he feigns paralysis of the legs to gain sympathy, and as a last resort he feigns the loss of his voice. His kinsmen repeatedly avow hypocritical love for him and continually frustrate his efforts to join their households. Finally the old man has to feign death. Then all those who did not want him when he was alive avow their love for him. Each son wants his father's body waked at his house. During all this squabbling the old man enters alive, shocking everyone. He goes off on his own to be with old friends and leaves the hypocrites with the Armenian adage of the title—it is easy to say you loved the dead.

I thought this play, with a nicely balanced cast of nine, would make a good vehicle for the Diocesan Players and staged it in November of 1979. An audience of six hundred packed the Kavookjian Auditorium, knowing they were to see a new play direct from Armenia. The problem of what to do with the elderly is of even more concern to Armenians in this country than in Armenia. Other plays that I saw in Armenia that do not involve ideological differences between the Soviet Union and the United States, could also be staged here. This kind of cultural interchange between the diaspora and the homeland may help sustain the Armenian ethnic theatre in the United States when interest in ethnicity and new immigration wane.

NOTES

1. Charles A. Vertanes, "Introductory Outline of the History of the Armenian Theater, in *Two Thousand Years of Armenian Theater* (New York: Armenian National Council of America, 1954), p. 13.

2. Ibid.

3. Interviews with Mugerdich Noorian, October and November 1978.

4. Krikor Zarian, *Hovhannes Zarifian* (Yerevan, Soviet Armenia: Armenian Theater Union, 1977, in Armenian).

5. Interview with Mary Derderian Azarian, October 1978, assisted by Alice and Charles Kasbarian.

6. Elia Kimatian, "The Armenian-American Colony and the Armenian Theater," *Hairenik Monthly* 41, no. 9 (September 1963); 41, no. 10 (October 1963); 41, no. 11 (November 1963); 41, no. 12 (December 1963); 42, no. 4 (April 1964); 42, no. 5 (May 1964).

7. Playbill for Krikor Vahan's *Wheel of Fortune*, produced by The Sevan Theatrical Society, 1968.

8. From the playbill.

9. In *The Armenian Church*, 21, no. 1 (Winter 1978).

10. For more on the play and playwright see Alexandre Shirvanzade, *For the Sake of Honor*, trans. and with an introduction by Nishan Parlakian (New York: St. Vartan's Press, 1976).

11. Edward Allworth, "The Modern Drama of the Transcaucasus," introductory essay to Alexandre Shirvanzade, *Evil Spirit*, trans. Nishan Parlakian (New York: St. Vartan's Press, 1980).

12. Vertanes, "Introductory Outline," p. 6.

13. Ibid., p. 7.

14. *Armenian Mirror-Spectator*, November 15, 1975.

15. November 6, 1975, p. 7.

16. *The Armenian Reporter*, February 15, 1973, p. 10.

17. Ibid., February 12, 1970.

18. Ibid., February 15, 1973, p. 10.

19. In a letter, February 14, 1975.

20. *The Armenian Weekly*, June 11, 1977.

21. Ibid.

22. Ibid.

23. Ibid.

24. *Armenian Mirror-Spectator*, February 24, 1979.

25. Pierre Papazian, "No Man Is An Island . . ." *Outreach* (a publication of the prelacy of the Armenian Apostolic Church of America) 2, no. 9 (January 1980).

BIBLIOGRAPHY

Books

Gyowldowdaghyan, S. *Shirvanzade's Linguistic Cultivation*. Yereven, Soviet Armenia, 1966. A work in Armenian on the linguistic concerns of Armenian playwright Alexandre Shirvanzade.

Hachverdian, Levon. *The History of the Armenian Theater: 1901–1920*. Yereven, Soviet Armenia: Art Institute of the Soviet Armenian Academy of Science, 1980. In Armenian. Provides considerable accounts of the lives and works of Levon Shant, Hagop Bavonian, Gabriel Sundakian, Alexandre Shirvanzade, and others.

Shirvanzade, Alexandre. *For the Sake of Honor*. Translated, with notes on the play and its author, by Nishan Parlakian. New York: St. Vartan's Press, 1976.

———. *Evil Spirit*. Translated, with preface and notes, by Nishan Parlakian. New York: St. Vartan's Press, 1980. This book contains an introductory essay by Edward Allworth, "The Modern Drama of the Transcaucasus," which outlines modern Armenian drama from the mid-nineteenth century, including some of the playwrights represented on the Armenian ethnic stage.

Stepanian, Karnig. *The Outline of Western Armenian Theater*. Yereven, Soviet Armenia: Art Institute of the Soviet Armenian Academy of Science, 1962. In Armenian.

Tamrazian, Hrant. *Shirvanzade.* Yereven, Soviet Armenia: Haypethrat, 1961. The best biography and analysis of Shirvanzade's works in Armenian.

Zarian, Krikor. *Hovhannes Zarifian.* Yerevan, Soviet Armenia: Armenian Theatrical Union, 1977. Covers the life and work of a man who spent the better part of his professional life in the Armenian ethnic theatre of New York.

Articles

Donabedian, Kevork. "The Theater and Dramatic Arts in Armenian History." *Armenian Review* (Summer, Autumn, Winter 1970 and Spring 1971). A work on the ancient and premodern Armenian theatre.

Kimatian, Elia. "The Armenian-American Colony and the Armenian Theater." *Hairenik Monthly* 41, no. 9 (September 1963); 41, no. 10 (October 1963); 41, no. 11 (November 1963); 41, no. 12 (December 1963); 42, no. 4 (April 1964); 42, no. 5 (May 1964). A history of Armenian ethnic theatre in the Armenian language.

Parlakian, Nishan. "Shirvanzade Revisited." *Ararat* 15, no. 1 (Winter 1974).

Vertanes, Charles A. "Introductory Outline of the History of the Armenian Theater." An "additional essay" in *Two Thousand Years of the Armenian Theater.* New York: Armenian National Council of America, 1954. A general account of Armenian ethnic theater. The booklet in which this essay appears is a digest in English of George Goyan's monumental Russian-language work of the same title, published in Moscow in 1952. Vertanes's essay contains brief entries on the major playwrights of the modern Armenian drama, including Sundukian, Shirvanzade, and Baronian.

2

Black Theatre

EDWARD G. SMITH

The cultured white race owes to the soul-expressions of its black brother too many moments of happiness not to acknowledge ungrudgingly the significant fact that what the Negro has achieved is of tremendous civilizing value. . . . We have to acknowledge not only that our civilization has done practically nothing to help the Negro create his art but that our unjust oppression has been powerless to prevent the black man from realizing in a rich measure the expression of his own rare gifts.[1]

Blacks have been part of the American stage since the 1700s, but very little of any of this long theatre tradition has been recorded in the standard histories of American drama—a notable omission.

White America was introduced to the performing ability of African slaves as early as 1664. The deck of the English slaveship *Hannibal* served as a stage for the imprisoned slaves, whose "daily exercise" was to be forced to sing and dance for the crew. The crew found them highly entertaining, as did the slave masters who later purchased them. But the habits, customs, and emotions that the slaves expressed in this entertainment showed that they were a people with a rich heritage; the demands of survival would have a significant impact on their contribution to American culture.

In the past ten years the Afro-American artist has gained recognition on the American stage: James Earl Jones and Trazana Beverly have won Tony Awards; Ashton Springer and Woodie King are well-known producers on the Broadway stage; and Richard Wesley, Melvin Van Peebles, and Charles Gordone are prominent Broadway playwrights. Black musicals are now images of black life styles, instead of hand-me-down white musicals. A supportive and developing black audience has arrived. Black theatre courses and plays are part of the curriculum now being offered by many colleges and universities. Black theatre has come a long way, but has still a much longer way to go.

Less than forty years ago this race of people could not sit on the main floor of most Broadway houses and could not perform on the same stages with whites. They were not allowed to present their own heritage on the American stage, but were stripped of their songs, dance, and identity. This same race of people made profits for white playwrights, producers, and directors. But though this race stepped on the American stage as buffoons, sambos, and Mr. Bones, it remained to play Emperor Jones, Othello, the Lord, and King Lear. It, too, found its heroes, loved ones, and makers of dreams. Theatre produced by the blacks themselves, and its plays and actors and actresses, are what this chapter is about.

THE BEGINNINGS

The Afro-American was introduced to the American stage in 1769 in the play *The Padlock*, with a West Indian slave named Mungo who played a profane clown of little authenticity, not a joyful, happy-go-lucky clown, but a nonsensical imbecile without poise or direction. *Robinson Crusoe* and *Harlequin* opened in 1786, depicting the black performer in the same negative way. In 1792 *The Yorker's Stratagem* by J. Robinson was greeted with universal applause. It described a New Yorker disguised as a rural Yankee trying to win the hand of a West Indian mulatto heiress, and the blacks in the production were not natives of the United States. In 1795 *The Triumph of Love* by John Murdock presented a native black as "Sambo"—a shuffling, cackling, allegedly comic servant who is freed by his master (which in itself must have caused considerable comment at the time). These plays were written, produced, directed, and acted out by white companies to a white audience, making the black performer most uncomfortable in his hideous roles. Thus the few blacks that were seen on the American stage were portrayed as intellectually and aesthetically empty characters.

It was not until 1776 that the American black was shown in the true light of the times through John Leacock's play *The Fall of British Tyranny*. The American government had discharged blacks from the army in 1755, and the British promised immediate freedom and equality to all blacks who joined their troops. Thousands of black men fled their masters and were recruited, trained, and armed by the British. These black troops in return agreed to kill their masters, which was reenacted on stage. Leacock gave the black performers positive images of themselves during those changing periods in American history. The Americans claimed that this gesture was the beginning of a "race war," and eventually blacks were welcomed back into the U.S. Army.

William Wells Brown (1815?–1884), who was born a slave in Lexington, Kentucky, was the first black man to write a novel, a drama, and a book of travel. He also became a lecturer and historian and is claimed to have written the first black play in America. *The Escape*, or *A Leap to Freedom*, was based on his personal experiences. This sharp satire on the institution of slavery has been characterized as "a hodge-podge with some humor and satire and much melodrama."[2]

In 1857, the United States Supreme Court held that a man once defined as property could not shed the title of property merely by walking about in "free territory" but had to be returned to his original owner. The Dred Scott decision reaffirmed the sanctity of property. In 1859, John Brown, angered and impatient with federal law and order, attacked Harper's Ferry in what he hoped would be the beginning of protracted guerilla warfare—protracted until the conscience of America could distinguish men from property. . . . Taking his plot from man-as-property and his viewpoint from abolitionism, William Wells Brown published *The Escape*.[3]

The play was never staged, but readings of it by Brown were warmly received. Doris Abramson, who uncovered the lost play at the Boston Atheneum Library and found that it had been published in Boston in 1858, wrote that it was "an interesting document both from a social and theatrical point of view."[4]

While the American stage continued to portray blacks as comic, shuffling, thank-you-sir servants, the African Grove Theatre was being founded by a West Indian black named James Hewett. Hewett had gained prominence as the first of the Negro tragedians—he was the first black to perform Othello and Richard III. This new black theatre company was started as early as 1821 in lower Manhattan, at Bleeker and Mercer streets. It performed Shakespearean drama, originals and readings, and musical recitals before mixed audiences. But the whites in attendance would shout derisive remarks at the actors, ridiculing their performances. Ultimately the theatre built a partition to accommodate white audiences only, yet they continued to harass the performers.

Loften Mitchell, prominent historian, professor, and playwright, wrote that "the police joined the attacks on the African Company. They raided the place repeatedly, interrupted performances and dragged actors off to jail. . . . What the police could not do was done by white hoodlums. They wrecked the African Theatre."[5] In 1823 it was forced to close its doors, but this determined group of actors continued to perform in other rented localities. James Hewett gave a stunning Shakespearian reading *Proud Heroes* in 1826 at a location near the by then defunct African Grove Theatre.

Ira Aldridge was the second Negro tragedian. He was born July 24, 1807, in New York and as a teenager played Rollo in Richard Sheridan's *Pizarro*, which was produced privately with an all-black cast. Aldridge was an intimate friend and colleague of James Hewett and often took leading roles at the African Theatre. Aldridge would perform Shakespeare there during the day, but at night he did clown roles on the uptown stage.

With the destruction of the African Grove Theatre, Aldridge sailed for England in 1824. In Europe he was hailed for his Othello and later was acclaimed by royalty. Edmund Kean and Aldridge became good friends, and Kean later played Iago to Aldridge's Othello in a series of productions. Aldridge's performances in *Merchant of Venice*, *Macbeth*, *Titus Andronicus*, and *King Lear* were also highly acclaimed. In non-English-speaking countries he performed in English while the local actors spoke in their own language. Foreign audiences loved him; he received many honors and decorations and was a member of several learned societies in Sweden. Others of Aldridge's close friends were Alexandre Dumas and Leo Tolstoy. Aldridge had just completed arrangements for his return to New York after a very successful tour when, with his health failing, he died on August 7, 1867, at Lodz, Poland.

James Weldon Johnson was a gifted songwriter, an author, a professor, and a field secretary in the NAACP. He wrote lyrics for some of his brother Rosamond Johnson's black musical productions. His important contributions were *God's Trombones*, *The Autobiography of an Ex-Coloured Man*, and *His Black Manhattan* and the words of music to "Lift Every Voice and Sing," the "Negro national anthem." In 1828 he formed a Committee of Concerned Black Americans to raise funds for the endowment of the Ira Aldridge Memorial Chair in the Shakespeare Memorial Theatre at Stratford-on-Avon, where thirty-three chairs honor great actors of the world. The bronze plaque honoring Aldridge describes him as one of the greatest Afro-American tragedians in history.

Next in popularity to the minstrels on the American stage were the "Tom shows," which usually focused on the antislavery theme. It has been said that these portrayals helped bring about the Civil War. Such plays as *The Branded Hand*, which appeared in 1845, and *The Captured Slave*, the theme of which was the arrest of a white man in New Orleans, his enslavement, and his escape, depicted the evils of slavery. In 1852 Harriet Beecher Stowe's novel *Uncle Tom's Cabin* was presented in play form at the National Theatre in New York, where it ran for a year to capacity houses, sometimes giving three performances a day. At one time, four companies were playing it simultaneously in New York. Stowe could not protect her dramatic rights because of her religious beliefs, and soon other versions appeared. This gave a number of black singers an opportunity to work on the American stage for the first time; they would sing the plantation songs behind a scrim (a transparent theatre drop) as little Eva went to heaven, or the bloodhounds chased Eliza across the ice. Uncle Tom and Topsy were always played by white actors made up sooty black. The black performers were usually "a passel of darkies and a brace of hounds." They were selected for their singing voices. Some of the touring companies would advertise "genuine Negroes and real bloodhounds."

In 1853 the National Theatre announced a special section in the theatre for black audiences. The first film version of *Uncle Tom's Cabin* (produced in 1903), presented a white actor as Uncle Tom. It was not until thirty years later that a black man played this role. The play did enjoy long years of popularity across the country, as the black performers did what whites thought they could do best— sing and dance.

Uncle Tom's Cabin is another example of the irony and the inconsistency of the Negro's role in American life. For one thing, its major character was based on a man named Josiah Benson, a minister, who escaped from slavery and took an active part in the underground railroad. He was in reality a militant, courageous man, but he became the prototype for Mrs. Stowe's leading character. . . . History came full cycle. Negroes began to resent the character Uncle Tom, and his name became a source of contempt on the lips of black people. An "Uncle Tom," "Tom," or "Uncle," is the most inflammatory, insulting thing a black man can be called.[6]

THE MINSTRELSY

The Minstrelsy could be called the "embryonic force" behind the rip-off of black art in America. African Americans were the originators of this form of entertainment, which was eventually taken to the American stage by Edwin Forrest—the first to cork his face black and imitate the singing and shuffling of the African American.

Charles Matthews first built Negro characterization on detailed observation of black Americans. While attending a performance of the African Theatre Company, a resident Negro theatrical troupe in New York City, Matthews heard the audience demand that the black actor playing Hamlet stop his soliloquy and sing "Possum Up a Gum Tree." Matthews' use of this song in his act, "A Trip to America," was the first certain example of a white man borrowing Negro material for a blackfaced act.[7]

Minstrelsy is said to have begun around the 1840s, focusing on the song, dance, and humor of humble black characters. The theme seldom altered, and many of the stereotypes are still being recognized today: flashy dress, big lips, nappy hair, shiftlessness, laziness, dice playing, fondness for watermelon and chicken, wine and gin drinking, scratching of the head and privates.

By 1828 blackfaced white performers were touring the country in their new art form. One popular minstrel performer of that era was Thomas "Daddy" Rice, author of the *First Ethiopian Opera.*

Thomas D. Rice while on tour in 1828, saw an old Negro, his right shoulder deformed and drawn up high, his left leg gnarled with rheumatism, stiff and crooked at the knee; doing an odd-looking dance while singing; "Weel About and Turn and Do Jus So;/Ebery Time I Weel About, I Jump Jim Crow." Aware that any peculiar song or dance had great public appeal, Rice recognized this as excellent material for a stage act. He learned the song and dance, added new verses. "Quickened and slightly changed the air," made himself up to look like the original—even to wearing his clothes—and took to the stage. His new act created a public sensation and took him on a triumphant tour of major entertainment centers, including dancing "Jim Crow" in New York City in 1832 and in London in 1836.[8]

It was not until 1865 that black minstrel troupes began to appear with recognition: the Georgia Minstrel Troupe toured the northeast, and soon one of its three companies toured England; the Lew Johnson Plantation Company grew to twelve companies in twenty-five years, claiming Bert Williams among its early members; and the Hyer Sisters Troupe drew its dramatic and operatic subjects from black history.

For a while black minstrel companies were flourishing businesses, some with black owners and managers, such as McCabe and Young, Pringles Georgia Minstrels, and the Hicks and Sawyer Minstrels. Charles Hicks took his troupe to Europe in 1870. However, white businessmen were soon to take over the ownership and management of the more successful minstrel companies. Some of the stars to emerge from minstrelsy were Sam Lucas and James Bland, composers of "Carry Me Back to Old Virginny" and "In the Evening by the Moonlight"; Billy Kersands, the most famous black star before Bert Williams; Tom McIntosh and George and James Bohee, who were lauded as the greatest banjo players in the country; and the Clowns of Primrose and West, who created jazz tunes, jigs, and dances and toured with white and black performers. W. C. Handy, known as the father of the blues, toured with minstrel troupes throughout the south, leading a band or as a sideman. Minstrelsy seemed to be the only form of entertainment that blacks could be identified with, and for that reason many of the black artists rushed at the opportunity to join traveling troupes. Minstrels were also paid and were treated as celebrities by their own people. Mitchell states:

Minstrelsy was troublesome to Negroes. The inherent stereotypes have already been noted. True, it offered theatrical training to Negro performers. It left us vaudeville monologues, dance routines and the double forms of music—described by Isaac Goldberg as "Music of the Heels" and "Music of the Heart." Minstrelsy was also the first authentic American theatre form. But it was troublesome.[9]

THE TURN OF THE CENTURY: BLACK MUSICALS

The black musicals, or "coon shows," had their genesis in the "Uncle Tom" and "minstrel" tradition. Just when the black artists were beginning to find a way of projecting their true image, whites took control. They made farcical caricatures of blacks that only they could enjoy.

In 1890 black producer Sam Jack cast the musical burlesque *Creole Show* with some of the prettiest black show girls around—something completely unique. It opened in Chicago during the World's Fair and ran for five seasons in New York. John W. Isham was a black producer whose performers had trained singing voices. Their operatic solos and choruses were performed successfully in his 1895 production of *The Octoroons*. During this same period, black actor-dramatist Bob Cole and performers from the coon and minstrel shows set out to destroy the negativity of the black image that was being focused on the American stage by their white constituents. Their musical, *A Trip to Coontown*, broke the minstrel tradition in 1898.

That same year Will Marion Cook, a composer, conductor, and violinist who had attended the Hochschule in Berlin and was responsible for writing over a dozen musical comedies for black shows, composed the music and Paul Lawrence Dunbar wrote the lyrics to *Clorindy*, the origin of the cakewalk (dance). Dunbar became one of America's renowned Negro Poets.

Bob Cole was one of the most versatile men in theatre: a singer, dancer, actor, writer, producer, and director. He played several instruments. Rosamond Johnson was a composer who had received his musical training at the New England Conservatory of Music in Boston and who traveled the vaudeville circuit. He wrote the music to the song "Lift Every Voice and Sing," which, as mentioned earlier, became popular in America as the "Negro national anthem." Cole and Johnson wrote the first black operetta, *The Shoofly Regiment.*

In 1902 blacks made history on the Broadway stage. *In Dahomey,* a satire of the American Colonization Society's "back to Africa" movement, was the first all-black musical that ever reached Broadway. It established the team of Bert Williams and George Walker as the top black stars in America and also in England, where it toured the following year. One cannot omit Bert Williams from the pages of theatre history, though he did everything on stage except the serious roles he always wanted to do. The Williams and Walker partnership soon became the strongest theatrical comedy team ever assembled. They had introduced and popularized the cakewalk and had been seen in several mediocre revues before *In Dahomey.*

This musical was written by a black team that went on to destroy the minstrels for the big musicals that were to follow at the end of the nineteenth century. The author, J. A. Shipp, was a member of the Primrose Minstrel Company, which toured with a mixed troupe and later contributed much to the development of black musical comedies. The music was written by Cook and the lyrics by Dunbar.

Others who helped diminish the minstrel pattern included John W. Isham, producer of *The Octoroons* and of *Oriental America.* His productions did away with the walkaround, or cakewalk, for the finale, substituting an operatic medley. Alex Rogers was the composer of many of the Williams and Walker songs of the time, including "I May Be Crazy" and the popular Williams show stopper, "Nobody." S. H. Dudley was part of the movement to big musicals, and he was also a producer and writer, best remembered for his outstanding show *The Smart Set.*

Williams and Walker were seen again in 1906 in the hit *In Abyssinia,* of which Loften Mitchell has written:

Abyssinia was troublesome to the critics. They liked it, but they stated bluntly that it was a little "too arty." It was too Caucasian; some critics said, too serious. In other words, they wanted a fast-moving "darky show."[10]

Bandana Land opened on Broadway in 1908, again with Williams and Walker. This was to be their last show, as Walker died three years later. "George Walker [was] the sleek, smiling, prancing dandy, and Bert Williams [was] the slow-witted, good-natured, shuffling darky."[11]

After his colleague became ill, Williams joined the famous Follies in 1910. Although he performed in blackface, he was the only black in an all-white company. His songs kept audiences roaring with laughter: "I'm in the Right Church but the Wrong Pew," "Oh Death Where Is Thy Sting?," "Come after Breakfast, Bring Along Your Lunch, and Leave before Suppertime." His acts ran less than half an hour, and he earned a salary equal to that of the president of the United States; yet on tour Williams had to live in third-rate segregated hotels, had to ride the freight elevator and take his meals in his room. He became ill while on tour with *Under the Bamboo Tree* and died in New York at the age of forty-seven.

Aubrey Lyles and Flournoy Miller were responsible for the birth of *Shuffle Along,* the biggest black musical success to hit Broadway in 1921. They were prolific writers and a comedy team that popularized vaudeville and revues. *Shuffle Along* played for over a year and toured two years. Its excellent cast included (1) Florence Mills, who became a star with her dancing and with a song called, "I'm a Little Blackbird Looking for a Bluebird"; (2) Josephine Baker, who later moved to Paris and became a theatrical success there, (3) William Grant Still, an oboist in the orchestra who was called the "dean" of black classical composers for his Afro-American Symphony and for being the first black to conduct a major American orchestra, the Los Angeles Philharmonic; and (4) Hall Johnson, who played first violin and viola in the orchestra, formed the famous Hall Johnson Choir, and recorded plays as musicals as choral director for RCA. *Shuffle Along*'s succession of unforgettable songs includes "Love Will Find a Way," "Bandana Days," and "I'm Just Wild About Harry" (later Harry S. Truman's presidential campaign song).

Two more talented composers to emerge in the early twentieth century were Noble Sissle and Eubie Blake. Sissle was noted for his lyrics and easy way of singing, Blake for his composing and ragtime jazz piano. Blake had this to say about the Broadway theatre:

I don't know but three (blacks on Broadway). The purse makes Broadway. Williams and Walker, Cole and Johnson, and Ernest Hogan, they were the big time shows. They played Broadway before, but it *wasn't* Broadway because it was dollar top (top price is $1.00). It didn't class as Broadway until it gets to two dollars and fifty cents. They played the same theatres, but it wasn't Broadway.[12]

Blake went on to say that he had started in show business at the age of nineteen with a traveling medicine show that was hitched to a horse and wagon. He had had to sing "them Tom songs" with his partner, Preston Jackson, for three dollars a week plus room and board. Blake and Sissle teamed up in *Chocolate Dandies,* which opened on Broadway in 1924.

Black musicals began to open up one after another. Lyles and Miller wrote *The Oyster Man* and *The Mayor of Dixie* for Ernest Hogan, a well-known actor, singer, and composer of that period. Lyles and Miller had to provide their own backing for the musicals, because whites were not interested in an "all darky show" that was conceived primarily for black audiences. Irving C. Miller, a brother of Flournoy Miller, produced the successful musical comedy *Put and Take* in 1921. The first play by Flournoy Miller and Lyles, *The Mayor of Dixie*, was rewritten and used as the book for *Shuffle Along*. They also wrote *Running Wild*, which popularized a new dance among blacks—the Charleston. The Plantation Revue opened first in a Harlem nightclub and then moved to Broadway starring Florence Mills. After that success, Mills appeared in *Dixie to Broadway*. In 1926 she opened in Harlem with *Blackbirds*, written especially for her by Eubie Blake with the wonderful song, "Memories of You."

Other musicals still kept coming: *Rang Tang* in 1927, *Keep Shuffling* in 1928; *Hot Chocolates* in 1929. In 1927–28 the black and white Florenz Ziegfeld production of the Jerome Kern musical *Showboat* had 572 successful performances before touring the country. *Showboat* featured "Ol' Man River," sung in the revival and in London by Paul Robeson. It should be noted here that the renowned jazz pianist Fats Waller wrote several of the musicals of that time, including *Keep Shuffling* and *Hot Chocolates*. Eileen Southern, in her book *The Music of Black Americans*, wrote: "According to Eubie Blake, there were so many all Negro shows on Broadway during the 1920s that two white song writers wrote a song entitled, "Broadway's Getting Darker Every Year."[13] Although these shows were written by black artists, on Broadway they were produced by whites. The audiences were predominantly white for Broadway houses, since blacks were not welcome to the downtown theatres. Many of these shows did play in Harlem theatres also.

UPTOWN AND DOWNTOWN: THE HARLEM RENAISSANCE

Theatres and night life flourished in Harlem in the twenties during the period known as the Harlem Renaissance, when blacks were in vogue. Alain Locke called it the "New Negro" period. It was the beginning of cultural and intellectual awakening, philosophical and sociological thought, and political awareness. Harlem was attracting young black artists and intellectuals from all around the country. Such names as Marcus Garvey, Bessie Smith, Aaron Douglass, Zora Neale Hurston, Countee Cullen, Langston Hughes, and Fletcher Henderson were talked about. Serious drama received as much attendance as vaudeville and musicals, and blacks, as subject matter for plays being written by blacks, were receiving recognition on the Broadway stage and in Harlem. Artists were working as never before. This period in the life of the black artist generated future developments for the American stage.

All-black musicals and vaudeville were still popular on the Broadway stage at this time, even though they were beginning to fade out. Harlem began attracting the crowds from downtown. James Weldon Johnson called this the "third theatrical period." The first period had begun after the Civil War, when blacks entered the professional stage, and the middle period had come in 1890, when blacks entered minstrel shows. From 1914 to 1930 Harlem saw more theatrical activity than at any other time until the 1960s. The move was to Harlem, but many artists were still living on the West Side between 50th and 70th streets. The Hotel Marshall on West 53rd Street became the pivitol point of the black artist's life. Actors, dancers, comedy teams, and jazz groups could always be found there in rehearsal, and most of them would take their acts to Harlem for performances. The thrust was Harlem. Johnson described life in the Harlem theatre as follows:

The Negro performer in New York, who had always been playing to white or predominantly white audiences, found himself in an entirely different psychological atmosphere. He found himself freed from a great many restraints and taboos that had cramped him for forty years. . . . So, with the establishment of the Negro theatre in Harlem, coloured performers in New York experienced for the first time release from the restraining fears of what a white audience would stand for; for the first time they felt free to do on the stage whatever they were able to do.[14]

One of the first theatres to open in Harlem in 1909 was the Crescent Theatre, located at 135th Street and Lenox Avenue. Its producer was a young writer and actor named Eddie Hunter, whose first comedy show was *Going in the Rages*. It was such a success that the theatre management asked him to do more. His reputation began to spread, and other artists began producing their plays with him. The Lincoln Theatre, which did vaudeville and movies, was down the street from the Crescent. Since the Lincoln emphasized films only, with low rates, the Crescent was soon forced to close.

Another black theatre that had been held in high esteem because of its productions and history was the Lafayette Theatre, founded in 1912 and located at 132nd Street and Seventh Avenue. This theatre presented plays that the middle-class Harlemites were quite proud to see. Although this house had to open its doors to vaudeville for financial reasons in 1913, it brought in one of the biggest successes, *Dark Town Follies of 1913*. This was the making of a new theatre. Productions from the Lafayette Theatre began touring in black houses in Washington and Philadelphia. In 1915 *Darkydom*, by Flournoy Miller and Aubrey Lyles, opened at the Lafayette to rave reviews. A critic wrote that "it looked like a Broadway opening."[15] This was the beginning of the movement of the theatre into its own communities, where stronger cultural relations would emerge during the soon-to-come Harlem Renaissance.

In April 1917, outside the Harlem district, white playwright Ridgeley Torrence's *Three Plays for a Negro Theatre* opened downtown at the Garden Theatre. This was the first time that a white writer wrote plays with any substance on the dramatically undeveloped potentialities of black life style. *Granny Maumee*, *The Rider of Dreams*, and *Simon the Cyrenian*, each in one act, made up an evening of plays geared for a Negro theatre. Johnson explained:

It was the first time anywhere in the United States for Negro actors in the dramatic theatre to command the serious attention of the critics and the general press and public. . . . The acting was fine; in several of the roles it was superb. . . . The praise of the critics was enthusiastic and practically unanimous.[16]

Loften Mitchell wrote:

Torrence's dramas must have played better than read. Certainly the opinions of such authorities as James Weldon Johnson and Edith Isaacs are not to be discounted. But Mr. Torrence's written text is embarrassingly clumsy, his Negro speech earthbound, and his themes seem remote from the actual experience of black people on this continent. While Torrence may have assisted in paving the way for the Negro to re-enter the downtown theatre, he also assisted in fathering a long line of neostereotype characters that ranged from the Emperor Jones to Abraham to Porgy to those of the present. Apparently, Torrence struck a norm that appealed to white theatregoers.[17]

Following is a scene from *The Rider of Dreams*. Husband (Madison) enters room. He is talking to his wife (Lucy).

Madison: (After a survey of the situation) What de boy do?

Lucy: He steal, dat what he do.

Madison: Um. What he steal?

Lucy: Mush. I tole him not to tech it.

Madison: Well, he was hongry, weren't he?

Lucy: Dat ain' de p'int. 'Tweren't his till I give it to him.

Madison: (Places the bag carefully by the doorway, throws his hat upon it, then seats himself at the table)
           Bring on dat mush. I'm tid'hd of dese fool doin's. Day ain't no git ahead wif um. If de boy wants mush let him git mush.[18]

The show opened on April 5, the day before the United States declared war against Germany. With the stress of war so great, attendance fell, and the show closed after only several weeks of running.

RACIAL AWARENESS IN THE THEATRE

Three worthy efforts were made previous to the Torrence plays. In 1910 Edward Sheldon had written *The Nigger*, which was produced in New York with an all-white cast. In this play the life depicted was of the white Southerners instead of black people, but the play increased awareness of the racial situation in America. In 1913 a play that was a historical pageant of black life, *The Star of Ethiopia*, was written and produced in New York by W.E.B. Du Bois, educator, editor, and director of publicity for the National Association for the Advancement of Colored People (NAACP) and author of *The Souls of Black Folk, An ABC of Color* and his *Autobiography*, which are still widely read today. Du Bois was the organizer of the Krigwa Players, a community theatre in Harlem during 1924–1927. His philosophy for this and other black performing groups was: (1) a theatre about us, (2) a theatre by us, (3) a theatre for us. In 1916 the Drama Committee of the NAACP and Du Bois produced *Rachel,* a three-act play on race by Washington, D.C., English teacher Angelina Grimke. The announcement on the program at the Neighborhood Playhouse in New York read: "This is the first attempt to use the stage for propaganda in order to enlighten the American people relative to the lamentable condition of ten millions of colored citizens in this free republic."[19] Here is one of the strong speeches from *Rachel.* Tom, brother of Rachel, is talking to his friend and Rachel.

Today, we colored men and women, everywhere—are up against it. Every year, we are having a harder time of it. In the south, they make it as impossible as they can for us to get an education. We're hemmed in on all sides. Our one safeguard—the ballot—in most states, is taken away already, or is being taken away. Economically, in a few lines, we have a slight show—but at what a cost! In the north, they make a pretense of liberality: they give us the ballot and a good education and then—snuff us out. Each year, the problem just to live, gets more difficult to solve. How about these children—if we're fools enough to have any?[20]

As the war continued, theatre work was on the decline for some, particularly in race and propaganda plays. By 1919, however, the Lafayette Theatre was beginning to glow again. The first production there under new producer Lester Walton, *The Octoroons,* introduced the Lafayette Players, a talented and explosive new company whose popular and original plays, as well as musical performances, did not take seconds from any companies around. But in 1921 the Lafayette Theatre again brought in vaudeville and motion pictures, leaving little work for the theatrical companies.

Three years after the Torrence plays, another white playwright was receiving criticism for his excellent play *The Emperor Jones.* Eugene O'Neill's production appeared at the Provincetown Playhouse in Greenwich Village in 1920. Mitchell commented on O'Neill and the play as follows:

This play, while offering one of the most magnificent roles for a Negro actor in the American theatre, is the first of a long line to deal with the Negro on this level. O'Neill obviously saw in the Negro rich subject matter, but he was either incapable or unwilling to deal directly with this matter. He chose, therefore, the Negro who would do the same things whites would do under similar circumstances—namely, establish an empire and exploit the people.[21]

Charles Gilpin played the Emperor. He was no stranger to theatre audiences; he had played with Williams and Walker, the Lafayette Players and the Chicago Company. The show was successful and later moved uptown for many months. O'Neill received honors for his play, and Gilpin was named one of the ten best actors in the New York theatre that year. But when the long run of the play ended, so did Gilpin's dramatic career, and he went back to his usual occupation, running an elevator.

O'Neill's career was just beginning. He went on to write other expressionist dramas: *The Hairy Ape* and *All God's Chillun Got Wings*, the latter with Paul Robeson and Mary Blair in the leads. Robeson was one of the most admired and well-known figures of his time. A scholar, actor, singer, and athlete, he played in *The Emperor Jones* on the stage and in the film production. Robeson also gave concerts of spirituals both at home and abroad. In 1930 his encounter with fascism moved him to become a spokesman for all oppressed people. As a result of his controversial political beliefs, he was blacklisted, his passport was revoked, and he spent over twenty years as a political exile.

All God's Chillun Got Wings does not deal with the problems of economics and militancy usual in plays on black subjects. Essentially the drama was about the social problems of a black intellectual lawyer who fell in love with a white gangster's mistress. Socially she was considered "white trash"; she tried to drag him down to her level by preventing him from becoming a lawyer. The script was published before the play was produced, causing newspapers to write outlandish articles in an attempt to discredit and destroy it. The opening audience was tense, and the critics disliked the work. John Gassner, in *Masters of the Drama*, stated:

At the time of production in 1924, as O'Neill noted, he received "anonymous letters which ranged from those of infuriated Irish Catholics who threatened to pull my ears off as a disgrace to their race and religion, to those of equally infuriated Nordic Kluxers who knew I had Negro blood, or else was a Jewish pervert masquerading under a Christian name in order to do subversive propaganda for the Pope."[22]

A year before the opening of O'Neill's play at the Provincetown Playhouse, a one-act play of black life was written by a black writer, Willis Richardson. *The Chip Woman's Fortune* opened on Broadway in May 1923. This was said to be the first serious play written by a black person for the Broadway stage. It was successful, but critic Alexander Woolcott wrote that a Negro folk theatre could never expect real recognition until it was able to offer a full program of satisfactory plays of Negro life. Also in the show were "jazz" interpretations of *The Comedy of Errors* by Shakespeare and *Salome* by Oscar Wilde.

In 1924 white playwright Paul Green won a Pulitzer Prize for *In Abraham's Bosom*, starring Rose McClendon and Frank Wilson. Green wrote more plays about blacks than any other white writer at the time. He collaborated with Richard Wright for the play adaptation of *Native Son* (1941). *Appearances* (1925) by Garland Anderson, was the first full-length black play to hit Broadway, but it had a short run. The huge cast of *Porgy* (1927) included McClendon and Jack Carter.

By the end of the twenties, new theatre groups had been organized: the Howard University Players, the Toussaint Players, the Harlem Experimental, and the Negro Art Theatre (which was located at the Abyssinia Baptist Church of minister and congressman Adam Clayton Powell). All these community-based theatre groups felt they could identify better with their own communities, especially because black audiences were still unwelcome in the downtown houses.

ENTERING THE DEPRESSION

Although the Depression of the 1930s ended many of the theatres in Harlem, the artists continued their work making the thirties an exciting and yet more creative period. The thirties started off in good fashion for the black performer. A cast of over a hundred was seen in white author Marc Connelly's Pulitzer Prize–winning hit, *The Green Pastures*. Sixty-five-year-old Richard B. Harrison headed the cast as "de Lawd." He learned the southern dialect from a white coach and made 1,568 straight performances. However, many blacks felt the play was abusive and disparaging to them and to religion. Mitchell had this to say:

The work, labeled "an attempt to see certain aspects of a living religion," describes a southern Negro child's image of the creation. God, for the child, is "de Lawd"—a frock-coated, ten-cent cigar smoking preacher, witnessing the fish fry, the crap-shooters, sinners, and Noah wanting a second keg of liquor to balance his Ark.[23]

The Green Pastures had an unusually long run of three years on Broadway and then toured the United States and Canada. It should be remembered that Jim Crow laws required black performers to room in third-rate houses and black audiences to occupy segregated seating in theatres. The large cast of *The Green Pastures* consisted of actors with established, recognized credentials: J. A. Shipp, Inez Richardson Wilson, Ivan Sharp, and musical director Hall Johnson and his choir. To many degrees this was a step backwards; "de Lawd" was considered a transmuted Uncle Tom, and minstrelsy had returned with black masks. No matter how degrading this racist play was, however, it did provide work for many black actors. In 1936 *The Green Pastures* was made into a film featuring Rex Ingram as "de Lawd" and Frank Wilson as Moses.

In 1933, while *The Green Pastures* was packing them in, the Negro Theatre Guild produced *Louisiana* by Augustus Smith. It also had a religious theme, but was more realistic, in that it depicted religious forces in the black area of Louisiana. *Run Little Chillun* by black dramatist Hall Johnson was a successful religious play staged on Broadway in 1933. It had 126 performances and a 1935 revival in Los Angeles to enthusiastic audiences for almost a year.

The wave of left-wing radical protest during the depression years strongly affected several white playwrights who saw the blacks in relation to American life and to their jobs and unions. *They Shall Not Die*, by John Wexley, was a dramatization of The Scottsboro Case. *Stevedore*, by Paul Peters and George Sklar, was a success downtown in the Village in 1934. It depicted the relation of blacks to their white labor union. Ingram, Carter, and Al Watts performed the leads in this protest melodrama. Mitchell wrote: "The play was so convincing that it is said tap dancer Bill Robinson while witnessing a performance, became so involved that he jumped to the stage and joined the dockhands in stoning the mob."[24]

LANGSTON HUGHES, 1902–1967

James Mercer Langston Hughes was probably the most prolific and influential black writer of our time. He devoted his life to writing and lecturing. His poetry, short stories, autobiography, song lyrics, plays, and books for young people have been widely read. Cultural and art institutions have been named in his honor. Hughes wrote about the places and people he knew—Harlem and its people. His poem "Notes on Commercial Theatre" best sums up his belief and has given direction for future black artists:

> You've taken my blues and gone
> You sing 'em on Broadway
> And you sing 'em in Hollywood Bowl
> And you mixed 'em up with symphonies
> And you fixed 'em
> So they don't sound like me. . . .
> But someday somebody'll
> Stand up and talk about me
> And write about me
> Black and beautiful
> And sing about me,
> And put on plays about me!
> I reckon it'll be me
> Me myself!
> Yes, it'll be me.
> 1936.[*][25]

Hughes's exemplary works are widely cited and his contribution to the black American theatre is unfathomable. He was the first black American writer to earn a living from writing. Hughes began seriously writing during the Negro Renaissance. He founded three little theatres: the Harlem Suitcase Theatre in New York; the Negro Art Theatre in Chicago, and the Skyloft Players in Los Angeles. He published his first play, *The Gold Piece*, in 1921. In 1935 *Mulatto* opened on Broadway. This was the longest running Broadway play by any black writer (373 consecutive performances). Other successful plays were: *Little Ham* (1935); *Troubled Island* (1936); *Simply Heavenly* (1957); *Tambourines to Glory* (1963); *Jericho-Jim-Crow* (1964); *The Prodigal Son* (1965). *Black Nativity* (1961)

---

[*] "Notes on Commercial Theatre," Copyright 1948 by Alfred A. Knopf, Inc. Reprinted from *Selected Poems of Langston Hughes*, by Langston Hughes, by permission of the publisher.

was produced for the Festival of the Two Worlds at Spoleto, Italy, and toured Europe in 1962, 1963, 1964, and 1965.

Vinette Carroll, artistic director of the Urban Arts Corps, directed *Black Nativity*. She talks about being asked to direct the play:

And Langston, of course had a big, big influence on me. He really gave me my first opportunity to direct because the theatre still hasn't gotten to the place where black directors direct white plays. Now, I don't mean to get to attaching any kind of value to it one way or the other. But Langston Hughes asked me to direct *Black Nativity*. That was the first commercial success that I had. [26]

Hughes was preparing to produce two new plays in 1967 just before his death. Woodie King, Jr., producer and director, was adapting Hughes's collection on Jesse B. Simple for the stage. King states in an article,

I finished the play, Simple's Blues, on April 3, 1967. Langston called me April 13, 1967 from the Hotel Wellington. At the time, he was working on a project for Harry Belafonte. He moved into the Wellington because, there, he could get away from the phone. It also gave him a chance to read the play immediately. He liked the play but felt it had too many characters. It would cost over $15,000. The producer had only $20,000 for the two plays, *Ask Your Mama* and *Simple's Blues*. . . . I understood what he was indirectly telling me and went to work on rewrites. I finished them on May 6, 1967. I called Langston immediately. He was in the hospital. He died May 22, 1967. [27]

PORGY AND BESS

In 1935 *Porgy and Bess* opened on Broadway. It was said by many critics to be the first American folk opera. Adapted from the novel to a play and then a musical by Dubose and Dorothy Heyward, *Porgy and Bess*, with music by George Gershwin, became an enormous success, running to 124 performances and tours around the country. It was revived successfully in 1942, 1953, and 1977. *Porgy and Bess* was considered by many blacks at that time, and even now, as degrading, exploitative and accepting of white paternalism. Yet others saw it as a hit; it meant "working." Todd Duncan, a music instructor at Howard University, played Porgy; Ann Brown, who held a fellowship at the Julliard School of Music, played Bess; and comedian and dancer John Bubbles was cast in the role of Sportin' Life. They were excellent, along with their huge cast. In an interview in *New Theatre*, Edward Morrow asked Duke Ellington why he said the music of *Porgy and Bess* was "grand." Ellington replied:

Why shouldn't it be? It was taken from some of the best and few of the worst. Gershwin surely didn't discriminate; he borrowed from everyone from Liszt to Dickie Wells (a jazz trombonist who was described as a "musician of romantic imagination"). [28]

Morrow then asked Ellington if he would ever write an opera or a symphony.

No, I have to make a living and so I have to have an audience. I do not believe people honestly like, much less understand, things like *Porgy and Bess*. The critics and some of the people who are supposed to know have told them they should like the stuff. So they say it's wonderful.[29]

Loften Mitchell reported himself unable to discuss the opera objectively, while Emory Lewis, in his book *Stages*, says this about it: "Touted as the first American folk opera, it was rather a tired, stereotyped musical of never-never land natives, happy with 'plenty of nuttin'."[30]

THE FEDERAL THEATRE

Although the thirties started out in a good fashion for black shows, they soon became "plenty of nothin" for black performers and the American theatre. It was estimated that more theatres closed around the country between 1935 and 1940 than ever before. Of course, the black artist was even harder hit.

Finally the picture changed. President Franklin D. Roosevelt and his wife Eleanor were concerned about the plight of the theatre and the unemployment that plagued its professionals. In 1935 the Federal Theatre was founded as part of the Work Projects Administration (WPA). Hallie Flanagan, a former professor of drama from Vassar, was the national director. The aim of the Federal Theatre was to employ theatre workers who were on public relief, in theatre-related jobs at salaries averaging $24 per week. Many black artists and workers were assigned to the Federal Negro Theatre, The Negro Youth Unit, The African Dance Unit, and the Lafayette Theatre. These special units gave black actors an opportunity to express and interpret their own culture.

Rose McClendon was chosen to direct the Lafayette Theatre unit; however, she felt she could do better as a performer and that the group needed more experienced direction. John Houseman, Broadway producer and president of the Phoenix Theatre, was then selected for the position. Houseman later teamed up with Orson Welles.

The first Lafayette Theatre production was Frank Wilson's *Talk Together, Chillun.* This show ran for twenty-nine performances, to over ten thousand people. Over the next two years the project came to pride itself on its costume, carpentry, and lighting departments; its backstage crew; and its house staff, custodians, and firemen. Oftentimes there was a directoral staff and a play-reading committee. The theatre provided apprenticeships in all areas of theatre. One distinguished playwright to emerge from its workshops was Theodore Ward, who wrote *The Big Fog,* one of the Lafayette Theatre's most powerful plays. It was produced in Chicago just prior to the dissolution of the Federal Theatre Project by Congress in 1939. It was again produced in New York but by Ward's Negro Playwright Company, which he formed in response to the loss of the backing for the Federal Theatre.

Houseman's second production, which opened in March 1936, was *Conjur*

Man Dies, by a well-known Harlem physician and novelist, Rudolph Fisher. The song, "I'll Be Glad When You're Dead, You Rascal, You" came from *Conjur Man Dies*, which eventually drew eleven thousand excited playgoers. Dooley Wilson played the lead, and Joseph Losy directed the comedy-mystery production. Wilson later starred in *Cabin in the Sky* (1941) with Ethel Waters, and in 1943 he was in *Casablanca* with Humphrey Bogart, where he played Sam. In *Casablanca* he made a song hit of "As Time Goes By."

"In Harlem's opinion, the Federal Negro Theatre's project production of *Macbeth*, at the Lafayette Theatre, was an eminent success."[31] On April 14, 1936, thousands of blacks celebrated this grand opening; this was one production for which white and black patrons stood together in line. Orson Welles directed *Macbeth*, and Jack Carter, remembered for his characterization in *Stevedore* and as Crown in the original production of *Porgy*, was Macbeth. Edna Thomas played Lady Macbeth and Canada Lee was Banquo, in a cast of 175. *Macbeth* eventually played to audiences of over ninety-eight thousand.

The Federal Theatre Chicago unit opened with *The Swing Mikado*, an adaptation from Gilbert and Sullivan that was later brought to Harlem. The popular comedians Bill Robinson and Eddie Green played the leads. Many new plays were being written and adapted for black audiences and supported by both races. But the WPA project did not last long enough for solid writers to be developed in the black units.

Canada Lee, a former boxer who had won acclaim from the Lafayette Theatre production of *Macbeth*, was cast as Bigger Thomas in Richard Wright's *Native Son*, which Orson Welles also directed. The strong disagreements between the writers and the producer of this controversial show are described in Houseman's book, *Run-Through*.[32] Two picket lines appeared at the final preview of *Native Son*. One, from the Urban League, was protesting the squalor of the book and the way it would shame black people; the other picket was from the Communist party, which could not forgive Wright for having defied party orders and refusing to rewrite certain sections of his book at its request.

Despite the protests, the play opened in March 1941 without incident. "Though it was excessively mechanical and coarse-textured, the play bared the fury and despair of a scorned and rebuked black man in more powerful images than Broadway was accustomed to."[33] Some of the cast from Welles's movie *Citizen Kane* and some from the Lafayette Theatre were in this huge production; there were three dozen stagehands and more than ten different stage sets. The show had 114 performances and received a nomination for the Drama Critics Award.

Othello with Paul Robeson was staged in August 1942 in Cambridge, Massachusetts, with Uta Hagen as Desdemona and Jose Ferrer as Iago, as a backers' production. Mary Webster, director of the play and a friend of Robeson, felt that if the play were done in America, it would be a landmark in American theatre. She, too, felt the prejudice of American audiences, but she persisted until she received backing for the play to open in Cambridge. Robeson was no stranger to

Othello, having performed it in London in 1930 with Peggy Ashcroft as Desdemona and promising actor Ralph Richardson as Roderigo.

Opening night of the Cambridge *Othello* was highly laudatory. The critics were enthusiastic.

Terming the Broadway production as staged by Margaret Webster "magnificent," John Chapman wrote, "it is an Othello of depth and body and rich sound, and in its title role Paul Robeson has majesty, . . . a voice whose resonance and deepness almost pass belief. . . . This new Othello with a Negro in the title role making love to a white Desdemona, is worlds apart from being a cheap theatrical trick. There is nothing cheap or titillating about it. It presents a black man of dignity and intelligence in the role of a black man of dignity and intelligence."[34]

Othello moved to Princeton, New Jersey, then to Boston and Philadelphia, all for two-week engagements. In October 1943 Robeson opened as Othello on Broadway, as "he brought the moor to life"[35] in 296 performances, a record for Shakespeare on Broadway. In 1959, at the age of 61, Robeson played *Othello* again in England.

THE AMERICAN NEGRO THEATRE

In spite of the advent of World War II, the black artists struggled to keep theatre alive in Harlem. The Rose McClendon Players, which Dick Campbell founded, offered a subscription series of three plays a year by black writers. Members were Frederick O'Neal, Helen Martin, Maxwell Glanville, and Ossie Davis; playwrights were Loften Mitchell, Abram Hill, and George Norford. The theatre closed in 1942. This led Hill, O'Neal, and Austin Briggs-Hall to organize the American Negro Theatre (ANT). Their first production of *Striver's Row*, by Hill, was an instant hit in Harlem; other productions of the ANT were *Natural Man*, by John Brown; *Garden of Time*, by Owen Dodson, and *Walk Hard*, by Hill. Harry Belafonte and Sidney Poitier were also members of this company.

The biggest hit for ANT was its 1944 Broadway-by-way-of-Harlem hit, *Anna Lucasta*, a play originally about Polish people, written by Philip Yordan. When the play did not go on the American stage, it was given to Hill's company. He adapted it to a black family situation, and it opened successfully in Harlem. *Anna Lucasta* had a successful Broadway run of almost three years with a cast completely different from the one that had opened in Harlem, including Ruby Dee, Canada Lee, Ossie Davis, Poitier, Maxwell Glanville, and Frank Silvera. *Anna Lucasta* was made into "two" motion pictures: the first was with an all-white cast—Paulette Goddard as lead—and the second with an all-black cast starring Eartha Kitt.

Next to follow *Anna Lucasta* was *Walk Hard*, which had a successful Broadway run. *Deep Are the Roots*, directed by Elia Kazan, successfully toured London. Ossie Davis opened in *Jeb*, by Robert Ardrey, which folded immediately. *Strange*

Fruit, by Lillian Smith, also saw sudden death. A black version of *Lysistrata* on Broadway also failed. *Street Scene,* by Langston Hughes, music by Kurt Weill, had a considerable run. In December 1947, ANT opened with *Rain* and *Almost Faithful,* directed by Harry Gribble. *Set My People Free* opened on Broadway with Canada Lee, Juano Hernandez, William Warfield, and William Marshall. *Our Lan',* by Theodore Ward, also opened in 1948, at the Henry Street Settlement, but moved to Broadway for only fourteen performances. The Henry Street Settlement, on the New York Lower East Side, is still in existence under the direction of Woodie King, Jr. *What the Winesellers Buy* and *For Colored Girls Who Have Considered Suicide/When the Rainbow Is Enuf* started at King's theatre before moving uptown and becoming off-Broadway and Broadway hits. The 115th Street People's Theatre in Harlem presented *Spring Beginning* by Oliver Pitcher, featuring many American Negro Theatre members: Maxwell Glanville, Ruby Dee, Austin Briggs-Hall, and Clarice Taylor.

THE NEW MUSICALS

Black musicals were prevalent in the first third of the century, but they became scarce on Broadway following the Depression. The forties had very few black musicals. Only three of any major significance were on Broadway: *Cabin in the Sky, Carmen Jones,* and *St. Louis Woman.*

Cabin in the Sky was the most outstanding, although it, too, repeated the familiar black stereotypes, in a story heavily laden with a religious theme, songs, dance, and comedy. The talented cast consisted of Ethel Waters, Rex Ingram, Todd Duncan, Dooley Wilson, Dick Campbell and the astonishing Katherine Dunham Dancers. *Cabin in the Sky* ran for 156 performances and a cross-country tour. Many of the songs from this musical have become standards, "Taking a Chance on Love," "Happiness Is Just a Thing Called Joe," and "Cabin in the Sky."

Five years later *St. Louis Woman,* by Arna Bontemps and Countee Cullen, was produced. It had a large cast, with Juanita Hall, Ingram, the dancing Nicholas brothers, Pearl Bailey, and Ruby Hill in the lead. Receiving mixed reviews the show had a short run.

The opera *Carmen Jones* was an all-black version of Bizet's opera *Carmen,* transplanted to the contemporary south. It had 231 performances and was later made into a motion picture starring Dorothy Dandridge. In the original cast were Luther Saxon, Napoleon Reed, Carlotta Franzell, Glenn Bryand, and drummer Cozy Cole. Although it delighted Broadway audiences, Loften Mitchell stated:

For all of its success and acclaim, *Carmen Jones* troubles me. Actually, it seems that in the adaptation, the Negro stereotype is sought. I feel this is more insidious than many other works that perpetuated the stereotype. *The Green Pastures, Porgy,* and *Porgy and Bess* seem to me to be works created by people who didn't know anything about Negroes.[36]

Other black musicals from the forties were *Mamba's Daughters* and *The Hot Mikado*. A few musicals with black performers in bit parts need mention here: *South Pacific*, with Juanita Hall cast as Bloody Mary; *Bloomer Girl*, with Dooley Wilson singing "Railroad Song"; and *Kiss Me Kate*, with Lorenzo Fuller singing "Too Darn Hot."

Broadway was hurting the uptown theatres. The forties were coming to an end and so was the American Negro Theatre and the 115th Street People's Theatre. Broadway had succeeded in taking black actors into "white" plays. The excitement that generated from the Black Theatre in the forties ended on a sour note, and it was not until the sixties that black musicals began their upswing.

THE 1950s THROUGH THE 1960s

The fifties and the first half of the sixties saw many all-black shows and major playhouses fold. The rise of television crippled the American theatre just as the film industry had when it was introduced to the American way of life. Broadway had begun to lose interest in the black protest theme, and some major playhouses were no longer profitable.

Not a single major commercial playhouse has been built on Broadway since 1932, but in the 1950s alone, dozens of opulent new playhouses were constructed by colleges and universities. Their promise for the future cannot be over-estimated."[37]

Virginia State College, Shaw University, Howard University, Morgan College, and Lincoln University were among the black colleges and universities offering courses in theatre training and playwrighting, a concept that was originated in the thirties by Randolph Edmonds, who was a member of the Intercollegiate Dramatic Association of North Carolina.

One of the oldest commercial theatres to survive this turmoil was the Karamu Theatre in Cleveland, Ohio. Founded in 1916 as the Gilpin Players, its Broadway stage alumni included Leonard Parker, Ivan Dixon, Melvin Stewart, Ron O'Neal and Robert Guillaume.

Black artists were moving away from Harlem and closer to the commercial scene. Blacks in the performing arts suffered a serious decline, as black plays were decimated on Broadway and moderated in the off-Broadway areas.

The Member of the Wedding opened in New York in 1950. Ethel Waters received star billing even though her role was that of a "glorified maid," but her performance became a hit. In March 1950 on Broadway, Helen Hayes headed a cast that included black actors in *The Wisteria Trees*, which was a watered-down adaptation of *The Cherry Orchard*. In April of the same year, Katherine Dunham and her dance troupe did remarkably well on Broadway. Off-Broadway saw Frank Silvera, one of the prominent black actors from the Harlem group, playing the lead in *Nat Turner*, a play that was well received and soon moved to Harlem to larger audiences.

The extent of work for the black actor was minimal. It was said that the black actor worked more regularly during the Depression than in the fifties. However, in October 1951, the Committee for the Negro Arts, composed of representatives from four Harlem drama groups, generated an awareness of black culture and helped support theatres in the area by exchanging mailing lists, costumes, and scenery. Its production calendar helped prevent scheduling conflicts. A group that parallels this committee today is the Black Theatre Alliance in New York City. These groups were responsible for several productions, all in Harlem. *A Medal for Willie*, by William Branch; *A World Full of Men* and *The Other Foot*, by Julian Mayfield; and *Alice in Wonder*, by Ossie Davis, were only a few.

The Apollo Theatre is a legend and a landmark, known worldwide as the Negro entertainment house for live music, dance, comedy, and big band shows. Sarah Vaughan and Ella Fitzgerald were a few of its weekly amateur night winners. The Apollo produced and staged *Detective Story* and *Rain*, starring Sidney Poitier in the latter.

Roger Furman organized the Negro Art Players in Harlem in 1952 and staged *Mooney's Kid Don't Cry*, by Tennessee Williams, and *The Quiet Laughter*, by Furman. The Negro Art Players included the late Roy Allen, Ed Cambridge, Ruby Dee, and Leon Bibb (the set designer); except for Allen, who became a television network technician, all of these members have become known for their excellence on the American stage. Furman is still in Harlem and heads the New Heritage Repertory Theatre.

Maxwell Glanville and Julian Mayfield formed the American Community Theatre, a theatre workshop that still exists in Harlem's YMCA, and presented Mayfield's *The Other Foot*.

It should be noted here that these groups formed in Harlem could not afford to pay their actors the minimum fee, and many of them had to take other jobs and hope for an off-Broadway, Broadway, or hit show that could come from their theatre group.

In September 1953 a Broadway play that involved blacks arrived. Louis Peterson's *Take a Giant Step* was an immediate success. Peterson was an actor turned playwright who had been a member of Clifford Odets's playwrighting workshop. His cast was made up of members of several of the theatre groups in Harlem: Frederick O'Neal, Helen Martin, Maxwell Glanville, Pauline Myers, Estelle Evans, and a high-school basketball player named Louis Gossett.

In October 1954 the off-Broadway Greenwich Mews Theatre presented William Branch's *In Splendid Error*. The Mews Theatre was known for its black productions; it also opened with *Trouble in Mind*, by Alice Childress, in 1955. In March 1957 the Mews Theatre produced Loften Mitchell's *A Land Beyond the River*, which was developed around the May 17, 1954, U.S. Supreme Court school desegregation decision, *Brown v. Board of Education of Topeka, Kansas*. *A Land Beyond the River* ran for over a year, and Glanville produced it in Brooklyn and in Newark, New Jersey.

On Broadway *Simply Heavenly*, a folk musical based on Hughes's book *Simple*

Takes a Wife, opened to a predominantly black audience but had only sixty-two performances.

Two important plays that changed the scope of black theatre in America were Lorraine Hansberry's *A Raisin in the Sun* and Jean Genet's *The Blacks. Raisin in the Sun* opened in New York in March 1959, after tryout runs in Chicago, Boston, and Philadelphia to rave reviews. *Raisin in the Sun* was written by a black female and had a black cast and a black director. It became the longest-running black play on Broadway since Langston Hughes's *Mulatto.* As a matter of fact, Hansberry chose the title from a Hughes poem, "Montage of a Dream Deferred." *Raisin in the Sun* was not just a play about a black family's situation and problems; the controversy became, Is it a black family show or a play that is universal? The play won the New York Drama Critics Circle Award over *Sweet Bird of Youth,* by Tennessee Williams. The all-soon-to-be-star cast consisted of Poitier, Dee, Diana Sands, Claudia McNeil, Gossett, Ivan Dixon, Lonnie Elder III, and Douglas Turner Ward and was directed by Lloyd Richards. The play had numerous tours and revivals and was soon made into a motion picture with many of the original Broadway cast.

The St. Mark's Playhouse, located on Manhattan's Lower East Side, is now the home of the Negro Ensemble Company. This playhouse used to be the scene of some exciting and trenchant black theatre, with such plays as *Funnyhouse of a Negro,* by Adrienne Kennedy; *The Slave* and *The Toilet,* by Leroi Jones; *Day of Absence* and *Happy Ending,* by Douglas Turner Ward. However, it was Jean Genet's *The Blacks* that attracted the theatregoers.

Genet stated in the introduction to his play that it was written by a white man and was intended for white audiences. His play opened in May 1961 and attracted enthusiastic audiences for over two years. Highly criticized and controversial, the play was so avant-garde and poetic that it took serious classical skills for black actors to pull it off. The cast that was selected did just that. Often Mitchell wrote that the show was more of a freak than a play, written with a sense of abandon and staged hostility.[38] The most talented cast of black performers was brought together, including James Earl Jones, Roscoe Lee Browne, Lou Gossett, Helen Martin, Cicely Tyson, Godfrey Cambridge, Raymond St. Jacques, Cynthia Belgrave, Maya Angelou, Charles Gordone, Vinnie Burrows, and Ethel Ayler. Many more came as replacements.

This was the beginning for young black writers; it was time to think seriously about their future on the American stage. Gordone began the framework for his future hit, *No Place to Be Somebody.* Burrows started her one-woman show on the black heritage. Peter DeAnda, who joined the cast later, started writing *Ladies in Waiting.* Robert McBeth, another cast member, went on to found the New Lafayette Theatre, and James Earl Jones later won a Tony Award for his performance in *The Great White Hope.*

Ossie Davis, an alumnus of the Negro Art Theatre and the Rose McClendon Players, wrote *Purlie Victorious,* which opened on Broadway in 1961. Davis and his wife, Ruby Dee, played the title roles. Their supporting cast of Godfrey

Cambridge, Helen Martin, Sorrel Boke, and Alan Alda received good reviews. Their efforts brought in the black audiences; they visited churches, socials, and fraternities urging support. *Purlie Victorious* was made into the film *Gone Are the Days* and into the smash musical *Purlie*. In the play Purlie remarks in the funeral service epilogue for Ol' Cap'n, "Being black is a thing of beauty, a joy, a strength, be loyal to yourself, your skin, your southern speech," and the blacks in the audience applauded. Purlie goes on to say, "Keep freedom in the family, do what you can for the white folks." Here some blacks in the audience booed, because they were tired of doing for the white folks when nothing was being done for them.

The civil rights movement played a major part in the Afro-American theatre and had a great impact on its performers. Rioting erupted; blacks and black leaders were being assassinated; busing was a major issue; and the Black Panthers were urging blacks to take up arms. In short, a sense of identity was being searched for, and blacks simply refused to be used by whites. Whites were unwelcome at black meeting places and social events.

Black artists were also seeking ways to define the world in their own terms. Two plays that deserve recognition for such definition are James Baldwin's *Blues for Mr. Charlie* and Leroi Jones's *Dutchman*, the latter receiving an Obie Award. Both plays opened in white downtown theatres and therefore, by the "black power" tenet, would not be considered black plays. These plays, written by blacks but geared for white audiences, castrated the oppressors and shouted obscene vulgarities at them like, "Hate you and hope you die, Whitey," while the black members of the audience remarked, "right on." Whites were confused, disaffected with the blacks they remembered from *Raisin*, *Purlie*, and *Porgy and Bess*. These black artists were seeing a new meaning for themselves in the sixties. No more, "Yas Sir," "Thank y'mam." The age of the revolutionary theatre was here; no more conked hair, cork, cake makeup, masks. Blacks became real people with real concerns and problems that could only be understood by their own people.

After a successful run off-Broadway, Leroi Jones headed for Harlem to take over what became the Black Arts Theatre. His two one-act plays had received harsh reviews at the St. Mark's Playhouse, and Jones felt that Harlem was where he should have been. The revolutionary concept was being heard. Jones said that the revolutionary theatre should force change; poet Haki R. Madhubuti (Don L. Lee) wrote, "We must destroy Faulkner, Dick, Jane, and other perpetuators of evil," while Robert McBeth was saying, "The only thing that we could possibly do as black artists is something new." Leroi Jones, who soon changed his name to Amiri Baraka, took his art to Harlem. He received funds from an antipoverty program to help establish his Black Arts Theatre in a brownstone house on 130th Street and Lenox Avenue. Baraka took his plays, poetry of black writers, black music, and dance to the neighborhoods in Harlem, performing in the streets, on the corners, wherever there were people. Two groups that have continued this concept with modifications are the Jazzmobile and Dancemobile in New York.

Baraka's concept of a black art theatre began to spread in the other Harlems of the country. Baraka became what white critics called an "angry young man," a racist, a revolutionary. The press first attacked his plays, *The Toilet* and *The Slave,* and after he moved uptown, they attacked his theatre revolutionary ideas of an all-black show (black actors painting their faces white to play white characters—minstrelsy in reverse). The Black Arts Theatre produced Baraka's plays *Dutchman, Experimental Death Unit #One, Black Mass,* and *Jello,* the latter about Jack Benny and Rochester.

Then the hawks from the OEO moved in and chopped off the funds. Again, this [misappropriation of funds] should have been expected. . . . And later, because of internal problems, the theatre was forced to close. But the Black Arts Group proved that there was a definite need for a cultural revolution in the black community.[39]

Black artists were beginning to develop a "black aesthetic" for this new black arts movement. Maulana Karenga from the West Coast set a ground of cultural ideologies together to give the black artist a set of criteria to live and work by. He felt that without a culture, black people were only a set of reactions to whites. With this movement, black theatre was beginning to pick up where the forties left off, with its social and "need to be with each other" hierarchy. Black social, or now revolutionary, plays were beginning to be produced in the small, dilapidated storefronts and loft spaces that were called black theatre.

Even the experimental off-Broadway playhouses were interested in producing some of these plays. The off-Broadway houses produced *Junebug Graduates Tonight,* by jazz musician Archie Shepp; *Who's Got His Own,* by Ron Milner; *The Amen Corner,* by James Baldwin (which eventually went to Broadway for a short run); and *The Prodigal Son,* by Langston Hughes. Woodie King made his debut as a producer in 1969, when in cooperation with the Chelsea Theatre Center, he produced *A Black Quartet* off-Broadway. He followed this with four black plays by Ed Bullins, Ben Caldwell, Leroi Jones, and Milner.

In 1967 a team of artists who had been working together in *Day of Absence* and *Happy Ending* came together and formed the Negro Ensemble Company. Douglas Turner Ward, Robert Hooks, and Gerald S. Krone leased the St. Mark's Playhouse for the company, with the help of funds from the Ford Foundation. Their season opened with a play by white author Peter Weiss, *Song of Lusitanian Bogey.* Many of the revolutionary artists attacked the playhouse for using a white writer and calling their theatre "Negro," but the company continued producing. The theatre grew in attendance because of the workshops in playwrighting, acting, and directing, a kind of growth that had not taken place since the days of the Lafayette Theatre in the thirties and forties.

The Negro Ensemble Company is still alive and has produced several plays that have reached Broadway, including *River Niger* and *First Breeze of Summer.*

Some of the best playwrights have had an opportunity to make their start there; Lonnie Elder, Jr., Paul Carter Harrison, Philip Hayes Dean, Joseph Walker, Leslie Lee, and Steve Carter are just a few. Many performers who are now on Broadway, in films, and on television were part of this splendid company of actors: Esther Rolle, Hooks, Roxie Roker, Clarice Taylor, Moses Gunn, Denise Nicolas, and Rosalind Cash.

Another black professional theatre, which also started in 1967, was the New Lafayette Theatre, located in the center of Harlem next door to the old Lafayette. Its founder and director, Robert McBeth, said the theatre kept the mood of the black revolutionary movement in the late sixties, "to raise the consciousness of the black people through our art." The theatre employed writer Ed Bullins, who was in residence at the Black Arts/West in San Francisco, an offshoot of Baraka's Black Arts Theatre. (The Black Arts/West was part of the Black House, which later became headquarters for the Black Panther Party for Self Defense. Huey Newton was a bit actor with this theatre group.) The New Lafayette Theatre opened its season with two revivals, *Who's Got His Own* and *Blood Knot*, by white South African playwright Athol Fugard. Fire destroyed the theatre, and while waiting for a new place, Director McBeth staged three of Bullins's plays at the off-Broadway American Place Theatre: *A Son, Come Home; The Electronic Nigger;* and *Clara's Ole Man*. Bullins, who was one of the most prolific writers of this period, won the 1968 Vernon Rice Drama Desk Award for this trio of plays. In December 1968 the New Lafayette Theatre reopened with Bullins's new play, *In the Wine Time*. It has been said of Bullins that seventeen of his plays were produced in one night during 1970. His plays have been presented at Lincoln Center, the New York Public Theatre, off-Broadway, and in various theatres around the country. In the early 1980s Bullins was conducting a writers' workshop at the New York Shakespeare Festival Public Theatre.

The New Lafayette Theatre performed ritual-type productions like those of the National Black Theatre, under the direction of actress Barbara Ann Teer. Black ritual productions would bring the audience and performers together through dance, song, sounds, or the spoken word, responding to one another with the emotions and feelings seen in black church services or musical jam sessions. The New Lafayette Theatre also produced two films and ran an agency for black writers. For some unknown reason, however, the theatre closed its doors in 1972, forcing its talented actors to go elsewhere. Some who later did well on Broadway, in films, and in television were Richard Wesley, playwright, and actors Whitman Mayo, James Gaines, Rosco Orman, Bette Howard, and Gilbert Moses.

The sublimation of the black theatre movement in the sixties could easily be transcribed as a recurrence of the black theatre movement of the forties. The sixties were producing new writers who were having their plays produced in new black theatres around the country: *Who's Got His Own*, by Ron Milner; *Ceremonies in Dark Old Men*, by Lonnie Elder, Jr.; *Requiem for Brother X* and its companion play, *Family Meeting*, by William Wellington Mackey. Black theatres in the sixties also began producing works of Nigerian playwright Wole Soyinka, including *Trials of Brother Jero* and *The Strong Breed*. The Negro Ensemble Company did his *Kongi's Harvest*, while South African Fugard was having success off-Broadway with his *Blood Knot*. White writers were capitalizing on black subjects for plays such as *Great White Hope*, by William Sackler, and Martin Duberman's *In White America*. Black performers were working, if not in black plays then plays with black characters, such as *Scuba Duba, Hair*, and the all-black production of *Hello Dolly*.

THE PAST AND THE FUTURE

By the end of the sixties and the beginning of the seventies, black theatre had gone through many phases and changes—some were good, while some left scars, as, in the forties. Black musicals of the sixties and seventies were more successful on Broadway than they had been in the fifties, returning to the forties' trend. To study the history of this exciting time, it would be imperative to compare the forties with the sixties (a book would be needed for the sixties alone); the seventies should be compared with the fifties. In both periods salvation for black theatre was found to come from the government, the guidelines for which were complicated and nebulous for the artist. But with all the glorification of *No Place to Be Somebody, Sty of the Blind Pig, River Niger,* and *The Wiz*—black theatre will still be considered "a sometime thing." If the past is a reliable guide to the future, white theatre historians will ignore the writer-turned-producer who had two productions on Broadway simultaneously, *Ain't Suppose to Die a Natural Death* and *Don't Play Us Cheap*—Melvin Van Peebles; the black producers of the Broadway productions of *The Wiz* (Ken Harper), *Bubbling Brown Sugar* (Ashton Springer), and *For Colored Girls Who Have Considered Suicide/When The Rainbow Is Enuf* (Woodie King, Jr.). History will forget the accomplishments of the few black directors that reached the Broadway scene—Gilbert Moses, Michael Schultz, and Lloyd Richards (who is now dean of Yale University's theatre department).

If black theatre in America is to survive, it must be both self-supported and community-supported. Black theatre, as with all ethnic theatre, should be part of the curriculum of all theatre schools in America; if not, it will continue to be underrated and continue the vicious circle of its struggle to exist. Black writers and their plays are still being exploited by white producers. Black performers are still seeking their identity both on and off stage. As long as white producers interpret the black experience as they see it and not the way it is written by black artists, the black theatre will remain the same. In the seventies white theatre establishments were getting more funds to produce black plays than black establishments, such as the Negro Ensemble Company, the New Federal Theatre, the Afro-American Total Theatre, and the National Black Theatre. The seventies delivered better-trained actors, technicians, and writers, but black theatre is at the same place as it was in the forties, fifties, and early sixties. Why? As long as white producers are paying for the ride, black artists will remain passengers who cannot understand where they have been, where they are now, and where they are going. But with all the fear, black theatre will wake up to say, like the character Tim in Ron Milner's play, *Who's Got His Own:*

Nothing's changed. Nothing important. Not a goddamn thing. But don't you worry, ol' man. Gone be a whole lotta' changes here. Soon. Damn soon. Yeh. You jus' keep watchin', ol' man. They gon' know we come from a long line of men—and got a long line comin', damn right. Damn right. Damn right.[40]

NOTES

1. Alain Locke, *The New Negro* (New York: Atheneum, 1969), pp. 23–24.

2. Sterling A. Brown, *Negro Poetry and Drama* (New York: Atheneum, 1969), p. 109.

3. James V. Hatch and Ted Shine, eds. *Black Theatre, USA: Forty-Five Plays by Black Americans, 1847–1974* (New York: Free Press, 1974), p. 34.

4. Doris M. Abramson, "America's First Negro Playwright," *Educational Theatre Journal* 20, no. 3 (October 1968), p. 375.

5. Loften Mitchell, *Black Drama* (New York: Hawthorn Books, 1967), pp. 33–34.

6. Ibid., pp. 33–34.

7. Robert C. Toll, *Blacking Up* (New York: Oxford University Press, 1974), pp. 26–27.

8. Ibid., p. 28.

9. Mitchell, *Black Drama*, p. 40.

10. Ibid., p. 51.

11. James Weldon Johnson, *Black Manhattan* (New York: Atheneum, 1975), p. 108.

12. Taped interview with Eubie Blake, Toronto, Canada, April 28, 1978, for Station WBFO Public Radio, Buffalo, New York.

13. Eileen Southern, *The Music of Black Americans: A History* (New York: Norton and Company, 1971), pp. 440–41.

14. Johnson, *Black Manhattan*, pp. 171–72.

15. *The New York Age* (newspaper) (August 1942), p. 531.

16. Johnson, *Black Manhattan*, pp. 175–76.

17. Mitchell, *Black Drama*, p. 69.

18. Alain Locke, *Plays of Negro Life* (New York: Harper & Bros., 1927), p. 29.

19. Ibid., p. 414.

20. Hatch, *Black Theatre USA*, p. 56.

21. Mitchell, *Black Drama*, p. 75.

22. John Gassner, *Masters of the Drama* (New York: Dover Publications, 1954), pp. 650–51.

23. Mitchell, *Black Drama*, p. 94.

24. Ibid., p. 98.

25. Langston Hughes, "Notes on Commercial Theatre" from *Selected Poems of Langston Hughes* (New York: Alfred A. Knopf, 1948).

26. Loften Mitchell, *Voices of Black Theatre* (Clifton, N.J.: James T. White Company, 1975), pp. 203–4.

27. Woodie King, Jr., "Remembering Langston," *Negro Digest* 18, no. 6 (April 1969): 95–96.

28. Roy Ottley, "The Negro Theatre, *Macbeth*," *New Theatre*, May 1936, p. 5.

29. Ibid., p. 18.

30. Emory Lewis, *Stages* (Englewood Cliffs, N.J.: Prentice-Hall, 1969), pp. 151–52.

31. Ottley, "The Negro Theatre," p. 24.

32. John Houseman, *Run-Through: A Memoir* (New York: Simon and Schuster, 1972).

33. Lewis, *Stages*, p. 155.

34. Dorothy Gilliam Butler, *Paul Robeson, All-American* (Washington, D.C.: New Republic Book Company, 1976), p. 109.

35. Langston Hughes and Milton Meltzer, *Black Magic* (New York: Bonanza Books, 1967), p. 202.

36. Mitchell, *Black Drama*, p. 120.

37. Garff B. Wilson, *Three Hundred Years of American Drama and Theatre* (Englewood Cliffs, N.J.: Prentice-Hall, 1973), p. 440.

38. Mitchell, *Black Drama*, p. 186.

39. Larry Neal, "The Black Arts Movement," *TDR Drama Review* T40 (Spring 1968): 32.

40. Ron Miller, "Who's Got His Own," in Woodie King, Jr., and Ron Miller, *Black Drama Anthology* (New York: New American Library, 1971).

BIBLIOGRAPHY

Books

Brown, Sterling A. *Negro Poetry and Drama*. New York: Atheneum, 1969. A historical study of poetry, drama, and fiction by African-American artists from 1700 to the 1930s.

Butler, Dorothy Gilliam. *Paul Robeson, All American*. Washington, D.C.: New Republic Book Company, 1976. Paul Robeson's biography in a new perspective.

Gassner, John. *Masters of the Drama*. New York: Dover Publications, 1954. A comprehensive and critical study of the drama from primitive times to the halfway mark of the present century.

Hatch, James V., and Shine, Ted, eds. *Black Theatre, USA: Forty-Five Plays by Black Americans, 1847–1974*. New York: Free Press, 1974. An anthology of forty-five black plays from 1847 to the present.

Hughes, Langston and Meltzer, Milton. *Black Magic*. New York: Bonanza Books, 1967. A pictorial history of black entertainers in America. Stories of artists, musicians, and performers from the plantation days to the mid-1960s.

Johnson, James Weldon. *Black Manhattan*. New York: Atheneum, 1975.

Lewis, Emory. *Stages*. Englewood Cliffs, N.J.: Prentice-Hall, 1969. The development of American theatre in each decade. Covers plays; playwrights, actors, and directors; Broadway, off-Broadway, and off-off-Broadway.

Locke, Alain. *Plays of Negro Life*. New York: Harper and Brothers, 1927.

———. *The New Negro*. New York: Atheneum, 1925, 1969. An anthology of fiction, drama, poetry, and music written by scholars of the Harlem Renaissance.

Miller, Ron. "Who's Got His Own." In Woodie King, Jr., and Ron Miller, Black Drama Anthology. New York: New American Library, 1971.

Neal, Larry. "The Black Arts Movement," *TDR Drama Review* T40. Spring 1968. A special quarterly from TDR Publications dedicated to the black theatre movement. Edited by Ed Bullins, with short one-act plays and commentaries from black artists and scholars.

Southern, Eileen. *The Music of Black Americans: A History.* New York: Norton and Company, 1971. History of black music in America from 1619 to the present, from the African heritage to the performers in symphony orchestras.

Toll, Robert C. *Blacking Up.* New York: Oxford University Press, 1974. A comprehensive history of minstrelsy and minstrel shows in the nineteenth century.

Wilson, Garff B. *Three Hundred Years of American Drama and Theatre.* Englewood Cliffs, N.J.: Prentice-Hall, 1973. This book combines the history of drama and theatre, showing the relationship between the two and how both were influenced by general historical events.

Articles and Interviews

Abramson, Doris M. "America's First Negro Playwright." *Educational Theatre Journal* 20, no. 3 (October 1968).

Blake, Eubie. Taped interview, Toronto, Canada, April 28, 1978, for Station WBFO Public Radio, Buffalo, New York.

King, Woodie, Jr. "Remembering Langston." *Negro Digest* 18, no. 6 (April 1969).

Mitchell, Loften. *Voices of Black Theatre.* New Jersey: James T. White Company, 1975. A series of taped conversations with performers, writers, directors, and producers of black theatres in the twentieth century.

Ottley, Roy. "The Negro Theatre, *MacBeth.*" *New Theatre,* May 1936.

3

Byelorussian-American Theatre

VITAUT KIPEL AND ZORA KIPEL

The topic. "Byelorussian Theatre in the United States" is without a doubt an entirely new subject in theatrical literature. Although Byelorussians have lived in the United States for many generations, their characteristics, views, needs, activities, and interests (theatre being one of them) have gone almost unnoticed in the literature or have very often been misinterpreted. The major cause of this situation has been that the group has often been confused or erroneously associated with the neighboring Slavic groups, Poles and Russians. Well, these are mistakes of the past. The picture is changing and past mistakes, wherever possible, are being corrected. Certainly the subject treated here, Byelorussian theatre," will help to identify Byelorussians, make some of their interests understood, and characterize their activities. The materials assembled here are mostly new and have been collected from Byelorussian-language publications, newspapers, publicity flyers, and so on, and also from interviews and from manuscripts of producers, performers, and community leaders who were involved in stage productions at various times in various places. Most of these primary documents are kept in the archives of the Byelorussian Institute of Arts and Sciences.

Because Byelorussia and Byelorussians are relatively little known in America, a short historical note seems appropriate here.

THE HOMELAND

Byelorussia is one of the three East Slavic nations located in the area in Eastern Europe bordered by Poland in the west and Russia in the east, Lithuania in the northwest, Latvia in the north, and the Ukraine in the south. Byelorussian history begins in the ninth century, when historical sources mention the tribal duchies of the Dryhavichy and Palachanie. These, as well as some other tribal states, developed during the tenth, eleventh, and twelfth centuries into a series of principalities, among which those of Smalensk, Turau, Pinsk, and Polack are prominent. It was then that the ethnic, cultural, and national characteristics of the Byelorussians were crystallized.

The thirteenth and fourteenth centuries witnessed the gradual process of consolidation of Byelorussian principalities and territory into the newly emerging state, the grand duchy of Lithuania. This state, in the course of time, became a true Eastern Slavic Empire, also incorporating some non-Slavic lands such as Samoigitia and others. In the Grand Duchy of Lithuania, the Byelorussian culture and language were the essential factors. In 1386 the Union of Kreva was concluded between the Grand Duchy of Lithuania and Poland. Thus Byelorussia shared the external political history of the Grand Duchy of Lithuania from 1386 until 1795, when the entire Byelorussian territory, as a result of the partitions of the Polish-Lithuanian Commonwealth, was occupied by Russia. Although the Byelorussian culture was predominant in the Grand Duchy of Lithuania and the Byelorussian language was the official language of the duchy, Polish cultural influences spread widely into Byelorussian territory, and toward the end of the seventeenth century, the Polish language replaced the Byelorussian and Polish cultural influence on all the Byelorussians was strong. With the takeover of Byelorussian territory by the Russians, an enormous process of Russification began. The Eastern Orthodox Church and the recently established secondary schools became the major tools of Russification. As a result of these cultural influences from the West and the East, the Byelorussian people lost their upper classes almost totally. The masses, however, remained almost intact and untouched by these foreign cultural influences and thus maintained their strong Byelorussian ethnicity.

In the second half of the nineteenth century, the process of national political revival was begun. The movement was at first primarily literary; however, beginning with the years 1861–1863, during the uprising in Byelorussia under the leadership of Kastus Kalinouski, strong voices resounded in favor of Byelorussian self-determination. The Byelorussian revival gained momentum in 1905–1906, when the Byelorussian political parties were formed and Byelorussian newspapers began to appear in Vilna. The national revival made considerable progress during the decade preceding the revolution of 1917. Byelorussian patriots, led by the brothers Luckievich and others, spread their influence all over Byelorussia and became active political forces bent upon the establishment of an independent, modern Byelorussian state that would comprise all territories inhabited by Byelorussians. The independence of Byelorussia was proclaimed March 25, 1918. Nine months later, or January 1, 1919, the Soviets proclaimed their own Byelorussian state, the Byelorussian Soviet Socialist Republic. A struggle followed between the two groups. However, although the national Byelorussian movement did not lack momentum, it could not resist the overwhelming power of the Red Army. As a result of the events of World War I, the Byelorussian territory was divided among several states, the major parts being in Poland and in the Soviet Union. In 1939 both sections of Byelorussia were united in one Soviet republic, and in 1945 the Soviet Republic of Byelorussia became a charter member of the United Nations and has been a UN member ever since. Today Soviet Byelorussia has a population close to 10 million, with over 1,250,000 in its capital, Minsk.

BYELORUSSIANS IN THE UNITED STATES

Byelorussians settled in this country even in colonial times. Although many of them contributed substantially to cultural development in America, they did not project a special visibility and were not recognized as a distinct ethnic group; in fact, many of them were identified with other ethnic groups. For example, Thaddeus Kosciuszko, well known as a Polish patriot, was born of a Byelorussian family in Byelorussia; Francis Dzerozhynski, one of the founders of the Catholic educational system in the United States, was born in Eastern Byelorussia and was a teacher in many Byelorussian towns before coming to the United States; Henryk Dmachouski, well-known sculptor who created the busts of Kosciuszko and Thomas Jefferson in Washington and General Pulaski's monument in Georgia, was born near Vilna in the Byelorussian territory.

The mass migration of Byelorussians to the United States began at the turn of the century and reached its climax shortly before World War I. Russian records show that about .7 million Byelorussians came to this country during the time of mass immigration, from the Vilna, Minsk, Brest, Pinsk, Grodno, Vitebsk, Bialystok, Mogilev, Gomel, and Smalensk regions. Unfortunately, U.S. immigration statistics and census data categorized Byelorussians as "Russians," "Poles," or "others," and lately as emigrants from the "USSR," instead of listing them as a separate ethnic group. Post-World War II Byelorussian immigrants, about .1 million of them, have had some degree of success in correcting past mistakes and injustices towards the Byelorussian ethnic group. They succeeded, for example, in identifying Byelorussia as their country of birth on their U.S. passports, rather than Russia, or USSR, or Poland. But this is only a small fraction in comparison with what remains to be done.

Presently the largest concentrations of Byelorussians are in New Jersey, New York City, Cleveland, Detroit, Chicago, Los Angeles, Maine, Indiana, and Pennsylvania.

BYELORUSSIAN THEATRE

There is something in the sensitive, romantic nature of Byelorussians that has always indicated a need for drama. From the earliest pre-Christian times, various religious rites and ceremonies and folk customs, such as Zavivannie Biarozki (rite of spring), Kupalle (midsummer festivities), Dazhynki (harvest feast), Kalada (winter celebrations), Dziady (feast to commemorate the dead), were dramatized. The traveling musicians, or *skamarokhi*, were the earliest performers. They wandered from town to town and from village to village, accompanied often by trained animals, chiefly bears, entertaining the people and enticing them to participate.

In spite of the advance of Christianity, the traditional pagan rites, though adapted to fit the Christian holidays, still retained strong pagan overtones, which remain until the present time, for example, *kaladoushchyki* (carollers) during Christmas time; *valachobniki* during Easter celebrations; Kupalle (Kupala's

Night), corresponding to St. John's Eve festivities or midsummer festivals; and other less important ones. The Christian era brought some new aspects for dramatization. Purely religious nativity scenes, the Adoration of the Magi, and the shepherds were first played in the church. Then these activities were transplanted to the churchyard, to the village square, and to the streets. This was the beginning of the oldest form of the Byelorussian theatre, batlejka, the puppet show.

The name Batlejka derives from the name Bethlehem. In the beginning Batlejka shows were strictly religious, depicting Biblical scenes and Biblical personalities. As time passed Batlejka began to add some attractions: interludes, scenes from everyday life. The setting of the Batlejka shows was simple: a large wooden box built like a doll house, one to three stories high and with a steeple. The wooden puppets, painted and dressed up, were moved along slits in the floor. Byelorussian ethnographers of the nineteenth century, such as Romanov, Shein, and others, describe different types of batlejkas, their characteristics, and their distribution and provide texts of the puppet shows, costumes of the dolls, and so on. These books are available at large research libraries in the United States, such as the New York Public Library, the Library of Congress, Harvard University, and others. The development of the batlejka theatre was at its peak in the eighteenth and nineteenth centuries, and it continued, though not prominently, until the Bolshevik Revolution. Almost at the same time as batlejka theatre developed, another form of Byelorussian theatre emerged: the school drama.

SCHOOL DRAMA

With the establishment of universities, academies, and monastery schools in the sixteenth century, drama as an instructional aid was introduced in these schools. The plays, first chiefly in Latin with religious, didactic themes, were supplemented soon by the *intermedyi* (interludes). These interludes were in Byelorussian and usually were light satires on everyday life, humorous sketches, comic acts, or jokes. The texts of these school plays and interludes were also used in Batlejkas. Batlejka, incidently, was also very often performed by students during vacations.

In the eighteenth century court theatres, sponsored by the Byelorussian nobility, flourished in the Byelorussian territory and produced elaborate shows. These theatres employed professional actors, singers, and dancers imported from Italy, France, and Germany, but most of the talent was drawn from the local people. The most famous court theatres were in Niasvizh and Sluck, sponsored by the Radzivills; in Horadnia (Grodno), sponsored by the Zizenhaus; and in Slonim, sponsored by the Aginski.

The onset of the nineteenth century marks the beginnings of the modern Byelorussian theatre, and Vincuk Dunin-Martsinkevich could and should rightly be called its father. A writer, playwright and poet, Vincuk Dunin-Martsinkevich was also an actor and director-producer. His opera *Sialanka* (The Peasant Woman), written in 1846 and put to music by Stanislaw Moniszko, was performed for the first time in Minsk in 1852. The author-composer also directed and produced the opera. Dunin-Martsinkevich's play *Pinskaya Shlakhta* (The Nobles of Pinsk) is considered a classic and has become the best known and most popular Byelorussian play. Even up to the present time it is successfully presented and well received in Byelorussia and by the Byelorussian community in the United States.

The development of Byelorussian theatre and Byelorussian culture was at a standstill almost half a century after the insurrection of 1861–1864, led in Byelorussia by Kastus Kalinouski. Although the Byelorussian language had been banned in 1839, a few years preceding the insurrection, and again after the insurrection and manifestation of Byelorussian cultural life was practically eradicated, this period in Byelorussian history was described by one British journal as follows:

Such is the picture of a people living in Europe, in the gloomiest spot of dark Russia. Yet it was these very people who after the subjugation of the Ukraine by the Tartars, and the ruin of the northern Republics by the Muscovites continued from the 16th Century uninterrupted intercourse with Western Europe, yea even transplanted the latter's Reform ideas into its own soil. To these people who for long had been a centre of culture for Russia, up to the time of the great Lomonosow, are now denied their most sacred rights. They are kept in the deepest darkness, possessing at present under the iron rule of the White Czars a smaller number of schools than they had in the 16th Century. Indeed, the people of White Russia have been pushed back by the Muscovite regime to three centuries before the 16th Century, so that today they exist in purely Middle Age conditions.[1]

The beginning of the twentieth century, however, brought enormous changes to Byelorussia. The ban on the Byelorussian language was lifted in 1905; Byelorussian newspapers began to appear; elementary texts were allowed to be published; and Byelorussian political parties were formed. The rebirth of Byelorussian culture began in earnest. This period is considered the most fruitful in modern Byelorussian history and is called the period of *Nasha Niva,* the name of the newspaper that contributed the most to the awakening of Byelorussian national identity. Development of drama and theatre followed. In 1907 Ihnat Buinitski formed an amateur Byelorussian theatre, which in 1910 became a professional theatre.[2] He traveled with this theatre from Vilna to Petersburg, from Warsaw to Polack, and to almost all cities in Byelorussia. Also in Vilna, Francishak Alachnovich, the most prolific playwright and most distinguished theatre historian, formed a drama club and performed in various Byelorussian cities. Alachnovich, Buinitski, and a couple of years later Uladyslau Halubok opened the way to the formation and development of a wide network of Byelorussian theatres. The repertories of the first Byelorussian theatres were rather diversified, and in addition to presenting original Byelorussian plays, they included many translations from the works of the Russian playwright Anton

Chekhov, the Polish playwright Elisa Orzeszkowa, and others.[3] The performances were supplemented often by folk singing, folk dancing, and poetry reading. Soon Byelorussian dramatic theatrical repertory began to appear in abundance; Alachnovich wrote numerous plays; Janka Kupala wrote *Paulinka, Raskidanaje Hniazdo* (Ruined Nest); and then a whole series of new writers and new theatrical talents began to appear and the modern Byelorussian theatre emerged.[4]

Byelorussian independence was proclaimed March 25, 1918, as a result of the intensive political activities of the Byelorussian National Intelligentsia, concentrated chiefly in Vilna and other large cities. They were led spiritually by Jazep Losik and the powerful group of intelligentsia from Petrograd University. Although this aspect is as yet barely analyzed, the revival and activities of the Byelorussian National Theatre during this political process from 1905 to 1907, when Buinitski and Alachnovich began their theatres, certainly played a very important role. The theatre had a great influence on the development of the national consciousness of the Byelorussians. With the proclamation of the Byelorussian independent state, the Byelorussian Democratic Republic, the theatre continued to grow. New leaders, such as Usevalad Fal'ski, Flarian Zhdanovich, Eustignei Mirovich, and others appeared.

The growth of the Byelorussian theatre continued when the Byelorussian Soviet Socialist Republic was proclaimed January 1, 1919. During the first decade of the Soviet regime, the leadership of the Byelorussian Soviet Republic was still nationality conscious. The prime objective of the national Communists was to develop and build a Byelorussian national state with cultural and economic independence. National art and culture were flourishing. The theatre was advancing rapidly. In the early twenties the First Byelorussian State Theatre was opened in Minsk; then the Second Byelorussian State Theatre was established in Vitebsk; and numerous studios and smaller theatres were formed. The Byelorussian repertory was at its peak; this was the true period of renaissance for the Byelorussian theatre. However, the strong resurgence of Byelorussian nationalism, with its tendencies toward separatism in future development of culture as well as in the state, did not coincide with the views of the party, and thus in the years after 1930, a systematic suppression of Byelorussian national art and theatre followed. Most of the plays written during the twenties and many of the authors have disappeared, and the Byelorussian theatre forcefully and gradually became another Soviet theatre, with only insignificant elements of Byelorussian national culture surviving.

The theatre in Soviet Byelorussia today, although with a repertory rather limited in nature and very censored politically, continues to grow. One of the latest guidebooks to the Minsk theatres describes the following: The Janka Jupala Byelorussian State Academic Theatre, the State Academic Bol'shoi Theatre of Opera and Ballet of the B.S.S.R., the Gorky State Russian Drama Theatre of the B.S.S.R., the Republican Young Spectators' Theatre, the State

Puppet Theatre of the B.S.S.R., and the Minsk State Musical Comedy Theatre of the B.S.S.R. This book also provides an extensive listing of the theatres' repertories.[5] According to the Byelorussian Soviet Encyclopedia published in 1973, there are fourteen active theatres in the B.S.S.R.[6]

Byelorussian theatre outside of Soviet Byelorussia was active in Germany, especially during the 1940s and early 1950s, when several theatrical groups were performing throughout Germany and two theatrical studios were in operation in Bavaria. Also, in France, Byelorussian theatrical performances were initiated in the late 1940s by one man, Auhen Kavaleuski, former artist and student of the Minsk State Theatre. In association with the Society of Byelorussian Youth in France, he organized a theatrical studio, and they performed in several cities. Kavaleuski was also a very gifted playwright and published numerous plays. Unfortunately he died at an early age.[7] Byelorussian theatrical activities in Great Britain, Belgium, Austria, and Australia were associated exclusively with the school programs. Professional and semiprofessional Byelorussian theatres are active in Canada and the United States.

BYELORUSSIAN THEATRE IN THE UNITED STATES

It is hard to tell exactly when Byelorussian-sponsored stage performances began in the United States. It is certain, however, that theatrical performances oriented toward Byelorussian immigrants in large industrial cities, primarily New York, Chicago, Philadelphia, Baltimore, Pittsburgh, Detroit, and Cleveland, were given in the early decades of this century.[8] Theatrical pieces by Gogol, or such as *Zaporozhets za Dunajem*, were understood and liked by Byelorussians as well as Ukrainians, who were the ones most instrumental in staging these shows. From interviews with Byelorussians of the pre-World War I period of immigration, it appears that Byelorussians preferred the Ukrainian plays to the Russian classics because the former were closer to their understanding. Only when the Russians presented some popular plays did the Byelorussians attend. To attract them to these shows, the advertising aimed at Byelorussians usually stressed Byelorussian geographical names with the explanation that the show would remind them of the old country or that their countrymen were members of the cast.

The earliest Byelorussian-sponsored stage performances, so far as we could determine, began to appear in the middle 1920s in Chicago.[9] Chicago in the early twenties became the center of Byelorussian political and cultural activities because of the great concentration of Byelorussian political leaders who came there after World War I. One such early performance was held on March 7, 1926, and was sponsored by the White Russian National Association of America. The stage show included a play, *Farmer's Wedding,* in addition to a concerto program and reading of Byelorussian poetry. Similar shows were organized in the

1930s and later years. [10] Byelorussian shows were also organized in New York, Philadelphia, and Baltimore. The emphasis in these shows, however, was on poetry and dramatic reading.

The war years witnessed more Byelorussian variety shows in which dancing and singing were included. The economic factor was the driving force in presenting Byelorussian theatre and variety. Initiated mostly by Soviets or pro-Soviet elements among older Byelorussians, these shows were followed by solicitations of financial gifts to help occupied Byelorussia and to help the Soviets to liberate the Byelorussian Republic. Such an approach was quite successful, and the Soviets were able to collect substantial sums of money.

The post-World War II period opened a new page in the history of the Byelorussians in the United States. As a consequence of the events of the war, about .1 million Byelorussians came to the American shores. These were people from all walks of life: cultural, political, industrial, and agricultural. Almost 100 percent of them had either high school or university educations. There was no question of their joining the existing organizations, consisting mostly of Byelorussian membership but wearing Russian or Slavic titles. The new immigrants began to form their own organizations. One must say, however, that at the beginning, for instance in the years 1950–1953, although strong attempts were made to find a common language with the older countrymen, larger contacts were never established. Hundreds of thousands of Byelorussians remained in the Russian-labeled organizations and churches. Many of them were hostile to the newcomers, and many were leftist.

The lack of closer contacts between the two waves of Byelorussian immigration was due chiefly to the reasons for leaving Byelorussia. The new wave of immigration was for political reasons, whereas the first wave of Byelorussian immigration had been almost entirely for economic reasons. The Byelorussian immigrants of the pre-World War I period were almost illiterate; the immigrants of the post-World War II period were almost all educated. New immigrants, through their organizational activities and to a certain degree through the theatre, were trying to show the American public the struggle of Byelorussian ethnicity and nationalism against advancing Russification in Soviet Byelorussia. They were also advocating the ideal of a Byelorussian independent state. During the late forties and early fifties, new Byelorussian immigrants formed organizations in several states and major cities of most industrial states, such as New Jersey, New York, Ohio, Illinois, and Michigan, which had large concentrations of these people. The theatrical activities went hand in hand with the organizational activities, and very often shows were arranged to mark the formation of a new organization.

Formation of theatrical groups was controlled mainly by the availability of professional leadership and numbers. What made the job easier was that prior to coming here many Byelorussians had been in displaced persons (DP) camps in Germany, where theatrical activities were at a high peak, and these people were aware of the available resources. An additional advantage was that the post-World War II wave of immigration consisted mostly of younger people who had gone to Byelorussian schools, many of whom had participated in theatrical activities in Byelorussia or in Germany. The leadership of these groups consisted mostly of experienced professionals or semiprofessionals. From the beginning, however, it was clear that the Byelorussian theatre could not support a permanent professional group. The community was not large enough and not sufficiently concentrated in any one locality to be able to provide adequate financial support for such a group. Thus part-time theatre groups were more practical and viable.

BYELORUSSIAN PROFESSIONAL ARTISTS AND WRITERS IN THE UNITED STATES

As a consequence of the events of World War II, many Byelorussian artists from the Minsk State Theatre and other Byelorussian theatres migrated to the United States. They settled in various cities, which had varying concentrations of Byelorussians, and for very practical reasons they could not form a Byelorussian professional theatrical group. However, they became catalysts and leaders in the organization of Byelorussian theatrical activities where they lived.

Alimp Mialencieu was one of the first Byelorussian artists to arrive during the late 1940s. He started as an actor in Minsk in the early 1920s and for a while was working with the Byelorussian Traveling Theatre (Halubok's theatre). Mialencieu's entire family was also connected with the theatre. In California the Mialencieus organized a theatrical ensemble that was mostly a variety group, presenting only incidental stage dramatic pieces. Nevertheless, their dramatic readings and presentations of short theatrical plays were very popular among Byelorussians and other Slavic groups. Mialencieu's group, which lasted until the middle 1950s, was also very warmly received by Byelorussians in New Jersey and New York.[11]

The activities of Mikola Kulikovich-Shchahlou, a well-known Byelorussian composer and arranger who settled first in New York, then in Cleveland, and later in Chicago were also very successful. In each city he organized theatrical and stage groups and left impressive records of his activities. He died in Chicago in 1969.[12] Other professional artists were Barbara Verzhbalovich, who helped a great deal in organizing a theatrical youth group in New York City; and Natalia Chemerisova, also in New York; Nadzeia Grade-Kulikovich in Chicago; and Lidzia Janushkevich-Nedwiga in Passaic, New Jersey. A large number of former Byelorussian artists settled in South River, New Jersey. Among them were Viachaslau Selach-Kachanski, former director of the Byelorussian State Theatre in Minsk; his wife Olga, a professional dramatic actress; Irene Zhylinski-Cupryk; Vila Sauchanda-Lewczuk; and Vera Zarutskaja, all of the Minsk Theatre, and Piatro Niadzviedski, well known to the Byelorussian community for his theatrical activities in Germany. All of these professionals have helped to organize Byelorussian stage and theatrical activities.[13]

The Byelorussian community was also fortunate to have among the post-

World War II immigrants many professional writers who helped a great deal with the repertory. Among these were Natalla Arsiennieva-Kushel, a Byelorussian poet who first published in Vilna in 1921. Her latest collection of works was published in New York in 1979; Michas Kavyl, a well-known Byelorussian poet who spent several years in a Soviet concentration camp for his ideas; Janka Zolak, poet and editor of many Byelorussian publications; Ales Zmahar, prolific writer of children's plays; Janka Juchnaviec, romanticist poet and playwright; Mikola Celesh, novelist and playwright; and others. The help of these people with the new repertory was substantial.

SEMIPROFESSIONAL THEATRE

South River, New Jersey

The history of the post-World War II Byelorussian theatre in the United States begins in 1950 with the production of Shchaslivy Muzh (Happy Husband), a classic by Alachnovich. The production was sponsored by the Byelorussian Theatrical Studio, which was affiliated with the United Byelorussian-American Relief Committee. The studio and the first performance were the results of the untiring work of Viachaslau Selach-Kachanski.[14] After arriving here from a DP camp in Germany, Selach-Kachanski organized the Byelorussian Drama Club. Soon he enlarged the club and formed a theatrical studio, for which he recruited over fifty members. He gave theoretical lectures on theatre arts, history of the Byelorussian theatre, characteristics of the Byelorussian stage, and classes on stage performance, mime, voice, and intonation. He also began to work on the play, and in the fall of 1950 he had his first performance in the United States. This comedy in four acts had first been played in Vilna in 1922 and has since been a frequent production on the Byelorussian stage. The performance was excellent, a complete sell-out of about five hundred tickets. Its success was largely attributed to the presence of Olga Kachanski and Irene Cupryk, both professional artists from Byelorussia.

Selach-Kachanski's next big production was another Byelorussian classic by Vincuk Dunin-Martsinkevich, Pinskaia Shlachta, which was first performed in Byelorussia in 1886. In South River Pinskaja Shlachta was staged on June 19, 1955.[15] Selach-Kachanski himself played the key role of Kutorha, although he also had a replacement in the person of Wital Cierpicki. Again his production was very successful, and the play was repeated several times. He also presented a vaudeville show, Niasmiely Zhanich, which featured the well-known performers Cupryk, Ihar Scors, Vala Vojciechowski, Michas Sienka, and Luba Uryuski, and another excellent show depicting harvest ceremonies in Byelorussia.[16] All performances were held in Shack's Hall which over the years became a landmark for the Byelorussian community in South River.

The success of Selach-Kachanski's plays is certainly due to his high profes-sional standards and requirements for both the stage and the artists. (One of the authors of this article was a member of his theatrical group in Germany.) But the success must also be attributed to the enthusiasm and dedication of young Byelorussians, who wanted to do their best to popularize Byelorussian culture. Many of the South River performers had been with Selach-Kachanski in his theatrical group in Germany. Among the early performers were Sienka, Kastus Worth, Lavon Shurak, Vera Kous, Cupryk, and Zina Sapanienka. All the stage designs in South River, for Selach-Kachanski's performances as well as for a multitude of later ones, were prepared by the very talented artistic couple, Luda and Aleh Machniuk. The original designs were constructed for *Pinskaia Shlachta*. Selach-Kachanski's work with the studio continued, although more along choreographic lines.

While Selach-Kachanski was working on his plays, another theatrical variety group was formed in South River under the leadership of Peter Niadzviedski.[17] This group, however, did not last too long. In the years after Selach-Kachanski's departure from South River, the theatrical leadership there was taken over by Irene Cupryk, under whose direction the South River Byelorussian Theatrical Studio has successfully produced many Byelorussian classics and new plays. Cupryk also has successfully ventured into writing several skits depicting problems of modern America and the adaptability of new Byelorussian immigrants to this country. The audience at these performances has been composed almost entirely of new immigrants, and the success of these plays has been tremendous, but Cupryk, continuing the tradition of the professional theatre, has always been quite demanding in her role as director. Cupryk's studio also performed in Glen Spey, near Monticello, New York. Over the years the following plays were performed under Cupryk's direction: *Nu i Ameryka* (Well, this is America), South River, 1960; *Mikitau Lapats* (Mikita's Shoe), a Byelorussian classic by Michas Charot, South River, 1965; *Matador*, a comic skit, South River, 1967; *Granny*, a one-act English-language play, South River, and Glen Spey, 1968; and *Shchaslivy Muzh*, a well-known Byelorussian play, South River, and Glen Spey, late 1960s.[18]

While Selach-Kachanski's plays were strictly Byelorussian-language plays, Cupryk has also used some English-language passages and plays. The casts for her plays have been largely recruited from the younger generation, and over the years she has recruited over sixty young players. Among the leaders in Cupryk's group were Nata Kirkevich, Zhenia Ciarpickaja, Michas Paluchovich, and Vala Kaminkova, as well as the veterans of Selach-Kachanski's performances, Vera Kous, Wital Cierpicki, Luda and Aleh Machniuk, Michas Sienka, Ihar Scors, Lavon Shurak, Renia Kasciuk, and Cupryk's long-time friend and coartists from Minsk, Vila Sauchanka-Lewczuk.

The South River Byelorussian Theatrical Studio was never formally disbanded; however, because many younger members moved elsewhere after finishing college, its membership diminished substantially and it became inactive. Cupryk, however, is still active in working with the school group and was very much involved in production of drama pieces in the Byelorussian Heritage

Festivals, which were held at the Garden State Arts Center, Holmdel, New Jersey, in 1976, 1977, and 1979. With the changing conditions, the group may revive again.

New York City

One of the earliest Byelorussian stage performances recorded in New York City was a concert given on 6th Street on February 2, 1952.[19] This concert was organized and sponsored by the Byelorussian Women's Association in the United States in conjunction with the women's division of the Byelorussian-American Association. The concert also included several dramatic plays, and these, as well as the entire program, were directed by Ipalit Palanievich. The dramatic plays at that concert included one by Natalla Arsiennieva-Kushel; *Expensive Dollar*, and two comic skits, *Kathryn and Steve* and *Vazhnaja Fiha*, by Jadvihin Sha, a well-known Byelorussian writer from the early days of this century. This concert gave impetus to the formation of a Youth Drama Club. As Palanievich recalls:

The Youth Drama Club under my leadership was composed of young amateurs, boys and girls who, with the exception of a few, never had any experience with the stage. Two of them, Tusia Kulikovich and Halina Hancharenka, whose parents were performers and closely connected with the stage in Byelorussia and Germany, were very helpful and also very gifted. I had much patience to work with all these youngsters under very unfavorable conditions; we lacked money and even a place to meet. More often we were meeting in a rented apartment downtown on Delancey Street. Our spirits, however, were high. In a relatively short time we were able to produce several plays and to achieve gratifying results on the stage. During 1953 and 1954 we produced such plays as "Majski Zhuk [The May Bug][20] and "Zbaulennie" [Deliverance] by Auhen Kavaleuski, "Chort i Baba" [The Devil and the Woman] by Francishak Alachnovich, "Zbiantezhany Sauka" [Embarrassed Sauka] by Leopold Rodzievich, and several other skits. We selected comedies and comic skits because we and the plays were very well received by the public and were successful financially. All our profits, however, went into the Byelorussian community fund. Our audience consisted mostly of new Byelorussian immigrants, but when we performed downtown, the older Byelorussian immigrants also came. Over these years some of the Club's members, N. Kulikovich-Kushel, H. Hancharenka, V. Bartul, B. Daniluk, and N. Zamorski, developed into almost professional artists and were eager to work. I must say, however, the one play we were unable to stage because of technical difficulties was "Paulinka" by Janka Kupala. Although we spent much time in rehearsing it, we couldn't coordinate and adjust the musical part, which we regretted very much. In 1954 the Club began to disintegrate; some of the members went to study, some took jobs overseas, and some got married. I couldn't keep it going because I had a very sick person in the family to care for. However, I must say that this Club was very successful and had the potential to develop into a permanent theater."[21]

Almost simultaneously with Palanievich's activities, another drama club began to emerge under the leadership of Natalla Orsa. This club was associated with the Byelorussian American Youth Association, the membership of which ranged in age from eighteen to twenty-five. The club had its inauguration on March 25, 1954, at the Byelorussian independence day celebration. This first performance was given at Washington Irving High School in Manhattan, and over six hundred tickets were sold.

The club presented the stage version of a famous Byelorussian literary work, *Kurhan*[22] (Burial Mount), by the classicist Janka Kupala. The play is a very complex allegorical piece, and the performance of the artists is crucial. The artists performed very well. The key role of Husler (Dulcimer) was played by Nick Zamorski. The other main character parts were performed by Halina Hancharenka, Tusia Kulikovich-Kushel and Barys Daniluk.

The club became very successful over the years and performed on many important occasions, the biggest being at the twentieth anniversary conference of the Byelorussian-American Association in 1969, when it presented the already-mentioned play *Chort i Baba.* The play was very successful, and by popular demand it was repeated again in Glen Spey, New York, in August 1969. The club also performed such well-known Byelorussian plays as *Zbiantezhany Sauka,* mentioned before, a variety of comic skits, and many adaptations of Byelorussian literary works.[23] Artists have come and gone over the years, but Natalia Orsa remains. She recalls that the key roles in many plays were performed by Kastus Vierabej, Alicia Kuryllo, Francis Bartul, Barys Daniluk, Vera Bartul, Ala Orsa-Romano, Vicka Palanievich, Anatol Aleksandrovich, and Orsa herself. Orsa's club also performed in South River, New Jersey. The stage designs for the club were often made by George Azarko and George Kuryllo.[24]

Cleveland

The Byelorussian Youth Drama Club in Cleveland was formed in 1951.[25] Its organizers were young people who were active in drama clubs in Byelorussian schools in Germany before coming here. The first performance of the Cleveland group was held on March 25, 1951. The club, under the leadership of Michas Bielamuk, produced a Byelorussian patriotic play, *Kastus Kalinouski,* by Natalla Arsiennieva-Kushel. The performers were Sciapan Kisiel, Alex Haroch, and Chviedar Pahuda. As Bielamuk recalls:

We all participated in the drama clubs in the Byelorussian schools in Germany, thus we were familiar with the play and we liked to present it in Cleveland. The play was a success and we decided to keep the club going. Our repertory consisted mostly of patriotic Byelorussian plays and we performed on various holidays.[26]

The group became more active and more professional with the arrival in Cleveland of Mikola Kulikovich-Shchahlou in 1953. Although Kulikovich stressed choreographic activities, he paid close attention to dramatic performance also. He was a consultant, and under his leadership the Cleveland drama group staged such plays as *Zbiatezhany Sauka; Praloh u Buduchyniu* (Prologue to Future), by N. Tal, *Kupalle*[27] (Midsummer Festival), an ethnographic musical arranged and produced by Kulikovich, and several smaller skits.

The Cleveland drama club performed in Rockford, Illinois, and Chicago also, under the leadership of Konstanty Kisly, a well-known Byelorussian musicologist and choir director who had come to Cleveland from Belgium in 1956. This club was active well into the 1960s. Recognizing that there was a shortage of repertory for Beylorussian drama clubs, the Cleveland Youth Association published a collection of plays as well as a series of musical revues.[28]

Detroit

The Byelorussian Drama Club of Detroit was formed in the late 1950s and was a semiprofessional society with bylaws, dues, and the like.[29] It was organized and led by Mikola Prusky. The goals and the program of the society were to popularize and advertise Byelorussian culture with emphasis on the stage and theatrical traditions. An interesting fact about this group is that Prusky was able to recruit Byelorussians of several generations, who worked together for several years. The club concentrated on Byelorussian repertory and in a relatively short period of time after its formation produced the well-known Byelorussian play *Paulinka,* which was favorably received not only by the Byelorussian community but also by Ukrainians, Russians, and Poles. It was reviewed by many critics and was of interest to the general public because of its specially printed programs with summaries of the play and the key roles in English.[30]

After several performances in Detroit, the club performed also in Chicago, Cleveland, Toronto, and London (Canada). One of the performers, Sviatlana Pleskacz, wrote a short note about their activities in the club.

Paulinka, a play by the famous Byelorussian playwright and poet Janka Kupala, was presented in Detroit, Chicago, and Toronto by the Byelorussian Drama Club of Detroit. The play was a great success, and the audiences all over were very receptive and seemed to enjoy the play very much. After months and months of hard work and many, many rehearsals, the play was first staged in Detroit, two weeks later in Chicago, and a week later in Toronto. Actually, only the participants can realize the hard work and tremendous effort that goes behind staging and presenting a play. The players were working on a very tight schedule, and the long trips by car were exhausting. However, the moral satisfaction was very great, because this group kept the Byelorussian spirit, culture, and heritage alive.

It must be kept in mind that this group is made up strictly of amateurs, mainly married people plus students both in high school and college. This group is also comparatively new, and we still need a lot of work to get better. However, only through more active participation and more work are we, in Detroit, going to be able to better ourselves and put on more and more plays. Although the Byelorussian population is small in comparison with other populations in other cities, we have made our presence known here in Detroit, and we feel that this is still only a beginning, leading to greater and better things in the future. We certainly need more active Byelorussians as these, and we need more plays, concerts, and other Byelorussian activities promoted all over the United States, Canada, and other countries, for who else will uphold the Byelorussian heritage, culture, and tradition than the Byelorussian people themselves?[31]

This was a very successful club, both culturally and financially.[32] Unfortunately it was short-lived. In a recent interview in which we asked Prusky, who now resides in Grand Rapids, Michigan, why the club did not continue this work, he replied,

I moved from Detroit because of my job. Many younger people left also, some to go to college. But, I hope one day to revive the club again, because theoretically we are still alive, we have our by-laws, our books, etc. We are waiting for the right time, and I am looking for the right play; and there are so many excellent plays, that I am sure we will be back on stage soon.[33]

Prusky notes also that all the proceeds from their performances were given to the Byelorussian community in Detroit at the time the community was acquiring a new church building and new property.

This concludes the review of Byelorussian semiprofessional theatrical groups active in the United States during the post-World War II period. These groups were working with Byelorussian repertory almost entirely, but their goals were to reach larger audiences not necessarily of Byelorussian descent. Their leaders were professional, either former artists or people who had been closely connected with the stage in Byelorussia; the performers in these groups were mostly Byelorussian-born Americans.

SCHOOL THEATRES AND YOUTH STAGE GROUPS

This form of Byelorussian theatre is still very active in the United States. School theatres have been formed for the purpose of teaching children Byelorussian customs, language, and culture; therefore they are primarily teaching aids, having the secondary purpose of developing theatrical skills and a taste for drama in the children. These theatres are associated, sponsored, and administered by Byelorussian supplementary schools. Most of their activities and repertory are related to school programs and holidays such as Easter, Christmas, Mother's Day, Veterans Day, and Halloween. Youth theatre groups are associated mainly with youth organizations such as the Byelorussian-American Youth Organization, Byelorussian American Youth of Illinois, and Byelorussian American Youth Association. The goal of the youth theatrical groups is to raise money for their organizations and to keep active programs.

Both school theatres and youth theatres are for amateur performers, ranging in age from six to fourteen in the schools and from fourteen to twenty-five in the youth groups. The repertories of these theatres could be grouped into themes such as customs and traditions, patriotic and historical Byelorussian plays, American plays, and adaptations or translations of classic juvenile plays into Byelorussian. The language of the plays and performers is mostly Byelorussian, although the leaders of these groups complain that it is harder and harder to get good Byelorussian-speaking youth. Often the group leaders and children compromise by translating passages of plays into English, thus producing a new form of bilingual play. A language conflict between the younger and older children is not an uncommon phenomenon. The older children, more proficient in Byelorussian, refuse to perform with the younger children, especially if the older children have to be dressed like animals or flowers.

Usually these theatres have no financial problems, but an enormous problem exists in costuming. As a rule the costumes are made by the parents. There is a nominal admission charge, but the profits go into the school fund or to the sponsoring organization. The audience is usually limited, but the shows are very warmly received and professional deficiencies are usually overlooked. The leadership of both groups consists of teachers, parents, or persons who once were connected with the stage—usually older interested persons. As with semiprofessional theatre, Byelorussian youth and school theatrical groups were organized mostly in the early 1950s in places where there were sufficient concentrations of Byelorussian immigrants. Many of these groups did not last long; however, several are still active.

Passaic, New Jersey

Somewhat regular supplementary education of Byelorussian children in Passaic, New Jersey, was begun in the early 1950s. Children were taught the Byelorussian language and some elements of Byelorussian culture. Theatrical activities followed, with school performances organized in Garfield, Lodi, Wallington, and Passaic. The plays dealt mostly with Byelorussian customs and with frequent adaptations of Byelorussian literary works. The leadership of the Passaic group consisted of Uladzimer Dutko, Symon Zemojda, Ivan Bendzierau, and Maria Kipel.[34]

New York City

The theatrical group in New York City, which was sponsored by the Byelorussian Sunday School and the student organization, dates back to 1952.[35] A dramatic montage depicting the life and activities of the Byelorussian National Poet Janka Kupala, was organized by the then director of the school, Natalla Orsa. The montage dedicated to Kupala was entitled *Piasniarskim Shlacham* (The

Bard's Way).[36] The occasion was the tenth anniversary of Kupala's tragic death. The entire program of the event was organized by the Byelorussian Institute of Arts and Sciences, and the school and youth groups were invited to stage the show. Later the New York school performed various plays, tales, elaborate customs adapted to the stage, and so on. Over the years the group performed dozens of plays, and it has remained active until the present time. In 1971 the older students translated into Byelorussian the well-known American newspaper editorial "Yes, Virginia, there is a Santa Claus" and adapted it for the stage, presenting it at Christmas time.

New Brunswick, New Jersey

The drama club associated with the Byelorussian-American Youth Organization in New Brunswick, New Jersey, was organized in the late 1950s by Byelorussian community leaders Uladzimier Kabushka, his wife Vera, and Vasil Stoma. These people, amateurs of the stage and once associated with amateur groups in Byelorussia, have written and produced several plays. The first one, a skit entitled *Deaf Tom*, was written by Kabushka. The unfortunate and untimely death of the author prevented him from seeing it produced. This play, as well as another, a comedy by Halina Puch entitled *I Have to Ask My Mother*, were produced by Vera Kabushka and Vasil Stoma, who took the leadership of the group after the death of Kabushka. Both plays were performed at the annual youth convention in 1959 in New Brunswick. As Stoma recalls, "It wasn't an easy task. Both plays were in Byelorussian, and it was difficult for the children to understand and speak and act at the same time. That was the time when even children who came here as infants in the late forties were beginning to speak only English."[37]

In describing his activities with the group, Stoma recalls that the problems were not of a linguistic nature only. In 1960 he was working on a patriotic musical drama, *Bielarus* (Byelorussia), which was performed in the same year in the Presbyterian church on Livingston Avenue in New Brunswick. Knowing that the children had problems with Byelorussian, Stoma assigned the major role in this play to a narrator, using music, light, and sound effects to minimize the need for spoken portions by the children. Modifications of some set designs were necessary because of objections by the church. After all these adjustments the play was very successful, and it was repeated again in 1970, with many more design modifications because the Byelorussians had acquired their own building by that time.

Over the years the group has performed many different plays on a more or less regular basis. In the sixties the leadership of the group was taken over by Alina Lysiuk, with the continuous help of Vera Kabushka and Stoma.[38] The New Brunswick youth group is still in existence. However, its theatrical activities are mostly associated with the school program and the Byelorussian church, which sponsors the school.

South River, New Jersey

One of the earliest school performances in the South River, New Jersey, community took place in the early 1950s under the leadership of Irene Cupryk, and an original play was written by Sviataslau Kous.[39] Youth theatre and school performances took great advantage of the availability of local professions such as Cupryk, Vila Sauchanka-Lewczuk, and two Byelorussian poets, Michas Kavyl and Anton Danilovich. In the sixties a great number of plays and theatrical shows were directed by Ludmila and Xavery Borisovets and Nina Orsa. In addition to traditional Christmas customs, the youth and school theatrical groups performed such plays as *Santa Claus Retires*, by Michas Kavyl, which reflects the social issues of modern America; *The Orphan-Hanula*, by Natalla Arsiennieva-Kushel, which depicts the father figure, rabbits, and wolves and their relationship. The music for this play was written by Dmiter Weresov and the choreography was done by Vila Sauchanda-Lewczuk. The group also staged Anderson's tales, translated into Byelorussian and adapted to the stage by Cupryk. The South River group is still active and performs on various occasions.[40] The performances sponsored by the Byelorussian-American Association began in 1951.[41]

Detroit

Theatrical activities in the Byelorussian supplementary school in Detroit began in 1953 and were sponsored by the Detroit chapter of the Byelorussian-American Association. These activities were slightly different from those in other cities. Because of the relatively small Byelorussian population in the Detroit area, the group had difficulties supporting its own theatre. Ultimately it turned for help to the International Institute of Detroit, which later included the Byelorussian productions in its own programs. Through the efforts of Tatiana Pleskacz, it also obtained assistance from several Detroit public schools, which included presentations of Byelorussian customs in their own performances. In addition, from 1954 to 1963 the Byelorussian supplementary school presented "The Christmas Season in Byelorussia" in cooperation with the Greenfield Park School. Pleskacz directed these shows, in which about twenty Byelorussian children participated. The performances given in English were supplemented by carolling in Byelorussian. The audience usually was English-speaking, but the performances could truly be called bilingual. They had a tremendous effect in promoting American multiculturalism. The Detroit school group is still active, although not on a regular basis. The Byelorussians of Detroit have acquired their own church building, where all performances are now held.[42]

Los Angeles

Byelorussian programs have been included in school performances in Los Angeles since the late 1950s. Alimp Mialencieu organized children to present Byelorussian Christmas customs at the city hall; ever since, Byelorussian Christmas customs have become part of annual Christmas programs showing customs from around the world. Over the years these shows have been directed by Juzefa Najdziuk, Katia and Alex Winnicki and Joseph Archiuch.[43]

Chicago

Although Chicago was the first large American city to present Byelorussian-sponsored stage performances, as early as the 1920s, it was not until the mid-1950s that more permanent theatrical activities took place. These were associated with the establishment of organizations such as the Byelorussian Youth Association in Illinois, the Byelorussian Orthodox Church in Maplewood, and later the Byelorussian Catholic Center at 3107 West Fullerton Avenue. Theatrical performances of the Byelorussian supplementary schools in Chicago are also associated with Byelorussian customs and patriotic plays. The activities were coordinated initially by Vaclau Panucevich and later by Vera Ramuk and William Puntus. Larger performances were organized in the mid-1960s by the Byelorussian Catholic Center. Examples of these were Syn i Maci (Son and Mother) and Kupalle, well-known Byelorussian plays. While he lived in Chicago, Mikola Kulikovich-Shchahlou also contributed a great deal to the promotion of theatrical performances in the Byelorussian schools.

The Christmas plays always attracted large audiences. One such play that was performed several times was The Ladder to Heaven, written by Teresa Tarasevich, in which a young child dreams of Jesus coming from heaven. The play was in English, but the carols were in Byelorussian, English, and French. The Chicago schools also presented Batlejka (The Puppet Show). Panucevich published several pamphlets of children's plays, thus enriching this repertory. The Chicago group is still active in giving school performances, associated mostly with events such as the international exhibition in Chicago, the Christmas Tree in the Museum of Science and Technology, and the like.[44]

Cleveland

The Byelorussian school in Cleveland, sponsored by the St. Mother of Zyrovicy Parish of the Byelorussian Autocephalic Orthodox Church and the Byelorussian-American Association, was organized in the mid-1950s. The school has a very extensive educational curriculum and from its beginning was actively participating in celebrations of various Byelorussian festivities. The emphasis in the performances was, however, on choreography and music. The staff of the school soon realized that several children in the school were very interested in the theatrical activities, and therefore the staff thought it would be better to have an independent school theatre club. One of the teachers, Irene Kalada-Smirnof, became the founder and leader of this club. The club operated independently from the school activities but was officially part of the school activities.

Kalad-Smirnof, herself a product of the Cleveland school system, in a 1978 interview recalled:

I formed the club with the purpose of bringing children closer to the stage and developing their artistic qualities while helping the ethnic heritage. Being involved with the stage since my early childhood, I knew from my own experience how hard it was sometimes to combine the school activities and the stage interests. Thus, I wanted to help children and the school. I felt that I could get better quality performances and involve the students more by making the club an independent operation.[45] From the very beginning Kalada-Smirnof secured the help of the most interested parents and of Ales Zmahar, a known Byelorussian writer and publicist who was then residing in Cleveland. It was a very productive cooperation. The parents assisted her in costuming and decorating needs; the school provided administrative help; and Zmahar wrote numerous plays, adaptations of tales and literary works, and arranged translations. The repertory of the club was very extensive: Byelorussian customs, tales, patriotic plays, and literary adaptations. Kalada-Smirnof feels that the valuable work done by Zmahar and the assistance of older children, members of the Byelorussian-American Youth Organization, contributed to the success of the theater club.

When asked what plays the children like the most, Kalada-Smirnof replied: "They liked them all, but most of all they enjoyed the tales, such as The Repka Tale. (Repka is a turnip)." The story of this well known Byelorussian tale is rather simple: Grandfather is trying to pull the repka out of the ground, but he cannot do it. He calls for help one after the other to the grandmother, his grandson, his granddaughter, the cat, the dog, and finally the mice. Finally, with the help of the mice, they are all able to pull the repka out of the ground. The moral of the tale is very clear—unity gives strength (there is strength in numbers). In addition to its moral aspects, this tale has the virtue of being very suitable for the stage because of the variety of costumes and the number of the performers, which can be as many as there are performers. Often, in addition to the cat and dog, the grandfather can call for help to a rabbit, a fox, and so on. This tale, incidentally, is also very popular in Byelorussia. The Cleveland Byelorussian School Theater Club has captured the attention not only of the Byelorussian community but also of American, Polish, and Ukrainian newspapers. The most extensive coverage of the Cleveland School Theater Club appears in the Byelorussian Voice, Toronto, Canada.

Byelorussian-American Youth Organization

The Byelorussian-American Youth Organization, the largest in the United States, has initiated and participated in many theatrical shows. One of its bylaws states that the organization should promote Byelorussian culture and pride in the Byelorussian heritage. Thus practically all members of this organization have had Byelorussian schooling here since early childhood and have been actively involved in many Byelorussian programs, lectures, festivals, and of course theatrical activities. In 1973 the organization initiated an annual talent show, the purpose of which was to encourage, promote, and develop artistic talents among youngsters of Byelorussian extraction. Variety programs and dramatic plays were both presented in these shows. One of the plays, *Jak Zhyts, kab Zdarovym Byts* (How to Live and Be Healthy), had an excellent reception in 1973.[46] The play is simple and didactic, instructing young people about cleanliness and hygiene, and is very characteristic of the plays given in Byelorussia. The organization is presently very active, especially in the production and administration of the Byelorussian Heritage Festivals at the Garden State Arts Center in Holmdel, New Jersey.[47]

REPERTORY

The repertory of the Byelorussian theatre in the United States is very diversified. The types of plays can be divided into several groups: original plays, classic Byelorussian repertory, translations of plays from English and German into Byelorussian and from Byelorussian into English, and adaptations of English-language plays to the interests of the Byelorussian community.

Original Plays

By original plays, we mean those written and produced in the United States. This category includes patriotic plays, adaptations of Byelorussian literary works to stage performance, plays depicting everyday life and comedies, and plays based on Byelorussian customs and tales. Patriotic plays and adaptations of literary works are probably the largest in number. This is because there are many active Byelorussian writers, such as Natalla Arsiennieva-Kushel, Michas Kavyl, Janka Zolak, Ales Zmahar, Kastus Akula, and Janka Juchnaviec living in the United States and Canada. The patriotic plays promote Byelorussian identity and pursue the goal of the Byelorussian state. The main plot in the plays is always the oppression of Byelorussia and the struggle of its people to regain independence from the oppressors. They depict the glorious, happy past, with Byelorussian kings and statesmen; rich Byelorussian culture since destroyed by enemies from the east and west (Russia and Poland); the foreign yoke of present Byelorussia; and the inevitable emergence of an independent Byelorussian state. Situations, rather than individual heroes, are characteristic features of these plays. Lately, however, individual historical episodes, such as the Sluck uprising of 1920 and the uprising of 1863–1864 under the leadership of Kastus Kalinouski, the national Byelorussian hero, are treated rather frequently also.

Kalinouski emerges as the prototype of the Byelorussian freedom fighter. Because of a lack of sufficient plays, adaptations of patriotic literary works such as the Byelorussian classics of Janka Kupala, Jakub Kolas, and Aloiza Ciotka is one means of increasing the repertory.

It is difficult to interest the English-speaking community in many of these subjects, with the possible exception of two plays: the one dramatic play by Todar Lebiada, *Zahublennaje Zhyccio* (The Lost Life), and *U Haspodzie Paduanskaj* (In Padua), by Arsiennieva-Kushel.[48] While *Zahublennaje Zhyccio* was never successfully put into production—although attempted by the South River studio—it depicts life in Soviet Byelorussia in the 1930s and could be adapted to represent almost any other location in the Soviet Union. The play, produced for the first time in Minsk in 1944, was published in Canada. The strength of the personages and of the action in this play makes it almost a masterpiece, reflecting a very difficult period of life in the Soviet Union. *U Haspodzie Paduanskaj*, describing the life and study of a Byelorussian scholar, Francisak Skaryna, who received his medical degree in the sixteenth century in Padua, Italy, has a subject that might be of interest to the general reader.

In the category of original plays are several comedies and sketches depicting everyday life. The author of most of these plays was Auhen Kavaleuski, formerly of the Minsk Theater, who resided in France. Kavaleuski's plays were original, easy to put on, and well liked by all audiences because their plots were of general human interest. In some sketches the passages are in two languages, and these plays are almost bilingual in effect.

Translations characterize the school theatre for the most part, the reason for this being that children have difficulty understanding Byelorussian but parents and teachers want to familiarize them with Byelorussian themes. The theatre is indeed one of the best tools for teaching the language, and in many instances the children have learned quite a bit of Byelorussian through this medium.

Plays dealing with the colorful, diverse, Byelorussian customs are also numerous, because their theatrical characteristics make them easily adaptable for the stage. These plays are very vivid, incorporating singing and dancing, and are understandable by all generations. One also finds several generations participating as performers. These plays are very popular in the schools, because they teach the children about Byelorussian heritage and give them an opportunity to learn the language and also to learn about the theatre. Many customs are adapted for the stage through literary works in which individual writers describe Byelorussian customs and relate them to patriotic themes. Such, for example, is Kupala's *Na Kucciu* (Christmas Eve). The Christmas theme is, incidentally, the most vividly treated on the Byelorussian stage for the reason that the Christmas season in Byelorussia is very rich in activities. Besides in community plays, the Byelorussians use Christmas customs in various international shows; for example, the Byelorussians in Chicago and California stage Byelorussian Christmas plays in various places almost annually.

Next to the Christmas customs, the Easter customs are rich and adaptable for the stage, and also Kupalle and Dazhynki, the midsummer and harvest festivals, are very colorful themes, diversified in action and requiring many performers. Although the decorations sometimes present a problem, the plays are relatively easy to stage.

Dramatization of Byelorussian Folklore

Adaptations of Byelorussian tales for the stage are also very numerous, for the reason that these stories are exceptionally appropriate for this medium. As one authority on Byelorussian tales has phrased it:

During every period of history, oral tales were the living voices of the people. Byelorussian folk stories reflect the ideals and moods of the people. Byelorussian folk tales have in their liveliness, uniqueness and beauty nothing comparable to them. The magical tales which revealed the hopes and aspirations of the people are characterized by a determined moral-philosophical attitude. The characters of these tales are connected with the unique nature of the Byelorussian woods and marshes. Stories dealing with mighty heroes are typical of Byelorussian folklore. The wealth of topics and subjects in Byelorussian fairy tales is unsurpassed. The tales which deal with the daily life of the people are mostly social satires. The animal tales are really the pearls of the Byelorussian folklore.[49]

Thus Byelorussian tales were adapted for the stage in almost all Byelorussian supplementary schools and were performed on many occasions, not only for Byelorussian children, but also in regular American schools. In addition to Byelorussian tales, several school stage directors have adapted the tales of other countries to the Byelorussian language for the Byelorussian community; for example, as we have seen, Anderson's tales were translated by Irene Cupryk and performed in South River, and "Yes, Virginia, there is a Santa Claus," adapted in the school in Brooklyn and entirely translated into Byelorussian by the oldest class of the year in 1971.

BYELORUSSIAN CLASSIC REPERTORY

The classic repertory is made up of plays written by Byelorussians that were very popular in Byelorussia. Some of them, like *Paulinka, Pinskaia Shlachta, Mikitau Lapats,* and others, have been presented repeatedly over half a century. They have typical Byelorussian characters, some degree of comic element, and plots of general human interest. These plays are relatively easy to obtain, and their production almost always guarantees success.

PERFORMANCE, ACTORS, AND AUDIENCE

To a certain degree the repertory has influenced the style of performance on the Byelorussian stage in the United States. The fantastic, allegorical fairy tales and folk customs inspired romanticism in the style of production and the interpretations of the roles. The patriotic plays employed a great deal of pathos. Plays based on everyday subjects required a naturalistic or realistic approach. Byelorussian theatre in general relies heavily on musical, choral, and choreographic accompaniment, which undoubtedly adds to its romanticism. Thus, it is safe to assume that the style of Byelorussian theatre in America is not well defined, nor has it any specific characteristics. It is, rather, a mixture or a combination of romantic naturalism and realism with emphasis on the romantic.

About 90 percent of the actors are of Byelorussian descent; however, among young groups non-Byelorussian performers are not unusual. This situation often happens in cases where a boyfriend or girlfriend not of Byelorussian background joins the Byelorussian community. Non-Byelorussian performers are also frequently found in school theatres where non-Byelorussians belong to Byelorussian churches.

Costuming in the Byelorussian theatre is not always an easy task; the number one problem is research into the costumes. Usually the research is done in libraries, although much is learned by asking older people who knew how a particular personage was dressed on stage or how the hero was supposed to have been dressed in real life.

The next problem is financing: as a rule the financing of the costumes is the responsibility of the sponsoring organization or the individuals who play the particular roles. The most expensive costumes are in children's shows. Usually the expense is covered by the parents or by the church parents' groups. After the shows the costumes may be given to the organization or kept by the person who played the role. Recently, however, the Byelorussian Institute of Arts and Sciences formed a bank of Byelorussian costumes, which are kept in one place and can be borrowed when needed.

Of the members of the audience for Byelorussian shows, 60 to 80 percent are Byelorussian. For some shows attendance might be as high as five to seven hundred, but usually it is not larger than one hundred and fifty to three hundred, and school shows have a much smaller attendance. It is found, however, that audiences at theatrical shows are much smaller than at general festivals or musical shows. The audiences at the Garden State Arts Center festivals in Holmdel, New Jersey, reached over three thousand.

Publicity is usually through the mail, newspapers, and announcements in churches and clubs. Advertising is normally done in both Byelorussian and English, and local English-language newspapers are used for advertising as well as other Slavic and Polish, Russian, and Ukrainian newspapers. For larger shows local broadcasting stations are also used.

BATLEJKA THEATRE

The survey of the Byelorussian theatre would not be complete without a review of the batlejka theatre, or Puppet Show. This form of Byelorussian theatre is very old in Byelorussia and presently is almost nonexistent.

The organizer of the first Byelorussian Batlejka show in the United States was Maria Stankievich, a former school teacher and an active member in the YMCA movement. Involved in work with various youth groups, Stankievich decided to familiarize the community with the oldest theatrical tradition in Byelorussia. Here is what Stankievich has written about the organization and the first Batlejka show:

I knew about the Batlejka shows from Bielarus and I decided to show this Byelorussian tradition to the American public. I went to the New York Public Library and borrowed a book about the Batlejkas in Byelorussia. I copied the parts pertaining to the Nativity play. Then I contacted members of the Women's organization to help me with dressing the puppets. We needed shepherds, angels, kings, magicians, peasants, gypsies, a horse and a clown. The costumes were made soon; the king in a black velvet robe, the peasants in embroidered Byelorussian national costumes, etc. I distributed the roles among the Girl Scouts with whom I was then working. The first performance, given at the YMCA on State Street in Brooklyn, was making the puppets bow and throw kisses to the public at the end.

The show was a great success. This was January 11, 1958. Attendance was excellent. We had done excellent publicity through mail, telephone, and local newspapers. Invitations were sent to Byelorussians and non-Byelorussians asking both little and big to come punctually, because our time was limited. Byelorussian women from the neighboring Byelorussian Orthodox Church helped a great deal. We needed help in painting, making costumes, acting, and vocalizing. To paint the peasants' homes we even got help from an experienced professional painter.

The Nativity play was not only religious, it also contained various scenes from different ways of life. The first scene began with a starlit heaven, shepherds and angels. The next scene was in the King's palace, his inquiry of the magicians and his cruel orders. The king was punished when death drew him to Hell. The choir lamented the weakness of humanity and admonished the people to live good lives. The next scenes depicted dialogues between the peasant and the doctor, the life of the gypsies, and, last, the clown singing various popular songs and saying good-bye to the people. Because the Christmas Batlejka was so successful, we decided to continue with the theater. During the Easter season we organized another show. In addition to "The Little Red Egg," we enlarged our repertory to include a puppet show "Alice in Wonderland" translated into Byelorussian. Here again the women's organizations gave us great help with decorations and costumes. The Byelorussian Community Center in Brooklyn was full on the day of the show.

The acceptance and the great pleasure with which the shows were received gave us the idea to make them more or less permanent, especially because we were receiving so much help from the youth groups. We repeated the Batlejka show many more times during the next few years in New Brunswick, N.J., and in Hawthorne, N.J. In the late 1950s we decided to put some plays on tape. Thus, we have the Batlejka show and Alice in Wonderland on tape. Alice in Wonderland was also played in the summer camps at the Byelorussian resort Belair-Miensk in Glen Spey, N.Y.[50]

In addition to the puppet shows, Batlejka shows were also presented live by students in the Byelorussian schools in Chicago, South River, and New Brunswick, and on occasion they emerge again.

CONCLUSIONS

As expected, Byelorussian theatrical traditions and forms were transplanted by immigrants to the United States. The development of the Byelorussian theatre in the United States was controlled primarily by the following factors: availability of competent professionals, presence of a sufficient number of Byelorussian immigrants, and availability of the repertory. The Byelorussian theatre in the United States is deeply ethnic and rather local, with little material that it can export to other communities, with a few exceptions. Emphasis in the American Byelorussian theatre is on ethnic and social aspects, with a great proportion devoted to historical plays. In that respect it differs strikingly from the theatre in Soviet Byelorussia, where Byelorussian historical plays are almost nonexistent. The American Byelorussian theatre also preserves a very important part of Byelorussian traditional culture: religious plays, which are not allowed in Soviet Byelorussia. One can safely say that the Byelorussian theatre in the United States preserves some forms and topics of theatre that have almost disappeared or are forbidden in Soviet Byelorussia.

Some difficulties are real and very serious for the Byelorussian theatre in the United States. One of them is the decreasing proportion of Byelorussian-speaking performers; the other is the dearth of new repertory. During the last few years Byelorussian dramatic theatre in the United States has been on the decline and the variety show is on the rise. This is due primarily to the fact that the younger, American-born generation chooses this more colorful form of expressing its ethnicity. The most striking examples of such variety performances are the Byelorussian festivals at the Garden State Arts Center, where several generations of performers and thousands of viewers are brought together.

The continuation of Byelorussian theatre in the United States depends upon its potential audience, new immigrants from Byelorussia, or it will switch entirely to the English language. The role of assimilation cannot be denied. At the appropriate time, however, the Byelorussian drama theatre may revive.

Appendix: Listing of Plays Performed by Byelorussian Theatres in the United States

Name of Show	Author	Producer	Date	Place
Sialianskaie Viaselle		Ivan Sauchuk	3/7/26	Chicago
Zaparozhats za Dunajem	Music by Semen Hulak-Artemovski		2/16/30	Chicago
Shchaslivy Muzh	Francishak Alachnovich	Viachaslau Selach-Kachanski	10/15/50	South River, N.J.
Kastus Kalinouski	Natalla Arsiennieva	Michas Bielamuk	3/25/51	Cleveland
Piesniarskim Shlacham	Janka Kupala	Natalla Orsa	6/30/51	New York
Christmas Night	Rev. Sviataslau Kous	Irene Cupryk	12/25/51	South River
Byelorussian Christmas	Uladzimir Dutko et al	Uladzimir Dutko	12/25/52	Passaic, N.J.
Darahi Dalar	Natalla Arsiennieva	Ipalit Palanievich	2/2/52	New York
Zbaulennie	Auhen Kavaleuski	Ipalit Palanievich	2/2/52	New York
Kaciaryna i Sciapan		Ipalit Palanievich	1952	New York
Mushka-Zielanushka	Maksim Bahdanovich	Natalla Orsa	5/30/53	New York
Chort i Baba	Francishak Alachnovich	Ipalit Palanievich	1953/54	New York
Majski Zhuk	Auhen Kavaleuski	Ipalit Palanievich	1953/54	New York
Kaladny Viechar	Natalla Arsiennieva	Uladzimir Kabushka	1/12/54	New Brunswick, N.J.
Byelorussian Christmas	Folk legend	Tatiana Pleskacz	1/54	Detroit
Kurhan	Janka Kupala	Natalla Orsa	3/25/54	New York
Byelorussian Easter	Folk customs	Uladzimir Dutko	4/54	Passaic
Zbiantezhany Sauka	Leapold Rodzievich	Natalla Orsa	11/6/54	New York
Christmas-Kuccia	Folk customs	Uladzimir Dutko	12/54	Passaic
U Kaladni Viechar	Anna Akanovich	Natalla Orsa	1/8/55	New York
Pinskaja Shlachta	Vincuk Dunin-Martsinkievich	Viachaslau Selach-Kachanski	6/19/55	South River

(continued)

Name of Show	Author	Producer	Date	Place
Varona i Lisitsa	Folk tale	Natalla Orsa	1/56	New York
Tym, Shto Pajshli . . .		Mikola Kulikovich	1956	Cleveland
Malamounaja (skit)	Mikola Kulikovich	Mikola Kulikovich	1956	Cleveland
Niasmiely Zhanich		Viachaslau Selach-Kachanski, Irene Cupryk	12/8/57	South River
Dazhynki, Piesa	Irene Cupryk	Viachaslau Selach-Kachanski	12/57	South River
Praloh u Buduchyniu	N. Tal	Mikola Kulikovich	1957	Cleveland
Malamounaja (skit)	Mikola Kulikovich	Mikola Kulikovich		Rockford, Ill.
Batlejka Theater	Folk customs	Maria Stankievich	1/11/58	New York
Pryhody Alonki	Natalla Arsiennieva	Maria Stankievich	4/20/58	New York
Zmaharny Shlach		Konstanty Kisly	3/25/58	Cleveland
Malamounaja (skit)	Mikola Kulikovich	Mikola Kulikovich	1958	Detroit
I Have to Ask My Father		Vasil Stoma	1959	New Brunswick
Deaf Tom	Uladzimir Kabushka	Vasil Stoma	1959	New Brunswick
Sniazhynachki	Uladzimir Kabushka	Vera Kabushka	12/25/59	New Brunswick
Byelorussia	Vasil Stoma	Vasil Stoma	3/25/60	New Brunswick
Paulinka	Janka Kupala	Irene Cupryk	Summer 1960	South River
Sluchchaki	Vasil Stoma	Vasil Stoma	11/60	New Brunswick
Christmas Eve	Customs	Jusefa Najdziuk	12/60	Los Angeles
Byelorussian Christmas	Natalla Arsiennieva	Ksenia Tumash	1/7–8/61	New York
Holy Night	Vasil Stoma	Vasil Stoma	1/61	New Brunswick
Paulinka	Janka Kupala	Mikola Prusky	4/30/61	Detroit
Matchyna Dola	Natalla Arsiennieva	Ksenia Tumash	5/14/61	New York
Zhuraviel i Capla	Maksim Tank	Irene Kalada	5/14/61 10/29/61	Cleveland
Kupalskaja Noch	Ales Zmahar	Irene Kalada	6/61, 8/61	Cleveland
Paulinka	Janka Kupala	Mikola Prusky	6/61	Cleveland
Paulinka	Janka Kupala	Mikola Prusky	6/61	Chicago
Paulinka	Janka Kupala	Mikola Prusky	6/61	London, Ont.
Repka	Folk tale	Irene Kalada	10/29/61	Cleveland
Cudounaja Noch	Michas Mickievich	Irene Kalada	1/14/62	Cleveland
Paklon Bielaruskich . . .	Vasil Stoma	Vasil Stoma	Christmas 1962	New Brunswick
Christmas Eve	Ales Zmahar	Irene Kalada	Christmas 1962	Cleveland
Sabaka, Kot, Myshka	Folk tale	Irene Kalada	1/62	Cleveland
Mid-Summer Festivities	Irene Kalada	Irene Kalada	9/62	Cleveland

(continued)

Name of Show	Author	Producer	Date	Place
Byelorussian Christmas	Folk customs	Tatiana Pleskacz	12/63	Detroit
Christmas in Byelorus	Ales Zmahar	Irene Kalada	1/11/64	Cleveland
Christmas play	Folk legend	John Tarasevich	1/64	Chicago
Santa Claus	Vera Kabushka	Vera Kabushka	1/64	New Brunswick
Well, This Is America	Irene Cupryk	Irene Cupryk	2/29/64	South River
Niasmelaja Niaviesta	Irene Cupryk	Irene Cupryk	2/29/64	South River
Jak Viasna Pryjshla	Natalla Arsiennieva	Zina Stankievich	Spring 1964	New York
Capla i Zhuravel	Folk tale	Zina Stankievich	Spring 1964	New York
Mother's Day	Ales Zmahar	Irene Kalada	5/64	Cleveland
Song of the flowers	Ales Zmahar	Irene Kalada	6/64	Cleveland
Matador	Irene Cupryk	Irene Cupryk	1964	South River
Shchaslivy Muzh	Francishak Alachnovich	Irene Cupryk	1964	South River
Christmas in Byelorussia	Literary adaptations	George Kalada	1/65	Cleveland
Christmas Eve (Na Kucciu)	Janka Kupala	Natalla Orsa	1/65	New York
Baika-Kryzhachok	Folk tale	Zina Stankievich	1/10/65	New York
Andrej za usich mudrej	Folk tale	Irene Cupryk	1/65	South River
Animals	Hans C. Andersen	Irene Cupryk	2/65	South River
Syn i Maci	John Tarasevich	Vera Ramuk	3/25/65	Chicago
Shlach da 25 Sakavika	Ales Zmahar	Irene Kalada	3/27/65	Cleveland
Batlejka Show	Folk customs	Maria Stankievich	Summer 1965	Glen Spey, N.Y.
Mikitau Lapats	Michas Charot	Irene Cupryk	7/3/65	South River
Shchaslivy Muzh	Francishak Alachnovich	Irene Cupryk	Summer 1965	Glen Spey
Nativity	Folk customs	Auhen Lysiuk	1/66	New Brunswick
In Bethlehem	Adaptations	Zina Horoshko	1/66	New York
Maminy Pamochniki		Zina Stankievich	5/21/66	New York
Kupalle	Vaclau Panucevich	Vera Ramuk	6/26/66	Chicago
Batlejka	Folk customs	Maria Stankievich	1/67	Hawthorne, N.J.
Batlejka	Folk customs	Maria Stankievich	1/67	New York
Piknick for Father	Vera Ramuk	Vera Ramuk	1967	Chicago
Granny	Irene Cupryk	Irene Cupryk/Vila Lewczuk	7/2/67	Glen Spey
Maryl'chyna Znachodka	Michas Kavyl	Irene Cupryk	1967	South River
Santa Claus Retires	Michas Kavyl	Irene Cupryk	1/19/69	South River

(continued)

Name of Show	Author	Producer	Date	Place
U Kaladni Viechar	Anna Akanovich	Natalla Orsa	1/19/69	New York
Chort i Baba	Francishak Alachnovich	Natalla Orsa	5/31/69	South River
Our Summer/ Mother's Day	Michas Kavyl	Irene Cupryk	5/69	South River
Sirotka Hanulka	Natalla Arsiennieva	Irene Cupryk	6/69	South River
Chort i Baba	Francishak Alachnovich	Natalla Orsa	8/16/69	Glen Spey
U Kaladni Viechar	Anna Akanovich	Natalla Orsa	1/19/70	New York
Lasnaia Kazka	Michas Kalachynski	Natalla Orsa	5/10/70	New York
Yes Virginia, There Is a Santa Claus	Translation	Natalla Orsa	1/17/71	New York
Belarus	Vasil Stoma	Vasil Stoma	3/25/71	New Brunswick
To Byelorussian Mother	Natalla Arsiennieva	Natalla Orsa	6/20/71	New York
Christmas Eve	Janka Kupala	Natalla Orsa	1/16/72	New York
Dazhynki/Harvest	Folk customs	Natalla Orsa	10/22/72	New York
Jak Zhyts, Kab Zdarovymbyts'		Zina Stankievich	7/73	South River
Syn i Maci	Janka Kupala	Zina Stankievich	6/23/74	New York
Mushka-Zielanushka Ka-maryk-Nasaty Tvaryk	Maksim Bahdanovich	Zina Stankievich	6/15/75	New York

NOTES

1. Heb Palisander, "The White-Russians, A Nation Driven Back into the Middle Ages under Muscovite Rule," *The Anglo-Russians*, London, Dec. 1904, p. 876.

2. *Byelorussian Soviet Encyclopedia* (Minsk: Ak. Navuk BSSR, 1975), Vol. 8, p. 401.

3. Anatol Semianovich, *Relaruskaia dramaturhiia* (Byelorussian Drama) (Minsk: Ak. Navuk BSSR, 1961), p. 101.

4. Uladzimir Hlybinny, "Backa naveishaie belaruskaie dramaturhii i teatru" (The Father of Modern Byelorussian Drama and Theatre), *Belarus* (New York) 5, no. 29 (Mar. 1953): 3.

5. *Theatres of Minsk* (Minsk: Belarus Publishers, 1973), pp. 3–21.

6. *Byelorussian Soviet Encyclopedia*, p. 370.

7. "In Memoriam Auhen Kavaleuski," *Byelorussian Youth* (New York) 19 (1963); 16; and "Auhen Kavaleuski, 1921–1963," *Backaushchyna* (Munich) 11, no. 611 (Oct. 1963): 3.

8. From interviews by Vitaut Kipel with older Byelorussian immigrants in New York: A. Sakadynski, Aug. 1959; I. Budyka and I. Chubar, Oct. 1961; A. Kalotka, July 1976.

9. *White-Russian National Association of America*, "Grand Performance, Concert and Ball." Chicago, Mar. 7, 1926, 29 pp.

10. "American Whiterussian Program of Whiterussian Day," Chicago, Feb. 16, 1930, 9 pp.

11. "In memoriam Alimp Mialencieu," *Backaushchyna* 7–8, nos. 621–622 (July 1964): 7; poster announcing Mialencieu's concert, Feb. 3, 1951, South River, N.J.

12. "Adyishou vydatny maistra" (An outstanding artist passed away), *Belarus* 144 (April 1969): 5.

13. Viachaslau Selach-Kachanski (Byelorussian People's Artist), *Byelorussian Word* (Ludwigsburg, Germany) 8, no. 29 (Sept.-Oct. 1955): 1; "In memoriam Selach-Kachanski," *Byelorussian Thought* (South River, N.J.) 20 (1976): 22; "In memoriam Lidzia Niadwiha," *Belarus* 145 (May 1969): 5; "Selach-Kachanski, The Triumph of Byelorussian Theater," *Byelorussian Youth* 21 (1964): 4–6; M. Kulikowich, "In Memoriam Barbara Verzhabalovich," *Belarus* 118 (Feb. 1967): 3.

14. *Byelorussian Tribune* (New York) 1, no. 1 (Aug. 27, 1950): 4; 1, no. 2 (Nov. 5, 1950): 3.

15. "Nie darma pratsuiuts" (They Work Not for Nothing), *Byelorussian Word* 7, no. 28 (July-Aug. 1955): 3.

16. "Spektakl-kancert Dazhynki" (The Harvest Show), *Carkouny Svietac* (South River, N.J.) 1, no. 8 (1957): 29–30.

17. *Carkouny Svietac* 2, no. 3 (1952): 15.

18. "Mikitau Lapatz," *Byelorussian Thought* 9 (1966): 31–32; "Performances at Belair-Miensk," *Belarus*, Sept. 1967, p. 5; Interviews with Irene Cupryk, South River, N.J., Oct.-Nov. 1978.

19. "Pryemnaie z karysnym" (Useful and pleasant), *Backaushchyna* 7–8, nos. 86–67 (Feb. 24, 1952): 6.

20. See review, *Belarus* 23, no. 47 (Mar. 6, 1954): 4.

21. Letter to Zora Kipel from Ipalit Palanievich, New York, N.Y., Dec. 17, 1978.

22. "Sakavikovae sviatkavannie u New York" (March 25 in New York), *Backaushchyna* 18, no. 200 (May 9, 1954): 3.

23. Review of *Zbiantezhany Sauka*, *Belarus* 4, no. 50 (Dec. 20, 1954): 8.

24. Letter to Zora Kipel from Natalla Orsa, New York, N.Y., Dec. 19, 1978; interviews with Natalla Orsa, Jan. 1979.

25. *20 Years of Byelorussian American Youth Organization* (Cleveland: BAYO, 1970), pp. 104–5.

26. Interview with Michas Bielamuk, Cleveland, Ohio, January 29, 1979.

27. *Kupalle* (Midsummer Festival, *Belarus* 3, no. 49 (Aug. 1, 1954): 8.

28. *Zbornik P'esau i Pesen* (Collection of plays and songs) (Cleveland: Byelorussian-American Youth Organization, 1953), 30 pp.

29. "Programs Sponsored by the International Institute in Detroit," Detroit, Mich., flyer addressed to St. Vladimirovsky Youth Group in Cleveland, Aug. 1959, p. 50.

30. "Pavlinka, a Review," *Ukrains'ka Hazeta* 6, no. 60 (June 1961): 4; Mikola Kulikovich-Shchahlou, "Paulinka z Detroitu," *Backaushchyna* 22, no. 557 (May 28, 1961): 4.

31. Sviatlana Pleskacz, "A Letter," *Byelorussian Youth* 10 (1961): 9.

32. Mikola Prusky, "Vialikaia padziaka" (A big thank you), *Svet* 2, no. 21 (1961): 8.

33. Interview with Mikola Prusky, Detroit, Sept. 1978; letter, Mikola Prusky to Vitaut Kipel, Detroit, Sept. 18, 1978.

34. "Jalinka u Passaiku," *Byelorussian Word*, 1–2, nos. 23–24 (Jan.-Feb. 1955); interview with Ul. Dutko, Passaic, N.J., Feb. 1979.

35. Letter from Natalla Orsa to Vitaut Kipel, New York, N.Y., Jan. 20, 1979.

36. Review of *The Bard's Way*, VICI, *The Herald* (New York) 1 (1952): 21.

37. Letter from Vasil Soma to Vitaut Kipel, New Brunswick, N.J., Oct. 28, 1978.

38. *20 Years of Byelorussian American Youth Organization*, pp. 101–3.

39. Interview with Sviataslau Kous, South River, N.J., Nov. 18, 1978.

40. Interviews with Irene Cupryk and Michas Sienka, South River, N.J., Oct. 20, 1978.

41. "Kupalle in South River, New Jersey," *Byelorussian Tribune* (New York) 4, no. 7 (July 29, 1951): 3.

42. Letter from Basil Pleskacz to Vitaut Kipel, Detroit, Feb. 14, 1979.

43. Letters from Jusefa Najdzuik and Joseph Arciuch to Zora Kipel, Los Angeles, Calif., Nov. 27 and 29, 1978.

44. Letter from Vera Ramuk to Vitaut Kipel, Chicago, Ill., Feb. 20, 1979.

45. Interview with Irene Kalada-Smirnof, Cleveland, Ohio, Oct. 16, 1978.

46. "The Byelorussian-American . . . ," *Sentinel* (South River, N.J.), May 30, 1973; Nina Zaprudnik, "Talent Show 1973," *Byelorussian Youth* 30 (summer 1973): 17.

47. "Byelorussian Heritage Festival, Report," Holmdel, N.J., April 1979, p. 2.

48. Natalla Arsiennieva-Kushel, *U haspodzie Paduanskaj* in *Between the Shores* (New York: Byelorussian Institute of Arts and Sciences, 1979), p. 184. Adapted to the stage by Nina Orsa, 1952.

49. Raisa Stankievich, "Byelorussian Folk Tales," *Byelorussian Youth* 34 (Summer 1974): 8–10.

50. Letter from Maria Stankievich to Vitaut Kipel, Hawthorne, N.J., Jan. 18, 1979.

BIBLIOGRAPHY

Books

Baryshau, Guryi, and Sannikau, Alex. *Belaruski narodny teatr batleika* (Byelorussian Folk Theater: Batleika). Minsk: Ministerstva Asviety, 1962. An authoritative monograph on the development of the batleika theatre; extensively documented.

Byelorussian Soviet Encyclopedia (BSE). 12 vols. plus index volume. Minsk; BSE, 1969–1976. Several volumes contain extensive information on the development and present state of Byelorussian theatre. Excellent illustrations, bibliographies.

Ciechanowiecki, Andrzej. *Michal Kazimierz Oginski und sein Musenhof zu Slonim.* Koeln: Boehlau Verlag, 1961. In the series: *Beitraege zur Geschichte Osteuropas,* Band 2. A scholarly work about the Slonim court theatre.

Dunin-Martsinkevich, Vincuk. *Vybranyia tvory* (Selected Works). Minsk: Ministerstva Asviety, 1957. Biographical data, short analysis of activities, and texts of major plays: *Hapon, Pinskaia Shlakhta, Zaloty,* and so on.

Miller, Antoni. *Teatr Polski i muzyka na Litwie jako straznice kultury zachodu, 1745–1865* (Polish Theatre and Music in Lithuania . . .). Vilna, 1936. Discussion of theatres on Byelorussian territory; survey and analysis, discussion of repertory and chronological development, extensive illustrations, references.

Niafiod, Uladzimir. *Belaruski teatr* (Byelorussian Theatre). Minsk: Akademiia Navuk BSSR, 1959. Scholarly monograph on the development of the Byelorussian theatre; the Soviet period is stressed but some important data and names are omitted.

————. *Suchasny belaruski teatr* (The Modern Byelorussian Theatre). Minsk: Ministerstva Asviety, 1961. Analysis of Soviet Byelorussian theatre. References.

Romanov, Yevdokim. *Belorusskii sbornik* (Collection of Works on Byelorussia). 9 vols. Kiev, 1886–1912. The most authoritative treatise on Byelorussians, their customs, songs, and life in the nineteenth century.

Seduro, Vladimir. *The Byelorussian Theater and Drama.* New York: Research Program on the USSR, 1955. The most complete and authoritative work on the Byelorussian theatre in English. Excellent documentation, illustrations, bibliography.

Semianovich, Anatol. *Belaruskaia dramaturhiia* (Byelorussian Drama). Minsk: Akademiia Navuk BSSR, 1961. Development of Byelorussian drama, repertory, performers.

Shein, Pavel. *Materialy dlia izuchenia byta . . .* (Ethnographical Materials). St. Petersburg: Akademiia Nauk, 1887–1902. *Sbornik,* vols. 41, 51, 57, 72. Extensive treatise on Byelorussian ethnography, customs, origins of songs, and so on. Excellent reference work on Byelorussian ethnography.

Theatres of Minsk. Minsk: Belarus Publishers, 1973. Guidebook to Minsk theatres in Byelorussian, English, and German. Extensively illustrated.

20 Years of Byelorussian American Youth Organization. Cleveland, BAYO, 1970. Analysis of different youth drama groups.

Zbornik p'iesau i pesen (Collection of Plays and Songs). Cleveland, Byelorussian-American Youth Organization, 1953.

Articles

"Advishou vydatny maistra" (An Outstanding Artist Passes Away). *Belarus* 144 (April 1969). Life and activities of Mikola Kulikovich-Shchahlou.

Arsiennieva, Natalla. "U haspodzie Paduanskaj." In *Between the Shores* (New York: Byelorussian Institute of Arts and Sciences, 1979), pp. 184–85.

"Auhen Kavaleuski, 1921–1963" [no author]. *Backaushchyna* 11, no. 611 (Oct. 1963). Life and activities of Auhen Kavaleuski, playwright, director, actor.

"Sv. Pam. Auhen Kavaleuski" (In Memoriam). *Byelorussian Youth* 19 (1963). Biography and review of his theatrical career. Portrait.

Budzimier, Uladzimir. "Uladyslau Halubok—narodny artyst Belarusi" (U. Halubok—People's Artist of Byelorussia). *Backaushchyna* 15–16, nos. 94–95 (Easter 1952). An extensive biographical sketch and review of his theatrical activities.

Ettinghof, B. "The National Theatres in the USSR." *VOKS Bulletin* (Moscow) 11, no. 5 (1931): 87–96. Analyzes the development of the Byelorussian theatre.

Fernald, John. "*King Lear* by the Minsk theatre Company." *VOKS Bulletin* 6, no. 83 (November-December 1953): 84–85. Review of the performance.

Hlybinny, Uladzimir. "Backa naveishaie belaruskaie dramaturhii i teatru" (The Founder of Modern Byelorussian Theater and Drama). *Belarus* (New York) 5, no. 29 (March 1953). Life and activities of Franchishak Alachnovich and his role in the history of Byelorussian theatre.

Kulikovich, Mikola. "Pamiatsi Barbary Verzhbalovich" (In Memoriam). *Belarus* 118 (Feb. 1967). Biographical data and theatrical career, photograph.

————. "Paulinka z Detroitu" (Paulinka from Detroit). *Backaushchyna* 22, no. 557 (May 28, 1961). Compares the performance of Paulinka in Chicago with the performance in Soviet Byelorussia. Very favorable review.

————. "Sto hod belaruskai opery" (The Hundredth Anniversary of Byelorussian Opera, 1848–1948). *Backaushchyna* 1, no. 45 (Jan. 2, 1959). An authoritative review of Byelorussian opera and operas on the Byelorussian stage.

Markov, P. "White Russian Theatre." *VOKS Bulletin* 1, no. 11–12 (1930): 15–17.

Sv. Pam. Alimp Mialenciseu" (obituary). *Backaushchyna* 7–8, nos. 621–22 (July 1964). Extensive review of his life and career. Mialetseu wrote an entirely new version of *Kupalle* (Midsummer Festival).

"Narodny artyst BNR: Viachaslau Selach-Kachanski." (Byelorussian People's artist). *Byelorussian Word* (Ludwigsburg, Germany) 8, no. 29 (Sept.-Oct. 1955). Extensive review of Kachanski's life and artistic career.

"New Byelorussian Plays." *International Literature* 12 (Dec. 1939). The repertoire of Byelorussian theatres in Minsk and Vitebsk.

Orlov, Dmitry. "Shakespeare on the Byelorussian stage." *VOKS Bulletin* 6, no. 83 (Nov.-Dec. 1953).

Prusky, Mikola. "Vialikaia padziaka" (A Big Thank You). *Sviet* (Detroit) 2, no. 21 (1961). Prusky expresses his thanks to all the people who helped with the performance and lists their names.

Rakhlenka, L. "The First White-Russian Theatre." *Soviet Culture Review* 7–8 (1933). Development of Byelorussian theatre from 1917 to 1920 and the establishment of the First State Byelorussian Theatre, September 1920.

Selach-Kachanski, Viachaslau. "Pamiatsi Lidzia Niadwiha" (In Memorium). *Belarus* 145 (May 1969). A portrait of the professional career of Lidzia Nedwiga.

————. "Tryumf belaruskaha teatru" (The Triumph of Byelorussian Theatre). *Byelorussian Youth* 21 (1964). The former director of the First Byelorussian Theatre in Minsk provides extensive information on the development of Byelorussian theatre under the Soviets. Most of this data is omitted from Soviet publications. Rare photographs.

————. "Selach-Kachanski, V." (In Memorium). *Byelorussian Thought* (South River, N.J.) 20 (1976). Professional career and biographical data.

Vasilevich, A. "Francishak Alachnovich." *Backaushchyna* 14, no. 296 (April 1, 1956). Extensive biography and account of his theatrical career.

4

Danish-American Theatre

CLINTON M. HYDE

DANISH NATIONAL THEATRE

Comedy and satire characterized the Danish National Theatre until the 1930s. Almost the entire production of immigrant theatre in the Danish-American colonies has also been comedy, satire, vaudeville, or musical revue. From the first satires of Ludvig Holberg (1684–1754), there was little Danish drama performed on the stage in Denmark. Naturally there were Danish translations of serious plays, which were well respected in the Royal Theatre in Denmark, but Holberg's comedies in the style of the French playwright Molière (1622–1673) set the trend for some time. Holberg's moralizing social satires are still performed today in Denmark.

One of the best examples of Danish satire to follow Holberg's lead was Johan Herman Wessel's (1742–1785) *Kaerlighed uden Strømper* (Love Without Stockings) (1772), a parody of the French tragedies of the time. It has often been noted that the Danish parody could follow the night after a straight performance of one of Voltaire's tragedies. One night the audience would applaud the serious, and the next night everyone would laugh at the comical version of the same. Apparently there was no intended criticism of the French manner of tragedy; the Danes have never resisted the temptation to make full use of a good sense of humor.

The tradition of Danish comedy was well developed and perhaps best utilized by the romantics and realists of the 1800s. Danish romanticism meant a return to Nordic themes of history and heroic figures. The Danish realists of the latter half of the nineteenth century found the interest in *Danskhed* (Danishness) in the milieu of the comedy, that is, in the everyday life of the common people of the northern countries. Situational comedy is something that can be identified in everyone's life. The comedies of the 1800s dominated the Danish theatre. The few dramas of a romantic nature were less well received, at least in the Danish-American communities. For example, *Axel og Valborg* (1809), a drama by Adam Oehlenschläger (1779–1850), was attempted once in Minneapolis but ended in a miserable failure.

In the 1860s the Danes flocked to the newest imitation of the Parisien *café chantants*.[1] Women sang songs in coffee houses and in the summertime in open pavilions. With the addition of a few more singers and a satirical plot with lyrics, the Danish *revy*, or musical revue, was born. Interest in theatre had been stimulated, creating a great demand for private theatre performances, when the king of Denmark turned over the Royal Theatre to the people in 1849. Students performed satire and parody for themselves and anyone who was interested. Interest in writing plays and especially comedy revues grew. The *Revy* has become a folk tradition that lives today in Denmark.

This is by no means a complete history of Danish National Theatre, but it can serve as an outline of the theatrical heritage of Danish immigrants of the nineteenth and early twentieth centuries. They brought with them memories of performances and scripts of Ludvig Holberg's satires, the comedies of the Danish romantics, and the student-life comedies and musical revues of the 1840s through the end of the 1890s.

By the 1930s Danish playwrights had begun producing serious drama, but this was little noticed in the Danish-American theatre, which selected its repertoire from the nineteenth century. A few attempts at Danish drama, such as *Ordet* (1926), by Kai Munk (1898–1944), were made by Danish immigrants between the world wars, but for the most part the Danish Americans have performed only comedies or revues from the past or plays they have written themselves.

AREAS AND EXTENT

Of the various Danish-American organizations that have performed regularly, there is a considerable amount of material available on those in Chicago, Minneapolis, and Seattle. Considering the history of Danish immigration in this country, it is particularly appropriate to look at these three colonies. Chicago and Minneapolis represent the earlier stages of Danish immigration to the Midwest during the second half of the nineteenth century. The theatrical activities in these colonies must have been typical of those in all the early settlements throughout Illinois, Iowa, Wisconsin, Minnesota, and Nebraska. The only difference would be the scale of the production in relation to the size of the colony. Chicago's Danish theatre bloomed particularly after 1900, for instance, but Minneapolis's Dania Hall was busiest in the last century. Seattle's Danish theatre, coming to life in the early 1900s, seems to have been typical of the later migration to the West Coast, either directly from Denmark or from Danish colonies in the Midwest. The zenith of Danish dramatic performances was in the 1920s and 1930s in Seattle and the other West Coast Danish colonies, from Vancouver to Los Angeles.

The history of Danish theatre in the United States can be dated to the earliest plays of the 1870s in Chicago and Minneapolis, up through the 1950s in the Midwest and on the West Coast. No doubt there have also been Danish theatre groups in New York and on the East Coast.

In the 1920s Danish dramatic societies were known to travel as far as from

Chicago or Seattle to Los Angeles. Guest performers from Denmark who have toured the United States have been mostly opera singers or poets. Apparently there have been very few professional or amateur theatre groups visiting the Danes abroad. An exception to this was a production of Johan Ludvig Heiberg's (1791–1860) Elverhøj (1828) in San Francisco in 1939, but this performance was in English.

Occasionally Danish plays are still performed by children's groups and in the Danish-American colleges, Dana College in Blair, Nebraska, and Grand View College in Des Moines, Iowa. As recently as April 1979 there was a production of a famous Danish musical, Genboerne (Neighbors), in the Danish Lutheran Church in Los Angeles. However, the Danish-American theatre that was known to many Danish immigrants in the period 1870–1950 is gone. Those who performed regularly in Danish in the 1920s and 1930s get together occasionally for songs and parties, but they no longer perform.

THEATRICAL GROUPS

Immigrants naturally take care of their needs in order of importance. First they find employment, find a church, and then form a social circle. In meeting these needs, immigrants often form organizations of mutual benefit. Besides establishing churches with services in their own language, the Danes in America developed fraternal and sororal organizations: the Dansk Brodersamfund (Danish Brotherhood) and the Dansk Søstersamfund (Danish Sisterhood), the Dania Lodge, and various literary circles, dramatic societies, and glee clubs.

In Chicago Dansk Ungdoms Foreningen (Danish Young People's Society) included theatrical productions besides its other church-oriented activities. Often the pastor of the local Danish Lutheran Church would lead the production in the church basement. When the audience appreciation grew, the local theatre or brotherhood hall was used to accommodate audiences of four to eight hundred. Chicago's Danish Young People's Society was led by Orla and Ove Knudsen and Orla Juul in an organization called Det Danske Teater from about 1914 to 1945. They performed in the Garrick Theater, the Northside Turner Hall, and later in Harmonien's Hall. There were always requests for guest performances in the Danish colonies around Chicago, such as in Racine, Wisconsin. (For a list of plays performed, see the fourth section of the appendix to this chapter.)

From 1870 to 1908 in Minneapolis, various Danish-Norwegian groups organized for the sole purpose of performing Danish comedy: Norsk Dramatisk Forening, Skandinaviske Forening, Den Danske Dramatiske Klub, and Den Dansk-Norske Dramatiske Forening. The Danish Young People's Society of 1905 and other groups presented over thirty-five plays in the period 1906–1915.[2] The plays were performed in the Pence Opera House, Turner Hall, the People's Theater, and Dania Hall. (For listings of the plays, see the second and third sections of the appendix to this chapter.)

The Danish Folk High Schools (Folkehøjskole) in the Midwest, such as in

Tyler and West Denmark, Minnesota, and Nysted and Blair, Nebraska, and at Grand View College all had student groups that performed regularly. The Grand View *Unge Kräfter* traveled to several Danish towns in Iowa after spring graduation.

In Omaha, Nebraska, the Young People's Society was particularly active in the 1920s under the direction of Pastor F. O. Lund in the Danish Evangelical Lutheran Church. Volunteers built a stage in the fellowship hall of the church. Lund had performed professionally in the Odense Theatre in Denmark as a child and in his youth. One of the guest performances in the Omaha church was by a young people's society from Marquette, Nebraska. They performed a play that undoubtedly was written in this country: *Den som gaar Køkkenvej*, which deals with an immigrant coming to live on a farm on the prairie. This play was later produced by the Danish Young People's Society in the Danish church in Seattle.

Gudrun Lund, the wife of F. O. Lund, remembers her first experience with Danish theatre in this country in a personal letter.

In the Fall of 1908 and the Spring of 1909 in Askov, Minnesota, I first experienced the fun of theater. The Danish colony was new and still had the name Partridge. They did not yet have a church nor a resident pastor. But several of the people that moved there had been to "Højskole" [adult education] in Denmark. The station master, Mr. Nortvig, was from Copenhagen. They decided to give a play. It was to be "Soldaterløjer" [Soldier Pranks] by Hostrup. Mr. Nortvig was the instructor and Aksel Berntsen, my father, taught the melodies of the songs by playing them on his violin. At the performance in the old town hall they sang without the use of instruments. The men built the stage and the ladies sewed the costumes. Over the stage they painted a sign that said, "Ej blot til Lyst" [Not for amusement alone]. The plays I remember from those first years of the colony are "Soldaterløjer" by Hostrup, "Fastelavnsgildet" [Shrovetide Fest] and "Et Uhyre" [A Monster] by Erik Bøgh, "En Nat i Roskilde" [A Night in Roskilde] by Hans Christian Andersen and a Revy written by Mr. Nortvig.[3]

In Seattle the Danish Young People's Society became known as Dagmar in the first decade of this century. Later the Danish Dramatic Club became known as Harmonien. While the Young People's Society continued to perform in St. John Lutheran Church on an occasional basis, Harmonien entertained regularly in the Danish Brotherhood lodge, Washington Hall, for almost fifty years. Danish summerschool for children, organized by Danish Lutheran churches in many parts of the country, presented skits and comedies in Danish.

ACTORS AND PRODUCERS

Danish-American theatre has been strictly amateur. However, judging from the success of many groups in performing for forty-five to fifty years before large audiences on a regular basis, the quality of the comedies and revues must have been high. In 1925 Harmonien in Seattle gave the profit of $161 from one performance to the building fund of the Northwest Danish Home.

The directors of theatre groups and individual plays in the Danish communities have often been Lutheran pastors, school teachers, or persons of some scholarly, theatrical background, but this is only the rule. In Minneapolis, for example, besides painter Peter Clausen, professional actress Sophie Oulie, and postmaster F. A. G. Moe, there once was an occasional laborer by the name of Hansen who "only worked summers." Two successive winters he financed his expensive taste in clothes and cigars by organizing and playing a comedy. His supporting actors, however, only let him run off with the box office receipts once.

The actors in Minneapolis were cigar manufacturer Theodore Darum; consul Snedorph-Christensen; lieutenant A. C. Nielsen, pioneer L. A. Andersen; the goddaughter of playwright and poet Jens Christian Hostrup (1816–1892), Mrs. Gunnet; police officer Holger Faurschou; sign painter Carl Neumann; printer Waldemar Kriedt; and many more.[4] Apparently the Danish theatre in Minneapolis had more life in it than the Norwegian. In 1900 the Norwegian actor Anton Sanness and his Danish wife joined the Danish Dramatic Society after moving from Chicago to Minneapolis. Although many of the actors are not identified, it is clear that the majority were skilled laborers or white collar workers who had an ethnic and esthetic interest in the theatre.

In Askov, Minnesota, it was the stationmaster, Nortvig, who got everyone together to perform the comedies known to those who had gone to the Folk High School in Denmark. No doubt among the actors were some farmers, who also had attended the "high school" during the winter months of their youth in Denmark, because the philosophy of N. F. S. Grundtvig's "school for life" was education for the masses. Through these former students the appreciation of theatrical arts for everyone was transplanted to the woods of Minnesota and the prairie of the Midwest. The performers in the folk high schools of Iowa and Nebraska were the same farmers' children, who returned to their communities and churches to continue the tradition wherever they could get enough Danes together for theatre.

Through fifty years of intense activity, the guiding force of Seattle's Danish dramatic society, Harmonien, was a woman of immense creativity, Elfrida Pedersen, nee Jensen, wife of plumber Hans Pedersen, who had proposed marriage to her behind the curtains during one of Harmonien's performances. She had no formal theatrical background; yet Elfrida Pedersen wrote enough lyrics to revue songs and playscripts to rightfully be called Seattle's Danish poet laureate. Her lyrics for the introductory song of *Seattle Revyen 1924* give a very good overview of the active members of the Danish community.[5] The song tells of an eighteen-year-old immigrant who crosses ocean and continent to land in Seattle. He gets a list of prospective employers in town and finds Dr. Sorensen, baker Rasmussen, Jensen who owns a fish shop, tailors Fries and Tagholm, butcher Hansen, painter Madsen, dairy owner Sam Olsen, mill owner Lehmann (also honorary Danish consul), plumber Pedersen, and milkman Mikkelsen.

Many of Harmonien's members were recruited from the boardinghouse in

Washington Hall, the Danish Brotherhood hall on Fourteenth and Fir Street, lovingly called Trine's Pensionat. The newest immigrants lived directly behind the stage in Washington Hall. For many the hall was an immediate introduction to the entire Danish colony. Several blocks away from Washington Hall there was a stage in the basement of St. John Lutheran Church, built in 1925 for the Danish Young People's Society productions. The attached parsonage housed the children of the colony in dormitory style for the Danish summerschool through the twenties, thirties, and forties. The children's plays obviously served to interest the students in Danish language and culture.

In the 1960s Emanuel Danish Evangelical Lutheran Church in Los Angeles was still performing occasionally in Danish under the Lund's direction. As recently as April 1979 the ever-popular *Genboerne*, by Hostrup, was presented in the Los Angeles church.

COMEDY, SATIRE, AND REVUE

Except for an occasional serious drama, almost all the Danish plays written and/or performed in the United States have been comedy, satire, or revue. Most of the full-length comedies were brought over from Denmark in the memories of the immigrants, although some groups purchased the scripts from the Danish press, Danskboghandelsforlag, in Ceder Falls, Iowa. The shorter skits, of course, were written and typed locally. Elfrida Pedersen kept 125 *lejlighedsdigte* (occasional poems) and songs from the active years of Seattle's Harmonien.[6] Many of them she had written herself. Several were printed for distribution to the audiences. The texts of these songs reveal the tradition of the *Revy* and the American immigrant experience. A *Revy* can include a simple plot, which is often repeated as a framework. The songs can be reworked again and again. *Seattle Revyen 1924*, presented by Harmonien in Washington Hall, included a good selection of such songs. They describe the daily life of the Danish newcomer to Seattle, the kind of work he or she could find, the social groups and the Danish Lutheran Church, and the Northwest Danish Home. They tell which Danes have been elected to office or have succeeded in public life. Besides the local references, the song texts show Americanization of the language for the sake of rhyme and meter, for example, *Plumberen* instead of *Blikkenslager* and expressions such as "you bet."

From adult-level comedy, the Danish-American theatre expanded in later years to the dramatization of Hans Christian Andersen fairy tales. *The Emperor's New Clothes, The Steadfast Tin Soldier*, and adaptations of *Ole Lukeøje* have been performed by and for the younger generation, often the children of the dramatic society. Although some of the skits had been presented in Danish to increase interest in the language among the young, the later performances, in 1950–1960, were in English.

In spite of the fact that Danish-American theatre has been almost entirely amateur, photographs show that there was often an attempt to use full sets and costumes. This was especially true in organizations such as Harmonien in Seattle, which had its own stage and room for storing props. If all the ethnic groups were staging plays as often as the Danes were in the twenties and thirties, the costume rental companies must have been very busy.

Except for the ever-popular comedies of Ludvig Holberg, the Danish-American theatres preferred comedies and *Revy* written in Denmark in the nineteenth century. Holberg's *Jeppe paa Bjerget* has been seen on the stage almost anywhere there has been a Danish theatre. This social-moralizing comedy in the vein of the French playwright Molière has some characteristics that would especially appeal to the Danes. Holberg's use of various dialects denoting the social status of the characters has a comic effect. There is the colorful language of the local drunk, Jeppe, who drinks himself into an impossible situation only to find it is a dream; he doesn't realize it is actually a trick played on him by the local baron. In a Pygmalion experiment, Jeppe is taken in a drunken stupor to the baron's estate. On his waking, the servants treat him as royalty, heeding his every command, which becomes rather ridiculous. After he passes out again, he is led to believe he is dying by hanging. He laments his life and his poor treatment of Nille, his wife. They are reunited when she convinces him he is not dead. The fact that Holberg's comedy has become a classic and has been played repeatedly in Denmark explains the appeal of *Jeppe paa Bjerget* to the Danish Americans. The content and the comedy situation lend themselves well to amateur performances.

The two most popular playwrights in Danish-American theatre, however, have been Jens Christian Hostrup (1816–1892) and Erik Bøgh (1822–1899). In the fifty years of its existence, Harmonien presented a Hostrup play no fewer than six times. In Minneapolis between 1870 and 1915, eleven of his comedy revues went over the stage.

A teacher and casual poet, Hostrup was best known by students for his drinking songs. In 1844 he wrote *Genboerne*, which besides being extremely popular in Denmark, is probably the Danish *Revy* that has been repeated most often in the United States. (See appendix to this chapter for dates of performances.)

Genboerne has a thin plot about students and bourgeoisie living close together. The students represent idealism and the bourgeois materialism. The uniting of the two is expressed in the marriage of the blacksmith's daughter, Rikke, to the student, Basalt. Along the way the actors sing numerous *Revy* numbers with allusions to authors and philosophers who were contemporaries of Hostrup, such as Hans Christian Andersen, Søren Kierkegaard, and N.F.S. Grundtvig.[7] The songs have been reworked over the years, true to the tradition of the *Revy*, and the Danish immigrants have no doubt all produced their own versions.

In 1847 Hostrup wrote *Eventyr paa Fodrejsen* (1847), the second most popular of his comedies. The plot, again only enough to connect the humorous songs, is a typical case of confused identities, which were popular also in the novels of the 1800s.

Erik Bøgh has been acclaimed for inventing the Danish *Revy*. With the performance of his *Nytaarsnat 1850*, Bøgh began his career as director of the Casino Theatre in Copenhagen and playwright of over a hundred *sangspil*, or musical comedies.

Harmonien in Seattle produced eight of his revues, and in Minneapolis there were at least six productions of his comedies in the period 1880–1900. In appealing to the masses, Bøgh went further than Hostrup in uniting the materialistic with the idealistic. He felt that poetry was to be enjoyed and turned his back on the academic excesses of the romantics.[8] In making the poetry of the *Revy* songs accessible to the masses, the universal recognition of the Danish "comedy with songs" among the immigrants in America is understandable.

The third most popular playwright of Danish-American theatre would have to be the Danish immigrants themselves. All the members and directors of the Danish dramatic societies in the United States contributed to the songs and skits performed in the Danish comedies. It is difficult to give credit where it is due, since the local authors of the revues are rarely mentioned on the programs printed for those occasions.[9]

ROLE OF DANISH-AMERICAN THEATRE

The first Danish-American theatre in the Scandinavian colony of Minneapolis was for the entertainment of the approximately two thousand Danes, Norwegians, and Swedes in 1870. The same can obviously be said for the Danish farming communities of the Midwest and the growing colonies on the West Coast by 1900. By the 1920s the cultural importance of Danish theatre was recognized, especially by those first-generation Danes who understood the language spoken on stage. The Danish Young People's Society in each church could use the entertainment value of the comedy in the fellowship hall as a means to "preserve the Danish language and cultural heritage." A tribute to Hans Christian Andersen in 1930 on the 125th anniversary of his birth was especially important for recognizing the world-famous Dane.

The stages in the Danish Brotherhood lodges and Dania halls across the nation provided as natural a gathering place as the Danish Lutheran Church. That Washington Hall in Seattle was filled with several hundred people for three or four evenings a year is a good indication of how popular Harmonien's productions were.

By the 1920s and 1930s, Danish Americans discovered the organization. Everyone was going to meetings of this or that club. Radio and television had not yet begun to paralyze the American brain in the evening hours after the hard eight-hour day. Elfrida Pedersen had the energy to coach, encourage, feed, and dress the performers of Harmonien. In a letter to a historian, Pedersen remembered taking the streetcar to downtown Seattle in the twenties to meet her husband, Hans the plumber, with clean clothes. He would disappear in the underground washrooms under the Pergola on Pioneer Square to change. When he emerged they would catch the next streetcar up to the Brotherhood Lodge on Capital Hill.[10]

In the most active years of the Danish theatre groups, there was a tidy profit in performing regularly. Harmonien in Seattle turned all its earnings over to the local Danish organizations. If the money was not sent to the Danish Brotherhood and Sisterhood Health Insurance Fund, it went to the building fund for the Northwest Danish Old People's Home (all performances from 1924 to 1931) or for the building of a church (1917–1919). During the Depression, Harmonien was the main financial supporter of the Danish organizations in Seattle.

In 1930 and 1931 the Danish dramatic societies of the United States pooled their earnings to help bring the Danish team to the Olympics in Los Angeles. This constituted the most political, if it can be called that, motivation to be found in Danish-American theatre. There may have been political messages in some performances in the early years of the Danish Brotherhood, but no record of this has been found.

Harmonien in Seattle celebrated its fiftieth anniversary on September 23, 1961, with a performance of *En Søndag paa Amager*, by Johanne Louise Heiberg, the same vaudeville the club had staged in the beginning, on November 11, 1911. The actors were second-generation Danes and newer immigrants of the fifties, but the original cast of Harmonien, the Danish Dramatic Club, was no longer on stage. Elfrida Pedersen had directed, arranged, and coached everyone through a glimpse of the past. She wrote the program, including a short history of Harmonien. Her speech on that day lamented the toll on entertainment that television and radio had exacted. Danish-American theatre had run its course. Interestingly enough, the theatrical creations of the Danish immigrants could not completely "preserve the Danish language and culture" in the American society. Rather, the attempt in the form of songs, skits, and so on continued a Danish tradition of amateur comedy and *Revy* while recording the process of Americanization of the Danish immigrants.

Appendix A: Productions of Harmonien in Seattle, Washington, from 1906 to 1961

Year Performed	Title of Play*	Type of Play	Author (if known)
1906	Fastelavnsgildet (The Shrovetide Fest)	revue	Erik Bøgh (1822–1899)
1909	Den Ene eller Den Anden eller: En af Dem Skal Giftes (The one or the other: one of them must marry)	comedy	P. Engel
1910	Haandvaerkernes Fest (The Craftmen's Fest)	one-act vaudeville	Louis Angely
1910	Valbygaasen (The Goose of Valby)	revue	Bøgh
1911	Haandvaerkernes Fest (The Craftsmen's Fest)	one-act vaudeville	Angely
1911	En Søndag paa Amager (A Sunday on Amager)	one-act revue	Johanne Louise Heiberg (1812–1890)
1912	Ikke en Smule Jaloux (Not a Little Jealous)	one-act comedy	Engel
1912	Fastelavnsgildet (The Shrovetide Fest)	revue	Bøgh
1912	Lille Nitouche (Little Nitouche)	n.a.	P. Fristrup
1912	Slaegtningerne (The Relatives)	one-act vaudeville	Henriette Nielsen
1913	Eventyr paa Fodrejsen (1847) (Adventure on Foot)	sangspil in four acts	Jens Christian Hostrup (1816–1892)
1913	Charles' Tante og Charlotte's Onkel (Charles' Aunt and Charlotte's Uncle)	burlesque	Reck
1913	Aars Revy eller Udflugten til Maple Grove Park (Annual Revue or the Outing to Maple Grove Park)	revy	local (Probably Elfrida Pedersen)
1913	Et Enfoldigt Pigebarn (A Simple Girl)	two-act vaudeville	Bøgh
1914	En Søndag paa Amager (A Sunday on Amager)	one-act revue	Johanne Louise Heiberg
1914	Studeprangeren (The Cattle Dealer)	two-act comedy	C. Andreasen
1915	Svinedrengen (The Swineherd)	fairy tale	Hans Christian Andersen (1805–1875)

110

1915	Valbygaasen (The Goose of Valby)	revue	Bøgh
1915	Revyen 1915 (1915 Revue)	revue	local
1915	Til Saeters (To the Mountain Pastures)	comedy	P. C. Riis
1917	En Tale (A Speech)	comedy with songs	C. M. Wengel
1917	Piperman i Knibe (The Piper in a Fix)	one-act farce	translated from French
1917	Slaegtningerne (The Relatives)	one-act vaudeville	Henriette Nielsen
1918	Den Dag Jeg Første Gang Dig Saa (The Day I Saw You for the First Time)	n.a.	Martin Halse
1918	I Pensionatet (In the Boarding House)	comedy with songs	n.a.
1920	Fyret ved Vesterhavet (The Lighthouse on the North Sea)	comedy with songs	Adolph Recke (1820–1867)
1920	Den Tredje (The Third)	comedy with songs	Hostrup
1921	Feriegaesterne (The Vacation Guests)	comedy with songs	Hostrup
1922	Den Graa Paletot (The Gray Palet)	two-act vaudeville	Bøgh
1923	Aegtemandens Representant (The Husband's Representative)	two-act vaudeville	Bøgh
1923	I Amors Kontortid (Love's Office Hours)	one-act farce	Holger Gundelach
1923	Et Enfoldigt Pigebarn (A Simple Girl)	two-act vaudeville	Bøgh
1923	Rasmines Bryllup eller Høkeren og Blikkenslager (Relatives Wedding or the Huckster and the Plumber)	four-act comedy	Axel Frisce and Robert Schønfeld
1924	Den nøgne Sandhed eller Seattle Revyen 1924 (The Naked Truth or the Seattle Revue 1924)	three-act revue	local
1924	Generaldirektør (General Manager)	two-act comedy	Verner Nielsen
1925	Paa Dydens Vej (The Way of Virtue)	two-act comedy	Elfrida Pedersen?
1925	Et Fremtidsbillede eller Alderdomshjemmet 1935 (A Picture of the Future or the Old Folks Home 1935)	skit	John Pedersen
1925	Haandvaerkernes Fest (The Craftsmen's Fest)	one-act comedy	Engel
1925	Det grønne Haab (The Green Hope)	drama with songs, four acts	Holger Drachman (1846–1908)
1925	Familiens Skraek (The Shock of the Family)	two-act comedy	n.a.
1926	Vaekkeuret (The Alarm Clock)	n.a.	Villian

*There are no official translations of these plays, including the few that have been translated in their entirety, e.g. *Jeppe paa Bjerget* by Holberg, which I will simply refer to as *Jeppe*, a man's name. The meaning of the full title, Jeppe paa Bjerget is, literally Jeppe on the hill. Those titles composed of proper names would most often remain untranslated or changed (i.e., anglicized, unless necessary).

(continued)

Year Performed	Title of Play	Type of Play	Author (if known)
1926	Nøddebo Praestegaard (The Noddebo Parish)	five-act comedy	adapted by Elith Reumert (1855–1934) from the short story "Ved Nytaarstid i Nøddebo Praestegaard," by Henrik Scharling
1927	Studeprangeren (The Cattle Dealer)	n.a.	Andreasen
1927	Slaegtningerne (The Relatives)	one-act vaudeville	Henriette Nielsen
1927	Naar Aegtemaend Filmer (When the Husband Films)	comedy	translated to Danish from Wilhelm Rechendorf
1928	Under Hammeren (Under the Hammer)	n.a.	Peder R. Møller
1928	En Børsbaron eller Den glade Kobbersmed (A Baron of the Stock Exchange or the Happy Coppersmithie)	n.a.	n.a.
1929	Tordenskjold i Dynekilen (Tordenskjold at the Battle of Dynekile)	three-act romantic drama	Carit Etlar (1816–1900)
1929	Sofaen (The Sofa)	n.a.	Reumert
1929	En Bryllupsaften (An Evening Wedding)	one-act comedy	Peter Nansen (1861–1918)
1929	København—Aarhus, Tur og Retur (Copenhagen—Aarhus, Round Trip)	n.a.	n.a.
1930	The Valiant	English performance by the Junior League	
1930	Harmonien's Sports Revy (Harmonica's Sports Show)	revue	local
1930	Harmonien's tribute to Hans Christian Andersen on the 125th Anniversary of his birth:		
	The Emperor's New Clothes	fairy tale performed in English by the Junior League	
	Princessen paa Aerten (The Princess and the Pea)	fairy tale performed by Harmonien	
1930	Min egen Dreng (My Own Boy)	five-act drama	n.a.
1931	Spar Jert Nye Tøj (Spare Your New Clothes)	party skit	Elfrida Pedersen
1931	Den Standhaftige Tinsoldat (The Steadfast Tin Soldier)	fairy tale	Andersen
1931	Barn i Kirke (Child in Church)	four-act farce	Peter Sørensen
1932	Sparekassen eller Naar Enden er God, er Alting Godt (The Savings Bank, or All's Well That Ends Well)	comedy	Henrik Hertz (1797–1870)

Year	Title	Type	Author
1932	Rasmines Bryllup (Relatives Wedding)	n.a.	Frisce and Schønfeld
1933	Lille Nitouche (Little Nitouche)	n.a.	Fristrup
1933	Jeppe paa Bjerget (Jeppe)	five-act satire	Ludvig Holberg (1684–1754)
1934	Soldaterløjer (Soldier's Pranks)	comedy	Hostrup
1935	Indkvartering eller Han Drikker (Lodging or He Drinks)	n.a.	n.a.
1935	Tvillingerne (The Twins)	four-act comedy	Reumert
1935	Peters Julegave (Peter's Christmas Gift)	four-act Christmas play	Rigmor Falk Rønne
1936	The 1936 Revy, or The All-Wave Radio Broadcast		n.a.
1936	En Søndag paa Amager (A Sunday in Amager)	one-act revue	Johanne Louise Heiberg
1937	Min Egen Dreng (My Own Boy) (performed by Harmonien in Seattle, Enumclaw, and Livermore, California, for 1,000 persons)	five-act drama	n.a.
1938	De Pokkers Studenter (Those Darn Students)	one-act comedy	Lars C. Ringholt
1939	Elverhøj (Elf Hill) (Elfrida Pedersen made a professional performance in this play in San Francisco in the War Memorial Opera House, together with Danish professionals such as Aksel Schiøtz, Ellen Malmberg, and Johannes Meyer, who appeared as guests from Denmark.)	romantic operetta	Johan Ludvig Heiberg (1791–1860)
1940	What a Week	revue in English	n.a.
1940	Naar Katten er Ude (When the Cat's Away)	n.a.	n.a.
1941	I Amors Kontortid (Love's Office Hours)	one-act comedy	Gundelach
1942	Valbygaasen (The Goose of Valby)	vaudeville	Bøgh
1948	Haandvaerkernes Fest (The Craftsmen's Fest)	one-act vaudeville	Angely
1948	Paa Dydens Vej (The Way of Virtue)	two-act comedy	Elfrida Pedersen?
1949	Tante gaar paa Maskarade (Auntie at the Maskarade)	n.a.	Rønne
1951	Genboerne (The Neighbors)	three-act comedy	Hostrup
1952	Skjul Intet for din Kone (Hide Nothing from your Wife)	three-act comedy	A. C. Wendsy
1954	De Flyvende Hatte (The Flying Hats)	n.a.	n.a.
1961	En Søndag paa Amager (A Sunday in Amager) (Harmonien's Fiftieth Anniversary)	one-act revue	Johanne Louise Heiberg

Appendix B: Plays Performed in Minneapolis, Minnesota, by Various Danish/Norwegian Groups, from 1870–1910

Year Performed	Title of Play	Type of Play	Author (if known)
1870	En Søndag paa Amager (A Sunday on Amager)	one-act revue	Johanne Louise Heiberg (1812–1890)
1873	Slaegtningerne (The Relatives)	one-act vaudeville	Henriette Nielsen
1874	Et Uhyre (A Monster)	one-act comedy	Erik Bøgh (1822–1899)
1874	Valbygaasen (The Goose of Valby)	revue	Bøgh
1878	Axel og Valborg (1809) (Axel and Valborg)	romantic drama	Adam Oehlenschläger (1779–1850)
1880	Pepita (Pepita)	n.a.	n.a.
1881	En Søndag paa Amager (A Sunday on Amager)	one-act revue	Johanne Louise Heiberg
1883	Valbygaasen (The Goose of Valby)	revue	Bøgh
1883	Eventyr paa Fodrejsen (1847) (Adventure on Foot)	four-act vaudeville	Jens Christian Hostrup (1816–1892)
1884	Store Bededagsaften*	n.a.	n.a.
1885	Hr. Volmer i Sorø (Mr. Volmer in Sorø)	n.a.	n.a.
1885	Intrigerne (The Intrigue)	vaudeville	Hostrup
1885	Soldaterløjer (Soldier's Pranks)	vaudeville	Hostrup
1886	De Nygifte (The Newlyweds)	vaudeville	Johan Ludvig Heiberg (1791–1860)
1886	Abekatten	n.a.	Johanne Louise Heiberg
1886	Den Tredje (The Third)	comedy with songs	Hostrup
	(A telegram was sent to Hostrup on the date of the performance in honor of his seventieth birthday, May 20, 1886)		

Year	Title	Type	Author
1886	En Nat i Roskilde (A Night in Roskilde)	satire	Hans Christian Andersen (1805–1875)
1888	Soldaterløjer (Soldier's Pranks)	vaudeville	Hostrup
1889	I Mørke (By Dark)	n.a.	n.a.
1889	Soldaterløjer (Soldier's Pranks)	vaudeville	Hostrup
1889	Jeppe paa Bjerget (Jeppe)	satire	Ludvig Holberg (1684–1754)
1890	Fastelavnsgildet (The Shrovetide Fest)	revue	Bøgh
1890	En Søndag paa Amager (A Sunday on Amager)	one-act revue	Johanne Louise Heiberg
1890	Store Bededagsaften	n.a.	n.a.
1891	Abekatten	n.a.	Johanne Louise Heiberg
1891	Slægtningerne (The Relatives)	one-act vaudeville	Henriette Nielsen
1892	Tordenskjold i Dynekilen (Tordenskjold at the Battle of Dynekile)	three-act historic drama	Carit Etlar (1816–1900)
1896	Om Forladelse (For Forgiveness)	n.a.	n.a.
1896	En Søndag paa Amager (A Sunday on Amager)	one-act revue	Johanne Louise Heiberg
1896	Et Enfoldigt Pigebarn (A Simple Girl)	two-act vaudeville	Bøgh
1896	Den Tredje (The Third)	revue	Hostrup
1897	Store Bededagsaften	n.a.	n.a.
1899	En lille Datter (A Little Daughter)	n.a.	n.a.
1899	Store Bededagsaften	n.a.	n.a.
1899	Intrigerne (The Intrigue)	vaudeville	Hostrup
1900	Tordenskjold i Dynekilen (Tordenskjold at the Battle of Dynekile)	three-act drama	Etlar
1900	Verdens Herkules (The Hercules of the World)	n.a.	n.a.
1900	Jeppe paa Bjerget (Jeppe)	satire	Holberg
1905	Valbygaasen (The Goose of Valby)	revue	Bøgh
1906	Genboerne (Neighbors)	three-act comedy	Hostrup
1907	Nej (No)	n.a.	Johan Ludvig Heiberg
1907	Nytaarsdag 1907 (New Years Eve 1907)	revue	local?
1909	En lille Datter (A Little Daughter)	n.a.	local?
1910	Jeppe paa Bjerget (Jeppe)	satire	Holberg

*The name of a church holiday, which to my knowledge, exists only in Denmark. Literally it means "the big day of worship." One of the pragmatic kings of Denmark made all the church holidays into one—reducing the number of days not worked by the peasants.

Appendix C: Plays Performed by the Ungdomsforening af 1905 in Minneapolis, Minnesota, from 1906 to 1915

Year Performed	Title of Play	Type of Play	Author (if known)
1906	Husets Folk (The People of the House)	n.a.	n.a.
1906	Gammel Kaerlighed ruster ikke (Old Love Rusts Not)	n.a.	n.a.
1908	En Prøveklud (A Sample)	n.a.	n.a.
1908	Deklarationen (The Declaration)	n.a.	Christian Richardt
1909	Min Svigersøn (My Son-in-law)	n.a.	n.a.
1909	En Søndag paa Amager (A Sunday on Amager)	one-act revue	Johanne Louise Heiberg (1812–1890)
1910	Kvikmans Kvaler (The Woes of Kvikmans)	n.a.	n.a.
1910	Den pantsatte Bondedreng (The Mortgaged Farmer Boy)	satire	Ludvig Holberg (1684–1754)
1911	Kvikmans Kvaler (The Woes of Kvikman)	n.a.	n.a.
1911	Naar Katten er Ude (When the Cat's Away)	n.a.	n.a.
1911	Store Bededagsaften	revue	local?
1911	Vaekkeuret (The Alarm Clock)	one-act farce from French	
1912	Piperman i Knibe (The Piper in a Fix)	vaudeville	Jens Christian Hostrup (1816–1892)
1912	Intrigerne (The Intrigue)	n.a.	Bentzonich
1912	Guldkareten (The Golden Carriage)	n.a.	n.a.
1912	Jensen Kommer (Jensen's Coming)	n.a.	Johanne Louise Heiberg
1914	Abekatten	n.a.	n.a.
1914	Betsy (Betsy)	n.a.	n.a.
1914	Jomfruen (The Virgin)	n.a.	n.a.
1915	Eventyr paa Fodrejsen (1847) (Adventure on Foot)	four-act vaudeville	Hostrup

Appendix D: Performances in Chicago by the Danish Young People's Society, from c. 1914 to 1945

Year Performed	Title of Play	Type of Play	Author (if known)
n.a.	Jeppe paa Bjerget (Jeppe)	satire	Ludvig Holberg (1684–1754)
n.a.	Ambrosius (Ambrosius)	n.a.	Christian K. F. Molbech
n.a.	Molboerne (The Molbo Folks)	comedy	n.a.
n.a.	Gøngehøvdingen (1853) (The Chief of Gonge)	historical novel dramatized	Carit Etlar (1816–1900)
n.a.	Elverhøj (1828) (Elf Hill)	romantic operetta	Johan Ludvig Heiberg (1791–1860)
n.a.	Bro over Havet (Bridge Over the Sea)	n.a.	n.a.
n.a.	Erasmus Montanus (Erasmus Montanus)	n.a.	Holberg
n.a.	Den forvandlede Brudgom (The Bridegroom's Metamorphosis)	n.a.	Holberg
n.a.	Rasmines Bryllup (Rasmine's Wedding)	four-act vaudeville	Axel Frisce and Robert Schønfeld
n.a.	Ebberød Bank (The Banks of Ebberød)	n.a.	n.a.
n.a.	Et Enfoldigt Pigebarn (A Simple Girl)	two-act vaudeville	Erik Bøgh (1822–1899)
n.a.	Første Violin (First Violin)	n.a.	Gustav Weid?
n.a.	Faedrenes Jord (Our Parents Earth)	n.a.	n.a.
n.a.	Et Opgør (A Conclusion)	n.a.	Weid
n.a.	Eventyr paa Fodrejsen (1847) (Adventure on Foot)	four-act vaudeville	Jens Christian Hostrup (1816–1892)
n.a.	Sofus (Sofus)	revue	Poul Hoff Kunst (in Chicago)
n.a.	Han sidder ved Smeltediglen (He is Sitting at the Melting Pot)	drama	Kai Munk (1898–1944)
n.a.	Egelykke (Egelykke)	drama	Munk
1945	Tvillingerne (The Twins)	four-act comedy	Elith Reumert (1855–1934)
1945	Et Opgør (A Conclusion)	n.a.	Weid

NOTES

1. *Dansk Litteratur Historie* (The History of Danish Literature) (Copenhagen: Politiken Forlag, 1976–1977), vol. 3, p. 487.
2. *De Forenede Staters Danske Almanak* (Danish Almanac for the United States) (Seattle, Wash.: Danish Publishing House on the Pacific Coast, 1916), pp. 85–90.
3. From a letter of personal memoirs in the possession of the author, by permission of Gudrum Lund.
4. *De Forenede Staters Danske Almanak*, 1916, pp. 88–91.
5. Printed song sheet entitled,, "Den nøgne Sandhed eller Seattle Revy 1924" ("The naked truth or Seattle revue 1924"), Archives and Manuscripts, Suzzallo Library, University of Washington, Seattle.
6. Archives and Manuscripts, Suzzallo Library, University of Washington, Seattle.
7. *Dansk Litteratur Historie*, vol. 3, pp. 489–90.
8. Ibid., vol. 3, p. 495.
9. For an excellent bibliography of Danish-American plays, see *Danish-American Life and Letters, A Bibliography by Enok Mortensen* (Des Moines, Iowa: Grand View College, Committee on Publication of the Danish Evangelical Lutheran Church in America, 1945).
10. Elfrida Pedersen Collection, Archives and Manuscripts, Suzzallo Library.

BIBLIOGRAPHY

Literature and Theatre History

Aumont, Arthur and Collin, Edgar. *Det danske Nationalteater, 1748–1889.* Copenhagen, 1896–1899. Vols. 1–3. A history of Danish Theatre 1746–1889.
Dansk Litteratur Historie. Copenhagen: Politikens Forlag, 1976–1977. Vols. 1–3.
Swendsen, Lauritz. *De Københavnske Privateteatres Repertoire 1847–1919.* 1907–1919. Vols. 1, 2.

Danish-American History

Den danske-amerikanske Historie. Copenhagen: Vanity Press, 1937.
Hartwick, Sophus. *Danske i California.* San Francisco, n.p., 1939, pp. 395–97.
Hall-Jensen, Arne. *Danske-Amerikanske Portraetter.* Copenhagen, 1928.
Mortensen, Enok. *Danish-American Life and Letters, A Bibliography by Enok Mortensen.* Des Moines, Iowa: Committee on Publications of the Danish Evangelical Lutheran Church in America, 1945.
Solomons Almanak, De Forenede Staters Danske Almanak. Seattle, Washington: Danish Publishing House of the Pacific Coast. (See especially 1916, pp. 85–95.) Copies can be found in the Northwest Collection, Suzzallo Library, University of Washington, Seattle.

Manuscript Collections

Dana College, Blair, Nebraska. Collection includes the college newspaper, library, archives, and church publications.
Elfrida Pedersen Collection. Archives and Manuscripts, Suzzallo Library, University of Washington, Seattle.
Grand View College, Des Moines, Iowa. Church publications, library, college newspaper.
Udvandrearkivet, Danes Worldwide Archives, Aalborg, Denmark.
See Enok Mortensen's bibliography above for a more complete listing of collections up to 1945.

5

Finnish-American Theatre

TIMO R. RIIPPA AND MICHAEL G.
KARNI

Beginning in the 1880s, ever-increasing numbers of Finns joined the great European migration to America. Their reasons for emigration were similar to those of other nationalities: the population explosion of the 1800s, famine, a shortage of arable land, the lure of adventure, and political repression. Finland had been a semiautonomous grand duchy of Czarist Russia since 1814. At the turn of the century, Finnish nationalism ran on a collision course with the pan-Slavist policies of the Russian authorities, resulting in large numbers of Finns choosing to leave their homeland. Between 1880 and 1914 close to three hundred thousand Finns emigrated to the United States, settling in large numbers in Michigan, Minnesota, Massachusetts, Washington, and Oregon.[1]

ORGANIZATIONAL LIFE AND THE THEATRE

Beginning in the 1890s, the Finnish-American immigrant communities experienced a great emergence of organizational activity. The only social outlets available to the earliest immigrants had been saloons and boardinghouses. As ever-greater numbers of immigrants arrived at the turn of the century, the temperance movement and the labor movement emerged to meet their social needs. Although people were also attracted to the ideologies of the organizations, it was the social activities, like drama, athletics, and dances, that brought and held organizational life together. A prominent figure in the Finnish-American labor movement, looking back at organizational life, estimated that "80 per cent of the membership in socialist chapters were mainly active in cultural and recreational activities like theatre; 20 per cent, or less, were engaged in political or ideological matters."[2] The Finnish-American immigrant theatre, then, must be understood as a significant part of Finnish-American organizational activity.

The first priority of any newly organized temperance society or workers' club was construction of its own hall. At their simplest these halls were rectangular wooden frame buildings, usually with a simple stage at one end. The larger halls, like the Socialist Opera in Virginia, Minnesota, were much more elaborate. The New York Finnish Labor Temple, for example, was built in 1921 at a cost of $325,000 and included a large stage and auditorium, meeting rooms, a restaurant, a roof garden for dancing, a pool room, a sauna, and a swimming pool.[3] As these "Finn halls" grew into centers of social and cultural life, amateur drama came to occupy the central place in the hall activities.

Within any Finnish community, there was no single representative theatre in which all interested Finns participated. Rather, each of several organizations within the community had its own theatre. In Astoria, Oregon, in the 1920s, the Finnish Brotherhood mutual benefit lodge and the local chapter of the Finnish Workers' Federation had their own theatres, each with a very high level of activity.

During their existence, these immigrant theatres were never professional, in the sense that they did not use actors and actresses who made their livelihoods by performing on the stage. Except for paid directors and occasional guest artists, all the actors and actresses were volunteers. After working all day at their regular jobs, they would spend two or three nights a week at rehearsals and weekends at performances. In industrial areas, where employees worked the shift system at factories or mines, the theatre personnel would get home from work at midnight, eat and change clothes, and then head for the hall for rehearsals that lasted into the early morning hours.[4]

Love for the theatre went back to a unique tradition for amateur theatre in Finland, where in the latter half of the nineteenth century a nationwide romantic and nationalist movement called the National Awakening had promoted the enlightenment and self-education of the populace. The work of education was carried on through young peoples' societies, workers' associations, temperance societies, and peoples' enlightenment societies. Finnish theatre had its origins in small town and provincial amateur theatre groups rather than in a royal theatre. By the late 1890s hundreds of amateur theatres existed in the country's rural and urban areas. This fondness for and tradition of theatre came over to America with the immigrants. Helmi Mattson, a Finnish-American playwright, observed in her memoirs: "The immigrant Finns have been accustomed since childhood to plays, just as they have to the sauna. Therefore, it is only natural that the older Finnish generation wouldn't have been without either in the new surroundings." In addition, it is important to note that the Finnish-American immigrant theatre was not an isolated phenomenon but was closely tied to the development of the amateur theatre movement in Finland, where the great majority of the plays originated.[5]

The popularity of amateur drama activity meant that the theatres became lucrative for their sponsoring organizations. In fact, the stage was the primary source of income of Finnish-American societies and provided the funds for the construction of halls and clubs. "Our stages have been built for the purpose of making money," said a famous director from the socialist theatre.[6] The fund-raising aspect of theatrical activity was not unique to the United States but also common in Finland. Nowhere in the old country, however, was the principle applied so consistently and methodically as it was in the United States during the great expansion of Finnish-American organizational life.

During the years of peak activity, all temperance, mutual benefit, and labor organizations with any dramatic activity generally staged at the very least one full-length play and several one-act plays each year. The level of activity depended largely on the talents and resources available. Large socialist theatres in New York and Massachusetts, for example, were able to stage over thirty large productions each theatre season.

Since organizational amateur theatre depended on shifting memberships, the available talent varied from season to season. The activity of the Seattle, Washington, Finnish Brotherhood Lodge serves as a typical example of the variables involved. A drama club started in 1918 amid a burst of enthusiasm. The group performed one-act plays, as well as several popular full-length productions such as Teuvo Rakkala's classic *Tukkijoella* (The Lumberjacks) and Minna Canth's *Murtovarkaus* (The Burglary). Interest lagged for several years but revived again in 1922 when young and talented members joined the lodge. Again activity lagged, and in 1924 only one play was shown. In 1925 the group benefited from an influx of new members and talent from the local Finnish Workers' Federation chapter, which had been disbanded during the political reorganization of the Workers' Party of America. Activity revived as four full-length plays were presented. In 1926 a part-time director was hired and four full-length productions were shown. In 1928 the groups performed ten full-length plays under the direction of a new paid director. With the coming of the Depression, activity began to decline as members moved away from the Seattle area to search for work. After 1933 only one play was performed each year.[7]

Obviously only the theatres with full-time directors and large reserves of acting talent were able to sustain a consistently high level of activity year after year. Only the theatres of the workers' movement achieved this level of activity. The stage was the central element in the social life of the Finnish-American labor movement, and the ambition of most socialist, industrial unionist, and communist theatres was to perform new plays as often as possible. Rather than sporadic, seasonal activity, the larger theatres of the labor movement staged new plays at least once a month for nine to ten months out of the year.

Although the audiences came to expect this pace of activity, not all theatregoers or actors were satisfied with it. In New York in 1914 an acting group went on strike because its members felt their efforts were being taken for granted. Although one writer boasted that the New York Finnish socialist stage in 1918 was producing a new play "almost every week and the artistic quality has risen," a director from the nonsocialist stage regretted the pressure that organizations (socialist chapters) exerted on their theatrical groups to perform as many plays as possible during the theatre season. Speaking ostensibly from concern, but perhaps also from envy, he wrote that two or three plays well done were preferable to more numerous productions poorly practiced and poorly staged.

"The current practice," he wrote, "only encourages that group of numb-skulled performers who aren't ashamed to step in front of an audience although they can't get their lines straight *even* with the prompter's help." Nevertheless, the demands of the audiences and the ever-present financial needs of the organization dictated the faster pace of activity. Apparently the situation did not change much over the years; eleven years later another theatre figure issued a similar appeal to organizations to raise the overall quality of productions by not overtaxing the drama societies. But the audiences who came to be entertained did not seem to mind the less-than-perfect productions. They wanted new plays and they expected them often. The various organizations did their best to accommodate their audiences.[8]

TEMPERANCE THEATRE

The earliest theatrical activity among Finnish Americans took place at the turn of the century on temperance stages. Among the very first temperance theatres, the Alku (Beginning) society of Maynard, Massachusetts, began a drama club in 1895 and the Sovittaja (Conciliator) society of Worchester, Massachusetts, started one two years later. One of the most famous of all temperances stages in the United States, the Uljas Koitto (Heroic Sunrise), in Quincy, Massachusetts, had spacious facilities and undertook many large productions.[9]

Although the temperance societies were secular organizations, their ideals attracted large numbers of clergy and church members, especially in the Midwest, and a conservative-liberal split over social policies and clerical influence soon occurred within the movement. The more conservative faction reflected the church's bias against not only drinking, but also dancing, card playing, and theatregoing. In 1898 a writer for this faction accused plays of instructing innocent people in "murder, theft, adultery and 'terrible love adventures.' " A minister writing in an 1898 temperance journal condemned theatres as "satanic hell-holes" that proliferated evil. Actors, according to him, were "the poorest examples of humanity on the face of the earth."[10]

Nevertheless, among the more liberal temperance societies, many of which were located in New York and Massachusetts, drama was by far the most popular form of entertainment. Reflecting the cultural and educational heritage of the Finnish National Awakening, these temperance advocates saw theatre as being "a golden gem in Finnish American intellectual and spiritual development" that, among many other benefits, provided an "edifying pastime for young people," one that "broadened people's social and intellectual horizons."[11]

The available evidence suggests that the overall scope of most temperance theatrical activity was limited to light entertainment for special occasions. The East Coast was an exception. The Alku society, in Maynard, appears to have been performing plays on an almost monthly basis in the mid-1920s. The activities of the Tähti (Star) society in New York City and the Uljas Koitto, in Quincy, suggest monthly dramatic activity during the theatre season between

1914 and the early 1920s. Elsewhere, the activity of the temperance drama clubs seems to have been more sporadic. In Hibbing, Minnesota, the minutes of the club either were not kept or were not preserved, although its theatrical activity shows up occasionally in the temperance society's general minutes. The Virginia, Minnesota, temperance society minutes from 1907 to 1909 record only the money taken in by the theatre. The minutes do not record the names of the performers or the plays. [12]

Because the dissension in the temperance ranks occurred simultaneously with the growth of the socialist movement, many Finns were attracted to the alternative secular activity that the socialist chapters offered. In fact, many temperance societies became socialist chapters, which retained the temperance ideals and social activities, particularly the theatre, but were oriented to secular social pursuits. For example, disagreement in the Hibbing temperance society in 1897 over the propriety of the play *Kovan Onnen Lapsia* (Hard Destinies), by the nineteenth-century Finnish feminist playwright Minna Canth, split the society, with the play advocates establishing a workers' club that later became a socialist chapter. [13]

LABOR THEATRE

According to estimates, from a fourth to a third of all Finnish immigrants in the United States were in some way affiliated with the Finnish-American labor movement. This affiliation can be traced in part to Finland, where liberal, nationalistic reformers established workers' clubs during the National Awakening to promote education for the working class. At the turn of the century a Marxist class consciousness developed within these clubs in Finland, as well as in similar clubs in the United States. In 1906 Finnish-American workers' associations and socialist clubs throughout the country united into one national organization, the Finnish Socialist Federation, which at the peak of its strength boasted 13,000 members in 273 chapters, 107 of which had drama clubs. [14] In 1914 and 1920 the federation underwent ideological splits that were to have a profound effect on the labor theatre. The first split involved the socialists and the industrial unionists (Industrial Workers of the World or IWW). In the second, the socialists split with the Communists. This political fragmentation brought about an increase in the number of workers' theatres, as well as an increase in the proletarian drama literature from each of the factions. [15]

In 1928 a famous Finnish-American actor and playwright, Lauri Lemberg, wrote an article entitled "The Finnish American Amateur Theatre," in which he observed: "Finnish American dramatic activity was born in and developed from the social activities of the immigrant workers." [16] Of all the organizations that supported dramatic activity, the labor movement developed the most advanced and sustained level of activity, which brought with it over a period of time an artistic and technical expertise that gave the productions a very high artistic quality.

In addition there was a general regard for theatre as an important cultural phenomenon instead of a form of light entertainment. Rather than engaging in sporadic activity, labor theatres staged plays throughout a theatre season. During the best years of the Finnish socialist stage, an estimated three thousand performances were given during the year and around five hundred thousand admissions to these performances were sold. The larger theatres, which sometimes had two separate acting crews, had the services of paid, full time directors, most of whom had had experience in professional theatres in Finland. The large workers' halls in cities like New York and Detroit were built with the theatre in mind and featured lavish facilities, with seating that accommodated over eight hundred people.[17] The drama groups were also concerned with the development of the art of acting. Drama classes for beginners were established under the direction of professional actors and directors from Finland such as Eero Boman and Faarlo Nissinen, both of whom were graduates of the drama school of the Finnish National Theatre.[18] In 1919 the Finnish Socialist Federation established a drama league with a centralized play library to assist and improve the quality of the federation's local drama clubs, especially the smaller ones.

It was on the East Coast that the labor movement had its most impressive dramatic activity. For example, in 1925 and 1926 the socialist theatre in Fitchburg, Massachusetts, staged thirty-six full length productions a year and averaged 15,000 paid admissions, taking in $6,000 both years. Fitchburg and New York City both had large drama groups with reserves of acting talent and the facilities for undertaking ambitious full-length productions. In 1926 Fitchburg adapted *Il Trovatore* and set it to speaking parts with solos and choruses. This was followed the next year by Gilbert and Sullivan's *Pirates of Penzance*, translated and adapted by the well-known journalist Frans J. Syrjälä. At a time when directors could only count on filling the theatre on two nights at the most, operettas like Kalman's *Gypsy Princess* and *Countess Maritza* and Franz Lehar's *Merry Widow* played up to three nights to capacity audiences, after which they usually toured. In 1923 the New York socialist theatre hired Finnish actor and director Aarne Orjatsalo, who staged *Othello, The Merchant of Venice,* and *Hamlet,* playing the leads himself. *Hamlet* got close to 1,000 paid admissions, a new record for the time. *Hamlet* was subsequently also performed on the New York Communist stage with great success, as Aarne Linnala gave an unforgettable performance in the lead role.[19]

Contributing to the high level of activity on the East Coast was the fact that the larger theatres had paid, full-time directors during the 1920s. Theatres in New York City (socialist and Communist) and Brooklyn, New York (Communist) and in Massachusetts in Maynard (socialist), Gardner (socialist), Fitchburg (socialist), and Worcester (socialist and Communist) were directed by permanent personnel.[20]

By virtue of the fact that the larger theatres had professional directors, performed full-length plays once or twice a month during a theatre season, and sometimes had enough members to form two separate acting crews that alternated the monthly productions, these theatres cannot be considered "ordinary" amateur theatres. Though the actors and actresses were certainly amateurs and volunteers, many talented people emerged from their ranks over the years. They became seasoned veterans of the stage, and only the limitations of language and the restrictions of the ethnic theatre kept them from going on to professional theatres.

The high level of activity in the labor theatres sparked an ongoing ideological debate in theoretical journals and newspapers. From the very beginning, the "bourgeois" character of many of the popular comedies, tragedies, and operettas provided an ideological problem. Everyone agreed that a workers' theatre should promote the teachings of Marxism, but because of the pressure to stage as many plays as possible during a theatre season, often almost any play, as long as it was not hostile to Marxism, was acceptable. The theatre was a source of income for the local chapter, and it was expected to make money. When a chapter acquired a paid director, it was spending money to make money. The fact that the director was expected to make the theatre a profitable venture put enormous pressure on decisions such as play selection. Most directors were cautious and selected plays that were certain box office winners. The theatre, they felt, had to be responsive to the tastes of the audience. Eero Boman, a professional actor and director from Finland, suggested in an article that audiences as well as actors would find a steady stream of proletarian plays too heavy and burdensome. The theatre "must be concerned with the creation of something invigorating and entertaining," Boman concluded.[21] He realized that if the theatre was used simply as a political and educational tool, it stood to lose its audience. Boman also knew that the immigrant actors' only reward was the sense of satisfaction that comes with doing well, something that is directly gauged by audience appreciation.

The opposing viewpoint was taken by Moses Hahl, a writer, novelist, playwright, and Marxist theoretician, who argued for strict ideological criteria for the theatre. At one point Hahl even suggested that acting classes be abolished and classes on dialectical materialism and the basics of the class struggle be made mandatory for all the actors and actresses. Already in 1915 Moses Hahl and Eero Boman had argued over the proper function of the workers' theatre in the pages of a theoretical journal.[22] Both had agreed that the theatre was a cultural device that should educate and entertain. Hahl, and later Kalle Rissanen, a theoretician who set ideological criteria for the Finnish-American Communist stage in the 1930s, emphasized ideology and saw the theatre primarily as a propaganda vehicle, a secondary function of which was entertainment. Directors like Boman, on the other hand, saw the theatre as a source of entertainment that could simultaneously instruct people ideologically. The distinction may seem academic, but it was a very real one to the theatre people, who tended to resist any dogmatic views that threatened to restrict their repertoire.

In the final analysis, all theatres sought to keep a balance between "heavier" didactic plays and "lighter" entertainment, but in many clubs the criteria for acceptable plays were often rather fluid and reflected the financial needs of the club or the personal preferences of the actors rather than ideological concerns. The continuing demand in the annual conventions of the Socialist Federation and later the Workers' Federation for more proletarian plays is an indication of the abiding popularity of the old favorite comedies, tragedies, and musicals.

MUTUAL BENEFIT SOCIETIES AND THE COOPERATIVE MOVEMENT

In addition to temperance societies and workers' clubs, plays were also staged by Finnish mutual benefit organizations. In the larger areas of Finnish settlement in Washington, Minnesota, Michigan, and New York, the lodges of the Knights and Ladies of Kaleva frequently presented plays.[23] However, since few lodges had theatre facilities of their own, the plays had to be performed in rented halls. Full-length plays were limited to special celebrations, festivals, or fund raisers. The same type of activity also characterized the Imatra mutual aid society of New York. A more accelerated pace of activity, however, took place among the Finnish Brotherhood fraternal benefit lodges on the West Coast. Lodges in Seattle, Washington, and Astoria, Oregon, had especially large theatre groups in the mid-1920s. Both cities benefited from an influx of talent from the theatres of the Finnish Workers' Federation after the closing of the federation's halls in 1925 during the reorganization, or "Bolshevization," of the Workers' Party of America. Although affected by shifting membership and adverse economic conditions, the theatrical activity in both Seattle and Astoria reached a peak in the mid- and late 1920s, when the theatres even had the resources to hire paid directors.[24]

Finnish-American theatre was not exclusively an urban activity. In farming areas it was common to find small theatre groups staging plays in rural temperance society or Communist halls. Sometimes plays were performed in grange or township halls. After its establishment in 1917, the cooperative movement in the Midwest sponsored dramatic activity that lasted into the 1930s. Through its Education Department, the Finnish Cooperative Wholesale, based in Superior, Wisconsin, produced its own dramatic literature in Finnish and English, consisting of one- to three-act plays designed to entertain and educate audiences in cooperative principles. One of the most memorable productions was A Gala Day in a Cooperative Store, a musical comedy complete with vaudeville routines and chorus girls, which successfully toured the Midwest in the mid-1920s. The drama department of the Northern States Women's Coops Guild sponsored playwriting contests and distributed short plays like A Woman's Way, which urged leaders to strike at what they considered unfair trade practices; The Potato War, which made the point that the cooperative was the best place to market potatoes; and Arpanumero (The Lottery Number), a cooperative comedy set in a farm home. Numerous plays promoting the cooperative movement were written by Edith Koivisto, a well-known actress and director in the Midwest. She also translated plays from Finnish into English and wrote radio skits and musicals for which she composed her own music.[25]

REPERTOIRE

The Finnish-American audiences that attended the immigrant theatre did not differ greatly from other theatre audiences. The theatre provided a means of escape from daily life into other realms of existence and experience. The plays transcended everyday life and idealized the thoughts and feelings of the immigrants about life, society, and human nature. Proletarian themes idealized and justified the struggle and cause of the labor Finns. The audiences enjoyed visually spectacular historical dramas and melodramatic romantic tragedies. They especially enjoyed Finnish folk plays that romanticized Finland's rural life and stereotyped its regional characteristics, dialects, and traditional rivalries. They liked comedies and farces. And everyone liked musicals and operettas, especially if they depicted the carefree and song-prone Gypsies.

Plays for the Finnish-American stage came primarily from Finland. The majority were either Finnish in origin or Finnish translations of foreign plays. Of 605 plays listed in a Finnish Workers' Federation Drama League catalogue from the 1920s, approximately 70 percent were Finnish in origin, while about 24 percent were Finnish translations of foreign plays. Only 6 percent could be identified as having been written by Finnish Americans.[26]

Of the 605 plays in the catalogue, 54 percent were comedies, 26 percent dramas and folkplays, 10 percent musicals and operettas, and 10 percent proletarian plays. The overriding popularity of comedies, followed closely by that of dramas, is substantiated by spot-checks of Finnish-American newspapers. Of 103 plays performed in the eastern district of the Finnish Socialist Federation (Ohio to New York) from January 1 to March 30, 1918, and advertised in the Massachusetts-based *Raivaaja* (The Pioneer), 43 percent were comedies, 42 percent dramas, 11 percent musicals, and 5 percent proletarian plays. Of 66 plays staged in the federation's central district (Minnesota to Illinois) during the same time period and advertised in the Wisconsin-based *Tyomies* (The Worker), 41 percent were comedies, 30 percent dramas, 18 percent musicals, and 11 percent proletarian plays.

Prominent among the plays that formed the core of Finnish-American stage repertoire from the late 1890s through the 1920s were classics from the Finnish theatre. All the major plays of Aleksis Kivi, the father of Finnish drama, were performed: *Kullervo*, *Nummisuutarit* (The Cobblers on the Heath), *Kihlaus* (The Betrothal), *Margareetta*, *Karkurit* (The Fugitives), and *Leo ja Liisa*. Minna Canth, a nineteenth-century Finnish feminist who was strongly influenced by Ibsen, was very popular and controversial. All of her comedies and problem plays were performed at one time or another, but of these *Murtovarkaus*, *Papin Perhe* (The Clergyman's Family), and *Työmiehen Vaimo* (The Worker's Wife) were the most frequently performed. Teuvo Pakkala's musical folkplay, *Tukkijoella*, would probably head any list of all-time favorites, followed closely by Artturi Jarviluoma's *Pohjolaisia* (The Bothnians). Among the historical dramas that were frequently performed were Z. Topelius's *Regina von Emmeritz*, J. J. Wecksell's *Daniel Hjort*, and Gustav von Numers's *Elinan Surma* (Elina's Tragedy). Many theatres performed Schiller's *The Robbers*, as well as Gerhart Hauptmann's *The Weavers*, Strindberg's *The Father*, Ibsen's *Ghosts* and *A Doll's House*, Holberg's *Jeppe of the Hill*, and numerous sentimental comedies by August Kotzebue, in Finnish. A good farce like *Carleyn Täti* (Charley's Aunt) always drew well and could be counted on to bolster box office receipts.[27]

Musicals were by far the best loved and best attended form of theatrical entertainment; yet because most musicals were large productions requiring much talent, resources, and time, they were performed less frequently than other types of plays. Most theatres sought to stage at least one big musical a year. Among the many forms the musical took were operettas, musical comedies, musical folkplays, musical proletarian plays, and even adaptations from grand opera like *Tosca* and *Il Trovatore*, staged at Fitchburg in the 1920s.

PLAYWRIGHTS

Only a very limited number of plays were written by the Finnish-American immigrants themselves. Most of these are proletarian plays. In fact, except for a handful of nonpolitical dramatists, most Finnish-American playwrights belonged to one of the three factions of the Finnish-American left.[28] Even the most famous of the nonpolitical dramatists, Lauri Lemberg, began his stage career in the socialist theatre. "The left wing immigrants were apparently much more active as poets and authors than the right wing and those not interested in politics at all," a Finnish historian has noted. "The fact that there were three labor movements and that each needed poetry, novels and plays suited to its ideology probably goes far in accounting for (their) energy."[29]

This also explains why the majority of their plays fall into the category of didactic, political melodrama, as many of their titles suggest: *Hehkuva Tulivuori* (The Glowing Volcano), *Yleislakko* (The General Strike), *Luokkaviha* (Class Hatred), *Joukkonyrkki eli Perkeleen Valtakunta* (The Fist of the Masses, or Satan's Kingdom). But whether the plays date from the early days of the socialist movement or from the 1930s, all of them sketch vivid portraits of the social conditions of their time as seen by the workers. If they are lacking in technique and sophistication, they lack nothing in ambition and political fervor. What they may lack in artistic merit, they more than make up for in sociopolitical interest. Themes were obtained from Finnish-American surroundings: from mining strikes and logging camps and from the actions of the authorities, for instance. Frequently the misery of life in Finland was recalled and the plays pointed out defects in Finnish society.[30] Drama that depicted the immigrants' heart-rending farewell to the homeland or described their typical difficulties with customs and language in the New World does not appear to have been very prevalent among the Finns. Moses Hahl's *Siirtolaiset* (The Immigrants), a full-length play based on his book *Maansa Hylkäämiä* (The Exiles), contains a searing indictment of a society that drives unemployed immigrants into alcoholism and prostitution. Aku Paivio's *Ajan Laulu* (The Song of Time) touched on the experience of leaving the homeland, but it is hardly a comic or sentimental account of the emigration process. The emphasis of the play is squarely on the class struggle and the deficiencies of capitalistic society in the Old World as well as the New.

In 1930 a burst of amateur playwriting activity occurred among the Finnish-American Communists, after the Komintern took the Finnish American workers' movement to task for being ideologically too lax in their social activities. In an open letter in the Finnish Communist press, the Komintern labeled the comedies, dramas, and operettas shown on workers' stages as "bourgeois trash" and advised that such plays be replaced with "interesting, beneficial, and modern" proletarian plays.[31] The new revolutionary line for the theatre was taken up by Kalle Rissanen, a journalist, writer, and playwright who, in numerous published articles, set about its immediate implementation. For a time in the 1930s, many of the old favorites disappeared from the stages of the Communist halls and were replaced by new, often crudely written, proletarian plays that were deemed more suitable. Contests were held by the central drama league to solicit new plays, and a lively criticism was carried on in newspapers and other publications over the artistic and technical merits of the new productions. Later many felt that the Komintern directive had been interpreted too narrowly, because in the fervor with which it was carried out, many of the old favorites in the drama league library had been destroyed.[32]

Subject matter for the new plays was drawn from the Finnish civil war, the Spanish civil war, and life in the Soviet Union, particularly in Soviet Karelia, which borders Finland. The poverty and social unrest of the Depression in the United States also provided themes. Most plays, in one way or another, dealt with the evils of the Depression and the cold-heartedness and inhumanity of bankers, government officials, and law officers.

An interesting and above-average play from this period is Hilja Koski's *Äiti Smith* (Mother Smith), where the central character is a strong-willed, sympathetic, and unselfish mother who has dedicated her life to political activism and to the class struggle. Her husband died years ago in an industrial accident due to faulty safety standards, and now she has a son fighting in the Spanish Civil War in the international brigade. Through letters she encourages him to do his part for the cause, even as she herself is carrying on the fight on the home front. The play gives a vivid portrayal of the woman's role in the class struggle and of a mother's responsibility in teaching class consciousness to her children. Mother Smith's one problem is another son who is reluctant to accept her revolutionary ideals. By the play's end, however, the questioning son is converted; the wounded volunteer returns from Spain; and all dedicate themselves with renewed vigor to the final victory over fascism.[33] Unlike many of the lesser plays from this period and genre, *Mother Smith* does not end with the actors and the audience joining in singing the "Internationale."

Among the playwrights of the Finnish-American labor movement were many prolific and well-known figures: Moses Hahl, Eemeli Parras, Anna Stein, Mikael

Rutanen, Helmi Mattson, Niilo Terho, and Fanny Ojanpaa. Perhaps the two best-known and most representative of all Finnish-American playwrights were Felix Hyrske and Lauri Lemberg. Both were leading figures of the Finnish immigrant stage, and their wide experience, talent, and prolific writing place them in the forefront of all Finnish-American playwrights.

Felix Hyrske was a professional actor-director-playwright who already had fourteen years of stage experience in Finland when he arrived in the United States in 1907. He excelled in the classical repertoire, especially in portraying heroic figures. His *Dr. Jekell and Mr. Hyde* was said to have been unforgettable. In addition to acting and directing for over twenty-five years, during almost all the major stages of the Finnish-American labor movement, Hyrske wrote over twenty plays, both comedies and dramas, adapting and translating many of them from contemporary literature.[34]

Hyrske considered the cultural education of the worker to be one of the most important functions of the labor movement. This theme is prominent in his play *Farmikodin Vastuksia* (Difficulties of a Farm Home), one of the better examples of Finnish proletarian writing to come out of the 1930s.[35] Though not artistically outstanding by any means, the play is an interesting examination of the priority of cultural values against a background of pressing economic need. Set in the 1930s, the play is about a poor Finnish-American family struggling to stay solvent and survive as the threat of foreclosure of their mortgage hangs over their heads. The overall theme is similar to themes found in the writings of Steinbeck and Dos Passos in the thirties, namely, that human values are destroyed by monopolistic capitalism, but workers will triumph when they learn to unite.

In addition, woven into the play is a lesson on the educational aspects of Finnish socialist hall activity, a feature that casts the play into a familiar Finnish framework. Even before the founding of the Finnish Socialist Federation, the socialists believed that hall activities enlightened and edified the individual members and steered them clear of such evils of capitalistic society as drunkenness, gambling, and prostitution. In *Farmikodin Vastuksia* the son of the family, Juho, is forbidden by his parents from attending socialist hall functions. Consequently he succumbs to the evils of the pool hall and gambles away the family's savings.

The play displays the socialist emphasis on the importance of a good humanistic and cultural education. It also reflects the typical Finnish immigrant's fixation on the need for education. Despite its economic deprivation, the family wants to get a piano and books for the children. The mother says:

Attending school isn't enough. "We must also have opportunity for musical pursuits, . . . additional education, and above all, our children must have literature. It's our responsibility to see to it that they have all of these. In this home we haven't devoted ourselves to cultural pursuits.

The father, though faced with financial ruin, agrees.

Music, song and studies as well as literature all have their place and I wouldn't want to prevent my children from having them."

But then he goes on to explain how the first consideration of a worker is to have enough food on the table. What the parents do not realize at this point in the play is that all of the cultural pursuits they desire for their children are available at the local workers' hall. Hyrske suggests that in an economic system that deprives people of their livelihoods, the hall is the one place where workers' families can pursue cultural activities.

Hyrske's play contains a strong indictment of a society that leaves people economically and culturally impoverished. Yet, unlike many other writers, Hyrske brought a restrained, sensitive touch to proletarian plays, avoiding the heavy melodramatic elements that typically characterized plays of this type. Also visible in this play is the kind of "Americanization" of Finnish-American drama that occurred from the 1920s onward. The Finnish family depicted in the play seems to have become an American family. The only thing that suggests its Finnishness is the names. The family does not even own a sauna, something that the grandmother in the play would like to see the family spend its money on instead of cultural "foolishness."

The same process of Americanization can be seen in the plays of Lauri Lemberg written in the same period. Though the plays were written in Finnish, the settings as well as the characters are American. Lauri Lemberg was a talented and innovative actor-director-playwright, who got his start in acting and directing in the socialist and IWW theatre.[36] His four earliest plays from the 1920s, *Shakaalit* (Shakels), *Salaliitto* (The Plot), *Phoenix*, and its sequel, *Bruno Titus*, deal with industrial unionist themes. *Salaliitto* was dedicated to Joe Hill, and like all of the plays it bristles with indignation at the oppressive machinations of evil factory owners and law officers.

Lemberg was masterful at orchestrating the action in his plays, in several of which he employed techniques reminiscent of movie serial "cliff-hangers." The ending to the second act of *Phoenix* is such a case. The hero, Bruno Titus, is an IWW organizer who just happens to love the same woman as the owner of the factory in which he works. The lady is a vivacious woman who is very interested in the social and economic issues of the day. Mr. Dexter, the unscrupulous factory owner, decides to rid himself of Titus, the troublesome organizer and romantic rival, by framing him on the charge of sabotaging the factory and, he hopes, killing him in the process. Dexter's men capture Titus and bring him to the factory office, which they are going to blow up, making Titus appear responsible and thereby allowing Dexter to collect insurance. As the curtain slowly begins to fall on the second act, the hero, who has been knocked unconscious and tied in a chair, gradually awakens and is horrified to find a dynamite charge sputtering on the floor next to him. Titus struggles, manages to free himself, and attempts to reach the window, but the bomb explodes, filling the stage with smoke and flames. The curtain drops, leaving the audience wondering about the hero's fate.

While Lemberg was writing plays for the IWW stage, he was also writing romantic comedies, farces, dramas, and musical folk plays. This was the creative direction in which he turned after 1924 and for which he is best remembered. His detective comedy, *Herttaviitonen* (The Five of Hearts), was staged by the National Theatre of Finland in 1921, thereby earning him membership in the Finnish Dramatist League and entitling him to collect royalties on behalf of the league on Finnish plays that were performed in the United States. Lemberg's later comedies included *Aatami ja Eeva* (Adam and Eve); *Parisangyt* (Twin Beds), which he adapted from a movie; *Laulu Vaaleanpunaisesta Silkkipaidasta* (The Song about the Pink Silk Shirt), a farce he adapted from an obscure American movie, which became one of the all-time favorites of the Finnish-American stage. It was followed by *Hääkellot* (Wedding Bells), which one noted director considered the best Finnish-American musical comedy of its kind. Among his romantic comedies and dramas were *Järki ja Sydän* (Reason and the Heart), *Kevätromanssi* (Spring Romance), *Vihreä Viitta* (The Green Cloak), and *Raha ja Onni* (Money and Fortune).

Lemberg was especially gifted in the musical folk play genre. His Argentinian folk play, *Haihtuvia Pilvia* (The Fading Clouds), was toured through the Midwest and the East Coast by Aarne Orjatsalo, the noted professional Finnish director, who worked in New York. Lemberg's gypsy musical, *Mustalais Manja* (Manja the Gypsy), and his Hungarian folkplay, *Kuuden Kylän Impi* (Impi from Six Villages), were both very successful "formula" musicals. The last two musicals were written under his pen name, Antonio Morosco. Lemberg also adapted *Carmen* into a four-act play and *The Count of Monte Cristo* into a five-act production.

In 1920, at a time when all the plays had to be ordered from Finland, Lemberg hired a staff of typists and began a successful play rental service in Duluth, Minnesota, that catered to all Finnish theatre groups in the United States and Canada. The play service was so successful that Lemberg gave up his job as a linotypist and worked at it full time for four years. Lemberg's only competition was the Finnish Workers' Federation Drama League, with which he had frequent encounters because, in the absence of international copyright laws, the drama league refused to pay Lemberg royalties on Finnish plays.[37]

Lemberg was prolific, well known, and well liked. He was the only Finnish-American playwright to have a play staged by the National Theatre of Finland in Helsinki and the only Finnish American who belonged to the Finnish Dramatist League. Few, if any, Finnish-American playwrights left as distinctive a mark on Finnish immigrant theatre activity.

GOLDEN AGE AND LEGACY

The Finnish-American immigrant theatre was primarily a first-generation phenomenon; its "golden age" lasted from shortly before World War I into the 1930s. An overview of the socialist theatre compiled in 1910 revealed that over half of the actors and actresses were between the ages of twenty-five and thirty.

A fourth were between thirty and forty, and another fourth were under twenty-five. This means that in the 1930s the majority were over fifty. This is significant because after 1930 theatre activity began to decline noticeably, as the immigrants grew older and as most of the second generation lost interest in the hall activities of their parents. The minutes of the socialist theatre in Gardner, Massachusetts, for example, reflect a growing sense of exhaustion among the drama club members in the late 1920s. The older members of the group declined to accept large roles anymore and refused to tour neighboring cities as in the past. Efforts to recruit new talent from among the young people were only partially successful. Interests outside the Finnish ethnic community drew many of the young people away from the hall activities. Although the large Finnish theatres still had steady activity throughout the 1930s, World War II finally marked the end of all large-scale theatre activity.

During its existence, Finnish theatre provided a major creative as well as social outlet for the immigrants. The plays that were performed filled various needs: they introduced contemporary social issues; they entertained; they strengthened the sense of Finnish identity; and they kept alive the sentimental bond to the homeland and the past. They acquainted many immigrants, few of whom had much formal schooling, with a large number of classics from Finnish and world theatre literature. In the words of Lauri Lemberg, the Finnish immigrant theatre left a rich legacy because "from its many participants, it developed people with wide cultural interests—singers, musicians, speakers and poets—who, in addition to their dramatic activities, enriched all other social and cultural activities of the Finnish American community."[38]

NOTES

1. John I. Kolehmainen, A History of the Finns in Ohio, Western Pennsylvania, and West Virginia (New York Mills, Minn.: Parta Printers, 1977), p. 6.

2. John Wiita [Henry Puro], "Cultural Life of the Finnish American Labor Movement," unpublished manuscript in the John Wiita Collection, Immigration History Research Center, University of Minnesota.

3. Onni Kaartinen, "The Workers' Clubs in the Greater New York Finnish American Community," in A History of Finnish American Organizations in Greater New York 1891–1979, edited by Katri Ekman et al. (New York Mills, Minn.: Greater New York Finnish Bicentennial Planning Committee, 1979), p. 232.

4. Sirkka Tuomi-Lee, "Stage Life Recollections," presentation at Finn Forum '79: an International Conference on the History of Finnish Immigration to North America, Toronto, Ontario, Canada, Nov. 2, 1979.

5. Ritva Heikkilä, "The Theatre," in Finland: an Introduction, edited by Sylvie Nickels et al. (New York: Praeger Publishers, 1973), pp. 261–62; Helmi Mattson, "Kuiskarin Muistelmia," Naisten Viiri, Nov. 28, 1942.

6. Eero Boman, "Näytämötaide ja Työväenluokka," Kalenteri Amerikan Suomalaiselle Työväelle 1915, p. 81.

7. Y.S.K.V. ja S-Liiton 50 vuotishistoria—Muistojulkaisu (Duluth, Minn.: Finnish Daily Publishing Company, 1937), pp. 178–84.

134   TIMO R. RIIPPA AND MICHAEL G. KARNI

. "Näytelmäseura," in *Viisitoista Vuotta New Yorkin Suomalaisten Sosialistien Historiaa 1903–1918* (Fitchburg, Mass.: Suomalainen Sosialistinen Kustannusyhtiö, 1918), p. 86; Vili Väre, "Näytämötaide Amerikan Suomalaisten Kesken," *Kalevainen* 3 (Feb. 1917): 51–52; Lauri Lemberg, "Amerikan Suomalaisten Seuranäytämö," *Tie Vapauteen* 5 (April 1928): 15.

9. *"Alku" Raittiusseuran 50-vuotis Juhlajulkaisu 1895–1945* (Hancock, Mich.: Suomalainen Luterilainen Kustannusliike, 1945), pp. 43–44; H. H-n, "Uljas Koiton Näyttämöltä," *Idän Suomalaisen Raittiuskansan Liiton Joulujulkaisu 1919*, pp. 75–78.

10. "Sananen teatterista," *Kirkollinen Kalenteri 1914*, pp. 54–58; "Teatterista," *Raittiuskalenteri 1899*, pp. 107–8.

11. E. W. Karjalainen, "Muutama Sananen Näytelmätaiteesta," *Idän Suomalaisen Raittiuskansan Liiton Joulujulkaisu 1919*, p. 61.

12. Edith Koivisto, "Lupaus: Hibbingin Suomalaisen Raittiusliikkeen Historia 1895–1957," unpublished manuscript in the Edith Koivisto Collection, Immigration History Research Center, University of Minnesota, p. 19.

13. Hans R. Wasastjerna, ed., *Minnesotan Suomalaisten Historia* (Superior, Wis.: Cooperative Publishing Association for the Minnesota Finnish American Historical Society, 1957), p. 600.

14. Douglas Ollila, Jr., "From Socialism to Industrial Unionism (IWW): Social Factors in the Emergence of Left-Labor Radicalism among Finnish Workers on the Mesabi, 1911–19," in *The Finnish Experience in the Western Great Lakes Region: New Perspectives* (Vammala, Finland: Institute for Migration, Turku, Finland, 1976), p. 157.

15. Michael G. Karni, "Yhteishyvä—or, For the Common Good. Finnish Radicalism in the Western Great Lakes Region 1900–1940" (Ph.D. diss., University of Minnesota, 1975), p. 92; Ollila, "From Socialism to Industrial Unionism," p. 157, note 9.

16. Lemberg, "Amerikan Suomalaisten Seuranäytämö," p. 15.

17. Elis Sulkanen, *Amerikan Suomalaisen Työväenliikkeen Historia* (Fitchburg, Mass.: Raivaaja Publishing Company, 1951), pp. 111–12. The figures Sulkanen quotes represent the combined activities of all three factions. The figures are substantiated by a report of the Finnish Workers Federation Drama League in 1920, which reflected only the nationwide theatrical activity of the communists. They had shown 325 different plays during the year with a total of 1,600 presentations. When the socialist and industrial unionist theatres are counted, the 3,000 figure is easily reached.

18. One of the problems that professional directors faced was that many Finnish-American actors and actresses spoke their lines with noticeable dialects. Standard Finnish was taught in the drama classes.

19. Frans J. Syrjälä, *Historia-aiheita Amerikan Suomalaisten Työväenliikkeesta* (Fitchburg, Mass.: Raivaaja Publishing Company, 1925), pp. 107–8; Victor Rautanen, "Finnish American League of Democracy, New York City Branch," in *A History of Finnish Organizations in Greater New York*, p. 209; "Amateur Theatre Movement of the Finnish Immigrants," *70th Anniversary Souvenir Journal 1903–1973 Tyomies* (Superior, Wis.: Tyomies Publishing Company, 1973), pp. 106–7.

20. Syrjälä, *Historia-aiheita*, pp. 106–7.

21. Eero Boman, "Sosialistinen Teatteri," *Säkeniä* 9 (Oct. 1915): 458.

22. Moses Hahl, "Sosialistinen Teatteri ja Työläisnäyteliä," *Säkeniä* 9 (September 1915): 398–407; Boman, "Sosialistinen Teatteri," pp. 458–59.

23. Lemberg's play rental service sent plays periodically to Kaleva lodges in these states in the 1920s. Lauri Lemberg Papers, Minnesota Historical Society, St. Paul, Minn.

24. *Y.S.K.V. ja S-Liiton Muistojulkaisu*, pp. 178–84; Walter Mattila, *The Theatre Finns* (Portland, Oreg.: Finnish American Historical Society of the West, 1972), p. 53; William Mannila, "Muistelmia Astorian Näyttämöltä," *Veljeysviesti* 44 (Dec. 1967): 43.

25. "'All the World's a Stage'—Immigrants and the Performing Arts," *Spectrum* 2 (April 1976), p. 6; Edith Koivisto Collection, Immigration History Research Center, University of Minnesota.

26. *Finnish W. Federation Näyttämö- ja Näyttämöväline Luettelo* (n.p., n.d.).

27. This list was compiled in part from "Meidän Sosialistiset Näyttämöt," *Raivaajan Työvainiolta* 6 (1910): 183–200, and "Saiman Näyttämö Fitchburgissa," *Siirtokansan Kalenteri 1948*, pp. 60–67.

28. In his Finnish-American bibliography, Dr. John Kolehmainen lists seven early nonpolitical plays by Finnish-American playwrights. One of these, *Kosiat* (The Suitors), written in 1897 by Aug. Korhonen, is the earliest-known Finnish-American play in existence. Despite the amount of theatre activity in the eastern temperance societies, only five plays have been identified as having been written for their stages. All of them were written by Ilmari Junno, an actor-director at the Alku temperance society in Maynard, Massachusetts. There is no way of knowing whether or not any of the plays dealt with temperance themes.

29. Reino Kero, "Finnish Immigrant Culture in America," in *Old Friends-Strong Ties*, edited by Vilho Niitama et al. (Vaasa, Finland: Institute for Migration, Turku, Finland, 1976), p. 124.

30. Kero, "Finnish Immigrant Culture," pp. 125–26.

31. *Taistelu Oikeistovaaraa Vastaan: Kominternin Opetuksia Amerikan Suomalaiselle Työväestölle* (Superior, Wis.: n.d.).

32. "Kulttuuritoimintamme pääsemässä uuteen nousukauteen," *Työmies*, Oct. 2, 1937.

33. Taru Sundsten, *Amerikansuomalainen Työväenteatteri ja Näytelmäkirjallisuus Vuosina 1900–1939* (Vaasa, Finland: Institute for Migration, Turku, Finland, 1977), pp. 61–62.

34. Syrjälä, *Historia-aiheita*, p. 111; Kalle Rissanen, "Feidias Veistää Henkilokuvia," unpublished manuscript, Immigration History Research Center, University of Minnesota, p. 168; "Meidän Sosialistiset Näyttämöt," p. 199.

35. *Työmies* Collection, Folder 39, Immigration History Research Center, University of Minnesota.

36. Lauri Lemberg Papers, Minnesota Historical Society, St. Paul, Minn.

37. Wasastjerna, *Minnesotan Suomalaisten Historia*, pp. 342–43.

38. "Saiman Näyttämö Fitchburgissa," p. 67.

BIBLIOGRAPHY

Books

Lindewall, Arvo, *Rosalie*. Yonkers, N.Y.: Kansallinen Kustannus Komitea, 1957. A thinly disguised, fictionalized biography, based on actual diaries, of Lauri Lemberg's first wife, Rosa Clay— actress, director, and Finnish-American "songbird." Her mother was African, her father English, and Rosa was raised by Finnish missionaries in Southwest Africa, eventually coming to the United States by way of Finland. The book gives an essentially accurate picture of the Lembergs' activities on the West Coast, when both Rosa and Lauri acted at the Astoria, Oregon, Socialist Theatre.

Mattila, Walter. *The Theatre Finns.* Portland, Oreg.: Finnish American Historical Society of the West, 1972. An excellent monograph on the theatre activities of the socialists, the Communists, and the Finnish Brotherhood in Astoria, one of the largest Finnish settlements on the West Coast.

Sulkanen, Elis. *Amerikan Suomalaisen Työväenliikkeen Historia* (The History of the Finnish American Labor Movement). Fitchburg, Mass.: Raivaaja Publishing Company, 1951. Sulkanen's history contains an excellent section on the amateur theatre that identifies individual theatres, actors, actresses, directors, and playwrights.

Sundsten, Taru. *Amerikansuomalainen Työväenteatteri ja Näytelmäkirjallisuus Vuonna 1900–1939* (The Finnish American Workers' Theatre and Theatre Literature 1900–1939). Vaasa, Finland: Institute for Migration, Turku, Finland, 1977. The first academic thesis published on the Finnish immigrant theatre. An excellent historical survey of the labor stage and analysis of Finnish-American proletarian literature.

Syrjälä, Frans. J. *Historia-aiheita Amerikan Suomalaisesta Työväenliikkeestä* (Historical Themes from the Finnish American Labor Movement). Fitchburg, Mass.: Raivaaja Publishing Company, 1925. Syrjälä was one of the leaders in the socialist movement and editor of the socialist newspaper, the *Raivaaja.* He devotes an entire chapter to theatre activities, focusing on the eastern socialist theatres and specifically on the Saima theatre in Fitchburg, Massachusetts.

Articles

Boman, Eero. (1) "Näytelijälle" (To the Actor), *Säkeniä* 9 (Mar. 1915): 133–36.

———. "Näytämötaide ja Työväenluokka (The Art of Drama and the Working Class)," *Kalenteri Amerikan Suomalaiselle Työväelle 1915,* pp. 79–88.

———. "Sosialistinen Teatteri" (The Socialist Theatre), *Säkeniä* 9 (Oct. 1915): 458–59. Essays by a theatre professional from Finland on the theory and reality of the Finnish socialist amateur theatre in America.

Hahl, Moses. "Sosialistinen Teatteri ja Työläisnäyteliä" (The Socialist Theatre and the Worker as Actor), *Säkeniä* 9 (Sept. 1915): 398–407.

———. "Työväennäytelmät ja Työläisnäyttelijät" (Proletarian Plays and Worker-Actors), *Säkeniä* 14 (April 1920): 147–52 and (May 1920): 201–207.

———. "Amerikan Suomalaiset Sosialistiset Näyttämöt" (America's Finnish Socialist Theatres), *Nykyaika* 16 (Dec. 1922): 10–12. In the essays from 1915 and 1920, Hahl developed the idea that the socialist stage was first and foremost a propaganda tool and that the repertoire should primarily, if not entirely, consist of proletarian plays. In the 1922 essay he admits the extremeness and impracticality of his earlier views and reminisces about socialist theatre activity on the East Coast.

H-n, H. "Uljas Koiton Näyttämöltä" (From the Uljas Koitto Stage). *Idän Suomalaisen Raittiuskansan Liiton Joulujulkaisu 1919,* pp. 75–78. A brief history of one of the largest temperance theatres in the United States.

Karjalainen, E. W. "Muutama Sananen Näytelmätaiteesta" (A Few Words about the Art of Drama), *Idän Suomalaisen Raittiuskansan Liiton Joulujulkaisu 1919,* pp. 61–62. A treatise on theatre as a form of cultural edification from the liberal temperance perspective.

Koivisto, Edith. "Lauri Lemberg—Näytelmäkirjailia" (Lauri Lemberg—Playwright), *Industrialisti,* Jan. 28, 1975. An excellent short biography of Lemberg, written in the form of a personal reminiscence by a woman who acted under Lemberg's direction on several Minnesota labor stages. It focuses on Lemberg as playwright and director.

Lemberg, Lauri. "Amerikan Suomalaisten Seuranäyttämö" (The Finnish-American Amateur Theatre), *Tie Vapauteen* 10 (April 1928): 15–16. A historical essay about the amateur theatre that anticipates its eventual decline and urges theatres to stress quality and "art for art's sake" in the years remaining.

Mattson, Helmi. "Kuiskarin Muistelmia" (Reminiscences of a Prompter), *Naisten Viiri*, Nov. 28, 1942. An amusing essay on one of the most essential but underrated jobs in the immigrant theatre, by one of the best-known playwrights from the Communist stage.

"Meidän Sosialistiset Näyttämöt" (Our Socialist Theatres), *Raivaajan Työvainiolta* 6 (1910): 183–200. A valuable overview of theatres and acting personnel in 1910. The article includes biographical sketches of forty actors and actresses, complete with dates of arrival in the United States, acting experience in Finland and the United States, and a list of the plays in which they performed as well as their favorite roles.

"Näytelmäseura" (The Drama Club), in *Viisitoista Vuotta New Yorkin Suomalaisten Sosialistien Historiaa 1903–1918* Fitchburg, Mass.: Suomalainen Sosialistinen Kustannusyhtiö, 1918, pp. 83–89. A detail-rich history of the New York Socialist Theatre up to 1918, affording a close look at the typical activity of a large theatre.

Rissanen, Kalle. "Näytelmäkirjallisuudestamme" (About Our Theatre Literature), *Viesti* 4 (April 1934): 166–72. This critique of proletarian plays is a good example of the effort to bring drama into line with the Komintern's directives.

"Saiman Näyttämö Fitchburgissa" (The Saima Theatre in Fitchburg), *Siirtokansan Kalenteri 1948*, pp. 60–67. A well-written short history of one of the most famous Finnish immigrant theatres in the country. Although the article was written anonymously, subsequent research has revealed that its author was Lauri Lemberg.

"Sananen Teatterista" (A Few Words about the Theatre), *Kirkollinen Kalenteri 1914*, pp. 54–58. The view of the Finnish American Lutheran church toward the theatre—the "few words" are all negative.

"Teatterista" (About the Theatre), *Raittiuskalenteri 1899*, pp. 103–11. An antitheatre article that typifies the view of the conservative temperance societies.

"Uuterimmat" (The Industrious), *Kalenteri Amerikan Suomalaiselle Työväelle 1915*, pp. 118–35. A series of biographies on actors and actresses active in socialist theatres throughout the country.

Väre, Vili. "Näytämötaide Amerikan Suomalaisten Kesken" (The Art of Drama among Finnish Americans), *Kalevainen* 3 (Feb. 1917): 51–52. A curiously idealistic essay concerned with the quality of Finnish-American theatre. Väre suggests that organizations should wind down the hectic pace of their theatre activity so that the art of drama can be properly cultivated.

Newspapers

All of the newspapers of the Finnish-American workers' movement are valuable sources of information. The *Toveri* (Comrade), *Työmies* (Worker), *Eteenpäin* (Forward), *Raivaaja* (Pioneer), and *Industrialisti* (Industrialist) contained weekly ads for plays that were being presented at workers' halls throughout the country. Correspondents would report on events from the various communities, and these columns would usually contain descriptions of plays that were going to be shown as well as reviews of the plays afterwards. Occasionally one even finds critical reviews, but they are the exception.

From 1928 onward the *Työmies* devoted a page per month entirely to the theatre. This contained descriptions of new plays, general discussions of stagecraft, and theoretical discussions about the function of a workers' theatre.

The conservative *New Yorkin Uutiset* (New York News) also ran play ads, mainly for the temperance societies and fraternal organizations that staged plays in the city.

Unpublished Sources

The Lauri Lemberg papers at the Minnesota Historical Society, St. Paul, Minnesota, contain not only typescripts of Lemberg's plays, but also play registers that record which plays were lent out, when they were lent, and to which theatres they were sent.

The Minnesota Finnish American Historical Society Archive Collection at the Immigration History Research Center, University of Minnesota, contains two essays by Lemberg. One is entitled "Minnesotan Näyttämötaiteen Historiaa" (Some History on the Minnesota Theatre), while the other is a longer essay entitled "Näyttämötaiteesta ja Seuroista" (About Theatre Art and Organizations).

A number of other collections at the Immigration History Research Center also contain a variety of materials dealing with Finnish theatre.

The Helmi Mattson papers include typescripts of all of the plays of this Finnish-American dramatist, as well as a photo album with over fifty photos of theatrical productions. In her autobiography she describes her activities as head of the Finnish Workers' Federation Drama League play library. Over four hundred plays that were once part of this library are now included in the center's *Työmies* collection.

The Edith Koivisto papers contain typescripts and music for the production of *Carmen*, which Koivisto adapted and toured through the Midwest in the 1920s. Also included are play reviews and several short plays that she wrote.

The John Wiita papers contain personal reminiscences of Finnish theatrical activity and several personal letters that shed light on theatre as a part of hall activity.

The center also has on microfilm the minutes of the Gardner, Massachusetts, socialist chapter, and these include the minutes of the Gardner Drama Club for 1911 and from 1915 to 1932, when its activity died out.

6

French Theatre in Louisiana

MATHÉ ALLAIN AND ADELE CORNAY ST. MARTIN

The area that is now the state of Louisiana has undergone many political changes. Claimed for France by Robert Cavelier, Sieur de la Salle, in 1682 it was settled by the French, who made New Orleans the capital in 1722. The area was ceded to Spain in 1762 after the French and Indian War and returned to France in 1800, when Napoleon conquered Spain. Finally, in 1803, the area was taken into the United States through the Louisiana Purchase. Reinforced by more than four thousand French settlers from Canada, the Acadians, who arrived in the late eighteenth century, the French-speaking population maintained its cultural identity after Louisiana became part of the English-speaking United States. French-language theatre was, and remains, an expression of that identity.

THE FIRST PERFORMANCES

Early Louisiana theatrical history is shrouded in conflicting testimonies and speculation. Some historians speak of a play, Le Père indien, given in 1753, supposedly at the mansion of Governor Pierre François de Rigaud, marquis de Vaudreuil de Cavagnal. The "Grand Marquis," as Vaudreuil was known, introduced many courtly graces to the rather primitive Louisiana social scene, but there is no documentary proof that theatrical activities were included. The earliest performance on record was in 1764, when a comedy was presented for Jean-Jacques d'Abbadie, director-general of the colony. The play, probably the first performed in the Mississippi Valley, was discovered by H. Gaston Hall of the University of Warwicke, England, who presented the volume to the Mississippi Department of Archives and History.[1] D'Abbadie, who had been sent to New Orleans after the French and Indian War, presided over a peace celebration that included public illuminations, casks of wine, and a ball at the governor's mansion, climaxed by what he described as a "successful performance" of L'Amant, Auteur et Valet by young townspeople.[2]

It seems likely that there were other amateur productions in private homes. The French and the Spanish were very fond of drama, and private theatricals played an important role in château social life. One only needs to recall the productions staged by Voltaire at Ferney or Madame de Staël's histrionic prowess at Coppet. Whatever nonprofessional activities took place in Louisiana, however, went unrecorded except for "two comedies . . . presented by individuals from the nobility and the armed forces" mentioned in the minutes of the cabildo, May 8, 1789.[3] The theatrical history of New Orleans actually begins on October 4, 1792, when Louis-Alexandre Henry, a Parisian, opened a small theatre situated approximately at what is now 732 St. Peter Street.[4]

At the Théâtre de la Rue Saint-Pierre, performances began "promptly" at 5:30 in the afternoon and the audience was strictly forbidden to interrupt "by shouting, whistling, or behaving in any way that might force an actor to be silent or to repeat his lines."[5] The building itself Baron Joseph-Xavier Delfau de Pontalba described as "small, but quite pretty," with twelve loges, a balcony, a pit, and a gallery.[6] The level of acting in 1792 left much to be desired, as might be expected from rank amateurs: Henry, who doubled as director and actor, was a carpenter by trade, and Madame or Mademoiselle Claretie, who played the female lead, was a milliner. The theatre consequently did not prosper, and between September and October 1793 Henry surrendered the property to his brother Jean and the direction to a Madame Durosier, who immediately introduced a new development: quadroon actresses, perhaps professionals from Santo Domingo, including the celebrated Minette, who had delighted Cap-Français and Port-au-Prince audiences until the Haitian slave uprising of 1791.[7]

In 1793 the little theatre of the Rue Saint-Pierre became embroiled in political controversy. News that Spain had declared war on France raised hopes among some of the more militant that Louisianians might rise against Spanish rule. The "Marseillaise" and other Jacobin songs were sung at performances, arousing such revolutionary fervor that Francisco Luis Hector, barón de Carondelet, Spanish governor of the province, outlawed anything resembling revolutionary music and martial dances at the theatre.[8] He was particularly incensed, understandably, about a song the words of which, he complained to the cabildo, were written by a well-known lady. It was sung to the tune of "La Carmagnole":

> Quand nous serons Républicains,
> Nous punirons tous ces coquins.
> Cochon de lait le premier
> Sera guillotiné. *[9]

The pun cochon de lait/Carondelet offended the governor, but the wily baron succeeded nonetheless in containing the agitation. The Théâtre de la Rue

---

* "When we become republicans, we will punish all these scoundrels. Suckling pig (cochon de lait) the first shall be guillotined."

Saint-Pierre continued its performances, which improved greatly in 1794 when a few professional actors from Santo Domingo joined the existing company.[10]

New Orleans' first theatre enjoyed sporadic success until 1803, when it was deemed unsafe:[11] "The said hall is ready to fall in ruins," stated the city council in its ordinance of December 20, 1803.[12] The theatre had been closed for some time, apparently because of a dispute over seating.[13] John Sibley, who visited the house in 1802 while it was closed, left an unfavorable description: "The Scenery is very ordinary and wants Variety, the whole House is Roughly Built and now Looks Shabby, the Paper that once covered the Rough work is peel'd off in spots and very much defac'd."[14]

Shabby though it might have become after eleven years, the Théâtre de la Rue Saint-Pierre had established certain traits that would characterize New Orleans stage history throughout the nineteenth century. From the very beginning, legitimate and lyric dramas were inextricably mixed in the Crescent City. In 1796, the first year for which play titles are recorded, there were successive performances of L'Honnête Criminel, a five-act drama by Charles-Georges Fenouillot de Falbaire (May 8); Sylvain, a one-act comic opera by André Ernest Grétry and Jean-François Marmontel (May 22); Blaise et Babet, a comic opera by N. Dezèdes and Jacques Marie Boutet, dit Monvel (July 17); and finally Eugénie and Le Père de famille, two five-act dramas, the first by Pierre Caron de Beaumarchais, the second by Denis Diderot, performed on November 4 to celebrate the feast of St. Charles Borromeo, patron saint of Charles III of Spain.[15] One can only marvel at the attention spans of colonial audiences.

During these early years another aspect of the New Orleans theatre was the association between dramatic productions and carnival balls. The love of dancing of the Creoles (the descendants of the first European settlers, French, German, and Spanish) and their terpsichorean skill elicited comments from virtually every visitor to the city. From the outset it seems to have been customary to attend a ball after a theatrical performance, hence the 5:30 curtain. Ballrooms were later built as parts of the theatres, and until the recent construction of the Theater for the Performing Arts, the New Orleans Municipal Auditorium served for both carnival balls and theatrical productions. Thus the history of theatre in Louisiana is bound with that of opera, music, and Mardi Gras celebrations.

It is also closely tied to the history of the black population, free people of color, quadroons, octoroons, and slaves. The presence of quadroon actresses has already been noted; blacks were also represented in the audience from the first. In 1802 Sibley mentioned the existence of galleries, "the upper one for People of Colour who are never permitted to mix with White People."[16] The "colored" balcony, a feature of Southern movie theatres until the Civil Rights Act, had its origin in colonial days, when blacks were part of the audience, although separated from whites. When even slaves were routinely admitted to the plays and operas, it is hardly surprising that the affluent and educated free people of color of the nineteenth century should have developed a dramatic tradition so vigorous that one of Louisiana's most prolific and successful playwrights, Victor Séjour, would come from their ranks.

Even before the closing of the Théâtre de la Rue Saint-Pierre in 1803, the need for a new building had been obvious for some time. The September 4, 1802, issue of the *Moniteur de la Louisiane* carried an eloquent apostrophe entitled "Lafon to the Public." Barthélemy Lafon, the author of the appeal, opened with a ringing defense of the theatre:

It cannot be doubted that besides providing entertainment the theater has a profound influence on morals. It develops the empire of reason and nurtures feelings of decency; it represses follies and corrects vices. To doubt these truths is to claim that men are insensitive to shame and contempt.

He argued that

the theater plays the same role towards vice and ridicule as the courts which judge it and the scaffold which punishes it play toward crime.

and therefore proposed a public subscription to erect a new "salle de spectacle."[17] Despite his grandiloquent appeal, public response seems to have been lukewarm, since no more was heard of Lafon's venture.

CULTURAL CONFLICT

The little theatre on St. Peter Street was to have a reprieve. A newly arrived French actor, Jean-Baptiste Fournier, obtained permission to repair it, and its reopening was authorized on November 28, 1804. At the same meeting the city council issued regulations intended to curb the obnoxious behavior of some playgoers. The theatres had probably been scenes of cultural confrontation between Creoles and Americans, because the ordinance specified that "the orchestra of the hall cannot be subject to fanciful demands to play this or that tune; the management binds itself to satisfy the public's demand by the rendition of national airs."[18] Since the transfer of Louisiana to the United States in 1803, several balls had degenerated into brawls when the Creoles demanded that the orchestras play French dances while the *Américains* requested reels. The city fathers were taking steps to insure orderly performances unmarred by such cultural clashes. Apparently they were successful; December 20, 1804, the first anniversary of the transfer, was celebrated with a performance undisturbed by rowdiness, and Governor W.C.C. Claiborne reported that both factions attended the theatre "in perfect harmony."[19]

The American governor found himself involved quickly, however, in another cultural conflict centered around the theatre. In June 1805 the abbess of the Ursuline nuns complained that "in a later performance at the theater their community had been held up to the Public as an object of derision."[20] The governor was caught in a dilemma: as an American official sworn to uphold the Constitution, he could not very well violate the First Amendment and close the play simply because it offended someone. On the other hand, as he wrote the abbess, he deplored "that a Representation at the Theatre should have been marked with indecency and disrespect toward your Amiable community."[21] But how does one explain such constitutional niceties to religious women born and bred under the *ancien régime?* Claiborne neatly side-stepped the issue and asked James Pitot, the mayor of New Orleans, whose purview it really was, insisted the governor, to use his "influence and authority" to check the "offensive" performance.[22]

The "offensive" play seems to have been an opera, *Les Visitandines*, by François Devienne. Besides that controversial opera, the Théâtre de la Rue Saint-Pierre presented at least twenty-two performances from June 1805 to February 1806, including sixteen different operas by nine composers. Historian Henry Kmen points out that it was "an amazing record for a town which as yet boasted only twelve thousand people."[23]

COMPETING THEATRES

This amazing activity was only the beginning, for in 1805 there appeared on the scene the brilliant actor-director from Santo Domingo, Louis Tabary. He quickly wrested control from Fournier and took over the Théâtre de la Rue Saint-Pierre. Not satisfied with this modest house, he immediately issued a call for the shareholders and proposed a new theatre. He placed full-page ads in *Le Moniteur*, purchased land, hired an architect, the famed Hyacinthe Laclotte, who had built a theatre in Bordeaux, and gained endorsements from prominent officials. On October 6, 1806, Tabary laid the first brick for what would become the celebrated Théâtre d'Orléans.[24]

Fournier, on the other hand, did not surrender easily. Having regained control of the Théâtre de la Rue Saint-Pierre, he resumed operations. In the meantime Bernard Coquet, a stage-struck ballroom operator, decided to transform his establishment into a theatre, which opened its doors on January 30, 1808, as theThéâtre de la Rue Saint-Philippe. For nearly two years, until December 9, 1810, when the Théâtre de la Rue Saint-Pierre gave its last performance, New Orleans had two competing theatres. And during that time work was proceeding, albeit in a desultory fashion, on the new Théâtre d'Orléans.

By the time the Théâtre de la Rue Saint-Pierre gave up the battle and closed, the first theatre in New Orleans had accumulated an impressive record. For opera alone, Henry Kmen counts between March 1, 1805, and December 10, 1810, "at least three hundred and fifty-one performances of seventy-six different operas."[25] The theatre had also performed numerous plays, including the premiere and only performance of the first extant play written in Louisiana, a tragedy entitled *La Fête du petit blé ou l'Héroïsme de Poucha-Houmma.*

6.1   The Théâtre d'Orléans.   (Courtesy of the Historic New Orleans Collection, New Orleans, Louisiana.)

LOUISIANA'S FIRST PLAY

Louisiana's first play was performed on February 11, 1809, as part of a double bill. The *Moniteur* announced it as depicting a "trait of fatherly love" and promised a lavish production with "Indian marches, new costumes, and generally everything that can contribute to the beauty of the spectacle."[26] The play, based on an event that had taken place in 1750, concerns the heroic conduct of Poucha-Houmma, chief of the Houmma nation. His son Cala-be has murdered a Choctaw in a fit of drunkenness and therefore, according to Indian law, must die to expiate his crime. Poucha-Houmma, however, saves his son's life by dying in his place. The author, Paul-Louis LeBlanc de Villeneufve, had just arrived in Louisiana as a sixteen-year-old *enseigne-à-pied* when Poucha-Houmma laid down his life. Detached among the Choctaws for seven years, which he later described as "the most beautiful" of his life, LeBlanc knew Cala-be personally and often conversed with him about his father's sacrifice.[27] Years later the aged, retired officer turned back to this episode of his youth when he heard newly arrived Frenchmen make derogatory remarks about the Indians. The so-called "savages" might have degenerated under the corrupting influence of the French, but before encountering European "civilization" the Louisiana Indians had been proud, independent, brave, enduring, with a deep sense of personal worth and dignity. LeBlanc wrote a play to prove it.[28]

The play was dedicated to Madame Marie-Anne Peborde de Laussat, the gracious wife of the colonial prefect Napoleon had sent to Louisiana in 1803 to transfer the colony from Spain to the United States. LeBlanc was seventy years of age when Madame de Laussat appeared on the New Orleans social scene, but the years that "might have been supposed sufficient to refrigerate at least, if not extinguish, his poetical ardor" had dampened neither his admiration of the "noble savage" nor his fondness for women. The man whom Claiborne called "the old Gentleman" became an enthusiastic admirer of the fair lady.[29] She won his admiration when she displayed compassion toward destitute Indians, and he remembered her in 1809 when he composed his tragedy.

LeBlanc's work is a classical tragedy in five acts, written in alexandrine verse in the best baroque tradition. The slender plot, however, hardly suffices for five acts, and rhetorical declamations, lamentations, recriminations, and apostrophes replace character development and dramatic intrigue. The play has been dismissed with patronizing remarks, often by critics who seem not to have read it. Although hardly a masterpiece, it was obviously composed by a cultivated man who had read the major French writers and knew the rules of classical tragedy. Louisiana's first play had a didactic, humanitarian purpose, justifying the grand rhetoric of Lafon's apostrophe "To the Public" several years earlier.

The first Louisiana play paid tribute to the native American. The next original work produced on the New Orleans stage honored an American hero, thus symbolizing the gradual reconciliation of the Creoles to their new nationality. July 4, 1811, saw the world premiere of *Un Trait de Washington, ou la France et l'Amérique,* a "heroic comedy, never before presented on any stage."[30] Alexis Daudet, a French-born actor, was the author, and the ubiquitous Louis Tabary played George Washington. M. Auguste was Lafayette, and a Mademoiselle Laurette, identified in the *Moniteur* as "a young peasant," took the part of "America."

While the Théâtre de la Rue Saint-Philippe thus continued to provide entertainment, work proceeded slowly on the Théâtre d'Orléans, which finally opened on October 19, 1815, with an opera by Pierre Gaveaux, *Un Quart Heure de silence.*[31] The theatre was destroyed by fire the following summer, but rebuilding began immediately. When it reopened three years later, Tabary was still manager but the impresario behind the Théâtre d'Orléans was John Davis, who became a major force in the New Orleans French theatre until 1837.[32]

THE THÉÂTRE D'ORLÉANS

John Davis was an enterprising individual who loved the stage. His many business ventures, such as hotels, ballrooms, a cigar manufacturing business, an import-export company, and gambling rooms, all served to subsidize his theatre, which was costly. Never satisfied with less than the best, he brought in performers from Paris. For the 1819 opening, two agents went to France and brought back two actors, one for opera and one for comedy; two actresses, one of whom was also a singer; a conductor; and several musicians. A characteristic of the Théâtre d'Orléans was that the performers were usually singers as well as actors, which must have insured an exceptional level of operatic acting. Normally the performers who were mainly actors sang in the chorus for opera or in minor roles, whereas the singers took the secondary roles in legitimate plays.

The theatre, which had cost $80,000 and had a seating capacity of thirteen hundred, was small, but it was considered elegant. Its façade had Doric columns for the first story, Corinthian composite columns for the second. The hall featured a parquet, two rows of boxes, galleries, and latticed boxes similar to the *baignoires* of French houses, for people in mourning who did not want to be seen at the theatre. The full architectural complex included Davis's hotel and the Orleans Ballroom. Henry Kmen comments:

Thus was the Orleans theater, the famous home of French Opera in antebellum New Orleans, built and launched. It resembled its two predecessors in owing its birth to the efforts of ballroom promoters, and its nourishment, at least in part, to the money provided directly and indirectly by New Orleans' passion for dancing.[33]

The brilliant opera double bill of its opening night, François-Adrien Boieldieu's *Jean de Paris* and Henri Berton's *Les Maris garçons,* was a prelude of things to come. Every year Davis recruited more personnel in France. In 1822 he brought the first regular ballet troupe to New Orleans.

Dramatically and musically the Théâtre d'Orléans was a triumph; financially, however, it was another story: without the ballroom and the gambling room, Davis could not have afforded his elaborate productions. Part of the problem was the competition from the Théâtre de la Rue Saint-Philippe, which still gave performances occasionally, and from the American Theater, which had opened on Camp Street in 1825, the first building in New Orleans to be lighted by gas.[34] The chief culprit, however, was the long hot summers, during which the affluent New Orleans residents most likely to patronize the theatres fled to cooler and healthier climes across the lake or in the North. Davis, never daunted by difficulties, found a solution: he took his company on a northern tour.

In two excellent articles, Sylvie Chevalley has told the story of those northern tours.[35] From 1827 to 1833 the Théâtre d'Orléans visited the large cities of the Atlantic seaboard, playing New York, Philadelphia, Boston, and Baltimore, usually to large audiences and critical acclaim. "The company," said the Philadelphia *Albion* of July 21, 1827, "is as good as is generally met with in the largest provincial cities of France, and much better than it has been our good fortune to see in any of the capitals (out of France) of Europe."[36] The tour repertoire drew heavily on opera and vaudeville, but included comedies such as Molière's *Tartuffe;* melodrama; and tragedies Jean Racine's *Andromaque,* Pierre Lebrun's *Marie Stuart,* and Jean-François Ducis's adaptation of *Hamlet.*

The Théâtre d'Orléans was opening in Philadelphia during its 1830 tour when news reached the city that Paris had overthrown the Bourbon king, Charles X. The French and American flags, the revolutionary tricolor of course, had floated all day in front of the Chestnut Theater, where the New Orleans company was appearing. That evening, between the two plays on the program, related a French eyewitness,

The orchestra struck up a national tune, the curtain rose, and the entire company wearing tricolor cockades and carrying tricolor flags appeared . . . singing "la Marseillaise." . . . At the first violin sound, at the first words, every French heart throbbed, . . . and the electrified parterre joined the actors for the famous refrain "Aux armes, citoyens!"[37]

The northern tours failed to solve the financial problem. The company had gained much acclaim, but the expenses of a touring troupe of over fifty performers were staggering. Davis's problems increased in 1825 when John Caldwell, an American impresario, introduced Italian opera at his new theatre on St. Charles Street. The challenge presented by the St. Charles Theater was epitomized by the operatic duel that took place in 1835, when the Americans were the first to present the American premiere of Giacomo Meyerbeer's *Robert le Diable.* The production, which the American critics praised lavishly, the French critics universally found wanting. A few weeks later the Théâtre d'Orléans offered the city its version of Meyerbeer's masterpiece, in a production the American critics denigrated but the French critics found "an epoch in the French theater of New

Orleans."[38] The chauvinistic clashes left from the territorial period were milder but had not disappeared.

The duel meant also that in a three-month period New Orleans had fifteen performances of the same opera by two different companies. It might have been an opera lover's dream, but it was a shareholder's nightmare. The financial backers finally announced that the Orleans Theater Company would take over the administration of the theatre, and on April 15, 1837, John Davis relinquished the reins he had so long held. The impresario, who had been ailing for some time, retired to a home across Lake Pontchartrain. When he died two years later, the city gave him a magnificent funeral. Immense crowds turned out; companies of the Louisiana Legion marched in the procession; and at the St. Louis Cathedral the entire company from the Théâtre d'Orléans sang a requiem composed for the occasion.[39]

THE THEATRE AS A SOCIAL CENTER

From 1840 to 1859 the Théâtre d'Orléans was under the direction of Charles Boudousquié, who continued Davis's tradition of hiring performers in France. The theatre continued to be the center of social life in the Creole city. "Not to be a subscriber, or at least a regular attendant at the opera," states an old New Orleans guidebook, "was tantamount to being ignored by society and looked upon as a person greatly lacking in taste."[40] It was fashionable for the cream of Creole society to fill the elegant playhouse on Thursday and Saturday nights in the Crescent City. Full evening regalia was *de rigueur* even in the parquet, where the gentlemen sported white kid gloves and full dress coats. The dress circle, which consisted of stalls, was filled with the most beautiful women in New Orleans, some would say in the world. The stalls were usually occupied by parties of four, "a young lady and her male escort, invariably attended by her mother or some elderly friends; as in no case was it considered allowable for an unmarried girl to appear in public without her 'chaperone' or some of her male relatives of nearest kin." The wide aisles permitted easy access to stalls and latticed boxes, and during intermissions the young men thronged the corridors, rushing to pay their respects to the "fair occupants." The families in mourning who occupied the latticed boxes, however, were visited only upon special invitation.[41]

The old guidebook waxes eloquent over "the jet black hair, the sparkling eyes, the pure complexions, the superb costumes with low-cut corsages and showing the round, beautiful arms, the gay and animated features" of the fair operagoers. "Never overdressed, and generally wearing white or some other light color, with purest camellias half hid amidst their brilliant masses of jet black hair, they resembled in grouping and appearance the beautiful conception of the artist, Winterhalter, in his celebrated painting of the Empress Eugenie and the ladies of her court."[42]

The theatres, needless to say, did not close on Sundays. In fact, that was the day when they drew some of their largest audiences. Incoming "Americans," however, were deeply shocked by the Creoles' disregard of Sabbath observance. Timothy Flint, who visited the city in the early 1820s, commented: "They fortify themselves in defending the custom of going to balls and the theatre on the Sabbath by arguing that religion ought to inspire cheerfulness and that cheerfulness is associated with religion."[43] But, as he reported, strict Protestants disagreed. He tells of seeing the French playbills for the Sunday performance posted at street corners on Sunday morning. Later in the day he observed a similar paper, but in English, posted under the French bills. It contained appropriate scriptural quotations, with a bold heading: "Remember the Sabbath day to keep it holy."[44] But it would have taken more than Biblical verses to deter New Orleans society from Sabbath breaking, and some twenty years later Bishop Henry Benjamin Whipple observed no fewer than twenty flagrant violations, including "two theatres open" and "French opera with ballet dancers."[45]

Central as the theatre was in New Orleans life, it was second to dancing. Dancing supported the theatre; dancing drew audiences into the theatre; and after the theatre, proper New Orleans residents went dancing. Concerts were often coupled with balls; plays and operas were followed by balls, often right in the theatre; and as Kmen points out, "Even the stellar performance of Mr. Church, who did bird imitations and sword balancing, and who capped all by playing the violin on his back on a slack wire in full swing, had to be combined with a ball!"[46]

To attract audiences, the theatre managers usually scheduled light musicals and vaudevilles on the same bill as grand operas, and assorted music hall acts were frequently featured with serious theatricals. It was not unusual to pair operas with what Kmen aptly calls "bizarre acts"; a trained horse, a strong man, a lady who did Spanish dances on a tight rope, jugglers, Tyrolean minstrels, an automated trumpeter, and even a team composed of an anaconda and a boa constrictor.[47]

Even with such attractions, the days of the Théâtre d'Orléans were numbered. In 1859 it was purchased by a Frenchman named Parlange, and soon Boudousquié withdrew from the management of the theatre and formed another association to erect a new opera house.

THE OPÉRA FRANÇAIS

The new theatre was designed by James Gallier, Jr., later one of New Orleans's most famous architects. The work, begun on April 9, 1859, was completed on November 28. On December 1 the Opéra Français opened with a gala performance of Gioacchino Rossini's *William Tell*.

The Opéra Français was a magnificent theatre. The entire house was painted white, with four gracefully curved balconies, each receding from the line of the other. The first two tiers, or dress circles, were divided into boxes, the front of which were decorated in gold. In the rear of each dress circle was the inevitable row of latticed boxes, and on each side of the proscenium were ample stage boxes. The other boxes, as in the Théâtre d'Orléans, were planned for four occupants. The third tier, without divisions or boxes, provided inexpensive seats for whites, and the fourth tier was reserved for nonwhites.[48]

In 1859, as in earlier days, free people of color as well as slaves regularly attended the theatre. In the Théâtre de la Rue Saint-Pierre, the free people of color had sat in the second loges, whereas the slaves had been admitted into the amphitheatre for fifty cents. At the Théâtre d'Orléans there were at first no provisions for slaves, but the impossibility of keeping bondsmen out was such that by 1822 the third balcony was reserved for them and the free colored sat in the second. In the Théâtre de la Rue Saint-Philippe, where there was no third balcony, a section of the second was partitioned for the slaves. Slaves were excluded, however, just as were the whites, from the Théâtre de la Renaissance, established in 1840. This theatre was, as its administration reminded the public, "established for [free] persons of color. These will be admitted exclusively."[49]

The nonwhite audience, on the other hand, was not admitted to the luxurious lounge rooms of the Opéra Français. The main salon, called the "crush room," was sixty feet in length, opening on a gallery. Besides, there were club rooms, several parlors, rooms for the ladies, a cloakroom and a boudoir, the most luxurious theatre parlors anywhere in America.[50]

Under the capable directorship of Charles Boudousquié and his assistant, John Davis, Jr., the Opéra quickly established itself as the new center of New Orleans social and cultural life. In the second half of the nineteenth century, everyone in New Orleans went to the performances, rich and poor, black and white, socialites and working people. In her sprightly memoirs, Eliza Ripley reminisced about the old opera house and told how the little seamstress who came and sewed "all day like wild for seventy-five cents" had never missed a Sunday night performance, no more than had the "dusky Henriette Blondeau" who came, "her *tignon* stuck full of pins" to do the ladies' hair.[51] Eliza's family went on Tuesdays and Saturdays.

The second season of the Opéra Français was notable for the debut of a young soprano who later became a legendary prima donna. Of the two lead singers hired for the season, one fell ill, the other broke a leg. The conductor, Max Strakosh, was married to Amelia Patti, a fine contralto with an eighteen-year-old sister. The younger woman learned the lead role in a week, and thus it was that on December 19, 1860, Adelina Patti made her world debut on the New Orleans stage in Gaetano Donizetti's *Lucia di Lammermoor*. She made her formal debut at the Royal Italian Opera House in New Orleans a year later, but it was in the Crescent City that her career had been launched.[52]

The 1860–1861 season was exceptionally brilliant. Grand operas, comic operas, light operas, comedies, and dramas alternated at the Opéra Français. The season ended early, however. War was brewing, and on April 10, 1861, the Opéra closed its doors, not to reopen until December 21, 1865, barely eight months after Lee's surrender at Appomattox. The 1865–1866 season was quite brief, less than two months, but it was a symbol of the city's determination to recover.

During the next few years the Opéra Français presented mixed seasons of plays and operas. The year 1866 saw the appearance of the celebrated *tragédienne*, Adélaïde Ristori, who gave twelve performances.[53] From 1872 to the beginning of 1875 the manager was L. Placide Canonge, one of New Orleans's most successful playwrights. Under his direction the repertoire leaned heavily toward the spoken drama. There was no opera during his first season, but he soon learned that even though opera cost a great deal more to produce than plays, it also drew far larger audiences.[54] Under the series of directors who followed him, the number of lyric productions increased and fewer and fewer plays were produced.

SARAH BERNHARDT'S VISIT

The year 1880 marked a notable event, Sarah Bernhardt's first visit to the Crescent City. Despite the exorbitant prices of the tickets, $270 for the best box seats for all nine performances, there was not an empty seat in the house when the curtain went up for the first performance of *Frou-Frou*, by Henri Meilhac and Ludovic Halévy. "La Divine," as she was known, returned to New Orleans during her many "farewell" tours, the last one in 1917 as an invalid who had to be wheeled on stage. But she was still indomitable, and despite her age and the inclement weather, she insisted upon participating in a Liberty Loan parade. When a threatening downpour was suggested as a reason for her not to participate, she scoffed: "My soldiers in France are standing knee-deep in blood and grime. I shall ride in the parade if none else does."[55]

One of her great pleasures in New Orleans was alligator hunting in the nearby swamps. Accompanied by Capt. Louis Rapho, a celebrated huntsman, she set out after performances and, according to the huntsman's reminiscences, never exhibited fatigue. Yet the performances she gave must have been quite demanding. During her first visit she went through a repertoire consisting of Racine's *Phèdre*, Victor Hugo's *Hernani*, Alexandre Dumas fils's *La Dame aux Camélias*, François Coppet's *Le Passant, Adrienne Lecouvreur* by Eugène Scribe and Ernest Legouvé, and *Le Sphinx* by Octave Feuillet. New Orleans saw her in some of her famous roles such as Edmond Rostand's *Cyrano de Bergerac* and *L'Aiglon;* Victorien Sardou's *Tosca* and *La Sorcière.* She also appeared in that grand melodrama, Alexandre Bisson's *Madame X*, during which, John Smith Kendall reminisces fondly, the brilliant actress, simply by manipulating her veil, stole a scene in which she uttered not a word, yet monopolized the attention of the audience.[56]

The Opéra Français closed its doors again for World War I. It had barely reopened when it burned to the ground on December 4, 1919. Officially it was a fire of "undetermined origin." F. Edward Hebert, the crusty congressman from Louisiana (1941–1977), who had been a reporter for the *New Orleans States* at the time, insists in his memoirs that "most of the *States'* staff knew who was responsible for the demise of that symbol of upperclass decadence. Jim Crown burned the opera house."[57] The gentleman from Louisiana relates how "a bunch of drunks" gathered in the patio of a cabaret adjoining the opera house. Maj. James E. Crown, a reporter who would become editor and managing editor of the *States* in 1937 and who went through three or four packs a day, and Roy Aymond, a cigar-smoking cartoonist, kept flicking their ashes in brandy barrels still packed in straw. The smouldering ashes eventually burst into flames. "One of them started that fire, flipping their ashes into those barrels,"[58] and so, if we can believe the former reporter, this is how the Opéra Français went up in flames and professional French theatricals in New Orleans came to an end.

AMATEUR THEATRICAL GROUPS

Amateur groups did keep French theatre alive in New Orleans and in the rural parishes.[59] Already in the nineteenth century, Canonge had organized two amateur theatrical groups, Le Club Dramatique Louisianais and Le Club Dramatique Orléanais. During the twentieth century two new groups were established, La Renaissance Française, which produced plays from November 1930 to June 1934, and Les Comédiens Français de la Nouvelle-Orléans, which began in September 1934. Founded by Gabrielle Lavedan, who directed and acted many of their early productions, Les Comédiens continue to perform a wide repertoire drawn from both classic and modern theatre and occasionally tour other Louisiana cities.[60]

THEATRE IN THE RURAL PARISHES

In the rural parishes, French theatrical activities have tended to be scanty, with the notable exception of touring companies from New Orleans, which are mentioned from time to time in Baton Rouge, Opelousas, Donaldsonville, New Iberia, and St. Martinville, both before and after the Civil War. In the last years of the nineteenth century and the early years of the twentieth, there is mention of visits to rural towns by the Opéra Français, usually performing vaudeville, operettas, or comic operas. In 1903 it cancelled its performances in New Iberia, where it had been appearing since 1895.[61] In December of that year the little town on the Bayou Teche was shocked when *Le Premier Mari de France*, a French farce which the local paper describes as of "questionable morality," was substituted for a scheduled opera.[62] It is unclear whether those performers came from the Opéra Français, but after this offense to local sensibilities, there seems to have been no more French opera or other theatricals in New Iberia.

The Opéra Français performed for a longer period of time in other towns of southern Louisiana. Elderly residents of Lafayette and St. Martinville reminisce fondly about visits of the famed company to St. Martinville, and at least once in

Lafayette in 1909 the Opéra Français performed Edmond Audran's operetta *La Mascotte*.[63]

St. Martinville, a small, picturesque town on the banks of Bayou Teche and also the site of Longfellow's *Evangeline*, had an active theatrical life. The town has for a long time prided itself on being "le petit Paris de l'Amérique" because the aristocratic refugees from the French Revolution settled there and tried to reconstitute along the Teche the civilization they had known on the banks of the Seine. The town tradition also claims that St. Martinville had opera before New Orleans. In any event, there is evidence that a one-act comic opera by a New Orleans composer, Eugène Chassaignac, was performed in 1850 at the Théâtre de St. Martinville.[64]

Later in the century the little village experienced considerable theatrical activity when the cultivated attorney and gifted playwright Félix Voorhies organized the C.C.C. (coffee, chocolate, and cake), a dramatic society that performed regularly in Duchamp Hall, giving mostly Voorhies's own plays. The group at first had to reinstate the Elizabethan tradition of using boy actors for female parts: theatricals were not considered respectable for "nice" girls. Eventually, however, the local gentry softened and Voorhies found himself with a full company of actors and actresses. Voorhies often composed incidental music for his dramatic works, and as in New Orleans, play performances were followed by balls.[65]

Today the French theatre is kept alive by the Comédiens Français, who perform two plays a year; by many high schools, which present one-act plays for the Foreign Language Festival;[66] and by a company formed in 1977, Nous Autres, which tours southern Louisiana with plays written in the Acadian French dialect spoken in the region.

THE REPERTOIRE FROM FRANCE

During the nineteenth century the French theatrical repertoire in New Orleans closely paralleled that of Paris. Charles I. Silin, who has studied the various works performed in New Orleans from 1806 to 1859, found that a staggering 1,320 of them were produced in these fifty-three years. He discovered that the most popular form was vaudeville, with 638 performances; then came comedies, 464; operas, 443; and dramas, 214. Melodrama accounted for 87 titles, and tragedy, the least popular genre, for only 49. The classical writers were not popular on the banks of the Mississippi; according to Silin there were only two tragedies by Corneille and five by Racine in the New Orleans repertoire. For light musicals the favored authors were Charles-Simon Favart, Michel-Jean Sedaine, François André Denican Philidor, Pierre-Alexandre Monsigny, Nicolas Dalayrac, and André Ernest Grétry.[67]

During the 1830s the romantic drama engulfed the New Orleans stage, which was seldom far behind the Parish fashion. Victor Hugo and Alexandre Dumas père dominated the repertóire: all of Hugo's dramas except *Cromwell* and *Les Burgraves* and thirty-four by Dumas were produced. Their popularity, however, was eclipsed by that of Eugène Scribe, whose "well-made plays" were to become New Orleans' all-time favorites. Within thirty years the Creole city saw 147 of his plays, some of them repeatedly.[68]

At the same time, the socially conscious plays of Emile Augier and Dumas fils entered the repertoire. As one might expect, *La Dame aux Camélias* was a favorite, in both its spoken and operatic versions. Toward the end of the nineteenth century operatic taste in New Orleans turned increasingly to grand opera, favorite composers being Halévy, especially *La Juive*, and Donizetti, Rossini, and Giuseppe Verdi, all sung in French. Meyerbeer's *Huguenots*, a New Orleans favorite, was in fact the last opera performed at the Opéra Français.

THE NATIVE REPERTOIRE

The nineteenth-century Louisiana stage was not limited to productions from France. Rather, a number of original plays by natives of Louisiana and by transplanted Frenchmen were also produced. Nor was the exchange one way; several Louisiana-born writers established themselves in Paris, where they enjoyed successful careers.

A contemporary of LeBlanc de Villeneufve was French-born Alexis Daudet, a reputable actor and occasional theatre manager who had come from Santo Domingo. The only one of his plays extant, *Bombarde ou Les Marchands de Chansons, Parodie d' "Ossian ou Les Bardes,"* was never produced in New Orleans, but the Crescent City did see his *L'Ecossais à la Louisiane*, probably the first original work performed in Louisiana, presented on June 22, 1808, a year before *Poucha-Houmma*. No copies of it are known to exist, however, Daudet was also the author of the heroic comedy *La France et l'Amérique*, which celebrated Louisiana's first Fourth of July as part of the United States.[69]

Le Moniteur tantalizes the theatre historian with its one mention of *Papa Simon ou les Amours de Thérèse et Janot*, "a creole vaudeville," which was announced for April 30, 1811. One would like to know the author of the play and the justification for calling it "creole."[70] Unfortunately no copy has surfaced yet, anymore than has the one-act play *Lafayette à la Nouvelle-Orléans*, which A. J. Guirot presented at the Théâtre d'Orléans during the general's visit in 1825.[71]

The influence of Hugo and Dumas père in the 1830s was not limited to performances of their plays; the French dramatists found imitators on the Gulf Coast. One of the earliest was Auguste Crébassol, who in 1838 wrote a drama, *Jeanne, petite fille de Robert le Diable*, which was rejected by the Théâtre d'Orléans but which shows that New Orleans kept up with the latest trends: *Hernani* had exploded onto the Paris stage in 1830.[72]

Crébassol's efforts were not rejected because the theatre's management was unfamiliar with the new romantic style, for the year before, on February 28, a five-act prose drama by Auguste Lussan had been produced: *La Famille créole*.

Lussan, born in France of peasant parents, had come to New Orleans as an actor with the Théâtre d'Orléans. His *Famille créole* was well received and was performed several times. He wrote three more dramas, *Sara la Juive; Les Martyrs de la Louisiane;* and *Trois Jours après Waterloo ou La Grande Chartreuse.* Although called a tragedy, *Les Martyrs* is really a romantic verse drama, the first literary treatment of the Revolution of 1768, during which the French colonists had risen against their new Spanish masters and driven out the governor who had been sent to take over the province. Lussan's play centers on the repression carried out by the next Spanish governor, General Don Alexander O'Reilly, and apotheosizes the leaders of the revolution as patriotic martyrs. Lussan died penniless in 1842 and was buried in Potters' Field in New Orleans.[73]

Charles-Oscar Dugué's *Mila ou La Mort de La Salle* also dramatized an episode of Louisiana history, the assassination of the explorer by one of his own men. In Dugué's drama the murderer is an Iago-type villain whose lust has been aroused by Mila, the beautiful Indian girl whom la Salle is to marry. (Obviously Louisiana-born Dugué had become a disciple of Chateaubriand while studying in France.[74])

Another native playwright contributed some dramas to the New Orleans stage. Sent to Paris by Judah B. Benjamin with letters for the Confederate mission, Henri Vignaud remained in the French capital, where he eventually became secretary of the American legation, a post he occupied for thirty-nine years. There he gained a considerable reputation for his studies of Christopher Columbus and the early discoveries, but before leaving his native city Vignaud had given two dramas to the stage, *Jane Grey,* performed at the Théâtre Française in 1851 when he was barely twenty-one, and *La Vieillesse des Mousquetaires,* performed two years later at the Théâtre d'Orléans.

Dumas père's musketeers provided the inspiration for another Louisiana drama, *La Mort de Porthos,* which Hippolyte de Bautte presented in 1851, not in New Orleans, but in the rural community of Donaldsonville. Born in France, de Bautte came to Louisiana in 1847 as a political exile and plunged into journalism and politics, finally dying of pneumonia, which he contracted while attending a meeting of the Democratic party. Another of his dramas, *Les Brigands de Bayou Lafourche,* was also performed in Donaldsonville. There is no record that his other play, *Boston et Québec,* was ever presented.[75]

Silin's analysis of the New Orleans repertoire indicated a preponderance of comedy and vaudevilles. It is not surprising that both genres should figure among the original works produced. One of the earliest comic works caused a small tempest. In 1846 the American army, led by Gen. Zachary Taylor, a Louisiana native, won a major victory over the Mexicans at Resaca de la Palma. Taylor became the man of the hour, especially in his native state. Félix de Courmont, a young lawyer born in the West Indies who had gained some fame in New Orleans for the biting verse satires he had published, made the mistake of writing a one-act comic opera that satirized one of the heroes of the battle, a certain Captain May, and treated Taylor himself with less than reverent respect.

The piece, at first titled *Resaca de la Palma*, was accepted by John Davis for the Théâtre d'Orléans and then withdrawn because of criticism. As expected, more criticism ensued, and the comic opera was finally given under the title *Le Capitaine May et le Général de la Vega sur les bords du Rio Grande*. Shortly after the performance, Courmont left New Orleans never to return, supporting the idea that it does not pay for an "outsider" to ridicule local heroes.[76]

Little is known of another comic opera composed about the same time by the prolific composer Eugène Chassaignac. Born in Brittany, Chassaignac studied with Halévy, then in 1849 came to Louisiana, where his one-act comic opera *La Nuit aux échelles* was performed in St. Martinville in 1850.[77] Similar obscurity surrounds *Une Femme en loterie*, a vaudeville by Edouard de Lauc-Maryat, who used the interesting pseudonym of Edouard Zéro. The play was produced in 1850, but nothing is known of it except for a review.[78]

Most nineteenth-century Louisiana playwrights preferred glamorous settings such as Paris or Venice. A local setting was used for two comedies published around the middle of the century, Ernest Legendre's *Deux Parisiens en Louisiane* and the delightful one-acter published in the *Almanach de la Louisiane* in 1864, *Les Deux Rivaux ou Un Mariage au bayou*. Well plotted and entertaining, the latter play uses skillfully the comic possibilities of the three types of French spoken in Louisiana: the modern French of the educated Creole, the Cajun of the rural dweller, and the creole dialect of the blacks. This good-humored comedy in no way reflects the bitterness and anxieties that plagued Louisiana at the time that it was written.[79]

Louis-Xavier Eyma was born in Martinique and died in France. It would be difficult to claim him as a Louisiana playwright had not his two visits to New Orleans, where his father resided, been crucial to his writing career. Most of the studies, novels, and travel accounts that poured from his fertile pen had the New World as their theme. Three of his vaudevilles were presented in Paris theatres: *Capitaine . . . de quoi*, *Le Renard et les raisins*; and *Le Mariage au bâton*.[80]

There can be no doubt, however, about claiming Victor Séjour as a Louisiana playwright, although this talented and prolific free man of color spent most of his productive life in Paris. Born in New Orleans in 1817, Séjour was sent to Paris in 1836 to pursue his studies and to remove him from the racial prejudice and ambiguous status that were his in New Orleans. In Paris he met Dumas père and Augier and embarked upon a theatrical career. His first play, *Diégarias*, was performed in 1844 at the Théâtre Français and his second, *La Chute de Séjan*, in 1849. All in all, twenty-one of his plays, most of them dramas, were given in Paris. His success and popularity can be gauged by the fact that when his *André Gérard* was given at the Odéon, Frédéric Lemaître, the most famous French actor of his day, played the lead role.[81]

A fervent Bonapartist (his first published work had been a poem in praise of Napoleon I), Séjour was said to have been greatly appreciated by Napoleon III, and his brilliant career ended with the fall of the Second Empire. He left only two comedies, *L'Argent du diable* and *Le Paletot brun*, a delightfully witty, albeit cynical, one-acter that was revived successfully in 1976 by Les Comédiens Français de la Nouvelle-Orléans. Only one of his plays uses a Louisiana theme, *Les Volontaires de 1814*, which treats the battle of New Orleans. Despite his fame and success, Séjour died quite poor and lies today in the Père-Lachaise cemetery in Paris.[82]

A contemporary of Séjour was another prolific and successful New Orleans playwright, L. Placide Canonge. Son of a distinguished New Orleans judge, Canonge studied in Paris at the College Louis-le-Grand. He returned to Louisiana, worked for several newspapers, and went back to Paris, where he published a series of articles in Emile Girardin's *La Presse*. He came back to New Orleans and until his death wrote for numerous newspapers. The theatre was his passion; he wrote theatrical columns, composed plays and libretti, acted, founded two amateur theatrical groups, and for a while was director of the Opéra Français. His dramatic compositions include several libretti: *Le Lépreux*, an opera with music by Gregorio Curto, a prolific New Orleans composer; *Louise de Lorraine*, an opera with music by Mme. Alonzo Morphy; and *Blanche and Renée*, an operetta with music by Eugène Prévost, which was performed by the young ladies of a finishing school.

He also wrote several dramas: *Le Comte de Monte Cristo*, based on Dumas's novel; *Juan ou Une Histoire sous Charles-Quint*; *Un Grand d'Espagne*; *L'Ambassadeur d'Autriche*; *France et Espagne ou la Louisiane en 1769*, another version of the 1768 revolution; and finally his most successful work, *Le Comte de Carmagnola*. The play was extremely well received in New Orleans, and according to James Wood Davidson, it was performed a hundred times in Paris.[83] Canonge also left a charming proverb in the manner of Alfred de Musset, *Qui perd gagne*.[84] Deft, well written, witty, and engaging, Canonge's comedy would have been worthy of his mentor's pen.

Canonge was probably the most influential figure in New Orleans theatrical life during the second half of the nineteenth century. Short-tempered, he was, says Davidson, "small but well formed. His features are classical, without a single faulty line; and as soon as one beholds his high, broad, smooth, perpendicular, beaming forehead, and large, lustrous, contemplative black eyes, the idea at once suggests itself that he must be a poet."[85] Canonge died in 1893, and with him, generally speaking, died the professional French theatre in New Orleans.

Canonge was the last New Orleans playwright of importance whose works were performed in his native city. Two brothers, Albert and Edouard Delpit, moved to Paris, became French citizens, and had some success on the French stage. A prolific novelist as well as playwright, Albert Delpit was awarded the 1880 Vitet prize by the French Academy for the whole of his work. His brother Edouard was equally prolific although less successful, but neither had any contact with New Orleans after moving to Paris.[86]

The playwrights who persevered in the Creole City had their works published rather than performed. So it was, for example, with the biting comedy penned by Charles Chauvin Boisclair Deléry in 1877, *L'Ecole du peuple*. In this one-acter Deléry, a pugnacious and opinionated man, cruelly satirized the black legislators of Reconstruction, singling out two by name, "Caius César" Antoine and "Percy Bysshe Shelley" Pinchback. Because of the inflammatory subject, the performance was not permitted in New Orleans.[87]

Alfred Mercier was a distinguished novelist and founder in 1876 of the Athénée Louisianais, an organization for the perpetuation of French language and culture. He wrote several plays, none of which was ever performed—nor do they seem to have been written with performance in mind. *L'Ermite du Niagara* is a long poetic dialogue, reminiscent of Lamartine and the early romantic poets. *Paracelse* could be classified as a romantic closet drama. So could another of his dramas, *Fortunia*, which treats the supremacy of fate in human life. Mercier's plays, moreover, are indicative of a trend that developed at the end of the nineteenth century among the Louisiana playwrights: whereas the early writers had been in close contact with literary developments in Paris, the turn of the century saw New Orleans authors gradually losing touch and writing in increasingly outmoded styles. As they were engulfed by the Anglo-Saxon tide, the Creoles struggled to maintain their heritage; the journal Mercier kept until his death sadly chronicles the gradual encroachment of English.[88] L'Athéné Louisianais kept meeting and publishing its *Comptes rendus*, but it increasingly became a beleagured bastion.

The *Comptes rendus de l'Athénée Louisianais* during these last years of the nineteenth and early years of the twentieth century became the chief means of expression of the Louisiana French playwrights. Thus they published Marie Joséphine Augustin's pleasant little *comédies de salon*, written for female casts, *Les Vacances de Camille* and *Le Dernier bonnet d'âne*. In 1901–1902 the *Comptes rendus* published a romantic drama by Joseph A. Maltrait, *Elizabeth à Corfou*, which deals with Elizabeth of Austria, the mother of the archduke who killed himself at Mayerling. The beautiful and unhappy empress retired to the island of Corfou to muse upon her fate. This static drama, more suited for reading than acting, was never performed.

In St. Martinville Félix Voorhies kept penning delightful, well-turned plays for his amateur company. A couple were published in the *Comptes rendus*, but most, after a few local performances, were relegated to oblivion. The *Revue de Louisiane–Louisiana Review* has undertaken a program of publication of the judge's plays, one of which, *Le Petit Chien de la veuve*, was successfully revived in 1975. This deftly written one-act comedy, a French version of Chekhov's celebrated *Boor*, is as lively, cynical, and entertaining as the Russian original.[89]

Some French in New Orleans continued writing. Recalling the early days of the Comédiens Français, Gabrielle Lavedan remembers Charles Boisset who composed three plays for the group, and Mme. May who also gave them three comedies. None of them has ever been published, nor have they ever been performed again.[90]

CONTEMPORARY FRENCH THEATRE

The history of the French theatre in Louisiana is not over. In 1968, in recognition of the state's French heritage and the need to preserve and develop this human resource, the Louisiana legislature established the Conseil pour le Développement du Français en Louisiane (CODOFIL). With the encouragement of this agency, a veritable renaissance has taken place in the French-speaking part of the state, especially among the "Cajuns," the descendants of the Acadians exiled by the English from Nova Scotia in 1755, and of the many groups, English, Spanish, German, Irish, absorbed into the Francophone culture of South Louisiana.

The renaissance of the language has been accompanied by a revival of theatrical activity and productivity. Nous Autres, a troupe composed of natives of Louisiana as well as French, Belgians, and Quebeçois, has been performing original plays written by and for French-speaking Louisianians. The plays utilize the rich folkloric heritage of the region. The first one, *Jean l'Ours et la fille du Roi*, written by the actors under the direction of Barry Jean Ancelet, coordinator of the University of Southwestern Louisiana's Center for Creole and Acadian Folklore, tells the story of a folk hero, Jean l'Ours, a penniless but clever, resourceful, and somewhat impudent peasant boy who wins the king's daughter with the assistance of his supernaturally gifted friends. The second play presented by Nous Autres, *Martin Weber et les Marais-Bouleurs*, is also drawn by Barry Ancelet from South Louisiana tradition.

The third, *Mille Misères: Laissant le bon temps rouler en Louisiane* was written by a young attorney, David Emile Marcantel, writing under the pseudonym of Marc Untel de Gravelle. Enthusiastically received, it was taped for Canadian and French television. *Mille Misères* concerns the plight of a Cajun trying to preserve his identity in the modern world and avoid assimilation in the great American melting pot, not because his way of life is superior but because it is his. Judging from the response of the audiences, the French language will survive in the Bayou State, and along with it, the French theatre.

NEED FOR RESEARCH

This cursory survey of the French theatre in Louisiana has raised many questions and has pointed out many avenues that should be explored. There is a great need to study carefully the nineteenth-century French theatrical activities in small towns such as Breaux Bridge, St. Martinville, Donaldsonville, New Iberia, Opelousas, and Lafayette. The existing studies have concentrated on the English-language theatre. Only in New Orleans have French theatrical activities been studied with any care, and even there the work has concentrated on opera. The activities of the theatres that catered exclusively to free people of color, such as the Théâtre Marigny and the Théâtre de la Renaissance, also need to be investigated.

Above all, there is a need to collect and study the works of the playwrights. The distinguished historian of colonial Louisiana, Charles O'Neill, has been at work for some years on a study of Séjour. Similar studies should be undertaken on Canonge, the Delpit brothers, Dugué, Lussan, Eyma, and Voorhies. It is unlikely that a careful study of provincial French drama will uncover a hitherto unrecognized genius, a Racine of the bayous or a creole Molière. But examination of the readily available texts suggests that such a study would considerably enrich our understanding of the Louisiana French experience. It would further enlarge our appreciation of the theatre and, as the present revival in the rural areas suggests, illuminate the relationship between drama and the sense of ethnic identity.

NOTES

1. *Mississippi History Newsletter* 20 (Jan. 1979).

2. A one-act play by Céron, first performed in Paris in 1746. See *A Comparative View of French Louisiana, 1699 and 1762: The Journals of Iberville and D'Abbadie* (Lafayette, La.: Center for Louisiana Studies, forthcoming).

3. Quoted in René J. Le Gardeur, Jr., "Les Premières Années du théâtre à la Nouvelle-Orléans," *Comptes rendus de l'Athénée Louisianais* (hereafter cited as *CRAL*), Mar. 1954, pp. 60–61.

4. René J. Le Gardeur, Jr., *The First New Orleans Theatre, 1792–1803* (New Orleans: Leeward Books, 1963), p. 3.

5. Quoted in Le Gardeur, "Les Premières Années," p. 62.

6. Le Gardeur, *First New Orleans Theatre*, p. 6.

7. Ibid., p. 10; Jean Fouchard, *Le Théâtre à Saint-Domingue* (Port-au-Prince: Imprimerie de l'Etat, 1955), pp. 303–44.

8. James A. Padgett, ed., "A Decree for Louisiana Issued by the Baron of Carondelet, June 1, 1795," *Louisiana Historical Quarterly* (hereafter cited as *LHQ*) 20 (1927): 591.

9. Quoted in Stanley Clisby Arthur, *Old New Orleans: A History of the Vieux Carré, Its Ancient and Historical Buildings* (New Orleans: Harmanson, 1936), p. 100.

10. Pierre-Louis Berquin-Duvallon, *Vue de la colonie espagnole du Mississippi ou des provinces de Louisiane et Floride occidentale en l'année 1802* (Paris: Imprimerie expéditive, 1803), pp. 29–30.

11. Le Gardeur, *First New Orleans Theatre*, p. 38.

12. Quoted in Nellie Warner Price, "Le Spectacle de la Rue St. Pierre," *LHQ* 1 (Jan. 1918): 217.

13. Henry Arnold Kmen, *Music in New Orleans: The Formative Years, 1791–1841* (Baton Rouge: Louisiana State University Press, 1966), p. 59.

14. G. P. Wittington, ed., "The Journal of Dr. John Sibley, July–October, 1802," *LHQ* 10 (1927): 486.

15. Le Gardeur, *First New Orleans Theatre*, p. 21.

16. Wittington, "Journal of Dr. John Sibley," p. 486.

17. "Lafon au Public," *Le Moniteur de la Louisiane* (hereafter cited as *Le Moniteur*), Sept. 4, 1802.

18. Quoted in Price, "Spectacle de la Rue St. Pierre," p. 219.

19. Dunbar Rowland, ed., *Official Letter Books of W.C.C. Claiborne, 1801–1816* (Jackson, Miss.: State Department of Archives and History, 1917), vol. 3, p. 35.

20. Ibid., p. 84.

21. Ibid., p. 85.

22. Ibid.

23. Kmen, *Music in New Orleans*, p. 63.

24. Ibid., p. 64.

25. Ibid., p. 74.

26. *Le Moniteur*, Feb. 15, 1809.

27. Born around 1734 in the village of Crest in Dauphiny, LeBlanc lost his father at thirteen. In 1750, while Vaudreuil was governor, he arrived in Louisiana and was sent to live among the Choctaws. He had a long, distinguished military career, serving as Indian agent later on the northwest Louisiana frontier and engaging in fur trade in the Natchitoches region. He died in New Orleans, May 16, 1815. See Mathé Allain, ed. and trans., *The Festival of the Young Corn or The Heroism of Poucha-Houmma by LeBlanc de Villeneufve* (Lafayette, La., 1964), pp. 3, 7.

28. Ibid., pp. i–viii.

29. [Charles Gayarré?], "The Tragic Muse in Louisiana," *New Orleans Times Democrat*, Nov. 30, 1884.

30. *Le Moniteur*, July 2, 1811.

31. Kmen, *Music in New Orleans*, p. 79.

32. Born in Paris in 1773, John Davis emigrated to Santo Domingo, then went to Cuba. In 1809 he came to New Orleans, where he died in 1839. His son John Davis, Jr., also made important contributions to New Orleans theatre history, as will be seen later in this chapter.

33. Kmen, *Music in New Orleans*, p. 92.

34. Lucille Gafford, "Our Superb Gas-Lighted Drama," *New Orleans Times-Picayune Sunday Magazine*, May 16, 1926, pp. 1–6.

35. Sylvie Chevalley, "La Première Saison theâtrale française de New York," *French Review* 24 (1951): 471–79, and "Le Théâtre d'Orléans en tournée dans les villes du nord, 1827–1833," *CRAL*, Mar. 1955, pp. 27–71.

36. Quoted in Chevalley, "Le Théâtre d'Orléans," p. 35.

37. Quoted in ibid., p. 56.

38. Kmen, *Music in New Orleans*, p. 136.

39. Ibid., p. 150.

40. *Historical Sketch Book and Guide to New Orleans and Environs* (New York: Will H. Coleman, 1885), p. 135.

41. Ibid.

42. Ibid.

43. Timothy Flint, *Recollections of the Last Ten Years Passed in Occasional Residences and Journeyings in the Valley of the Mississippi . . .* (1826), reprint ed. (New York: Alfred A. Knopf, 1932), p. 295.

44. Ibid., p. 296.

45. Lester B. Shippee, ed., *Bishop Whipple's Southern Diary, 1843–1844* (Minneapolis: University of Minnesota Press, 1937), p. 119.

46. Kmen, *Music in New Orleans*, p. 5.

47. Ibid., p. 176.

48. Nathaniel Cortlandt Curtis, *New Orleans, Its Old Houses, Shops and Public Buildings* (Philadelphia: J. B. Lippincott, 1933), p. 195.

49. Kmen, *Music in New Orleans*, p. 235.

50. Lorelle Causey Bender, "The French Opera House of New Orleans, 1859–1890" (master's thesis, Louisiana State University, 1940), p. 10.

51. Eliza Moore (Chinn) McHatton Ripley, *Social Life in Old New Orleans, Being Recollections of My Girlhood* (New York: Appleton, 1912), pp. 68–69.

52. Bender, "The French Opera House," pp. 17–18.

53. Ibid., p. 22.

54. Ibid., p. 30.

55. John Smith Kendall, "Sarah Bernhardt in New Orleans," *LHQ* 26 (1943): 776.

56. Ibid., p. 776.

57. F. Edward Hebert with John McMillan, *Last of the Titans: The Life and Times of Congressman F. Edward Hebert of Louisiana* (Lafayette, La.: Center for Louisiana Studies, 1976), p. 74.

58. Ibid.

59. Louisiana is divided into parishes instead of counties.

60. See Gabrielle Lavedan, "Le Théâtre français d'amateurs à la Nouvelle-Orléans," *CRAL*, 1963, pp. 10–28.

61. *New Iberia Weekly Iberian*, Feb. 2, 1895; *New Iberia Enterprise*, Feb. 14, 1903.

62. *New Iberia Enterprise*, Dec. 23, 1903.

63. *Lafayette Daily Advertiser*, Dec. 28, 1909.

64. Auguste Viatte, "Complément à la bibliographie d'Edward Larocque Tinker," *Revue de Louisiane–Louisiana Review* 3, no. 2 (1974): 20.

65. Marcelle Frances Schertz, "The Plays of Judge Félix Voorhies, 1838–1919" (master's thesis, Louisiana State University, 1940).

66. From thirty to fifty high schools from throughout the state perform plays during the annual Foreign Language Festival, held on the campus of the University of Southwestern Louisiana. Most of them repeat these plays later for home audiences.

67. Charles I. Silin, "The French Theatre in New Orleans," *American Society of the Legion of Honor Magazine* 27 (1957): 127–30.

68. Ibid., p. 131.

69. *Le Moniteur*, July 2, 1811. For publication and performance information concerning Louisiana plays, see the bibliography to this chapter.

70. *Le Moniteur*, Apr. 30, 1811.

71. Edward Larocque Tinker, *Les Ecrits de langue française en Louisiane au XIXe siècle: Essays biographiques et bibliographiques* (Paris: Champion, 1932), p. 262. Unless otherwise noted, Tinker is the source for information on the nineteenth-century playwrights.

72. Viatte, "Complément," p. 49.

73. See Beverly Randolph Splane, "A Study of Auguste Lussan's *Les Martyrs de la Louisiane*" (master's thesis, University of Southwestern Louisiana, 1965).

74. Charles-Oscar Dugué, *Mila ou La Mort de La Salle*, CRAL, Oct. 1907, pp. 250–64; April 1908, pp. 320–38.

75. Viatte, "Complément," p. 21.

76. Tinker, *Ecrits*, pp. 94–97.

77. Viatte, "Complément," p. 20.

78. Ibid., pp. 24–25.

79. Ibid., p. 34. For *Les Deux Rivaux*, see Ethel Marie Bergeron Burleigh, "Selected One-Act Plays from the French Literature of Louisiana, Adapted for Use in Secondary Schools" (master's thesis, University of Southwestern Louisiana, 1961).

80. Tinker, *Ecrits*, p. 194.

81. Ibid., pp. 427–31; Daniel G. Van Acker, "Le Plus Boulevardier des Louisianais, Victor Séjour," CRAL, 1971–1973, p. 27.

82. Tinker, *Ecrits*, p. 431.

83. Ibid., p. 69; James Wood Davidson, *Living Writers of the South* (New York: Carleton, 1869), p. 82.

84. See Burleigh, "Selected One-Act Plays."

85. Davidson, *Living Writers*, p. 82.

86. Tinker, *Ecrits*, pp. 125–30.

87. Ibid., p. 120.

88. Gloria Noble Robertson, "The Diaries of Dr. Alfred Mercier, 1879–1893" (Ph.D. diss., Louisiana State University, 1947), pp. 228, 235–36, 342–44, 345, 388.

89. It was performed in Lafayette, La., in Nov. 1975 by students of Our Lady of Fatima High School as part of the Willis Ducrest Festival of French and Acadian Visual and Performing Arts.

90. Lavedan, "Le Théâtre français d'amateurs," pp. 13, 14, 19.

BIBLIOGRAPHY

Original sources are widely scattered. The Louisiana State Museum Library houses a rich collection of early music, libretti, and theatre programs. There are excellent microfilmed files of New Orleans newspapers in the New Orleans Public Library. The Louisiana State University Library has the most complete collection of Louisiana newspapers. The texts of plays are very rare, however; the most complete collection is in the Howard-Tilton Library of Tulane University. The plays of Victor Séjour, Louis-Xavier Eyma, and Albert and Edouard Delpit are in the Bibliothèque Nationale in Paris. Edward Larocque Tinker assembled a large library of Louisiana materials, which he left, along with his papers, to the American Antiquarian Society in Worcester, Massachusetts.

Bibliographies

Tinker, Edward Larocque. *Les Ecrits de langue française en Louisiane au XIXe siècle: Essais biographiques et bibliographiques.* Paris: Champion, 1932. Best and most complete bibliography of French writers in Louisiana. Extensive sketches of major Louisiana playwrights such as Canonge, Séjour, and the Delpits.

————. *Bibliography of the French Newspapers and Periodicals of Louisiana.* Worcester, Mass.: American Antiquarian Society, 1933.

Viatte, Auguste, "Complément à la bibliographie d'Edward Larocque Tinker," *Revue de Louisiane–Louisiana Review* 3, no. 2 (1974): 12–57.

Books

Allain, Mathé, ed. and trans. *The Festival of the Young Corn or The Heroism of Poucha-Houmma by Leblanc de Villeneufve.* Lafayette, La., 1964. Annotated translation of the first play published in Louisiana. The introduction covers the life of the author and the circumstances surrounding the composition of the play.

Armant, Fernand. *L'Opéra et ses hôtes, album illustré avec photographies et esquisses biographiques.* New Orleans: Du Croissant, 1881.

Arthur, Stanley Clisby. *Old New Orleans: A History of the Vieux Carré, Its Ancient and Historical Buildings.* New Orleans: Harmanson, 1936.

Asbury, Herbert. *The French Quarter.* New York: Garden City Publishing Co., 1938. Brief mention of the French theatres and opera houses (pp. 121–25).

Barde, Alexandre [Flavien de las Deümes]. "Aux Dames créoles." In *Nemesis Louisianaises.* New Orleans: Imprimerie de Gaux et Trosclair, 1843. A poem in which he appeals to the ladies to save the theatre by their attendance and support.

Baroncelli, J. G. de. *Le Théâtre Français à la Nouvelle-Orléans.* New Orleans: Imprimerie Geo. Muller, 1906. One of the earliest studies of the French theatre in Louisiana. Rather superficial and inaccurate.

Bernhard, Karl, duke of Saxe-Weimar-Eisenach. *Travels through North America during the Years 1825 and 1826.* 2 vols. Philadelphia: Carey, Lea and Carey, 1828. Bernhard, who spent some six weeks in New Orleans, left extensive descriptions of the theatres and the performances.

Berquin-Duvallon, Pierre-Louis. *Vue de la colonie espagnole du Mississippi ou des provinces de Louisiane et Floride occidentale en l'année 1802* Paris: Imprimerie expéditive, 1803. Gives a critical description of the early theatre in New Orleans and of the performances (pp. 24–32).

Bishop Whipple's Southern Diary, 1843–1844. Edited with an introduction by Lester B. Shippee. Minneapolis: University of Minnesota Press, 1937. Mentions flagrant violations of the Sabbath in New Orleans, including theatrical performances (p. 119).

Blassingame, John W. *Black New Orleans, 1860–1880.* Chicago and London: University of Chicago Press, 1973. Treats the participation of the black community in New Orleans operatic life.

Caulfield, Ruby Van Allen. *The French Literature of Louisiana.* New York: Institute of French Studies, Columbia University, 1929. Brief, general treatment.

Curtis, Nathaniel Cortlandt. *New Orleans, Its Old Houses, Shops and Public Buildings.* Philadelphia: J. B. Lippincott, 1933. A few pages about the theatre buildings (pp. 188–201).

Davidson, James Wood. *Living Writers of the South.* New York: Carleton, 1869. Includes sketches of several Louisiana playwrights: Placide Canonge (pp. 80–85), Charles Deléry (pp. 136–37), Adrian Rouquette (pp. 484–91), and Charles-Oscar Dugué (pp. 173–74).

De Menil, Alexander Nicolas. *The Literature of the Louisiana Territory.* St. Louis, Missouri: St. Louis News Company, 1904. Mentions French drama only in passing.

Desdunes, Rodolphe Lucien. *Our People and Our History.* Translated and edited by Dorothea Olga McCants. Baton Rouge: Louisiana State University Press, 1973. Study of the New Orleans free people of color and their accomplishments. Includes a brief sketch of Victor Séjour, the very successful playwright (pp. 28–32).

Dormon, James H. *Theater in the Ante-Bellum South, 1815–1861.* Chapel Hill: University of North Carolina Press, 1967. Excellent and complete history of antebellum theatre, with only passing references to French drama.

Flint, Timothy. *Recollections of the Last Ten Years Passed in Occasional Residences and Journeyings in the Valley of the Mississippi . . .* (1826). Reprinted. New York: Alfred A. Knopf, 1932. Flint traveled to New Orleans in the 1820s and described the theatres as well as the French-American cultural clash.

Fortier, Alcée. "The Literature of Louisiana." In *Biographical and Historical Memoirs of Louisiana.* (1892) 3 vols. Reprint. Baton Rouge, La.: Claitor's Publishing Division, 1975. Brief sketch (2:64–70) largely reproduces Fortier's article in *PMLA* 2 (1886): 31–60.

————. *Louisiana Studies: Literature, Customs, and Dialects, History and Education.* New Orleans: F. F. Hansell and Bro., 1894. The chapter on French literature reproduces the article in *PMLA,* 2 (1886): 31–60.

Fortier, Edouard J. *Les lettres françaises en Louisiane*. Québec: L'Action Sociale Limitée, 1915. Overview with some analysis. A few pages on the drama.

Fossier, Albert A. *New Orleans: The Glamour Period, 1800–1840*. New Orleans: Pelican Publishing Co., 1957. Deals with the French theatres. The chapter repeats the information in Baroncelli for the early period but quotes in full some interesting letters and articles from newspapers of the 1830s and 1840s (pp. 467–87).

Fouchard, Jean. *Le Théâtre à Saint-Domingue*. Port-au-Prince: Imprimerie de l'Etat, 1955. Although this monograph contains nothing about New Orleans or Louisiana theatre, it provides interesting background on the actors and theatergoers who sought refuge in Louisiana after the Santo Domingo revolution.

Gafford, Lucille. *A History of the St. Charles Theater in New Orleans, 1835–43*. Private edition, distributed by the University of Chicago Libraries, Chicago, Ill., 1932. The St. Charles performed only English plays; however, this study provides peripheral information on the French theatre.

Gaisford, John. *The Drama in New Orleans*. New Orleans: J. B. Steel, 1849. Extremely superficial and almost completely devoid of information.

Historical Sketch Book and Guide to New Orleans and Environs. New York: Will H. Coleman, 1885. Contains an excellent description (pp. 134–36) of the Théâtre d'Orléans and of the theatregoing public.

Jones, Howard Mumford. *America and French Culture, 1750–1848*. Chapel Hill: University of North Carolina Press, 1927. Includes a chapter (pp. 345–49) on French theatre in America with excellent, well-documented information on the New Orleans stage.

Kane, Harnett T. *Queen New Orleans: City by the River*. New York: Bonanza Books, 1949. One chapter deals with the theatre, although mostly with the contributions of Noah M. Ludlow and James H. Caldwell to the English-speaking stage.

Kendall, John Smith. *The Golden Age of the New Orleans Theater*. Baton Rouge: Louisiana State University Press, 1952. Exclusively concerned with English-language theatre, but mentions the French very briefly.

_____. *History of New Orleans*. 3 vols. Chicago and New York: Lewis Publishing Company, 1922. There is a brief mention of early French theatrical activities (2:727–41).

Kmen, Henry Arnold. *Music in New Orleans: The Formative Years, 1791–1841*. Baton Rouge: Louisiana State University Press, 1966. Seven of the twelve chapters deal with opera, which is mostly French. It does give an excellent history of the theatres in New Orleans during those years.

_____. "The Music of New Orleans." In *The Past as Prelude: New Orleans 1718–1968*. Edited by H. Carter, W. R. Hogan, J. W. Lawrence, and Betty Carter. New Orleans: Tulane University Publications, 1968. Includes an excellent sketch of the musical history of New Orleans, including the French opera (pp. 210–32).

Le Gardeur, René J., Jr. *The First New Orleans Theatre, 1792–1803*. New Orleans: Leeward Books, 1963. Invaluable study of the beginning of the theatre in New Orleans. Establishes the date and place of the first theatre, the actors, the performances, and some of the plays.

Ludlow, Noah M. *Dramatic Life as I Found It* (1880). Reprint. New York: Benjamin Blom, 1966. Most interesting, but not always accurate, personal memoir of the actor-manager. Although he produced only English plays, he provides valuable information about French theatrical activities in New Orleans, where he frequently brought his company.

New Orleans City Guide. Boston: Houghton Mifflin, 1938. Chapter on the theatres (pp. 123–130) includes a police ordinance (1804) that attempted to curb the boisterous behavior of theatergoers.

Norman, Benjamin Moore. *Norman's New Orleans and Environs* (1845). Reprint. Baton Rouge: Louisiana State University Press, 1976. Descriptions and pen sketches (pp. 176–80) of the midcentury theatres.

Reinders, Robert C. *End of An Era: New Orleans, 1850–1860.* New Orleans: Pelican Publishing Co., 1964. The chapter on the "public arts" (pp. 174–95) includes drama and opera. Very sketchy.

Ripley, Eliza Moore (Chinn) McHatton. *Social Life in Old New Orleans, Being Recollections of My Girlhood.* New York: Appleton, 1912. Charming and rambling memoires of New Orleans immediately after the Civil War. Casts interesting light on the importance of theatregoing and operagoing.

Rowland, Dunbar, ed. *Official Letter Books of W.C.C. Claiborne, 1801–1816.* 6 vols. Jackson, Miss.: State Department of Archives and History, 1917. Contains references to the *Visitandines* affair.

Smith, Sol. *Theatrical Management in the West and South for Thirty Years* (1868). Reprint. New York: Benjamin Blom, 1968. Memoirs of an actor-manager, which although concerned with the English-speaking stage, contain occasional information about French theatrical history in New Orleans.

Tallant, Robert. *Romantic New Orleanians.* New York: E. P. Dutton, 1950. Very sketchy treatment; gives dubious information about the early period (pp. 192–200).

Testus, Charles. *Portraits littéraires de la Nouvelle-Orléans.* New Orleans: Imprimerie des Veillées Louisianaises, 1850. Sketches, by a contemporary, of Louisiana French writers, including playwright L. Placide Canonge, who is judged rather severely.

Vetter, Ernest G. *Fabulous Frenchtown: The Story of the Famous French Quarter of New Orleans.* Washington: Coronet Press, 1955. Just a few pages (pp. 203–6), but relates an interesting anecdote.

Viatte, Auguste. *Histoire littéraire de l'Amérique française des origines à 1950.* Paris: Presses Universitaires, 1954. Standard history of French literature in America, with three chapters on Louisiana. Provides excellent information and some critical analyses.

Waldo, Lewis P. *The French Drama in America in the Eighteenth Century and Its Influence on the American Drama of That Period, 1701–1800.* Baltimore: Johns Hopkins University Press, 1942. Only a few pages about Louisiana.

Young, Perry. *The Mistick Krewe: Chronicles of Comus and his Kin.* New Orleans: Carnival Press, 1931. Really a history of Mardi Gras and the carnival organization, but because carnival balls were held in theatres, it overlaps with theatre history.

Journals and Newspapers

Allain, Mathé. "LeBlanc de Villeneufve in Natchitoches." *Louisiana Studies* 4 (1965): 41–46. Describes the activities of Louisiana's first playwright as a fur trader and gives examples of his fierce displays of temper.

Augustin, J. M. "Fifty Years of French Opera." *New Orleans Daily Picayune*, Oct. 24, 1909. Lengthy summary of French operatic performances in New Orleans, written for the fiftieth anniversary of the French Opera House. Very detailed list of personnel for each season. List of operas premiered in New Orleans.

Black, Elizabeth. "Allons à l'Opéra Français." *Theatre Arts Monthly* 15, no. 11 (Nov. 1931): 929–37. An evening at the Opéra Français, seen through the eyes of a child.

Bogner, Harold F. "Sir Walter Scott in New Orleans, 1818–1832." *Louisiana Historical Quarterly* (hereafter cited as *LHQ*) 21 (1938): 420–25. Concerns mostly English-language theatre, but because of the popularity of French opera based on Sir Walter Scott's novels (cf. *La Dame blanche*) it touches on French theatre also.

Chandler, Elizabeth. *Barbamouchi l'illustre de Félix Voorhies. Revue de Louisiane–Louisiana Review* IX, no. 1 (Summer 1980): 1–19. Edition with introduction of this unpublished one-act comedy.

————. *Le Guet-à-pens de Félix Voorhies. Revue de Louisiane–Louisiana Review* VIII, no. 1 (Summer 1979): 1–31. Edition with an introduction to this unpublished one-act farce.

Chevalley, Sylvie. "La Première Saison théâtrale française de New York." *French Review* 24 (1951): 471–79. Treats the visit to New York of the Théâtre d'Orléans, which performed sixty-four plays and comic operas from July 13 to September 22, 1827. Extremely well researched and complete.

———. "Le Théâtre d'Orléans en tournée dans les villes du nord: 1827–1833." *Comptes rendus de l'Athénée Louisianais* (hereafter cited as *CRAL*), Mar. 1955, pp. 27–71. Treats the tours undertaken by the Théâtre d'Orléans during the summer months when the New Orleans theatres were closed. The Théâtre successfully toured New York, Philadelphia, Boston, and Baltimore. List of plays performed is included.

Ditchy, Jay K. "Une Comédie en langue française au milieu du dix-neuvième siecle." *CRAL*, Mar. 1960, pp. 66–67. Brief summary and analysis of *Les Deux Rivaux ou Un Mariage au bayou*.

Eddy, Buddy. "Le Bigame ou l'Ecole des femmes jalouses by Félix Voorhies." *Revue de Louisiane–Louisiana Review* 4, no. 1 (1975): 1–21. Transcription with an introduction to this unpublished one-act comedy.

Fischer, David Barrow. "The Story of New Orleans' Rise as a Music Center." *Musical America* 19 (Mar. 14, 1914): 3–5. Includes a fairly detailed summary of opera in New Orleans, stressing the number of first American performances of important operas.

Fortier, Alcée. "French Literature in Louisiana." *Publications of the Modern Language Association PMLA* 2 (1866): 31–60. Treats the French theatre briefly (pp. 37–42).

———. "La Littérature française de la Louisiane." *CRAL*, Nov. 1892, pp. 208–19. Brief overview with a couple of pages on drama.

Fouchard, Jean. "Minette et Lise . . . Deux actrices de couleur sur les scènes de Saint-Domingue." *Revue d'Histoire des Colonies Françaises* 43 (1955): 186–219. These two actresses, children of a French colonist and a free woman of color, were highly successful on the Haitian stage. They disappear from records after the revolution and may have found their way to New Orleans.

Gafford, Lucille. "Our Superb Gas-Lighted Drama." *New Orleans Times-Picayune Sunday Magazine*, May 16, 1926, pp. 1–6. Sprightly summary of New Orleans theatrical history, emphasizing the contributions of Noah M. Ludlow and James H. Caldwell's Camp Street Playhouse, opened in 1824. It was the first building in New Orleans lighted by gas.

[Gayarré, Charles?] "The Tragic Muse in Louisiana." *New Orleans Times-Democrat*, Nov. 30, 1884. Brief sketch of LeBlanc de Villeneufve and his tragedy, *Poucha-Houmma*.

Grima, Edgar. "Municipal Support of Theatres and Operas in New Orleans." *Publications of the Louisiana Historical Society* 9 (1917): 43–45.

Isaacs, Edith J. R. and Gilder, Rosamund. "Gallic Fire: The French Theatre in America." In "An International Theatre: Made in America." Special Issue. *Theatre Arts* 28 (Aug. 1944): 457–64. Concerned with French theatre throughout the United States, but especially in New Orleans. Draws on well-known information.

Kendall, John Smith. "Sarah Bernhardt in New Orleans." *LHQ* 26 (1943): 770–82. Bernhardt visited New Orleans repeatedly from 1880 to 1917. Includes personal reminiscences of her performances in New Orleans.

Lafargue, André. "The New Orleans French Opera House: A Retrospect." *LHQ* 3 (1920): 368–72. Sorrowful lament for the passing of the Opéra Français, which had burned the year before.

———. "Opera in New Orleans in Days of Yore." *LHQ* 29 (1946): 660–78. Particularly valuable for the personal reminiscences of what opera meant to all classes of French society.

Lavedan, Gabrielle. "Le Théâtre français d'amateurs à la Nouvelle-Orléans." *CRAL*, 1963, pp. 10–28. Relates the activities of two amateur groups, La Renaissance Française, founded in 1930, and Les Comédiens Français, which succeeded the former in 1934.

Le Gardeur, René J., Jr. "En Marge d'une affiche de théâtre de 1799." *CRAL*, Mar. 1955, pp. 24–25. Describes a fragment of a poster for *Renaud d'Ast*, an opera in two acts by Jean-Baptiste Radet and Pierre-Yon Barré, music by Nicholas Delayrac. Poster dated Sept. 3, 1799.

————. "Le Premières Années du théâtre à la Nouvelle-Orléans." *CRAL*, Mar. 1954, pp. 33–72. Very carefully documented study, later enlarged into a monograph. Quotes at length from sources. This article explodes the myth that the New Orleans theatre was established in 1791 by refugee actors from Santo Domingo.

Lejeune, Emilie. "Reminiscences of the French Opera." *Publications of the Louisiana Historical Society* 9 (1917): 41–43. Describes the visit to the opera of the Grand Duke Alexis.

Lingg, Ann M. "Great Opera Houses. New Orleans." *Opera News* 25 (Dec. 10, 1960): 22–25. Brief sketch with mention of many French operas that received their first American performances in New Orleans.

Loeb, Harry Brunswick. "The Opera in New Orleans: A Historical Sketch from the Earliest Days through the Season 1914–1915." *Publications of the Louisiana Historical Society* 9 (1917): 29–41. Brief and superficial sketch. Interesting, however, in its discussion of the negative impact of opera on musical life in New Orleans.

McCutcheon, Roger P. "The First English Plays in New Orleans." *American Literature* 11 (May 1939): 183–99. Sketchy article covering the early years of English-language theatre. Shows how slowly the English-language theatre began, and gives some interesting information on the Franco-American cultural war.

McPeek, Gwynn S. "New Orleans as an Opera Center: A Vanished Era Is Reviewed." *Musical America* 74 (Feb. 15, 1954): 25, 136, 226. Sketchy summary of the heyday of New Orleans French opera, 1809–1919.

Moore, Lillian. "The Dupont Mystery." *Dance Perspective* 7 (1960): 5–103. Entire issue devoted to the career of Louis Dupont, a French dancer active in Baltimore, Philadelphia, and Charleston who danced from 1792 to 1796 with the company of Alexandre Placide. The company fell apart when "Madame" Placide (Suzanne Vailland) ran off with an actor, Louis Douvilliers. All except Dupont are associated with the history of the New Orleans stage.

Nott, George William. "Paris Acclaimed Louisiana Playwright Forgotten Here." *New Orleans Times-Picayune Sunday Magazine*, Feb. 6, 1927, pp. 3, 6. Brief sketch of the life and theatrical activities of L. Placide Canonge.

"Orleans Author, Composer Dies." *New Orleans Times-Picayune*, Sept. 10, 1948, p. 2. Obituary of Laure Castellanos May states that her French plays were performed at the Orleans Club.

Padgett, James A., ed. "A Decree for Louisiana Issued by the Baron of Carondelet, June 1, 1795." *LHQ* 20 (1927): 590–605. The decree itself concerns general police, bridge and road upkeep, and slave regulations, but the introduction mentions "Jacobin" songs sung in the theatres in 1793.

Peytavin, John Ludger. "Le Théâtre à la Nouvelle-Orléans et à Richmond pendant la Confederation." *CRAL*, Sept. 1890, pp. 178–85. Concerned mostly with theatrical activities in Richmond, but with a few paragraphs about Louisiana.

Price, Nellie Warner. "Le Spectacle de la Rue St. Pierre." *LHQ* 1 (Jan. 1918): 215–23. There is no record of a theatre built before 1806. Prior to 1806 a building was used that was designated as the Spectacle de la Rue St. Pierre (1793–1811).

Ritchey, David. "Robert de Lapouyade: The Last of the Louisiana Scene Painters." *Louisiana History* 14 (Winter, 1973): 5–20. Lapouyade did sets for theatres in New Orleans from 1902–1927, including the Opéra Français.

St. Martin, Gérard Labarre. "*L'Hôtel du Lapin Truffé* de Félix Voorhies." *Revue de Louisiane–Louisiana Review*, in press. Edition and introduction to this one-act play.

————. "*M. Bétinet de la Pincette* de Félix Voorhies." *Revue de Louisiane–Louisiana Review*, in press. Edition of the play, earlier entitled *Ça s'embrouille, ça s'arrange*.

Saxon, Lyle. "Fire leaves Famous Home of Lyric Drama Great Heap of Ruins." *New Orleans Times-Picayune*, Dec. 5, 1919.

Sloane, Karen Williamson. "Plays About Louisiana, 1870–1915: A Checklist." *Louisiana Studies* 18 (Spring 1969): 26–36. Includes only a few French plays.

Strauss, S. Noel. "An Interesting History of New Orleans Theaters." *New Orleans Times-Picayune,* May 9, 1920, Section 3, p. 13. Journalistic sketch of the theatres, with special attention given to the Théâtre d'Orléans.

————. "Old New Orleans and Its Opera, The Repertory, Theaters, Audiences." *New York Times,* Dec. 6, 1925, p. 10. Excellent article about New Orleans contributions to operatic history that stresses its primacy as an opera center. Gives a vivid reconstruction of operagoing in New Orleans at the time of Lafayette's visit (1825).

Swift, Mary Grace. "Dancing Belles and Beaux of Old New Orleans." *Revue de Louisiane–Louisiana Review* 7, no. 1 (1978): 49–63. Describes the theatrical dancing, mainly accompanying operas in New Orleans through the early 1820s. Excellent illustrations.

————. "Dancing Belles and Beaux of Old New Orleans." Part II. *Revue de Louisiane–Louisiana Review,* in press. Continues Part I into the 1840s.

————. "French Artists Experience *La Bonne Vie* at Sea." *Revue de Louisiane–Louisiana Review,* in press. Brief but informative article describing the 1835 ocean crossing of the French actors hired by John Davis for the Théâtre d'Orléans.

Van Acker, Daniel G. "Le Plus Boulevardier des Louisianais, Victor Séjour." *CRAL,* 1971–1973, pp. 14–30. Sketch of the life and works of Séjour, with analysis of some of the plays.

Wittington, G. P., ed. "The Journal of Dr. John Sibley, July–October, 1802," *LHQ* 10 (1927): 474–97. Sibley describes the New Orleans theatres in 1802.

Unpublished Theses and Dissertations

Bender, Lorelle Causey. "The French Opera House of New Orleans, 1859–1890." Master's thesis, Louisiana State University, 1940. Covers the history of French opera in New Orleans during the second half of the nineteenth century. Gives a complete list of French operas performed each season from 1859 to 1890.

Bradsher, Enolia. "The Transfer of Louisiana from France to Spain in Louisiana Drama." Master's thesis, Louisiana State University, 1935. Studies the treatment of the 1768 uprising against Spain in two plays in French: Auguste Lussan's *Les Martyres de la Louisiane* and L. Placide Canonge's *France et Espagne ou La Louisiane en 1769,* and one play in English, Thomas W. Collen's *The Martyr Patriots.*

Brink, Florence Roos. "Literary Travelers in Louisiana, 1803–1860." Master's thesis, Louisiana State University, 1930. Mentions descriptions of theatres and theatrical performances.

Burleigh, Ethel Marie Bergeron. "Selected One-Act Plays from the French Literature of Louisiana, Adapted for Use in Secondary Schools." Master's thesis, University of Southwestern Louisiana, 1961. Includes the texts of *Le Petit Chien de la veuve,* by Félix Voorhies; *Qui perd gagne* by Canonge; and the anonymous play, *Les Deux Rivaux ou Un Mariage au bayou.*

Cornay, Jeanne W. "A Survey of Amateur and Professional Theatrical Activity in Lafayette, Louisiana from 1870–1920." Master's thesis, University of Southwestern Louisiana, 1967. Lists the plays performed during that period, including the French ones, as reported in the *Lafayette Daily Advertiser.*

Finley, Katherine Price. "One-Act Plays by Louisiana Writers as Resources in Secondary School Classroom." Master's thesis, University of Southwestern Louisiana, 1959. Includes a one-act adaptation, in English, of LeBlanc de Villeneufve's *Poucha-Houmma.*

Gafford, Lucille. "Material Conditions in the Theaters of New Orleans before the Civil War." Master's thesis, University of Chicago, 1925. Chiefly concerned with the theatres that produced plays in English, but illuminates the material conditions for all theatrical performances.

Gray, Wallace Allison. "An Historical Study of Professional Dramatic Activities in Alexandria, Louisiana from the Beginning to 1920." Master's thesis, Louisiana State University, 1951. Theatrical activities, 1822–1920. No French play produced there professionally.

Hanley, Kathryn Tierney. "The Amateur Theater in New Orleans before 1835." Master's thesis, Tulane University, 1940. Contains valuable information concerning professional performances in which amateurs participated and all performances by amateur groups.

Lindsey, Henry Carlton. "The History of the Theatre in Shreveport, Louisiana to 1900." Master's thesis, Louisiana State University, 1951. French touring companies did not go as far north as Shreveport. The only mention of any French performers concerns a magician.

"Operatic Performances in New Orleans." (Compiled by the WPA in New Orleans, n.d.) On deposit in the Louisiana State Museum Library, New Orleans. Listing of performances, both French and English.

Primeaux, Beverly. "Annals of the Theatre in Lafayette, Louisiana, 1920–1940." Master's thesis, University of Mississippi, 1955. No French drama was performed during those years, but informants told the author in interviews about the visits of the French opera to St. Martinville during the summers.

Robertson, Gloria Noble. "The Diaries of Dr. Alfred Mercier: 1879–1893." Ph.D. diss., Louisiana State University, 1947. A few references to Mercier's own plays.

Schertz, Marcelle Frances. "The Plays of Judge Félix Voorhies, 1838–1919." Master's thesis, Louisiana State University, 1940. Introduction deals with the life of Voorhies and the performances of his plays. There are summaries of several plays and complete texts of two monologues in dialect: "Le Voyage à Gringalet," and "Gringalet à la Noce à Zozéphine."

Soileau, Maylan J. "A Study of Some Aspects of Louisiana French Literature (A Suggested Reader of Second-Year French in Louisiana)." Master's thesis, University of Southwestern Louisiana, 1958. Includes text of Marie Augustin, Les Vacances de Camille.

Splane, Beverly Randolph. "A Study of Auguste Lussan's Les Martyrs de la Louisiane." Master's thesis, University of Southwestern Louisiana, 1965. Includes the complete text of the play, a brief sketch of Lussan, and the historical background.

Teague, Oran. "The Professional Theatre in Rural Louisiana." Master's thesis, Louisiana State University, 1952. Deals with theatrical activities in small towns such as Opelousas and Thibodaux in the nineteenth century. A few French touring companies are mentioned.

Tilley, Ruth Emily. "The Life and Writings of Judge Félix Voorhies." Master's thesis, Louisiana State University, 1940. General information about Voorhies.

Varnado, Alban Fordesh. "A History of Theatrical Activity in Baton Rouge, Louisiana, 1819–1920." Master's thesis, Louisiana State University, 1947. Complete history of theatrical activities in Baton Rouge, including a few visits from the New Orleans French companies.

Original Louisiana Works

Ancelet, Barry Jean, et al. (1951–   ). Jean l'Ours et la fille du roi. Acadian play in three acts. Lafayette, La.: Center for Louisiana Studies, 1979. Performed Lafayette, La., Mar. 16, 1977, Griffin Hall Auditorium.

———. Martin Weber et les Marais-Bouleurs. Acadian play in one act. Performed Lafayette, La., Apr. 1, 1978, University of Southwestern Louisiana, Union Theater.

Armant, Fernand [On Sé Ki] (1849– ?). Les Patriotes. 1876. Read at l'Athénée Louisianais in May 1876 and performed in June.

Augustin, Marie Joséphine [Tante Marie] (1851– ?). Le Dernier bonnet d'âne. Comptes rendus de l'Athénée Louisianais (hereafter cited as CRAL). Jan. 1898, pp. 211–31.

———. Les Vacances de Camille. CRAL, July 1896, pp. 505–12; Sept. 1896, pp. 513–24.

Barde, Alexandre [Flavien de las Deümes; Maledict; C. Roques] (1816–1868). Un Bal d'enfants. Reviewed by Bienvenu Coco in La Renaissance louisianaise, Oct. 27, 1867.

———. La Dernière Nuit de Lafrenière. Play in verse performed by Canonge and mentioned in Barde, Histoire des comités de vigilance aux Attakapas. Saint-Jean-Baptist, Louisiane: Imprimerie du Meschacébé et de l'Avant-Coureur, 1861.

Bautte Hippolyte-Prudent [Prudent d'Artlys]. de (1821–1861). *Boston et Québec.* Patriotic drama in three acts. Mentioned in the *New Orleans Times Democrat,* June 25, 1893.

――――. *La Mort de Porthos.* Performed Donaldsonville, La., Oct. 14, 1851.

――――. *Les Brigands du Bayou Lafourche.* Drama in five acts. Performed Donaldsonville, Sept. 7, 1851.

B . . . C . . . (?). *Les Deux Rivaux ou Un Mariage au bayou,* comedy in one act. *L'Almanach de la Louisiane,* 1864. Reprinted in Burleigh, "Selected One-Act Plays."

Bernard, Pierre-Victor (1828–1911). *Un Début.* Comedy in one act. CRAL, Mar. 1, 1884, pp. 530–38.

Bouis, Amédée-Théodore (1821– ?). *Prenez mon aigle, ou La Révolution aux Iles Marquises, actualité.* In three tableaux. Paris: P. Masgana, 1899.

Canonge, Louis-Placide [René] (1822–1893). *L'Ambassadeur d'Autriche.* Drama in five acts. Mentioned by Charles Dimitry in the *New Orleans Times Democrat,* Jan. 22, 1893.

――――. *Blanche et Renée.* Operetta in two acts. Words by Canonge, music by Eugène Prévost. Written for Madame Burr and performed by the girls of her school in June 1871. Reviewed favorably in the *Renaissance louisianaise,* July 2, 1871.

――――. *Le Comte de Carmagnola.* Drama in five acts. New Orleans: Imprimerie du Courrier de la Louisiane, 1856. Performed New Orleans, June 6, 1852. Reviewed in *Le Carillon,* May 18, 1873.

――――. *Le Comte de Monte-Cristo.* Drama in five acts. *Revue louisianaise,* May 17, 24, 1846. Performed New Orleans, May 17, 1846, Théâtre d'Orléans.

――――. *France et Espagne ou La Louisiane en 1768 et 1769.* Drama in four acts. *Courrier de la Louisiane,* 1850. Performed New Orleans, June 1, 1850, Théâtre d'Orléans.

――――. *Gaston de Sainte-Elme.* Tragedy in five acts. New Orleans: Bibliothèque de la Société Historique, 1842. Performed New Orleans, May 17, 1840, Théâtre d'Orléans.

――――. *Un Grand d'Espagne.* Drama in four acts. *L'Orléanais,* April 1851. Performed May 30, 1847. Reviewed by Eyma in *L'Abeille,* June 1, 1847.

――――. *Juan ou Une Histoire sous Charles-Quint.* Drama in four acts. Performed New Orleans, May 20, 1849, Théâtre d'Orleans. Reviewed favorably in *La Violette,* May 1849.

――――. *Louise de Lorraine.* Opera in five acts. Words by Canonge, music by Mme. Alonzo Morphy. Mentioned by Charles Dimitry in an article on Canonge, *Times Democrat,* Jan. 22, 1893.

――――. *Maudit Passeport ou Les Infortunés d'une drogue.* Vaudeville in one act. New Orleans: Gaux, 1840. Performed New Orleans 1839, Théâtre d'Orléans.

――――. *Qui perd gagne.* Comedy in one act. *Courrier de la Louisiane,* 1849. Performed New Orleans, May 7, 1848, Théâtre d'Orléans. Reviewed harshly by Edouard de Lauc-Maryat [Edouard Zéro] in *L'Orléanais,* May 19, 1850.

Canonge, Louis-Placide, fils, and Raimondy, Rodolphe. *Un Coeur de Vendéenne.* Performed New Orleans, 1856, Théâtre d'Orléans.

Chassaignac, Eugène (1820–1878). *La Nuit aux échelles.* Comic opera in one act, 1850. Performed, Saint Martinville, La., 1850.

[Clement, ?]. *Papa Simon ou les Amours de Thérèse et Janot.* Mentioned in *Le Moniteur,* Mar. 21, 1807.

Courmont, Félix de. *Le Capitaine May et le Général de la Vega sur les bords du Rio Grande.* Comic opera in one act. Libretto by Courmont, music by Fourmestreaux. New Orleans, J. L. Sollée, 1847. Performed New Orleans, May 27, 1847.

Crébassol, Auguste. *Jeanne, petite fille de Robert le Diable.* 1838. Never performed.

Daudet, Alexis [L'Hermite du Bayou] (? –1822). *Bombarde ou les Marchands de Chansons, parodie d' "Ossian ou Les Bardes."* Lyric melodrama in five acts. Written in collaboration with Joseph Servière and François-Pierre-Auguste Léger. Paris: Mme. Cavanagh, 1804. Performed Paris, 30 messidor an xii, Théâtre de Molière.

――――. *Le Camp de Jackson ou Le Prix de la valeur.* Vaudeville in one act. New Orleans, 1815. Performed New Orleans, Jan. 28, 1815, Théâtre St. Philippe.

――――. *L'Ecossais à la Louisiane.* Comedy. Performed New Orleans, June 22, 1809.

———. *La France et l'Amérique ou un Trait de Washington.* Performed New Orleans, July 4, 1811.

Deléry, Charles Chauvin Boisclair (1815–1880). *L'Ecole du peuple.* Comedy in one act in verse. New Orleans: Imprimerie du Propagateur Catholique, 1877. Reviewed in *CRAL,* May 1887, p. 66.

Delpit, Albert (1848–1893). *Le Fils de Coralie.* Comedy in four acts in prose. Paris: P. Ollendorff, 1880. Performed Paris, Jan. 16, 1880, Gymnase Dramatique.

———. *Jean-Nu-Pieds.* Drama in four acts in verse. Paris: E. Dentu, 1875. Performed Paris, Aug. 9, 1875, Vaudeville.

———. *Les Maucroix.* Comedy in three acts in prose. Paris: P. Ollendorff, 1883. Performed Paris, Oct. 4, 1883, Comédie Française.

———. *Le Message de Scapin.* Comedy in one act in verse, 1876.

———. *Passionnément.* Comedy in four acts. Paris: P. Ollendorff, 1891. Performed Paris, Mar. 3, 1891, Odéon.

———. *Le Père de Martial.* Play in four acts. Paris: P. Ollendorff, 1883. Performed Paris, Apr. 20, 1883, Gymnase Dramatique.

———. *Les Chevaliers de la Patrie* (1876). Where no publication data are included, titles are all the author has. Titles were listed in Tinker, *Ecrits,* p. 128.

———. *Robert Pradel.* Drama in four acts, 1873.

———. *La Soeur de charité.* Paris: E. Dentu, 1875. Performed Paris, July 11, 1875, Vaudeville.

———. *La Voix du maître.* An À propos in one act in verse. Paris: Michel-Lévy frères, 1870. Performed Paris, Jan. 15, 1870.

Delpit, Edouard (1844–1900). *Constantin.* Drama in five acts in verse. Paris: Didier, 1877.

———. *La Sentinelle.* Play in one act in verse. Paris: E. Dentu, 1871.

Dietz, Auguste-Théodore (1798–1869). *Cléone ou La Prise de Navarin.* Tragedy in five acts. Act V, Scene 3 published in *L'Entr'acte,* Feb. 23, 1834.

Dugué, Charles-Oscar (1821–1872). *Le Cygne ou Mingo.* Tragedy. No known copy. Mentioned in newspaper announcements and in the *Cambridge History of American Literature* 5:592.

———. *Mila ou La Mort de La Salle.* Drama in three acts in verse. New Orleans: J. L. Sollée, 1852. Reprinted in *CRAL,* Oct. 1907, pp. 250–64, and Apr. 1908, pp. 320–38.

Duhart, Adolphe (?–1909). *Lélia.* Performed New Orleans, 1867, Théâtre d'Orléans.

Duquesnay, Adolphe Lemercier (1839–1901). *Le Mal d'Oreste.* Dramatic poem in *Essais littéraires et dramatiques.* Paris: Librairies-Imprimeries réunies, 1892.

Eyma, Louis-Xavier [Adolphe Ricard] (1816–1876). *Capitaine . . . de quoi?* Vaudeville in one act. Written in collaboration with Amédée de Jallais. Poissy: Imprimerie d'Arbieu, n.d. Performed Paris, June 21, 1850, Vaudeville.

———. *Le Mariage au bâton.* Comedy-vaudeville in one act. Written in collaboration with Saint-Yves. Paris: D. Giraud, 1853. Performed Paris, Feb. 26, 1853.

———. *Le Renard et les raisins.* Comedy-vaudeville in one act. Written in collaboration with Amédée de Jallais. Paris: Beck, 1851. Performed Paris, Feb. 2, 1851, Porte Saint-Martin.

Guirot, A. J. (1803–1871). *Lafayette à la Nouvelle-Orléans.* Play in one act, 1825. Performed New Orleans, 1825, Théâtre d'Orléans.

Lauc-Maryat, Edouard [Edouard Zéro] de *Une Femme en loterie.* Comedy. Published, but no copy available. Performed New Orleans, May 6, 1850, Théâtre d'Orléans. Reviewed by Canonge in *Le Vigilant,* Sept. 25, 1850.

LeBlanc de Villeneufve, Paul-Louis (1734?–1815). *La Fête du petitblé ou l'Héroïsme de Poucha-Houmma.* Tragedy in five acts. New Orleans: Imprimerie du Courrier de la Louisiane, 1814. Performed New Orleans, Feb. 21, 1809, Théâtre de la Rue St. Pierre. Published also in *CRAL,* Jan. 1909, pp. 421–32; Apr. 1909, pp. 443–64; Oct. 1909, pp. 529–36; Jan. 1910, pp. 13–30.

Legendre, Ernest G. *Deux Parisiens en Louisiane.* Comedy in two acts. *Le Messager,* June 27, 1859, and following issues.

Lussan, Auguste (?–1842). *La Famille créole.* Drama in five acts in prose. New Orleans: Fremaux, 1837. Performed New Orleans, Feb. 28, 1837. Théâtre Français.

————. *Les Martyrs de la Louisiane.* Tragedy in five acts in verse. Donaldsonville, La.: E. Martin and F. Prou, 1839. Performed New Orleans, May 10, 1839. Reprinted in *CRAL*, Jan. 1912, pp. 8–32; Oct. 1912, pp. 140–54; Jan. 1913, pp. 181–86; and Apr. 1913, pp. 202–20.

————. *Sara la Juive ou La Nuit de noces.* Drama in five acts. Donaldsonville, La.: T. F. Johnson and J. H. Philips, 1839. Performed New Orleans, June 5, 1838, Théâtre Français.

————. *Trois Jours après Waterloo ou La Grande Chartreuse.* Performed May 9, 1840.

Maltrait, Joseph A. [Joseph le Beuzit]. (1865–1937). *Elizabeth à Corfou. CRAL*, Nov. 1901, pp. 360–68; Jan. 1902, pp. 22–41; Apr. 1902, pp. 70–90.

Marcantel, David Emile [Marc Untel De Gravelle]. (1949–). *Mille Misères: Laissant le bon temps rouler en Louisiane.* Acadian play in three acts. Projet Louisiane. Document de travail no. 5. Quebec: Université Laval, 1979. Performed Lafayette, La., Mar. 13, 1979, University of Southwestern Louisiana, Union Theater.

May, Laure Castellanos (1867–1948). *Le Bouquet de fête.* Fantasy in one act.

————. *Les Dictatrices.* Comedy in four acts.

————. *France-Louisiane.* Comedy in three acts. Performed New Orleans, Dec. 11, 1934, Holy Name Hall.

Mercier, Alfred (1816–1896). *L'Ermite de Niagara.* A *mystère* in five acts. Paris: Jules Labitte, 1842.

————. *Fortunia.* Drama in five acts. New Orleans: Imprimerie Franco-Américaine, 1888. Reprinted in *CRAL*, Nov. 1888, pp. 179–234.

————. *Paracelse.* Dramatic dialogue. *CRAL*, Nov. 1890, pp. 190–218.

Monsieur Desjardins ou L'Habitant dans l'embarras. Private reading mentioned in *L'Argus*, Jan. 11, 1827.

Pérennès, P. E. *Guatimozin ou Le Dernier Jour de l'empire mexicain.* Tragedy in five acts in verse. New Orleans: J. L. Sollée, 1839. Performed in New Orleans, Aug. 6, 1863, Théâtre Marigny.

————. *Hicotengal*, a tragedy. Performed in New Orleans at the Théâtre Marigny.

Pitre, Glen (1950–). *Vampires and the Rh Factor, or The Rougarou Who Came from Bayou 'tit Caillou.* Acadian play in one act. Mimeographed. New Orleans: Côte Blanche Productions, 1979.

Séjour, Victor (1817–1874). *André Gérard.* Drama in five acts in prose. Paris: Michel-Lévy frères, 1857. Performed Paris, Apr. 30, 1857, Odéon.

————. *L'Argent du diable.* Comedy in three acts in prose. Paris: Michel-Lévy frères, 1854. Performed Paris, Mar. 27, 1854, Variétés.

————. *Les Aventuriers.* Drama in five acts. Paris: Michel-Lévy frères, 1860. Performed Paris, Apr. 12, 1860, Gaîté.

————. *La Chute de Séjan.* Drama in five acts in verse. Paris: Michel-Lévy frères, 1849. Performed Paris, Aug. 21, 1849, Théâtre de la République.

————. *Compère Guillery.* Drama in five acts in prose. Music by Alexandre Artus. Paris: Michel-Lévy frères, 1860. Performed Paris, Mar. 3, 1860, Ambigu-Comique.

————. *Cromwell.* Unpublished. See Tinker, *Ecrits*, p. 431.

————. *Diégarias.* Drama in five acts in verse. Paris: C. Tresse, 1844. Performed Paris, July 23, 1844, Théâtre Français.

————. *Les Enfants de la louve.* Drama in five acts. Written in collaboration with Théodore Barrière. Paris: Michel-Lévy frères, 1865. Performed Paris, Apr. 15, 1865, Gaîté.

————. *Les Fils de Charles-Quint.* Drama in five acts. Paris: Michel-Lévy frères, 1864. Performed Paris, Feb. 13, 1864.

————. *Le Fils de la Nuit.* Drama in three *journées.* Paris: Michel-Lévy frères, 1856. Performed Paris, July 11, 1856.

————. *Les Grands Vassaux.* Drama in three *époques* and in five acts in prose. Paris: Michel-Lévy frères, 1859. Performed Paris, Feb. 16, 1859.

————. *La Madone des roses.* Drama in five acts. Written in collaboration with Théodore Barrière. Paris: Michel-Lévy frères, 1869. Performed Paris, Dec. 5, 1868, Gaîté.

————. *Le Marquis caporal.* Drama in five acts. Paris: Michel-Lévy frères, 1865.

————. *Le Martyre du coeur.* Drama in five acts in prose. Written in collaboration with J. Brésil. Paris: Michel-Lévy frères, 1858.

————. *Les Massacres de la Syrie.* Drama in eight tableaux. Paris: J. Barbaré, n.d. Performed Paris, Dec. 28, 1860.

————. *Les Mystères du temple.* Drama in five acts. Paris: Michel-Lévy frères, 1862. Performed Paris, Aug. 12, 1862, Ambique-Comique. Analysis of the play in the *Renaissance louisianaise,* Sept. 21, 1862, signed Paul de Saint-Victor.

————. *Les Noces vénitiennes.* Drama in five acts in prose. Paris: Michel-Lévy frères, n.d. Performed Paris, Mar. 8, 1855.

————. *Le Paletot brun.* Comedy in one act. Paris: Michel-Lévy frères, n.d. Performed Paris, Dec. 28, 1859, Porte Saint-Martin.

————. *Richard III.* Drama in five acts in prose. Paris: D. Giraud and J. Dagneau, 1852, and New Orleans: Imprimerie A. Gaux et L. Dutuit, 1853. Performed Paris, Sept, 28, 1852, Porte Saint-Martin.

————. *La Tireuse de cartes.* Drama in five acts in prose. Paris: Michel-Lévy frères, 1860. Performed Paris, Dec. 22, 1850, Porte Saint-Martin.

————. *Le Vampire.* See Tinker, *Ecrits,* p. 431.

————. *Les Volontaires de 1814.* Drama in five acts. Paris: Michel-Lévy frères, 1862. Performed Paris, Apr. 12, 1862.

Vignaud, Henry C. (1830–1922). *Jane Grey.* Performed New Orleans, 1851, Théâtre Français.

————. *La Vieillesse des Mousquetaires.* Performed New Orleans, May 23, 1853, Théâtre d'Orléans.

Voorhies, Félix (1839–1919). *Ah, j'suis bien malheureux!* Dramatic monologue. Performed St. Martinville, June 10, 1888, Duchamp Hall. Handwritten copies of this and other Voorhies plays are in the archives of the Louisiana State library.

————. *Barbamouchi l'illustre.* Vaudeville, 1869. *Revue de Louisiane–Louisiana Review* VIII, no. 1 (Summer, 1979): 1–31.

————. *Le Bigame ou L'Ecole des femmes jalouses.* Comedy, 1875. *Revue de Louisiane–Louisiana Review* 4, no. 1 (1975): 1–21. Analysis in CRAL, May 1883, p. 364.

————. *Ça s'embrouille, ça s'arrange.* Comedy, 1870. Performed St. Martinville, June 1, 1889, Duchamp Hall. Appears in revised form as "M. Bétinet de la pincette."

————. *Ce que femme veut, Dieu le veut.* Comedy in four acts, 1870.

————. "Les Demi-confidences de Jean Gigoux." Comic scene, n.d.

————. "Gringalet à la noce de Zoséphine." Comic scene in dialect, 1878.

————. *Le Guet à pens.* Comedy in one act, 1869. *Revue de Louisiane–Louisiana Review* IX, no. 1 (Summer 1980): 1–19.

————. *L'Histoire de tous les maris.* Comedy in four acts, 1873. Translated by Voorhies as *All Husbands are Alike,* 1899.

————. *L'Hotel du Lapin Truffé.* Comedy in one act, n.d. *Revue de Louisiane–Louisiana Review,* in press. Erroneously listed in Tinker *Ecrits,* as "L'Hotel du lapin étripé."

————. *Le Jardinier grand seigneur.* Comedy in four acts. Louisiana State University Archives, n.d., unpublished.

————. "M Bétinet de la pincette." Comedy in two acts, n.d.

————. "Monsieur Vérité." Monologue, n.d.

————. "La Mort de Lubin." Comic scene, n.d.

————. "Ne pas lâcher la proie pour l'ombre, " Proverb in one act, n.d. CRAL, Oct. 1905.

————. *Les Noces d'argent du couple Néral.* Comedy in one act, n.d. CRAL, Jan. 1891.

————. "Petite fille et grand'mère." Proverb in one act, n.d.

————. "Presque pendu." Comedy in three acts and one tableau, 1863.

————. "Tribulations d'un garçon boulanger." Comic scene, n.d.

————. "Le Voyage à Gringalet." Comic scene in dialect, n.d.

7

German-American Theatre

CHRISTA CARVAJAL

The ethnic artistic effort that supported German-language theatre in its astounding variety of professional, semiprofessional, and amateur ventures in the
United States spans a time period of more than one hundred years. During the
third decade of the nineteenth century, German-language theatre "established
itself firmly on the East Coast and gradually spread into the interior, so that
finally it was found from Texas to Minnesota and from the head of navigation on
the Mississippi to its mouth."[1] As an important facet of American theatre
culture, it received its final public recognition in 1935, when along with the
Yiddish theatre and the Negro theatre, it became one of the specialized enterprises sponsored by the New York office of the Federal Theatre Project of the
Works Progress Administration.[2]

Reasons for the origin and the disappearance of German ethnic theatricals are
fairly easy to discern. Within the context of German immigration history, it is
hardly surprising that the founding of German-language theatres coincided with
the first major immigration waves, which brought to America many politically
motivated, educated Germans during the 1830s and 1840s. Nor is the final
disappearance of German-language theatres, which coincided with the beginning of the Second World War, too difficult to explain.

Between its recorded beginning and ending, however, the almost one hundred years of German ethnic theatre activities represent a phenomenon that is
difficult to interpret because of its complexity, especially since many of the
records are incomplete and pictorial materials are virtually nonexistent. Most
general treatments are, therefore, either incomplete or misleading. (See the
bibliography at the end of this chapter.) While several fine scholarly studies
exist that deal with specific theatres, a systematic cultural analysis of German-
language theatre in the United States has not yet been attempted. Such a study
would have to deal with both the theatre and the dramatic literature produced
by the German immigrants. It is the aim of this chapter to provide the groundwork for such an analysis.

The first recorded German-language theatre productions were staged in Philadelphia. There is some evidence that a farce entitled *Die Alte Jungfer* (The Spinster) was given there on September 16, 1807, in the Old Theater.[3] However, the first concerted effort to produce theatre in German by a German troupe can be traced back to September 1830, when the German Amateur Theatrical Society of Philadelphia "appeared for a few evenings in the Washington Theater on Old York Road in Philadelphia and performed a German play each night."[4]

For the years between 1830 and 1840 only amateur theatricals are recorded.[5] During the fifth decade of the nineteenth century, however, several important professional companies were formed, in addition to the many more amateur groups already flourishing. By the beginning of the Civil War, German theatres had been established in almost every state of the Union.[6]

It can be safely ascertained that the professional and amateur German theatres that came into being during the three decades after 1830 were sustained by the creative energy and enthusiasm of first-generation German immigrants. Considering the state of continental German theatre culture, the immigrants' successful theatrical endeavors in the United States after 1830, indeed their initial preoccupation with the performing arts as a major vehicle for ethnic cultural expression, is not surprising.

THE CONTINENTAL GERMAN THEATRE

In Germany during the early decades of the nineteenth century, the theatre had achieved a unique place in the consciousness of the people. The astounding number of standing professional theatre establishments in the German states brought dramatic entertainment to almost every city with more than 15,000 inhabitants.[7] Audiences were attracted from every class.[8] "The number of court and state theatres [had] . . . removed the drama, in the popular mind, further from mere amusement and into the realm of serious culture."[9]

Theatres in Germany had been established by the rulers of the German states throughout the eighteenth century, with Leipzig, Hamburg, Mannheim, and Weimar soon becoming the most important centers of dramatic activity. Generous aristocratic patronage and the contributions of such outstanding creative theatre artists and dramatists as Caroline Neuber, Gotthold Ephraim Lessing, Friedrich von Schiller, and Johann Wolfgang von Goethe thus created a national German theatre almost a century before the German states became a unified national, political entity. No other European country had, during the latter half of the eighteenth century, a theatre institution as well endowed, as well received, and as functional as the German one.[10]

The history of German dramatic literature during the middle and the latter decades of the eighteenth century shows an astounding wealth of native talent at work: the dramas of Lessing, Goethe, and Schiller, all of which were widely read and widely produced, marked for some time to come a peak in the literary life of Germany. Simultaneously, and continuing well into the nineteenth century, the "lesser" drama evolved, drama written for production on many a stage demanding novelty fare for large audiences.[11]

Of the lesser dramatists, August Friedrich von Kotzebue enjoyed the greatest popularity. His plays "combined sensational subjects, striking spectacle, and humanitarian sentiments so successfully that he helped to create the vogue for melodrama that was to dominate the 19th century stage."[12] Though many German literary critics referred to his plays as *Unterhaltungsliteratur* (literature for entertainment), the most accomplished actors and directors of Germany joined the audiences in their appreciation of Kotzebue's well-crafted dramas.[13]

The political and social crises that preceded the revolution in 1848 did not seriously interfere with the operation of German theatres. "By 1842, Germany had 65 permanent theatres employing about 5000 actors, singers, and musicians."[14] The theatres were subsidized with public funds, giving company members the status and security of civil servants.

In the memories of German immigrants coming to the United States during the 1830s and 1840s, the theatre was indeed a well-established element of cultural tradition. Thoroughly familiar with professional theatrical entertainment and, generally, well read in past and contemporary German dramatic literature, the first major group of German immigrants pursued the establishment of ethnic theatres as an important bridge between continental culture and life in the New World, with an initial emphasis on preservation of German customs and language.

Thus the theatre activities of German Americans were initiated and sustained by the enthusiasm and support of an ethnic audience, educated and appreciative of the performing arts, a circumstance that explains not only the *Spielpläne* (season bills) of German American theatres for many decades, but also its ultimately limited influence on American theatre. It was a *Liebhabertheater* (amateur theatre) throughout its duration, a sophisticated amateur effort, exceptional professional endeavors notwithstanding.

EARLY AMATEUR THEATRICS

During the middle decades of the nineteenth century, amateur German theatres usually followed a similar pattern of establishment, organization, and production. After a *Liebhaber Verein* (amateur association) was founded, goals and seasonal playbills were decided upon. Then volunteers from the ethnic community at large and from the membership of the association were solicited to study parts under the direction of a knowledgeable amateur. After due rehearsal time, play productions were presented in a suitable hall to the German-American audience. Admission was often charged, and the money thus raised was used for worthwhile projects in the ethnic community.[15]

The intent of early German amateur theatrics was clearly to encourage the perpetuation of the finer tastes of German immigrants, presumably threatened by contact with the harsh realities of the New World frontiers. Contemporary editorials in the German-language press stressed the civilizing and educational benefits to be derived from amateur theatrics. "Let these meager beginnings be a warning that . . . there are better things, . . . higher pleasures to be enjoyed than grubbing for the almighty dollar," wrote a critic in Columbus, Ohio, in 1855.[16] The meager beginnings of the Thalia Verein theatre in Columbus, in the form of a production of *Die Leibrente* (The Pension) and *Nachtwächter* (The Night Watchman), gave this critic hope that the theatre "would provide both art and relaxation, cultural deepening and individual stimulation."[17] Equally earnest, the editor of a small-town German newspaper in Texas wrote on the occasion of an amateur premier performance there: "We hope that the purpose of this endeavor will result in a full house of friendly people who will not forget . . . the all-involving educational purpose of the undertaking. . . . Therefore, let us encourage this beautiful effort."[18]

Studies dealing with regional German ethnic theatres in Texas, Iowa, Ohio, Missouri, and Wisconsin before the Civil War show that Kotzebue and other lesser dramatists were far more popular playwrights than Schiller and Goethe and, furthermore, that the seasonal play selections emphasized comedy over serious drama even during the initial period of German amateur theatrics.[19] The seriousness of effort, however, cannot be doubted. It gave the amateur theatre of the German immigrants a tangible highbrow flair, fostering an early impression among American neighbors "that the Germans were somehow the ethnic group in America that had a monopoly on culture."[20]

The chronological history of German amateur theatre activities after 1830, according to available documents and data, shows that amateur associations began regular theatrical seasons in the following locations:

1830 Philadelphia, Pennsylvania
1838 Canton, Ohio
1839 New Orleans, Louisiana
1840 New York, New York; Baltimore, Maryland
1842 St. Louis, Missouri
1843 Cincinnati, Ohio; Hermann, Missouri
1848 Highland, Illinois; Manitowoc, Wisconsin
1849 Louisville, Kentucky
1850 Fredericksburg, Texas; Milwaukee, Wisconsin; St. Joseph, Missouri
1853 Detroit, Michigan
1854 New Braunfels, Texas; Washington, Missouri
1855 Columbus, Ohio; Cleveland, Ohio; Davenport, Iowa; San Francisco, California
1856 Chicago, Illinois; San Antonio, Texas; Boonville, Missouri
1857 St. Paul, Minnesota
1858 Jefferson City, Missouri; New Ulm, Minnesota
1859 Lexington, Missouri; Madison, Wisconsin
1860 Kansas City, Missouri[21]

Undoubtedly, German amateurs mounted theatrical productions in many other locations as well. Undated references point to theatre activities after 1840 in Ithaca, Rochester, and Buffalo, New York; Pittsburgh and Reading, Pennsylvania; Belleville and Peoria, Illinois; Clinton and Plainview, Michigan; Denver,

Colorado; Omaha, Nebraska; Boston, Massachusetts; Indianapolis and Evans-ville, Indiana; and Galveston and Austin, Texas.

ETHNIC DRAMATIC LITERATURE

Many German amateur theatre associations showed a distinct preference for a certain group of contemporary dramatists, besides the aforementioned Kotzebue. Plays that appeared regularly on German-American playbills after 1840 were written by Theodor Koerner, Charlotte Birch-Pfeiffer, Karl-August Goerner, Gottfried Adolf Muellner, Karl F. Toepfer, Louis Schneider, Emil Pohl, Heinrich Boernstein, and Roderich Benedix.

Although performed successfully on continental German stages during the early decades of the nineteenth century, the works of these playwrights generally found little attention and even less praise from German critics and literary historians. Only Kotzebue, whose first drama *Menschenhass und Reue* (The Stranger, 1789) was produced at one time by almost every amateur or profes-sional German theatre in the United States, was considered worthy of serious criticism by contemporary German writers—his temporary international fame made it difficult to ignore him.

Already by 1800 Kotzebue's plays, first translated and produced by William Dunlap in New York, had gained "a celebrity hitherto unequalled except in the case of the immortal Shakespeare" with American audiences.[22] Kotzebue's suc-cess on American stages was rather short lived, however, perhaps because, according to American critics, his characters seemed to possess "more German nature than human nature." Managers of American theatres "were urged to present English plays instead of having recourse to the vile trash of Kotzebue."[23] The Teutonic flavor of Kotzebue's dramas was, of course, the very reason for his popularity with German-American audiences. Kotzebue's characters were often typical of continental middle-class German citizens and their everyday prob-lems, so the immigrants' identification with them lasted well into the final decades of the nineteenth century.

Historians of German-American theatres have dealt only in passing with the dramatic literature presented by German ethnic theatres during the nineteenth century. Consideration of the staged ethnic literature, however, might well contribute to the understanding of the uniqueness and specific flavor of Ger-man-American theatrics. The dramas of the popular playwrights mentioned above mostly belonged to the categories of *Volksstück* (folk drama), *Schicksalsdrama* (fate tragedy), or *Schwank* (farce).[24] The *Volksstück*, and the *Posse* (musical folk comedy), was both realistic and humorous and depicted the past and contemporary folkways of various German regions. As a genre it was related to the *Schwank*, although the latter often employed slapstick comedy and emphasized farce elements. The *Volksstück's* goal was a recognition of the special worth of the common German, the "little man."

Three regions in Germany brought forth identifiable and characteristic folk dramas of considerable originality: the areas surrounding Berlin, Frankfurt, and Munich. Each locale came to represent a specifically northern (Berlin), middle (Frankfurt), or southern (Munich) German way of life, sense of humor, and dialect in its respective *Lokaldichtung* (regional creative writing).[25] Any preference for certain authors of *Volksstücke* among German-American audiences and amateur performing groups may have indicated that the immigrants came from a particular region of the old country.[26]

A *Schicksalsdrama* was a pseudoromantic tragedy that often centered around an incident pitching members of a family or clan against one another. Its major idea rested on a concept linking individual guilt with tribal or family doom. Muellner's dramas *Der neunundzwanzigste Februar* (The Twenty-Ninth of February) and *Die Schuld* (The Guilt) were typical of this dramatic genre.

The *Schwank* had "as its only purpose laughter" and represented that particular type of drama in which simple-mindedness and innocence reign supreme:

The *Schwank* is a modern child of the *mimus* of antiquity. . . . It plays with things, not . . . with ideas. It has its roots in this world and does not know of metaphysics. It is ignorant of [the idea of] fate; . . . it is governed instead by the [dramatically effective] accident.[27]

Its most popular nineteenth century proponents were Kotzebue and Benedix, who were credited with the creation of many German *Schwank* stock characters. Birch-Pfeiffer's often-produced comedies, which were modelled after Kotzebue's plays, proved for some time the theatrical effectiveness of this genre.

Within the context of a consideration of theatrically popular and widely produced dramatic ethnic literature, it is important to keep in mind that all of the above-mentioned dramas had one element in common: they were written for professional productions on well-established theatre stages and for audiences who appreciated theatre entertainment as a professional endeavor. The plays left little room for experimentation or creative improvisation, even when transplanted onto amateur stages. They neither inspired new nor challenged accepted concepts of "German-ness." Instead, these dramas, particularly as played and viewed by German Americans, reinforced the respectability of a continental bourgeois culture—and the notion of permanence and familiarity in a foreign physical environment. By fostering that notion, the dramatic literature of German-American theatres served a useful purpose, yet ultimately contributed to the decline of an original, creative theatre effort.

PROFESSIONAL ETHNIC THEATRES

Of the many amateur troupes throughout the United States, only a few grew into professional and continuous theatre establishments. In four locations, however, the enthusiasm for theatre of faithful ethnic audiences and the presence of a number of professionally trained immigrant theatre artists contributed to the creation of viable and energetic *Stadttheater* (municipal theatre) companies, which left an artistic legacy of measurable importance to American theatre culture.

The German theatre in New York was, from its beginnings, destined to become a showcase of the German dramatic tradition. As no other city in the United States, New York remained connected with European cultural developments because of the continuous flow of immigrants to its port throughout the nineteenth century. Begun in January of 1840 as an uncoordinated amateur effort, establishment of the German theatre in New York was an extremely painful and protracted process that took the better part of two decades to result finally in a permanent, professional theatre.[28]

On September 4, 1854, the Alte Stadttheater, New York's first regular and dignified house for German drama, opened its doors for the first time.

A general survey of the Altes Stadttheater shows us that during the entire period of its existence its management was almost continually confronted by two alternatives, neither of which was highly attractive. The directors could choose either to give plays of real dramatic worth, in which case they very often ran the risk of drawing small audiences, or they could attract large gatherings to their hall, as a rule, however, only by plays of thoroughly inferior quality. How to offer habitually the finest dramas and how, at the same time, to keep up the attendance—that was for Hamann and Hoym a constant source of worry. And so the Stadttheater as a whole was but another aspect of that eternal conflict between irreconcilable antitheses to which the German mind likes to cling so tenaciously—the desire to unite aesthetic idealism with material success.[29]

Otto Hoym, a fine actor and director, and Eduard Hamann, the Stadttheater's financial benefactor, managed, however, to keep the theatre alive and growing, deftly mixing dramatic offerings of literary worth with the popular fare of the lesser dramatists. All plays were given in repertory, "offering different plays on successive nights."[30]

The Alte Stadttheater company included many professionally trained actors who had proven their talent on continental German stages. Of these, Hoym's wife, Elise Hoym-Hehl, became a favorite actress with New York German audiences. One of her strongest rivals was Karoline Lindemann.[31] Alexander Pfeiffer and Daniel Bandmann "thrilled audiences" in many leading roles.[32]

In only ten seasons, the first professional German-language theatre in New York created a solid foundation for the further flourishing and wide acceptance of a serious ethnic theater arts institution, resulting in the Neue Stadttheater at 45-47 Bowery, "described as one of the largest homes of drama that not only New York but the entire country could boast at the time."[33] From 1864 to 1872 the new Stadttheater staged productions that equalled in scope and professional execution the best offerings in the old country.

After the Neue Stadttheater, which burned down in 1883, the Irving Place Theatre became the representative German-language theatre in New York. From 1892 to 1907, under the management of Heinrich Conried, this theatre introduced to the United States the theatrical concepts of the Meininger,[34] the troupe of theatre artists under the tutelage of Georg II, Duke of Saxe-Meiningen, which had virtually revolutionized the German theatre with its new methods that aimed to create a naturalistic dramatic representation of life on the stage. The Irving Place Theatre was considered by some contemporary critics as one of the most outstanding professional theatres in America.[35]

At the Irving Place Theatre, ensemble work was stressed instead of the star system. A contemporary observer commented that the "superiority of Mr. Conried's company consists in objectivity, in harmonious work together, and in versatility."[36]

Mr. Conried believed that the public is not benefited by too sumptuous a stage-setting. The attention should be directed to the interpretation and the artistic efforts of the performers. The dramatic critic quoted above describes a contrast between German and English methods as shown in the performance of "Maria Stuart," a play which actresses, including Madame [Fanny] Janauschek, Madame [Helena] Modjeska, and Fanny Davenport, have acted on the American stage. "Modjeska's Mary is one of her most beautiful creations, the best Mary I have seen, but yet the play never moved me as it did at the Irving Place, because the whole cast there was so much better than Modjeska's ever is." The title role was played at the German theatre by a person much less gifted than Madame Modjeska, but the genius of the poet Schiller found expression instead, and the artistic effect was far superior to any ever produced by an actor, however famous. Conried nevertheless secured many artists of the first rank for his troupe, as Hedwig Lange, Marie Reichardt, Hedwig von Ostermann, Hermine Varma, Alexander Rattmann, Adolf Zimmermann, Gustaf von Seyffertitz, and many others. Distinguished actors from Germany have frequently appeared, as Adolf Sonnenthal, Ludwig Barnay, Ferdinand Bonn, Georg Engels, Marie Geistinger, Agnes Sorma, Helene Odilon.[37]

Another professional German-language theatre establishment of considerable importance evolved from amateur beginnings during the 1840s in St. Louis. The first performance there was initiated in 1842 by Rudolf Riese, "an actor of ability, originally from Berlin, [who,] in the course of a variegated existence, became stranded in St. Louis."[38] Riese claimed to have been the director of the German opera house in Philadelphia and, at one time, the managing director of the German theatre in New Orelans.[39] His theatre troupe, however,

was short lived. It could lay little claim to artistic or dramaturgical excellency. But it deserves recognition because it was epoch-making in the cultural history of the German element of St. Louis. From it may be traced the history of the institution, which, thru [sic] the vicissitudes of more than seven decades, has, without serious interruption, but with varying degrees of fortune continued . . . to fulfill a cultural mission.[40]

The theatre that followed Riese's venture was organized by Christian and Louise Thieleman, who had already directed and acted in New York, New Orleans, and Chicago. However, German theatre did not flourish in St. Louis until 1850, when playwright Heinrich Boernstein moved there. He had "come to America with a varied and rich experience, not only as a journalist, but more especially as an actor and impresario and playwright."[41] Boernstein founded the Philodramatische Gesellschaft (Philodramatic Association) in 1853 and succeeded through this organization in creating a lasting interest in professional German-language productions.[42] In 1859 Boernstein opened the St. Louis Opernhaus, but he was forced to close it in 1861. During this short time he established his company "as the best German theater in the United States," according to contemporary critics.[43]

After the Civil War the St. Louis German theatre continued to produce a repertory of classic and contemporary plays under several managing directors. In 1890 and 1891, Hermann Riotte introduced works by Hermann Sudermann and Henrik Ibsen to the German-American audience. But the "realistic drama failed . . . to gain approval. . . . Judging from the limited number of repetitions such plays received, they were not yet in favor with the public."[44]

In Cincinnati the professional German theatre began to establish itself after Boernstein's St. Louis troupe had given some outstanding guest performances in 1861.[45] "Even the English language newspapers were obliged to acknowledge these productions."[46] Like other cities with large German immigrant communities, Cincinnati already had German amateur theatrical productions during the early 1840s.[47] During 1844 and 1845 the Thielemanns made guest appearances with local amateurs.[48] Both tried to establish professional theatres during the following years but failed and consequently moved on to Chicago, "where they played a more important and happier role in the founding of German theatre."[49]

Not until after the Civil War did the German professional theatre enjoy wholehearted support from German audiences in Cincinnati. In 1869 Fanny Janauschek "created a storm of enthusiasm with her passionate interpretation" of Mosenthal's *Deborah* and Schiller's *Maria Stuart.*[50] The guest appearance of Marie Seebach in 1870 created a similar appreciation.

In 1871, sponsored by the German Turngemeinde (Association of Gymnasts), the Stadttheater in der Turnhalle (Municipal Theatre in the Gymnasium) began its first season with an exclusively professional troupe under the management of Julius Collmer.[51] From that year until 1876, this theatre functioned as a professional institution with reasonable success. After 1876, however, because of internal power struggles and intrigues, it lost the support of its sponsors and of the German audience.

For several years thereafter, the Deutsche Theatre in Robinsons Opernhaus (German Theatre in Robinson's Opera House) became the principal professional theatre for German-language productions.

The *Deutsche Theatre* was, from its beginning, a more consciously artistic institution than the theatre in the *Turnhalle*. It was meant to address the [refined] expectations of Cincinnati's [German] theatre art enthusiasts. Generally, it managed to succeed in that goal. . . . By the end of April 1881, however, an outbreak of Puritan religious fanaticism in the state of Ohio put an end to [the efforts of] the German theatre in Cincinnati.[52]

Throughout the final decades of the nineteenth century, opposition by the English-speaking population in Ohio to German Sunday entertainment constituted a major obstacle to the further growth of professional theatrics. Several theatre companies tried stubbornly either to ignore or to adjust to the Sunday laws, but the professional German theatre effort never recovered from the blow it received through the passing of laws that, among other sentiments, represented also the strong antitheatre feeling of most Ohioans.[53]

Perhaps the most outstanding and continuous professional German-language theatre in the United States was the Milwaukee Stadttheater, which later became the Pabsttheater. American and German theatre historians seem to agree that Milwaukee's German theatre represented not only the best of a German theatre tradition, but also, as no other theatre in the United States, was responsible for introducing the best modern plays by German playwrights.[54]

The reasons for the remarkable vitality of the professional German theatre in Milwaukee are manyfold.

Milwaukee, it seemed, was different [from many other northern European immigrant communities]. German was a required language in the public schools, and the German-English Academy, where German was a favored tongue, was much in vogue with the best people. . . . This "foreign atmosphere" went far below the surface of this peculiarly free and democratic city. It was more than a matter of cakes and beer and names . . . more even than a matter of language. [The Milwaukee Germans] . . . were adventurous, intelligent, independent, dignified, socially progressive men and women. They set the tone of Milwaukee's early civic life.[55]

They also prospered early. Milwaukee's German audiences not only supported their theatre with enthusiasm, but also with considerable monetary generosity. They were able to attract and keep the first professional ensembles, maintain well-equipped theatre facilities, and see to the professional management of their municipal performing arts institution.

Amateur theatrics began in Milwaukee in 1850.[56] Five years later, professional actors began to appear with amateur groups. During the Civil War, theatre activities decreased. In 1868, however, the Stadttheater opened and until 1884 regularly presented a varied repertory with competent professional actors.

"The year 1884 marked the most important turning point in the history of the Milwaukee stage."[57] That year Julius Richard, Ferdinand Welb, and Leon Wachsner took over the management of the theatre and began to establish its artistic and professional reputation.[58] Even during their first season, the managing directors presented a theatre bill with twenty important literary dramas. Interestingly, in their *Faust* production, Faust was portrayed by two different actors.[59] During the following years, the management of the Stadttheater was able to engage several well-known actors and actresses from Germany for guest performances, most notably Anna Haverland, a *königlich sächsische Hofschaus-*

pielerin (a title given to permanent members of the court theatre of Saxony), and Hedwig Raabe from Berlin.[60]

In the fall of 1890 the Stadttheater moved into the renovated old Grand Opera House, which Ferdinand Pabst had bought "to create a more beautiful and more spacious home" for the German theatre.[61] Here the modern naturalistic drama was regularly produced and, unlike in other German-American communities, well received by the ethnic audience. The plays of Sudermann, Ernst von Wildenbruch, and Gerhart Hauptmann created an awareness of the exciting theatre developments in continental Germany. There, during the two decades following the unification of the German states in 1871, a new literary movement had begun to change the drama and the theatre. Influenced by Ibsen and August Strindberg, the young dramatists of Germany proclaimed that the modern drama had to be "naturalistic," had to address the social problems of the day, and had to deal with the reality of a modern world. With the productions of Ibsen's *Ghosts* and Hauptmann's *Vor Sonnenaufgang* (Before Sunrise) in 1889, the director, Otto Brahm of the Freie Bühne (Free Stage) in Berlin, had ushered in a new era in German theatre history.

In the winter of 1891 Josef Kainz, Germany's most accomplished actor, appeared at the Stadttheater in Milwaukee. A former member of the Meininger,[62] Kainz had become an actor of astounding versatility. "Wherever he traveled, triumph followed him."[63] His repertory included Hamlet, Romeo, Ferdinand (*Intrigue and Love* by Schiller), and many modern roles in dramas by Ibsen, Sudermann, and other contemporary playwrights. He became Germany's art ambassador, playing with leading German troupes outside the Reich.

In 1895 the Stadttheater was totally destroyed by fire. However, toward the end of the same year, Pabst gave to the city of Milwaukee and its German community a new, splendid theatre, which was named after him. A beautiful, modern theatre facility, the *Pabsttheater* would house for decades not only one of the finest German professional acting troupes, but also a small resident opera and ballet company.

INFLUENCE AND CONTRIBUTION OF THE GERMAN-AMERICAN THEATRE

In retrospect, one wonders why the astonishing number of lively German ethnic theatres in the United States left seemingly scant evidence of a traceable German influence on the emerging American theatre. It has been pointed out that two global wars silenced the voice of the German-American community, finally forbidding an ethnic pride in that cultural tradition, which seemed tainted by the events of 1917 and 1939.

There is little doubt that in many frontier communities of the New World, German immigrants were often the first who produced and supported dramatic entertainment. It is difficult, however, to measure the influence that their theatre enthusiasm could have had on a growing American appreciation of the performing arts. With the construction of railroads, American touring companies were soon traveling everywhere in the United States, and before the turn of the century, English-language theatre productions were widely and enthusiastically viewed and appreciated by audiences from Washington to Texas.

In many cities, especially in the southwestern United States, German Americans were the first to construct adequate theatre halls and public buildings with stages and theatrical facilities, which they usually shared with or made available for English-language theatre productions, operas, or musical entertainment. Again, it can only be suggested that this must somehow have been important for a growing appreciation of theatre in America.

With the exception of the German theatres in New York and Milwaukee, the theatrical efforts of the German immigrants left few traces in American theatre history. There is no doubt, however, that German-language theatrics represented a serious effort by an immigrant group to establish and maintain an ethnic cultural identity and that, as such, they served the intended purpose well.

However, as no other artistic effort, the art of theatre depends upon a continuous and intimate involvement with a living language. It is not surprising therefore, that as German became a "second" language for the children and grandchildren of the immigrants, German ethnic theatres ceased to flourish. Eventually they became museums of a theatrical heritage rather than creative centers for an ethnic cultural expression.

Generally, the German immigrants adjusted well to the New World, met its challenges with great enthusiasm, and became American patriots and English-speaking citizens much faster than most other immigrant ethnic groups. Without doubt these fortunate circumstances eroded the vitality of the German theatre, diminishing its real impact on American theatre culture: the German-American theatre had no creative fountain of agony and protest.

However interesting as an historical phenomenon, the German theatre may be said to have existed in the memory of tragedy, not in the experience. Perhaps that, not the wars, rendered it obsolete.

NOTES

1. Hermann E. Rothfuss, "The Beginnings of the German American Stage," *German Quarterly* 24 (1951): 93.

2. Douglas McDermott, "The Odyssey of John Bonn: A Note on German Theatre in America," *German Quarterly* 38 (1965): 325.

3. Rothfuss, "The Beginnings," p. 96.

4. Ibid.

5. Ibid., pp. 96–98.

6. LaVern J. Rippley, *The German-Americans* (Boston: Twayne Publishers, 1976), p. 130.

7. Oscar G. Brockett, *History of the Theatre* (Boston: Allyn and Bacon, 1968), p. 409.

8. Ibid., p. 344.

9. Thomas Wood Stevens, *The Theatre from Athens to Broadway* (New York: D. Appleton and Company, 1933), pp. 159–60.

10. Brockett, *History of the Theatre*, pp. 400–415.

11. There are presently no studies in English dealing with German popular drama and melodrama.

12. Brockett, *History of the Theatre*, p. 350.

13. Ibid., pp. 348–50.

14. Ibid., p. 409.

15. Christa Carvajal, "German Theatres in Central Texas, 1850–1915" (Ph.D. diss., University of Texas, 1977), p. 38.

16. LaVern J. Rippley, "German Theatre in Columbus, Ohio," *German-American Studies* 1, no. 2 (1970): 80.

17. Ibid.

18. Carvajal, "German Theatres," p. 37.

19. No study exists at this point that compares the *Spielpläne* of German-American theatres.

20. Rippley, "German Theatre in Columbus, Ohio," p. 79.

21. Most studies are in agreement on the dates of founding German theatre efforts. However, some discrepancies do exist. I had to rely on published data and, in the case of conflicting information, on corresponding cross-references.

22. David Grimsted, *Melodrama Unveiled* (Chicago: University of Chicago Press, 1968), p. 9.

23. Ibid., p. 12.

24. Since no English-language studies treat the "lesser" German dramatists, I have relied on the few authoritative German studies of popular dramatic literature.

25. Karl Holl, *Geschichte Des Deutschen Lustspiels* (Leipzig: Verlagsbuchhandlung J. J. Weber, 1923), and Wilhelm Kosch, *Das deutsche Theatre und Drama seit Schillers Tod* (Leipzig: Vier Quellen Verlag, 1922), contain treatments of German regional dramatic literature.

26. No scholarly study exists that analyzes the *Spielpläne* within this context.

27. Holl, *Geschichte*, p. 282.

28. Fritz A. H. Leuchs, *The Early German Theatre in New York, 1840–1872* (New York: Columbia University Press, 1928), p. 75.

29. Ibid., p. 76.

30. Ibid., p. 81.

31. Ibid., pp. 103–13.

32. Ibid.

33. Ibid., p. 125.

34. Albert Bernhardt Faust, *The German Element in the United States* (Boston: Houghton Mifflin, 1909), Vol. 2, pp. 329–30.

35. Ibid., p. 329.

36. Ibid., p. 330.

37. Ibid., p. 331.

38. Alfred Henry Nolle, "The German Drama on the St. Louis Stage," *Americana Germanica* (Philadelphia: University of Pennsylvania, 1917), Vol. 32, p. 9.

39. Ibid., p. 11.

40. Ibid., p. 12.

41. Ibid., p. 15.

42. Ibid., p. 16.
43. Ibid., p. 32.
44. Ibid., p. 65.
45. Ralph Wood, "Geschichte des deutschen Theaters von Cincinnati," *Deutsch Amerikanische Geschichtsblätter* (1932), p. 11.
46. Ibid., p. 19.
47. Ibid., pp. 11–14.
48. Ibid., p. 14.
49. Ibid., p. 21.
50. Ibid., p. 21.
51. Ibid., p. 24.
52. Ibid., p. 43.
53. Ibid., pp. 63–82.
54. Henry A. Pochmann, *German Culture in America* (Madison: University of Wisconsin Press, 1957), p. 358.
55. "The German Theatre in Milwaukee," *Theatre Arts* 28 (1944): 465–66.
56. John C. Andressohn, "Die literarische Geschichte des Milwaukeer deutschen Bühnenwesens, 1850–1911," *German American Annals* 10 (1912): 65–88, 150–70.
57. Ibid., p. 150.
58. Ibid.
59. Ibid., p. 151.
60. Ibid., pp. 152–53.
61. Ibid., p. 156.
62. The Meininger was Germany's first naturalist theatre troupe, founded by the Duke of Saxe-Meininger, Brockett, *History of the Theatre*, p. 421.
63. "The German Theatre in Milwaukee," p. 468.

BIBLIOGRAPHY

Books

Faust, Albert Bernhardt. *The German Element in the United States*, Vol. 2. Boston: Houghton Mifflin Co., 1909. A general history of Germans in America that contains a scholarly but brief treatment of theatre.

Grimsted, David. *Melodrama Unveiled*. Chicago: University of Chicago Press, 1968. One of the finest cultural histories of melodrama in America, Grimsted's book could provide a model for any serious study of the *Spielpläne* of German-language theatres or the popular drama on German stages in the United States during the nineteenth century. Grimsted analyzes the popularity of playwright Kotzebue on American stages during the early years of the nineteenth century.

Leuchs, Fritz A. H. *The Early German Theatre in New York, 1840–1872.* New York: Columbia University Press, 1928. An outstanding study of regional theatre.

Pochmann, Henry A. *German Culture in America*. Madison: University of Wisconsin Press, 1957. A general history, including brief but scholarly treatment of theatre.

Pochmann, Henry A., and Schultz, Arthur R. *Bibliography of German Culture in America to 1940.* Madison: University of Wisconsin Press, 1953. A comprehensive bibliography, including listings of unpublished dissertations.

Tolzmann, Don Heinrich. *German-Americana: A Bibliography.* Metuchen, N.J.: Scarecrow Press, 1975. Another comprehensive bibliography, including listings of unpublished dissertations.

Articles

Andressohn, John C. "Die literarische Geschichte des Milwaukeer deutschen Bühnenwesens, 1850–1911." *German American Annals* 10 (1912): 65–88, 150–170. An outstanding study of German theatre in Milwaukee, in German.

Bowen, Elbert R. "The German Theatre of Early Rural Missouri." *Missouri Historical Review* 46 (1952): 157–61. A study of regional amateur theatre.

Frenz, Horst. "The German Drama in the Middle West." *German-American Review* 8 (1942): 15–17, 37.

Nolle, Alfred Henry. "The German Drama on the St. Louis Stage," *Americana Germanica.* Philadelphia: University of Pennsylvania, 1917, Vol. 32. An outstanding study of regional theatre.

Rippley, LaVern J. "German Theatre in Columbus, Ohio." *German-American Studies* 1, no. 2 (1970): 80–101. A detailed study of a regional amateur theatre.

Rothfuss, Hermann E. "The Beginnings of the German American Stage." *German Quarterly* 24 (1951): 93–102. A most thorough and scholarly study of the early German-language theatre.

Weisert, John J. "Beginning of German Theatricals in Louisville." *Filson Club History Quarterly* 26 (1952): 347–59. A study of regional amateur theatre in Louisville.

Wood, Ralph. "Geschichte des deutschen Theatres von Cincinnati." *Deutsch Amerikanische Geschichtsblätter* (1932), pp. 3–112. An outstanding study of German theatre in Cincinnati, in German.

8

Hungarian-American Theatre

THOMAS SZENDREY

Any account of Hungarian ethnic theatrical activity in the United States must take into consideration the cause, pattern, socioeconomic status, and cultural-educational level and interest of the Hungarian emigration to this country. This is necessary because the cultural activities and aspirations of the numerous waves of immigrants arriving here were substantially shaped not only by their backgrounds but also by settlement patterns, adjustments to American conditions, organizational and religious activities and organizations, and the desire—sometimes a serious consideration, in other instances only a fleeting concern of little consequence—to preserve a cultural heritage in an alien land. These variations of concern were also related to the reasons for emigration of the different waves of arriving Hungarians, as well as to the socioeconomic status and educational attainment levels of those who eventually settled in the United States.

An examination of the numbers of Hungarians arriving in the United States is of fundamental importance in understanding settlement patterns and the extent of Hungarian life, including entertainment and the theatre, since these were invariably the consequence of sufficiently large settlements of Hungarians. Most accounts of the immigration make note of the presence of Hungarians in the United States in the late eighteenth and early nineteenth centuries; however, they were not numerous enough to generate institutional or theatrical life.[1] The flow of Hungarian immigration to the United States in the latter nineteenth and early twentieth centuries, however, was sufficiently large for institutions supportive of cultural activities to be established.

The first significant number of Hungarian immigrants began arriving in this country in the 1870s and 1880s, and the apex was reached at the turn of the century, specifically the years 1890–1905. After this the rate of arrival slowed down until World War I and then was reduced to a trickle.[2] However, these immigrants established and sustained Hungarian cultural life for more than two generations. The interwar and post-World War II immigrants, who were mostly political refugees, sustained this heritage, built on this foundation, and added their own cultural values and aspirations to it. The theatre, whether amateur, semiprofessional, or professional, consistently exercised an impact on Hungarian cultural development in the United States. Indeed, in the estimation of numerous individuals concerned enough with this culture and language to write about it, the theatre, especially the amateur activity, was and still is considered to be an integral part of language maintenance efforts and a catalyst in nearly all other ethnic-consciousness-centered activities and organizational life.[3]

The Hungarian ethnic theatre in the United States served almost entirely for entertainment and language retention. The actual plays produced and presented were invariably forgotten by the audience and by historians of dramatic literature as well. These plays certainly did not consistently serve as a vehicle of cultural development, nor did this theatrical activity have a memorable and lasting effect, except in the nontheatrical areas of language maintenance and support for ethnic organizational activity. With very few exceptions, serious drama was rarely attempted in Hungarian ethnic settlements, because the educational and social level and the concerns of these settlements were not attuned to it. In most instances Hungarian ethnic theatre programs emphasized operettas and plays with a folk character. Serious drama and urbane comedies were placed on the programs of the Hungarian ethnic theatre only after the patterns of immigration and settlement produced audiences that desired and were willing to make the necessary sacrifices for such theatrical endeavors. However, the demand for such theatre was minimal, and only a very few presentations of serious drama can be found throughout the otherwise colorful history of the Hungarian ethnic theatre. In recent years, however, serious Hungarian drama has been presented in major cultural centers and university towns. A discussion of the major trends, personalities, plays, and related theatrical concerns as these have occurred in the history of Hungarian theatre in the United States should illustrate and confirm these more general observations.

THE DEVELOPMENT OF HUNGARIAN THEATRICAL ACTIVITY IN THE UNITED STATES

As soon as there was a sufficiently large number of Hungarian settlements in the United States, the larger communities witnessed the development of amateur theatrics. In the early 1850s the earliest manifestations of an organized cultural life by Hungarian immigrants became visible, and a significant first step was the establishment of a short-lived newspaper, *Magyar Száműzöttek Lapja* (Newspaper of Hungarian Refugees) in New York in 1853,[4] followed by *Magyar Amerika*, edited by Vilmos Löw, in 1879 and other papers, such as *Az Amerikai Nemzetőr* (The American Guardian) in 1884 and *Szabadság* (Liberty), edited by Tihamér Kohányi, in Cleveland in 1891.[5] The desire for organizational activity and a theatre was expressed in these newspapers. By 1869 the first Hungarian theatrical performance was presented in New York, followed by performances in Cleveland in 1888 and Chicago in 1889.

By 1865 some Hungarian cultural organizations had been established in New

York City, specifically the Magyar Egylet (Hungarian Association), and the first theatrical performance was related to the activities of this organization. A few young people in this organization decided to perform an amateur play, and their first production, the first Hungarian play presented in the United States of which records exist, was Ferenc Csepreghy's A szökött katona (The Escaped Soldier) at the Dramatic Hall on East Houston Street in the fall of 1869.[6] While a success, the initial performance must have exhausted the players, because no further performances were scheduled until 1877. The Hungarian newspapers wrote about no other performances until 1885, when Csepreghy's one-act comedy A kitünő vendég (The Esteemed Guest), was presented.[7]

These amateur presentations must have appealed to the audience, because the idea soon spread and deepened. In 1886 Henrik Miskolczy, an individual who had had theatrical experience in Hungary, arrived in New York and immediately organized a movement to establish a permanent amateur theatrical company. His efforts led to the establishment of the Hungarian Amateur Theatrical Society of New York on January 16, 1887. The first presentation by the group was held on March 15, 1887, in conjunction with a Hungarian patriotic festival. They presented Gergely Csiky's play A sárga csikó (The Yellow Colt).[8]

During the course of the same year the society presented a series of plays: in the spring Jenő Rákosi's Leánykérő (The Suitor) and Miskolczy's own attempt at writing for the theatre, Kicsike (The Little One), and in the fall A tót leány (The Slovak Girl). In addition to these activities, the company also obtained a musical director in the person of Károly Feleky and was also faced with competition from other amateur groups, which presented at least six more plays, drawn mostly from the works of Csepreghy, during 1887. This situation resulted in the merger of the various New York–based amateur groups the following year,[9] resulting in an increased level of involvement of Hungarians living in the New York area. One of the new amateur actors was Géza D. Berkó, active in 1888–1889, who later would become the editor of the Amerikai Magyar Népszava (American-Hungarian People's Voice) and one of the major supporters of the short-lived professional theatre company that would be organized by New York Hungarians in 1905.

In addition to this Hungarian-language theatrical activity in New York, there was also an association of Hungarian friends of music, under the leadership of Ferenc Korbay and his wife Ilona Ravasz, who presented musical and dramatic programs for a mostly American audience during the 1880s. Their activities represented one of the earliest attempts by Hungarians in the United States to present the culture of their homeland to American audiences, providing an example for such activity since that time.[10]

Hungarians who settled in other parts of the United States followed the lead of the New York Hungarians and soon established amateur theatrical groups of their own. Cleveland Hungarians were fortunate, because Miskolczy visited Cleveland in August 1888 and organized an amateur theatrical group there; after the necessary rehearsals A tót leány and Leánykérő were performed on September

8 and 9, respectively. Encouraged by the success of these presentations, the Hungarians established an association in February 1891, the Clevelandi Első Magyar Műkedvelő Társaság (First Hungarian Amateur Theatrical Society of Cleveland), and through the cooperation of Imre Fecső, a newspaper owner, it obtained a hall for its purposes.[11]

The pace of events was hastened by István Gábor, the secretary of the Verhovay Association, a Hungarian fraternal group, who issued the following plea in the *Amerikai Nemzetőr* of March 1891 for Cleveland Hungarians to foster theatrical life:

Yes, the time is here, you Hungarian brethren of Cleveland, that we open that coffin in which our greatest treasure, our true Hungarian sentiment and our language has lain for ages, and give this new life through our untiring effort and patriotism. . . . Come and let us struggle together so that we may enjoy together the vengeance against those who are enemies of the madonna of Hungarian culture. Hurry, and together with the previous members, take your place among us."[12]

Emboldened by this emotion-laden plea, the Cleveland amateurs presented an original Hungarian-American play by Kohányi entitled *The Greenhorns*, dealing with the difficulties encountered by Hungarian immigrants upon their arrival in this country.[13]

Since there was already a large number of Hungarians in Cleveland at this time and the number increased rapidly during the 1890s and early 1900s, this theatrical activity soon broadened in scope and involved many individuals, who established a number of organizations for theatrical purposes. Furthermore, the guest appearance of the outstanding Hungarian prima donna Ilka Pálmay in 1902 provided additional impetus; the Jókai Circle and the Önképzőkör (Society for Self-Culture) were organized during this time.[14] Two years later the St. Stephen Circle was formed by a group of young men. Their major interest was amateur theatrics, and their first presentation was a Christmas pastoral play on Christmas Day 1904.[15] A Hungarian Workingmen's Singing Club, also concerned with amateur theatrics, was organized on August 5, 1908, and this organization presented numerous amateur theatrical performances over the next fifty years.[16] All of this activity was recalled by a former participant, who later described the extent of it in the years before 1914. Most of the plays presented were operettas or folk plays.[17] This same emphasis will be found in the theatrical activity of Hungarians in the United States until 1948 and, with some minor changes, even later.

Hungarian-American theatrics soon spread to other cities with Hungarian populations. Chicago witnessed the first such amateur performance on April 6, 1889, when a group of young people organized into an amateur theatrical society and presented Csepreghy's *A szökött katona* in the North Side Turn Hall.[18] Some records have survived about Hungarian theatrical activity in other places as well, and there were numerous efforts that escaped the attention of chroniclers of Hungarian immigrant life. However, records have survived concerning the activity of Géza Osterhúber of Newark, N.J., who established Hungarian cultural activities in the Newark area in 1903 and, during the course of more than twenty years, produced more than 100 plays for a number of Hungarian organizations.[19] Hungarian theatrical activity was begun in Bethlehem, Pennsylvania, in 1892, and a music and drama group organized in 1905.[20] Similar activities in other Hungarian settlements throughout the United States were inevitably bound up with the establishment of churches, almost all of which supported and fostered theatrical activity. One of the best-documented examples of this has been the support of the Catholic churches of Toledo, Ohio, for the mummers' play that has been presented there every Christmas for more than fifty years.[21]

In addition to this widespread amateur theatrical activity, professional Hungarian actors were under contract with the Conried German theatrical company and others participated in professional American theatres. Noting that numerous Hungarian actors were living and working in New York (Lajos P. Borsodi, Etelka Utassi, Lajos Barnai, the Királyfi brothers, and Lajos Horváth) Gusztáv Erdélyi, one of the leading individuals in New York Hungarian circles and editor of *Nemzetőr*, proposed in his newspaper in 1889 that a permanent professional Hungarian theatre be established. This proposal was discussed for many years before a committee composed of Gábor Ágoston, Géza D. Berkó, Béla Perényi, and Gyula Róth undertook the necessary steps and made the financial commitments to bring this professional theatre into operation in 1906.

This year represented the high point of Hungarian theatre in New York. One or two presentations were held each week, and well-known guest artists such as Ilka Pálmay, the greatest Hungarian operetta star of that era, added additional luster to the program.[22] However, this pace of presentations was difficult to sustain, and in spite of the efforts of directors such as the Bányai brothers, Stanley Horton, Hugó Kardos, and János Skóthy, the theatre eventually failed. The memento addressed by the theatrical company to the Hungarian community indicated some of the reasons for this failure. One of these reasons was emphasized: "We Hungarian artists who have been in the new homeland for only a short time, sadly experience that we Hungarians are far behind the other nationalities in terms of our cultural institutions."[23] The memorandum went on to point out that, in spite of the untold sacrifices of the actors, there was not enough support for this theatrical venture. Although the company expressed its resolve to carry on, this was not possible because of serious financial difficulties, personal conflicts, poor management, and the excessively high fees paid to guest artists from Hungary. One of the actors involved in this first professional company, looking back from a perspective of more than thirty years, pointed out that the failure of the company forced the actors to turn to other professions or return to their homeland—as indeed some did. The result was renewal of amateur theatrics and greater reliance on semiprofessional touring companies, to satisfy the cultural needs of the Hungarian community in the United States, especially after World War I.[24]

While the failure of this New York-based professional company was not the end of Hungarian theatre in the United States, as the rather pessimistic professional actor Lajos Horváth believed, but it did return the initiative to the amateur and semiprofessional theatre that flourished during the interwar period. Indeed, a few short-lived professional theatres functioned after 1920, but the Depression era undermined even such professional efforts. Quite simply, the population patterns of Hungarian settlement in the United States divided the potential audience into many cities, which were thus able to support amateur theatrics and touring companies but not resident professional theatres. Nonetheless, what remained of the professional theatre provided an example of quality stagecraft and acting, which had a generally salutary effect on amateur theatrics; furthermore, many professional actors simply became producers and directors with the amateur troupes.

The amateur theatre, from its earliest days in 1869 and consistently until our own time, has also made many valuable contributions to Hungarian life in the United States by keeping alive the Hungarian national heritage and language, even among second-generation Hungarians, and by raising the cultural level of the immigrants, who were mostly of peasant background. It also brought Hungarians together and gave them a sense of collective identity, thereby promoting that organizational life that has fostered a Hungarian identity in the American mosaic and contributed to the resurgence of the sense of ethnicity in our own day.

THEATRICAL ACTIVITIES OF HUNGARIAN AMERICANS, 1914–1945

Built on the foundations established before 1914, the cultural life of Hungarian-Americans became more institutionalized and better established during the next thirty years. There had been a tentative character to Hungarian-American life and culture before the First World War, insofar as there was a reverse migratory flow back to Hungary; furthermore, the constant influx of new immigrants was not conducive to establishment of a stable pattern of life. This transitory state, coupled with the internal migration of Hungarian Americans to various parts of the country and the urbanization of a mostly peasant immigrant group, helped shape the social condition and cultural milieu of Hungarian Americans during this era and later.

Hungarian Americans' theatrical taste was related to their condition in this new land. The two major categories into which the repertoire of the Hungarian-American theatre divides itself, namely the folk play and the operetta, which comprised in approximately equal proportions 90 percent of all theatrical productions of record, is of significance. The folk play, based mostly upon peasant motifs in a patriotic setting, represented an interest in the immigrants' national and social origins, while the operetta, sometimes in the form of musical comedy, represented a romanticized escape from the burdens of urbanization and also provided that musical element so traditionally a part of Hungarian culture. More modern tendencies in the theatre and dramatic writing did not appeal particularly to this audience, nor were they suited to the ability of the mostly amateur performers. Cosmopolitan themes also had little appeal except to the highly educated element, which was quite small until the coming of political refugees in the 1930s, post-World War II immigrants, and subsequent political refugees. In all cases, however, cultural activities, including the theatre, served to maintain the language and culture as well as to entertain.

The increasing stability of Hungarian-American life, coupled with the growth of communities centered around churches and civic and fraternal organizations, provided a setting in which many cultural activities, including the theatre, found a home and means of support. The growth of organizations provided a home for the theatre, and in return the theatre provided a source of cohesion and an artistic expression of common values for these organizations. Professional and semiprofessional touring companies provided a link among the various Hungarian communities and often gave more polished and enjoyable performances than the amateur groups. Their performances were invariably the highlights of the theatrical season, especially in the smaller settlements. Furthermore, these professional companies sometimes attempted to present serious drama, which was generally beyond the capabilities of even the best amateur troupes.

One of the most striking characteristics of the Hungarian ethnic theatre during the interwar and immediate postwar eras was the large number of performances and of participants. Recalling the theatrical life of this era, some elderly Hungarians, including the second generation János Pulusics and Erzsébet Görgényi, have related that according to their recollection there were sometimes as many as eight or ten plays staged in Cleveland during some months in the 1930s and early 1940s.[25]

While Cleveland was undoubtedly the largest Hungarian settlement in the United States, a similar level of activity can also be found in New York and Chicago, and a lesser but nonetheless significant level in the smaller Hungarian settlements. The pages of the Hungarian daily Szabadság (which although published in Cleveland served as a daily paper for the entire Hungarian community in the United States) revealed that for the first nine months of 1934 there were about eighty-two amateur and professional performances, mostly operettas and folk plays, in twenty-two U.S. cities and towns, including not only cities with major Hungarian settlements, such as Cleveland, New York, Chicago, Detroit, Buffalo, Pittsburgh, and New Brunswick, New Jersey, but also towns and cities with smaller Hungarian populations, such as McKeesport, Homestead, Allentown, and Philadelphia, Pennsylvania; Garfield, Trenton, Kearny, Somerset, and Passaic, New Jersey; Columbus, Akron, and Canton, Ohio; Wallingford and Bridgeport, Connecticut; East Chicago and South Bend, Indiana; and St. Louis, Missouri.[26] Other volumes of this newspaper carried reports of theatrical activity by Hungarian Americans in Virginia, West Virginia, and California, in addition to the states named above. Furthermore, examination of newspapers published weekly and also local journals suggests that the incidence of theatrical activity was even higher.[27] Theatrical activity, with the exception of the Depression years, was generally sustained at this level throughout the interwar period, but a diminution occurred in the post-World War II era. Amateur theatrical activity has declined precipitously since then, and since a breakdown of most ethnic neighborhoods is impending in the foreseeable future, the decline should continue.[28]

The programs of these amateur and semiprofessional theatrical activities can best be seen by providing a few representative examples. In addition to the preponderance of operettas and folk plays, at least 85 to 90 percent of all plays presented were written in Hungary, and only a very small proportion of the program consisted of plays written by Hungarian Americans or individuals of other nationalities. Plays, especially comedies and operettas, from the theatrical periodical *Színházi Élet* (Theatrical Life), published in Hungary,[29] provided the bulk of the program. Indeed, the Zilahy-Heltay Hungarian Comic Theater of New Brunswick, N.J., a semiprofessional troupe that undertook more than twenty-five tours of Hungarian theatres throughout the United States and Canada, presented plays and operettas published mostly in the aforementioned journal.

The organizer and director of this troupe, Sándor Zilahy, was one of the major figures in Hungarian-American theatrical life. In addition to producing and directing numerous operettas, many of which were then also played by the amateur companies, he traveled throughout the United States teaching theatre arts to amateurs and second-generation Hungarian children. He also produced and directed amateur plays in Hungarian settlements in Trenton and other New Jersey towns and on more than one occasion staged Easter passion plays for the New Brunswick Hungarian Catholic church.[30]

The same operettas and folk plays were on the programs of amateur and semiprofessional theatres in other cities and towns. One of the earliest Hungarian touring companies, the Sándor Palásthy group, was active in the years immediately before and after World War I, employing a number of professional and guest artists as well as an orchestra and a large managerial staff. It regularly toured the larger Hungarian communities between New York and Chicago.[31] Many older Hungarians that I interviewed still recalled the visits of the Palásthy troupe to Cleveland, and they especially remembered the performance of Mici Hajós[32] in the operetta *Sári*.[33] This touring company did not fail to have an effect on amateur activity; many of the plays it produced were later presented by the numerous amateur companies. So popular were these operettas that amateur groups in Homestead, Pennsylvania; Cleveland; St. Louis; Trenton; and elsewhere followed the lead of these touring companies and presented operettas, such as *Maritza grófnő* (Countess Maritza), by Imre Kálmán, which was certainly beyond the capacity of these amateur troupes.[34]

Such ambitious theatrical projects, however, were better suited to the talents of the semiprofessional and professional touring companies. In addition to the

Zilahy-Heltay and Palásthy troupes, mention must also be made of the activities of Eugene Endrey and his Chicago Hungarian Theatre.[35] According to his own account, Endrey came to the United States sometime in the early 1920s with a professional theatre troupe he had organized. After the failure of this venture, which he considered to be a cultural mission, he established his own troupe in New York, composed of himself; his wife, called Lady Margaret in his memoirs; Gáspár Szántó, Adrienne Tomory; and a musical director, Julius Horváth. After a series of tribulations, vividly described in the memoirs, this small collective became the nucleus of the Chicago Hungarian Theatre, established in 1925.[36] After the resolution of difficulties with the Hungarian Actors Union and Sári Fedák, an eminent Hungarian actress on a U.S. tour at that time, the Chicago Hungarian Theatre opened with a performance of Ferenc Lehár's operetta *Blue Mazur* (in the estimation of Endrey a more serious work than the same composer's *The Merry Widow* or *The Count of Luxemburg*).[37]

After a successful opening season, the Chicago Hungarian Theatre went on tour in 1926 and 1927. After numerous intermediate stops it arrived in New York and presented an operetta by Béla Zerkowitz, entitled *Miss Innocent*, at the Cort Theatre on New York's West 48th Street. Endrey informs us that the play was an instant success and led to further theatrical ventures for his company.[38] He cites a whole series of testimonials from Hungarian and American newspapers concerning his theatrical company and also states that he received praise from the president of the Hungarian Overseas World Association, Imre Jósika-Herczeg.[39] In spite of these and some other successful ventures, the Endrey theatre was faced with numerous difficulties of a political and financial nature, which led to its demise in the early 1930s. Endrey himself, however, returned to New York and ventured into the American theatre and radio. The Endrey troupe had performed mostly operettas and musicals; however, it had also staged some of the works Endrey himself had written for the stage.

The operetta was the mainstay of the programs of these professional and semiprofessional touring companies, but the folk play occupied a central position on the programs of the amateur theatrical companies. Although the professional theatre was also motivated, at least in part, by a sense of cultural mission and desire to maintain the Hungarian language, it existed primarily to provide entertainment for people undergoing the trauma of rapid urbanization. The amateur theatre, on the contrary, was very much concerned with the goal of language maintenance and was quite obviously permeated with a sense of cultural mission, augmented by a desire for cultural self-improvement. The very name given to many of these organizations engaged in the sponsorship of amateur theatrics, *önképzőkör* (society for self-culture), lends credence to this judgment.[40] The involvement of large numbers of people in these productions, the audience as well as the active participants, helped to sustain and foster Hungarian-American organizational life. The involvement of the churches in this theatrical activity was a significant example of their ability to influence their congregations, thereby augmenting their traditional religious role.

A reasonably comprehensive account of this amateur theatre necessitates identification of numerous groups and organizations. Obviously no listing could be complete, given the often fragmentary, sometimes contradictory, and invariably chaotic status of the preservation of the records of the immigrant heritage in general and especially of the smaller ethnic groups. Nonetheless, even an incomplete listing will affirm the extent and impact of this amateur theatrical movement, and an analysis will tell us something about its artistic and cultural concerns, which will not change fundamentally as additional Hungarian-American amateur theatre history comes to light. Amateur theatrical groups were found wherever a sufficient number of Hungarians had settled, and some of these organizations could trace their origins back to the period before 1914. However, these groups became widespread and very active in the 1920s and 1930s. In the 1940s and after, their number and level of activity declined, but some form of amateur theatrics has been sustained with varying degrees of success in the larger centers of Hungarian-American life.[41]

Hungarian amateur theatre was most active in Cleveland, Chicago, and greater New York-New Jersey. In the Chicago area the number of Hungarians had grown from approximately 3,600 in 1890 to 70,000 in 1920. To satisfy the cultural needs of this expanding population, organizations were soon established that drew on local talent and provided numerous forms of entertainment, including a great deal of theatre. This was augmented by the Hungarian touring companies, which played to large crowds.[42] In 1926 Chicago Hungarians established the Thália Amateur Theatre Circle, under the leadership of Pál Berák, a resident Hungarian playwright. Irma Petrovics, Mór Wottitz, and József Pfeifer.[43] Although the circle was quite active in Chicago Hungarian cultural life, its records, in a publication entitled Szinházi Ujsag (Theater News), published by the Chicagoi Magyar Szinház (Chicago Hungarian Theatre), edited by Joseph Viz, are not available.[44] There are, however, records of some amateur theatrical activity in Chicago in the Hungarian daily paper Szabadság, which reported that the South Side Association amateurs presented Berák's play A téli napsugár (The Winter Sunshine) on April 29, 1937, and the Hungarian radio hour presented a play adapted for the radio by József Gál entitled János úrfi leánykérőben (Master John Goes Courting), directed by Ferenc J. Kovách.[45] All indications, however, point to the fact that the activities of the Chicago amateurs were much more extensive than this.

Probably the greatest number of amateur theatrical companies and the most active amateur theatrical life were in Cleveland, the major settlement center of Hungarians in the United States, with an estimated Hungarian population of 80,000 to 100,000 in the 1930s. According to figures compiled by the Nationalities Service Center of Cleveland, 105,000 Hungarians or individuals of Hungarian ancestry lived in Cleveland in 1974.[46] At least nine amateur and semiprofessional theatrical groups were active here in the 1930s, among them the American-Hungarian Choral Society (also known as the Workers' Choral Society), the Self-Culture Circle, the St. Stephen Chorus, St. John's Church

Amateur Theatre Society, St. Margaret Dramatic Club, the Cser Theatre, The Workers' Home Society, St. Elizabeth's Church theatrical group, the Bethlen Hall company, and the amateurs associated with the West Side Lutheran Church.[47]

The first of these amateur theatrical organizations was associated with St. Elizabeth Church. This troupe presented its first production, a folk play entitled *Kósza Jutka,* in 1898 and was still active in 1947, presenting a play entitled *A katona őrmester* (The Army Sergeant), directed by Sándor István.[48] Their productions were presented in the church hall built for this purpose, which was last used for a theatrical performance in the early 1960s. Other church groups were also active in theatrics, presenting folk plays such as Pál Vidor's *Vörös Sapka* (The Red Hat), *Másodvirágzás* (Second Flowering), and *Erdők királya* (King of the Forest), as well as Ede Szigligeti's *A cigány* (The Gypsy), which was directed by Károly Tomási, one of the most active directors of amateur plays in Cleveland.[49]

Another organization actively involved in amateur theatrics in Cleveland was the Workers' Choral Society, which presented mostly operettas and musical pageants. In the 1930s and 1940s, under the direction of Károly Kocsándy, János Mátyás, and Mihály Parlagh, it presented numerous operettas, including *Érik a buzakalász* (The Ripening of the Wheat), by György Ujházi and Dezső Kellér; *Aranyvirág* (The Golden Flower), by Jenő Huszka; *Májusi muzsika* (The Music of May), by Imre Farkas; and many others, including some folk plays.[50] This level of activity was sustained until approximately 1950, after which many of the original members became too old for active participation and the second and third generations were not sufficiently interested to maintain such a level of theatrical activity. The arrival in Cleveland of approximately 10,000 Hungarians in the early 1950s and almost 8,000 more in the aftermath of the Hungarian Revolution of 1956 resulted in a minor resurgence of theatrical activity, but the major Hungarian settlement, which had provided the broad base of support for theatrical activity, has been either eroding or dispersing throughout the greater Cleveland metropolitan area since the early 1960s. Activities since 1950 will be discussed in the next section of this chapter.

Amateur and semiprofessional theatrical activity of the same character took place in many other towns and cities with considerable Hungarian populations, but on a smaller scale. Amateur theatrical activity in Detroit was inspired by the Hungarian poet György Kemény; furthermore, an association dedicated to amateur theatrics was established there, presenting mostly folk plays and the less demanding operettas. This amateur activity, here as elsewhere, was supplemented by the visits of semiprofessional and professional touring companies during the 1920s and 1930s.

The East Chicago and South Bend, Indiana, communities also had amateur theatrics, each with its own resident amateur company. In these two centers the major support came from the churches, and in the 1930s the companies presented a number of operetta performances. In the 1940s, in addition to the major

Hungarian cultural center in Cleveland, amateur groups in Akron, inspired by the activities and concern expressed by the leading Hungarian-American poet, Árpád Tarnóczy, and in Canton and Columbus, Ohio, presented mostly folk plays and attempted, especially in Columbus, to involve second-generation youth. There was also active Hungarian theatrical life in St. Louis, supported by the local Hungarian newspaper and the churches.[51]

In the Eastern states, similarly inspired amateur theatrical groups were to be found in even the smallest Hungarian settlements. In Pennsylvania amateur groups were concentrated in the Pittsburgh area, especially in McKeesport and Homestead. Further east, amateur groups were also found in Daisytown, Allentown, and Philadelphia, where a Workers' Choral Society presented operettas in the 1930s and 1940s.

There were and still are many Hungarian settlements in New Jersey. Almost all of these settlements supported at least one amateur theatrical company and also hosted the touring companies. New Brunswick was the major center for Hungarian cultural activities in New Jersey, due in large measure to the fact that approximately 25 percent of the population was of Hungarian birth or ancestry. Another reason for the significance of New Brunswick as a center of theatrical activity was the indefatigable work of Sándor Zilahy, who in addition to organizing his company, which toured the Hungarian-American communities regularly, also produced and directed amateur plays in New Brunswick and in other New Jersey cities.

There was also an amateur theatrical group in Garfield, known as the Theatrical Circle of the Hungarian House. The West Hudson Youth Circle, under the leadership of Ede Vaaly, was active in Kearny. In Trenton there was an amateur theatrical circle established by János Meleg, and theatrical efforts were supported by the fraternal groups and the churches of Newark.

The Hungarian theatre in Connecticut centered around the activities of Sándor Bihari. A professional actor, he had been instrumental in the establishment of the Thália Theatre in New York before 1914. After the war he settled in Bridgeport and later in Wallingford and was actively involved in the production of amateur plays in Connecticut for more than twenty years.[52]

The Hungarian professional theatre, especially the ideal of a permanent Hungarian theatre, failed any number of times, but the actors and other theatre professionals who participated in these numerous ventures did play a role in Hungarian cultural life, even if little is known about most of them. Brief biographical sketches of two Hungarian-American actors were published in two memorial volumes commemorating the role of Hungarian-Americans in this country.[53] One of these individuals was Aladár Zsadányi. From an international career, he came to the United States after World War I and became an Hungarian-American actor, playing leading roles with the Sándor Palásthy troupe. He established the first permanent Hungarian theatre in Detroit, and after this short-lived venture played with the Cser Theatre in Cleveland and participated in numerous theatrical efforts in New York. Among his accomplishments was the organization of the American-Hungarian Actors Union.[54]

The other actor of note in the Hungarian-American community was Gyula Szemere. After a career on the Budapest stage lasting more than a decade, he came to New York as a guest actor in 1926. Although he had a contract offer from the Hungarian National Theatre, he chose to remain in the United States. During his years here he became one of the most popular theatrical personalities in the Hungarian-American theatre both as actor and director, and his fame extended even to the American theatrical world.[55]

The multifaceted Hungarian-American theatrical world enjoyed the support of the Hungarian community, and without a doubt the theatre supported the organizational and cultural aspirations of that community. The amateur theatre was especially recognized and appreciated, not so much for its artistic merit or originality but for its role as a cultural catalyst, especially its suitability for fostering the maintenance of the Hungarian language among second-generation youth. This role of the amateur theatre was consistently emphasized not only by those who produced and directed the plays, but also by the Hungarian-American press. For example, the daily paper *Szabadság* offered the editorial opinion that the amateur theatre should be actively supported because, among other positive features, it affords an excellent opportunity for language maintenance.[56]

HUNGARIAN-AMERICAN THEATRICAL ACTIVITIES SINCE 1945

After a decline of activity during the war years, the theatrical efforts of Hungarian Americans reached their former, or prewar, level; however, the high level of activity characteristic of the prewar period was sustained for only a few years, certainly not beyond 1950. There are any number of reasons for this slowdown, in which theatrical activity was ultimately reduced to a mere trickle of performances. Among the factors that can be cited to explain this, the primary one was probably the advancing age of those whose activities as directors and actors had populated the amateur and professional stages. Their children and grandchildren, born and educated mostly in the United States, have not generally exhibited the same level of enthusiasm as the previous generation. Hence the concern about this second generation, often articulated by the participants in the amateur theatrical movement, was not unjustified, even if the results are not reflective of the older generation's effort and enthusiasm. The older generation still comprises a theatrical audience, but the new generation has not provided the amateur performances. The movement to the suburbs of many second-generation Hungarians also weakened those bonds of community that had sustained the theatre, especially the amateur theatre.

There was also increased competition of film as a medium of popular entertainment. The screening of Hungarian films, beginning in the late 1930s and increasing rapidly, especially after 1945, had a negative impact on the amateur theatre. Some locales used previously for the theatre were now being equipped for film. Many organizers of Hungarian cultural life, seeing the popularity of the new art form as well as the relative ease of presentation, turned to film in their efforts to sustain interest in their organizations.

The professional touring companies, however, could better withstand these negative pressures, since these companies provided a form of entertainment still strongly desired by large segments of the Hungarian-American community. They could still attract audiences, especially if a well-known film star accompanied the touring theatrical group. These phenomena can be illustrated by an analysis of the motion picture and theatre advertising in the Hungarian daily *Szabadság*, especially in the years after 1945. The number of announcements for the amateur theatre declined at least 50 to 70 percent, but the number of tours by professional theatre companies remained relatively stable, and the advertisements revealed that numerous well-known Hungarian actors and actresses, mostly guest artists from Hungary, accompanied these touring companies.

Two theatrical events from 1947 illustrate the changed situation. The paper *Szabadság* announced that on October 5, 1947, the Cleveland Hungarian theatre companies would host the eminent Hungarian actor Pál Jávor and that he would play the leading role in a play entitled *Délibáb* (Fata Morgana) by Ernő Vajda. The notice went on to state that the local actress Ilona Thury would also be in the cast.[57] Performances of this type proved successful not only in Cleveland, but elsewhere as well. Jávor later joined forces with the New York-based American-Hungarian People's Theatre, directed by József Galambos, and went on tour with that company.[58]

Seeing what the formula of success was, other groups, mostly New York based, were organized and went on tour. For example, the New York Operetta Theatre was organized under the direction of Mihály S. Sárossy, who gathered a number of professional actors[59] and went on a few nationwide tours, presenting mostly operettas, such as Mihály Eisemann's *Csak egy kislány van a világon* (There is but One Girl in the World) and works by Imre Kálmán, Imre Farkas, and Jenő Huszka.

Another commendable initiative was also taken in New York; Istvan Papp and Lilly Erdődy organized the American Hungarian Artists' Association and staged benefit performances to support aged Hungarian theatrical personalities.

These efforts, while innovative and valuable in themselves, did not assure continuation of a high level of theatrical activity. The late 1940s and early 1950s can best be characterized as a transitional period, with the decline of a broadly based theatrical life supported mostly by the older immigrants, who were very much involved with the theatre, and the constantly diminishing involvement of their descendants. The transitional period ended with the arrival of the new immigrants, displaced persons between 1948 and 1952 and refugees in 1956 and 1957, in both instances preceded and followed by the arrival of various kinds of political refugees. The early and mid-1950s were a time of adjustment for these newly arrived refugees; organizational and cultural activities became secondary concerns, and economic and political issues dominated their lives.

After the initial period of adjustment, the new groups developed their own patterns of organizational and cultural priorities and values, which were generally at variance with those of the earlier generations of Hungarian Americans. First these new arrivals attempted to provide for the education of their children; this was closely followed by involvement in political organizations concerned mostly with the situation in their homeland. This difference of concern and the lack of understanding between the old and the new immigrants, complicated by disagreements between the postwar displaced persons and the 1956 refugees, postponed the concern with building cultural institutions until the early 1960s. By this time the ethnic communities were generally breaking down, even if this process was accompanied by a resurgence of ethnic consciousness. This breakdown caused further disruptions in the Hungarian-American communities, placing the need to renew cultural institutions into the background again.

Dissatisfied with the cultural values of the older immigrants and faced with difficulties in political and economic adjustment, these new refugees organized their own cultural institutions, each wave in its own way. Since the major cultural interest of most of the new immigrants was in education and language maintenance, coupled with an obvious interest in sustaining the Hungarian identity of their children, the organizational structures established by them reflected those concerns. Thus the entertainment aspect of theatre was relegated to a secondary position, and the concern with the theatre as an instrument of teaching and preserving the Hungarian language became paramount.

Theatrical activity for the sake of language preservation was woven into the fabric of new immigrants' lives. Manifestations of this concern can be found in the cultural activities of the Hungarian scouting movement, which among other activities presents plays on special occasions, such as Christmas and patriotic feasts. Nor is the theatrical dimension missing from the program of Hungarian-language weekend and other schools and the activities of Hungarian youth groups of diverse backgrounds.[60] The Hungarian churches also play a role in fostering this amateur theatrical activity. Documentation concerning this aspect of the ethnic amateur theatre is difficult to obtain, as it must be sought in the uncharted maze of ethnic newspapers, journals, organizational and church bulletins, and personal reminiscences, and there are hardly any central and no regional or national repositories for such materials nor any effective means of bibliographical support for research work in such materials.[61] Nonetheless, the following few examples may serve as a preliminary account of this theatrical activity.

A Hungarian youth group in Cleveland, Ohio, under the leadership of Sándor Marady, affiliated initially with the Committee for Hungarian Liberation, presented its first theatrical production, Ferenc Herczeg's Gyurkovics lányok (The Gyurkovics Girls), in May 1963 with great success.[62] Building upon the reception accorded this performance, the group adopted the name Déryné Theater and presented a series of plays in Cleveland, Toledo, and Pittsburgh from 1963 to 1970, including an operetta by Imre Farkas, *Nótas kapitány* (The Captain of Song), in 1967[63] and Lászlo Németh's *Petőfi Mezőberényben* (Petőfi in Mezoberény) in 1968. The group eventually decided to open its own theatre in the former Moreland Theatre in Cleveland and after opening the rebuilt theatre building on June 8, 1969, hoped to provide a setting not only for amateur theatrics, but also for visiting guest artists from Hungary and elsewhere. However, the project soon collapsed, because a substantial minority of Hungarians were opposed to such cultural exchange and also because the Hungarian neighborhood on Cleveland's East Side was declining rapidly as a self-contained community.[64] Even though the attempt to establish a permanent theatre failed, the efforts to revive amateur theatrics were successful for a while under the leadership of György Gyékényessi, who established the Cleveland Hungarian Theatre and produced a number of plays in the late 1960s and early 1970s, including Zsigmond Móricz's *Sári biro* (Judge Sári) on June 7, 1970.[65]

All these efforts notwithstanding, there was a marked decline of the Hungarian amateur theatre in the 1970s. Organization of folk dance groups and sponsorship of literary and musical programs became much more widespread, not only in the larger, but also in the smaller Hungarian communities. Since the 1960s many individual artists, musicians, and scholars have toured the Hungarian communities with great success, but only a very few theatrical groups. In most instances such tours have been attempted only when well-known Hungarian artists visited, and then a complete program is put together. One of the most successful of these ventures was the performance of Imre Kálmán's *Marica grofnő*, organized by László Dékány, a Hungarian actor living in New York, on the occasion of the visit of János Sárdy, a well-known and liked Hungarian actor, to the United States in 1967. Similar occurrences have been rare since that time, and Hungarian-American cultural life has been characterized by folk dancing, literary programs, musical performances, and lectures, sometimes augmented by amateur and professional theatrical performances.

HUNGARIAN-AMERICAN DRAMATIC WRITING

Although almost all of the plays performed by the Hungarian-American theatre were written in Hungary, some were written by established Hungarian writers after their arrival in the United States and others by Hungarian Americans who became writers and dramatists here. A very few of the plays were reflective of the Hungarian-American experience. Furthermore, some successful Hungarian dramatists with established international reputations, such as Ferenc Molnár and Melchior Lengyel, eventually settled in the United States and wrote for the American stage.

The works of Molnár and Lengyel, and also Ernő Vajda, belong more properly to the history of Hungarian dramatic art and literature, and the account of the performances of their works in this country belongs to the history of the American theatre and of American-Hungarian cultural connections. The activities of some other dramatists, however, such as Pál Berák, belong more properly to the history of the Hungarian-American theatre.

The outstanding Hungarian-American playwright was undoubtedly Berák, born in Aszód, Hungary, in 1869. After a successful writing career in Hungary, where he wrote the dramas *Áldozatok* (Victims) and *Mátyás király* (King Matthew), he arrived in the United States in 1903 and settled in Chicago. During the course of a forty-three-year life in the United States, he was always actively involved in the Hungarian-American theatre as a director, producer, and writer, but achieving renown primarily as a dramatist. He presented his first play written here, *A biró lánya* (The Judge's Daughter) in 1905. It proved to be the most popular play in the repertoire of the Hungarian-American theatre.[66] Among his other plays were *Tévesztett utakon* (On Wrong Routes), *Bosszú* (Revenge), *Vándormadarak* (Migratory Birds), *Udvari bolond* (Court Jester), *Elcserélt menyasszony* (Bride by Mistake), and *Téli napsugár* (Winter Sunshine). This last-mentioned work was a musical comedy about the life of the Hungarian-American farmer (music by János Kurucz) and proved to be most popular.[67] Berák recognized the social significance of amateur theatrics and actively participated in them as long as he was able to do so.

Another Hungarian-American playwright whose activities included both Hungarian and American theatre was Stephen Linek, born in Budapest in 1893. His plays were produced in Hungary, Germany (by Max Reinhardt), and the United States before he began writing for the Hungarian-American theatre.[68] Another dramatist, Miklós Labanics, born in Monok, Hungary, in 1884, came to the United States in 1903 and settled in St. Louis. His writing career was confined to the years he spent in this country. He wrote approximately a dozen amateur plays in Hungarian, published mostly by the St. Louis Hungarian almanac, and one English-language play entitled *Escape to Freedom*, with autobiographical overtones.[69]

In addition to these individuals, who were primarily dramatists, other writers, including poets and journalists, also wrote dramas and occasional theatrical pieces. The journalist and indefatigable organizer of Hungarian-American life, Tihamér Kohányi, wrote *The Greenhorns*, already mentioned, depicting the problems faced by new immigrants upon their arrival in the United States; this play was quite popular at the turn of the century.[70] Another journalist, Ferenc Prattinger, editor of *Magyar Ujság* (Hungarian News), a Detroit-based Hungarian newspaper, wrote *Polgár-Császar* (Citizen-Emperor), which was presented in Kolozsvár, the former capital of Transylvania, a part of Hungary given to Romania according to the terms of the Treaty of Trianon, 1920. The author was condemned by the Romanian authorities because the play had an obvious irredentist dimension.[71]

Other Hungarian-American writers and theatrical personalities who contributed to the corpus of Hungarian dramatic literature, or at least dramatic literature concerned with Hungarian topics but written in English, included Ilona

Fülöp, a one-time director of Hungarian theatres in New York; Sári Dobó, who won numerous prizes for her English plays on Hungarian subjects; and Gizella Mészáros, who wrote an occasional play for the opening of the Hungarian Cultural Gardens in Cleveland in 1932. The outstanding poet of the Hungarian-American community, Árpád Tarnóczy, wrote a play entitled A *nagy örökség* (The Great Tradition) to commemorate the fiftieth anniversary of the Verhovay Fraternal Association. László Szabó wrote dramas in verse entitled *Irredenták* (Irredentists), published in Budapest in 1903, and *Pocahantas*, an Indian tale in eight acts published in the United States in 1955. All of these literary efforts had some minimal contact with Hungarian and American cultural life. However, the relationships among the Hungarian-American, Hungarian, and American theatres were more extensive than this; they included the role of Hungarian Americans in the relationship of Hungarian with American theatre.

RELATIONSHIP OF THE HUNGARIAN AND AMERICAN THEATRES

While in any event there undoubtedly would be cultural connections between Hungary and the United States, even within the confines of theatrical concerns, this cultural and theatrical contact has been influenced by the fact that large numbers of Hungarians have settled in the United States. References to the United States and its history and culture appear in Hungarian art and literature; however, specific references in the dramatic literature are quite rare, one example being a comedy dealing with nineteenth-century America by Julius Hay, *Das neue Paradies* (*The New Paradise*), published in 1931.[72]

There are two obvious aspects of the relationship between Hungarian and American theatre. One of these is the presentation of plays by Hungarian writers on the American stage, and the other is the visit of Hungarian theatrical personalities to the United States. These visits can be divided into two distinct categories: visits to the Hungarian ethnic theatre and involvement in American theatrical life. Some of these visits by Hungarian artists resulted in commitments to stay in the United States. Furthermore, individuals of Hungarian parentage born in the United States, or for that matter immigrants born in Hungary who were not connected with the theatre there, have also been involved in the development of the American theatre. Given all of these possibilities, the relationship of Hungarian with American life can be seen as multifaceted, and the extent and character of the mutual involvement can best be characterized by a series of examples.

The best-known involvement of Hungarian dramatic art in the American theatre, characterized by an anonymous writer as the Hungarian invasion of the New York stage,[73] was the presence of actresses of Hungarian birth or ancestry on the New York stage in the early twentieth century, including Mizzi Hajos, the Dolly sisters (Jancsi and Rozsika), Josephine Victor, Franciska Boros, Frances Cameron, and Olga Helvai.[74] Actors and actresses of Hungarian birth or parentage have continued to appear on the American stage. For example, in the 1930s the Hungarian actress Sári Fedák appeared not only on the stage of the Hungarian ethnic theatres, but also on the Broadway stage, mostly in roles that dealt with Hungarian themes.[75] Another well-known Hungarian actor, Ernő Király, who played mostly operetta roles, was a guest artist with Hungarian and American theatre companies in 1920 and 1923 and settled in the United States in 1928. After his arrival as a permanent resident he devoted his energies to the Hungarian-American theatre, directing and producing operettas and musicals.[76]

Active in New York during the 1940s, on both the Hungarian-language and American stages, were Ilona Thury, considered by many to be the leading Hungarian-American actress; Anna Gyenge, an excellent operetta performer; and Sándor Svéd, a world-famous Hungarian opera singer who joined the Metropolitan Opera.[77] Other actors and actresses of Hungarian birth or ancestry played a large role in the development of the American stage and some times also in the cinema; Paul Lukas, Lili Darvas (an internationally renowned dramatic actress, wife of Ferenc Molnár), Julia Keleti, Vilma Bánky, Martha Eggerth, Béla Lugosi, and Peter Lorre were better known for their cinema performances.[78] In addition to these performers, mention must also be made of the producers Martin Beck and Al Wood, both of Hungarian background, and Yolanda Mero Irion, one of the founders of the New Opera Company. The director of the Chicago Hungarian Theatre, Eugene Endrey, also directed a play slated for Broadway, Imre Kálmán's operetta *Sári*. It opened in Philadelphia, was praised by the reviewer for the *Philadelphia Inquirer*, but never reached Broadway.[79] Endrey was also involved in the Provincetown Playhouse in Greenwich Village, where he established a one-act variety theatre that boasted of some success for approximately one year.[80]

The major link between Hungarian and American theatre, however, was a group of outstanding Hungarian dramatists. Dominant among them was Molnár, whose works, fifty-three of them, were performed extensively on the New York stage between 1908 and 1940. Enro J. Gergely described this situation:

This activity represents a Hungarian-American cultural contact which for thirty-two years loosely linked the theatres of the two nations. Comparatively few people are aware of the extent of this "Hungarian invasion" of the American theatre. In the three years from 1923 to 1925, seventeen new Hungarian plays opened on Broadway, and from 1930 to 1933, twelve. During the entire period there were only six years all together in which no professional production of a Hungarian play was to be seen in New York.[81]

All of these works were presented in an adapted form, with the adaptation generally done by outstanding American writers and theatre professionals, including, among others, David Belasco, Benjamin Glazer, Ben Hecht, P. G. Wodehouse, and Edna St. Vincent Millay. These plays undoubtedly projected an image of Hungary and Hungarian life that was significantly better and more variegated than that entertained under the general ignorance and popular prejudice widespread in the United States before this time. The enhanced under-standing of Hungarian culture and civilization evident since that time must, at least in small measure, be attributed to this theatrical activity.[82]

As I have said, the major figure of this "Hungarian invasion" was Molnár. Attempts to explain his almost universal popularity and appeal have been made by numerous literary and theatre critics, producers, directors, and actors. For example, Louis Rittenburg, in his introduction to *All the Plays of Molnár*, states that Americans have been "singularly responsive to Molnár's plays,"[83] and Belasco, after providing an account of his productions of some of Molnár's plays, explains his attachement to the Hungarian dramatist:

From my first acquaintance with his writings I marked Molnár as a dramatist of original and fearless mind, whose work evinces lively contempt for hide-bound conventionality, quick apprehension alike of the humor and the pathos of human experience, keen sympathy with the wretched and miserable, extraordinary constructive faculty, unerring dramatic instinct and a satisfying, sinewy vitality of style.[84]

Molnár himself, in his memoirs, pointed out that there was a definite working relationship between Belasco and himself.[85] The memoirs of Molnár provide a rather extensive but rambling account of his involvement with the American theatre, especially after he settled in the United States. Without a doubt, he was a permanent fixture and respected participant in Hungarian, American, and international theatrical life, and ties of friendship attached him to many of the outstanding theatrical personalities of his age.[86] *Liliom*, Molnár's best-known and most-performed piece, was first produced in the United States by the The-atre Guild in 1921, with Joseph Schildkraut and Eva Le Gallience, and revived in 1940 by Vinton Freedley, with Burgess Meredith and Ingrid Bergman. Its musical version, entitled *Carousel*, a 1945 show and 1955 motion picture, with songs by Rodgers and Hammerstein, endeared Molnár to a very wide American audience and obtained for him a respected position in American cultural life.[87]

All of this certainly testifies to his stature in the world of American theatre, but his significance as a writer and dramatist and also his unique talents were best described by the outstanding Hungarian-American literary scholar and writer Joseph Reményi:

His international fame brought him to the top of the theatrical world, proving that as an "export" writer of plays he entertained not only audiences of various nations but called their attention to a Danubian country in which people speak and write a language that, although philologically and poetically isolated, can be used splendidly for the expression of universal sentimentality, gaiety, illusionism, and ingenuity.[88]

Without a doubt Molnár, together with some of the other Hungarian dramatists whose works were extensively performed on the New York and American stage in the first half of this century, such as Ernő Vajda, author of the much-praised play *Fata Morgana*,[89] László Bús-Fekete; Melchior Lengyel; Atilla Orbók; László

Fodor; Ferenc Herczeg; Lajos Zilahy; Dezső Szomory; and many others, exercised a tremendous impact on the American theatre and contributed to an enhanced understanding of Hungary in a world context.

In the post-World War II period Hungarian theatre has not enjoyed such a wide-scale reception as it did during that earlier era. However, since the late 1960s, through the efforts of Hungarian dramatists, coupled with the work of a generation of young Hungarian intellectuals in the United States and elsewhere, who are conversant with the cultural patterns and styles of the United States, Hungarian drama underwent a renaissance outside the borders of Hungary. The works of Lajos Zilahy, who has continued to write plays and novels, served as a bridge between the 1940s and the 1960s, and the plays of the current generation of Hungarian dramatists, such as András Sütő, Gyula Hernádi, and especially István Örkény, have been staged in the United States in excellent English translations.[90] Örkény's play The Tót Family has been presented at the Arena Stage in Washington, D.C., and his Catsplay has also been presented in the United States.[91] András Sütő's Star at the Stake, a historical drama about Calvin and Servetus with modern parallels, was staged in 1979 by the Threshold Theatre Company of New York.[92]

A careful reading of Hungarian theatrical and literary journals indicates that modern American dramas are presented by Hungarian theatres in Budapest and the provincial cities. All of these developments permit one to conclude that, although the institutional Hungarian ethnic theatre has seen more active days, the theatrical experiences of Hungarians, Hungarian-Americans, and other Americans of whatever heritage, still intersect in numerous ways.

NOTES

1. Information concerning the presence of Hungarians in the Americas before the U.S. Civil War can be found in Eugene Pivány, Hungarian-American Historical Connections from Pre-Colonial Times to the End of the American Civil War (Budapest: Royal Hungarian University Press, 1927), and Géza Kende, Magyarok Amerikában; Az amerikai magyarság története, 1583–1926 (Hungarians in America: The History of Hungarian Americans, 1583–1926), vol. 1 (Cleveland: Szabadság, 1927).

2. Immigration statistics must be used with caution, because there are numerous estimates with a sufficient variation to allow for doubt. I have relied upon John Kósa, "A Century of Hungarian Immigration, 1850–1950," American Slavic and East European Review 16 (Dec. 1957), pp. 501–14, and the information provided by the Hungarian Central Statistical Office in Hungary, Központi Statisztikai Hivatal, A Magyar Szent Korona országainak kivándorlása és visszavándorlása, 1899–1913 (Emigration and Remigration from the Lands of the Hungarian Holy Crown, 1899–1913), new series (Budapest: Magyar Statisztikai Közlemények, 1918), Vol. 67.

3. An excellent review of the efforts at language maintenance, together with excellent notes, is given by A. Joshua Fishman, Hungarian Language Maintenance in the United States (Bloomington: Indiana University Press, 1966).

4. Data concerning the Magyar Száműzöttek Lapja (Newspaper of Hungarian Refugees), can be found in Emil Lengyel, Americans from Hungary (Philadelphia: J. B. Lippincott, 1948), pp. 195–96.

5. Concerning Tihamér Kohányi, consult Kende, *Magyarok Amerikában*, Vol. 2, pp. 189–203.

6. Ibid., p. 123.

7. Ibid.

8. Kálmán Káldor, ed., *Magyar-Amerika irásban és képben (Hungarian-Americans in Writings and Pictures)* (St. Louis, Mo.: Hungarian Publishing Co., 1939), Vol. 2, p. 10.

9. Kende, *Magyarok Amerikában*, p. 126.

10. Géza D. Berkó, ed., *Amerikai Magyar Népszava Jubiléumi Diszalbuma, 1899–1909 (The Jubilee Memorial Volume of the American Hungarian People's Voice)* (New York: Amerikai Magyar Népszava, 1910), pp. 61–62.

11. Kende, *Magyarok Amerikában*, p. 126.

12. Ibid.

13. Ibid., pp. 127, 191.

14. Imre Sári-Gál, *Az amerikai Debrecen; Képek a clevelandi magyarság életéböl (The American Debrecen: Pictures from the Life of the Hungarians of Cleveland)* (Toronto: Pátria Publishing Co., 1966), p. 78.

15. Káldór, *Magyar-Amerika*, Vol. 1, p. 24.

16. John Körösföy, ed., *Hungarians in America* (Cleveland: Szabadság Publishing Co., 1941), p. 48.

17. Sári-Gál, *Az amerikai Debrecen*, p. 15, relates an account of a conversation with a Mrs. Galgányi, an individual quite active in amateur theatrical circles in Cleveland.

18. Kende, *Magyarok Amerikában*, p. 127.

19. Information concerning the activities of Géza Osterhúber can be found in Káldor, *Magyar-Amerika*, Vol. 2, p. 150.

20. Ibid., Vol. 2, p. 185.

21. Concerning church support for amateur theatre in Toledo, see the excellent article describing the mummers' plays by Raymond J. Pentzell, "A Hungarian Christmas Mummers' Play in Toledo, Ohio," *Educational Theatre Journal* 29 (May 1977): 179–98. A more general observation concerning the role of the churches in support of amateur theatre can be found in David A. Souders, *The Magyars in America* (New York: Doran, 1922), p. 91.

22. Berkó, *Amerikai Maygar*, p. 62.

23. Ibid., p. 65.

24. Káldor, *Magyar-Amerika*, Vol. 1, pp. 281–82.

25. An examination of the Hungarian press in the United States, especially the major daily *Szabadság (Liberty)*, confirms these recollections.

26. Based upon an examination of *Szabadság* for 1934 and 1937.

27. One of the major difficulties in writing about the life of Hungarian Americans in terms of specific concerns, such as the theatre, is the almost complete lack of bibliographic control and the haphazard and fragmentary preservation, at best, of ethnic newspapers.

28. Interviews with Sandor Zilahy in New Brunswick, N.J., in August 1963 and with Alexander Murady, director of the Déryné Theater in Cleveland, 1962–1970, during my association with him "in these theatrical endeavors."

29. Now generally unavailable in the United States. The Detroit Public Library at one time possessed an almost complete set, but upon application to use this I was advised that the publication had been withdrawn from the library collection. I have in my possession approximately ten volumes. The texts of some of the plays presented by the Hungarian-American theatre were first published in this periodical.

30. Details can be found in the 1934, 1937, and 1947 volumes of *Szabadság*, specifically the Feb. 12, 1934; Feb. 2, 1934; June 16, 1934; and Nov. 15, 1947 issues.

31. Fishman, *Hungarian Language Maintenance*, p. 9.

32. She also played on the American stage, as reported in an article signed only A. P., "The Hungarian Invasion," *Theatre Magazine*, Jan. 1913, p. 16.

33. Sári-Gál, *Az amerikai Debrecen*, p. 36.

34. References to these amateur operetta presentations are to be found in *Szabadság*, Feb. 11, 1934, Jan. 11, 1934, and March 29, 1934.

35. Much of this and the following paragraphs are based on the memoirs of Eugene Endrey, *Beg, Borrow, and Squeal* (New York: Pageant Press, 1963), a very personal and emotional account of his life, but difficult to use because the account is impressionistic and disdains the use of dates, even when citing newspaper articles.

36. Ibid., pp. 50–76.

37. Ibid., p. 88.

38. Ibid., pp. 109–10.

39. Ibid., pp. 113–19.

40. Conversations with individuals involved in such movements also confirms this characterization of purpose. Se note 28 for reference to Zilahy interview, and Theresa Gyulay (interviewed in 1961–1962), who was active in amateur theatre in Detroit and in Miami (the Kossuth Civic Center, from 1952–1970).

41. Among these larger centers of Hungarian life presently are New York City; New Brunswick and Passaic, New Jersey; Cleveland; Pittsburgh; Chicago; and Los Angeles, California. There are others, but the aforementioned are the largest centers of Hungarian population.

42. Barbara Schaaf, "Magyars of the Midwest," *Chicago Tribune Magazine*, May 6, 1979, p. 27.

43. Káldor, *Magyar-Amerika*, Vol. 1, p. 138.

44. This publication is mentioned in Joseph Széplaki, ed., *Hungarians in the United States and Canada, A Bibliography* (St. Paul, Minn.: University of Minnesota, Immigration History Research Center, 1977), but only a single number is listed as available, namely Vol. 2, no. 7 (1939).

45. Information can be found in *Szabadság*, Apr. 2, 1937, and Apr. 29, 1937.

46. Cited in Imre Sári-Gál, *Clevelandi magyar múzeum* (Cleveland Hungarian Museum) (Toronto: Amerikai Magyar Írók, 1978), p. 170.

47. Letter from John Palasics to Thomas Szendrey, April 13, 1979.

48. Information from *Szabadság*, Nov. 10, 1947, and Nov. 16, 1947.

49. Information from *Szabadság*, Oct. 27, 1947; Jan. 21, 1934; Feb. 20, 1934; and May 2, 1937.

50. Information from *Szabadság*, Jan. 28, 1934; April 27, 1937; and Nov. 22, 1947.

51. Based mostly on the back files of Hungarian newspapers, especially *Szabadság*, and also personal correspondence. Letter from János Pulusics to Thomas Szendrey, April 13, 1979. Also, conversations with Pulusics in Cleveland, summer 1979; with M. Károly Péterváry, Cleveland, 1966; Sándor Zilahy, Cleveland, 1963; and Dr. György Gyékényesi, Cleveland, 1965 and 1966. Events in Canton are described in *Szabadság*, Feb. 9, 1934; in East Chicago, Jan. 24, 1934; and in South Bend, Jan. 17, 1934, and April 22, 1937. For events in Columbus see Káldor, *Magyar-Amerika*, Vol. 1, p. 150.

52. Connecticut events are given in ibid., Vol. 2, p. 82; New Jersey events are given in ibid., Vol. 2, p. 97, and in *Szabadság*, Jan. 19, 1934, and Feb. 15, 1934. Information about theatrical performances in McKeesport, Daisytown, Allentown, and Philadelphia

can be found in *Szabadság*, March 13, 1934; Jan. 3, 1934; and Jan. 9, 1934; and Káldor, *Magyar-Amerika*, Vol. 2, p. 203. A report about a performance in St. Louis can be found in *Szabadság*, Feb. 6, 1934.

53. Káldor, *Magyar-Amerika*, Vol. 2, p. 203.

54. Ibid., Vol. 1, p. 134.

55. Ibid., Vol. 2, p. 35.

56. Editorial in *Szabadság*, Jan. 27, 1934.

57. Information from *Szabadság*, Oct. 4, 1947.

58. Information from *Szabadság*, Oct. 24, 1947.

59. Some of these actors and actresses were Margit Bodán, Manci Király, Lajos Horváth, and István Rátkai.

60. *Kossuth Polgári Kör 20 éves jubileum 1952–1972*, (Kossuth Civic Center, 20th Anniversary, 1952–1972, Ligonier, Pa.: Bethlehem Freedom Press, 1972). I also consulted my personal collection of programs from the New Brunswick, New Jersey, Hungarian weekend school and numerous numbers of *Magyar Cjerkész (Hungarian Scout)*, the monthly magazine of the Hungarian Scouting movement, published in Garfield, New Jersey. Also pertinent are records of the Déryné Theater of Cleveland, 1962–1970, in my possession.

61. The following discussion is based upon documents in my possession and a partial review of the ethnic newspapers and bulletins. Nonetheless, there remains much to be done before a definitive account of this aspect of Hungarian theatrical life in the United States can be written.

62. A review of the play was published by *Szabadság*, May 25, 1963. This play was adapted for the American stage by Edith Ellis with the title *The Seven Sisters* and was staged at the Lyceum Theatre in New York on Feb. 20, 1911. Details from Emro Joseph Gergely, *Hungarian Drama in New York; American Adaptations, 1908–1940* (Philadelphia: University of Pennsylvania Press, 1947), p. 186.

63. József Lendvay, "A 'Nótás Kapitány' Clevelandban," ("The 'Captain of Song' in Cleveland") *Képes Világhiradó* (Illustrated World Review) 10 no. 6 (June 1967): 17.

64. I was one of the organizers of that effort, and most of the documents and other materials pertaining to this theatre are in my possession. Included among these materials are the contract establishing the theatre, the opening day invitation and poster, and other posters and correspondence.

65. Sári-Gál, *Clevelandi magyar múzeum (Cleveland Hungarian Museum)*, p. 102, reproduces the playbill.

66. Concerning Berák's activities in the amateur theatre, see *Szabadság*, May 27, 1937.

67. Leslie Könnyű, *A History of American-Hungarian Literature* (St. Louis, Mo.: Cooperative of American Hungarian Writers, 1962), p. 46. Consult also Káldor, *Magyar-Amerika*, Vol. 1, p. 142.

68. Könnyü, *A History*, p. 45.

69. Ibid., p. 46.

70. I have not been able to locate a copy of this play, only a few brief references to it.

71. Káldor, *Magyar-Amerika*, Vol. 1, p. 197. Prattinger was imprisoned and eventually exiled.

72. Cited in Julius Hay, *Born 1900: Memoirs*, translated from German and abridged by J. A. Underwood (LaSalle, Ill.: Open Court Publishing Co., 1975), p. 377.

73. A. P., "The Hungarian Invasion," p. 15.

74. Ibid., pp. 15–16.

75. Concerning Sári Fedák, consult the following: Ágnes Kenyeres, ed., *Magyar Életrajzi lexikon (Hungarian Biographical Encyclopaedia)* (Budapest: Akadémiai Kiadó, 1967), Vol. 1, p. 476; Henry A. Phillips, "Hungary's Impress on World Theatre," *Theatre Magazine*, Aug. 1928, p. 56; and Endrey, *Beg, Borrow and Squeal*, pp. 85–86.

76. Kenyeres, *Magyar Életrajzi lexikon*, Vol. 1, p. 917.

77. Géza Domokos, *Modern Amerika és a magyarság élete (Modern America and the Life of the Hungarians)* (New York: Charles Brown Printing House, 1941), pp. 93–94.

78. Lengyel, *Americans from Hungary*, pp. 290–91.

79. Endrey, *Beg, Borrow, and Squeal*, pp. 167–71.

80. Ibid., pp. 209–12.

81. Gergeley, *Hungarian Drama*, 3.

82. Ibid., 186–90. A complete list of the plays, their authors, and their adapters and the particulars concerning the Broadway performances are given.

83. Ferenc Molnár, *All the Plays of Molnár* (Garden City, N.Y.: Garden City Publishing Co., 1937), introduction by Louis Rittenberg, p. xi.

84. Ibid., p. ix.

85. Ferenc Molnár, *Companion in Exile: Notes for an Autobiography*, translated by Barrows Mussey (New York: Gaer Associates, 1950), pp. 141–42.

86. Ibid., pp. 214–16, 245–47, 257–58.

87. Ibid., p. 176.

88. Joseph Reményi, *Hungarian Writers and Literature*, edited by August J. Molnár (New Brunswick, N.J.: Rutgers University Press, 1964), p. 362.

89. Ernő Vajda, *Fata Morgana*, translated by James L. A. Burrell and Philip Moeller, (New York: Theatre Guild, 1924).

90. *Catsplay*, by István Örkény, was translated by Clara Györgyey, and *Star at the Stake*, by András Sütő, was translated by Jenő Brogyányi. Information from Clara Györgyey and the playbill from *Star at the Stake* is in my possession.

91. Henry Popkin, "The Brilliance, Dazzle and Despair of the East European Stages," *New York Times*, July 31, 1977, pp. 4-D, and 18-D.

92. Playbill is in my possession.

BIBLIOGRAPHY

Books

Bakó, Elemér. *Guide to Hungarian Studies*, 2 vols. Stanford, Calif.: Hoover Institution Press, 1973. A comprehensive bibliographical guide to the works concerning Hungary that are to be found in major U.S. research libraries. Special attention in Volume 2 to Hungarians outside Hungary, including a section devoted to the cultural life of Hungarians in the United States.

Balogh, Joseph K. *An Analysis of Cultural Organizations of Hungarian-Americans in Pittsburgh and Allegheny County*. Ph.D. diss., University of Pittsburgh, 1945. A comprehensive study of Hungarian institutional life in the Pittsburgh area. Information concerning the theatre is limited to a few names.

Bardin, Hillel. *The Hungarians in Bridgeport*. Bridgeport, Conn.: University of Bridgeport, 1959. Information of a general nature. Contains only minimal data about cultural activities.

Berkó, Géza D., ed. *Amerikai Magyar Népszava Jubiléumi Diszalbuma, 1899–1909. (The Jubilee Memorial Volume of the American Hungarian People's Voice.)* New York: Amerikai Magyar

Népszava, 1910. One of the earliest memorial albums about Hungarian life in the United States. Contains significant information about theatrical activity in the 1880s and 1890s that is difficult to locate elsewhere.

Brown, Thomas Allston. *A History of the New York Stage: From the First Performance in 1732 to 1901*, 3 vols. New York: Benjamin Blom, 1964 (first published 1903). Useful information about the plays presented on the New York stage; some minimal information about Hungarians.

Carpenter, Niles. *Immigrants and Their Children, 1920. A Study Based on Census Statistics Relative to the Foreign Born and Native White of Foreign or Mixed Parentage.* Washington, D.C.: Government Printing Office, 1927. A statistical study useful for determining the extent of ethnic life in the United States at that time.

Cook, Huldah Florence. *The Magyars of Cleveland.* Cleveland: Citizen Bureau, 1919. Mostly general information about the settlement patterns and problems of Hungarians in Cleveland. Only minimal information about cultural concerns.

Csorba, Zoltán. *Adalékok az amerikai magyar irodalom történetéhez. (Contributions to the History of American Hungarian Literature.)* Pécs, no publisher given, 1930. Deals with the historical development of American Hungarian literature but is very sketchy in its treatment of dramatic writing.

Domokos, Géza. *Modern Amerika és a magyarság élete. (Modern America and the Life of the Hungarians.)* New York: Charles Brown Printing House, 1941. An account of Hungarians in America, based upon the author's experiences as a visitor to numerous Hungarian-American communities in 1939–1940. Contains some data on actors and the theatre.

Endrey, Eugene. *Beg, Borrow, and Squeal,* New York: Pageant Press, 1963. The memoirs of a Hungarian-American actor and producer who was actively involved in Hungarian theatrical affairs mostly in New York and Chicago. While the memoirs contain extensive information, it proves difficult to use as a source in most instances because dates are generally not provided.

Farkas, Pál. *Az amerikai kivándorlás. (Emigration to America.)* Budapest: Singer és Wolfner, 1907. This brief study of Hungarian immigration to the United States is based mostly upon Hungarian sources and does not deal directly with cultural concerns.

Fishman, A. Joshua. *Hungarian Language Maintenance in the United States.* Bloomington: Indiana University Press, 1966. A highly informative study of the means by which Hungarians have maintained their language in the predominantly English-speaking United States. While instructive in some of its theoretical concerns, the author also discusses the role of the theatre and cultural institutions in language maintenance efforts.

Gellért, I., ed. *Amerikai magyar karriérek albuma. (An Album of American Hungarian Careers.)* Cleveland: Szabadság Publishing Co., 1923. Brief biographical sketches of Hungarian Americans who have achieved prominence in either American or Hungarian-American life.

Gergely, Emro Joseph. *Hungarian Drama in New York: American Adaptations, 1908–1940.* Philadelphia: University of Pennsylvania Press, 1947. This most detailed study of the influence and impact of some Hungarian dramatists upon the New York theatre shows how Hungarian plays were adapted to the American stage. Fundamental for any study of Hungarian-American cultural relations. Contains valuable bibliographic citations.

Gerster, Árpád G. *Recollections of a New York Surgeon.* New York: P. B. Hoeber, 1917. These memoirs of a well-known and respected Hungarian surgeon, who spent most of his life in New York, shed some light upon the problems faced by those who engaged in or supported Hungarian theatrical activities in the United States.

Gracza, Rezsoe, and Gracza, Margaret. *The Hungarians in America.* Minneapolis: Minn.: Lerner Publications, 1969. This popular account of the Hungarians in America provides some pertinent information about Hungarian cultural figures, including actors and other theatrical and motion picture personalities.

Hay, Julius. *Born 1900: Memoirs,* translated from German and abridged by J. A. Underwood. LaSalle, Ill.: Open Court Publishing Co., 1975. The memoirs of this Hungarian dramatist, who was actively involved in leftist causes throughout his life, contain extensive information about Hungarian intellectual and cultural life in this century but only minimal information about Hungarian cultural life outside Hungary.

Hungary, Központi Statisztikai Hivatal. A Magyar Szent-Korona országainak kivándorlása és visszaván-dorlása, 1899–1913; Emigration et Retour des Emigrés des Pays de la Sainte Couronne Hongroise de 1899 à 1913. (Emigration and Remigration from the Lands of the Hungarian Holy Crown, 1899–1913.) Publications statistiques Hongroises, new series, vol. 67. Budapest: Magyar Statisztikai Közlemények, 1918. A compendium of basic statistical data on emigration and repatriation, published by the Hungarian government.

Incze, Sándor, ed. Magyarok Amerikában. (Hungarians in America.) Budapest: Szinházi Elet, 1921. An illustrated album containing extensive information about successful Hungarians, including some theatrical professionals, in the United States. The editor was also the publisher of the Hungarian theatrical periodical Szinházi Élet (Theatrical Life).

Káldor, Kálmán, ed. Magyar Amerika irásban és képben (Hungarian America in Writings and Pictures), 2 vols. St. Louis, Mo.: Hungarian Publishing Co., 1939. One of the most comprehensive collections of brief biographical sketches about Hungarians in the United States, together with information about churches and civic, fraternal, and cultural organizations. Also included are some biographical sketches of Hungarian-American actors and actresses.

Kardoss, John. Hungarian Theatre to the Twentieth Century. Brooklyn, N.Y.: Long Island University, 1967. This brief survey of twentieth-century Hungarian drama provides some of the basic necessary information about this subject.

Kemény, György. Élet könyve. (The Book of Life.) Detroit: Magyars in America, 1946. The author was one of the most active and outstanding literary figures in Hungarian-American life. This collection of his writings, mostly poetry, provides an understanding of the Hungarian-American cultural scene.

Kende, Géza. Magyarok Amerikában; Az amerikai magyarság története, 1583–1926 (Hungarians in America: The History of Hungarian Americans, 1583–1926), 2 vols. Cleveland: Szabadság Publishing Co., 1927. Still represents, if not in all its details, the most comprehensive story of the Hungarians in America as of the date of its publication. These volumes contain a few chapters on theatrical and cultural life; a never-published third volume was to have dealt with such concerns.

Kenyeres, Ágnes, ed. Magyar Életrajzi lexikon (Hungarian Biographical Encyclopaedia), 2 vols. Budapest: Akadémiai Kiadó, 1967–1969. This Hungarian biographical encyclopaedia contains some data about Hungarian theatrical personalities who had a reputation there before embarking for the United States. Some of the sketches also provide details about the American visits of Hungarian actors and actresses.

Könnyű, László. Az amerikai-magyar irodalom története. (A History of American-Hungarian Literature.) St. Louis, Mo.: Cooperative of American Hungarian Writers, 1961. This and the English-language version of the same book, cited below, contain a brief survey of Hungarian-American literature and excerpts from some of the writings. The work of some of the dramatists is also mentioned.

Könnyű, Leslie. A History of American-Hungarian Literature. St. Louis, Mo.: Cooperative of American Hungarian Writers, 1962.

Körösfőy, John, ed. Hungarians in America. Cleveland: Szabadság Publishing Co., 1941. Contains numerous short biographical sketches of Hungarian-Americans, including some theatrical personalities. Also provides information about some civic and religious organizations and their amateur theatrical ventures. The most comprehensive section deals with the Hungarians in Cleveland.

Kuné, Julián. Reminiscences of an Octagenerian Hungarian Exile. Chicago: published by the author, 1911. These memoirs of a Hungarian exile who emigrated not long after the failure of the 1848 revolution in Hungary provide the reader with a wide-ranging account of the conditions of Hungarian life in Chicago at that time.

Lengyel, Emil. *Americans from Hungary.* Philadelphia: J. B. Lippincott, 1948. This volume, part of the series edited by Louis Adamic, provides an overview of Hungarian-American life; some of the chapters deal with literature, art, and the theatre.

Lukács, György, ed. *Magyarok a kulturáért.* (*Hungarians for Culture.*) Budapest: A magyar-francia Kulturliga kiadása, 1929. This compendium of informative articles about various facets of Hungarian culture includes two relevant but brief essays, one dealing with the Hungarian theatre in general and the other with the reception of Hungarian drama outside Hungary.

Maksai, Miklós. *Ne vegyétek el a fiaimat: szinmű.* (*Do Not Take Away My Sons: Drama.*) Buffalo, N.Y.: Akcio Hungarika Könyvosztálya, 1963. This drama with a patriotic theme was typical of the type of drama that appealed to the Hungarian refugees in the 1960s.

Molnár, Ferenc. *All the Plays of Molnár.* Garden City, N.Y.: Garden City Publishing Co., 1937. The most complete collection of Molnár's plays available in English; contains a preface by David Belasco and information about the American adaptations and premieres of Molnár's plays.

————. *Companion in Exile: Notes for an Autobiography,* translated by Barrows Mussey. New York: Gaer Associates, 1950. These notes give the reader extensive and detailed information about Molnár's years in the United States and his relationships with American and international theatrical life.

Pivány, Eugene. *Hungarian-American Historical Connections from Pre-Colonial Times to the End of the American Civil War.* Budapest: Royal Hungarian University Press, 1927. Focuses mostly on political and intellectual connections; some minimal information about literary matters.

Reményi, Joseph. *Hungarian Writers and Literature,* edited by August J. Molnár. New Brunswick, N.J.: Rutgers University Press, 1964. This collection of writings by the most eminent Hungarian-American literary scholar provides testimony of the interaction of two cultures. His essay on Ferenc Molnár was very useful to this chapter.

Sári-Gál, Imre. *Az amerikai Debrecen; Képek a clevelandi magyarság életéből.* (*The American Debrecen: Pictures from the Life of the Hungarians of Cleveland.*) Toronto: Patria Publishing Co., 1966. These pictures of Hungarian life in Cleveland provide some information as well as some reminiscences about amateur theatrics by Cleveland Hungarians. Some information is also provided about visiting artists from Hungary in the early twentieth century.

————. *Clevelandi magyar múzeum.* (*Cleveland Hungarian Museum.*) Toronto: Amerikai Magyar Írók, 1978. A continuation of the previous work; however, the bulk of the information deals with more recent, mostly post-1945, events and personalities.

Souders, David A. *The Magyars in America.* New York: Doran, 1922. This study sponsored by mission groups provides information mostly about patterns of acculturation of Hungarians into American life; minimal data about amateur theatrics supported by church groups is given.

Szabó, László. *Irredenták, drámai költemény 8 felvonásban.* (*Irredentists, Dramatic Poem in 8 Acts.*) Budapest: Budapesti Hirlap, 1923. A literary work with a patriotic theme, written by a Hungarian-American writer and published in Hungary.

————. *Pocahantas, Indian rege 8 felvonásban.* (*Pocahantas, An Indian Tale in 8 Acts.*) Windbar, Pa.: Expert Printing Co., 1955. A play with an Indian theme by a Hungarian-American writer and poet.

Szántó, Miklós. *Magyarok a nagyvilágban.* (*Hungarians in the Wide World.*) Budapest: Kossúth Kiadó, 1970. A brief historical account of Hungarians outside Hungary, written by a specialist in such concerns; some information about theatrical topics.

Szécskay, György. *Öszi tarlózás ötven éves mezőn.* (*Fall Gleaming in a Fifty Year Old Field.*) Pittsburgh, Pa.: no publisher given, 1947. These poems and reminiscences of one of the most colorful Hungarians in the United States provide poetic images of Hungarian-American life, mainly in Pittsburgh.

Széplaki, Joseph, ed. *Hungarian Newspapers in Microform Available in the United States and Canada.* Youngstown, Ohio: Catholic Hungarians' Sunday, 1977. A bibliography and research guide.

————, ed., *Hungarians in the United States and Canada, A Bibliography.* St. Paul, Minn.: University of Minnesota, Immigration History Research Center, 1977. This guide lists some sources for the history of the theatre and also gives a descriptive record of some manuscript holdings.

Vajda, Ernő. *Fata Morgana,* translated by James L. A. Burrell and Philip Moeller. New York: Theatre Guild, 1924. The text of one of the most popular Hungarian plays presented on the New York stage. Information about its premiere is also included.

Articles

Crawford, Jack. "Broadway Throngs to Liliom," *The Drama* 2 (June 1921): 308–10. A brief article describing the popularity of Ferenc Molnár's play.

Hegedüs, Ádám de. "Hungarian Drama and Dramatists," *Theatre Arts* 14 (June 1930): 481–84. A brief survey of modern Hungarian drama intended to provide basic information to the English-speaking reader.

Jósika-Herczeg, Imre. "America's Ties with Hungary," *Current History Magazine* 14 (May 1921): 222–24. A brief, general statement about Hungarian-American relations by an individual interested in promoting such relations.

Kósa, John. "A Century of Hungarian Emigration, 1850–1950," *American Slavic and East European Review* 16 (December 1957): 501–14. One of the most compact and useful explanations of the phenomenon and character of Hungarian immigration to America; emphasizes more the point of departure rather than the point of arrival.

Marchbin, Andrew. "Hungarian Activities in Western Pennsylvania," *Western Pennsylvania Historical Magazine* 23 (1940): 163–74. A brief survey of the activities, mostly social and organizational, of Hungarians in this region. Minimal concern with cultural matters.

P. A. "The Hungarian Invasion," *Theatre Magazine,* January 1913, pp. 14–16. This listing and brief characterization of Hungarian dramatists and other theatrical professionals on the New York stage provides telling testimony to the interest in Hungarian drama by Americans in the early twentieth century.

Patric, John. "Magyar Mirth and Melancholy," *National Geographic* 73, no. 1 (Jan. 1938): 1–55. A general characterization of Hungarian life and popular culture, useful as background.

Pentzell, Raymond J. "A Hungarian Christmas Mummers' Play in Toledo, Ohio," *Educational Theatre Journal* 29 (May 1977): 179–98. Detailed study, discusses the relationship of the play as presented in the United States with its Hungarian origin.

Phillips, Henry Albert. "Hungary's Impress on World Theatre," *Theatre Magazine,* Aug. 1928, pp. 20–56 passim. A brief article documenting the impact of Hungarian theatrical professionals on the New York stage in the first quarter of the century.

Popkin, Henry. "The Brilliance, Dazzle and Despair of the East European Stage," *New York Times,* July 31, 1977, pp. 4-D, 18-D. The writer discusses contemporary Hungarian theatre and calls attention to its broader cultural significance; also stresses the extent of knowledge about the American theatre in Hungary.

Puskás, Juliana. "A magyar szervezetek Amerikában" ("*The Hungarian Organizations in America*"), *Törté-nelmi Szemle (Historical Review)* 13, no. 4 (1970): 528–68. The historical research of this writer concerning Hungarian organizations in the United States is significant in determining the profile and activities of numerous organizations, including some engaged in theatrical activity.

Schaaf, Barbara. "Magyars of the Midwest," *Chicago Tribune Magazine,* May 6, 1979, pp. 22–36 passim. This account of Hungarians in the greater Chicago area provides some information about theatrical activity in the 1920s.

Szendrey, Tamás. "Az emigrációs magyar irodalom válsága ("*The Crisis of Hungarian Emigré Literature*"). In János Nádas and Ferenc Somogyi, eds., *A XVI. Magyar Találkozó Krónikája. (The Proceedings of the 16th Hungarian Congress.)* Cleveland: Árpád Kiadó, 1977, pp. 30–32.

Speculates about the past and future of Hungarian literary efforts and consciousness outside Hungary.

Várdy, S. B. "Hungarians in America's Ethnic Politics." In Joseph S. Roucek and Bernard Eisenberg, eds., *America's Ethnic Politics*. Westport, Conn.: Greenwood Press, 1982. This well-researched account provides valuable and useful background for the study of cultural life in the Hungarian-American community.

Other Sources

In addition to the books, articles, interviews, and letters cited, this study is based upon unpublished sources in my possession concerning the Déryné Theater of Cleveland and interviews and correspondence with many individuals active in both professional and amateur Hungarian-American theatre with information about the theatre. I have also used the Hungarian paper *Szabadság* for the years 1934, 1936, 1937, 1946, and 1947 and other selected issues, as well as other Hungarian newspapers and periodicals, especially for the events of the past fifteen years. Mention should also be made of the Ferenc Molnár collection in the New York Public Library.

9

Irish-American Theatre

MAUREEN MURPHY

The Irish who came to America, even those who arrived before the Great Famine of 1845–1847, came without a highly developed native drama. While there are dramatic elements in early and medieval Irish literature, drama in the conventional sense grew as the result of English influence and the growth of towns. There was almost no theatrical activity outside Dublin in the seventeenth and early eighteenth century, and in Dublin even the Smock Alley Theatre did not encourage native drama as much as it offered fare from the London stage for the amusement of the Anglo-Irish ascendancy.[1]

During the nineteenth century the Irish in larger country towns were introduced to the theatre through visits of companies of traveling players. Amhlaoibh O'Súilleabháin mentions three such visits to Callan, County Kilkenny, in 1829, 1831, and 1832 in his remarkable journal *Cín Lae Amhlaoibh*.[2] It is likely, however, that most Irish country people did not see even those rural performances. For those living in the northern and eastern counties, there were mummers' plays, also introduced by British settlers. The plays, acted by boys and young men, involved a combatant's death and his revival. While they were traditionally performed at Christmas, some aspects of the plays—costumes and processions—were features of other Irish calendar festivals.[3]

Dramatic activities were frequently part of Irish weddings and wakes. Sean O'Sullivan describes such music, dance, storytelling, and games in *Irish Wake Amusements*. Two of the more elaborate imitative games, "Sir Soipín or The Knight of Straw," and "Nuala and Dáithí" even included improvisational dialogue and costumes.[4] O'Sullivan suggests that these wake traditions were survivals of the customs associated with the great fairs of Ancient Ireland, which originated at the funeral games for the high kings.[5] Although the nineteenth-century Irish, particularly the country people, may have been unfamiliar with the theatre, they were well acquainted with the popular pastimes of Irish rural society, the music, dance, storytelling, and recitations of local talent and of itinerant fiddlers, pipers, poets, propheciers, and storytellers. Prefamine fiction is full of examples of these figures. When the Irish came to America, they brought these traditional forms of entertainment; therefore the Irish became associated with music and dance in their portrayal on the American stage.

THE STAGE IRISHMAN

The development of Irish drama in America can be divided into five stages: the period before 1830, 1830–1860, 1860–1890, 1890–1918, and 1918 to the present. The Irish who emigrated before the famine were generally better prepared for American life than those who emigrated at midcentury. They usually had some education and some financial means and were emigrating to improve opportunity rather than to escape starvation. For the most part these Irish were quickly assimilated into eighteenth- and nineteenth-century American life. Indeed, when the stage Irishman made his first appearance in farces by English and Irish playwrights, he was an amusing caricature who bore little or no resemblance to the reality of the Irish in America. His type was best described by Maurice Bourgeois.

The stage Irishman habitually bears the generic name of Pat, Paddy or Teague. He has an atrocious Irish brogue, makes perpetual jokes, blunders and bulls in speaking, and never fails to utter, by way of Hibernian seasoning, some screech or oath of Gaelic origin at every third word; he has an unsurpassable gift of "blarney" and cadges for tips and free drinks. His hair is of a fiery red; he is rosy-cheeked, massive and whiskey loving. His face is one of simian bestiality, with an expression of diabolical archness written all over it. He wears a tall felt hat (billicock or wideawake) with a cutty clay pipe stuck in front, an open shirt-collar, a three-caped coat, knee-breeches, worsted stocking and cockaded brogue shoes. In his right hand he brandishes a stout blackthorn or a sprig of shillelagh, and threatens to belabor therewith the darling person who will "tread on the tails of his coat." For his main characteristic (if there is any such thing as psychology in the stage Irishman) are his swagger, his boisterousness and his pugnacity. He is always ready with a challenge, always anxious to pick a quarrel; and peerless for cracking skulls at Donnybrook fair.[6]

The stage Irishman appeared in a number of plays in the 1820s. *The Poor Soldier*, popular in New Orleans in 1820, was played in Brooklyn by "a respectable company" in 1826. *The Irishman in London; St. Patrick's Day; Love in a Camp, or Patrick in Prussia; Sons of Erin;* and *The Irish Widow* were also performed during the 1820s.[7] Richard Butler, the earl of Glengall's English farce *The Irish Tutor*, which made its American debut at the Park Theatre in New York in 1823, also had a New Orelans run. In addition to plays featuring the stage Irishman, James McHenry's portrayal of early Irish history, *The Usurper*, appeared in New York in 1827; the following year there were productions of James Sheridan Knowles's *Brian Boroihme, or The Maid of Erin;* of Richard Butler's *Brian the Brave;* and of George Pepper's *Ireland Redeemed.*

The early success of the stage Irishman in America prompted drama historian Margaret G. Maryoga's remark, "The stage Irishman is as old as America drama itself."[8] This figure, which appeared in plays set in Ireland, was one of a trio of

Irish types that developed between 1830 and 1860; the others were the stage Irish immigrant and a native American folk hero based on Irish immigrant antecedents. Stage Irishmen in plays like Samuel Lover's *Rory O'More*; Tyrone Power's *St. Patrick's Eve, or The Order of the Day*; and J. B. Buckstone's *The Irish Lion* continued to be in demand not only in the eastern United States but also along the frontier and in San Francisco, where twenty-eight such plays were performed between 1851 and 1859.[9] In part the success of such plays was based on their association with famous actors or actor-managers like Tyrone Power, John Brougham, Dion Boucicault, and Barney Williams, who made Irish comic characters their specialty.

The American stage Irish immigrant type, a character who shared many traits with the stage Irishman but who appeared in an American setting and whose humor, like much other ethnic humor, depended on the contrast between the speech and culture of the immigrant Irish and those of the native American, appeared in the plays of John Brougham (1810–1880). Said to be the original for Charles Lever's *Harry Lorrequer* and known for his portrayal of Hamlet with a heavy Irish brogue, Dublin-born Brougham made his American debut as Felix O'Callaghan in *His Last Legs* in 1842. Among his seventy-five plays and sketches, his Irish immigrant plays, *The Irish Yankee, or The Birthday of Freedom* (1840) and *Temptation, or The Irish Emigrant* (1849), were particular favorites. While the characters are stage immigrant types, the poor but honest character of Pat in *The Irish Emigrant* make the Irishman something more than burlesque. Another play, *The Game of Love* (1855), anticipated the lace-curtain Irish cartoon characters Jiggs and Maggie in its satire of a socially ambitious wife, who changes her name from Murphy to De Merfie when her husband makes his fortune.

The early acceptance of the stage Irishman and stage immigrant by both Irish and non-Irish began to change in the years between 1830 and 1860. They enjoyed great popularity on the American stage, but on the other hand, the types seemed to be cruel and crude caricatures, meant to represent, at some level of reality, poor Irish immigrants. For example, the *New Orleans Picayune* included several reports of court news in which writers compared the behavior of Irish immigrants in New Orleans with that of Irish stage characters.[10] Some began to protest this image of the Irish. J. C. Prendergast of *The Orleanian* wrote in 1853 that he had never met any Irish as poor or debased as the Irish immigrant characters in the Irish-Yankee sketches of Barney Williams and his wife Maria Pray.[11] In New York two Irishmen were ejected from the theatre for hissing during a revival of Tyrone Power's *O'Flannigan and the Fairies* (1837) in 1847.

MOSE THE BOWERY B'HOY

While the stage Irishman and the stage immigrant flourished in the American theatre, an original comic character, based on an Irish immigrant type, swaggered onto the stage in Benjamin Baker's *A Glance at New York* (1848). He was

Mose the Bowery B'hoy—boaster and brawler, heroic fire fighter, and guardian angel of the greenhorns and of Linda the Cigar Girl. Whether or not Mose was in fact based on Mose Humphrey, a printer for the *New York Sun* and a volunteer fireman with Lady Washington Engine No. 40, the character owes its origin to Irish firemen in city volunteer companies.[12]

The Irish were drawn to fire companies by the excitement, the camaraderie, the horseplay, and the prestige associated with company uniforms and equipment. The companies maintained fierce rivalries, raced one another to fires, and often fought over control of the water supply. Since the fireman was a well-known city figure, Mose was a great success in the decade between 1848 and 1858. *A Glance at New York* was followed with a number of Mose adventures, notably *A Glance at Philadelphia!* (1848), *The Mysteries and Miseries of New York* (1850), *New York as It Is* (1851), *Linda the Cigar Girl, or Mose among the Conspirators* (1856), and *Mose in California* (1857). In addition Mose inspired other fireman plays, including S. D. Johnson's *The Fireman* (1849), John Brougham's *Life in New York, or Tom and Jerry on a Visit* (1856), and Dion Boucicault's *The Poor of New York* (1857), which featured Dan the Fireman battling a blaze in a tenement. When municipal fire companies replaced the colorful volunteer companies and the steam engine came into service, the Mose figure vanished from the stage, but a heroic Irish fireman archetype lived on in Finley Peter Dunne's account of Chicago fireman Mike Clancy's last fire.[13]

By the mid-nineteenth century the Irish immigrants were beginning to fulfill the prophecy of Thomas D'Arcy McGee and others that, given the opportunity, they would take their places in American life among the leading citizens. The Civil War was a crucible for that integration; Irish volunteers on both sides helped destroy the anti-Irish, anti-Catholic nativism that manifested itself in the Know-Nothing party and in the signs, "No Irish Need Apply."

ROMANTIC NATIONALISM

Dion Boucicault

Irish drama in America between 1860 and 1890 reflects this change in its two major aspects, both comic: in the romantic nationalism of Dion Boucicault's Irish melodramas, particularly *The Colleen Bawn* (1860), *Arrah-na-Pogue* (1864), and *The Shaughraun* (1874), and in the realistic sketches of Edward Harrigan's urban Irish immigrants in the Mulligan cycle (1878–1884).

Dublin-born Boucicault made his London stage debut, under the name Lee Moreton, as Teddy Rodent, an Irish rat catcher in *A Legend of the Devil Dyke* (1838). When he arrived in America in 1853, Boucicault was known as an actor for his portrayal of rogue heroes and as a prolific playwright for a series of translations, adaptations, and original comedies and melodramas.

Boucicault's attitude toward Irish nationalism was careful. Aware that contemporary Irish plays like *Brian Boreimhe, or The Maid of Erin, Brian the Brave,*

Ireland Redeemed, and *The Red Branch Knight, or Ireland Triumphant* romanticized Irish history for the Irish immigrant, he wrote *The Raparee, or The Treaty of Limerick* (1870) and *Robert Emmet* (1884). The Emmet play is of particular interest because in addition to his usual romantic, melodramatic treatment, Boucicault recognized the symbolic importance of Emmet to Ireland and to Irish nationalism.[14] In writing *Arrah-na-Pogue* and *The Shaughraun,* however, Boucicault followed the practice he established in *The Octoroon* (1859), a play about slavery written two months after John Brown's raid. By both recognizing the injustice of slavery and sympathizing with the end of the way of life its loss threatened, he offended neither North nor South.

Boucicault treated Fenianism in much the same manner, with the result that *The Shaughraun* was received with equal appreciation in Dublin, in London, and in the United States.[15] While in *The Shaughraun* a Fenian rebel lands on the Mayo coast and there are references to Manchester and Clerkenwell, Boucicault defused the politics by teaming the English Captain Molinieux and the Fenian Robert Ffolliott against Squireen Corny Kinchela and the police informer, Harvey Duff. The play was not without its political message, which was humanitarian rather than partisan. Conn the Shaughraun's plea for the release of Irish prisoners from English jails was echoed in Boucicault's letter to Benjamin Disraeli. The letter asked for the same compassion in releasing Fenian prisoners as was manifested in the *deus ex machina* pardon that occurs at the end of the play.

Arrah-na-Pogue, set in Wicklow in 1798, balances the rebel heroes Beamish MacCoul, whose name suggests the Irish mythic hero Finn MacCoul, and Arrah-na-Pogue, a figure for Anne Devlin, the faithful servant who refused to betray Robert Emmet, with a sympathetic portrayal of the English military. Major Coffin is rigid and arbitrary, but he is just; the sergeant who guards Shaun the Post befriends him and gives him news of Arrah; and the British officers respect The O'Grady, an aristocrat of the old Gaelic order. However sympathetically Boucicault treated his English characters, however, Queen Victoria still banned singing of Boucicault's "The Wearing of the Green" from English performances of the play.

In both *The Shaughraun* and *Arrah-na-Pogue,* Boucicault relied on the melodramatic structure, which has as one of its conventions the restoration of order, to maintain a light hand in dealing with the English policy of treating Irish political activists as criminals. He shared this theme with writers of nineteenth-century Irish fiction, who made it the basis for serious social comment.

Boucicault's romanticism, which complemented his nationalism, was the romanticism of an Irish exile. As Beamish MacCoul thinks of leaving Ireland for the last time, his speech is full of emigrant ballad clichés, which nevertheless reflect the anguish of separation.

See, the morning is beginning to tip the heights of Mullacor; we must part. In a few hours I shall be on the sea, bound for a foreign land; perhaps never again shall I hear your voices nor see my native hills. Oh, my own land! Bless every blade or grass upon your green cheeks. The clouds that hang over ye are the sighs of your exiled children and your face is always wet with their tears. Eirne meelish, shlawn loth! Fare ye well! And you, dear Abbey of St. Kevin, around which the bones of forefathers are laid.[16]

Boucicault further dramatized the romantic image of Ireland with his blushing colleens, broths of boys, genial parish priests, neatly thatched cottages, carefree songs and dances—all lightly laced with *poitín* and patriotism.

Much of the success of these three Boucicault plays can be attributed to the clever peasant characters of Myles na gCopaleen in *The Colleen Bawn*, Shaun the Post in *Arrah-na-Pogue*, and Conn the Shaughraun. Some critics suggest their origin is in the parasite-slave of Roman comedy; however, Boucicault found the models for his Irish heroes in native American dramatic figures like Mose and the Yankee.[17] Neither rogues nor romantic heroes, these characters are distinguished by their inherent kindness and loyalty, which make them protectors but not suitors of the heroines, by their knowledge of traditional lore, and by their instinctive courtesy and nobility.

Edward Harrigan

Influenced by Boucicault, the early Irish plays of Edward Harrigan (1845–1911) were the derivative *Arrah-na-Brogue* (1873) and the melodramas set in Ireland, *Iascaire* (1876) and *The Logaire* (1878). At the same time Harrigan began work on a comic series based on Dan Mulligan, an Irish immigrant grocer. Harrigan's affectionate portrayal of Mulligan is an improvement over the earlier stage Irish figures. Although Mulligan is impulsive and given to drinking and fighting with little provocation, he is honest, generous, and loyal in his high-spiritedness. Harrigan's sketches differed from the plays of Brougham and Boucicault in that they did not portray the Irish in opposition to Yankee or English authority, but focused instead on those Irish who achieved some local status in ward politics (*The Mulligan Guard*, 1873). The competition between the Irish and black fraternal orders was the subject of *The Mulligan Guards and the Skidmores* (1875); further rivalry was introduced with the German butcher Gustave Lochmuller in *The Mulligan Guard Picnic* (1878, revised 1880).

The Mulligan sketches took more definite form in *The Mulligan Guard Ball* (1879), a play with a Romeo-and-Juliet plot involving the marriage of Tom Mulligan to Katrina Lochmuller. It was an instant success, and others followed: *The Mulligan Guard Chowder* (1879), *The Mulligan Guard Christmas* (1879), *The Mulligan Guard Surprise* (1880), *The Mulligan Guard Nominee* (1880), and *The Mulligans' Silver Wedding* (1891). Essential to the success of Harrigan's plays were the actors—Harrigan himself and his partner Tony Hart (Anthony Cannon)—and the humorous, sentimental songs written by Harrigan's father-in-law David Braham. Harrigan's plays were widely admired in their time. William Dean Howells, the American novelist, saw in the New York plays the beginning of American comedy.[18]

The last two Mulligan plays, *Cordelia's Aspirations* (1883) and *Dan's Tribulations* (1884), chronicle the rise and fall of the Mulligans: their move from Mulligan's Alley uptown to Madison Avenue, Cordelia's efforts to be accepted by New York society, and their return to their old neighborhood when their fortunes are reversed. In these transformations Harrigan more fully develops the characters of Cordelia and Dan Mulligan. Their loyalty and devotion to each other and their willingness to start over and work hard to rebuild their lives were attractive qualities in themselves and reinforced the growing image of the Irish in America as not only high spirited, but also responsible and trustworthy.

After the successful Mulligan series, Harrigan's later, less successful Irish plays turned from the immigrants who enjoyed local prestige and success to those involved in a more urgent reality. *Squatter Sovereignty* (1882), while an amusing study of social distinction among the poor, was a play about the legal rights to the shantytown at the foot of East 72nd Street. *The Leather Patch* (1886) was a study of New York "low life."

Harrigan and Hart parted in 1885; by 1895 Harrigan's popularity had declined. Large numbers of Irish were moving into the middle class and enjoying increased respectability. As the Irish attained more respectability, Harrigan's characters ceased to be recognizable. These Irish wanted to replace the images of the stage Irishman and stage immigrant with more appropriate images of Irish identity.

THEATRE AND POLITICS

Irish drama in the years between 1890 and 1918 reflected the growth of Irish political power. Not only did the Irish control urban politics in major American cities, but they also began to exert influence on national politics and, in their concern for Irish home rule, on international politics. Harrigan's *The Mulligan Guard Nominee*, a satire on then-current electioneering that set Dan Mulligan against Gustave Lochmuller for alderman, can be considered a forerunner of political drama in America. According to Caspar H. Nannes, political drama came late because few theatre managers were willing to risk controversial subjects on the stage until after 1890, when new sources of information made people more aware of political issues and playwrights and producers took advantage of this interest.[19]

Local elections were the substance of the political plays of the 1890s. In A. Gratton Donnelly's *A Tammany Tiger* (1896), rival candidates are competing not only for the same office but for the same girl. E. W. Townsend's *McFadden's Row of Flats* (1897) and the anonymous *McSorley's Twins* (1897), two Harrigan imitations, involve alderman contests, in the latter against a background of Irish-American songs, dances, and jokes.

Plays of the next decade focused on political leadership. George H. Broadhurst's *The Man of the Hour* (1906) was based on the story of New York mayor George McClellan, who sacrificed his political career in 1906 when he repudiated his backer, Tammany boss Charles Francis Murphy. Murphy also was the model for Boss Haggerty in James S. Barcus's *The Governor's Boss* (1914), a dramatization of the impeachment of New York governor William Sulzer in 1913. Michael Regan, the hero of Edward Sheldon's play *The Boss* (1911), is a labor leader, not a politician, but the loyalty required by both organizations is the same. Regan is a ruthless man but he has his own integrity. When Porkey McCoy, acting on Regan's orders, almost kills Donald Griswold, a Regan enemy, Regan accepts the responsibility.

At the national level Irish-American political involvement focused on the question of Irish independence. Between 1900 and 1910 Irish nationalist movements in the United States—both the constitutionalists, favoring home rule, and the physical force advocates, favoring total separation of Ireland from England—rebuilt their organizations. The result, according to Francis Carroll in his study *American Opinion and the Irish Question, 1910–1923*, was that Irish-American and sympathetic general American interest in the Irish question made the nationalist movement in Ireland far stronger than it would otherwise have been.[20] At no time in the history of Irish drama in the United States were drama and politics so closely involved.

As early as the 1880s the two nationalist positions were represented in Boucicault's *Robert Emmet* (1884), with its revolutionary hero, and in Harrigan's *The O'Regans* (1886), with its more moderate home rule advocate. Perhaps the best measure of the importance of drama to Irish nationalism is a description of the Irish pageant. This pageant was written by Anna Throop Craig and produced by the American Committee of the Gaelic League of Ireland in May 1913 at the Sixty-Ninth Street Regiment Armory in New York. The Irish Historic Pageant involved five-hundred participants: Gaelic societies, the Irish-American Athletic League, and members of the Sixty-Ninth Street Regiment. Divided into two parts, the Ireland of the Fianna and the Ireland of the sixth century, the Pageant was designed to present Ireland's past in the context of its aspirations for home rule.[21]

THE ABBEY TOUR

Given the strong Irish-American involvement in home rule and the concern about the image of the Irishman at home and in America, the 1911 tour by the Irish Abbey Theatre was the cause of some anxiety—indeed, hostility. Many Irish Americans felt that some of the Abbey plays, particularly John Millington's Synge's *Playboy of the Western World,* would jeopardize their hard-won respectability and political influence. The Abbey Players were not the first group of Irish actors to visit America. Some Dublin actors arrived at the St. Louis Exhibition in 1904 to stage AE's (George Russell's) play *Deirdre* (1902). The play was not a success. Since the company had nothing else to offer, the Irish company's effort was replaced after a few days by *An Irishman's Stratagem*. Dublin papers complained that "the hated stereotype of the 'stage Irishman'" had been substituted for the Dublin play.[22] *Deirdre* had failed because it was a weak play; however, *Playboy of the Western World*, denounced in Dublin for its immorality and anti-Irishness, aroused the same hostility in America.

As soon as the Abbey Players arrived in Boston on September 29, 1911, the controversy started. A series of articles appearing in the Jesuit weekly *America* during September, October, and November denounced the Irish theatre, and *Gaelic America* for October 14, 1911, carried this resolution from the United Irish-American Societies of New York:

Resolved—That we, the United Irish-American Societies of New York, make every reasonable effort, through a committee, to induce those responsible for the presentation of *The Playboy* to withdraw it, and failing in this we pledge ourselves to drive the vile thing from the stage, as we drove McFadden's Row of Flats and the abomination produced by the Russell Brothers, and we ask the aid in this work of every decent Irish man and woman, and of the Catholic Church, whose doctrines and devotional practices are held up to scorn and ridicule in Synge's monstrosity.[23]

Lady Augusta Gregory, one of the Abbey's directors, protested that the examples quoted as offensive had been cut, but the Irish-American Societies were determined to drive the *Playboy* from the American stage. *Playboy* performances were challenged in every city. Mayors' representatives or police officials attended the play to investigate charges against it. In Philadelphia, after a record audience at the last *Playboy* matinee, the Abbey Players were arrested for presenting an indecent play. The case was dismissed. When the company arrived in Chicago, its last stop, an "Anti-Irish Players League" claimed to have a petition signed by eight thousand people, but the protest did not trouble the *Playboy's* run. Irish-American organizations protested without success; the theatres were filled with Abbey enthusiasts, and Lady Gregory remarked after the tour, "We were never stopped for a single night; our curtain was never lowered till the end of the act."[24]

It would be an oversimplification to suggest that while theatres were packed for Abbey performances, all the Irish Americans demonstrated outside. Many appreciated the efforts of Lady Gregory and William Butler Yeats to produce plays that would add to Ireland's dignity. Mary Boyle O'Reilly's *Boston Sunday Post* review reflects this appreciation.

Lady Gregory and William Butler Yeats have trained their players to interpret to the children of Irish emigrants the brave and beautiful and touching memories which, through the ignorance of the second generation, have ceased to be cause for gratitude or pride.

Not this alone: by their fine art, the players have dealt a death blow to the coarse and stupid burlesque of the traditional stage Irishman, who has, for years, outraged every man and woman of Celtic ancestry by gorilla-like buffoonry and grotesque attempts at brogue.[25]

An outgrowth of the Abbey tour was the impetus the Irish players and playwrights gave to the development of the little theatre movement in America. Maryoga credits Yeats's visit to America in 1903–1904 with inspiring a group of New Yorkers under the direction of Joseph I. C. Clarke "to promote a movement for the endowment of an arts theatre."[26] Montrose J. Moses attributes the establishment of Mrs. Lyman W. Gale's little theatre in Boston directly to the Abbey tour.[27] Beginning in 1915 the works of Irish playwrights Lord Dunsany (Edward John Morton Plunkett), George Bernard Shaw, Yeats, and James Joyce were produced under the direction of Helen Arthur, Agnes Morgan, and Alice and Irene Lewisohn at the Neighborhood Playhouse on Grand Street, New York City. For a while the Irish Theatre of America made its home in the Neighborhood Playhouse.[28]

EUGENE O'NEILL

The most significant Irish-American connection with the little theatre movement was the association by Eugene O'Neill (1888–1953) with the Provincetown Players that began with the production of Bound East for Cardiff in 1916. Like his earlier "lost" plays, Bound East for Cardiff reflects the influence of the dramatists of the Irish literary revival, particularly the romantic naturalism of Synge and the Irish-American tradition of Boucicault and Harrigan. While some critics have viewed Bound East for Cardiff as a study in alienation and loneliness, Yank's isolation as he dies among indifferent shipmates is ameliorated by Driscoll's loyalty, a theme central to Irish drama.[29]

Since O'Neill's use of his Irish-American background has been the subject of major critical attention, this discussion will focus on the aspect of his Irish-American sensibility that he shared with other dramatists dealing with Irish Americans in the post-1918 period, the conflict between an individual's obligation to self, on the one hand, and the claims of family and of the Church, on the other. The increase in Irish-American prosperity and respectability, combined with the religious piety that characterized postfamine Irish Catholicism, produced an idealization of family ties, which were already strong. That idealization encouraged the young to sacrifice themselves for their families and the old to maintain control over their families to insure their own status and security in old age. Family pressure was reinforced by the Church. This tension between individual goals and family solidarity and respectability is focused most intensely in O'Neill's finest play, perhaps America's finest play, Long Day's Journey into Night. John Henry Raleigh's analysis of the autobiographical and cultural contexts of the play argues that New England Irish Catholicism provides "the folkways and mores, the character types, the interrelationships between characters, the whole attitude toward life that informs Long Day's Journey and gives it its meaning."[30]

Other playwrights of the post-1918 period have examined this conflict of loyalty between the individual and the Irish-American institutions of family,

Church, and politics. The secret marriage between Abraham Levy and Rose-Mary Murphy in Anne Nichols's popular comedy *Abie's Irish Rose* (1922) offers an example of that conflict. In Philip Barry's *The Joyous Season* (1934), a family of Boston Irish is provided with an understanding of the way family members' happiness is limited by the ideals of society and respectability. The lack of such understanding, frequently demonstrated by the lack of communication and the tension between family members, is the theme of plays like Frank Gilroy's *The Subject was Roses* (1965) and plays from Ireland that have been popular in America, like Brian Friel's *Philadelphia, Here I Come* (1965) and Hugh Leonard's *Da* (1978).

Although Raleigh characterizes the Irish and Irish Americans as excessively familial and noncommunal, the dominant themes in Irish and Irish-American plays reveal that other Irish-American institutions demand the same loyalty and subordination of the individual required by the family.[31] Emmet Lavery's *The First Legion* (1934) examines a young priest's loyalty to his superior over a question of belief in a miracle. For a chance to be mayor, Matt Stanton, the hero of William Alfred's play about Irish-American Brooklyn in the 1890s, *Hogan's Goat* (1965), betrays the loyalty of the two women who love him.

DRAMA SOCIETIES

Less well known than the professional productions of Irish and Irish-American plays, the work of Irish-American drama societies has had a more direct influence on the Irish-American community. The Thomas Davis Irish Players (TDIP) the oldest Irish drama group in New York, began its forty-eighth season in 1980.[32] Founded in 1933 by Irish students enrolled in evening high schools, the TDIP took its name from the Irish nationalist Thomas Davis (1814–1845), whose maxim "educate that you may be free" is the TDIP motto.

The founders, Daniel Danaher, John Duffy, Joseph O'Reilly, Mary Kelly, Thomas McDermott, Martin Walsh, and John Hughes, produced their first play, Edward McNulty's *The Courting of Mary Doyle*, in 1934. The following year the TDIP accepted an invitation to perform for the Parish Club of St. Barnabas Church; in this way, it established the precedent of appearing under local sponsorship at parish, school, and Irish-American fraternal activities throughout the New York region. As an organization with the goal of transmitting Irish culture through Irish drama, the TDIP has also participated in many special Irish-American cultural events. It has presented such plays as Daniel Corkery's *Resurrection* and Yeats's *Cathleen ni Houlihan* in several Easter Week commemorations, observances of the rising in Dublin that began on Easter Monday in 1916. It also performed plays in Philadelphia and Providence in 1976 for the Irish bicentennial organizations in those cities. It brought its production of P. H. Pearse's *The Singer* to the Comhairle na gCumann Gaeilge Drama Festival held at Iona College in 1966, a festival that featured plays in Irish as well as in English.[33] Pearse's life was the subject of an original TDIP play in

1979, written at the request of the American Patrick Pearse Centenary Committee.

The TDIP constitution restricts its productions to Irish or Irish-American plays. Selections of the two plays produced each season are based on audience appeal; most have been successful at the Abbey. Since the TDIP does not have a permanent theatre, feasibility as well as casting considerations are also part of the decision. Two plays particularly popular with their audiences have been John Murphy's *The Country Boy* (1960) and John B. Keane's *Many Young Men of Twenty* (1961), both of which involve emigration; an Irish emigrant's return to Ireland from America and a family's anguish about emigration to England in the 1950s.

In addition to the TDIP there are two other Irish-American drama groups, which were founded in New York in the 1970s: the Irish Rebel Theatre at the Irish Arts Center (1972), which produces four plays each year, two revivals and two original works of Irish or Irish-American writers, and the Committee on Irish Ethnicity's Travelling Theatre (1974), which offered one-act plays to New York audiences for a season before turning its efforts to establishment of a museum and folk center in New York City.

The larger role of drama in transmitting Irish culture that has been demonstrated by these Irish-American groups is a measure of the vitality of Irish drama in America today. Amateur and professional companies regularly offer plays by Irish and Irish-American writers; playwrights continue to write about the Irish and the Irish-American experience; and both Irish-American and non-Irish-American audiences support this theatre. Irish drama in the United States, in its growth in characterization of the Irish from the caricature in farce to the sympathetic hero of a realistic play, has informed American understanding of the Irish identity and of the Irish-American experience. In doing so, Irish drama in the United States has enlarged the ideal of the founders of the Abbey Theatre—to work for the dignity of Ireland—to include fostering Irish-American pride in the Irish heritage.

NOTES

1. William Philip's *St. Stephen's Green: or, the Generous Lover* (1699 or 1700) was the first Smock Alley production set in Dublin, but it was Charles Shadwell's Squire Dandle's speech about his maid in *The Hasty Wedding* that first urged the Irish to take pride in their heritage: "It is not above two years ago, sure she was taken out of an Irish Cabin, with her Brogues on, and yet begins to despise her own Country, and is fond of everything that's English." William Smith Clark, *The Early Irish Stage: The Beginnings to 1720* (Oxford: Clarendon Press, 1955), p. 159.

2. Tomás de Bhaldraithe, ed., *Cín Lae Amhlaoibh* (Baile Átha Cliath: An Clóchomhar, 1970), pp. 57, 92, 95.

3. Caoimhín O'Danachair, *A Bibliography of Irish Ethnology and Folk Tradition* (Dublin: Mercier Press, 1978), p. 42, lists several studies of Irish mummers' plays. The best is Alan Gailey, *Irish Folk Drama* (Cork: Mercier Press, 1969). A survival of a mummers' play was collected by Marie Campbell in Kentucky in the 1930s. Marie Campbell,

"Survivals of Old Folk Drama in the Kentucky Mountains," in Richard M. Dorson, ed., *Buying the Wind* (Chicago: University of Chicago Press, 1964), pp. 215–33.

4. Sean O'Sullivan, *Irish Wake Amusements* (Cork: Mercier Press, 1967), pp. 89–90.

5. Ibid., p. 164. In her summary description of the pagan rites of the festival of Lughnasa, Máire MacNeill suggests that ritual dance plays may have been part of the celebration of the Celtic harvest festival. Máire MacNeill, *The Festival of Lughnasa* (London: Oxford University Press, 1962), p. 426.

6. Maurice Bourgeois, *John Millington Synge and the Irish Theatre* (London: Constable, 1913), pp. 109–10. See also J. O. Bartley, *Teague, Shenkin and Sawney* (Cork: Cork University Press, 1954), and George C. Duggan, *The Stage Irishman* (London: Longmans, Green, 1937).

7. Earl F. Niehaus, *The Irish in New Orleans, 1800–1860* (Baton Rouge: Louisiana State University Press, 1965), pp. 14–15; William Sharp, A *History of the Diocese of Brooklyn 1853–1953* (New York: Fordham University Press, 1954), Vol. 1, p. 316, n. 43.

8. Margaret G. Maryoga, A *Short History of the American Drama* (New York: Dodd, Mead and Co., 1943), p. 247.

9. William Carson, *The Theatre on the Frontier* (New York: Benjamin Blom, 1932), pp. 202, 289, 297, 303, 313; Joseph Gaer, ed., *The Theatre of the Gold Rush Decade in San Francisco* (New York: Burt Franklin, 1970), pp. 30–31.

10. Niehaus, *Irish in New Orleans*, pp. 124–25.

11. Ibid., p. 126.

12. Richard M. Dorson, "Mose the Far-Famed and World Renowned," *American Literature* 15 (March 1943–January 1944): 288–300.

13. Finley Peter Dunne, "The Popularity of Firemen," in Charles Fanning, ed., *Mr. Dooley and the Chicago Irish: An Anthology* (New York: Arno Press, 1976), pp. 161–65.

14. See discussion in Harold Ferrar, "Robert Emmet in Irish Drama," *Eire-Ireland* 1 (1966): 19–28.

15. The first Fenian attempt to invade Canada occurred on June 1, 1866, and the Clerkenwell and Manchester episodes followed in England in 1867. Thomas D'Arcy McGee, who opposed Fenianism, was assassinated in Canada in 1868; he was Canada's first political martyr. There was a second unsuccessful Fenian attempt to invade Canada in 1870.

16. Dion Boucicault, *Arrah-na-Pogue*, in David Krause, ed., *The Dolmen Boucicault* (Dublin: Dolmen Press, 1964), p. 115.

17. Ibid., pp. 39–40. The most direct influence of Mose on Boucicault was in the character of Dan the Fireman in *The Poor of New York*.

18. William Dean Howells, "Editor's Study," *Harper's*, July 1886, pp. 315–16.

19. Casper H. Nannes, *Politics in the American Drama* (Washington, D.C.: Catholic University of America Press, 1960), p. 14.

20. Francis M. Carroll, *American Opinion and the Irish Question, 1910–1923* (Dublin: Gill and Macmillan, 1978), p. 192. See also his first two chapters, pp. 1–54.

21. "Irish Historic Pageant in New York," *Outlook* 104 (1913): 258–59.

22. Mary M. Lago, "Irish Poetic Drama in St. Louis," *Twentieth Century Literature* 23 (1977): 186.

23. The anonymous *America* articles were "The Irish Players and Playwrights," *America* 5, no. 25 (1911): 581–82; "Irish Opinion on the Irish Players," 5, no. 26 (1911): 614–15; "Further Opinion and the Irish Players," 6, no. 1 (1911): 11–12; and "Plays That May Not Be Patronized," 6, no. 7 (1911): 159–60. The United Irish-American

Societies resolution was reprinted in Augusta Gregory, *Our Irish Theatre: A Chapter of Autobiography* (Gerrards Cross: Colin Smythe, 1972), p. 222.

24. Ibid., p. 138.

25. Ibid., p. 254.

26. Maryoga, *Short History of American Drama*, p. 301.

27. Montrose J. Moses, *The American Dramatist* (New York: Benjamin Blom, 1964), p. 401.

28. Alice Lewisohn Crowley, *The Neighborhood Playhouse* (New York: Theatre Arts Books, 1959), p. 61.

29. Harry Cronin, *Eugene O'Neill: Irish and American: A Study in Cultural Context* (New York: Arno Press, 1976), p. 45.

30. John Henry Raleigh, "O'Neill's *Long Day's Journey into Night* and New England Irish-Catholicisms," in John Gassner, ed., *O'Neill, A Collection of Critical Essays* (Englewood Cliffs, N.J.: Prentice-Hall, 1964), p. 125.

31. Ibid., p. 128.

32. Conversation with Daniel Danaher, February 5, 1980.

33. The Irish plays were Leon O'Brion's *Labhartar Bearla Annseo* and an original play by Donegal-born Sean Dubh Ua Gallchobair Mac Potair, *Oir Chan Fhaigheann Sibh Braon.*

BIBLIOGRAPHY

Books

Boucicault, Dion. *The Dolmen Boucicault*, edited by David Krause. Dublin: Dolmen Press, 1964. An edition of Boucicault's most successful Irish plays, *The Colleen Bawn, Arrah-na-Pogue,* and *The Shaughraun,* with an excellent introduction by Krause.

Bourgeois, Maurice. *John Millington Synge and the Irish Theatre.* New York: Benjamin Blom, 1965. Chapter 5 discusses Irish drama before Synge and Synge's relationship to the Abbey Theatre.

Brougham, John. *The Game of Love.* New York: S. French, 1856.

————. *The Irish Yankee: or, The Birth-Day of Freedom.* New York: S. French, 1856.

————. *Temptation: or, The Irish Emigrant.* New York: S. French, 1856.

Clark, William Smith. *The Early Irish Stage: The Beginnings in 1720.* Oxford: University Press, 1955. The definitive study of Irish drama, particularly Dublin drama in the seventeenth and eighteenth centuries, with attention to the development of the Smock Alley Theatre. Some discussion of the origin of some Irish character types and themes. Excellent bibliography.

Cronin, Harry. *Eugene O'Neill: Irish and American. A Study in Cultural Context.* New York: Arno Press, 1976. The cultural context of Irish-American Catholicism in O'Neill's plays.

Gailey, Alan. *Irish Folk Drama.* Cork: Mercier Press, 1969. The texts of five Irish mummers' plays, with details of their production and an examination of Irish folk drama as it related to other Irish customs.

Gelb, Arthur, and Gelb, Barbara. *O'Neill.* New York: Harper and Row, 1960. The standard O'Neill biography.

Gregory, Augusta. *Our Irish Theatre: A Chapter of Autobiography.* Gerards Cross: Colin Smythe, 1972. Informal history of the Abbey Theatre. See Chapter 7 for the 1911 Abbey tour. Contemporary accounts in the press, pp. 222–56.

Kahn, Ely. *The Merry Partners: The Age and Stage of Harrigan and Hart.* New York: Random House, 1955. Popular biography of the theatrical team of Edward Harrigan and Tony Hart.

Niehaus, Earl F. *The Irish in New Orleans, 1800–1860.* Baton Rouge: Louisiana State University Press, 1965. Chapter "Irishmen on the Local Stage and in Humor, 1830–1862" is a valuable survey of Irish drama in New Orleans.

O'Neill, Eugene. *The Plays of Eugene O'Neill*, 3 vols. New York: Random House, 1964.
———. *Long Day's Journey Into Night*. New Haven: Yale University Press, 1956.
Potter, George. *To the Golden Door: The Story of the Irish in Ireland and America*. Boston: Little, Brown, 1960. Short theatre section. No references.
Quinn, Arthur Hobson. *A History of the American Drama: American Drama from the Beginning to the Civil War*. New York: Harper and Brothers, 1923. The standard history of American Drama, Chapter 13, Boucicault.
———. *A History of the American Drama: From the Civl War to the Present Day*. New York: F. S. Crofts and Co., 1943. Chapter 4, Harrigan. Chapter 21, O'Neill. Some theorizing about the relationships of culture to personality and about Irish and Irish-American dramatists.
Rourke, Constance. *American Humor*. New York: Harcourt, Brace and Co., 1931. The influence of American folk types on the formation of national character. See Chapter 4, "Strollers," for a discussion of folk types and American drama.
Shannon, William V. *The American Irish*, rev. ed. New York: Macmillan, 1966.

Articles

Anonymous. "Irish Historic Pageant in New York," *Outlook* 104 (1913): 258–59. A description of the Irish Historical Pageant, May 1913, produced by the American Committee of the Gaelic League of Ireland.
Anonymous. "The Irish Players and Playwrights," *America* 5, 25 (1911): 581–582; "Irish Opinion on the Irish Players," 5, 26 (1911): 614–15; "Further Opinion and the Irish Players," 6, 1 (1911): 11–12; and "Plays That May Not Be Patronized" 6, 7 (1911): 159–60. A series of hostile articles in the Jesuit weekly attacking the Abbey Players, particularly the morality of Synge's *Playboy of the Western World.*
Dorson, Richard M. "Mose the Far-Famed and World-Renowned," *American Literature* 15 (1943–1944): 288–300. A history of the figure of Mose the Bowery B'hoy from his first appearance in Benjamin A. Baker's *A Glance at New York* in 1848 until the 1860s, when the Civil War and the introduction of the steam fire engine made Mose obsolete. Checklist of Mose plays.
Ferrar, Harold. "Robert Emmet in Irish Drama," *Eire-Ireland* 1 (1966): 19–28. Survey of the dramatic use of the figure of Robert Emmet, including discussion of Dion Boucicault's *Robert Emmet.*
Lago, Mary M. "Irish Poetic Drama in St. Louis," *Twentieth Century Literature*, 23 (1977): 180–94. Account of the unsuccessful attempt to produce AE's *Deirdre* with a company of Irish actors at the St. Louis World's Fair in 1904.
Raleigh, John Henry. "O'Neill's *Long Day's Journey into Night* and New England Irish-Catholicism," *O'Neill, A Collection of Critical Essays*, edited by John Gassner. Englewood Cliffs, N.J.: Prentice-Hall, 1964, pp. 124–41. O'Neill's autobiographical play as an expression of New England Irish Catholicism.
Rossman, Kenneth. "The Irish in American Drama in the Mid-Nineteenth Century," *New York History* 21 (1940): 39–53. Survey of Irish playwrights and actors in the United States including John Brougham, Dion Boucicault, Tyrone Power, Barney Williams.
Wittke, Carl, "The Immigrant Theme on the American Stage," *Mississippi Valley Historical Review*, 34 (1953): 211–32. The pioneering study of the Irish on the stage.

Other Sources

The theatre collections of the New York Public Library and of Harvard University have particularly strong Irish and Irish-American theatre materials. The New York Public Library has microfilms of Edward Harrigan's typescripts and his scrapbooks (fourteen reels of typescripts, two reels of scrapbooks; news clippings, playbills, and letters.) The New York Public Library also has Dion Boucicault material. Harvard has an excellent collection of Mose the Bowery B'hoy material.

10

Italian-American Theatre

EMELISE ALEANDRI AND
MAXINE SCHWARTZ SELLER

Italian-American theatre arose in response to needs that were common to Italian-American immigrant communities throughout the nation. Therefore, although the names, theatre buildings, streets, and cities were different, the substance of Italian-American theatre was easily recognizable from one location to another. Impresarios toured with their own local companies to other immigrant communities around the country with great acceptance and recognition, and Italian-language dailies in one community often carried news items about theatre groups in other cities.

Because of the relative homogeneity of Italian-American theatre, and because of the paucity of scholarly research and the abundant but scattered nature of the sources, this chapter will focus upon two cities as case studies, New York and San Francisco. The part of the chapter about New York, by Emelise Aleandri, will explore nineteenth-century origins of Italian-American theatre. The part about San Francisco, by Maxine S. Seller, will describe the theatre at its peak in the opening decades of the twentieth century.

ITALIAN-AMERICAN THEATRE IN NINETEENTH-
CENTURY NEW YORK CITY

The history of Italian-American theatre remains consistent with the history of all theatre, in that it reflects the society and times that produced it. The special characteristics of this particular ethnic theatre in the nineteenth-century depended on the sociological patterns and makeup of the Italian immigrant community, in this case specifically in New York City. What follows is a historical investigation into the origins, initial development, and early progress of theatrical activity among resident Italian-American artists performing theatre in Italian for Italian-speaking audiences.

The Italian immigrant theatre in New York City originated and fluctuated, along with the Italian-American population, during specific and faily well-defined periods of immigration. For the purposes of this study, two separate blocks of immigration have been categorized: the whole period leading up to the unification of Italy in 1871 and the postunification period lasting until 1900.

Before 1870

Before the eighteenth century, little if any theatre was performed among Americans, native or immigrant, except the dance rituals of the American Indians, because of the tremendous hardships of the struggling new colonies and in the Northeast, the strong Puritan influence, with its stand against theatrical entertainments. A few Italian immigrants traveled to America at the request and inducement of the American colonies, which found themselves in need of Italian skills and labor, but the performing arts did not appear among them.

During the eighteenth century the reasons for Italian immigration reflected not only America's continuing need for Italian craftsmanship, but also political and religious pressures in Italy. In terms of theatre, the former reason brought scene designers to these shores, such as Charles Ciceri in 1794, who created the scenery for many productions in New York City's John Street Theatre[1] and Park Theatre.[2] But these theatres housed plays geared to Anglo-American, not Italian-American audiences.

During the eighteenth century, according to one author, there was an instance of Italian-American theatre. Pasquale De Biasi, in his chapter "I 50 Anni di Scene di Guglielmo Ricciardi" in Ricciardi's memoirs, provides the only mention of a performance specifically for Italian Americans, in 1765[3]: a Mr. Galluppi and a Mr. Giardini presenting a *commedia-ballata* (comedy ballet, or dance comedy). Theatre historian George C. Odell does not mention this production in his *Annals*, but when writing of this era he is concerned almost entirely with theatre presentations for Americans. None of our other sources for this time segment mention these performers, including the accounts by John Horace Mariono[4] and Howard R. Marraro.[5] Furthermore, De Biasi neglects to give his sources for this emphatic statement about an event at which he could not have been a witness. Hence this remains just a suspicion of a theatre beginning.

During the nineteenth century, political and religious pressures in Italy brought over Lorenzo Da Ponte, known extensively as Mozart's *librettista* and in New York City for his valiant attempts to initiate opera. Da Ponte affords us the first approximation of the Italian-American theatre. In order to promote study of the Italian language at what is now Columbia University, Da Ponte around 1808 wrote short plays in Italian to be performed by his students. He is, therefore; the first recorded Italian-American playwright. He even constructed a little theatre in his home, in which his students performed Vittorio Alfieri's *Mirra* for an audience of 150. But this ambitious attempt failed to spark much interest in continuing the project.[6]

The many Italian political refugees who emigrated from Italy as a result of the turmoil during the attempts at unification of the Italian principalities concerned themselves more with politics than theatre in this country. The other Italian performers who appeared on the New York City stage during the early part of the nineteenth century, such as Donegani's Tumblers, Falconi the Magician, the Bologna Dancers, and the numerous Italian opera singers with various companies, performed mainly for American audiences[7] and therefore fall short of being Italian-American theatre.

Of the approximately 4,000 Italian immigrants in the United States in 1850,[8] only 833 lived in New York State.[9] This small figure gradually increased within the next twenty years, to a total of about 20,000 in the United States by 1870.[10] But a dramatic immigrant theatre of any significance, by and for Italian Americans, had yet to emerge. Such a theatre finally began to take shape during the last thirty years of the nineteenth century.

ORIGINS OF ITALIAN-AMERICAN THEATRE, 1871–1900

An Italian immigrant theatre serving an Italian-American community finally began to evolve during the last thirty years of the nineteenth century. The significant events that serve as the rough boundaries to this time segment are the unification of Italy in 1871 and the beginning of the new great waves of immigration in the twentieth century.

The seeds of Italian-American theatre activity grew from the harsh realities of life in Italy, such as cholera, famine, and drought, rather than from a noble desire to propagate the theatrical tradition overseas. These unpleasant factors were related to the political situation of the fledgling Italian nation, unaccustomed to the problems of national unification. Political dissension resulted in the beginning of the socialist movement. The land in Italy was overworked and beset with drought, disease, and other problems. Farmers who had previously depended on their own local principalities now turned in vain to a disorganized and inept central government that was unable to provide for their welfare. In addition, the Italian population increased 25 percent during the years 1871–1905.[11] The statistics of the Italian census after ten years of unification revealed that the population had increased from 257 per square mile of usable land in 1881 to 294 people per square mile in 1901,[12] in spite of emigration to secure employment or to escape from the recurring cholera epidemics.

Numerous references were made during the decade 1881 to 1890 in New York City to special benefit performances for the needy people of Italy. The Circolo Filodrammatico Italo-Americano spent the proceeds of many of its productions in this manner. Special benefits were given for the cholera victims of an unnamed Italian city on November 23, 1884,[13] for the cholera victims of Messina on December 4, 1887;[14] for the earthquake survivors in Liguria on May 1, 1887;[15] and for the hurricane survivors in Sardinia on December 1, 1889.[16] Although this was the only drama group to give benefits of this nature, on

Sunday evening, November 8, 1885, in New York City at Steinway Hall, the "Gran Concerto Serale a beneficio dei colerosi di Palermo" was sponsored by the united Italian societies of New York, Brooklyn, Newark, and Hoboken. This benefit was organized "by some of the leading Italian gentlemen of this city,"[17] who Odell informs us were the Conte di Foresta and G. B. Raffo.[18]

Health and economic factors in Italy immediately effected a change in the ethnic fabric of New York City. For instance, from 1861 to 1870 the total Italian immigration to the United States numbered 11,728; it jumped to 55,759 from 1871 to 1880.[19] The year 1882 alone saw 32,160 Italian immigrants enter the United States,[20] and during 1891–1900, 651,899 Italians[21] came to these shores, the greater part of them settling in industrial cities in New York State, especially New York City.[22]

Upon arrival they congregated in ghettos, in which the chief places of social activity were the Church, the social clubs, and the coffee houses. These places saw the development of Italian-American theatre. No evidence has appeared to indicate that much theatre emanated from religious festivals or rites in New York. Odell makes one reference to the Italian students of the Catholic Church of San Francesco Saverio, who performed the Plautus comedy *Gli Schiavi*. The Italian title is misleading; the performance, with the assistance of Monsignor Satolli, was recited in Latin and therefore was not really Italian-American, in spite of the Italian-American audience and performers.[23]

Possibly the reason for this lack of religious theatre lies in the fact that New York City was a great metropolitan city during that quarter century, and as in most of the larger cities in Italy, churchgoing there was left to the women and children. In any event, it was the social clubs and cafe chantants[24] (*caffe concertos*)[25] that more readily provided the first theatrical activity for Italian Americans, while at the same time performing a very important community function.

Italian-American theatre developed fairly rapidly among the various social clubs of Little Italy. These local associations proved to be an integral part of community life. During this quarter century, these Italian societies and clubs *di mutuo soccorso* (of mutual benefit) met regularly and frequently. Membership in these various circles overlapped from one type of club to another, with the result that a great social web was forming, linking them all together.

The initial modest number of these organizations eventually swelled to an extensive list, filling many pages in the volumes of the *Brooklyn Daily Eagle Almanac*. Their number began to decrease toward the end of the first quarter of the twentieth century, with the decrease in immigration, until in 1929 the *Eagle* ceased to list the Italian societies. These social clubs' activities were also regular and consistent enough in the late nineteenth century for Odell to chronicle in his *Annals*.

These associations are noted here less for their initial avowed reasons for organizing than for their subsequent socializing, wherein lie the real beginnings of Italian-American repertory theatre in New York City. The nomenclature of these societies indicates a great diversity of activity: occupational, political, literary, dramatic, military, musical, choral, and nationalistic; but the social aspect was common to all. Their members enjoyed dances and balls, literary lectures, concerts, benefits, and the holidays, on which they could combine any and all of these activities, especially plays and/or parades for their marching bands and rifle clubs, which they invariably brought out each October 12 to celebrate the discovery of America.

They met consistently at places such as the Germania Assembly Rooms (also known as the Teatro Italiano), at 291-293 Bowery, and the Teutonia Assembly Rooms, at 144 East 16th Street, between 3rd Avenue and Irving Place; in the parks of Manhattan and the other boroughs during the appropriate seasons; or in the case of the smaller clubs, in the private homes of the members.

Il Circolo Filodrammatico Italo-Americano

Many of these societies eventually engaged in regular theatrical ventures and were known under the general title, *circolo filodrammatico*, especially in the twentieth century. But during the nineteenth century only one dramatic and social club the Circolo Filodrammatico Italo-Americano, was listed consistently in the *Brooklyn Eagle*. Although other groups produced theatre during this period, the Circolo Filodrammatico Italo-Americano was the only "club" listed as such. It was undoubtedly the first and provides us with the first instance of a bona fide play production.

The first mention Odell makes of a native Italian-American dramatic performance refers to October 17, 1880, when the Società Filodrammatica Italiana di New York performed the play *Maria Giovanna* at Dramatic Hall, 44-46 East Houston Street. It had previously met on September 26, 1880, at the home of the L. Jorio and G. Gazzoli, probably to rehearse.[26] The event of October 17 is notable in that it is the first recorded verifiable production by a regular Italian-American repertory company performing in Italian for an Italian-American audience. This play also has a subtitle and an alternate title: *Maria Giovanna ossia le Due Madri* (Maria Giovanna or the Two Mothers) or *Povera Giovanna* (Poor Giovanna). These were used in a subsequent production of the play by the Circolo Filodrammatico Italo-Americano on November 24, 1892.[27] The two titles together create an impression of melodrama.

Not only was the Società Filodrammatica Italiana the first on record, but under an assortment of names it enjoyed the greatest activity and longevity of any company in this period. There are records and dates of performances by this group that together outnumber the combined productions of all the other companies of this time. This drama company, composed mainly of amateurs, managed to remain together, giving performances on a regular basis from 1878 to 1894, when the files of *Il Progresso Italo-Americano* break down. But the *Brooklyn*

Eagle Almanac continued to list the group under the social clubs until 1902, with its headquarters located at 80½ Mulberry Street,[28] after which it drops out of history completely.

On February 9, 1878, a Circolo Italiano gave a musical-literary entertainment at the Teutonia Assembly Rooms.[29] This may have been a first budding attempt of the young company, but the information is too scarce to be certain. The first sufficiently documented recorded performance of this group as a regular theatrical company is the above-mentioned production of *Maria Giovanna*. The group performed under the name Società Filodrammatica Italiana di New York, the title by which it was first known, until October 2, 1881, when it began to call itself the Compagnia Filodrammatica Italiana,[30] and later, with what seems to have been a burst of satisfaction, la Nota (Noted) Compagnia Filodrammatica.[31] Finally, after four years of success with Italian-American audiences, the group adopted the permanent and sociologically significant title of Circolo Filodrammatico Italo-Americano with the February 22, 1885, performance of *La Mendicante di Sassonia* (The Beggar of Saxony).[32] Since this title remained with it throughout its history, I shall refer to it hereafter as such, regardless of the year under discussion.

After its beginning at the Dramatic Hall, the winter season of 1881 brought the company to the Teatro Vercelli, managed by J. Vercelli and also known as the Hotel di Roma, located at 152-154 East 42nd Street, for two performances only, on Sunday, October 2, 1881, and Sunday, October 9, 1881.[33] The Germania Assembly Rooms were the company's permanent home from the spring season of 1883 onward. Occupancy of this new and permanent "home" coincided exactly with the performance on February 21, 1883, when the group began to call itself the Nota Compagnia.[34] This seems to indicate that finding this location was no mean event in the group's opinion.

The Circolo also made a special excursion now and then, such as to the festival at Brommer's Union Park, at 133rd Street and the East River, on May 24, 1886, to commemorate Garibaldi's triumphal march into Palermo,[35] or to a special banquet at the Cliff Cottage Hotel on Staten Island on Sunday, July 6, 1890.[36]

The Circolo may have found a permanent station at the Germania Assembly Rooms, but by no means did it have exclusive use. The assembly hall was shared not only with other theatre companies, but with the rifle clubs, marching societies, music leagues, political organizations, and social circles of Little Italy and also with the German and French societies of New York City.

Business Arrangements

Management of the Circolo Filodrammatico Italo-Americano was conducted in a businesslike fashion. The files of *Il Progresso Italo-Americano* furnish the following information on election results and fiscal accountings: On November 23, 1884, the company reported a very uncomplicated management system. Two officers were listed, the president, a Mr. B. Bertini, and his secretary, a Mr.

A. Cartosio.[37] By March 12, 1886, a more complete committee was formed, reflecting the fact that during 1886 performances became more frequent and more regular than before, and this increased activity continued in the years that followed. The complete committee, as reported for March 12, 1886, reads as follows:

Presidente	Fausto D. Malzone
Tesoriere	G. Balletto
Vice-Tesoriere	A. Tassinari
Segretario	Eugenio Metelli[38]

It is interesting to note that this list of committee members included two actors, Metelli and Malzone. The previous president and secretary had not been recorded in any performance lists as actors.

On August 18, 1886, the secretary, Metelli, issued to the press the results of the company election of officers for the 1886–1887 season.

Presidente	Fausto D. Malzone
Vice-Presidente	G. Jacolucci
Tesoriere	G. Carbone
Vice-Tesoriere	A. Crocco
Segretario	G. Fossati
Direttore	E. Benzoni[39]

Again only two members of this administration were actors, Malzone and Eduardo Benzoni. Also noteworthy is the fact that the position of director was included on the "board of directors." The members seem to have served out their full terms for the entire season, and also for the next season, with the exception of Fossati, who was replaced by J. Burron, another actor, on January 8, 1888.[40]

On January 11, 1890, we note that "bouncers" were needed in the Germania Assembly Rooms; the bouncers were now part of the administrative committee, with the title Ispettori di Sala (room inspectors). The complete committee of 1890 was:

Presidente	Fausto D. Malzone
Segretario	F. Mele-Barense
Tesoriere	R. Vetere
Ispettori di Sala	Samuelo Rosselli
	Nicola Grill
	Valentino Morini
	Luigi Bicchierai[41]

Again two members of the committee were actors, Malzone and Mele-Barense. For the performance of July 14, 1891, the Circolo added a house doctor to its ranks, R. Asselta, with the title, Medico della Società.[42] By November 26, 1891, G. Burron was listed as ispettore di sala.[43]

Finally a poster dated April 4, 1893, indicated that the society considered itself prominent enough to name Tommaso Salvini honorary president for life. Malzone, Zumbo, and Catarsi were the actors on this committee:

Presidente Onorario a Vita	Commendatore Tommaso Salvini
Presidente	Fausto D. Malzone
Vice-Presidente	A. de Yulio
	A. Alvino
Segretario	N. Juzzolini
Tesoriere	D. Spinelli
Direttore	Lucio C. Zumbo
Ispettore di Sala	Dionisio Catarsi[44]

Only a brief mention in the *Brooklyn Eagle* listings for 1899,[45] with Malzone indicated as president, supplemented this last administrative note.

An agenda published in *Il Progresso,* with my translation, illustrates what the board of directors discussed at its Saturday conferences at the headquarters at 407 Canal Street on September 4, 1886.

Ordine del giorno	Agenda
Ammissione dei soci	Admission of the members
Lettura del verbale	Reading of the minutes
Proposta del dott. Guidone	Proposal of Doctor Guidone
Programma della recita pel 3 ottobre	Programme of the October 3 performance
A beneficio di che?	For whose benefit?
Distribuzione delle parti	Distribution of roles
Nomina dell'ispettore di sala	Appointment of a room monitor
Suggeritore e attrezzisto	Prompter and scene designer
Musica	Music
Nomina del medico	Appointment of a doctor
Festa del 20 settembre	Feast of September 20
Affari diversi	Other business[46]

Unfortunately only a small number of fiscal accountings of the early companies are available for this time period; most pertain to the Circolo Filodrammatico Italo-Americano. During the 1885–1886 season the Circolo donated $1,343 to various charitable causes. This considerable sum evoked much praise from the *Il Progresso* reporter.[47] In keeping with contemporary customs, the Circolo performed its share of benefits. The above-mentioned sum was divided during that season among the following causes: the Fondo Social (Community Chest), February 7, 1886;[48] the Italian hospital, January 10, 1886;[49] the Italian school, April 11, 1886;[50] and the Knights of Labor, April 18, 1886,[51] and May 15, 1886.[52]

On the agenda of the meeting for September 4, 1886, the subject for discussion, "Programme for the Performance of October 3rd" was followed by the question: "For whose benefit?" The committee must have decided that the Circolo Filodrammatico itself was now entitled to a benefit night. The accounting given to the press was as follows:

Tickets sold at the door—391 @ 25¢ each		$ 97.65
Reserved seat tickets—47		11.75
Total		$109.40
Expenses		
Theatre rental	$15.00	
stage manager and scenery	18.00	
music	18.54	
costumes	4.00	
printing and posters	19.00	
Total	$74.54	74.54
		$ 34.80
20% transferred to the Circolo		7.00
Net receipts		$ 27.86

The ever-anonymous *Il Progresso* reporter hastened to remark that if the Circolo expended any of its funds toward printing for advertising, no profit was enjoyed by *Il Progresso*, since the newspaper always made free space available to the Circolo regarding notices of performance.[53] The Circolo Filodrammatico seldom held benefits for itself. Most of its receipts from benefits were donated to charitable works, such as the aforementioned aid to cholera victims of Messina on December 4, 1887, the accounting for which was made public by the group's secretary, J. Burron.

Box office gross receipts	$134.00
Expenses: cost of theatre	
costumes	
scenery and scene designer	
printing	
transportation	
drinks	
copyist	
prompter	
	$ 74.40
Net profit	$ 59.60, sent January 1, 1888, to the mayor of Messina.[54]

The monument to Christopher Columbus that now stands in the center of Columbus Circle was erected in 1892, partly through the energies and benefits of the Circolo Filodrammatico Italo-Americano and other drama groups and social clubs of this period. The then secretary of the Circolo, F. Mele-Barense, released the accounting of the funds resulting from two such benefits, those of January 12, 1890, and January 20, 1890.

Box office from the two shows	$165.30
Expenses	111.13
Net profit	$ 54.17

This amount of $54.17 was added to the running tally kept by the newspaper for the monument fund and brought that fund to a total of $3,782.87. The *Il Progresso* reporter explained that the Circolo's donation would have been greater but for some mysterious incident, of which only he and his readers were aware. Apparently the Circolo had been found in violation of a Sunday blue law, which disrupted the first performance of January 12 to such an extent that the Circolo received gratis the use of the Germania Assembly Rooms and was obliged to give out free tickets to the second performance on January 20.[55] Also, the program for this second performance of *La Figlia Unica* (The Only Daughter) indicates that a special speech by Pulcinella preceded the performance and that the role of Domenico Castellani was performed by F. Mele-Barense.[56]

This limited evidence on expenditures indicates that the Circolo Filodrammatico Italo-Americano operated on a semiprofessional level. The actors were not recompensed, but they conducted their productions and their repertory company in a businesslike manner.

Directors, Actors, and Prompters

Without exception, all the directors of the Circolo were actors with the troupe as well. Unfortunately, of the 100 productions mounted by the Circolo, the directors of only eleven are known with certainty. Apparently the directors' individuality as artists was not considered important enough to warrant accreditation of their work in the press notices. Nor were they recompensed for their services, as the fiscal accounts indicate, although the prompter and scene designer did receive some, if meager, remuneration. Those directors of whom there are records for specific productions and dates are:

Eduardo Benzoni	November 23, 1884
	October 3, 1886
	December 5, 1886
	February 20, 1887
	May 1, 1887
Lucio C. Zumbo	January 12, 1890
	January 20, 1890
	Fall of 1890
	January 1, 1891
	December 24, 1891
	April 4, 1893
E. Boncetti	December 8, 1891
	December 24, 1891

Unfortunately, nothing is known regarding their methods, styles of directing or theories of theatre, or whether they had any such specifics in mind at all. We can infer that the directors simply took some responsibility for organizing the production along the guidelines decided upon by the administrative committee and that the twentieth-century concept of the director as the absolute unifying element of the production was not yet in vogue.

Cast lists, on the other hand, are more plentiful for the plays of the Circolo Filodrammatico. A large number of actors performed in the numerous plays staged over the years of the Circolo's history. Actors, like directors, received no salaries but donated their time, efforts, and talents. Many also acted and directed with other companies. The actors apparently had their artistic differences. For the February 7, 1886, performance of *I Timidi* (The Timid Ones), *I Due Sordi* (The Two Deaf People), and *The Rival Tenants*, a statement was made to the press that Luigi Zaganelli, Dionisio Catarsi, and Catarsi's wife, Argia Catarsi, would purposefully remain absent from that evening's performance for reasons of a personal nature.[57]

In private life the actors engaged in their own nontheatrical businesses and professions. From the numerous advertisements in the pages of *Il Progresso*, more is known about their business and social activities than about their expertise in acting or directing. We have data on the following members of the Circolo Filodrammatico Italo-Americano:

Eduardo Benzoni was a partner in an Italian restaurant at 148 Bleecker Street.[58]

R. Guidone, a pharmacist, was a partner in the Farmacia Italiana, at 242 Elizabeth Street, near Houston Street. Many flamboyant ads recommend his Guidone's Wonderful Elixir.[59] He was also first vice-president of the Società Italiane Militari Uniti.[60]

G. Selvaggi was a partner in the Cafè Eldorado, 24 Spring Street.[61]

Fausto D. Malzone was honorary vice-president of the Società Stella d'Italia,[62] of the Società Italiana dei Barbieri,[63] and of the Società Militare Sant'Arsenio Italo-Americana di Mutuo Soccorso di New York.[64] He resided at 88½ Mulberry Street[65] and maintained at 80½ Mulberry Street a small banking business and travel agency where he also sold imported wines.[66]

Dionisio and Argia Catarsi ran the Hotel Colombo at 135 Bleecker Street.[67] Another Catarsi sold wines and liquors at 134 Sullivan Street.[68]

Rocco Metelli, playwright, actor, and the only prompter on record,[69] was secretary of the Società dei Reduci delle Patrie Battaglie.[70]

Constantino Talamo Rossi had been a lieutenant in Nice of the cavalry of the Italian army.[71] These military titles were maintained even when the bearers left Italy and emigrated to another country.

Lucio C. Zumbo held the position of counselor in the Società Protezionista e di Mutuo Soccorso dei Barbieri Italiani di New York.[72] He resided at 23 Prince Street.[73]

Luigi Zaganelli was a prominent member of the Knights of Labor.[74]

Don Angelo Legniti was elected sixth member of the administrative council of the Instituto Italiano,[75] which still exists today at 686 Park Avenue. He ran a small banking business and travel agency at 89 Mulberry Street,[76] which he later relocated to 60 Mulberry Street.[77] Ricciardi described him with great respect in his memoirs, as an honored member of the Italian "colony." In 1900 Legniti introduced Ricciardi to Enrico Caruso, both his personal friends. Legniti resided at 12th Street and 2nd Avenune.[78]

Paolo Cremonesi performed some type of work with or on silk, somewhere in New Jersey.[79]

Finally, J. Burron was Secretary of the Società Stato Maggiore Bersaglieri d'Africa, located at 346 East 54th Street.[80]

Other than this biographical data, we know very little about the actors' style or talents, except that they were extremely popular. The reviews and coverage of performances in the *Il Progresso* are generally laudatory, with few if any adverse comments or theatrical theory of any value.

Many of the company's performers appeared with the other Italian-American groups in this history: A. Benna, Rosalia Miraglia, Giuseppina Menghini, and Carlo Neigre with the Compagnia Comico-Drammatica Italiana; Rosalia Miraglia, Francesco Ricciardi, Lucio C. Zumbo, A. Pasio Sapere, and Eleonora Paoli with the Compagnia Filodrammatica Napoletana; Rosalia Miraglia, Riccardo Bencetti, Carlo Brizzi, Giuseppina Menghini, Carlo Neigre, Icilio Delicati, and Rosa Franchi with the Compagnia Filodrammatica Carlo Goldoni; Rosalia Miraglia and Carolo Brizzi with the Compagnia Filodrammatica Galileo Galilei; A. Pasio Sapere, Riccardo Bencetti, and Amalia Cioni with the Gara Artistica Napoletana; Eleonora Paoli, Fausto D. Malzone, Bernardino Ciambelli, and A. Ciambelli with the Compagnia Drammatica; Argia Catarsi, A. Domenici, and L. Metelli with the Soceità Filodrammatica Tommaso Salvini; Carlo Brizzi and Vincenzo Badolati with La Scintilla; and Vincenzo Bellarosa with the Compagnia Filodrammatica Italiana Dante Alighieri.

One other type of performer deserves mention. A glance at the lists of performances and casts indicates that almost all performances included music and/or singing and that a dance or community ball inevitably closed each evening's festivities. The maestro, or band leader, was responsible for supplying this necessary addition of music and was paid for his labors. As the Italian word indicates, the maestro was more often than not a teacher, and on the evening of a performance his students would often fill up the ranks of the orchestra and sometimes perform solos during the intermissions.[81] The professor, as he was sometimes called, did not belong to the individual company but was "jobbed" in for the occasion, and he was shared not only with the other drama groups, but also with the marching societies and rifle clubs for their parades and feasts.

Musical figures who conducted at one time or another for the Circolo Filodrammatico Italo-Americano included Luigi Conterno, Gentile, Carmine Sanna, Pecoraro, Raffaele Codeluppi, D. Tipaldi, Vincenzo Rosati, and Gioacchino Norrito. Among these, Pecoraro either resided at or maintained a business at 11 East Broadway.[82] The instruments used either as part of the orchestra or for solos included the clarinet, trombone, zither, flute, cornet, piccolo, mandolin, harp, cello, violin, and piano. Magicians who sometimes supplemented the evening's entertainment were Giusberg and Edoardo Lopez.

On the technical nature of these productions we can find little information, except that a scene designer was employed and paid. The company apparently furnished its own costumes. The prompter, listed as another of the company's expenses, can be considered an element of the production of importance equal to that of the director. The only prompter of record with the Circolo Filodrammatico Italo-Americano was Rocco Metelli, who also served as an actor and playwright.

The prompters' manner of functioning was characteristic of the Italian-American theatre. They were a nonrealistic convention accepted by Italian immigrant audiences as a necessary intrusion. The prompter's presence during the production, always very much in evidence, can be likened to that of the black-hooded manipulators of the bunraku Japanese puppet theatre—an element vital to the proper staging of the play. An anonymous observer and critic of Italian-American theatre in the early twentith century provided a unique and clever description of the prompter's extremely important part in the production.

In the fashion of the more careless repertory theatres, where dozens of plays must be acted with pratically no rehearsals, the prompter was much in evidence. In fact on Thursday nights there were pratically three performances going on. . . .

The players themselves gave one with a wary eye on the prompter's box. The prompter gave another—complete, strongvoiced, and about two seconds ahead of the official rendition. And the audience managed to give a third—laughing, applauding, shushing noisy children, and hissing in a body. They never hissed the actors or the villains. They kept these indications of sentiment for those who delayed the play by laughing too long.[83]

Frequently the actors ignored or conveniently forgot the script, in which case the actor improvised and relied on the ever-present and indispensable prompter. It seems the directors did not insist on uniformity of performance or enforce a strict adherence either to a script or a set style of performance. The apparent lack of "discipline" by the members of the production made the role of the prompter essential to any play.

The Repertoire

With respect to the plays and playwrights, the Circolo Filodrammatico consistently and successfully produced an interesting and varied repertory, including a wide assortment of dramatic forms from both Europe and New York City: farces, comedies, dramas, romantic tragedies, melodramas, children's theatre, and verse dramas. Plays were never staged alone, but with a variety of embellishments and entertainments either during the intermissions or following the regular performances. These included magic tricks and acts, dancing skits, declamations and recitation, monologues and dialogues, grand marches and rifle demonstrations, prizefighting exhibitions, poetry readings, songs, and instrumental solos or duets. A typical complete evening, somewhat extended by dint of a special occasion or benefit performance, would follow the pattern of the following *serale beneficio* for the Italian cholera victims, which took place on Sunday, November 23, 1884, at the Germania Assembly Rooms:

L'Erede del Proscritto ovvero L'Arcano della Vendetta (The Exile's Heir or the Mystery of the Revenge), drama in five acts by F. Castelvecchio

Part I	Symphony from the opera *Guglielmo Tell* by Rossini
Part II	First act of the play
Part III	Famous concert Polonaise for the clarinet
Part IV	Second act of the play
Part V	"L'Incredula," polka for baritone written and performed by V. Palmieri
Part VI	Third act of the play
Part VII	"Les Sirenes," waltz by E. Valdteuful
Part VIII	Fourth act of the play
Part IX	"Pirata," aria arranged for the trombone by Bellini
Part X	Fifth act of the play
Part XI	Sextet from *Lucia di Lammermoor*, by Donizetti
Part XII	Special commentary for this occasion
Part XIII	"Il Pappacone," aria buffa
Community Dance[84]	

The Italian-American audience expected and received a full evening's entertainment. A *gran ballo* usually finished the evening, with music provided by one of the aforementioned *professori*.

The study of the plays and productions of this particular ethnic theatre reveals the character of the Italian-American audience in particular and the Italian immigrant society in general. The people of the "colony," as they considered themselves, patronized the various performances in family groups on Sundays in order to be entertained, to laugh, and to escape their dreary existence. The skill, versatility, and enthusiasm of the performers weighed more heavily than any other of the theatrical embellishments, and the audiences were vociferous in their approval or disapproval. As is evidenced by the existence of the prompter, talent was more important than a good memory or fidelity to the written script.

There are too few descriptions of the realism employed in the physical productions, but we know that naturalism was certainly not in vogue. The period of naturalism in Italy extends approximately from 1870 to 1920, which would adequately cover the time segment under discussion here. Although many Italian playwrights associated with the Naturalistic movement in Italy were produced by the Italians in America, especially the Circolo Filodrammatico Italo-Americano, the earlier fanciful and romantic plays of these otherwise naturalistic playwrights were the most popular and most frequently performed. These playwrights were

Paolo Giacometti, whose plays were most often mounted by the Circolo Filodrammatico, Paolo Ferrari, Giuseppe Giacosa, and Giovanni Verga.

Other playwrights from different periods of Italian literature were also very well received: F. Castelvecchio, Leopoldo Marenco, Carlo Goldoni, Vittorio Alfieri, Teobaldo Cicconi, Luigi DeLise, Luigi Camoletti, Carlo Roti, Vincenzo Monti, Valentino Carrera and Cletto Arrighi. Some French playwrights were also included in the repertoire: Fournier and Meyer, Jean-Francis Alfred Bayard and Jean-Louis Laya, Victorien Sardou, Augustin Eugène Scribe, George Ohnet, and Adolph Dennery.[85] Observations of the genres of these playwrights imported from the continent, which account for about 24 out of the 100 plays staged by the Circolo, reveal mainly melodramas and bourgeois dramas, romantic tragedies and medieval legends, the well-made play, and a Goldoni *commedia dell'arte*-style comedy. This choice of selections creates the clear impression of a middle-class audience, with appropriate tastes and values, and a world view that admits of good and evil, reward and punishment, religion and a God-inspired universe.

Since few of the Italian-American scripts remain, we must assume that they reflected a philosophy of life similar to that implied by the foreign selections. Many of the detailed titles of the Italian-American plays demonstrate no evidence to the contrary. More often than not, especially during the early years of its history, the play notices of the Circolo Filodrammatico Italo-Americano do not credit the playwright. Among the accredited Italian-American playwrights, Bernardino Ciambelli's plays were the most performed, and he often acted in them as well. A journalist with the Italian daily *Bollettino della Sera,*[86] Ciambelli wrote the following plays:

Figlia Maledetta (Accursed Daughter), a title that smacks of bourgeois drama (January 6, 1892);

Ramo d'Ulivo (Olive Branch), a children's theatre piece described as a "realistic scene of community interest written specifically . . . for the two children Laura and Ruggiero Catarsi," children of the aforementioned actors, Dionisio and Argia Catarsi May 30, 1892);[87]

Cuor di Fanciulli! (The Heart of Children!), described as a "contemporary sketch . . . dedicated to the F. D. Guerrazzi Tuscan League which has done so much to save the lives of the two unfortunate nationalists Rugani and Pertiga." This sketch was also recited by children. (April 4, 1893);[88]

I Misteri di Mulberry (The Mysteries of Mulberry Street), a drama in six acts (November 30, 1893, and March 26, 1894).

Rocco Metelli, the above-mentioned actor and prompter of this group, contributed one recorded play, *Chiara, la Condannata a Morte* (Chiara, Condemned to Die), staged by the Circolo Filodrammatico on October 8, 1887, at the Turn Hall Theatre, 66–68 East 4th Street, as a special benefit for Chiara Cignarale, a real-life semiheroine of the Italian-American community. The saga of Cignarale was chronicled in installments in the pages of *Il Progresso Italo-Americano*. Chiara was accused of murder in 1887. The crime was covered by *Il Progresso*, but those issues are missing.[89] What we do know about her, and consequently about the subject matter of Metelli's play, is simply that she was a young woman accused of the murder of her husband and subsequently convicted and sentenced to the death penalty. Odell tells us she later received a temporary stay of execution from the governor of New York.[90]

A. Balletto was a partner in an Italian printing shop at 178 Park Row with Gardella and F. L. Frugone,[91] another Italian actor with a different theatre company. Agostino Balletto's farce *Il Campanello dello Speziale* (The Chemist's Doorbell) was mounted May 15, 1886.

Nothing else is known about the other playwrights produced by this company and mentioned in the files of the *Il Progresso*, who were L. Gazzoletti, and M. Cuciniello. We cannot even be certain that they were Italian-Americans, although their names were not included among the better-known native Italian playwrights. This group might very well have been composed in part of obscure Italian playwrights of a particular Italian village, produced here through the efforts of an admiring entrepreneur from the home town, as was the case with Guglielmo Ricciardi and his company, discussed below. The titles of the plays give no clues, unlike Ciambelli's *I Misteri di Mulberry*, which geographically places the author. This group of artists only accounts for about fifteen productions. Not only are there playwrights who cannot be placed, but many plays remain anonymous as to authorship, most of them comedies, farces, and skits, with some serious *drammi*, actually melodramas, all of which we suspect are of Italian-American origin.

The Circolo performed on Sundays and holidays and at special events, often devising special skits to befit particular occasions, such as *L'Entrata di Garibaldi in Napoli*, performed on February 21, 1883, which, commemorated the anniversary of Garibaldi's triumphal entry into Naples. Garibaldi's successful marches proved a frequent inspiration for the Italian companies, as in performances by the Circolo on February 20, 1887, and May 24, 1886.

The following is a short compendium of the most repeated popular anonymous plays:

Maria Giovanna ossia Le Due Madri, an Italian import described as "an extraordinary performance" and alternately titled *Povera Giovanna*[92] (October 17, 1880, and November 24, 1892);

La Consegna è di Russare (The Instructions Are to Snore), a farce in several dialects (December 12, 1880; September 10, 1890; and January 1, 1891);

Il Segretario del Segretario d'un Segretario (The Secretary of the Secretary to the Secretary), a "brilliant comedy" (December 25, 1880, and March 13, 1881);

I Due Sordi, a "brilliant farce" (February 7, 1886, and May 24, 1886);

La Battaglia di Tolosa ovvero la Colpa del Cuore (The Battle of Tolosa, or The Weakness of the Heart), a historical drama that seems from the title to have melodramatic overtones (January 30, 1881, and February 13, 1881);

La Macchia di Sangue (Mark of Blood), sounding like a revenge melodrama of the blood-curdling French variety (April 10, 1881; October 2, 1881; and October 9, 1881): and

I Polli in Quarta Generazione (Chickens of the Fourth Generation), an "exhilarating farce" with an irresistible title, performed only once (December 1, 1889).

Pulcinello, a comedy skit, was another favorite sometimes performed by the Circolo. The Neopolitan character of Pulcinello is derived from the old Commedia dell'Arte scenarios of the sixteenth century and remains the same buffoon type in the Italian-American skits. Whereas the Commedia dell'Arte depended heavily on improvisational embellishment of the scenario, in America the Pulcinello farces were sometimes devised and written out by the acting companies or depended on an individual interpreter of the role who developed his own skits. The actor V. Romeo was the only interpreter of the Pulcinello role on record in the Circolo Filodrammatico Italo-Americano.[93] The skits created by the Circolo Filodrammatico were:

Pulcinello geloso della Moglie (Pulcinello Jealous of his Wife, January 9, 1881),

Pulcinello Prestidigitore (Pulcinello the Magician, February 6, 1881, and January 16, 1881), and

Il Flauto Magico con Pulcinello (The Magic Flute with Pulcinello, February 13, 1881, and March 27, 1881).

Although it produced some Pulcinello farces, the Circolo Filodrammatico was known less for Pulcinello productions than for regular comedies and dramas. The company of Francesco Ricciardi was more closely identified with the development of the Pulcinello character. He made a guest appearance with the Circolo as Pulcinello on October 5, 1893, in *Pulcinello medico a forza di bastonate* (Pulcinello, Doctor by Dint of Beatings).[94] Francesco Ricciardi is discussed with his own company, below.

The Circolo Filodrammatico Italo-Americano, then, was popularly successful, operated in a semiprofessional and businesslike manner, introduced the Italian-American audience to Italian and French continental works as well as original Italian-American plays, and functioned not merely for purposes of entertainment but as an intrinsic social force by reason of the benefits it staged for worthwhile social causes and community interests. Information about this company gives us a general picture of the activity of the other groups about whom less material remains.

La Compagnia Comico-Drammatica Italiana

The next dramatic troupe of interest to this chapter, the Compagnia Comico-Drammatica Italiana, was the first and only Italian-American theatre company in the nineteenth century that was founded and based in Brooklyn, catering primarily to Brooklyn audiences. The troupe performed contemporaneously with the Circolo Filodrammatico Italo-Americano, but the latter never invaded the territory of the former in South Brooklyn and thus represented no ostensible competition.

The Compagnia Comico-Drammatica provided the first intimation of a working professional theatre collective for which the theatre was a source of livelihood. It continued in the manner of the Circolo Filodrammatico Italo-Americano to introduce Italian-American audiences to Italian and French playwrights; it concentrated on Neopolitan plays, which catered to the tastes of the Neopolitan audiences of South Brooklyn and of other cities in the Northeastern part of the United States. Out of this company emerged Guglielmo Ricciardi, one of the most important figures in the Italian-American theatre of the nineteenth century because of his development as an actor of significance in the American theatre and cinema.

La Compagnia Napoletana

A distinctly Neopolitan flavor characterized the work of the band of actors known as the Compagnia Napoletana. As the Manhattan counterpart of the Brooklyn-based Compagnia Comico-Drammatica Italiana, the Compagnia Napoletana gave performances for basically Neopolitan audiences at approximately the same time as the Ricciardi-Savarese troupe and with the same degree of frequency and regularity. There are records of thirty-one of their productions. Their special product consisted almost exclusively of Pulcinello farces in the Neopolitan dialect, played to the Neopolitan audiences of Manhattan. As with the two previously covered theatre circles, the name the group used varied.

This society represented a certain degree of refinement of the work of the Italian-American theatre by virtue of its specialization. By almost exclusive selection and production of Pulcinello comedy skits and farces in the Neopolitan dialect, the company added a substantial number of performances to this ethnic theatre scene and apparently filled a gap left by the other theatre societies of the era. The popularity of Pulcinello also attests to the great need on the part of the Italian immigrant laborers for amusement and laughter as an escape from their crowded lives in the city that Guglielmo Ricciardi often called "la citta demente"[95] (recalling Dante's words) and Pasquale De Biasi, "il Babele di Manhattan."[96]

La Compagnia Comico-Drammatica Italiana A. Maiori e P. Rapone

In the nineteenth century the last of the four major companies of consequence to this chapter, the Compagnia Comico-Drammatica Italiana A. Maiori e P. Rapone, assumed great popular stature, which carried over well into the twentieth century and gave a classical dignity to the Italian-American stage. The Maiori-Rapone troupe, named after its cofounders, Antonio Maiori and

Pasquale Rapone, was the last of the major companies of the century to become organized and functioning, around 1892.

This troupe survived longer than its three predecessors; its theatrical enterprises formed a bridge into the next century. It mounted forty-three known productions, and there must have been many more.

The significance of the Maiori-Rapone troupe lies in its completely professional nature and especially in Maiori's introduction of Shakespeare to Italian-American audiences, who may never have seen Shakespeare produced before. The company emphasized productions of the classics and better-known serious European dramas, along with the comic farces of Pasquale Rapone. The availability of information about this group is evidence of its popularity and success, at least in the nineteenth century.

As for Maiori, his story continues, rather unsuccessfully, into the twentieth century. At first his theatre was successful, and he maintained other theatres on the Bowery, but eventually he was forced to go into the variety theatre business, which turned out to be a financial loss for him.

Other theatre companies that enjoyed a brief existence in New York City during the nineteenth century were La Società Filodrammatica Tommaso Salvini, La Compagnia Filodrammatica Galileo Galilei, La Compagnia Partenopea, La Compagnia Filodrammatica Italiana Dante Alighieri, La Compagnia Filodrammatica Carlo Goldoni, La Gara Artistica Napoletana, and Il Teatro Italiano (The Eighth Street Theatre).

Theatrical Theory and Criticism

Italian-American theatrical theory and criticism were virtually nonexistent in the nineteenth century. The sporadic attempts at critiquing hardly comprise sufficient criteria from which to create a poetics of theatre or a code of dramatic values. The desire of the Italian-American audience was for diversion and entertainment, pure and simple. The anonymous *Il Progresso* reporters, though perhaps more literate than other members of the audience, were nevertheless typical members of the Italian immigrant community, with the same middle-class values. Since no names were given for the reviewer(s) in *Il Progresso* throughout the nineteenth century, it cannot be ascertained whether or not the reportage was conducted by more than one. From the general tone of the writing and from reading through the entire *Il Progresso* dailies remaining from the nineteenth century, I have been able to make certain inferences. The reporter was a man. Whether or not more than one person wrote the commentary, the writing was done by someone familiar with the companies' activities. The reviewer also probably knew some of the theatre personalities.

The theatre column, if it can be called that, acted as a clearinghouse for information about theatre activity in New York City and its environs, before and after the theatrical events occurred.

From the small available sampling of critiques on the Italians by an Italian, we can only summarize a brief poetics of theatre: actors should know their parts well enough that the prompter's job does not overreach the actors'; actors should recite with enthusiasm and volume; directors should assess the limitations of their actors, especially the amateurs, and choose appropriate material, avoiding the more difficult Italian and French classic writers; playwrights should not attempt too much realism; and finally, the theatre is meant to delight and instruct.

Il Teatro delle Marionette

No discussion of Italian-American theatre would be complete without some mention of the popular Italian marionette theatres. The Teatro delle Marionette, located at 9 Spring Street, was only one of several Italian marionette shows presented in New York City during the nineteenth century. Giuseppe Cautela specifically indicated two others, one on Elizabeth Street, catering to Sicilian audiences in the Sicilian dialect, and another on Mulberry Street, performing in the Neopolitan dialect for Neopolitan audiences.[97]

The arrival of the Italian marionette show, a native Italian entertainment, coincided with the waves of immigration.[98] Because of the technical expertise required, the Italian marionette theatre was wholly an Italian import and not an Italian-American development. The marionettes provided the same necessary function of entertainment for the Italian-American immigrant community as did the regular theatre, but to a lesser degree.

The marionettes stood three feet high and weighed over one hundred pounds, according to Pisani[99] (forty to seventy pounds, according to Hutchins Hapgood).[100] The steel armor, helmets, and vizors in which the marionette figures were encased accounted for this great weight.[101] Silk and velvet fabric was used in the construction of other marionette costumes to the sum of $100 for each costume. In addition to the skill required to maneuver these heavy figures, the puppeteers also had to be able to memorize long passages from the Italian epic poets—no prompter here! This was no task for an amateur or a dilettante; the Italian puppeteers came to America full-blown in their professions, having been trained as boys for these roles.

Il Caffè-Concerto

Concurrent with the theatrical activity developing in the theatres, halls, assembly rooms, and other types of houses, the Italian-American theatre was also progressing in a different direction. A different form arose in the various cafes—café-chantants, caffè-concertos, Italian restaurants, bars, and smaller music halls located in Manhattan, Brooklyn, and West Hoboken. Guglielmo Ricciardi remembered that at least half a dozen sprang up in New York's Little Italy during the period 1895 to 1903.[102] We know now that there were several more.

A café-chantant was a coffee house or café-bar where, as in Italy, alcoholic beverages were served in addition to *caffè* (coffee) and where working-class Italian immigrants convened, usually on Sunday, their only leisure time. Like the theatre, the *café-chantant* proved to be a social affair and a sociological phenomenon. Friends, refreshments, and a singing guitarist performing favorite Italian folk songs and romantic ballads served to lessen the traumas of big-city living in a strange country. On Sundays such entertainment was advertised as a "sacred concert" to avoid difficulty with the civil authorities.

The most popular of these coffeehouses to become a place of entertainment was the Villa Vittorio Emanuele III, located on Mulberry Street near Canal Street and named for the then current king of Italy. The Villa Vittorio Emanuele III operated successfully from about 1892[103] (Ricciardi places it about 1895)[104] until about 1903.[105] The Villa Vittorio Emanuele III introduced Italian-American audiences to the famous impressionist Eduardo Migliaccio, one of the most popular individuals in the history of the Italian-American theatre in New York City. (See below for further discussion of Migliaccio's contributions.) The twentieth century was the period of his greatest activity and popularity, but his origins and first attempts began in the *caffè-concertos* of nineteenth-century Little Italy.

Around 1903 the *café-chantant* era came to a close. The heyday of the *café-chantant* or *caffè-concerto* was another important phase in the development of the Italian-American theatre. The *caffè-concerto* was essentially a commercial enterprise, entertainment providing the lure that boosted the business of the cafés and bars in the Italian communities.

Two important names emerged from the *café-chantant* period: Guglielmo Ricciardi, who progressed into a lucrative career in American theatre and films, and Migliaccio, who used the *caffè-concerto* as a springboard into the Italian theatres on the Bowery in the twentieth century. Although both men performed *macchiette* (character sketches) and sang Neapolitan songs, Ricciardi remained essentially Italian in his art forms, while Migliaccio succeeded in conveying the essence of the Italian immigrant experiencing America.

From the *caffè-concerto* grew Italian-American vaudeville-type entertainments, specifically Migliaccio's *macchietta coloniale*, a direct response to the process of Americanization undergone by the Italian immigrant in New York City.

Breaking Ground for the Twentieth-Century Stage

The Italians made no spectacular innovations in theatre architecture or dramatic criticism, the latter being virtually nonexistent, the former distinguished by the reuse of existing structures, both theatrical and nontheatrical.

In general, the Italian-American theatre of the last three decades of the nineteenth century represents a breaking of ground for the more ambitious theatrical endeavors of the twentieth century. The rudimentary base established during this period proved to be more than adequate preparation for the next great influx of immigrants, in the first two decades of the new century. This preliminary period of development would eventually flower into a prolific and culturally significant era.

The theatre of the new century is the subject of another study, now in preparation. The vitality of Italian-American theatre in New York City rose and fell in proportion to the statistics on Italian immigration to the city. A definite pattern is discernible. Each great wave of Italian immigration, resulting from political, religious, and economic pressures in Italy, invariably provided the impetus for theatre in New York City.

One significant result was the professional phase of the Italian-American theatre that developed. The following list serves to enumerate the best-known among the individuals and groups that have existed in New York in the twentieth century: the Filodrammatica Racalmuto, the Circolo Filodrammatico Polimnia of Attilio Carbone, the Circolo Filodrammatico Novelli, the Teatro Garibaldi of Gennaro Ragazzino, the Clemente Giglio Players, the Teatro D'Arte Company of Giuseppe Sterni, and companies headed by these impresarios: Giovanni di Rosalia, Silvio Minciotti, Francesco di Cesare, Paolo Cremonesi, Alberto Servilla, Angelo Glorio, Mario Siletti, Armando Cenerazzo, Alberto Campobasso, and Enzo dell'Orefice.

The opening decades of the twentieth century saw the beginning of professional Italian-American theatres in many cities other than New York as well, including the large West Coast concentration of Italian immigrant population, San Francisco.

ITALIAN-AMERICAN THEATRE IN SAN FRANCISCO*

Like its counterpart in New York City, professional Italian-American theatre in twentieth-century San Francisco had roots in earlier, informal entertainments in cafes, social clubs, and amateur dramatic societies. Unlike its New York City counterpart, however, San Francisco's professional Italian-American theatre was created and sustained almost single-handedly by one person, the energetic and talented Antonietta Pisanelli Alessandro. This essay will describe the development of this theatre and the activities of this remarkable woman.

Italians and Theatre In Nineteenth-Century San Francisco

Six thousand Italians, largely from northern and central Italy, had settled in California by the middle of the nineteenth century, earning their living as merchants, farmers, and fishermen.[106] In *Two Years Before the Mast*, Richard

*This material was previously published as Maxine S. Seller, "Antonietta Pisanelli Alessandro and the Italian Theatre of San Francisco: Entertainment, Education and Americanization," *Educational Theatre Journal* (now *Theatre Journal*) 28, no. 2 (May 1976): 206–19, and is reprinted by permission of the publishers.

Henry Dana described some of these earliest Italians in California, sailors "in blue jackets, scarlet caps, and various colored underclothes bound ashore on liberty, singing beautiful Italian boat songs all the way in fine chorus."[107]

As Dana's description suggests, Italians brought their love of music to California with them. As early as 1850 there was an attempt to establish an Italian theatre in San Francisco, already the entertainment center of the Gold Rush. On September 13, 1850, a Signor Rossi opened an Italian theatre on Kearney and Jackson Streets. He offered a variety show including magic tricks and a ventriloquist act, as well as music and dancing by his wife. The show brought good reviews and ran for four nights, until a fire closed down the theatre. Rossi reopened at a new location, only to have it destroyed by fire again. San Francisco at the height of the Gold Rush was a dangerous city for people whose livelihoods depended upon wooden structures; after a third, then a fourth, and finally a fifth fire, Rossi and his theatre disappeared permanently from San Francisco.[108]

In the decades that followed, there was no popular Italian theatre in San Francisco. Italian opera companies came periodically and were well received by fashionable audiences, which paid admissions of two dollars and up. At these prices, most of the Italian-born population could not afford to indulge its passion for opera, though according to Johnny Ryan, a call boy at Macguire's Opera House, this did not keep them from trying.

The greatest butters-in on grand opera are the Iytalian [sic] fishermen. They know their music, but haven't the price. Whenever we want singers for the chorus and hadn't time to train them, we used to go down to the wharf and get Iy-talian (sic) fishermen. You'd find every one of 'em knowing their scores and singing 'Erani' and 'Traviata.' You could use a limited number, but every evening they'd crowd in at the stage door. "I'm in the chorus!" "I'm in the chorus!" they'd say. We'd know they wasn't, but we'd let them in when no one was looking.[109]

Opera was Italian in language and cultural background, but the opulent opera houses of nineteenth-century San Francisco remained the province of the wealthy Anglo-Saxon population. Despite their love of opera and their knowledge of it, most Italian immigrants could never be more than, as Johnny Ryan put it, "butters-in"; the opera houses were not theirs. Popular Italian theatre, theatre that the majority of Italian immigrants could enjoy and feel at home with, had other roots. It began with the societe filodrammatiche, the informal amateur groups that sprang up spontaneously in San Francisco, as in other centers of Italian population throughout the country. Here Italian immigrants got together in any convenient place to play the mandolin or guitar, sing, perform pantomime, and in general to enjoy themselves and entertain one another. Sometimes these groups gave public performances, charging a small fee that was donated to a community charity.

It was the societe filodrammatiche, informal and democratic in both their performers and their audiences, that formed the base of the popular theatre introduced by Antonietta Pisanelli Alessandro—a theatre that would become the "dominant social institution" of Italian San Francisco.[110]

Antonietta Pisanelli and Professional Theatre

Antonietta Pisanelli was born in Naples in 1869 and immigrated to New York City. As a young woman, her knowledge of Neapolitan folk songs and her magnificent stage presence led her into the world of the *societe filodrammatiche* and then into New York's professional Italian theatres. Earning her living by singing, dancing, and acting, she went on tour to Philadelphia, New Haven, Chicago, and other industrial cities with sizable Italian populations. Pisanelli's success was marred, however, by a series of personal tragedies. First her mother died, then her husband, then her youngest child. Seeking a fresh start, she set out for California with her remaining child, a young son, and little else but her own talent and ingenuity.

Arriving in San Francisco in the spring of 1905, Pisanelli organized the first professional Italian performance since the ill-fated activities of Signor Rossi over a half-century before. She hastily assembled a group of amateur performers from the local *societe filodrammatiche*. Then she circularized the North Beach Italian community (the main Italian settlement in the San Francisco area) to let it know that on Sunday evening, April 9, there would be a Grand Serata Straordinaria, a *spettacolo variato* for the benefit of the *canzonettista signora* Antonietta Pisanelli. Reserved seats were priced at 50 cents; general admission was 25 cents. The performance was to be held at Apollo Hall, on Pacific Street near Stockton, an old building where "colored artists" had given a benefit performance for flood victims in 1862 and where, in the early twentieth century, the Italian clubs of the North Beach area were accustomed to meeting.[111]

The curtain opened to a full house. The program included songs by Pisanelli and by a local performer, Signor Luigi; two plays, *Cavalleria Rusticana*, with music from Pietro Mascagni's opera of the same name; a farce, *Prestemi tua moglie per dieci minuti* (Lend Me Your Wife For Ten Minutes); and a concluding spectacle, a grand ball. According to an observer, "settings were crude and liable to collapse or fall apart at any unlikely moment; so were the actors." Indeed, one actor did fall apart. The barber, who had been drilled in his part, the prologue of *Cavalleria Rusticana*, forgot his lines. He stood helplessly before the audience in a costume of knee breeches and false whiskers, paralyzed by the trauma of the moment. Ignoring the help offered by the prompter and the audience, he forgot even his native tongue. "Well, all right," he finally mumbled in English, and he walked off the stage.[112]

"Somehow we went through the play," Pisanelli told an interviewer in 1939, shaking her head in wonder at the recollection. "I don't know how, but we did.[113] Actually it was Pisanelli herself who saved the play with her spendid rendition of Santuzza. The entire performance was greeted with great enthusiasm, "happily punctuated with the 'ahs' and 'Benes' of the audience." Aside from the verve and talent of the star performer, there was another reason for the success of the evening. "The public was starved for the sound of its own tongue and would suffer anything as long as it was done in Italian.[114] The performance was a financial as well as an artistic success; Pisanelli cleared a profit of $150.

After a series of performances at Apollo Hall, Pisanelli leased another building, Berglieri Hall, on the corner of Stockton and Union, where she continued her career as manager, producer, director, and star in San Francisco's first successful professional Italian theatre. She supplemented local talent by bringing in such professional Italian companies from the East as the Rapone and Cesare companies. When the fire department closed her theatre because it violated city ordinances, she reopened it as the Circolo Famigliare Pisanelli. The new theatre was actually a café, with tables grouped around a small stage. There was no admission charge, but between the acts the admiring public bought drinks while Signora Pisanelli went from table to table, exchanging greetings and singing Neapolitan songs.[115]

The Circolo Famigliare Pisanelli became the main social institution of the North Beach Italian community—a combination opera, theatre, café, and club. The theatre was an instant success not only because of the quality of its entertainment, which was high, but also because it met the needs of a new and expanding Italian immigrant community.

The community that patronized Pisanelli's Circolo was very different from the one to which Signor Rossi's ill-fated theatre had played half a century earlier. Encouraged by the introduction of relatively inexpensive steamship transportation, a new and much larger wave of Italian immigrants had come to California at the turn of the century. In the nineteenth century the largest foreign-born communities in California had been the Chinese and the Irish. By the time Pisanelli's Circolo opened, the Italian community was the largest, outnumbering both the Chinese and the Irish. While there had been only 6,000 Italians in the entire state in the 1850s, half a century later there were over 35,000 in San Francisco alone.[116] San Francisco was the cultural and social center for California's growing Italian population, and the North Beach area, where Pisanelli's theatre was located, was the social and cultural center of Italian San Francisco.[117]

While the original Italian immigrants of California had come overwhelmingly from northern Italy, from Tuscany, Genoa, and the lake district, the twentieth-century population contained a larger proportion of the poorer, less-well-educated immigrants from southern Italy. Like earlier immigrants, the newcomers brought with them a love of good music and a need for good entertainment. Even more than earlier immigrants, they lacked the money, the formal clothes, perhaps even the desire to frequent the established English theatres and concert halls. Hence the great appeal of the Circolo, an informal, friendly, and inexpensive theatre where they could feel at home.

The Circolo offered entertainment in the language the newest immigrant could understand. It was located in the heart of the Italian quarter, and its prices were low. To the many single male immigrants, lonely for friends and family left behind, the Circolo offered companionship. To the immigrant family, the Circolo offered respectable entertainment that could be shared by women and even children. Many of the newer southern Italian immigrants were so badly educated that they could not keep in touch with their native language and culture through books or even through the Italian-language press. To these people the Circolo offered entertainment and culture that could be experienced directly through the spoken word, as it had been in the old country.

New immigrants and long-time residents, young and old, men and women, the prosperous and the poor, the entire spectrum of the North Beach Italian community, made it a habit to spend Sunday evenings at the Circolo Famigliare Pisanelli. Because of this the Circolo and the other equally popular theatres opened by Pisanelli within the next two decades were able to play a unifying role in the life of the immigrant community. They helped to unite the rapidly growing Italian population by providing immigrants from different parts of the homeland with a common meeting place and a common set of experiences. They helped to ease the problems of the "generation gap" by giving young people opportunities to appreciate the language and tradition of their parents. Finally, they helped the non-Italian population, many members of which were among their delighted patrons, to see the Italian immigrants in a favorable light and thus to accept them more readily as desirable neighbors.

Journalist J. M. Scanland described a typical performance; the account, though romantic in language, illustrates the Circolo's function as a social as well as an entertainment center in the Italian community.

The patrons of the Famigliare Circolo arrive slowly, for in the quarter there is plenty of time for everything and there is no need to be in a hurry when seeking amusement. About 8 o'clock the floor of the Circolo is dotted with groups of different types—men with their families; others without families, young men with their senorinas (sic), and still others who have no senorinas. . . . Gradually the circle is filled—perhaps there are six hundred in the two half circles—the two hundred in the gallery making themselves heard in the various dialects shouting "Let it go!" . . . In the first circle there is a hubbub of voices and bursts of merry laughter. All are talking, each coterie in their own dialect. There are greetings of friends, smiles from lovers, and mischievous glances from senorinas who are looking their sweetest in their costumes of various colors. . . . Suddenly the sweet soft strains of "Heart Bowed Down" from "The Bohemian Girl" or a gem from Rigoletto are heard. The hubbub ceases, and some who think they possess musical abilities accompany the orchestra by humming the chorus or whistling the airs. The orchestration is very artistic, and when the music ceases there are shouts of admiration.[118]

The rich musical and theatrical tradition of the Italian community was reflected in the wide range of programs offered at the Circolo. A different opera was presented every night; La Traviata, Rigoletto, La Boheme, and Otello were favorites. The simplicity of the staging of these operas and the limitations of space did not dampen the enthusiasm of the audience. Certainly this was the opinion of Scanland.

Italians look upon opera as a necessity and also strictly as an amusement, and they want it strong and good, artistically and musically. They care little for scenery—they want the acting, and upon this and the music everything depends. . . . This unique Circolo makes little effort at scenic effects—the artists are expected to make their own scenes and pictures in dramatic acting. At times the little stage is well crowded with characters, but there seems to be enough room for the most striking situations and dramatic scenes, and the auditors are satisfied without the aid of scenery.[119]

Equally well received by the Circolo's audiences were the simple comedy acts, Italian farce or vaudeville, known as *zarzuella*. Like the operas, these sketches were played with a minimum of scenery.[120] In the tradition of Italian popular comedy, the *Commedia dell'Arte*, the actors often worked without scripts, relying upon their own spontaneous wit and skill at improvisation. Often the audience could recognize the costumes, characters, or situations portrayed in these sketches as characteristic of particular districts in Italy—perhaps the district that was their former home, in which case their pleasure must have been doubled.

Between the acts of operas or *zarzuella*, the Circolo presented folk songs representative of the various areas of the old country, especially Pisanelli's own Naples. Whatever the program of the Circolo, the main attraction was always Pisanelli, who reserved the opening and closing appearances, as well as many choice spots in between, for herself. An admirer of the Circolo, Scanland was even more effusive in his admiration of Pisanelli herself. He leaves the following description, which though undoubtedly exaggerated, is at least suggestive of reality:

With the rise of the curtain Signorina (sic—Signora, unfortunately) Antonretta Pisanelli, the brightest star of the Circolo, trips out upon the stage amid bursts of applause. She is prettily dressed in black, the dress cut décolleté [sic], revealing shapely shoulders and the bust of a model. Her Neapolitan cameo face is stamped with intellectuality and refinement. Heavy brows arch her piercing velvety eyes—as black as midnight, yet flashing with the brightness of the diamond—the kind that drive men crazy. A profusion of coal black hair heightens the beauty of her classic face.[121]

Pisanelli was not only a good performer and a successful impressario, she was also an excellent businesswoman. To supplement the revenue from the sale of drinks at her café theatre, she sublet part of the building to local merchants. She obtained additional income by selling advertising space on the programs and on the theatre curtains. When patrons complained of the heat, she gave them paper fans covered with advertisements of local shops, saloons, restaurants, and banks. If the weather was cold, the patrons got the fans all the same. Finally, with what one writer referred to as "seismographic intuition," Pisanelli sold her theatre for $20,000 in 1906—less than a week before the great earthquake and fire that destroyed San Francisco. Using even this disaster to best advantage, she split her company into small groups and sent them on tour, advertising them as "survivors of the San Francisco earthquake."[122]

Received as heroes wherever they went, the "survivors of the San Francisco earthquake" were highly successful at the box office. Pisanelli herself had one bad experience while on tour in St. Louis. When the folksong "Carme" was performed instead of the opera *Carmen,* which had been erroneously listed in the program, the audience howled with rage and threatened to destroy the theatre. With her usual ingenuity, Pisanelli averted disaster. She pushed her young son on stage to quiet the audience with a childish rendition of "Wait' Til the Sun Shines, Nellie." While the delighted audience shouted "Bravissimo piccolina," Pisanelli's recently acquired second husband slipped out the back door to carry the evening's receipts to safety.[123]

The Peak Years—1907–1914

After the devastating earthquake and fire, the Italian section of San Francisco was the first part of the city to be rebuilt, thanks to the thrift of the inhabitants, most of whom had accumulated at least a little capital, and thanks to the skill of local Italian bankers.[124] Pisanelli, now using the name Alessandro acquired by her recent remarriage, rebuilt, too. With Mario Scarpa, a talented young man she had introduced to the theatre, she opened a series of small establishments called nickelodeons—the Iris, the Beach, and the Bijou. At these popular theatres the public could enjoy a vaudeville-type Italian variety show of farce, song, and one-act comedies for a nickel or a dime. An Irish priest tried to prevent the opening of the Beach theatre across the street from St. Francis Church. With her usual finesse, the resourceful Signora Alessandro was able to persuade an Italian-American, Mr. Calegari, on the city's board of supervisors to license the theatre at the location she had chosen. "The signora could go far; she had the local Italian colony in San Francisco solidly behind her."[125]

The nickelodeons were an instant success. One of them, the Bijou, became famous for its offering of Stentorello, a stock character from the popular comedy tradition of Tuscany. Over the centuries virtually every part of Italy had developed its favorite stock characters, who appeared in drama after drama. Stentorello was "the simpleton, the country bumpkin, the gluttonous servant, the crafty fruit vendor, the shiftless drunkard, the menial with an heroic heart, . . . the Florentine people.[126] Sometimes entire plays were built around the character of Stentorello. Sometimes Stentorello appeared for no apparent reason, interrupting a serious drama, perhaps by Shakespeare, to point at the actors, grimace, make a coarse gesture or comment, and leave the audience laughing hysterically. Arthur Godi of the San Francisco de Cesare Company, brought in by Alessandro from the East, had introduced Stentorello at the Circolo Famigliare Pisanelli, but it was at the Bijou that he developed the character fully, making it his permanent role. Delighted audiences "tumbled hysterically into the aisles" whenever he appeared.[127]

The years between 1907 and 1914 were the peak years of Italian theatre in San Francisco. Italian theatre was becoming so popular, both among the growing Italian community and among the general population, that Alessandro decided to move to larger quarters. She persuaded a local businessman, Abe Reuf, to advance her the capital to buy and remodel a large Russian church on Washington Square, the heart of the North Beach area. When she was unable to repay him in time, the church, now converted into a theatre, was rented to an American vaudeville company. As the signora undoubtedly had anticipated, the American vaudeville company did not last long in Italian North Beach. When it moved out, her Italian theatre moved in.[128]

The new theatre, named the Washington Square Theater, opened in 1909 with a seating capacity of a thousand. Like its predecessor, the Circolo, it soon became a dominant institution in the Italian community and an important part of the cultural life of San Francisco. In the words of a contemporary traveler, "Here the Italian Theater thrives—a large structure, clean and up to date. Except upon festival nights, it is a 10¢ show, but, I assure you, a good one. If you watch the programme, you can have anything you like."[129]

At the Washington Square Theater between 1909 and 1914 you could indeed have almost anything you liked. It was the only legitimate theatre in San Francisco to change its program every day, and twice on Saturday and Sunday! For an admission price of a nickel or a dime (later raised to 10 cents and 20 cents), the audience enjoyed a four-hour show. A mainstay of the program was opera, including grand opera brought in from New York by the Maori Company. There was Shakespearean drama, including *Othello*, *The Merchant of Venice*, *The Taming of the Shrew*, and *Hamlet*, and works by Dumas, Goethe, Sudermann, Sardou, and Jules Verne. There were also less prestigious works, plays written by the actors themselves. (Mario Scarpa's *Caino* and *Abele* was performed in 1909.) Popular plays were imported from Italy ([Valerio] Busnelli's *The Nun of Cracow* and [Luigi] Gualtiere's melodrama *The Mysteries of the Spanish Inquisition*, for example) or adopted from the American stage (*The Two Orphans* was popular). Even movies were shown at the eclectic Washington Square Theater. "Highbrow" and "lowbrow" entertainment were mixed indiscriminately on the same program and enjoyed equally by the audience. In January 1911 a performance of Beaumarchais's *Barber of Seville* was billed with a championship wrestling match. Reviewing the evening's program, an Italian newspaper devoted six paragrpahs to the wrestling match and only one paragraph to the play![130]

One-act comedy sketches remained as popular as ever. Stentorello moved from the Bijou to the Washington Square Theater, interrupting other dramas or starring in sketches of his own.

To give an example: a young modiste is decorating linings for bonnets; to her appear in turn three suitors: a decrepit but proud marquis with monacle and rheumatic legs, then an overdressed but handsome city chap, and finally Stentorello, the country clown dressed . . . in a sort of Watteauesque motley. . . . He's fond of cracking vulgar jokes, but withal has a certain peasant craftiness, getting the best of everybody, and finally, of course, outwitting his rivals and winning the pretty milliner.[131]

Farfariello

Other stock figures of Italian *Commedia dell'Arte* were introduced—Pulcinello, the Neapolitan clown, for example—but the most significant comic offering of the Washington Square Theater was a new figure, Farfariello. As Stentorello was Tuscan and Pulcinello, Neapolitan, Farfariello was American. He was created by Eduardo Migliaccio, an old friend of Signora Alessandro. Migliaccio immigrated to the United States in 1895 and worked in a New York garment sweatshop until he was fired for burning a hole in a pair of pants. At this point he was discovered by Pisanelli, still in New York, who was looking for a partner for her act in a little theatre on Mulberry Street. Pisanelli, brought him to the Mulberry Street theatre, where he created Farfariello, the archetype of the poor southern Italian immigrant. Farfariello was the street vendor, the rag picker, the organ grinder, the pick-and-shovel man, the uneducated "greenhorn," who murdered the English language as well as the Italian. Yet, like Stentorello, Farfariello was hero as well as clown, exposing the weaknesses of the wealthier, more pretentious people around him and somehow triumphing over them.[132]

Some of Farfariello's humor came from his abuse of language. He ridiculed the half-Italian, half-American vocabulary of the immigrant, who would transform "elevator" into "eveta," "car" into "carro," and "Van Ness" into "Vanessi." Much of the humor contained a strong element of social satire. Many of the sketches were parodies of famous people—Enrico Caruso, for example—or of easily recognizable Italian-American types—the fruit dealer, the grocer, the school girl, the nurse. They included shrewd comment on the class structure both of Italy and of the Italian-American colony in the United States. For example, a favorite song described the effect America had in dissolving the rigid class structure of Italy. The humor of the song lies in a pun on the title "la Sciabola," a word which meant "sabre" and thus had upper-class connotations in Italy but which had come to be used for "shovel" in Italian America.

> This new world is upside down
> And the cafone [poor person] here can smile
> For the coat of arms has no renown
> And callouses are in style
> There the signore raises his sabre (sciabola)
> When his sacred honor's hurt
> But here the shovel (sciabola) is used in labor
> And raises mostly dirt.[133]

When Farfariello appeared in New York, Luigi Lucatelli, New York correspondent for *Il Seccolo di Milano,* described him to readers in Italy:

Migliaccio, surnamed Farfariello, has created with words, music, costume, and makeup the most delightful colonial sketches that can be imagined. Every aspect—ironic, serious or gay, joyous or grotesque, of colonial life has traversed the art of this young man of genius.

From the little shopkeeper parvenu, decked out in the uniform of a general, to the cafone who comments on current topics and argues with the American who discredits the far-off fatherland, the simple and stubborn spirit, gayly bizarre, or a little veiled in melancholy comes to us through his art.[134]

Pisanelli had first discovered the comic genius of Migliaccio in New York, and now she brought him to San Francisco, where his Farfariello became the hit of the new Washington Square Theater. Indeed, so popular was Farfariello that Migliaccio took the act on tour to Italy—a theatrical present from the colonies to the homeland. The key to Farfariello's popularity in San Francisco, as in New York, was the fact that he served as a mirror—satirically distorted but a mirror nonetheless—in which the Italian immigrants could see the reflection of their own recent struggles, sufferings, and triumphs. However unpleasant life had been in the homeland, the process of immigration and adjustment to a new life was painful. Farfariello took this process, treated it with exaggeration, irony, and humor, and held it up for the new Italian-Americans to examine from the emotionally safe vantage point of the stage. Farfariello helped the Italian immigrant community to understand, laugh at, and thus transcend its own experience. Through Farfariello, Italian theatre contributed to the process of Americanization.

The Decline of Italian Theatre

Though it was not apparent at the time, the triumph of Farfariello marked the peak of popular Italian theatre in San Francisco and, at the same time, the high point of the career of Signora Alessandro. New Italian theatres came and went, some created by the energetic signora, some established by others, but none occupied the dominant position in the community enjoyed by the Washington Square Theater from 1909 to 1914. Beset with financial problems, Signora Alessandro lost control of the Washington Square Theater in 1914, and the building was converted into a movie house. Undaunted, she spent the next few years renting and erecting new theatres in North Beach and adjoining areas, including a Spanish theatre for the growing Mexican-American community and a Chinese theatre in Chinatown.

As Alessandro's new interests indicate, the population of North Beach was becoming more diverse with the passing years. Many Italians remained there, however, and she did not abandon her interest in them yet. In 1917 she gained control of the California Theater on Broadway "by an extraordinary manipulation of finances," renamed it the Liberty Theater, and, bringing in new companies, gave a new lease on life to Italian theatre. Stentorello and Farfariello returned for brief visits to the Liberty Theater, and on one occasion, a traditional Italian passion play was performed.[135] The support of the Italian community alone was not strong enough to sustain the theatre, however, or perhaps Signora Alessandro wanted to pursue her interest in Mexican theatre. Whatever the reason, she changed the Liberty Theater to Teatro Crescent in 1922, installed the

Spanish-speaking Compano de comedias variedades internacionales, and brought in a Mexican comedian, Romualdo Tirado. The new Crescent Theater offered both Spanish and Italian performances.

Antonietta Pisanelli Alessandro's last Italian theatrical venture was in 1924. She leased and remodeled an old church, rented the ground floor as a movie house, and in the remaining space opened the Teatro Italiano di Varieta. Almost immediately the new Italian theatre became known as the Teatro Alessandro Eden, taking on the name of its founder. Like the original Circolo, the Alessandro Eden was set up as a café. The arms of the chairs grouped around the stage opened up to make little tables for ice cream, cake, and coffee. The program, a mixture of opera, operetta, and comedy, was not as interesting as that of the earlier theatres. Stentorello and Farfariello were gone. Signora Alessandro had aged, of course, but her style remained as flamboyant as ever. On October 3, 1924, she held a grand opening ceremony, featuring an appearance of the noted tenor Tito Schipa, who was in San Francisco at the time. When the Italian community contemplated building a memorial to Dante (it was never built), she sold special programs to raise money for the cause. In these programs her own picture was only slightly smaller than Dante's.

As good a businesswoman as ever, Signora Alessandro updated her advertising with new slogans such as "Il riso fa buon sangue" (Laughter brings health).[136] Her handbills for the new theatre used a novel format, that of the comic strip. One showed a chic Italian "flapper" leaving her house, accompanied by her little dog. The Americanized teenager meets her mother, presumably a more traditional woman, and the conversation between them, written on balloons coming from the characters' mouths, is as follows:

MOTHER: Where are you going with that little dog? Don't you know you are making a hideous appearance?

DAUGHTER: Mama! But I have no other diversion!

MOTHER: Well, if it is a question of diversion, this evening I will take you to see Casta Susanna at the Alessandro Eden, and I am sure that you will be content.[137]

In April 1925 Signora Alessandro staged a gala spectacular at the Teatro Alessandro Eden to celebrate the twentieth anniversary of the opening of her first Italian theatre in 1905. She duplicated as exactly as possible the very first performance staged shortly after her arrival in San Francisco—the same songs, the same plays, even the same cast as far as possible. The celebration was really a gala farewell, however, because shortly thereafter, Signora Alessandro retired from active involvement with the Italian theatre.

Popular Italian theatre declined as the 1920s drew to a close, and within a decade it disappeared altogether. A small "art" theatre continued to give productions of the works of new Italian playwrights such as Pirandello and D'Annunzio, but these productions aroused no broad support or interest within the community.

Signora Alessandro's sudden withdrawal from the Italian theatre in the mid 1920s might be compared to her sale of the Circolo shortly before the San Francisco earthquake—perhaps there was an element of intuition in both decisions. There is a more rational explanation for the 1925 decision, however. Astute and closely attuned to the Italian community, Signora Alessandro was undoubtedly aware of the forces that were making Italian theatre as she had known it obsolete.

The popular Italian theatre established by Antonietta Pisanelli Alessandro had always functioned as an integral part of the North Beach community. During the first two decades of the century North Beach had been a social and cultural center of Italian life; indeed, a program had been put forth in 1910 to make North Beach into "un piccolo canto della patria," a small corner of the beloved Italian homeland.[138] Even before Signora Alessandro's retirement, however, this idea had been abandoned. As early as 1923 an article in the *San Francisco Examiner* described the demise of "Little Italy" both as a geographic reality and as a cultural ideal. "North Beach was once the Italian quarter, but more and more as they have been absorbed into the life of the city they have abandoned the idea of an Italian district and spread out through the city until they have homes and own property in almost every part of it. . . . A great many of them are simply American citizens who originated in Italy."[139]

Time, increasing affluence, and Americanization were breaking up the original North Beach community that had supported Italian theatre. As Alessandro's use of the Italian-American flapper in her advertising suggests, a new generation of American-born young people, now reaching adulthood, did not share the language, the preferences, nor the isolation that had led their parents to embrace Italian theatre so enthusiastically. In the 1920s new forms of entertainment were widely available—the movies, the radio—and these were popular not only with the younger generation, but with their increasingly acculturated parents as well. Italian theatre could not compete with the glamor of Hollywood.

NOW WHO'S UP THERE ON THE STAGE?

There were many Italian theatres outside New York City and San Francisco in the early twentieth century. In Philadelphia there were La Compagnia Italiana Stati Uniti, La Compagnia Filodrammatica Carlo Goldoni, Verdi Hall, and La Compagnia Filodrammatica Vittorio Alfieri. In New Jersey there were La Compagnia Filodrammatica di West Hoboken, La Compagnia Alessandro Manzoni, I Scintilla di West Hoboken, the Circolo Filodrammatico Felice Cavalotti di Paterson, and I Dilettanti Filodrammatici Vittorio Emanuele di Paterson.

Italian theatres in Boston included the Circolo Italiano, the George Washington Club, and the Sezione Filodrammatica of Club Aurora. In Cleveland there was the Italian Filodrammatic Club, in Tampa the Centro Asturiano Theatre, and in Cicero, Illinois, the Italian Dramatic Society. In the early 1920s Chicago had an Italian vaudeville and two legitimate theatres, one of which played Shakespeare and Victor Hugo as well as contemporary Italian dramas, and at least ten amateur theatres, including the Eleanora Duse Dramatic Club based at Hull House. In St. Louis two Italian theatre clubs were still active in the 1940s.

No doubt there were many other companies about which information is fragmentary or nonexistent, as Italian theatres could be found wherever Italians congregated—in New Haven, Los Angeles, Denver, New Orleans, parts of Vermont, and elsewhere.

In New York City, in San Francisco, and wherever they were found, Italian-American theatres filled a need in the immigrant community. Their greatest popularity coincided with the periods of heaviest immigration because they provided social life and entertainment for the recent arrivals. When those needs no longer existed, the decline and eventual demise of the Italian-American theatre in its original form was inevitable. Assimilation, the restriction on immigration passed in 1924, and the advent of radio, movies, and television—all contrived to make the popular Italian-American theatre obsolete and almost nonexistent by 1960.

Ironically, it had contributed to its own demise. It had eased the loneliness and cultural shock of immigration by providing something familiar to people who had been plunged into a strange environment. It had helped immigrants to understand and even to laugh at the changes that were taking place in their lives and had introduced them, gradually and painlessly, to aspects of American life. Finally, by helping immigrants and their children to feel good about their own heritage and experience, it had helped them move more confidently into their new American lives.

In spite of weak hopes on the part of some that it will relive its original popularity, the Italian-American theatre described here was a sociological phenomenon that will never be repeated in the same way, if at all. Other ethnic theatres that enjoyed popular vitality in the 1960s and 1970s, such as the black and Puerto Rican theatres, were responding to different needs. Although some Italian immigration continues, advances in technology, including the ready accessibility of television and movies (Italian movies at that), assure that popular immigrant theatre is no longer possible.

Pasquale De Biasi recounts an episode in which a veteran Italian-American impresarrio was visited in his old age by a young actor. The impresarrio asked the young man:

"Che se dice? 'O teatro che fa? Chi ce sta mo' 'ncopp' 'e scene?" ("What's new? What's happening in the theatre? Now who's up there on the stage?")
    "Nessuno." ("No one").[140]

NOTES

    1. George C. Odell, *Annals of the New York Stage* (New York: Columbia University Press, 1927), Vol. 1, pp. 346, 378, 381, 385.
    2. Ibid., Vol. 2, pp. 6, 8, 14, 18, 39.

3. Pasquale De Biasi, "I 50 Anni di Scena di Guglielmo Ricciardi" (The 50 Stage Years of William Ricciardi), in Guglielmo Ricciardi, *Ricciardiana: Raccolta di Scritti, Racconti, Memorie, ecc. del veterano attore e scrittore Guglielmo Ricciardi* (New York: Eloquent Press Corp., 1955), p. 152.

4. John Horace Mariano, *The Italian Contribution to American Democracy* (Boston: Christopher Publishing House, 1921).

5. Howard R. Marraro, "Italians in New York during the First Half of the Nineteenth Century," *New York History* 26, no. 3 (July 1945): 278–306.

6. Lorenzo Da Ponte, *Memoirs of Lorenzo Da Ponte, Mozart's Libertist*, translated with an introduction by L. A. Sheppard (New York: Houghton Mifflin Company, 1929), p. 316.

7. Odell, *Annals*, Vols. 1 and 2.

8. Mariano, *The Italian Contribution*, p. 210.

9. Marraro, "Italians in New York," pp. 278–306.

10. *The Brooklyn Daily Eagle Almanac: A Book of Information, General of the World and Special of New York City and Long Island* (New York: Press of the Brooklyn Eagle Book and Job Dept., 1908), p. 153.

11. Lawrence Frank Pisani, *The Italian in America: A Social Study and History* (New York: Exposition Press, 1957), p. 47.

12. Mariano, *The Italian Contribution*, p. 6.

13. *Il Progresso Italo-Americano*, Nov. 24–25, 1884, p. 1.

14. *Il Progresso Italo-Americano*, Jan. 8, 1888, p. 1.

15. Ibid.

16. *Il Progresso Italo-Americano*, Dec. 2–3, 1889, p. 2.

17. *New York Amusement Gazette: Record of Operas, Theatres, Concerts and Other Entertainments* 1, no. 9 (Oct. 31, 1885).

18. Odell, *Annals*, Vol. 13, p. 69.

19. *Brooklyn Daily Eagle Almanac*; p. 53.

20. Mariano, *The Italian Contribution*, p. 210.

21. *Brooklyn Daily Eagle Almanac*, p. 153.

22. Pisani, *The Italian in America*, p. 66.

23. Odell, *Annals*, Vol. 15, p. 655.

24. Giuseppe Cautela, "The Italian Theatre in New York," *American Mercury* 12, no. 45 (Sept. 1927): 106–12.

25. Ricciardi, *Ricciardiana: Raccolta di Scritti*, pp. 58–60.

26. Odell, *Annals*, Vol. 11, p. 302.

27. *Il Progresso Italo-Americano*, Nov. 24, 1892, p. 2. English translations for the Italian titles have been provided by the authors of this chapter where necessary.

28. *Brooklyn Daily Eagle Almanac*, 1902, p. 209.

29. Odell, *Annals*, Vol. 10, p. 433.

30. Odell, *Annals*, Vol. 11, p. 515.

31. Odell, *Annals*, Vol. 12, p. 78.

32. Ibid., p. 489.

33. Odell, *Annals*, Vol. 11, p. 515.

34. Odell, *Annals*, Vol. 12, p. 78.

35. Ibid., p. 70.

36. *Il Progresso Italo-Americano*, July 8, 1890, p. 1.

37. *Il Progresso Italo-Americano*, Nov. 23, 1884, p. 2.

272   EMELISE ALEANDRI AND MAXINE SCHWARTZ SELLER

38. Il Progresso Italo-Americano, Mar. 12, 1886, p. 2.
39. Il Progresso Italo-Americano, Aug. 18, 1886, p. 2.
40. Il Progresso Italo-Americano, Jan. 8, 1888, p. 1.
41. Il Progresso Italo-Americano, Jan. 11, 1890, p. 2.
42. Il Progresso Italo-Americano, July 14, 1891, p. 2.
43. Il Progresso Italo-Americano, Nov. 26, 1891, p. 2.
44. Theatre poster included on microfilm with the Sunday, October 16, 1892 issue of Il Progresso Italo-Americano, apparently in error and out of order. The poster was printed by the Eco d'Italia Press, 22 Centre Street. The above information is additionally documented in Il Progresso Italo-Americano, April 4, 1893, p. 2.
45. Brooklyn Daily Eagle Almanac, 1899, pp. 210–11.
46. Il Progresso Italo-Americano, Sept. 4, 1886, p. 2.
47. Il Progresso Italo-Americano, Aug. 18, 1886, p. 2.
48. Odell, Annals, Vol. 12, p. 69.
49. Il Progresso Italo-Americano, Jan. 9, 1886, p. 2.
50. Il Progresso Italo-Americano, Apr. 10, 1886, p. 1.
51. Il Progresso Italo-Americano, Apr. 17, 1886, p. 1.
52. Il Progresso Italo-Americano, Apr. 30, 1886, p. 2.
53. Il Progresso Italo-Americano, Nov. 8–9, 1886, p. 2.
54. Il Progresso Italo-Americano, Jan. 8, 1888, p. 1.
55. Il Progresso Italo-Americano, Feb. 9, 1888, p. 1.
56. Il Progresso Italo-Americano, Jan. 19, 1890, p. 1.
57. Il Progresso Italo-Americano, Feb. 8–9, 1886, p. 21.
58. Il Progresso Italo-Americano, Sept. 7, 1890, p. 2.
59. Il Progresso Italo-Americano, Sept. 4, 1886, p. 3.
60. Il Progresso Italo-Americano, Oct. 9, 1886, p. 2.
61. Ricciardi, Ricciardiana: Raccolta di Scritti, p. 21.
62. Il Progresso Italo-Americano, Jan. 24, 1888, p. 2.
63. Il Progresso Italo-Americano, Feb. 15–16, 1886, p. 2.
64. Il Progresso Italo-Americano, July 12–13, 1886, p. 2.
65. Il Progresso Italo-Americano, Aug. 14, 1890, p. 1.
66. Il Progresso Italo-Americano, Sept. 2, 1890, p. 3.
67. Il Progresso Italo-Americano, Sept. 4, 1892, p. 2.
68. Il Progresso Italo-Americano, Oct. 30, 1890, p. 2.
69. Il Progresso Italo-Americano, Nov. 23, 1884, p. 2.
70. Il Progresso Italo-Americano, May 22, 1886, p. 1.
71. Ibid.
72. Il Progresso Italo-Americano, May 14, 1886, p. 2.
73. Brooklyn Daily Eagle Almanac, 1908, p. 264.
74. Il Progresso Italo-Americano, May 14, 1886, p. 2.
75. Il Progresso Italo-Americano, Oct. 8, 1892, p. 2.
76. Il Progresso Italo-Americano, Aug. 14, 1890, p. 1.
77. Il Progresso Italo-Americano, Feb. 22, 1891, p. 2.
78. Ricciardi, Ricciardiana: Raccolta di Scritti, p. 39.
79. Il Progresso Italo-Americano, Dec. 6, 1892, p. 2.
80. Il Progresso Italo-Americano, 1888, date unclear, p. 1.
81. Odell, Annals, Vol. 11, p. 302; Il Progresso Italo-Americano, Nov. 24–25, 1884, p. 1.

82. *Il Progresso Italo-Americano,* Jan. 16, 1889, p. 2.

83. "Grasso, Great Italian Actor, and The Screen," *La Vedetta Artistica* 1, no. 7–8 (Oct.–Nov. 1921), p. 17.

84. *Il Progresso Italo-Americano,* Nov. 23, 1884, p. 2.

85. Odell, *Annals,* Vol. 14, p. 96.

86. Ricciardi, *Ricciardiana: Raccolta di Scritta,* p. 27.

87. *Il Progresso Italo-Americano,* May 29, 1892, p. 2.

88. *Il Progresso Italo-Americano,* Apr. 4, 1893, p. 2.

89. *Il Progresso Italo-Americano,* Jan. 6, 1888, p. 2; Jan. 15, 1888, p. 2; May 1, 1888, p. 1; May 2, 1888, p. 2; June 8, 1888, p. 2; June 28, 1888, p. 1; Dec. 23, 1892, p. 2.

90. Odell, *Annals,* Vol. 13, p. 495.

91. *Il Progresso Italo-Americano,* Sept. 4, 1889, p. 3; Oct. 16, 1892, p. 6.

92. *Il Progresso Italo-Americano,* Nov. 24, 1892, p. 2.

93. Odell, *Annals,* Vol. 12, p. 78.

94. *Il Progresso Italo-Americano,* Oct. 1, 1893, p. 2.

95. "The crazy city," in Ricciardi, *Ricciardiana: Raccolta di Scritta,* p. 17.

96. De Biasi, "The Tower of Babel, New York," and "Prefazione," in Ricciardi, *Ricciardiana: Raccolta di Scritta,* p. 5.

97. Cautela, "Italian Theatre in New York," p. 111.

98. Pisani, *The Italian in America,* p. 178.

99. Ibid.

100. Hutchins Hapgood, "The Foreign Stage in New York: 3. The Italian Theatre," *Bookman* 11 (Aug. 1900): 545–53.

101. Ibid.

102. Ricciardi, *Ricciardiana: Raccolta di Scritti.*

103. The name Villa Vittorio Emanuele III arouses some speculation. Since the dates I mention for the opening of this café extend from 1892 or 1895 until 1903 at the latest, the reason King Victor Emanuel III of Italy was chosen to be thus honored poses a problem. Victor Emanuel III did not become King of Italy until 1900, a year of the assassination of his father, Humbert I (who, incidentally, also had a *caffè concerto* in New York named for him). It is possible that the villa was thus named after one of its transformations and remodelings, which might have coincided with the ascendancy of the king in 1900. Another possibility is that the café, sometimes referred to as simply the Villa Vittorio Emanuele without the III, might have been named for the father of Humbert, King Victor Emanuel II, retained that name throughout the reign of Humbert, and then updated when the next Victor Emanuel became king. Nowhere is there any explanation or clarification of this point.

104. Ricciardi, *Ricciardiana: Raccolta di Scritta,* pp. 58–60.

105. Cautela, "Italian Theatre in New York," p. 106.

106. For further information on the Italian community of California, see Andrew F. Rolle, *The Immigrant Upraised: Italian Adventurers and Colonists in an Expanding America* (Norman, Okla.: University of Oklahoma Press, 1968), and Deanna M. Paoli, "The Italian Colony of San Francisco 1850–1930" (Ph.D. diss., University of San Francisco, 1970).

107. Rolle, *The Immigrant Upraised,* p. 252.

108. Lawrence Estavan, ed., "San Francisco Theater Research Monographs," Works Progress Administration, San Francisco, 1939, Vol. 10, p. 1. Unpublished manuscripts available in the San Francisco Public Library and New York City Public Library, Lincoln

Center. For general background on San Francisco as a center of culture and entertainment in the midnineteenth century, see Oscar Lewis, *This Was San Francisco* (New York: David McKay, 1962), and George MacMinn, *The Theater of the Golden Era in California* (Caldwell, Idaho: Caxton Printers, Ltd., 1941).

109. Pauline Jacobson, "Napoleon of the Theaters," *San Francisco Bulletin*, Aug. 18, 1917, p. 13.

110. Estavan, "San Francisco Theater," Vol. 10, p. 5.

111. Ibid., Vol. 15, p. 186.

112. Ibid., Vol. 10, pp. 6–10.

113. Ibid., Vol. 10, p. 10.

114. Ibid., Vol. 15, p. 186.

115. Ibid., Vol. 10, p. 11.

116. Paul Radin, *The Italians of San Francisco: Their Adjustment and Acculturation*, abstract from the SERA Project, Parts I and II (San Francisco: R and E Research Associates, reprint, 1970), pp. 27–39.

117. Paoli, *Italian Colony*, p. 48.

118. J. M. Scanland, "An Italian Quarter Mosaic," *Overland Monthly*, Apr. 1906, as cited in Estavan, "San Francisco Theater Research," Vol. 10, pp. 13–14.

119. Ibid., p. 12.

120. Ernest Peixotto, "Italy in California," *Scribner's* 48 (July 1910): 82. See also Estavan, "San Francisco Theater," Vol. 10, pp. 17, 21.

121. Ibid., Vol. 10, p. 14.

122. Ibid., pp. 12–20.

123. Ibid., pp. 20–21.

124. Winfield Scott, "Old Wine in New Bottles," *Sunset*, May 1913, as cited in Wayne Moquin, ed., *A Documentary History of the Italian Americans* (New York: Praeger Publishers, 1974), p. 137.

125. Estavan, "San Francisco Theater Research," Vol. 10, p. 22.

126. Ibid., p. 25.

127. Ibid., pp. 26–27.

128. Ibid., p. 27.

129. Ernest Peixotto, *Romantic California* (New York: Charles Scribner's Sons, 1910), p. 8.

130. Estavan, "San Francisco Theater Research," Vol. 10, p. 39.

131. Peixotto, *Romantic California*, p. 20.

132. Deanna Paoli Gamina, "Connazionali, Stentorello, and Farfariello: Italian Variety Theater in San Francisco," *California Historical Quarterly* 54 (Spring 1975): 29–36.

133. Estavan, "San Francisco Theater Research," Vol. 10, pp. 53–55.

134. Ibid., p. 52.

135. According to Estavan (ibid., p. 45), the passion play was making excellent progress until "the crucified Christ suddenly felt a sinking sensation. He glanced down and learned that he was sinking, that the block which supported him on the cross . . . was slipping down. . . . The actor began cursing heartily, . . . summoning his prototype to witness his predicament. Beneath the cross knelt Maria Magdalena and Veronica, their lamentations disturbed by the frenzied profanity of the martyred Christ. In the wings were the rest of the cast, bursting with suppressed laughter."

136. Ibid., p. 67.

137. Ibid., p. 68.

138. Paoli, *The Italian Colony*, pp. 45, 77. Paoli cites Ettore Patrizi, Gl'Italiani in California (San Francisco: tip. = Litogr. del Giornade l' (Italia), 1911), 33.

139. Robert H. Williams, "Little Italy," *San Francisco Examiner*, Nov. 25, 1923.

140. De Biasi, "Prefazione," in Ricciardi, *Ricciardiana: Raccolta di Scritti*, p. 7.

BIBLIOGRAPHY

The Brooklyn Daily Eagle Almanac: A Book of Information, General of the World and Special of New York City and Long Island. New York: Press of the Brooklyn Eagle Book and Job Department, 1886–1915.

Da Ponte, Lorenzo. *Memoirs of Lorenzo Da Ponte, Mozart's Librettist*, translated with an introduction by L. A. Sheppard. New York: Houghton Mifflin Company, 1929.

Estavan, Lawrence, ed. "San Francisco Theater Research Monographs," Vol. 10. Works Progress Administration, San Francisco, 1939. Unpublished manuscripts available in the San Francisco Public Library and the New York City Public Library, Lincoln Center. The best account, with illustrations, of the history of Italian theatre in San Francisco.

Mariano, John Horace. *The Italian Contribution to American Democracy*. Boston: Christopher Publishing House, 1921. A defense of the Italian Americans written during the immigration restriction controversy, this work contains valuable statistical data and other information on the early-twentieth-century Italian community in the United States.

New York Amusement Gazette: Record of Operas, Theatres, Concerts and Other Entertainments 1–13 (1885–90).

Odell, George C. *Annals of the New York Stage*, Vols. 1–15. New York: Columbia University Press, 1921. A standard and comprehensive theatre history.

Paoli, Deanna M. "The Italian Colony of San Francisco 1850–1930." Ph.D. diss., University of San Francisco, 1970.

Peixotto, Ernest. *Romantic California*. New York: Charles Scribner's Sons, 1910.

Pisani, Lawrence Frank. *The Italian in America: A Social Study and History*. New York: Exposition Press, 1957.

Radin, Paul. *The Italians of San Francisco: Their Adjustment and Acculturation*, abstract from the SERA project, Parts I and II San Francisco: R and E Research Associates, reprint, 1970.

Ricciardi, Guglielmo. *Ricciardiana: Raccolta di Scritti, Racconti, Memorie, ecc. del veterano attore e scrittore Guglielmo Ricciardi*. New York: Eloquent Press Corp., 1955.

Rolle, Andrew F. *The Immigrant Upraised: Italian Adventurers and Colonists in an Expanding America.* Norman, Okla.: University of Oklahoma Press 1968. Contains information on the early history of San Francisco's North Beach community.

Schiavo, Giovanni E. *The Italians in Chicago: A Study in Americanization*. Chicago: Italian American Publishing Company, 1928. An account of the Chicago community, including its theatres, by a noted early Italian-American historian.

Articles

Cautela, Giuseppe. "The Bowery," *American Mercury* 9, no. 35 (Nov. 1926): 365–68 and "The Italian Theatre in New York," *American Mercury* 12, no. 45 (Sept. 1927): 106–12.

Cunetto, Dominic. "Italian Language Theater Clubs in St. Louis, Missouri 1910–1950." M. A. thesis, University of Florida, 1960.

De Biasi, Pasquale. "I 50 Anni di Scene di Guglielmo Ricciardi." In Guglielmo Ricciardi, *Ricciardiana: Raccolta de Scritti, Racconti, Memorie, ecc. del veterano attore e scrittore Guglielmo Ricciardi*. New York: Eloquent Press Corp., 1955, pp. 152–54.

Gamina, Deanna Paoli. "Connazionali, Stentorello, and Farfariello: Italian Variety Theater in San Francisco," *California Historical Quarterly* 54 (Spring 1975): 29–36.

"Grasso, Great Italian Actor, and the Screen," *La Vedetta Artistica* 1, nos. 27–28 (Oct.–Nov. 1921): 17.

Hapgood, Hutchins. "The Foreign Stage in New York: 3. The Italian Theatre," *Bookman* 11 (Aug. 1900), 545–53. One of a widely read series of articles by a noted journalist.

Il Progresso Italo-Americano, Nov. 23, 1884 to Dec. 5, 1894. New York City Public Library, collection incomplete. Italian-language daily in New York City and an important source of information about early Italian-American theatre in that city.

Marraro, Howard R. "Italians in New York during the First Half of the Nineteenth Century," *New York History* 26, no. 3 (July 1945): 278–306.

Peixotto, Ernest. "Italy in California" *Scribner's* 48 (July 1910). Contains vivid contemporary descriptions of Italian vaudeville and comedy in San Francisco.

Scanland, J. M. "An Italian Quarter Mosaic, *Overland Monthly*, Apr. 1906. Enthusiastic and slightly romanticized, but useful, journalistic descriptions of Antonietta Pisanelli and her theatre, Circolo Famigliare Pisanelli.

Williams, Robert H. "Little Italy," *San Francisco Examiner*, Nov. 25, 1923. Article describing the beginning of the dispersion of San Francisco's Italian colony.

Other Sources

Most of the source materials on Italian-American theatre lie buried in microfilms and newspaper collections in the public libraries of cities that had large Italian immigrant populations. The Immigration History Research Center at the University of Minnesota has the personal papers of some important figures in Italian-American theatre.

11

Latvian-American Theatre

ALFREDS STRAUMANIS

There are several means by which the success and vitality of a theatre can be measured. An average Broadway producer will use the length of the play's run and the profits generated for the investors; the directors on the board of a nonprofit regional theatre will rely on the reviews praising the artistic achievements of their ensemble; and the actors in a community theatre will judge their success by how much fun they had doing a certain production. The down-to-earth theatre manager, however, will use the size of the potential audience of a given city as a measure of success or failure, and the manager's criterion will be the generally accepted and statistically proven fact that only 2 percent of the total American population attends theatre in a given year. According to this criterion, the Latvian theatre in the United States, since the first production of a play in the Latvian language in 1898, has been more than successful, and its vitality is undisputable.

There have been two definite waves of Latvian immigration to this country. The first started in 1888 and reached its peak around the end of World War I; the second started in 1948, reaching its climax during 1952 and stopping almost completely shortly before 1960. While in 1905 unofficial estimates show about five thousand Latvians in this country, the 1930 U.S. census figures indicate 38,091 and the 1970 census figures, 86,413 Latvians.[1]

Although the total Latvian population in this country has changed drastically, the percentage of those attending theatre in different time periods has remained almost constant. In 1909, when about 800 Latvians lived in and around Boston and on the average 233 of them attended the nine plays presented there that season, it was 28 percent.[2] In 1975, when *Princese Gundega un Karālis Brusubarda* (literally translatable as Princess Buttercup and King Bristlebeard), written in 1912 by Anna Brigadere (1861–1933), was produced in New York City, the three standing-room-only performances had 2,400 spectators, or 24 percent of the 10,000 Latvians living in the New York metropolitan area.

The high percentages in the given examples can be attributed to the large concentrations of Latvians in the two cities. It is true that the Latvians, although coming from a basically agricultural society in their homeland, have adapted themselves to city life here. They live and work mostly in and around the larger metropolitan centers on the East Coast, in the northern United States, and on the West Coast. Still, many have settled in smaller communities far removed from the major Latvian colonies. As these do not have their own theatre ensembles, they are served by traveling companies out of the larger centers. These companies tend to visit as many small communities as possible, and quite frequently they travel from coast to coast. As their scope seems to be nationwide, statistics on the size of their total audience may yield a more realistic percentage.

In 1956 one such company, under the auspices of the now defunct Association of Latvian Theatre Friends, traveled out of New York City to thirty-one locations as far west as Sioux Falls, South Dakota, covering about 25 percent of the territory of the United States. The four-character play *Jaunās asinis* (The Young Blood), by émigré writer Voldemārs Kārkliņš (1906–1964), had varied numbers of spectators: the one performance in Chicago had 650, as opposed to only 30 at the performance in Elkhart, Indiana. The total number of those who saw this production, however, was more than ten thousand. Taking the highest-known Latvian count in the United States—the eighty-six thousand of the 1970 census—as a base, we still have an attendance of almost 12 percent, without regard for the number of Latvians in the total population who were of age to appreciate the theatre.

I could go on citing statistics, as well as relating personal experiences, such as meeting people who had traveled three hundred miles from their residences just to see the above-mentioned play, for which, besides playing a role, I was the stage manager. The point is that the Latvian theatre in the United States has remained a successful and vital institution throughout the more than eighty years of its existence. This sustained activity puzzles the historian because theatre is a communal experience, while the Latvian people are strongly individualistic, and because there have been two entirely different groups of Latvians in the United States, the result of two waves of immigration.

The first wave, which started late in the nineteenth century, consisted of people who were seeking better economic conditions than those in the Baltic provinces of the Russian Empire as well as of those with religious persuasions not pleasing to the czarist regime, such as the Latvian Baptists. A smaller percentage of the first wave was made up of hard-core revolutionaries who had either been exiled or had escaped from the penal expeditions the czar had sent into Latvia during and after the 1905 revolution. According to some accounts their number reached about four thousand; however, only about a thousand of these were socialists, as far as their political allegiance was concerned.[3] This small but very active and outspoken segment of the Latvian immigrants before and during World War I defended the cause of Soviet Russia, as opposed to that of an independent Latvia. Their ability to agitate and organize among their ethnic group members has created a somewhat distorted impression about the "old Latvians"[4] in the eyes of Americans and in the minds of the Latvian immigrants of the second wave. Many of the "old Latvian" socialists had become Communists and had joined the American Communist party or returned to Soviet Russia early in its existence. Thus, when the second wave of Latvian immigrants arrived, they expected, according to the pronouncements of their nationalistic leaders, to meet the "red Latvians."

The second wave of immigration started after World War II, and it brought to America Latvians who had been instrumental in creating a free and independent Latvia by fighting the German as well as the Soviet armies. They and their children had seen a period of prosperity in Latvia between the two wars, but they had also been witnesses to killings and deportations of their countrymen during the first Soviet occupation of Latvia in 1940–1941. When the second occupation became imminent at the end of World War II, they fled their country and were settled in West German displaced persons' camps, hoping to return after the war as soon as the Western powers would have forced the Russians to leave the occupied lands. This did not happen, however, and the displaced persons were given a choice of emigrating to the United States, among other countries. The status of a displaced person was not the most promising, and although urged by their leaders not to leave Europe, many Latvians immigrated to the United States as a stopgap measure.

The two waves of immigrants were on ideologically opposite sides, and their reasons for immigrating were completely different; therefore it is surprising to find theatre as a popular institution in both groups. This chapter will describe the theatres of the old and the new Latvian immigrants as separate entities, which they were. However, recognizing that for both groups theatre was a vital institution, an attempt will be made to determine the common denominator of its genesis as well as the forces that helped to sustain it.

BIRTH OF THEATRE IN LATVIA

The tribes that later became the Latvian nation are known to have inhabited the area east of the Baltic Sea since at least the beginning of our era,[5] but only during the latter part of the nineteenth century was a conscious effort begun to solidify this nation and free the land of its ancestors from the two oppressors, the German barons and the Russian czar. At that time the Latvian theatre was born, and the way in which this birth occurred partially explains its persistence among the two Latvian-American societies—congeneric, though on opposite sides philosophically and politically. The Latvian theatre was not established because of a dormant need for an aesthetic experience; it was created to enable the leaders of the National Awakening to legally assemble large crowds. All meetings in the Baltic provinces of the Russian Empire were forbidden unless an authorization from the government was expressly given. Thus at its very beginning the Latvian theatre was utilitarian in nature, an institution with a definite purpose, as the history of its development clearly indicates.

Until 1868 the Latvians did not have national organizations. The Russian governor, influenced by the German barons, declined to authorize such organizations, which in his opinion could become sources of unrest against the existing order. In 1867 crops were bad in Finland and Estonia and famine followed; the Latvian leaders used this occasion to organize a Latvian Relief Committee, for which they were able to secure an authorization from the governor.[6] In order to raise money this committee organized lectures and concerts; also a play in the Latvian language, *Žūpu Bērtulis* (Bertulis the Drunkard) was performed.[7] Compared with the concerts and lectures, the first show in Latvian was an unexpected success. This induced the Latvian leaders to develop the medium, which could easily be used for propaganda as well as for education. A second play, this time a translation of F. L. Schroeder's *Stilles Wasser, tiefes Wasser*, was produced shortly after.

With this play the translator made a bad choice; for the Latvians there are many better and more suitable plays. . . . The theatre ought to be like school, in which the human being is physically and spiritually elevated and taught to choose the correct way of living. Comedy is the trend now, but even comedy can show how foolishness and vice fight with knowledge. The theatre is the place where our language can be developed, and that it needs development is evident.[8]

This reviewer also insisted that plays in which the Latvians would be able to recognize themselves as characters and learn from their deeds should be presented on stage. But he conceded that "it is quite hard to write plays; the Creator has not given this capacity to everyone."

As if following this advice to develop the Latvian language, Richards Tomsons (1834–1884), a member of the theatre section of the newly formed Latvian Relief Committee of Riga, wrote an original one-act play, *Vecais Jurka* (The Old Jurka). This play was produced not only in Riga but also in Jelgava. About the presentation on April 27, 1869, we read: "A play in the Latvian language . . . was something extraordinary. . . . After the show in the streets of Jelgava one could hear the Latvian language spoken freely for the first time.[9]

For us this emphasis upon "the Latvian language spoken freely" is important. It shows that a theatre is able to awaken national pride. The Latvians who lived in the cities were economically well situated; as artisans and merchants they were better off than the Germans and the Russians. But culturally these same Latvians had adopted the way of living and the language of the Germans. Now, after the first show in their native language, these people became conscious of their nationality. However, one should not overestimate the quality of the first original play in Latvian, since it was written by a man who was an amateur in literature as well as in theatre.

ĀDOLFS ALUNĀNS

On June 24, 1869, a play, *Paša audzināts* (Self-tutored), by Ādolfs Alunāns (1848–1912), was presented in connection with the erection of the building for the Latvian Association of Riga (Rīgas Latviešu Biedrība) (formerly the Latvian Relief Committee [Latviešu Palīdzības Komiteja]). The author participated in the production and at once became popular as a writer and actor in the Latvian theatre.[10] He had studied acting early in his life at the German theatre in Jelgava. In 1866 he had established himself as an actor in German troupes in Tallinn, Tartu, Narva, and St. Petersburg, but he switched over to the newly created Latvian theatre at its infancy.

Paša audzināts was presented in many towns and communities. These presentations stimulated the organization of theatre groups in Bauska, Allaži, Vecpiebalga, and other towns. While he was director of the theatre section of the Latvian Association of Riga, Alunāns traveled to other communities to help organize these groups. In the first fifteen years of his activities, Alunāns produced about 250 plays.[11] After twenty-five years of acting and directing in the Latvian theatre, he became known as the father of Latvian theatre.[12]

Besides acting and directing, Alunāns continued to write plays, and to translate them from German and Russian. During the first ten years of the Latvian theatre, some forty individuals tried writing plays. Eight of the new playwrights were teachers; one was an actor; and one was the owner of a factory.[13] Most of these playwrights produced adaptations and localizations, and only occasionally was an original written. Although Alunāns directed these plays as well, his credo was to build a purely national theatre. His ideas about such a theatre were expressed by a reviewer as follows: "Theatre has always developed and strengthened the national consciousness. Therefore, we have to produce plays which are structured according to our bones, the flesh of which is like our flesh, where the characters act and talk like the Latvians do.[14]

In order to achieve his goal, Alunāns proceeded step by step. A reviewer had written that "comedy is the trend now,"[15] and Alunāns wrote comedies, such as *Paša audzināts* and the operetta *Mucenieks un muceniece* (Mr. and Mrs. Cooper) for the single intention of attracting an audience. In these comedies he showed life on the estates, where the new Latvian farmers lived still influenced by the barons. This life was still well remembered by the spectators. The characters were realistic; the language used in the plays was the same as the Latvians used in their conversations. In *Mucenieks un muceniece* Alunāns used Latvian folk songs for the musical numbers and devised the plot around these songs. Everything seemed familiar to the audience: the songs, the folk costumes, the dances. Thus those in the new Latvian theatre audience felt that the theatre was part of their lives and accepted it as such.

After his success with the comedies and the operetta, where the folk songs were used in order to acclimate the new audience with the art form, Alunāns started to write plays with more elaborate plot and characterization. He did not, though, reject the folk song and the folk tale as a basis for his plays. He merely concentrated upon a specific song or tale and devised the plot around it, keeping in mind the theme, the mood, and especially the ethical maxim this song or tale contained. In 1887 the play *Kas tie tādi, kas dziedāja* (Who Were Those Who Sang) was written in this manner, and the first line of a folk song became the title of the play. The same method was used also in *Visi mani radi raud* (All My Relatives Are Crying), only here the plot was based on a folk tale about a poor laborer who falls in love with a boyar's daughter. A very theatrical play, written in 1889, was *Seši mazi bundzenieki* (Six Little Drummers), which also had for its title the first line of a folk song. It contained elements of the Latvian wedding ritual.

Only when the Latvians had accepted theatre as part of their existence did Alunāns become a fighter for the ideas of the Juanā strāva (New Current) a literary movement that had been started in 1890 by the editors of *Dienas Lapa* (Daily Bulletin), at a time when the national awakening had begun to lose its purpose and direction. A character in *Kas tie tādi, kas dziedāja*, for example, tells a baron about the national pride the Latvians possess:

Sir, our little nation has just awakened from a long and deep sleep. This nation has lost plenty: its songs, its gods, and its freedom. But a small jewel, well hidden from the robbers, is still in its possession. Through centuries it glitters brighter than gold or diamonds. Even today this jewel is in the heart of every Latvian. We call it honor. Sir, I'm willing to loose my land, never my honor.[16]

In two dramas, *Pārticība un nabadzība* (The Fortunate and the Poor) and *Lielpils pagasta vecākie* (The Aldermen of Lielpils), Alunāns explores tbe ideas of national awakening and national unity to the utmost. "As the author of these two plays Alunāns has ceased to be an objective observer of life. He is imbued with an aggressive desire to comment on it."[17] His last play, *Mūsu senči* (Our Ancestors), written in iambic verse, is the synthesis of all his strivings. It is the culmination of his patriotic, aesthetic, humanistic, and social ideas. The theme is taken from Latvian legends, partially recorded,[18] and the story is about the Latvian ancestors fighting the Teutonic Crusaders. The ritual of the summer solstice is shown in all its splendor in this play. When a Latvian leader, Imants, is killed by a scheme of the German sympathizer, Kaupo, the daughter of another Latvian leader takes the sword and leads the fight. In the play her father, Acons, tells the Germans, "We've decided to be the masters in our land again. We, all Latvians, by this are telling you and all your friends that from now on we want the fruits of our land for ourselves.[19]

Mūsu senči was produced on the eve of the revolution in 1905, a revolution that was the climax of the efforts of the Juanā strāva. At that time Alunāns had retired from active involvement with the theatre, but his work was carried on by others.

THE NEW DRAMATISTS

The first three decades of the Latvian theatre were spent under the hegemony of Alunāns, but in 1893 the situation changed. This was partly due to the rise of new and better dramatists, such as Rūdolfs Blaumanis (1863–1908), Anna Brigadere, Jānis Rainis (real name, Jānis Pliekšāns, 1865–1929), and Aspazija (real name, Elza Rozenberga-Pliekšāns, 1868–1943), and partly to the achievements of Pēteris Ozoliņš (1864–1938), the new theatre director of the Latvian Association of Riga. Ozoliņš had studied drama and the art of directing at the conservatory of Dresden and had also acted in Germany for two years. He sought and found a purely national art in the plays of Blaumanis. With the production of Blaumanis's *Pazudušais dēls* (The Prodigal Son) in 1893, he started a new era in the history of the Latvian theatre.

The new dramatists generally differed in their style of writing. Some of them, such as Rainis and Aspazija, who had first begun writing in the German language, tried to write Latvian plays in the manner of German *Volksstücke*. However, the Latvian audiences, already excited about the national awakening and the renaissance of the folk ritual, reacted negatively to everything not purely nationalistic. When the same Rainis started to write his symbolic dramas based upon the legends of ancient Latvians, in which he reconstructed the folk ritual and inserted ideas of the national awakening, his success was instantaneous. The New Theatre of Riga (Jaunais Rīgas Teātris) opened in 1909 with his *Zelta Zirgs* (The Goldon Steed)[20] and until its closing due to World War I produced five of Rainis's symbolic dramas.

A symbolist movement was quite popular in Western Europe at the end of the nineteenth century, and Rainis and his contemporary Latvian playwrights may have borrowed techniques of using symbols from such dramatists as Maurice Maeterlinck. Their symbols, however, were not of a kind that could be universally understood; they were developed from a specifically Latvian folk tradition. The primary reason for using this kind of symbolism was the need to hide the deeper meaning of an intended message from the censors whose authorization was required for producing a given play. Thus in *Uguns un nakts* (Fire and Night) Rainis, in order to emphasize the ongoing fight between the Latvian people and their oppressors, used the character of the Black Knight. For the censor the Black Knight was just an evil soldier, but for the Latvian spectator it became a symbol of all the forces that had subjugated the nation for seven hundred years.

The new dramatists used other devices that achieved symbolic meaning. Brigadere, in the aforementioned *Princese Gundega un Karālis Brusubarda* uses Latvian proverbs such as "When night is the darkest, a new day starts." The line was intended as a promise to the Latvian people, and it was taken as such symbolically by the audience. As a matter of fact, all plays of the period under discussion were permeated by such symbolic devices. Arvīds Ziedonis, Jr., while talking about Rainis, aptly says:

All of his plays . . . were created for the inspiration and the guidance of his people toward political and spiritual maturity and understanding. Against the background of legendary and historical dramas, based on the nation's folklore, through symbolism and verse, Rainis created a powerful medium for the expression of his contemporary aspirations. In this way he bridged the past, the present and the future, giving old truths a new meaning.[21]

Rainis's wife, Aspazija, also used legends and folklore motifs for her plays. She elevated her characters to symbols in line with the ideas of the New Current. Jānis Rudzītis (1909–1970), a literary critic, having in mind Aspazija's *Sidraba šķidrauts* (The Silver Veil),[22] wrote:

Aspazija became the most glaring figure among the neo-romanticists, full of buoyance, passionate temperament, verve and pathos. Her pseudonym and mental disposition remind us of the famous wife of Pericles. Her heroes, especially women, are inclined to the absolute emancipation, "where the human spirits are united in harmonious feelings, and a stream of light flows undisturbed forever."[23]

In *Sidraba šķidrauts*, which was produced on the eve of the 1905 revolution, the heroine, Guna, calls for absolute emancipation, and it is no wonder that Guna became the symbol of this revolution.

The five above-mentioned dramatists wrote in a variety of styles and covered the whole range of experiences and aspirations of the now nationally solidified people. The folk comedy, started by Alunāns, was continued and improved upon by Blaumanis, whose writing was realistic in the best sense of the term. Blaumanis also wrote dramas exposing the changes in society, and with a deep psychological insight showed conflicts between characters that represented the old and the new. Powerful dramas, such as *Ugunī* (On Fire), *Pazudušais dēls*, and *Indrāni* (The Indrāns) dealt with the rift between the individual and the society or parents and children.

Brigadere, besides exploring the work ethic in her fairy tale plays, was an objective observer of society in the small towns. In the first case she used a slightly romantic, and in the second a realistic approach, though avoiding the melodramatic. Melodrama was the trademark of Aspazija, who excited her audiences with symbolic as well as realistic plays such as *Zaudētas tiesības* (Lost Rights). In this play, besides denigrating the former masters of the land, the barons, she fought diligently for the emancipation of women. While Alunāns ended his career with the romantically nationalistic *Mūsu senči*, Rainis started his with romantically symbolic plays such as *Uguns un Nakts*.

The second generation of Latvian dramatists had learned from the best examples of Western drama: Shakespeare, Schiller, Goethe, Lessing, Hauptmann, and Ibsen, among others. They had been translated, quite often by the dramatists under discussion themselves, and produced by the Latvian theatres. At the beginning of the twentieth century, Russian authors, such as Tolstoy and Gorky, also saw light on the Latvian stages. But whatever their style or dramatic know-how, all these dramatists wrote about their own people and included easily identifiable folklore motifs in their plays. In such a way they were able to give impetus to the dissemination of the ideas of the national awakening, to the solidification of the aspirations of the people, and to the identification of Latvians as a group. These dramatists were able to evoke the appropriate emotional attitude in their audiences and attract great numbers to the theatres. In doing so, they fulfilled the primary goal of the first generation of dramatists: to make theatre the place for large gatherings.

The popularity of the new institution, the Latvian theatre, is evidenced by statistics. In 1881, when in Riga there was only one Latvian theatre, thirteen performances were given with 5,500 in attendance; in 1900 the same theatre gave seventy-three performances with 43,000 attending. During 1901 there were 523 performances in Latvian given in Riga; in 1905 the number dropped to 454 (during the 1905 revolution Latvian theatres were closed by governmental decree as instigators of unrest), but it rose to 654 in 1907, to 1,329 in 1910, and to 1,460 in 1911. The total audience in 1910 had reached 190,000, and it increased to 195,000 the following year, when Riga had half a million inhabitants.[24] The high audience figure is even more surprising if we consider the large number of inhabitants of other nationalities, such as Lithuanians (they had their own theatre in Riga), Russians, Poles, and Estonians—all attracted to Riga because of its industrial growth—and Germans and Jews, both of which groups had their own theatres in the city.

The newly created love for theatre did not cease to exist even during World War I, when many Latvians were forced to leave their country and settle in different parts of the Russian Empire, some as far as Siberia. There were many theatre performances in Latvian language throughout Russia during the war years, and the Latvians remaining in Soviet Russia after the war had their own theatre ensembles until the Stalinist purge in 1937. One of them, Skatuve (The Stage), founded in Moscow in 1919, became a professional state theatre, with considerable artistic fame among the other minority theatres, which gathered for yearly "Olympiads" in Moscow.

This theatre tradition was also renewed by the Latvian immigrants to the United States. Presumably love for theatre must be present in order to sustain this form of art; however, immigrant theatre should be seen from a different perspective, where love is the apex supported by more basic ingredients, which sustain the human existence in a new and still unfamiliar land.

OLD LATVIAN THEATRE

It must have been love for the art that prompted the pioneers of the Old Latvian theatre to spend many hours after a hard day's work in preparing the first U.S. productions in the Latvian language. This love must have existed before they arrived in the United States, as is indeed apparent from the scant evidence found in some oral histories and even in obituaries that have appeared in the

American Latvian press. Advertisements in Latvian newspapers of the day indicate that some immigrants had had theatre education, or at least experience,
such as Vilija Jansone-Schlossberg, who offered "dramatic training in Latvian
and German, including stage speech, mimicry, and gestures."[25] Jansone-
Schlossberg was the wife of a well-established Latvian actor of Riga, Roberts
Jansons (1864–1899), and she immigrated to the United States after her husband's death. Mīce Niedze, who came here in 1906 and had acted for many years
with the New York Latvian ensembles, had previous acting experience in Riga,
together with Jānis Sauleskalns, who had arrived earlier. Niedze later became
quite prominent among the Latvian actors and directors.[26] Alberts Munkens
(1871–1948), who in his obituary is credited with producing the first play in the
Latvian language in the United States, also had previous experience: he had
worked with Alunāns and other prominent theatre personalities of Riga as an
actor and had written drama criticism for progressive Latvian newspapers.[27]

Munkens arrived in 1902, settled in Philadelphia, and in the same year,
according to the obituary, organized a Latvian theatre production. Although an
organization of Latvians, the Society of Free Letts, had existed in Philadelphia
since 1892, there is no mention of this production in its archives. Thus we have
to assume that the first production was done by individuals not associated with a
club or organization, and there is no factual evidence regarding the play's title
and the place it was produced.

The obituary informs us further about Munkens' activities: he moved to San
Francisco and founded a theatre group there, but in 1910 he was in Boston,
where he participated in the Latvian Socialist Workers Union theatre group as
an actor and director. He spent the last twenty-five years of his life in New York
City, where he took part at least in one production of Aspazija's *Vaidelote* (The
Vestal), as well as in "living newspaper" productions, probably those produced
under the auspices of the Federal Theatre Project. Munkens also wrote plays.
Their descriptions indicate an allegience to socialist causes, and his *Šuvējas*
(Seamstresses) has been produced in New York and Philadelphia. His two
known plays in English, *Death Sentence* and *The Nail*, have been staged in New
York.

The excitement about theatre that was constantly growing in Latvia was
carried across the Atlantic to the new land; it prevailed among participants and
spectators alike. An additional need for a dramatic experience in the native
language was created by the new environment the immigrants encountered. It
was not easy for them to change their former life styles suddenly; in most
instances they had to learn new skills or at least new approaches, while working
in more technically advanced situations than in the industry of their homeland.
Most of the Latvian immigrants were able to speak German and Russian besides
their native Latvian, but the inability to communicate in English created an
obstacle to acceptance by the "melting pot" society. Thus the gatherings for
rehearsing a play in Latvian or at least attending a performance, where the

language they knew the best was used, helped to fight the loneliness, which in turn could lead to feelings of inferiority.

It has been difficult for the second-wave Latvian immigrants to learn about the experiences and feelings of those in the first wave. As Osvalds Akmentiņš relates, it was almost impossible for individuals of these two groups to communicate or for those in the second wave to have an insight into the working and social conditions experienced by the first immigrants. When Akmentiņš asked about their theatres, however, the "speaker's face lit up, the vestiges of distrust disappeared and the beautiful memories came back." The speaker, in this case Ludmila Karlsone, a former actress of the Boston Latvian theatres, is quoted as saying, "Yes, yes, I did it too! . . . We youngsters didn't talk politics, . . . we just wanted to have good times. . . . We always liked productions with music and songs. We even created our own dances."[28]

ORGANIZATIONAL SUPPORT

When the ethnic organizations offered their sponsorship, the old Latvian theatre really started growing. Such support is mentioned in the minutes of the November 5, 1905, meeting of the Latvian Society of Boston (1889–1966), the oldest Latvian organization in the United States. A theatre committee announced that it had rehearsed a lengthy play, although it was unable at the time to present it to the public. Still, it asked the society to organize a presentation of the play with a dance afterwards, in the next February on the evening before Washington's birthday.[29]

At the above-mentioned meeting, the leaders of the society actually had planned a concert and a play production for the society's sixteenth birthday. Such a plan reminds us of similar activities in the Baltic provinces under the czar, where concerts and theatre performances were used to attract as many people as possible. In other words, the organization was not so much interested in "art for art's sake" as in the utilitarian values of art. We do not find the title of the play in the minutes, and there is no mention of the actors or the director. Nevertheless, the organization's plan was faultless; the presentation brought in a profit of one hundred dollars.

The Latvian Society of Boston, as most of the first Latvian organizations in the United States, was concerned with the physical and economic welfare of its members. It helped in settling the new immigrants and provided financial help in case of illness, as well as death benefits. The second-oldest organization, the Philadelphia Society of Free Letts (still in existence), was concerned with arranging for a place for social gatherings, and as soon as a building was acquired, two billiard tables were its first "capital investment." As mentioned earlier, there were many immigrants who had left Latvia for religious reasons. This segment formed church groups, where the sustaining of faith joined the welfare considerations. It is evident that the goals and aspirations of these organizations were not conducive to theatrical activities. If such activities were sponsored, they were expected to accomplish only one thing: to raise money for the organization.

The Revolutionaries of 1905

The situation changed drastically when the revolutionaries of 1905 started arriving. They formed their own socialist workers' clubs and societies or, after joining the existing organizations, took over their leadership. The welfare organizations became political entities; they were tools in the hands of the hard-core revolutionary leaders for promoting the socialist-communist causes. As had been the case during the Latvian national awakening, these leaders understood the value of theatre as a medium for agitation and propaganda.

Branches of the Socialist Workers Society were founded in almost all major Latvian colonies; the most active were those in Boston; New York; Philadelphia; Elizabeth, New Jersey; Chicago; Detroit; Cleveland; and San Francisco. All of these branches had theatre groups associated with them, either directly under their control or, as separate legal entities, under their influence. Very seldom did one of these groups have a strong director who was allowed to make artistic decisions. Such decisions were made by a theatre committee, and quite often the plays were chosen by the ideological leaders of the branches or societies. For this reason many agit-prop-type plays found their way to the stage. If such plays were not available, they were written by local authors. Among them we find *Maija svētki* (Celebrating May), by Dāvids Bundža (1873–1901), produced in 1908 in New York, and *Viņi uzvarēs* (They Will Overcome), by Sīmanis Berģis (1887–1943), published in *Strādnieks* in 1912. The latter deals with a strike in Massachusetts and was meant for the Latvian immigrant youth.

Besides theatre these societies had another powerful tool in their hands. They published newsletters, magazines, and newspapers, through which they not only propagandized their ideologies but also disseminated information concerning current events. These publications helped the theatre by advertising the times and places of performances, as well as generating interest in the plays by describing them and including the names of the participants, and so on. When the theatre group was associated with the club publishing the newsletter or newspaper, the promotion would be free. Still, there were theatre groups, such as the one associated with the Chicago branch of the Latvian Socialist Party, that published their own materials. An example is the *Teātra Grupas Vēstnesis* (Theatre Herald), which was published starting with the first seasons of the group, founded in 1907. It informed not only about the plays presently in production but also about forthcoming plays and events concerning or connected with theatre.

As far as can be determined from the rare playbills still in existence, there were at least two theatre groups in Chicago, because two Latvian socialist or workers' groups with the same goals had different theories about how these goals could be reached. Such a rift among the socialists existed well into the twenties, until the most fervent leaders had died or returned to Europe. Some of them went to Soviet Russia and some to independent Latvia, but in both instances they failed to receive a heros' welcome. Besides the revolutionary Latvian immigrants, there were two other major segments: the nationalistic immigrants, who cherished the idea of a free and independent Latvia, and a third group organized according to their religious persuasions, mostly Lutherans and Baptists. These segments also had publications expressing their points of view. The nationalistic publications were noncommittal toward theatre, but the religious ones quite often warned their readers about the "devil's institution called theatre."[30]

Play Selection

Play selection for productions seems to have been the major concern during the entire life of the old Latvian theatre in the United States. The plays had to please or at least satisfy everybody. The political leaders wanted drama that was ideologically appropriate to their goals; the sponsoring organizations wanted plays that would attract large audiences and bring in money; the actors looked for plays with good roles; and the critics insisted on drama that was geared more to educating than entertaining the spectators. All the spectators wanted was to be entertained in their own language, although there are accounts regarding audiences' behavior that indicate their ability to entertain themselves by chatter and catcalls during the performances, regardless of what kind of play was presented.

Because of so many differing demands, rarely could a theatre group plan an entire season, although such effort is evident from some documents describing the organization of the groups. All members of the group were asked to read a given number of plays, make comments, and propose the best of them for production. These comments very often were hilarious and themselves became a comment upon the taste, the intelligence, the dramatic know-how, and especially the political outlook of the readers. (The director of the quite extensive drama holdings of the Philadelphia Society of Free Letts, Niklāss Lazdiņš, takes pleasure in reading these comments to the visitors of the library.) The plays were ordered from Latvia after the theatre committee of a group appropriated funds, and they could not be checked out for reading by the general public until they were either produced or found unfit to be shown on stage.

There were requests from some groups for plays ordered from Soviet Russia, and those also were fulfilled. However, the Latvians who remained in the Soviet Union after World War I and had been successful in establishing a professional theatre in Moscow were desperate for new plays themselves. From that period only one play, *Riežu plāvēji* (Tillers of Their Masters' Land), by Sīmanis Berģis (1887–1943), that had been produced by Skatuve, the professional Latvian theatre in Moscow, was chosen for production, in Philadelphia.

The author, a revolutionary of 1905, had lived in the United States for some years and had participated in the socialist movement in Boston. Berǵis practiced what he taught; when in 1917 the communist revolution spread to Latvia, he returned home and became a functionary in the Communist Party. When the nationalist government succeeded in establishing independent Latvia, Berǵis moved to Moscow and lived there until his death. His works, as were those of other progressive Latvian writers living in Russia or Latvia, were published by Prometejs, the Latvian publishing house in Moscow.

In comparison with the playbills of the theatres in Latvia before World War I, as well as with those of independent Latvia, the only difference in Latvian theatres in the United States was the lapse of time of some ten years before the same plays were produced. Plays that contained elements pleasing to the social-ist leaders were produced sooner here, among them plays by Rainis and Aspazija. The father of Latvian theatre, Ādolfs Alunāns, was well represented with plays, such as *Mūsu senči, Kas tie tādi, kas dziedāja,* and *Seši mazi bundzenieki.* It is interesting to note that when the Society of Chicago Latvian Workers, the only remaining old Latvian organization in Chicago, celebrated its fiftieth anniversa-ry of "stage activities" on April 28, 1957, at the Harmony Hall, 1053 N. Kostner Avenue, it did so with a performance of *Seši mazi bundzenieki.* The performance started at four in the afternoon and was followed by other fes-tivities, including a dance. This fact not only indicates the longevity of the Latvian ethnic theatre in a city as vibrant as Chicago, but also suggests the closing of a circle, begun with a simple folk comedy presenting characters with which the Latvians at the beginning of their theatre tradition could identify and, embellished by the folk songs and folk dances that had first attracted audiences to the theatre and instilled love for dramatic art. There were only two more known productions staged in 1958 by the old Latvians in Chicago, both musicals. Already in 1951 the second-wave immigrants had occupied the Hull House theatre, where many old Latvian shows had been staged.

In a different way a circle was also closed by the Society of Boston Latvian Workers at their May celebration in 1948. The program started with the singing of "Internationale," included a speech between some musical numbers; and ended with a one-act play, *Neļaujiet aiziet* (Don't Let Them Leave), by Anna Kupše (pseudonym of Anna Brodele, 1910–1981), which had not yet been shown in Soviet Latvia. The play was written during World War II. The plot deals with the German occupation of Latvia; some of the characters collaborate with the Germans, and some oppose them. Many of the first-wave immigrants were fighting the oppression of the German barons, and in this way—seeing a renewed fight—the circle closed for them, especially because the drama sees the events from the communist point of view. This seems to have been the last old Latvian performance at the society's house, at 23 Kenilworth Street, Roxbury, Boston; in the fifties the house was purchased by Daugavas Vanagi (the Hawks of Daugava), the largest welfare organization of the second-wave Latvian immigrants.

Effect of Socialism on the Old Latvian Theatre

As stated earlier, the old Latvian theatre became very active with the arrival of the 1905 revolutionaries, and the most fervent period was between 1912 and 1917. During those years the socialist leaders were the most energetic in promoting their causes; therefore the plays chosen for production discussed social issues and promoted freedom of choice and freedom from oppression. Rainis and Aspazija both had been part of the New Current group in Riga before their forced emigration to Switzerland in 1905, and their plays were reflections of their strivings and ideology. It is no wonder that most of the plays of Rainis and Aspazija were produced by the socialist immigrants, many of whom had been associated with the authors in Riga.

When Aspazija's *Zaudētas tiesības* had been produced in Riga during the 1894 season, *Dienas Lapa*, the New Current's newspaper, widely publicized the play. This newspaper, while explicating the socialist concept of social justice, also commented on aesthetic principles, relating them to art in general and drama in particular. In March 1908 the play was produced in New York City.

In December of the same year, another play by Aspazija, *Vaidelote*, opened in New York, where her *Sidraba šķidrauts* and *Zeltīte* (Goldie) were produced in 1913. Another of her plays, *Neaizsniegts mērķis* (Unattained Goal), was staged in 1916 in Minneapolis. All the above-mentioned plays were staged repeatedly in major Latvian communities until the end of World War I. From that time Aspazija's popularity diminished; however, as late as 1932 her *Zaudētas tiesības* and as late as 1942 her *Neaizsniegts mērķis* were played in Boston.

The production history of Rainis's plays parallels that of his wife, Aspazija. Thus his *Zelta zirgs*, first produced at Christmas 1909 in Riga, was on the stage of the Ebeling Casino, 156th Street and St. Ann's Avenue, New York City, on February 2, 1913. His *Pūt vējiņi* (Blow Wind), with "new costumes and sets created according to the models from the *New Theatre of Riga*,"[31] opened on January 9, 1915, in Boston's Kossuth Hall. It was repeated in Boston in 1931 and in 1939. Other Latvian communities also staged this folk play, which requires rich, ethnographically appropriate costumes and scenery.

Somehow the old Latvian theatres neglected other plays by Rainis, considered the greatest poet and dramatist by Latvians of all walks of life without regard for political allegiance. Only another minor play, *Pusideālists* (Half an Idealist), written early in the dramatist's career in the fashion of the German *Volksstück*, was produced in its entirety, as was *Girts Vilks*, an unfinished play that was shown in San Francisco and New York in 1916. Scenes have been excerpted from one of Rainis's greatest plays, *Uguns un nakts*, based upon the Latvian national epic, *Lāčplēsis* (The Bearslayer), but the entire play was never produced. It could be argued that this failure to produce Rainis's plays was because of artistic and technical inability to produce plays of such stature, but it may also have been because when Rainis and Aspazija returned to independent Latvia in

1922, they were thought of as having renounced in the United States the unchanging socialist causes of the 1905 revolutionaries.

Considering all the plays, originals and translations, produced during the six decades of old Latvian theatre in the United States reveals a trend: the revolutionary drama, as represented by symbolic as well as by agit-prop plays, slowly gave way to social drama based in realism. This drama at first contained theses or messages, but it later became a vehicle for depicting psychological realities, thereby facilitating a deeper understanding of character motivations and relationships. Also, a move from the tragic to the comic genre can be detected. Tragedy, melodrama and serious drama dominated the playbills until World War I; since then comedy and even farce have been the fare.

Rūdolfs Blaumanis

Rūdolfs Blaumanis, with his realistic dramas and comedies about country life and people in Latvia, fit the changing trend ideally. His play Indrāni, discussing a generation gap in a changing society that leads to a tragic conclusion, was produced during the 1912–1913 season in Boston and New York. According to the reviews, the spectators identified extremely well with the characters and were pleasantly surprised to see the traditional Latvian sauna on stage.[32] Blaumanis's rustic comedy Zagļi (Thieves) was produced in Boston the next season, and on Christmas 1914 his children's play Pamāte (Stepmother) was shown at Szabo Hall in Cleveland. On November 25, 1914, Zagļi was produced by the Elizabeth (New Jersey) Latvian Socialist Workers branch, and his Ugunī opened at Kossuth Hall in Boston, October 12, 1914. It was also produced in San Francisco's Sokol Hall on December 24, 1916. Indrāni was staged by the Newark branch of the Latvian Socialist Workers on March 17, 1917, and April 19 of the same year, Pazudušais dēls played on the Dudley Opera House stage in Boston. Boston's old Latvians also witnessed performances of Blaumanis's Ļaunais gars (The Evil Spirit), and it was the first play in Latvian ever produced on the Hull House stage in Chicago, September 12, 1908.

Indrāni received a new production in Boston on December 3, 1920, and the announcement of this event supports my thesis on the utilitarian nature of Latvian immigrant theatre.

Latvian workers for years have understood the importance of their press and have supported it morally and financially. The workers' newspapers have always suffered from lack of money. Recognizing this fact, the Society of Latvian Workers together with the publishers of Rīts have organized four days of festivities the proceeds of which will be used to support the newspaper. . . . December 3rd, Blaumanis' The Indrāns, without doubt artistically the most accomplished Latvian original drama, will be presented. . . . Real art gathers its strength from nature and life itself as from an eternally fertile soil. The Indrāns, with exquisite simplicity and naturalness depicts the Latvian peasantry of a certain historic period. Reading and seeing the play forces one to imagine the peasants' paradise the bourgeois government of present Latvia promises to recreate based on private property laws.[33]

As the above quote suggests, even drama with superior artistic qualities had to serve as a vehicle for propaganda. That the spectators of this production really could perceive a warning of the dangers of having "a corner of land one could call his own"[34] is debatable, as that question is never raised by the dramatist. If anything, the readers of the announcement were reminded of the recent agrarian reform law instituted by the republican government of Latvia, parceling the huge estates once owned by the German barons and distributing the land to former farmhands and sharecroppers. This action actually fulfilled the basic goal of the 1905 revolutionaries, who wanted to be masters of their ancestors' land, as Alunāns suggested in his last play, Mūsu senči. This goal, though, had been modified with the passage of time, especially under the influence of the Bolshevik revolution of 1917, which called for communal land ownership. Such ownership has become reality since the creation of the kolkhozes and sovkhozes in today's Soviet Latvia.

The tendency to attach a sociopolitical meaning to every play produced by the old Latvians is ironic in light of another play by Blaumanis, staged by the same Society of Latvian Workers in 1947. The play, Skroderdienas Silmačos (Tailors' Days at Silmači), deals with life on a rich, estate-like farm in Latvia at the turn of the century and extols the goodness and compassion of its owner towards the carefree and happy farm workers. There is an abundance of folk motifs, emphasizing the nationalistic qualities of the characters in the play. What sociopolitical message this production could contain at a time when the goals of the old Latvian socialists-turned-communists had been fulfilled by the establishment of Soviet Latvia, one can only guess. It could be that the setting was changed to a modern kolkhoze and the rich owner had become the director of a collective farm.

Whatever the interpretations, the fact remains that all full-length plays by Blaumanis, including a rustic comedy, Trīnes grēki (The Sins of Lizzy), have been produced in the old Latvian theatres all over the United States. The one-act Pēc pirmā mītiņa (After the First Rally), satirizing overzealous socialists, also has been produced in some colonies. His dramas were played most frequently during the twenties, and his comedies remained on the playbills through the forties.

Other Dramatists

In comparison with the other four major first-generation Latvian dramatists, Anna Brigadere was not popular in the old Latvian theatres. One of her realistic comedies, Kad sievas spēkojas (War of the Wives), was produced in 1933 in Boston, but there is no information about this or her other plays being staged elsewhere. Only her classic fairy tale play, Sprīdītis (Tom Thumb), surprisingly was shown at two places at the same time. The advertisements section of the December 18, 1917 *Strādnieks* announced that the Society of Latvian Socialist Workers would present the play at its clubhouse, 51 Dudley Street in Roxbury, at half-past-three in the afternoon of December 25, 1917. The play was listed as a fairy tale in five scenes, and the admission charge was thirty cents. Below this ad is another, informing us that at four in the afternoon the same play, only listed as a children's play in three acts, would be presented by the Latvian Socialist Branch of Roxbury at the Dudley Opera House, 113-19 Dudley Street, Roxbury, Boston. General admission was thirty-five cents, children admitted free. Both events were meant to be children's festivals, with dancing after the shows, and both lasted until midnight. At the time of the Bolshevik revolution the tension between the different branches of the same organization must have run high, to allow this duplication of effort to please the children of the same immigrant colony.

Plays by the next generation of Latvian dramatists started to appear shortly before World War I. They had been produced in Riga and, due to the Latvian mass migration into Russia during the war, also in Moscow, St. Petersburg, and other places throughout the crumbling empire. The works of some of these playwrights found their way to the old Latvian stages in many Latvian-American colonies, including one-act plays by Jānis Jaunsudrabiņš (1877–1962), his children's play, *Sapnis saulītē* (Dreaming in Sunshine), and his full-length comedy, *Jo pliks, jo traks* (Poor and Crazy); drawing room comedies by Edvards Vulfs (1886–1919), such as *Meli* (Lies), and his one-act *Greizsirdība* (Jealousy) and *Linis murdā* (Caught in a Trap), satirizing small-mindedness and bourgeois morality; and one-act comedies by Jūlijs Pētersons (1880–1945).

Quite popular was Jānis Akurāters (1876–1937), who at the beginning of his literary career had been excited about the 1905 revolution and had written some revolutionary songs, among them "Ar Kaujas saucieniem uz lūpām" (With Battle Cries on Our Lips), which became a rallying song for striking workers. His one-act *Laupītāji* (Robbers) was produced quite often, as were his full-length plays, such as *Priecīgais saimnieks* (The Happy Landowner), *Ķēniņa meita* (The King's Daughter), and *Kurzemē* (In Courland). After spending some years in Sweden and Norway in order to escape persecution by the czarist regime, Akurāters returned to Latvia at the beginning of World War I and joined the Latvian Rifles to fight the attacking German army. At that time he had renounced the ideas of the New Current by stating that art should be apolitical. As if foreshadowing this action by Akurāters, a critic described his play *Lāča bērni* (Bear Cubs), produced in 1914 in Boston, as devoid of ideology. This drama about the life of farm hands, observed the critic, was not written according to the socialist norm.

We are slaves and slaves we will remain. We have to bow to our destiny, carry our cross until death will save us. This is the only idea that can be detected in the play. That the struggle of an individual will not bring a brighter future, that the chains of slavery can be broken only by fighting together with commrades of one's own class, the author does not show.[35]

When Akurāters's *Kurzemē* was produced in 1927 by a socialist front organization, the New York Latvian Educational Society, a reviewer asked if it actually did not make fun of the socialist movement.

No fun was ever made of the socialist movement by two other Latvian dramatists, Leons Paegle (1890–1926) and Andrejs Upīts (1877–1970). Both were devout Marxists all their lives and as such propagandized socialist ideologies in their plays, which were written according to the best socialist-realist precepts. In their early works they developed their themes bluntly and created their characters as socialist heroes or bourgeois villains, in dramatic actions designed for agitation-cum-propaganda. In their later works, however, they were able to achieve a quality that places their plays among the best in Latvian dramatic literature. It is surprising that these plays were never considered by the old Latvian theatres. Instead, Paegle was represented by his agit-prop play *Gadu simteņu sejas* (Faces of Centuries), depicting the struggles of the working class in four different historic periods. The purpose of producing this particular play during the 1922 May Festival in New York becomes clear from the admission prices announced in the newspapers: fifty cents, but all unemployed workers could enter free of charge.

Upīts's one-act plays, such as *Amacones* (Amazones), *Lapas viesulī* (Leaves in a Storm), and three under the common title *Pārcilvēki* (Supermen), all satirizing the bourgeois society, were produced as early as 1913 and as late as the 1940s. His *Viens un daudzie* (One and the Many), a four-act tragic comedy, was produced in 1913 in Boston, where his last known full-length play ever produced in the United States, *Apburtais loks* (The Magic Circle), was also staged in 1937. Upīts's four-act comedy *Kaijas lidojums* (Flight of a Seagull), a caricature of the upper-class society of independent Latvia, arrived in New York with surprising speed: it had been produced in Riga in 1926, and it opened in New York early in 1928. It is unfortunate that his artistically superior historic tragedies, *Mirabo* (Mirabeau) and *Žanna d'Arka* (Joan of Arc), produced in independent Latvia in 1926 and 1930, respectively, could not have been enjoyed by the old Latvians. The same could be said about Paegle's monumental *Dievi un cilvēki* (Gods and Men), a historic verse drama showing an uprising in ancient Egypt.

Playwrights who had started their careers in independent Latvia were produced in the United States only rarely. Among those the more enduring were Elīna Zālīte (1898–1955) and Hugo Krūmiņš (1901–), who has sometimes written under the pseudonym Gunispers. Zālīte's *Svešas asinis* (Strange Blood) and *Maldu Mildas sapņojums* (Reverie of Wandering Milda) were staged at the same time in 1940 in Boston and New York, resulting in reciprocal guest performances. As far as it can be ascertained, her comedy *Bīstamais vecums* (Critical Age) presented in 1948 by the Latvian Workers Society of Boston, was the last production of this group.

Between the two world wars, Krūmiņš had several of his comedies performed by the old Latvian theatres. Two of them stand out because of the circumstances surrounding their productions. The first one, *Vecpuiši precas* (Bachelors' Wedding) was staged in New York and advertised as a play "without ideological message," suggesting that the general public might have grown tired of the constant prodding with socialist slogans. The second, *Vecpuiši* (Bachelors), after being produced in different Latvian communities, was played in Chicago by the drama club of the old Latvian Workers Society in 1954, at which time the author, as a second-wave immigrant, was already in the United States.

There were also some writers among the old Latvians whose plays reached beyond local consumption. The pioneer of the American Latvian theatre was Alberts Munkens. Besides his already mentioned plays, he wrote a five-act drama about the life of workers, *Upuri* (Victims), which was first produced in 1913 in Boston. Sīmanis Berģis (1887–1943), whose agit-prop play *Viņi uzvarēs* (They Will Overcome) was produced in 1913 when the author still lived in Boston, became one of the few Soviet Latvian writers produced in the United States while living in Moscow, where he had gone early in the twenties. His *Riežu pļāvēji*, which he had started in Boston but completed in Moscow, was produced in the late twenties in Philadelphia. Each Latvian community seemed to have somebody with dramatic ability, but besides children's plays and plays written for specific events, these literati did not enjoy wider popularity.

Some of the more active groups produced up to twenty plays in a season, and it is evident that the relatively young Latvian dramatic tradition could not supply enough new plays, especially because of the particular selection process, which favored plays that would present the capitalist class in a bad light. Thus it was necessary to turn to plays of other nations, which were available in translation. These plays were selected according to the best tradition of the free theatre movement that was started during the 1880s in Europe. Most of these plays were realistic, many even naturalistic, and in accordance with the famous doctrine pronounced by Emile Zola, they depicted life at its worst.

In many instances minor plays by now-forgotten playwrights were selected only because they expounded socialist ideologies and during the translation process could be adapted to fit a specific need of a given group. However, many classics also were produced, among which were such plays as *The Weavers, Before Sunrise,* and *The Sunken Bell,* by Gerhardt Hauptmann; *All Souls* and *The Good Hope,* by Hermann Heijermans; *Enemy of the People,* by Henrik Ibsen; *The Robbers* and *William Tell,* by Friedrich Schiller; *The Power of Darkness,* by Leo Tolstoy; *The Blue Bird,* by Maurice Maeterlinck; *The Marriage* and *The Inspector General,* by Nikolai Gogol; and *The Broken Jug* by Heinrich von Kleist. Among the plays oriented more to social themes were *Honor,* by Hermann Sudermann; *The Stream,* by Max Halbe; *The Red Robe,* by Eugène Brieux; *The Lower Depths,* by Maxim Gorki; and *Moral,* by Ludwig Thoma. Soon after its American premiere Eugene O'Neill's *Anna Christie* was also shown in Latvian on the old Latvian stages, as were plays by John Galsworthy, Ferenc Molnár, and the

Russians Leonid Andreyev, Boris Lavrenyov, and Anton Chekhov, though only one-act plays by the latter were produced.

It is surprising to find so few plays from the English dramatic literature. Even Shakespeare was granted only one production of *King Lear,* and George Bernard Shaw, the "superman" among social critics, was neglected completely. More understandable is the absence of the American dramatists, who started to be concerned with social and political issues only in the thirties, when the revolutionary spirit of the old Latvians was already "played out."

The total number of productions, done by more than twenty different groups during the more than fifty years of the old Latvian theatre, can be only guessed. The most active producing groups, in Boston, Chicago, and New York, sometimes with two or more ensembles, staged as many as twenty plays in a season during their most productive years. At the same time, groups in smaller Latvian communities succeeded in producing one or two plays yearly. If it is assumed that on the average only two plays were produced by the about twenty groups in each of the fifty years of the old Latvian theatre, that would be two thousand productions. With a minimum average of five characters in each play, ten thousand roles would have had to be filled—by people for whom acting was only an avocation.

Actors and Actresses

In the old playbills some names appear repeatedly, though many others appear only once or twice. The name of Jānis Sauleskalns appears the most frequently. Besides acting and directing in different New York groups, he participated in some productions in Boston as guest actor. Mīce Niedze, according to her own count, played some four hundred roles on the old Latvian stages in New York. Still, reading the journal entries of some theatre group meetings, gives the impression that a sufficient pool of actors was not always available. Steps had to be taken to attract new faces. As early as 1909 the Latvian Association of Boston had created a theatre fund, in which 15 percent of the profits generated by public performances were deposited. This fund was kept by the theatre committee, and prizes to the best actors were awarded in the amounts of $1.50 for first place, $1.00 for second, and $.50 for third—a pittance indeed, according to today's standards.[36] The different groups in Philadelphia must have suffered from a shortage of actors during the latter part of the twenties. This problem was solved at least temporarily by consolidating all the theatre groups into one, which became known as the Theatre Group of the Progressive Organizations (1928–1937). This group also established an actors' fund, though it is not known what purpose the fund served.

Another inducement to participate in play productions was a tradition established by the Latvian Association of Boston in 1897. Its records indicate that in order to attend a performance "the members who participate in the theatre group pay half price, and non-members who participate are admitted without charge."[37] This was especially pleasing to the many theatre enthusiasts who did not care for the politics of the various organizations but were willing to partici- pate for the love of theatre itself. This tradition also seems to have had an impact upon the longevity of the old Latvian theatres. When in the late twen- ties the polarization among the various organizations had become less drastic, it was only natural that those involved in theatre productions were the first to unite.

Another factor promoting unification was the fact that only the strongest organizations had been able to acquire their own houses. The Latvian Workers Association of Boston was one of them, and its house at 23 Kenilworth Street in Roxbury, Boston, with a medium-sized stage and an auditorium seating over four hundred, became a factor in forming a strong ensemble.

The minutes of this group have been preserved by the theatre archives of Daugavas Vanagi,[38] indicating the size of the membership between 1928 and 1948. In the 1928–1929 season, during which the group produced seven full- length and six one-act plays and prepared an additional play for a guest perfor- mance in New York, there were thirty-four members. The membership re- mained at a relatively constant level until 1934. By the beginning of 1935, however, there were sixty-four members. The membership declined steadily after 1937, sinking to twenty-three in 1948, when the last known production took place.

At the beginning of the period described above, the consolidated Phila- delphia group included between twenty and twenty-four members. The Chicago group, as determined from a photograph taken after what seems to be a presenta- tion of Rainis's *Pūt vējiņi,* had fifty-three members at that time. A versatile actress, Berta Karkone, who had directed many productions as well, was part of that group.

It is impossible to ascertain the number of people who were involved with theatre in New York, where there is no evidence of a joint effort to establish only one theatre group. Although a building fund had been established by the oldest organization, none of the old Latvian clubs and associations had acquired a house in order to have a centralized place for their various activities, including theatre productions. The fund still exists, but the Latvian Association of New York has been taken over by the immigrants of the second wave. Regardless of this shortcoming, the New York community seems not to have suffered a short- age of acting talent. There are several indications of that fact, one being a playbill of the fourteenth "living newspaper" as presented by the united council of the Latvian organizations in New York and its suburbs on January 28, 1928. Part 6 of the "living newspaper" is listed as "voices from the public and the critics," and it tells us that the spectators were willing to become participants in a production even if their participation was only improvisational in nature. The idea of the living newspaper, well developed by such Latvian dramatists as Paegle and Linards Laicēns (1883–1938), both revolutionary activists in the Latvian republic and in Soviet Russia, seems to have been the only contribution to the American theatre by the old Latvians. Although a connection cannot be established at this time, the fact remains that this concept was used by the Latvians long before the Federal Theatre Project developed its living newspapers.

Additional benefits to the members of various theatre groups were lectures delivered in many colonies about dramatic structure, character analysis, and new trends in drama. These lectures were prepared by the socialist leaders and were considered part of the ideological education of the working classes. Some theatre groups organized more practical learning experiences, such as technique classes for improving stage speech, gestures, and application of makeup. Even more appealing were the "actors' evenings," during which the participants "emptied several barrels of beer and smoked many dozens of cigars," accompaniments that might have induced a wider participation in productions, but that certainly added to the fervor of many church leaders in condemning theatre as the devil's instrument.[39]

Directors

Two kinds of directors have developed since their emergence from the German duchy of Saxe-Meiningen. The first is a director as traffic policeman, who tries to achieve order without causing an accident; the second is a creative artist and a leader, who inspires the actors and evokes their creative powers by more subtle means than a shrill whistle. The old Latvian theatre directors, however, as shown by the available information, would not fit into either of the above categories.

At the beginning these directors were nothing but enthusiasts with some acting experience in amateur troupes. They performed leading roles in the same plays they directed, which is reminiscent of the actor-managers in the English and early American theatres. Later their authority was minimized by the statutes of the various sponsoring organizations, as well as by the rules devised by the theatre committees. As far as the records indicate, the Theatre Group of the Progressive Organizations in Philadelphia had assigned all the powers to a seven-member committee, which designated the director for each play by a vote. When Gogol's The Marriage was put up for production and a director was duly assigned by vote, the committee also wanted to distribute the roles without consulting the director. Understandably the director resigned, and the group had to call a meeting, at which it was decided that a set of statutes was needed defining the duties and responsibilities of all concerned. These statutes, if they were ever written, have not been preserved, but already in 1916 the theatre group of the Latvian Workers Association of Boston had issued an eight-page booklet with its statutes. This booklet prescribed that only plays with progressive content would be produced and that selection of directors would be done by vote. A director's duties and rights were defined as falling in three categories: (a) staging the play by giving directions to the actors and defining the activities of the others involved in the production, (b) making a list of all the properties and artifacts needed for the production and communicating it to the theatre committee not later than two weeks before the opening night, (c) replacing any actor who was incapable of creating the assigned character or who did not attend rehearsals or refused to learn the role properly. The director was obligated, however, to inform the theatre committee about replacements he made.[40]

Scenery

The above-mentioned duties and rights did not include a conceptualization of the production's visual elements that would involve scene and costume designers. As a matter of fact, a designer very seldom is mentioned in the preserved playbills. The locale of the dramatic action, however, is consistently specified in the playbills for each act or even scene, suggesting that the design elements that might have been used were not sufficient to create as complete an illusion of time and place as required for a given play. It further suggests that the wings and backdrops permanently installed on the stages used by the old Latvian theatres were adapted to suit any and all plays.

There have been instances when scenery was designed and built for a particular production. This must have been an extraordinary accomplishment, because the novelty was not only mentioned in the promotional materials but also talked about at length by the reviewers. Once, in 1917, a professional scene designer, Jānis Kuga, was asked to design a production of Aspazija's *Sidraba šķidrauts*. Kuga, who was the first important Latvian scenographer and had gained prominence while designing sets for the New Theatre of Riga, was in Moscow during World War I. There he was contacted by the play's director, Vilis Eksteins, and when the scene and costume design sketches were completed, they were brought to the United States by a bookstore owner, Augusts Raņķis. The sets and costumes were built in Boston at the cost of seven hundred dollars. Kārlis Siliņš, who reviewed the play, seems not to have been impressed. "Not much can be said about the costumes and scenery; they fit the play, and the sets for the last act were an artistic success."[41]

A mention that scenery and costumes "fit the play" would please every scenographer of today; however, the unwillingness of the reviewer to discuss the visual aspects of the production in detail suggests that the dialogue of a play was considered a primary concern. Also, the inability of the producers to spend much money on scenery and costumes had made them minimize their importance. There were complaints about the stages of the rented halls, such as that "the name itself of Dudley Opera House is full of pride but its stage lacks even the elementary scenery," or "when the producers needed a simple forest scene, they had to bring in their own trees."[42] There were also great plans to improve the design elements, as during the production of Lavrenyov's *The Battleship Aurora*, which took three months to be mounted and for which on the stage a "very realistic ship will be built and theatrical machinery installed that will give a complete illusion of moving waves and clouds, as well as the sounds of the ship's noises." Whether the stage of the Bohemian Benevolent Association of New York City (Narodny Budowa, 321 East 73rd Street) was fit to accommodate such wonders is not known, but the reviewers failed to be excited about the physical production and discussed in detail only the play's content, its messages, and the actors portraying the heroic sailors.

Critics

Besides dramatists, actors, directors, and designers, the critic is an important ingredient if a theatre is to be considered at least a quasi-institution. The old Latvian theatre was not lacking writers who reviewed and criticized its productions, although their abilities were as diverse as the quality of the different productions mounted in the many Latvian communities. While in a small community actors not participating in a given production wrote reviews praising their colleagues, in larger cities people with erudition in drama and theatre criticized every production thoroughly. The years of the most fervent criticism of old Latvian theatre were between 1910 and 1920, and the critics often contradicted one another. Some accepted the American norm and discussed the productions as a form of art, and others insisted upon the utilitarian nature of theatre for advancement of ideologies of the working class and education of the spectators, minimizing the value of entertainment.

Thus the most common kind of criticism that filled many pages of the socialist press was strong exposition that discussed the play itself and emphasized the theme, characters, and actions as appropriate for the proletariat. The appreciation and evaluation part of the review reflected the norm established by the particular critic, and the success or failure of the production was always assigned to the selection of the play. The plays had to be selected, the critics insisted, according to the precepts of "historical materialism," and the contents had to be modified in order to fit the progressive ideologies. When in 1914 Schiller's *William Tell* was produced in Boston, certain scenes were deleted and the visual elements—scenery, costumes, and lighting—were minimal. A critic, Schüter-Klein, saw a degradation of art in such an approach. One of the most prolific socialist critics, Siliņš, who as his writings attest was well-versed in the art of dialectics, was quick in answering and pointing out the reasons for socialist-realist criticism.

The works of the best dramatists, except some plays by Shakespeare, are not shown here [in the United States] on the stage. Everything that is full of vitality, deep in thought and contains the spirit of protest is not liked by the majority of the theatre public. Thus the local theatre syndicates mold their art according to the taste of the spectators, like fitting a shoe to the public's foot.[43]

In the above quote, besides suggesting an agreement with the definition of progressive criticism, as had been proposed a year earlier by Vilis Dermanis in his essay "Modern Proletariat and Art,"[44] Siliņš pinpoints the utilitarian aspect of the immigrant theatre: only in their own midst are Latvians able to create and enjoy an art that is not alien to them; the art offered by the English-speaking population of the country is not fit to be consumed.

Importance of Old Latvian Theatre

The old Latvian theatre lasted for three generations. This cohesiveness was due to many factors, social, historical, and cultural. Even with the pressures of the "melting pot" environment and a willingness to adapt themselves to the new country, it was not easy for the new citizens to accept an alien culture overnight. The idea of not belonging has destroyed many immigrants, from all ethnic groups; and the Latvians were fortunate to find in their theatre a safe island, where they were welcome, where their native language could be freely spoken, and where they could find refuge from their daily struggles. In the homeland the old Latvian theatre had served as a gathering place during the period of National Awakening; it served as a gathering place for many Latvians in the United States as well, a home away from home. Thus when the socialist group leaders needed a medium for the dissemination of their ideas, theatre was a natural choice, given its established tradition.

The theatre also performed other functions in the immigrant community. First-generation Latvians in the United States were very much concerned with the perpetuation of their kind; this had been a strong tradition among their ancestors, whose land had been ravished by conquerors from every direction. The theatre helped serve this cause by bringing Latvian youth together for rehearsals and performances, resulting on many occasions in in-group marriages. A good example of this fact is the playbill *Seši mazi bunzenieki* on April 28, 1957, when the theatre group of the Latvian Workers Society of Chicago celebrated its fiftieth jubilee. On the bill we find Rachel and Carl Velvels and Melanie and Eduard Sarapus playing roles, Emma Hartman on stage and her husband Fred in the prompter's box, and Jack Mednis designing the sets while his wife Elsie played the leading role and directed the play.

The most pleasing utilitarian effect of the old Latvian theatre, however, at least to me, was its ability to sustain the Latvian language. When five actors from the Soviet Latvian Riga Drama Theatre visited Chicago at the end of April 1979, their audience consisted of old as well as new Latvians, and all of them conversed freely in their mother language although many of the old Latvians had never set foot in Latvia.

After more than six decades[45] of turbulent activity, the old Latvian theatre slowly dissipated during the 1950s, leaving its art, if not its heritage, to be carried along by the theatre groups of the new Latvians.

NEW LATVIAN THEATRE

Among the second-wave Latvian immigrants to the United States, which took place after World War II, were more than fifty actors and actresses, eight directors, five scenographers, two light designers, three theatre administrators, five playwrights, and a number of composers and movement/dance consultants. All of them had worked for years in the Latvian professional theatres in cities such as Riga, Liepāja, Jelgava, and Daugavpils or, after graduating from theatre schools during the war, were ready to enter the profession. With them came many opera and operetta singers, some well known throughout Europe, as well as a dozen dancers from the famous Riga Opera ballet. Such a number of trained artists certainly could have met the prerequisites for a professional Latvian theatre in the United States; but these people had not immigrated as theatre artists. Even with the liberal displaced persons' quotas, they had to sign up for jobs their sponsors were able to provide, and those jobs ranged from janitor of a large apartment house to cleaning lady in an office. Those who could work as hostesses in restaurants or as bank tellers were very fortunate.

The newly immigrating actors and other theatre workers were products of the theatres of the post-World War I independent Latvia. A number of Latvian patriots had declared the independence of their country on November 18, 1918, while the western part of the country was still occupied by surrogates of the former German barons, who had enslaved the Latvian nation for seven centuries, and the eastern part by supporters of the newly established Soviet government in Russia. Nevertheless, in 1919 the first Nacionālais Teātris (National Drama Theatre) was founded in Riga, followed by the Dailes Teātris (Riga Art Theatre). Very early in the history of free Latvia, both theatres received state subsidies as institutions supporting the new cultural policies of the nation.

Many of the leading actors and directors, as well as playwrights and critics, had had experiences that made them unique in the new theatre: they had learned the Stanislavski system at its very beginning while spending their war years in Russia, and they had been exposed to the best of Western drama while exiled to Scandinavia and other Western European countries. There were many theatre artists who, though quite openly endorsing the Communist cause, came back to independent Latvia and added their knowledge of the agitation and propaganda aspects of theatre to the whole. During the 1920s the capital of the new republic, Riga, became the meeting point of artistic activities between the East and the West, and names like Michael Chekhov, Feodor Chaliapin, and Max Reinhardt, among others, were common there.

In the early twenties new professional theatres also opened their doors in larger provincial towns such as Liepāja, Jelgava, and Daugavpils, and they all received state subsidies. Similar support was granted to some ensembles that rehearsed in Riga but traveled throughout the country with performances.

The Nacionālais Teātris produced mainly the classics of the Latvian drama, at the same time encouraging new dramatists to submit their plays or dramatizations. In this theatre the emphasis was on the play itself, and due to this approach the Nacionālais Teātris became known as the literary theatre. The Dailes Teātris experimented with plays from all over the world, and its repertory included classics as well as recently written plays in the many new styles evolving at the beginning of the century. Under the leadership of Eduards Smiļģis

(1886–1966) and Jānis Muncis (1886–1955) the Diales Teātris became a theatre of form, declaring that a play becomes a work of art only on stage in front of
an audience.

In a very short time the new Latvian theatre was able to reach a quality that
was recognized by theatre specialists of other nations. André Antoine wrote
about the scenography of the Riga Art Theatre shown at the International
Exhibition of Decorative Arts in Paris of 1925 as follows:

In my opinion, a production of the Riga Art Theatre would be as educational and
pleasurable as one staged by Stanislavsky. If we want to be inspired by foreigners, the
Latvian exhibition is a fertile source of experience, because it discards nothing from the
past but routinism and really opens up a vast expanse for other forms.[46]

Muncis was instrumental in arranging the models for the said exhibition, and he
received a Grand Prix from the exhibition for his efforts.

Another connection with the West, as well as with the East, was Anna Lācis.
She was a member of the Riga Workers Theatre (Strādnieku Teātris), which was
supported by Communist-front organizations (the Communist party was outlawed in Latvia). Lācis traveled to Germany to work with Erwin Piscator and
Bertolt Brecht, learning the rudiments of the Epic Theatre at its very beginnings. She used this knowledge in staging agit-prop plays for the Latvian workers, but when the government closed the Workers Theatre, she emigrated to the
Soviet Union.

When an authoritarian government came to power in 1934, large outdoor
spectacles became popular. One such spectacle, The Song of Renaissance
(Atdzimšanas dziesma), employed 3,500 participants, including 300 actors and a
100 ballet dancers. It was performed three times, for an audience totalling
160,000. It was staged by Muncis, who had recently returned from the United
States, where he had studied at the Occidental College of Los Angeles and had
designed and directed for two years at the Pasadena Playhouse. Such spectacles
drew attention from other European countries, and an Italian journalist, Alex-
andro Pavolini of the Corriera della Sera, called them the best vehicle for establishing contact between the government and the people.[47] There is no doubt
that these spectacles were political in nature, but they did excite a patriotic
fervor.

While the art of acting, directing, and scenography had reached a high level
of excellence and the theatres, such as the one at Jelgava, could boast of having
the best technically equipped stages in Eastern Europe, the original dramaturgy
remained quite parochial. In preference, dramatizations of novels and translations of foreign plays were produced. Only in the 1930s were new dramatists able
to break away from the traditional folk play and the shallow drawing room
comedy.

Until 1934, during the parliamentary government, the theatres were free to
chose their repertories, as the government mostly was concerned with economic development. When the authoritarian government was instituted,

however, definite policies were imposed upon all cultural and educational activities. Besides the large outdoor spectacles, theatre was used in schools and
organizations sponsored by governmental agencies, as a tool for educating the
masses and disseminating ideas. The 4-H clubs (modeled after the American
organization), the Boy Scouts, and the Home Guards frequently held playwriting competitions for works that would fit their needs. These contests drew a
large participation from established writers, from journalists, from teachers, and
even from the members of the various organizations. The winning entries were
produced in community halls and schools, and very often professional actors or
directors were hired to stage them. The plots of these plays very often were based
on legends, folk tales, or recent historic events. Their open or hidden messages
were designed to boost patriotism and love for the current leaders. Undemocra-
tic though this might seem to American readers, this approach helped to bring
theatre to the grass-roots level. There was no "black list" of foreign plays that
could not be translated and published, and foreign plays were read freely in
schools and at home. There was no official (prior) censorship as in the Russian
Empire or the Soviet Union. Very rarely, and only after the fact, were published
plays banned for dissemination, and only in one instance was the run of a play
cut short at the Nacionālais Teātris by an edict of the minister of education.

During the Depression, the effects of which also reached Latvia, the theatres
started producing operettas and musical comedies, in such a way adding a new
dimension to the acting and directing training and techniques. Most of the
theatres were able to survive economically and keep their personnel intact.

Foreign Occupations of Latvia

A setback occurred during the first Soviet occupation, in the 1940–1941
season. Many actors, directors, and designers were released from their theatres
and sent to others in different cities. Whatever the reason behind this action, it
destroyed the established ensembles, and many plays that had been in the
repertory for a long time could not be performed anymore. But the new government was not interested in the old plays. New ones were quickly translated from
Russian, all of them bluntly propagandistic, filled with slogans pronounced by
two-dimensional characters who were excessively good (according to Soviet
standards) or very bad, but never truly human. The plays of Latvian dramatists
Andrejs Upīts and Leons Paegle, who were Marxist in their allegiance, seemed
far superior to the new Soviet plays, and they too found their way to the stage
during the first Russian occupation.

The German occupation (1941–1945) that followed was not better, only
different as far as play selection was concerned. The theatres renewed or created
new productions of the old German classics, and in order to accommodate the
German soldiers on leave in Riga, they produced a large number of situation
comedies and operettas.

When the second Russian occupation became imminent at the close of World

War II, many actors left Latvia, mainly to escape the injuries their war activities could bring, and moved to Germany. Many also found themselves in troop theatres moving west with the retreating German army. At the end of the war, approximately half of all professional Latvian actors had reached displaced persons' camps in West Germany. There, in the fall of 1945, they produced plays that were enjoyed by many thousands of refugees. The actors had hoped to return to their homeland, but after four years of continuous performances in the camps, they were forced to emigrate to England, Australia, or the United States.

In the United States

The dream of some former theatre administrators and directors to create a professional theatre in the United States encountered a major obstacle: each former theatre worker, often burdened by family responsibilities, saw as his or her first duty to serve out the contract signed with the sponsor and to establish a firm economic basis. However, love for the art remained strong, and as early as 1950, theatre groups were formed in many new Latvian colonies.

The actors from the former Nacionālais Teātris, the Dailes Teātris, and the theatres at Jelgava and Liepāja had settled on the East Coast. Thus the American Latvian Theatre was formed, with ensembles in New York, Boston, and Washington, D.C. The New York ensemble, under the direction of Osvalds Uršteins (1910–1980), a versatile actor who before the war had directed at the Nacionālais Teātris after graduating from the Polish directing school at Warsaw, opened on January 8, 1950, with Ķīnas vāze (Chinese Urn), by Mārtiņš Zīverts. Under Uršteins's direction this ensemble produced one to three plays annually until 1955, when Uršteins returned to Germany as a member of the Voice of America team. Under the same name, however, the ensemble, with constantly changing personnel, continued to produce plays. Besides directing and acting in the ensemble, Uršteins conducted an actors' studio for the younger generation.

The Boston ensemble was founded in September 1950, and its first production, No saldenās pudeles (Sweet Wine of Love), by Rūdolfs Blaumanis, opened on January 6, 1951. The ensemble had chosen Jānis Lejiņš and Kārlis Veics as its artistic leaders and Jānis Kājiņš as the administrator. Lejiņš had been associated with Nacionālais Teātris as an actor, director, and playwright; Veics had been one of the principal actors and directors of the Dailes Teātris. The set design for the first production was executed by the dean of the Latvian scenographers, Jānis Kuga.

According to its twenty-fifth anniversary booklet, by 1976 the Boston ensemble had presented 115 performances, in 17 different Latvian colonies, to more than 41,000 spectators, as well as prepared and participated in various commemorative activities honoring great Latvian playwrights and theatre artists.[48] Most of the productions were directed by Lejiņš, and some by Veics and Valfrīds Streips, who with his wife, Ance Rozīte, had been the principal actors at the former Jelgava Theatre, and during the last ten years mainly by Reinis Birzgalis, who had started his career at the Dailes Teātris. Birzgalis had also directed the production of *Skroderdienas Silmačos*, the classic by Rūdolfs Blaumanis, as a collaborative effort of the American Latvian Theatre and the DV (Daugavas Vanagi) Jaunais Teātris Bostonā (DV New Theatre at Boston) in connection with the Latvian Song Festival 1978, held in Boston, a traditional event visited by more than thirty thousand Latvians from all over the world.

Osvalds Uršteins returned to the United States and settled in Washington, D.C., where on March 18, 1960, the Washington ensemble opened with *Klauns Fiasko* (Clown Fiasco), by Zīverts. Since then it has produced one play annually, mostly new plays by dramatists in exile. Due to self-imposed standards regarding the quality of the productions, as well as because the actors were working on other jobs during the day, rehearsals have sometimes extended through a four- to five-month period. The ensemble has found fewer than four hundred spectators in its home town, so it has also given guest performances in other towns. All this has demanded considerable effort and time, making it impossible to prepare more than one production yearly.

Another theatre "with respectable ability," as Anšlāvs Eglītis wrote in connection with its production of Arthur Miller's *View from the Bridge*, its seventeenth play in ten years, is the San Francisco Little Theatre, the heart and soul of which are Laimonis and Brigita Siliņš.[49] They both had received theatre education in American colleges and practical experience in California community theatres, and although since 1966 they have produced one or two plays annually in their theatre, they find time to participate in American productions as well. Both are also the only known Latvian actors in exile who were invited to perform on the stage of the Nacionālais Teātris.

The idea of a permanent professional Latvian theatre in the United States was tried once more by Jēkabs Zaķis, who besides acting in many ensembles in Liepāja and Riga, had been the artistic director of the Jelgava Theatre for fifteen years and the director of Radio Riga for ten years. Under the sponsorship of the American Latvian Association, the Teātra draugu biedrība (Society of Latvian Theatre Friends) was established in 1952 to raise capital for a permanent traveling company. Although one could become a "friend" by supporting this venture with as little as one dollar, only by January 21, 1955, was enough money raised to allow the new ensemble to start its tour with *Indīgā efeja* (Poison Ivy), by Voldemārs Kārkliņš (1906–1964), a novelist and translator who had turned playwright after leaving Latvia. In 1956, this time organized by Jānis Šāberts, formerly an actor with the Nacionālais Teātris, a new ensemble of four actors was formed. Lilija Štengele, who frequently had been billed as a star in Russia and Latvia in the 1930s, was brought out of retirement, and a play, *Jaunās asinis* (Young Blood), was written specially for her by Kārkliņš. The play was directed by Kārlis Veics of Boston.

As the actors were paid weekly salaries plus travel expenses and the star took a percentage off the top, no profit was realized at the end of the tour. And although the production received good notices in all thirty-one of the Latvian communities it visited, additional support for the Teātra draugu was not forth-coming. Šāberts found another four-character play, Pēdējā laiva (The Last Boat to Freedom), by Zīverts, by now a well-established and popular playwright, and organized another tour in 1958. At that time, however, Zīverts's plays had been produced repeatedly throughout the exile communities. Pēdējā laiva dealt with a subject matter too painful for the new Latvian immigrants, and also the produc-tion was not conceived in the best professional manner. The reviews, including one by me, were not complimentary; and it was said that the critics "sunk" the production, together with the Teātra draugu.

Šāberts found another star, Ādolfs Kaktiņš, and organized the last tour of the society in 1960. Kaktiņš, who had played the Latvian mythical hero Lāčplēsis in the original production of Uguns un nakts at the New Theatre of Riga and later had become a celebrated opera singer at the Riga Opera, as well as at other prominent opera houses in Western Europe, celebrated his seventy-fifth birth-day with this tour, performing the principal character. The play, Pēc kaut kā cēla, nezināma (Something Noble and Unknown), was written especially for this occasion by Eglītis, a short story writer, novelist, and playwright presently living in the United States. Besides Kaktiņš, Šāberts, and Ksenija Brante, who was an operetta singer from the former Folk Theatre (Tautas Teātris) at Riga, Alma Mača, one of the few Latvian actresses performing on Canadian television, participated in this tour. It visited thirty-six cities from coast to coast, including five in Canada.

It is interesting to note that the new Latvian immigrants settled in the same areas where the old Latvians were living. The reasons were twofold: the old Latvians became sponsors of the newcomers, and living and working conditions in the North and Midwest were more similar to those in Europe than living conditions in the South. Sizable colonies developed around Cleveland, Detroit, Indianapolis, Minneapolis, Milwaukee, and Chicago, besides those previously mentioned.

The Chicago Latvian Theatre was founded on November 26, 1950, on the initiative of Otto Krolls, former owner of an arts agency in Latvia. He attempted to establish a similar enterprise in the United States and persuaded a former director of one of the companies he had managed in Latvia, Valdis Hermanis, to settle in Chicago and prepare the first production of the new theatre, Ķīnas vāze, by Zīverts. It opened on May 26, 1951, on the Hull House stage.

The next day, May 27, 1951, the first ensemble under the sponsorship of a new Latvian organization opened with No saldenās pudeles, by Blaumanis, in Milwaukee. This group was the theatre ensemble of the Latvian Society of Wisconsin, with an experienced director, Pēteris Ozols, at its helm. Six months later the welfare organization Daugavas Vanagi started another theatre in the same city under the direction of Millija Valtere-Einberga. This theatre included a youth ensemble producing plays for children. Competition for actors as well as for audiences seemed to develop, and the quality of the productions suffered. Therefore a new ensemble, this time independent of any organization, was formed in 1954; it was known as the Milwaukee Actors Group. It opened with *Indrāni*, by Blaumanis, under the direction of Gustavs Amols. As most of the actors from the ensemble of the Latvian Society of Wisconsin joined the new group, the ensemble's theatrical activities ceased with the production of *Vīna raugs* (Wine Yeast) by Teodors Zeltiņš (1914–) on July 9, 1955. During the 1950s, two different Latvian Lutheran churches in Milwaukee produced plays with their young parishioners as actors, and even a sports club organized theatre performances.[50] Such an overextension has hurt the Latvian theatre in Milwaukee, and during the last fifteen years new productions have been realized only sporadically by the Daugavas Vanagi ensemble.

The above-mentioned Chicago Latvian Theatre was able to sustain itself for a longer period. It produced twenty plays in ten years, and its ensemble, sometimes counting up to fifty participants, remained stable. However, in the spring of 1961, with the production of *Deguns* (Nose), by Zeltiņš, this theatre closed. The main reason for closing seemed to be the demolition (for reasons of urban renewal) of the former Hull House theatre auditorium, where the Chicago Latvian Theatre had had a permanent home. Other reasons were the retirement of Otto Krolls from its administration and his death, as well as the death of Valdis Hermanis.

Subsequently a theatre was sponsored by the Chicago Latvian Association, but as writes Māra Antēna, a still active actress turned director and theatre educator, "while in 1951 there were over fifty individuals who wished to act, ten years later less than ten actors could be found."[51] The association imported directors from other colonies, among them the aforementioned Jānis Šāberts and Valfrīds Streips, as well as Ansis Tipāns, who had studied under the famous Russian actor-director Michael Chekhov, but the venture was not successful partly due to a clash of personalities, partly because of lack of permanency in leadership. It produced only four plays, among them two new Latvian originals, *Kā zaglis naktī* (Like a Thief in the Night), a controversial play by Zīverts, and *Zīmes smiltīs* (Signs in the Sand), by Artūrs Voitkus.

Among the other ensembles sponsored by various organizations during the 1950s, some have survived for more than twenty-five years; others have ceased to exist as soon as their originators—former professional actors or directors—have left the community or died. As early as March 29, 1951, the Daugavas Vanagi sponsored the New Latvian Theatre in Boston. It started its work as a studio for young theatre enthusiasts under the guidance of Kārlis Veics, who had left the Boston ensemble. In six years he succeeded in creating a group of able young actors, who since 1957 have also taken part in the productions of the American Latvian Theatre. The most praised production of the New Latvian Theatre was Shaw's *Pygmalion*, which opened May 2, 1959, under the direction of Valfrīds Streips. Daugavas Vanagi also has theatre ensembles in Cleveland, San Francisco, and Minneapolis. The last one, as the DV Theatre in Minnesota, celebrated its twentieth birthday in 1977 with a production of *Tautieša Zupēna atmoda* (The Awakening of Landsman Zupēns), by Gunārs Grieze, directed by Jēkabs Vērenieks, who in the early fifties had his own theatre group in Minneapolis.

The North American Latvian Association

When in the mid-1960s the theatre movement of the new Latvians seemed to have reached a period of recession and many of the smaller groups had disappeared, an attempt to revitalize it was made by establishing the North American Latvian Theatre Association. The goals of the association were to facilitate an exchange of talent and provide a wider exposure to all ensembles by organizing theatre festivals. Only about half of all theatre groups in the United States and Canada joined the association at its inception and only one more or less professional-quality ensemble, the San Francisco Little Theatre, became a founding member. The three ensembles of the American Latvian Theatre were not interested in joining because "only amateurs were in the leading positions of the organization."[52] As of this writing the association has organized six festivals in Toronto (a Daugavas Vanagi theatre ensemble from Toronto is a member), Chicago, San Francisco, Minneapolis, and Cleveland. Although bylaws governing the organization's activities were made and guidelines established according to which a festival jury should award the top prize (named after the Father of Latvian Theatre, Ādolfs Alunāns) to the ensemble presenting the best production, they have not always been adhered to. This has created disenchantment, and as of 1978 the San Francisco Little Theatre had cancelled its membership until definite guidelines should be established and followed. The distances some groups would have to travel to the festival locations have created hardships in some cases. Also, selection of the participating ensembles has often been below par as far as the quality of their productions was concerned.

Nevertheless, the association successfully held a week-long theatre camp in Michigan during the summer of 1978. There some formerly professional actors and directors, some theatre teachers of Latvian descent from American universities, and young theatre enthusiasts were able to exchange views and acting and producing techniques. Also the newsletter and a journal, *Skatuve* (Stage), which the association publishes, though not regularly, help to disseminate information about Latvian theatre activities and new plays.

Scarcity of new original plays has been an important factor in the life of the new Latvian theatre. Some new playwrights emerged during the first years of exile in Germany, but they were produced mainly because of their previous achievements as prose writers or poets. Among them were Eglītis, Ģirts Salnais, Kārkliņš, and Zeltiņš. Voldemārs Richters, Osvalds Liepa, and Hugo Krūmiņš, who had written many plays for the amateur theatre in Latvia, were not able to achieve a wider popularity, but Lejiņš had his plays produced in Latvia and also in the United States. However, at the beginning of the new Latvian theatre, only Zīverts was considered worth playing in colonies all over the country. Thus the new ensembles relied upon the classics the actors and directors were familiar with from their former theatres.

Hungry for their ethnic culture, the spectators were satisfied with what they saw, as the plays reminded them of their past experiences in the homeland. But because of the need to adapt themselves to the new environment, a craving for a different kind of drama eventually became evident. Although Zīverts was considered a master craftsman, too much of the same seemed to become tedious. The classics also required expensive productions, and not all ensembles could afford them. The playwrights tried to help the situation by writing plays with small casts requiring only one set. Such an approach infringed upon the quality of the plays, and although play contests were organized, not many of the winning entries were chosen for production.

The American Latvian playwrights, such as Eglītis, Kārkliņš, Grieze, and Skaidra Pence-Neimane, used comedy as their form of expression, and for a while their plays pleased the audiences, who were willing to laugh about themselves in the comedies showing the pitfalls of adapting to a new environment and mores. Serious drama appeared from the pen of Voitkus, a minister by occupation, whose Jūdass (Judas) and Zīmes smiltīs received good notices. Jānis Viesiens, a new author living in Sweden, fell into the same category, notably with his Jānis Reiters, a historical drama about the first Bible translator into Latvian. Uldis Siliņš, living in Australia, wrote some comedies that were produced in the United States, but his best play, Pilsoņa Avota lieta (The Matter of Citizen Avots), dealing with the relationship between an exile and the Soviet Latvian functionaries, has not as yet been produced by an American Latvian theatre. The Sydney Latvian Theatre, however, has toured the United States with this play. Serious drama, Tagad ir citādi, Ābeles kungs (It's Different Now, Mr. Abele), by myself, was produced by the Washington ensemble in 1972; and Eglītis has also done some serious though sarcastic, playwrighting. His latest tend to border on the absurd, and not all in the Latvian audiences appreciate this kind of drama. An exciting production of his Leo, depicting a Latvian scientist in search of the perfect life style, was done by the San Francisco Little Theatre in 1976, but the audience, as well as the jury of the theatre festival at Minneapolis, was divided in its judgment.

The lack of new plays is made even more serious by the cultural policies of some organizational and theatre leaders in the Latvian ethnic group, who refuse to recognize the new playwrights of Soviet Latvia. Only one play, Kamīnā klusu dzied vējš (In the Fireplace the Wind Sings Quietly), by Harijs Gulbis, has been produced in the United States. The blatant praise of the system in the Soviet Latvian drama has almost completely disappeared since the 1960s, giving way to social criticism and in-depth study of individuals attempting to sustain their national identity. The old Latvians seem to have been braver—they produced plays written in independent Latvia, even if they had to be edited to fit the socialist aesthetic.

What the North American Latvian Theatre Association has attempted only with partial success, namely, the bringing together of all Latvian theatre practitioners—former professionals, avocational actors, and those who have been able to become part of the American theatre either as actors, designers, or teachers—

in order to sustain one of the most cherished cultural activities of the Latvian nation, seems to be working in two other instances. These are productions of plays in connection with Latvian song festivals and in the ethnic Saturday/Sunday schools and children's and youth camps during the summers.

Song Festivals

Every time a song festival is organized, theatre is invited to participate. The expected large number of spectators allows the production budget to be very liberal. Sets and costumes can be designed and built in a professional manner, and a technically well-functioning theatre is usually rented for such an occasion. One of the most popular directors (and, if possible, one who agrees with the "cultural policies" of the organizers) is hired to select a well-known play and produce it with local actors. Sometimes, however, the actors, as well as a topnotch designer, have to be imported from other Latvian communities. For the all-American Latvian Song Festival 1978 in Boston, *Skroderdienas Silmačos*, a folk play by Blaumanis, was chosen. It was directed by Reinis Birzgalis, and Ēvalds Dajevskis, a member of the American Scenic Artists who had designed sets for the professional theatres in Latvia, was hired to do the scenography. One scene of the play takes place on the traditional Latvian St. John's Day, and Iraida Jansone, the dance consultant, choreographed it in spectacular fashion, using dancers and singers dressed in folk costumes with dazzling colors and silver applications. Another production, using young actors from New York, was based on the classic *Sprīdītis*, by Anna Brigadere, this time with music by Andrejs Jansons. Both productions were well attended; *Sprīdītis* was completely sold out for both performances.

A regional song festival at San Francisco in 1979 included a play by Eglītis. Actually a dramatization of the author's novel, *Omartija kundze* (Mrs. Omartijs), it was directed by Laimonis Siliņš. Almost at the same time, Osvalds Uršteins directed *Daugava* (The River Daugava), by Jānis Rainis, on Gotland Island, where a song festival was organized and attended by Latvians from all over the free world.

It is evident that in order to prepare spectacular shows, the director needs as many actors as possible. A mixture of professionals and avocational actors, old and young, is inevitable, and while all attempt to generate a feeling of national togetherness and ethnic pride in their audiences, they themselves are molded into an ensemble with a definite purpose: the sustaining of the Latvian theatre tradition.

Theatre for Latvian Youth

The future of Latvian theatre in the United States is even more assured by its use in promoting and revitalizing the immigrants' ethnic heritage. Drama is used in the many schools under the aegis of ethnic and church organizations, starting with the primary grades and extending through high school. Plays are specially written for different educational levels in order to teach the language and acquaint the children with Latvian character traits. The sources of subject matter and plots are mostly Latvian folk tales and *dainas* (folk songs). Classic Latvian dramas written for youth theatre are produced repeatedly with young actors in order to perpetuate the speaking of their mother tongue. A proponent of such activities is Artūrs Rubenis, who holds a master's degree in drama from Boston University. He was the initiator and first president of the North American Latvian Theatre Association, and he presently teaches and directs at the United Latvian Parish School in Cleveland. He has written, "In a Latvian theatre presentation we listen, hear, feel and think in Latvian. It is the best way to perceive the Latvian worldview, the best way to sustain the spiritual strength in our lives."[53]

Productions originating in the ethnic schools are popular with students and audiences alike. From them a pool of young actors with respectable abilities has been developed and youth ensembles formed in cities such as Seattle, Indianapolis, and Los Angeles. These ensembles produce plays in Latvian, either independently or sponsored by organizations or church groups. Two of these groups have gained prominence in the total Latvian theatre movement.

The Minnesota Latvian Youth Theatre was founded in 1958 in Minneapolis and still produces plays, under the directorship of Edgars Šulcs, with Jānis Dimants, Jr., as its administrator. It uses students from the Minneapolis/St. Paul Latvian schools in all production areas, and the active involvement of their parents makes each play a community affair, with preparation often lasting for more than half a year. During the time used for rehearsing a play, meticulous attention is paid to correct usage of the language, character development, and costume details. The ensemble accepts new talent every year; however, the basic idea of sustaining the ethnic heritage and strong goal orientation are the ingredients that have made it a permanent institution. The theatre has built a portable stage, which is installed in the Latvian House for each production. The production of Brigadere's *Maija un Paija* in 1976 has been considered its major success.[54]

While the Minnesota Latvian Youth Theatre can pride itself on its endurance through time and minor organizational obstacles, the more slowly developing new talent on the East Coast can boast about its quality. When in 1957 the Newark Latvian school produced *Pūt vējiņi*, by Rainis, the director, Paulīne Brekte, had cast a high school student, Vilnis Baumanis, in the major role. He and the other cast members, as I have witnessed, were able to deal eloquently with the poetic images, which were borrowed by the author entirely from the Latvian *dainas*. Eighteen years later the same Baumanis played the major role in a production that, according to Rasma Birzgale, was the "most grandiose Latvian theatre production in the thirty years of exile."[55] Birzgale, who started as an avocational actress in the Boston ensemble and has developed into a well-rounded theatre critic, writes in superlatives about the 1975 production of

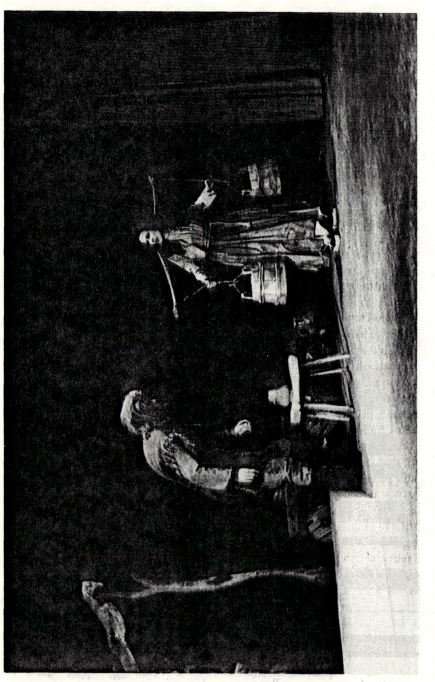

11.1 *Princese Gundega un Karālis Brusubārda*, by Anna Brigadere, Beggar's hut. (Production photograph by Bruno Rozītis, New York, New York.)

Brigadere's *Princese Gundega un Karālis Brusubarda.* (See Figure 11.1.) It was directed by Ņina Lagzdiņa, designed by Dajevskis, and produced by the New York ensemble of the American Latvian Theatre. Original music was written by a second-generation Latvian-American composer, Guntars Gedulis. Most of the roles were played by young actors who had been working with the director while attending the Latvian schools in New York. There were also actors who had studied under Uršteins, as well as former professional actors, some of them traveling to rehearsals from as far as Boston. The role of Gundega was played by Andra Lagzdiņa Ozols, the daughter of the director and a celebrated actor, Kārlis Lagzdiņš (1896–1960) from the Nacionālais Teātris. Many parents and teachers, such as Paulīne Brekte from Newark, helped with the technical aspects of the production, making the producing organization almost one hundred members strong.

It should be emphasized that Latvian ethnic theatre in the United States is not a professional, community, or educational institution, but all of them together. The element that unites them is the cultural heritage of the participants. It consists of the common language, folk traditions, mores, destiny, and world views. The above-described production is an excellent example of ethnic theatre in its ideal state. If such an achievement is possible after thirty years in a new environment, then one must be optimistic about the future of the "new wave" Latvian theatre in the United States. Even pessimists cannot deny it at least thirty more years, following the sixty-year precedent of the old Latvian theatre.

NOTES

1. Osvalds Akmentiņš, *Latvians in Bicentennial America* (Waverly, Iowa: Latvju Grāmata, 1976), p. 21.

2. Osvalds Akmentiņš, "Pieminot veclatviešu teātri Amerikā," in *Raiņa un Aspazijas gada grāmata* (Västeräs, Sweden: Ziemeļblāzma, 1973), pp. 90–102.

3. Osvalds Akmentiņš, *Amerikas latvieši: 1888–1948, fakti un apceres* (Lincoln, Nebr.: Vaidava, 1958), p. 107.

4. The term *veclatvieši* (Old Latvians) was coined by the press of the second-wave Latvian immigrants in order to delineate the two ideologically different groups.

5. An account of the prehistory of the Balts can be found in Marija Gimbutas, *The Balts* (New York: Frederick A. Praeger, 1963).

6. Arveds Švābe, *Latvijas vēsture 1800–1914* (Uppsala, Sweden: Daugava, 1958), p. 399.

7. A German minister, Alexander Johann Stender, had adapted it from a Danish comedy, *Jeppe paa Bjerget,* by Ludwig Holberg, and it was published 1790 in Jelgava.

8. Latvian newspaper *Mājas Viesis,* no. 45, 1868. All translations from Latvian and other languages, if not otherwise noted, are by the author.

9. Latvian newspaper *Baltijas Vēstnesis,* no. 35, 1869.

10. Artūrs Bērziņš, *Ādolfs Alunāns latviešu teātrī* (London: Latpress, 1954), pp. 26–28.

11. Ibid., p. 146.

12. Ibid., p. 138.

13. Ibid.

14. J. Velme in the Latvian magazine *Austrums* 4 (1887).

15. Baltijas Vēstnesis 35 (1869).

16. As quoted in Bērziņš, *Ādolfs Alunāns*, p. 198.

17. Ibid., p. 205.

18. James A. Brundage, *The Chronicle of Henry of Livonia* (Madison: University of Wisconsin Press, 1961).

19. Bērziņš, *Ādolfs Alunāns*, p. 207.

20. See a recent translation of the play in Alfreds Straumanis, ed., *The Golden Steed: Seven Baltic Plays* (Prospect Heights, Ill.: Waveland Press, 1979). See also Andre Sedriks, "The Metamorphosis of the Antiņš Character in Latvian Drama 1909–1973" (Ph.D. diss., Southern Illinois University at Carbondale, 1977). The protagonist of *The Golden Steed*, Antiņš, has become the "bringer of sun" symbol for the Latvians.

21. Arvīds Ziedonis, Jr., *The Religious Philosophy of Jānis Rainis* (Waverly, Iowa: Latvju Grāmata, 1969), p. 321.

22. See a recent English translation by Astrid Stahnke, "Aspazija and *The Silver Veil*" (master's thesis, Southern Illinois University, Edwardsville, 1977).

23. Jānis Rudzītis, "Literature and Drama," in *Cross Road Country Latvia*, edited by Edgars Andersons (Waverly, Iowa: Latvju Grāmata, 1953), p. 259.

24. Švābe, *Latvijas*, p. 717.

25. *Strādnieks* (The Worker, a weekly newspaper, published in Boston, Mass.), Apr. 15, 1908.

26. Akmentiņš, *Raiņa un Aspazijas gada grāmata*, p. 92.

27. *Amerikas Latvietis* (American Latvian, a semimonthly newspaper, published in Boston since 1940), Sept. 11, 1948.

28. Akmentiņš, *Raiņa un Aspazijas gada grāmata*, p. 91.

29. Ibid., p. 94.

30. Osvalds Akmentiņš, "Pirms piecdesmit gadiem" (Fifty Years Ago), *Tilts* (Minneapolis, Tilta apgāds), Nrs. 42/43 (1961), p. 55.

31. *Strādnieks*, 1914.

32. *Strādnieks*, Jan. 9, 1914.

33. Rīts (Morning), Nov. 27, 1920. Published by the Boston Society of Latvian Workers.

34. This is a paraphrase of *Savs kaktiņš, savs stūrītis zemes* (One's Own Corner, One's Own Piece of Land), title of a story by Jānis Purapuķe (1864–1902), a writer who promoted the idea of private property as means toward a better life and who therefore was called the "propagandist of the ideology of one's own corner" by the New Current writers.

35. L. Stein in *Strādnieks*, Oct. 23, 1914.

36. Akmentiņš, "Pirms piecdesmit gadiem," p. 55.

37. Ibid., p. 53.

38. Daugavas Vanagi, Inc., is the largest welfare organization of the second-wave Latvian immigrants, and it maintains a theatre library in Boston.

39. Akmentiņš, "Pirms piecdesmit gadiem," p. 54.

40. Ibid., p. 55.

41. *Strādnieks*, Dec. 18, 1917.

42. Ibid., Sept. 15, 1914.

43. Ibid., Nov. 10, 1914.

44. Vilis Dermanis, "Modern Proletariat and Art," *Domas*, nos. 1–2 (1913). *Domas* was a literary magazine published in Riga by members of the New Current.

45. As relates Akmentiņš ("Pirms piecdesmit gadiem," p. 53), the first signs of a production in Latvian can be detected from a journal entry by the first Latvian organization in the United States, the Latvian Association of Boston, in 1895. A theatre committee was established consisting of five members: J. Šitke, E. Randau, F. Kairit, J. Beitlec, and B. Biederman. The minutes mention that nonmembers could also participate in play production; however, nothing is known about any play actually produced before 1898, the year of the organization's tenth birthday.

46. Quoted in Felix Cielēns, The Latvian Drama (Stockholm: Latvian P.E.N. Centre, 1950), p. 5.

47. Roberts Kroders, Le Théâtre des Fêtes Lettonnes (Riga: Pagalms, 1937), p. 27.

48. Rasma Birzgale, et al., eds., Amerikas Latviešu Teātris (Boston: ALT Bostonas Ansamblis, 1976).

49. Anšlāvs Eglītis, "Gatavības apliecība desmit gados," Laiks, October 30, 1976.

50. Raimonds Čaks, "Latviešu teātŗa darbs Milvokos," Skatuve un Dzīve, no. 1 (September 1959), pp. 7–9.

51. Personal letter to Alfreds Straumanis, July 7, 1968.

52. Kaspars Strūga, "Piezīmes teātŗu dienās," Tilts, nos. 154, 155 (December 1976), p. 70.

53. Quoted in Jānis Liģeris, "Teātra izrādes skolās—mācības viela," Laiks, May 1, 1971.

54. Kaspars Strūga, "Vēl cīņa nav galā," Tilts, nos. 154, 155, p. 40.

55. Rasma Birzgale, "Sudraba kalēji," Tilts, nos. 154, 155, p. 30.

BIBLIOGRAPHY

Books

Akmentiņš, Osvalds. Amerikas latvieši: 1888–1948, fakti un apceres. Lincoln, Nebr.: Vaidava, 1958. Facts and opinions about fifty years of Latvian immigrants in America.

_____. Latvians in Bicentennial America. Waverly, Iowa: Latvju Grāmata, 1976. Informative sketches and photographs from various Latvian communities in the United States.

Andersons, Edgars, ed. Cross Road Country Latvia. Waverly, Iowa: Latvju Grāmata, 1953. Contains articles about the Latvian people, geography, economics, history, sciences, and arts. Selected bibliography.

Bērziņš, Artūrs. Ādolfs Alunāns. London: Latpress, 1954. Comprehensive discussion of the "father of Latvian theatre."

Brundage, James A. The Chronicle of Henry of Livonia. Madison: University of Wisconsin Press, 1961. A translation with introduction and notes.

Gimbutas, Marija. The Balts. New York: Frederick A. Praeger, 1963. An account of the prehistory of the Balts.

Kroders, Roberts. Le Théâtre des Fêtes Lettonnes. Riga: Pagalms, 1937. A treatise dealing with the philosophies and history of nationalistic theatre spectacles in independent Latvia.

Straumanis, Alfreds, ed. Baltic Drama: A Handbook and Bibliography. Prospect Heights, Ill.: Waveland Press, 1981. Estonian, Latvian, and Lithuanian drama overviews, biographies of major playwrights, more than 4,600 play titles, including synopses and annotations, index of titles in the original and English, index of authors, bibliographies of sources.

_____. Confrontations with Tyranny. Prospect Heights, Ill.: Waveland Press, 1977. Anthology of six Baltic plays with introductory essays.

_____. The Golden Steed: Seven Baltic Plays. Prospect Heights, Ill.: Waveland Press, 1979. Anthology of seven Baltic plays with introductory essays.

Švābe, Arveds. *Latvijas vēsture 1800–1914*. Uppsala, Sweden: Daugava, 1958. History of a period in Latvia depicting the national awakening and societal change.

Ziedonis, Arvīds, Jr. *The Religious Philosophy of Jānis Rainis*. Waverly, Iowa: Latvju Grāmata, 1969. Includes synopses and discussions of Rainis's plays. Bibliography.

Theses and Dissertations

Šedriks, Andre. "The Metamorphosis of the Antiņš Character in Latvian Drama: 1909–1973." Ph.D. Diss., Southern Illinois University, Carbondale, 1977. Study of dramatic characters in plays by Rainis, Paegle, Putniņš, Zīverts, and other Latvian dramatists.

Stahnke, Astrid. "Aspazija and *The Silver Veil*." Master's thesis, Southern Illinois University, Edwardsville, 1977. Includes a translation of *Sidraba šķidrauts*, by Aspazija.

Straumanis, Alfreds. "Latvian Theatre: The Synthesis of Ritual and National Awakening." Master's thesis, Hofstra University, 1964. Includes a translation of *Sestdienas vakars* (A Saturday Evening), a one-act play by Blaumanis.

Valters, Juris. "Anšlavs Eglītis: A Changing Artist." Master's thesis, Southern Illinois University, Carbondale, 1978. Includes a translation of *Ferdinands un Sibila* (Ferdinand and Sybil), by Eglītis.

Periodicals and Pamphlets

"Amerikas Latviešu Teātris." Boston: ALT Bostonas ansamblis, 1976. Pamphlet commemorating the twenty-fifth year of the American Latvian Theatre in Boston.

Amerikas Latvietis. A semimonthly newspaper published in Boston since 1940.

Austrums. A scientific literary monthly published in Moscow, Jelgava, Riga, and Cēsis from 1885 to 1906.

Baltijas Vēstnesis. A semiweekly paper from 1869, weekly from 1870, and daily from 1880, when it merged with another Riga paper, until 1906.

Cielēns, Felix. "The Latvian Drama." Stockholm: Latvian P.E.N. Centre, 1950. Pamphlet in English describing the history and tendencies of Latvian drama.

Dienas Lapa. A daily newspaper published in Riga from 1886 to 1905, at times supporting the New Current, with its liberal and Marxist ideologies.

Domas. A monthly literary magazine published in Riga from 1912 to 1915.

Laiks. A Latvian newspaper, published twice a week by Grāmatu Draugs, Brooklyn, N.Y., since 1949.

Mājas Viesis. A weekly newspaper published from 1856 to 1910 in Riga.

Raiņa un Aspazijas gada grāmata. Yearly calendar, published since 1967 by Raiņa un Aspazijas Fonds (RAF) in Västeräs, Sweden. Contains articles about Rainis and Aspazija, including discussion of their dramatic works.

Rīts, nos. 1–48. Weekly magazine for science and literature, published in St. Petersburg during 1907.

Skatuve un Dzīve, nos. 1–13. Published in Chicago by Otto Krolls between 1959 and 1962. A magazine of Latvian theatre in exile.

Strādnieks. A weekly newspaper published between 1906 and 1919 in Boston by the American Latvian Socialist Organization.

12

Lithuanian-American Theatre

BRONIUS VAŠKELIS

Lithuanians began to arrive in the United States in larger numbers during the second half of the nineteenth century. By the end of the century about fifty thousand Lithuanian immigrants had settled mainly in the coal mining regions of Pennsylvania. Some of them also settled in cities such as Boston, Brooklyn, Baltimore, Newark, Philadelphia, Cleveland, and Chicago.

THE FIRST PERFORMANCES

Theatrical amateur groups appeared as soon as the first social and religious organizations, parishes, and newspapers were founded. The first attempt to produce a play in Lithuanian was made in 1885–1887 in New York City. The first successful performance took place on December 31, 1889, at the People's Theater in Plymouth, Pennsylvania, when a group of twenty-six persons produced Antanas Turskis's three-act play *Be sumnenės* (Without Conscience). On February 12, 1890, a "Lithuanian dramatic company" of eighteen persons gave a "Lithuanian performance" in three acts at Kaier's Opera House in Mahanoy City, Pennsylvania.[1] The next Lithuanian play, *Kova po Grunvaldu* (Battle at Grünwald), written and directed by Jonas Grinius, was produced on June 4, 1892, at the Vorwaerts Turner Hall in Chicago. Seventy-one actors, fully dressed in medieval attire and armor, participated on the stage in a huge battle scene. These three groups, pioneers of Lithuanian theatre, were disbanded soon after the performances, with the exception of Grinius's dramatic group, which produced two more plays in 1894.

News of Lithuanian theatrical activities spread quickly throughout the Lithuanian colonies. During the 1894–1895 season, eight dramatic amateur groups, recently formed in the Pennsylvania cities of Plymouth, Pittston, Shenandoah (two groups), Scranton, Philadelphia, and Pittsburgh and in Newark, New Jersey, gave eighteen performances of fifteen plays. During the following five years, eleven new drama groups were formed.[2] At the turn of the century, of the twenty-four spontaneous and short-lived groups formed during the first decade of theatrical activities, fourteen remained active, eight enjoying four to five years of existence. During this decade there were in all eighty-seven performances of thirty-five plays by Lithuanian and foreign authors.

The members of these groups were unskilled laborers, working in mines, factories, and clothing shops, most of them with no previous acting experience. Theatre was viewed by émigré leaders not merely as entertainment for their countrymen, but as a patriotic and educational activity capable of awakening national consciousness and pride. The plays, mainly comedies, farces, and melodramas, were based on the social, moral, and national problems prevalent in Lithuania. They appealed to the sentiments of the homesick, lonely, uprooted immigrants, and therefore the performances were very well received. According to newspaper accounts, immigrants of other nationalities, such as Germans, Jews, Poles, and Slovaks, attended Lithuanian performances in Chicago; Plymouth; Shenandoah; and Waterbury, Connecticut.

The organizers and directors of Lithuanian drama groups and societies came from different walks of life. They included three organists of Roman Catholic churches, three priests, two journalists, one physician, and several unskilled workers. Grinius and Mykolas J. Stupnickis (1857–1945) stand out by virtue of their activities and devotion to the theatre. Starting in 1892 Grinius devoted fourteen years of his time and energy to the promotion of Lithuanian theatre. He worked as an actor, director, producer, and playwright. After producing three plays in Chicago, he moved to Spring Valley, Illinois. There he organized a dramatic troupe and staged two plays in 1896. In 1898 he formed a new troupe of players and toured Lithuanian communities in Cleveland; Mahanoy City; Plymouth; Pittston; Forest City, Pennsylvania; and Brooklyn, New York. In 1900–1904, with a new group of actors, he gave several performances in Waterbury; New Britain, Connecticut; and Brooklyn, New York.

Stupnickis, a physician by profession, wrote or adapted from other foreign languages six plays, including an original melodrama, *Kankinimas Kataliku Lietuvoje* (Torture of Catholics in Lithuania), which met with popular success and was performed by eight acting groups in 1895–1897. He also formed theatrical groups in Plymouth, Pittston, and Shenandoah, and under his direction each produced one or two plays. After 1895 he directed plays in Chicago for two dramatic groups and for several fraternal organizations that occasionally staged their own plays.

During the twentieth century Lithuanian immigration continued to grow. By 1910 there were over 200,000 Lithuanians in the United States, and by 1915 there were 300,000. The majority chose to settle in cities where Lithuanian communities had already been established in the nineteenth century. A larger number of the new immigrants had had some schooling, especially those political refugees who came after the 1905 revolt in Lithuania. Second- and third-generation Lithuanians who had integrated themselves into the American mainstream as professionals and civil servants were still very active in the social, cultural, and political life of the American-Lithuanian communities.

GROWTH OF THEATRE: THE EARLY TWENTIETH CENTURY

The changes that took place in the Lithuanian diaspora affected theatrical activities a great deal. Drama groups were multiplying, and by 1907 one or more existed in every sizable Lithuanian community. Theatrical entertainment became an integral part of social and cultural émigré life. Theatre groups were competing for members and also for theatregoing public. For instance, socialist drama groups, with their fighting fervor and their more interesting performances, lured members of groups sponsored by Roman Catholic parishes. Groups without any affiliation, such as independent drama societies and choral-dramatic ensembles, grew stronger and appealed to a wider audience, and soon they became in every sense theatres of the community; by their theatrical achievements they stood high above the parish, socialist, and other more specialized theatrical groups.

Although they appealed mainly to the members and friends of their organizations and gave only sporadic, occasional performances, parish and socialist theatre groups played significant roles in some of the communities. For instance, in Brooklyn, Baltimore, Boston, and Chicago from 1907 to 1916, there were permanent socialist groups that gave two or three performances regularly every year. In 1914 socialist actors gave eighty-seven theatrical performances.[3]

Parish theatre groups were less active and less numerous; however, the drama society Varpas (Bell), working under the auspices of the Lithuanian church in Baltimore, gave about twenty theatre performances in 1914–1916. The repertory of parish groups consisted mainly of religious plays and domestic comedies. The socialists tended to offer more social comedies and farces, as well as plays with political or antireligious undertones. While paying lip service to the notion that a theatre is a weapon in the workers' movement, several socialist theatre groups, among them groups in Boston, Waterbury, and Philadelphia, produced patriotic historical plays without any social or revolutionary content.

Until 1907 choral groups very seldom staged their own plays; yet they often presented several songs between acts at the performances of the dramatic groups. The situation was radically changed by the arrival in the United States of the composer and chorus master Mikas Petrauskas (1873–1937). He began to give musical performances while touring the Lithuanian communities. Then, staying in each city for months or sometimes years, he formed musical and dramatic societies in Brooklyn, Detroit, Boston, Chicago, and Scranton. The repertory of these societies-choruses consisted primarily of his own melodramatic musical comedies and operettas, but many plays were staged as well. For example, of the sixteen works presented on the stage by the dramatic and choral society Birutė of Chicago during its first three seasons in 1908–1911, ten were plays. The Theater and Song Society of Cleveland, formed in 1909, produced more than thirty plays during 1909–1916. The musical and dramatic society Gabija, founded in 1914 in South Boston, at one time featured plays and operettas weekly.[4] Petrauskas's performances lured thousands, becoming the most popular form of entertainment among Lithuanians.

The most serious and significant dramatic performances, however, were given by independent drama groups and societies. During 1900–1919 they existed in every larger Lithuanian community, giving full evening programs of serious plays, acted by experienced amateur players. These differed from the other theatrical groups by their regular and permanent activities, by their repertory, and by the quality of their performances. For instance, members acting over a long period of time together were of professional quality, and performances given by societies in Baltimore, Brooklyn, and Chicago were of high artistic merit. From 1901 to 1914 the Lithuanian Dramatic Association of Baltimore, under the direction of Vincas Nagornoskis (1869–1939), produced over thirty plays, among them *Mindowe* (about Mindaugas, the king of Lithuania), by Juliusz Slowacki, *Kiejstut* (about Kęstutis, prince of Lithuania), by Adam Asnyk; and *Živilė* (about a legendary Lithuanian heroine), *Pilėniečiai* (The Defenders of the Pilėnai), *Rutvilė* (about a Samogitian girl), and others, by Nagornoskis. Historical plays and plays of a serious nature were also performed with great success from 1903 to 1916 by the S. Daukantas Theatrical Society of Brooklyn. However, the drama societies in Chicago and its suburbs particularly distinguished themselves by their serious intent, scope, and artistic ventures. The highest peak of achievement of the Lithuanian émigré stage may be considered to have been during the period 1908–1919 in Chicago.

The first important effort to raise the Lithuanian theatre to a higher artistic level was an undertaking in Chicago in 1908 by Bronius Laucevičius (1884–1916). Having assembled a group of experienced amateur actors, he formed the Dramatic Circle. At first it functioned under the auspices of the Lithuanian Socialist Party, but within a year it became independent. Under several directors it performed serious plays and light comedies for a fee to various organizations and groups, with great success, for more than a decade.

At the same time two dramatic troupes of a similar nature were performing in Chicago. The Youth Theatrical Circle, founded in the town of Lake (now part of Chicago) in 1910, directed by Marija (Mary) Dundulienė (1874–1953) and since 1913 by Jonas Žalpys-Zolp (1885–1972), gave seventy-eight performances over the span of twelve years. The Theatrical Amateur Society of Roseland, established by Dundulienė in 1911, performed more than forty plays to various clubs and organizations during a ten-year period. About two-thirds of the plays were domestic comedies. To improve the skill of its members, the society established a fund for talented persons to attend drama schools, and in 1921 a course was offered for its members on acting and on the theatrical arts. Dundulienė also had a drama studio. These three troupes were able to pay a nominal fee to their directors for each of their rehearsals and performances.

In 1915 professional actors established the Lithuanian Theater Company. Benediktas Vaitekūnas was in charge of a drama section, Petras Sarpalius of a music section, and V. Brusokas of monologue and jokes section. The company gave two vaudeville-type performances on Saturdays and seven on Sundays throughout the year of 1915 at the Lithuanian theatre Milda in Bridgeport, Connecticut.

To raise the level of theatrical performances in the United States, Laucevičius edited and published the monthly magazine *Veidrodis* (The Mirror). Its eleven issues, published in 1914 and 1915 in Chicago, primarily dealt with theoretical problems of theatre, acting, and criticism.

By 1913 Lithuanian theatrical activities in the Chicago area had become numerous and complex. There were about fifteen active groups. Sometimes they staged the same plays at the same time, two or even three performances on the same day. In order to coordinate theatrical activities and to stage better and larger plays by concerted efforts, in 1914 the leaders of seven drama societies formed the Alliance of Lithuanian Dramatic Societies. Laucevičius was elected its general director. The alliance presented several plays in 1914–1915 with great success, and the profit from the performances was used to aid war victims in Lithuania.

Several attempts were made to form a traveling troupe. For example, H. Mockus formed a group of actors in Chicago, and in 1907 he toured Lithuanian communities in the coal region of Pennsylvania. Because of its poor acting and the low quality of its one-act farcical pieces, the troupe failed to arouse much attention among Lithuanians and was soon disbanded.

The most successful troupe of this kind was formed by Aleksandras Vitkauskas (1887–1943) in Boston. With a repertory catering to the lower tastes of audiences, such as Jerzy Żulawski's *Mirtų vainikas* (The Wreath of Myrtle) and Kazys Puida's *Gairės* (Landmarks), he successfully toured about thirty Lithuanian communities in 1916–1917. Vitkauskas had studied the dramatic arts in St. Petersburg and Moscow, and in 1911–1914 he had had a traveling troupe in Lithuania. During his sojourn in the United States, aside from his activities with the touring troupe, he also organized drama groups in Boston, Waterbury (Connecticut), New York, Chicago, and Philadelphia and presented more than a dozen plays. The largest and best-known venture was the performance of Marcelinas Šikšnys's historical play *Pilėnų kunigaikštis* (Prince of Pilenai) in 1918 in Waterbury. It was performed outside by a cast of some 150 persons, to an audience of over 5,000, many members of which were of other ethnic groups.

Around 1916 young members of the Knights of Lithuania, largely college students and graduates, began to form theatrical groups. Within two years there were thirty-six such groups. Drama troupes of the Knights of Lithuania in Brooklyn, Cleveland, Baltimore, Chicago, and Waterbury were more active, producing two or three plays of religious and patriotic nature each year. Five groups in the Chicago district formed an alliance, and through concerted effort presented full evening programs, including such plays in Lithuanian as William Shakespeare's *Hamlet*, Henrik Ibsen's *Nora*, Asnyk's *Kiejstut*, and Johann Schiller's *Wilhelm Tell*.

The repertories of drama groups between 1900 and 1919 predominately contained realistic plays and farcical comedies, translated from foreign authors or written by authors living in Lithuania. Among nearly twenty immigrant playwrights, four were especially prominent and were well received by audiences. Nagornoskis, a tailor by profession, wrote nine historical plays in Lithuanian and two in English. Despite their amateurish and melodramatic nature, his plays were performed time and again on Lithuanian-American stages. Also, two of them were produced by amateur groups in Lithuania, one in Riga, and one in St. Petersburg. Laucevičius, whose pen name was Vargšas (Poor Fellow), wrote twelve plays. They deal mainly with the lives and social problems of the peasants and workers in Lithuania. Although his plays were not of high dramatic quality, they were performed with popular success by Lithuanian-American groups and several were even performed in Lithuania. Dundulienė, who is now almost forgotten as a playwright, wrote more than a dozen plays for the amateur stage. Many of them she produced herself from manuscripts; published ones were performed by parish groups and groups of the Roman Catholic Women's Alliance and the Progressive Women's Alliance. Žalpys-Zolp, who held two degrees in dramatic arts and music from American schools, wrote about twenty plays. His realistic plays, with simple plots and vividly drawn characters, had a great appeal to the audience. Of the four published Žalpys plays, Valkata (The Tramp) was staged with success in Canada and Lithuania as well as the United States.

THEATRE AFTER WORLD WAR I

After World War I the former dramatic societies showed very little activity. New theatrical groups, short-lived and of no apparent significance, presented predominately trite, domestic comedies by Juozas Čepukaitis and didactic plays by Juozas Židanavičius. The plots of the latter were drawn from the lives of saints, from the Bible, or from history.

When the majority of Lithuanian socialists joined the Communist Party of America in 1919, the activities of socialist theatrical groups were discontinued. In 1935–1939, however, several performances of dramatic importance were produced by Jonas Valentis, who at that time, worked at the Lithuanian Folk Theatre in Brooklyn, a subordinate of the Lithuanian Proletarian Fine Arts League. Valentis, a tailor by profession, had attended Michael Chekhov's Drama Studio and for a while had worked at the Civic Repertory Theatre in New York City.

Between the wars Lithuanian theatre underwent a powerful resurgence, induced by visits and prolonged tours of professional actors from Lithuania. One of the more prominent visitors was Juozas Vaičkus (1885–1935), founder of the professional theatre in Lithuania, who came to Brooklyn in 1923 and formed a drama studio. After a year of unsuccessful efforts to form a permanent theatre, he moved to Chicago, where he succeeded. The nucleus of his theatre consisted of talented and experienced amateur actors, half of them American born. At first he gave performances at halls in the Lithuanian community, and during 1925–1926 the performances were at Jane Addams's social settlement, Hull House. He also had a drama studio and toured larger Lithuanian communities. During the fall of 1928 Vaičkus's troupe presented four plays a week at Goodman Theater, among them Slowacki's *Mindowe*, Schiller's *Cabal and Love*, and Hieronim Drucki-Lubecki's *Taip mirdaro lietuviai* (This Way Lithuanians Died). The audiences dwindled and the performances incurred financial losses. Vaičkus tried in vain to make some money by performing plays at various halls of Lithuanian parishes. Nevertheless, the troupe was disbanded at the end of the year. Vaičkus left for Hollywood.

At that time a vaudeville variety touring troupe known as the Dzimdzi-Drimdzi attracted crowds in every community. The troupe was formed in 1924 by Antanas Vanagaitis (1890–1949) and three other professional actors who came from Lithuania. The troupe presented songs, satirical sketches, and dramatic skits in Lithuanian communities every season until 1931.

Stasys Pilka (1898–1976), another professional actor from Lithuania, worked for a while with the Vanagaitis touring troupe. In 1927 he formed a dramatic group in Chicago and in 1928 in Brooklyn as well. His more noteworthy performances during these two years, included Molière's *Goerges Dandin*, Sofija Čiurlionienė's *Aušros sūnūs* (The Sons of Dawn), and Petras Vaičiūnas's *Tuščios pastangos* (Futile Endeavors) and *Sudrumsta ramybė* (Quietness Disturbed).

Working with amateur actors, Vaičkus and Pilka raised the level of acting and staging, and the repertory as well. However, there was no apparent improvement or lasting result in the activities of dramatic groups afterwards. The theatrical doldrums continued from 1931 for about twenty years, until a considerable number of professional actors appeared as a result of the influx of 35,000 new immigrants in 1947–1951.

NEW IMMIGRATION AFTER WORLD WAR II

Actors who fled the Soviet occupation of Lithuania and settled in the United States immediately began to form drama groups and studios. In 1949 amateur theatre ensembles of greater significance were given performances in Boston, Baltimore, Chicago, Cleveland, Detroit; and Los Angeles. Each group had several experienced actors among its members. Performances were also directed by formerly professional actors or directors. All of the members of these groups were recent immigrants.

By 1964 there were about twenty such theatre groups, and more than thirty directors were producing plays.[5] From that time, however, the activities of Lithuanian émigré theatre took a downward course. By 1968 half of the groups formed in the fifties showed no theatrical activity, and only a few new groups have been formed. Among those worth mentioning are Antras kaimas (Second Village), established in 1963, and the Youth Theater of Chicago in 1968.[6] In order to revitalize theatrical activities, four Lithuanian theatre festivals were organized, but the festivals did not bring about the desired results. Six Lithuanian-American amateur groups participated in 1968, two in 1971, three in 1974, and three in 1977. By the end of 1979 only two permanent theatre groups, one in Los Angeles and one in Chicago, were giving performances annually or on a regular basis.

The repertory of these postwar amateur theatre groups was also new; they did not produce the works of earlier immigrant playwrights or plays that had enjoyed popular success during 1900–1919. Most of the groups presented sentimental and didactic plays written either in independent Lithuania or abroad by émigré playwrights, such as, Vytautas Alantas, Jurgis Gliauda, Stasys Laucius, Anatolijus Kairys, and Anatas Rūkas. Many of them were geared for the amateur stage. The most popular and widely performed plays were by Kairys (1914–), an émigré writer. His apparently appealed to the sentiment of immigrant audiences, with themes such as patriotism, national pride and loyalty, and the need to preserve the Lithuanian language.

Some directors, such as Jurgis Blekaitis (1914–), Algimantas Dikinis (1922–), Vytautas Valiukas (1916–), and Antanas Škėma (1911–1961), tended toward experimental and creative ventures. They undertook mainly modernistic works of both Lithuanian émigré and foreign authors in translation. The dramatic idiom and ideas of the modern theatre drew a smaller, but nevertheless appreciative, audience. It was a real challenge, and sometimes too difficult a task, for the amateur actors to bring to the stage the structurally and stylistically complex works of Lithuanian-American playwrights such as Škėma, Algirdas Landsbergis (1924–), and Kostas Ostrauskas (1926–). For instance, the complex themes and philosophical issues of Ostrauskas's plays, amidst generally simple plots and laconic dialogues, are conveyed by different structural levels as well as linguistic juxtapositions; because of this, few attempted to stage them. The existentalist themes and problems of Škėma's plays are dealt with by cruel, harsh, at times incompatible theatrical techniques. Some in the audience were shocked, and thus were critical of the author and actors as well.

Despite avant-garde comic and sometimes surrealistic stage techniques, however, Landsbergis's plays met with considerable popular success in every larger Lithuanian community; their portrayal of the grotesque and of the comical in contemporary life is subdued by humor and a lyrical tone. Landsbergis's play *Penki stulpai turgaus aikštėje* (Five Posts in the Market Place) was also staged by English-language dramatic groups in Chicago in 1961, New York City in 1961, Toronto in 1966, and Carbondale, Illinois, in 1975.

CENTERS OF POST-WORLD WAR II DRAMA

During the postwar period, Chicago again became the center of Lithuanian immigrant theatrical activities. Here the largest number of professional actors and stage directors had settled. Over a span of thirty years, at least ten amateur theatrical groups gave performances at one time or another, directed by more than twenty different directors. Between 1949 and 1953 several groups distinguished themselves by performances of professional quality. For example, the performances directed by Blekaitis and Valiukas were welcomed by theatre critics and sophisticated audiences for their scenic innovations and artistic achievement. Among Blekaitis's staged plays were *Rocket to the Moon*, by Clifford Odets; *Anna Christie*, by Eugene O'Neill; *The Imaginary Invalid*, by Molière; the comedy *Svetimos plunksnos* (Foreign Feathers), by Vineas Adoménas; and the historical play *Živilė*, by Škėma. Valiukas produced *Antigone*, by Jean Anouilh; *Glass Menagerie*, by Tennessee Williams; and *Kanarėlė* (The Canary), by Ostrauskas (Figure 12.1).

Pilka (1898–1976) and Rūkas (1907–1967) gave traditional performances of plays they had been accustomed to presenting while working in Lithuania or Germany. Plays such as *Naujieji žmonės* (New People), by Petras Vaičiūnas; *Tėvas* (Father), by Juozas Grušas; *Bubulis and Dundulis*, by Rūkas; *Valdovas* (The Ruler), by Vincas Mykolaitis-Putinas, met with great success, especially among older audiences who had seen them performed in Europe. For instance, *Naujieji žmonės* ran ten performances in Chicago and a dozen more in other Lithuanian communities.

The Association of Dramatic Artists (1954–1972) gave fifty-five perfor-

12.1   Kazys Vasiliauskaa as Rokas and Leonas Karamazinas as Jokubas in *Kanarėlė*, by Kostas Ostrauskas, New York, New York, 1962. (Production photograph by Vytautus Augustinas, courtesy of the author.)

mances of twelve plays, staged by six directors. Among the plays directed by Dikinis, which were highly acclaimed, were *Barzda* (Beard) and *Vėjas gluosniuose* (Wind in the Willows), by Landsbergis; *Street Kid*, by Daria Niccodemi; *Bubulis and Dundulis*, by Rūkas, and a dramatization of Kristijonas Donelaitis's poem *Metai* (Seasons). Birutė Pukelevičiūtė's fairy tale comedy in verse, *Aukso žąsis* (Golden Goose), directed by the author herself, was also a significant production.

Since 1963, Antras kaimas, which has fostered comic and satiric theatre, has given about 150 performances to Lithuanians throughout the United States and Canada. The troupe took its model from Second City, a professional American troupe popular in Chicago in 1963. The repertory consisted of a number of brief comic and satiric sketches written by Lithuanian émigré writers. Algirdas T. Antanaitis (1927–) has been heading the troupe since 1968.

The Lithuanian Community Players in Brooklyn, formed by Vitalis Žukauskas (1919–) in 1951, produced ten plays, mainly by Lithuanian émigré writers, with popular success in several Lithuanian communities. One of its most noteworthy performances was the play *Laikas* (Time), by Škėma and Žukauskas, presented in concert with a Lithuanian choir and a folk dance group at the Brooklyn Academy of Music in 1961. Among the performing actors were Rūta Lee-Kilmonytė, a television and film star, Pilka, Škėma, and Žukauskas. Žukauskas is known also as a comedian. He has presented about 400 performances by his so-called Theater of One to Lithuanians in the United States, Canada, and Australia.

In 1953 a drama studio was formed in New York City by Blekaitis, Henrikas Kačinskas, and Škėma. Its students presented A. J. Cronin's play *Jupiter Laughs*, directed by Blekaitis. In New York City Blekaitis also directed Malakov's play *Refugees*, produced by the New Russian Theater, and Giraudoux's *Amphitryon 38*, produced by Showcase, an American group. After a ten-year interval Blekaitis staged Ostrauskas's *Pypkė* (The Pipe) and *Duobkasiai* (Gravediggers) in Chicago.

In 1961–1965 Valiukas's group was giving highly artistic performances of contemporary Lithuanian-American plays in Queens, New York. Among them were Škėma's *Vienas ir kiti* (The One and the Others), Ostrauskas's *Kanarėlė*, and dramatizations of Vincas Krėvė's works.

The Amateur Drama Troupe of Detroit (1949–1968) presented over fifty original and translated works, directed by Zuzana Arlauskaitė-Mikšiene (1889–1973), a former actress of the Kaunas State Theatre. Among the more noteworthy performances were *Vieną vakarą* (One Evening) by Škėma, *Vincas Kudirka* by Kazys Inčiūra, *Tėvas* by Grušas, *Naujieji žmonės* by Vaičiūnas, *Petro Caruso* by Roberto Bracco, *Nora* by Ibsen, *Street Kid* by Niccodemi, and *Glass Menagerie* by Tennessee Williams. Of the 100 performances, half were presented by tours to Lithuanian communities in the United States and Canada.

Aleksandra Gustaitienė (1905–), a veteran of the Lithuanian stage, formed the Lithuanian Drama Troupe in Boston, and under her direction (1952–1969)

12.2   Vytautas Juodka (left) and Algirdas Kurauskas in *Pypkė*, by Kostas Ostrauskas, Chicago, Illinois, 1963. (Production photograph by Algimantas Kezyz, courtesy of the author.)

the troupe gave about sixty performances of thirteen plays, among which were an adaptation of *A Christmas Carol* by Charles Dickens, *Red Wine* by Erneste Karlinš, *Vincas Kudirka* by Inčiūra, *Maniakas* (Maniac) by Kazys Saja, *The Stranger* by August Strindberg, and *Nuodemingas angelas* (Sinful Angel) by Vaičiūnas. The Lithuanian theatre Vaidila in Cleveland (1952–1968) was headed by Petras Maželis. It produced fourteen plays, mainly by Lithuanian authors,

12.3   Algimantas Dikinis (left) and Vytautas Juodka in *Duobkasiai,* by Kostas Ostrauskas, Chicago, Illinois, 1967. (Production photograph by Algimantas Kezyz, courtesy
of the author.)

among which were *Atžalynas* (The Young Generation) by Kazys Binkis, *Vincas
Kudirka* by Inčiūra, *Penki stulpai turgaus aikštėje* by Landsbergis, *Kęstučio mirtis*
(Death of Kęstutis) by Jonas Mačiulis-Maironis, and *Tėvas* by Grušas.

The Lithuanian Drama Troupe of Los Angeles, established in 1949, presented
over thirty plays, mainly by Lithuanian émigré writers, written for the amateur
stage. The activities of the troupe were intensified when Dalila Mackialienė
became its director in 1962. She was able to assemble a number of young and
talented amateur actors and to raise the level of the troupe's performances. It
performed with popular success in Chicago, Toronto, and even in Sydney and
Melbourne, Australia (1979).

LEVELS OF THEATRICAL ACTIVITY

This brief survey shows that during ninety years of Lithuanian immigrant
theatre activities there were two peaks, 1907–1919 and 1949–1966, and two
doldrums, 1931–1949 and from 1970 on. The peaks occurred when the highest
numbers of immigrants were entering the United States, and the doldrums when
most immigrants had merged into the mainstream of American life.

The Lithuanian theatre, like many other immigrant organizations and institutions, was a part of the various Lithuanian communities in the United States, having few contacts with American theatre life. Actors working with the amateur theatrical groups had to earn a living doing jobs totally unrelated to the theatre. They also had to learn new skills or even new professions. Gradually their theatrical activities became an avocation.. In pursuit of better jobs or positions, some of them moved away from their ethnic communities and away from the émigré theatre as well. The few remaining theatrical groups are run by experienced amateur actors, but the majority of their members are college students and other stage enthusiasts who stay for a short period of time and want to act without learning rudimentary acting skills.

NOTES

1. *Tri-Weekly Record* (Mahanoy City, Pa.), Feb. 11, 1890.
2. New groups were formed in Chicago (1895); Mahanoy City, Pa. (1895); Waterbury, Conn. (1895); Spring Valley, Ill. (1896); Mt. Carmel, Pa. (1896); Chicago (a second group, 1898); Cleveland, Ohio (1898); Elizabeth, N.J. (1898); Minersville, Pa. (1898); and Waterbury (a second group, 1899).
3. "1914 metai Amerikoje ir Lietuvoje," *Jaunoji Lietuva* (Chicago), Jan. 1915, p. 739.
4. Antanas Kučas, *Lithuanians in America* (Boston: Encyclopedia Lituanica, 1975), p. 227.
5. Vitalis Žukauskas, "Teatrinio klausimo anketa-III," *Margutis* (Chicago, Ill.), June 1964, p. 25.
6. The Youth Theater started work as a drama studio, to teach young people the rudiments of the actor's skill and diction and of the Lithuanian language. Soon, under the direction of Darius Lapinskas (1934–), its students started producing plays.

BIBLIOGRAPHY

Books

Primary source materials for this chapter are mostly in Lithuanian periodicals. The list of books embraces only the more important works that portray life and activities related to theatre of Lithuanian Americans.

Ambrose, Aleksas. *Chicagos lietuvių istorija* (History of Chicago Lithuanians). Chicago: Lithuanian American Historical Society, 1967. Extensively records Lithuanian theatrical activities in the Chicago area.

Baltrušaitis, Juozas. *Teatras žmonijos gyvenime* (Theatre in Life of Humanity). Pittsburgh, Pa.: Baltrušaitis Bros., 1912.

Budreckis, Algirdas M., ed. *The Lithuanians in America 1651–1975*. Dobbs Ferry, N.Y.: Oceanna Publications, 1976. Articles on Lithuanian immigrant cultural and social life.

Encyclopedia Lituanica, 6 vols. Boston: Lithuanian Encyclopedia Press, 1974–1978.

Fainhauz, David. *Lithuanians in Multi-Ethnic Chicago*. Chicago, Ill: Lithuanian Library Press, 1977.

Jonas, Jr. (Jonas Žilius). *Lietuviai Amerikoj* (Lithuanians in America). Plymouth, Pa.: Susivienymas Lietuviuc Amerikoge (Lithuanian Alliance of America) 1899. The first attempt to record Lithuanian life in the United States.

Kučas, Antanas. *Lithuanians in America*. Boston: Encyclopedia Lituanica, 1975. A broad survey of the cultural, artistic, and economic activities of Lithuanian immigrants.

Lietuvių enciklopedija (Lithuanian Encyclopedia), 36 vols. Boston: Lietuvių Enciklopedijos Leidykla, 1953–1969.

Maknys, Vytautas. *Lietuvių teatro raidos bruožai* (Outline of Lithuanian Theatre Development). Vilnius: Mintis, 1972. Includes an extensive survey of Lithuanian theatre in the United States.

Mažoji lietuviškoji tarybinė enciklopedija (Small Soviet Lithuanian Encyclopedia), 3 vols. Vilnius: Mintis, 1966–1971.

Michelsonas, Stasius. *Lietuvių išeivija Amerikoje 1868–1961* (Lithuanian Immigrants in America). Boston: Keleivis, 1961.

Milukas, Antanas. *Amerikos lietuviai XIX šimtmetyje 1868–1900* (Lithuanian Americans in the Nineteenth Century). Philadelphia: Keleivis, 1939. Records cultural activities of Lithuanian immigrants.

Šilbajoris, Frank R. *Perfection of Exiles: Fourteen Contemporary Lithuanian Writers.* Norman: University of Oklahoma Press, 1970. Among the fourteen Lithuanian émigré writers, the three leading Lithuanian playwrights are presented and analyzed: Algirdas Landsbergis, Kostas Ostrauskas, and Antanas Škėma.

Širvydas, Vytautas, et al. *Juozas O. Širvydas: biografijos bruožai 1875–1935* (J. O. Širvydas: Biographical Notes). Cleveland, 1941. The most extensive and detailed presentation of Lithuanian-American life. Includes a section of bibliographies of prominent personalities.

Straumanis, Alfreds, ed. *Confrontations with Tyranny.* Prospect Heights, Ill.: Waveland Press, 1981. The collection of Baltic dramas contains Algirdas Landsbergis's play *Penki stulpai turgaus aikštėje,* as well as an introduction.

Periodicals

Aidai (Echoes), cultural magazine, Brooklyn, N.Y., since 1950. Includes poetry, prose, and drama as well as articles about various cultural and social aspects of the lives of Lithuanian immigrants.

Akiračiai (Horizons), monthly review of cultural and political affairs, Chicago: Viewpoint Press, since 1968.

Draugas (Friend), daily Catholic newspaper, Wilkes-Barre, Pa., 1909–1912; Chicago, since 1912. One of the most widely read dailies among the Lithuanian immigrants. Since Nov. 24, 1924, the Saturday supplement has been published, for topics in education, literature, art, and theatre.

Kova (The Struggle), weekly Socialist newspaper, Philadelphia, Pa., 1905–1918. Included announcements and reviews of performances.

Lituanus (A Lithuanian), Lithuania quarterly journal of arts and sciences in English, Chicago: Lituanus Foundation, since 1954. Presents articles and reviews pertaining to the countries and peoples of the Baltic States, particularly Lithuania.

Margutis (Easter Egg), monthly magazine, Chicago, 1928–1964. Contains a number of articles and reviews of literature, art, and theatre.

Metmenys (Outlines), cultural magazine, Chicago, Ill.: AM&M Publications, since 1959. Presents selections of new works in belles-lettres, drama, and arts by Lithuanian authors abroad, as well as articles, book reviews and evaluations of public activity in the Lithuanian diaspora.

Veidrodis (Mirror), monthly magazine of theatre, Chicago, Ill., 1914–1915. Contains reviews of plays and performances staged in Chicago.

Vienybė (Unity), oldest existing Lithuanian newspaper, until 1920 *Vienybė Lietuvninkų* (Unity of Lithuanians), Plymouth, Pa., 1886–1920; Brooklyn, N.Y., since 1920. The most extensive source of information on Lithuanian immigrant theatre.

Vytis (The Knight), monthly magazine of the Lithuanian-American Catholic organization Knights of Lithuania, Chicago, 1915–1932. Contains reviews of performances, as well as articles on art and theatre.

Libraries and Archives

Alka, American-Lithuanian Cultural Archives, Putnam, Conn. A large collection of plays and periodicals pertaining to Lithuanian immigrant theatre.

American Lithuanian Theater Archives, Vitalis Žukauskas, 88-58 75th Street, Wood Haven, N.Y. A large number of plays, playbills, reviews of performances, and articles and books about Lithuanian theatre.

Library of Kent State University, Kent, Ohio. A large collection of Lithuanian immigrant periodicals and books.

Van Pelt Library, University of Pennsylvania, Philadelphia, Pa. The largest depository of Lithuanian books and periodicals in the United States.

13

Mexican-American Theatre

JOHN W. BROKAW

Mexican Americans, in contrast with all but one other ethnic group in the United States, preceded the English colonists to these shores. Today they rank second in numbers among U.S. minorities and in certain locales form a majority of the population. Despite their historical importance to the development of this country in agriculture, mining, art, and industry, to most Americans the Mexican Americans remain a mystery wrapped in Anglo ignorance and indifference.[1] The rise of Chicano theatre in recent years has motivated theatre historians to examine its antecedents, and the process revealed a mine of information, not only about a rich tradition of Spanish-language theatre in the Southwest about which we knew next to nothing, but also about a cultural tradition that still functions in the Mexican-American community today.

THE PROBLEM OF NOMENCLATURE

Any study of Spanish-language culture in the southwestern United States runs rather quickly into the problem of nomenclature. There is a bewildering list of descriptive terms for the people in this group and no easy way to resolve the disagreements as to which is most appropriate. Even the people themselves disagree. Some of them, especially in New Mexico and Colorado, prefer to be called Spanish Americans or Hispanics. Those who emigrated from Mexico during the first quarter of this century and their descendents might be offended by such an emphasis on the Spanish, and they prefer to be called Mexican Americans. Those who immigrated more recently prefer to be called Mexicans, and still others prefer to be known as Chicanos.[2] No one term finds universal appeal or acceptance in the barrios, or Spanish-language neighborhoods.

This chapter will use the terms in a historical sense only. That is, from 1598 until 1823, during the colonial period, all Hispanics residing in what became the southwestern United States were "Spanish"; between 1823 and 1845 they were "Mexicans"; and since 1845 they have been "Mexican Americans."

This method has some limitations, despite its apparent neatness. For example, even prior to the wars of independence, some "Spaniards," especially among the *criollos*—descendents of Spanish conquistadors born in this hemisphere—thought of themselves as "Mexicans," and after independence some "Mexicans," especially among the residents of what became New Mexico, continued to think of themselves as "Spaniards." Moreover, after the Treaty of Guadalupe Hidalgo (1845), many "Mexican Americans" continued to think of themselves as "Spaniards" or "Mexicans" despite their new citizenship status. Be all this as it may, the Mexican Americans technically came into being with the ratification of the treaty, although one would have a difficult time isolating differences between the "Mexican" culture of 1844 and that of the "Mexican Americans" in 1845.

SPANISH SETTLEMENT

The features of that culture derive in large part from the nature of the land settled by these hardy pioneers. Coronado was the first, in the 1540s, when his armed reconnaisance party wandered through the Southwest, the borderlands, in search of the Seven Cities of Gold.[3] Although he did not find them, he found promising locations for settlement. For half a century expeditions traversed the borderlands, but they always returned to the south or simply disappeared, the victims of a hostile environment. In 1642 Diego de Vargas managed to establish settlements around the old pueblos at the headwaters of the Rio Grande in northern New Mexico.[4] Those settlements and others that grew from them remain to this day, and until the Second World War they suffered an almost splendid isolation, first from New Spain and Mexico and then from the rest of the United States.

"Isolation," writes Carey McWilliams, "is the key to the New Mexico environment." Travel between the settlements took months, and the trip was not made often. The settlements were

isolated from Mexico, Texas and Arizona; isolated by deserts, mountains, and hostile Indian tribes. It would be difficult to imagine an isolation more complete than that which encompassed New Mexico from 1598 to 1820. For its isolation was multiple and compound: geographic isolation bred social and cultural isolation; isolated in space, New Mexico was also [isolated] in time.[5]

The northern provinces, therefore, maintained a society that in most ways resembled the seventeenth rather than the nineteenth century.[6] But when the isolation was broken, however slightly, the contact came not with Mexican provinces to the south but with the Yankee traders who blazed the Santa Fe Trail from St. Louis. Along this trail, many emigrants from the United States came to the Southwest.[7] Opposition to the influx of Americans came not so much from Mexico City as from the hostile Indians in the area, especially the Comanches.

Patterns of Spanish settlement in the Southwest show considerable influence from Indians, especially hostile ones such as the Kiowas and Comanches in Texas and the Apaches in New Mexico and Arizona. The Spaniards could move armed parties almost anywhere they wished, but settlements could only flourish among the relatively peaceful pueblo Indians of northern New Mexico and along the California coast, where equally peaceful natives offered little resistance. Only after 1848 were the more resistant native peoples suppressed and new settlement made freely in other parts of the Southwest.[8]

ANGLO-AMERICANS AND MEXICAN AMERICANS: THE NINETEENTH CENTURY

During the decades immediately following the Napoleonic Wars in Europe, Spain began losing colonies in this hemisphere at an alarming rate. A few Anglo settlers on the fringes of the empire, therefore, attracted little attention. In fact, the last Spanish viceroy in Mexico City had encouraged immigration to the northern provinces in hopes of creating a buffer of Anglos loyal to Spain against the advance of the United States.[9] After Mexico won independence, the new government found itself faced with northern provinces, particularly Texas and California, that had more Anglos than Hispanics. Worst of all, the loyalty of those provinces was not nearly as enthusiastic as the government in Mexico might have wished.

The fledgling regime in Mexico City, however, could do little to slow the Anglo tide. The government contented itself with imposing on the provinces economic sanctions in the form of high tariffs on exports and imports, sending troops to collect them and as a consequence producing implacable opposition among most of the citizens of Texas, Hispanic as well as Anglo. By trying to make matters difficult for the Anglo settlers, the central authorities also made them worse for the Hispanics.[10] In 1835 the citizens of Texas rose in rebellion against Mexico and, after a sharp and bloody war, established an independent republic. The figures are untrustworthy, but the estimate of the Anglo and Hispanic populations at that time is 30,000 of the former and 5,000 of the latter. When Texas was admitted to the Union in 1845, these Hispanics and their descendents became the first Mexican Americans, followed shortly afterward by the Hispanics of New Mexico, Arizona, and California.

Because of their relative isolation from the larger population of Anglos, however, the Hispanics maintained a distinct culture. In Texas, for instance, most were located south of the Nueces River, near the border. By contrast, in New Mexico most of the 60,000 Hispanics were found in the northern reaches of the state. Arizona had only around 500 in 1848, and most of these were scattered through the mountains of the south or along the Santa Rita valley. The haciendas of California held perhaps as many as 10,000, and they were almost exclusively located from San Luis Obispo south to the border.[11]

After the Mexican War, Anglo-Americans flooded into the new territories. The gold rush (1849) in California brought hundreds of thousands into the state. The other states along the way to California saw their populations grow because of those who stopped before they reached the gold fields and those who returned after their dreams of bonanza collapsed. Throughout the remainder of the nineteenth century, both Anglos and Mexican Americans fought against tenacious Indians and against natural forces and other hardships, to make the Southwest what it is today. There remains, however, despite the proximity of the two groups, an unfortunate ignorance of the Hispanic culture among the Anglos. The language barrier contributes to this, as does a feeling of cultural self-sufficiency in both groups. But there are historical factors as well.

In California and New Mexico, the Mexican-American residents lived in tightly knit and rather exclusive communities from the first; this kept alive their sense of ethnicity. Anglos treated them with indifference or ignored them. In Texas "the economic development of the Lower Rio Grande did not get under way," Carey McWilliams reminds us, until 1904.

Thus, for more than a hundred years the *Tejanos* [Texans of Mexican descent] lived a life apart, cultivated their own customs and traditions. Even after 1848 they knew very little about what was going on in the United States and cared less. When they traveled they went to Mexico. If they attended school, they were instructed in Spanish language; if they read a newspaper, it was printed in Spanish.[12]

To maintain their strong sense of community, Mexican Americans cultivated several arts. Most Americans are familiar with their design, music, and cuisine. To some extent these have become part of the dominant culture, widely appreciated and enjoyed, at least in their commercial forms.

Most Mexican-American arts came under close scholarly scrutiny during the 1960s and 1970s and are, or will soon be, widely accessible. One thinks immediately of the work of Américo Paredes in his meticulous study of the border folk song tradition, *With a Pistol in his Hand,* which illuminates so many of the Mexican-American community's values and beliefs.[13] By the 1970s there was an increasing number of exhibits of Mexican-American weaving, wood sculpture, and other arts that reflect that community's tastes and attitudes. Such distinctive cultural emanations have allowed the Mexican Americans to maintain an identity quite separate from the larger American amalgam.

Over the years their culture has changed to reflect the changing perceptions and attitudes of the Mexican Americans themselves. The development of the culture is nowhere clearer than in their theatrical history. There have been four major periods in the development of Mexican-American theatre. The first began with the treaty of Guadalupe Hidalgo and ended in the late 1870s. The second began in the late 1870s and ended with the Mexican Revolution of 1910. The third began in 1910 and ended with the Great Depression. And the last, preceded by a hiatus of almost thirty years, began in 1965 and continues to this day.

EARLY THEATRE: THE BIBLICAL NARRATIVES

The absorption into the United States of those resident in the territories ceded by Mexico in 1848 created the Mexican Americans.[14] These people continued to live much as they had before their change in citizenship; their culture was largely as it had been before the change, and therefore the period from 1845 to roughly 1875 can be characterized as a continuation of the colonial culture of the beginning of the nineteenth century, especially in New Mexico, but also in Texas and California. Almost all theatrical activity during these years centered around the Biblical narrative, performed by amateurs under the supervision of the parish priests.

The plays, for the most part improvised around a scenario, were performed particularly at Christmas and Easter. These pieces are still seen today in the Southwest, but since the Second World War and the advent of radio, movies, and television, the number of productions has suffered a precipitous decline and the plays have been substantially altered. As late as 1940 these plays could be seen in every town that had been originally settled by the Spanish.[15] In addition to these religious pieces, secular plays were occasionally performed that dealt with historical events. These latter usually had Spanish rather than Mexican subjects. For example, one of the most popular was about the expulsion of the Moors from Spain.

The most popular of these amateur pieces, still to be seen today, was called *Las Pastorelas*.[16] Rubén M. Campa tells us it began as an anthology of four plays: (1) *El coloquio de San José*, which recounted the events of the wedding of Joseph and Mary and their journey to Bethlehem; (2) *La pastorela*, or *El auto del Niño Dios*, which opened with the shepherds being addressed by the angel, showed their visit to the manger, and ended with their worship of the Christ; (3) *Los reyes magos*, which depicted the story of the three Magi; and (4) the fourth play, which had no title that Campa could find and had nothing to do with the Christmas season but represented the meeting of Jesus and the scholars at the temple in Jerusalem. After the 1940s many changes in these pieces occurred. They were condensed, for example, and combined into a single play. The fourth piece is rarely seen any more. The Magi, who used to bring gifts, which they distributed to the children in the audience, rarely do now: Santa Claus does that honor.

Despite these changes, however, some aspects of the play remain as they always have been. For example, songs continue to play an important part in the performance, and for the most part these are traditional airs. Also, actors still improvise much of the action. As a consequence of the improvisation, change comes readily to the productions. On the one hand, they thus become a reliable indicator of the participants' current attitudes and emotions and, by implication, those of the community at large, but on the other, it is difficult to trace the patterns of change since little is written down.

Nevertheless, several inferences can be drawn as to the nature of theatre in the early Mexican-American period, based upon what is known about these productions today. First, theatre then was almost exclusively an amateur activity, conducted by and for the local population for its own instruction and amusement.

Second, the emphasis on religious subject matter and the uniformity of that subject matter indicate the influence of the clergy over production. This assured that the performances would reflect a uniform moral and ethical code, fostered by the Church but expressing normative values of the community as a whole and therefore serving to bind the individuals closely together in shared beliefs.

Third, since the traditions that informed this type of drama extended back to the Middle Ages and had been introduced by the Spanish missionaries, there is little in the plays that might be attributed to or that is reflective of a distinctly Mexican culture; the plays transcended nationality.[17]

In 1848 the Mexican Americans were in effect severed from a growing Mexican culture before many had become a part of it. The Mexican-American culture at that time had more in common with the seventeenth century than it had with the nineteenth, but also more in common with that of Mexico than with that of the United States. Between 1848 and 1875 Mexican-American theatre steeped itself in the traditions of previous centuries, while the Anglo theatre moved swiftly west of the Mississippi, leaped to the California gold fields, spread through the Great Plains along with the railroads, and finally reached into the deserts of the Southwest as towns and cities grew there. For this theatre, the lure of markets brought touring companies of professional actors performing the most popular plays from the metropolitan centers of the eastern seaboard. By contrast, Mexican-American audiences held few attractions for professional companies from Mexico until the 1870s.

PROFESSIONAL TROUPES FROM MEXICO

In that decade the itinerant Mexican troupes, which plied their trade among the settlements of northern Coahuila, Tamaulipas, and Nuevo León, began to cross the border into Texas.[18] Prior to that time, although people apparently had crossed the frontier constantly without hinderance, one must assume that there had been insufficient demand among Mexican Americans for professional theatre. Until the twentieth century even those troupes that performed for Mexican-American audiences found most of their business on the Mexican side of the frontier; nevertheless, from the 1870s until the Great Depression of 1929, an increasing number of such troupes performed in the United States for at least a part of their season each year. As a consequence, (1) Mexican American audiences acquired access to a professional theatre and, moreover, it was a Mexican one, rather than one of their own; (2) sufficient demand for such troupes had grown in the United States to warrant their meeting it; and (3) during the first decade of the twentieth century, demand in the United States had exceeded the demand in Mexico to the point that several of these troupes performed more often in the United States than in Mexico. The amateur productions held their own in the face of this growing professional theatre, but they were influenced by it, especially in those areas of Texas close to the frontier, where the professionals were seen most often. According to eyewitnesses, amateur performances would reflect acting features of the more popular professional actors; that is, certain gestures, poses, and vocal techniques were mimicked by the amateurs.[19]

Records of these touring troupes remain fragmentary, and much work remains to be done before the precise nature of their activities will be known. Variations must have existed among them with respect to quality of performance and in other matters, but it seems reasonable to assume that they had much in common. The principal source of documentation about these troupes is the archive of the Compañía Dramática de Hernández-Villalongín, which was donated to the University of Texas by members of the family.[20] On the basis of this evidence, generalities can be inferred about the repertories, organization, rehearsal, touring, and method of operating of these companies.

Although Mexican, they demonstrated a splendid disregard for the international border. They moved back and forth at will after 1875 and for the first time brought to Mexican-American audiences the standard repertory of the Mexican stage. The Hernández-Villalongín troupe, a group that began its career in 1849 and continued active service until 1924, maintained 146 plays in its stock.[21] Not all remained active throughout the career of the troupe, but at least 123 of them date from the period after 1880. In other words, of the plays we know about, most were selected after the company began performing in the United States. As to the plays themselves, ninety-three came from non-Mexican sources—one from Belgium, two from Germany, three from Italy, seven from France, and eighty from Spain. The rest were from the Mexican stage. This preponderance of foreign titles implies that the troupe sought to attract an audience from among the elite class and those who had pretensions to that class. Among the dramatists represented in this repertory were Schiller, Echegaray, Benevente, Sudermann, Sue, and Zorilla, along with many popular melodramatists from the Spanish and French stages. As to the plays themselves, eighty-four are tragedies, dramas, or melodramas, and sixty-two are comedies; most of them favor the romantic style, although some contain realistic material. All but eighteen of the titles had been produced in Mexico City before this company staged them; these eighteen seem to have been commissioned by the company from authors both in Mexico and, after 1910, in the United States.[22]

Because of the relative stability of the repertory, the troupe had constant demands made on it with respect to production requirements. The organization of the company reflects this quite clearly. For example, not all members of the company were members of the Hernández or Villalongín families, but most were. Members of those families played the leading roles, while the nonmembers were cast in secondary and tertiary roles. The generally applicable arrangements in stock companies in Mexico and abroad also obtained in this company: namely, actors had a line of business that they performed throughout their careers;

once roles had been assigned, the actors held them for as long as they remained with the company, and all roles were assumed to be ready for performance on short notice.

As to the acting, the quality must have varied from company to company, but that of the Hernández-Villalongín company was legendary. Eyewitnesses tend to remember only this company by name, although they recall several others touring southern Texas at the same time.[23] It must be concluded, therefore, that this troupe was held in high esteem among the audiences of this period. In part the troupe's excellent reputation for acting skill may have derived from the constant association of the children with the performances. They attended all the performances, sat in the front row, and learned the business of acting from their parents. When they grew old enough, they were cast and began the long process of training for the stage.

If the supporting casts were well trained and if the unity of production revolved around the mutual trust and confidence of the cast members, the polish came from the meticulous rehearsal process under the supervision of the manager. Even when the company traveled, rehearsals continued without interruption. An actor was expected to have the lines memorized before rehearsals began. The agenda for the rehearsals consisted of arranging the entrances and exits, the byplay of the cast, the business of the scenes, and the dramatic effects to insure a moving performance. Most of the plays in the repertory, of course, had been largely arranged for previous performances; however, if a long time had passed between performances, the piece would be rehearsed to bring it back to an acceptable level of readiness.[24]

Ordinarily, since the bill changed every day, the company had several plays in rehearsal simultaneously. During a single rehearsal period, from 10:00 in the morning to 1:00 or 2:00 in the afternoon, the actors might rehearse as many as three plays in sequence. If a new piece were in preparation, most of the time would be devoted to it; if all the pieces were revivals, then the one requiring the most time would receive it.

The tours themselves occupied most of the year. Until 1910 the troupes were constantly on the move, although the Hernández-Villalongín families maintained homes in Montemorelos to which they repaired during the winter months when travel was impossible. The company was preceded by an advance man, who made the necessary arrangements for licenses, fees, and facilities. He provided for advertisements of the troupe's offerings and for the settings and met other technical requirements. The latter were usually a number of kerosene lamps, called "quinques" after the Frenchman who had invented them. No small part of the troupe's success depended on these advance men.

Prior to the 1870s the troupes wended their ways through the mountains of northern Mexico and across the valleys and deserts, from one town to the next, playing for single performances a bill of various entertainments.[25] The bill offered a long play followed by one or two short plays and incidental entertainment including songs and dances or monologues, all done by one or more of the actors. The incidental entertainment was the usual way for the youngsters in the family to begin performing. They would rehearse their specialty numbers until their parents believed they were ready for public exposure and then be introduced, bringing an appropriate glow to the hearts of the audience. During the songs and the monologues the audience was encouraged to join in, thus producing conviviality and fellow-feeling that were remembered years later.[26]

With respect to the manner of performance, the provincial troupes generally followed the lead of the metropolitan companies in Mexico City. The evidence we have from eyewitnesses indicates that the performances seen by Mexican Americans conformed to a long-established tradition of professional acting that had had its origins in Europe, had flourished there, and had been brought to Mexico by the Spaniards. That tradition was based upon the classic definition of drama as an "imitation" of an action. The actors set about their imitation, not by actually creating a "real" character in "real" events, but by using a number of conventional signs and symbols, including certain postures and attitudes in which they placed their bodies, certain gestures and expressions, and certain vocal techniques in order to refine their characterizations and thus make them artistic creations. All of this required the actors to develop considerable technical skill. Once mastered, however, that skill allowed the actors to build their performances upon a firm foundation, one recognized and understood by audience and fellow actors alike. Quite clearly such a system of performance required a good deal of training. Only the troupes themselves had the expertise and the opportunity to provide such training; thus actors in the professional companies tended to be the sons and daughters of the actors, willing to learn while being paid little or nothing.

During the years from 1900 to 1910, at least some of the troupes began to perform in the United States more often than in Mexico. For example, the Hernández-Villalongín company had achieved such a reputation among both Anglos and Mexican Americans that they were invited to perform at the opening of the San Antonio Opera House in 1900. From that event on, the troupe increased the number of its performances on this side of the frontier, until by 1910 their Mexican dates were down to nine out of thirty-two weeks.

FROM IMMIGRANT TO RESIDENT TROUPES: THE EARLY TWENTIETH CENTURY

In 1910 revolution broke out in Mexico, and as a consequence of the social upheavals, tens of thousands of Mexicans streamed north across the frontier. With them came the acting companies. In Texas many of the immigrants settled in San Antonio and other centers of Mexican-American culture south of the Nueces River. Here several of the troupes sought patronage, but most sank quickly into oblivion. At one time there were three Mexican companies performing regularly in San Antonio, but soon only one remained—la Compañía Dramática de Carlos Villalongín.

This company continued to operate much as it had during its touring days—
six to twelve actors, a small technical staff, and a traditional repertory. Shortly
after his opening of a repertory regime at the Teatro Aurora, Villalongín discovered that he needed to increase the number of plays in the repertory. He
found two sources for the new pieces: Mexico City and local writers. It is
particularly significant that under these new circumstances he turned to local
playwrights, since this reflected an attempt to bind the company closer to the
community. Prior to 1910 these troupes had been Mexican in nature and character. They had brought Mexican culture across the border, stayed briefly in
Mexican-American communities, and then moved on. They were welcome
guests, perhaps, but not members of the community; hence, they could not—
even if they had wished to—comprehend the Mexican American way of life or
culture. After 1910, however, the troupes became members of the Mexican-
American communities.

Little is known about the impact of the new immigrants on the relatively
small Mexican-American community after 1910. The infusion of new arrivals
from Mexico no doubt made it more "Mexican" than "American" for a time;
hence the popularity of the Mexican troupes. The repertory continued to feature
frequent performances of such thematic plays as El cinco de Mayo and Los heroes
de Tacubaya. Perhaps many of the immigrants entertained thoughts of one day
going back to Mexico to resume their interrupted lives, but as the years passed
those hopes must have dimmed; they became accustomed to their new lives and
adjusted to the Mexican-American culture.

The companies also adjusted their manner of operation under these new
circumstances, notably in the matter of casting. In San Antonio the Villalongín
troupe began casting local residents on a regular basis. To be sure, while touring
the company had also employed locals for supernumerary roles. This built a
speedy and effective rapport with the townsfolk, but it made little difference to
the quality of the performance or to the nature of the troupe's operation. When
a stock company begins to employ locals, however, there is a perceptible change
in both aspects of performance. First of all, the manager has time to select the ad
hoc performers carefully, to use them in a variety of roles depending on their
talent and skill, and finally to augment the company's own resources with those
of the community at large. This last has the potential for building something
more than a superficial rapport; it can establish close ties of a mutually beneficial
kind between troupe and community. For example, the Villalongín troupe discovered at least two local residents who became valuable members of the company; one of these, a Miss Newman, is reported to have had a Mexican-American mother. At all events, these and others had the opportunity to rehearse with
the troupe, become familiar with its manner of production, and contribute
substantially to its popularity.[27]

From 1910 on, then, the troupe was increasingly influenced by its new home.
The use of local actors, the practice of leasing a theatre building and performing
for the most part in one town, and that of commissioning local writers to

compose plays are three important examples of this assimilation. Even going on tour in the early summer became a necessary but not very pleasant part of the business after 1910, whereas before it had been a way of life.

Other, less fortunate, troupes continued to tour. In Del Rio, Texas, for example, El Teatro Juarez booked a number of such troupes between 1919 and 1929, including those of Sarita Contla and Ignacio Iglesias, who toured combinations arranged around themselves as stars, and Lucha Altamiran, whose attraction was in such plays as *La Mujer X* (Madam X), *La Llorona* (The Weeping Woman), and *Los Tres Gorriones* (The Three Sparrows). For a two- or three-year period in the 1920s, this theatre had a resident stock company managed by Hilario Altimirano and his brother Nacho. Juan Tenorio was the assistant producer. The last major event at this theatre occurred in 1929, when Virginia Fabregas brought her Mexico City company to Del Rio for a single performance. After that the theatre was given over to vaudeville or *carpa* (a uniquely Mexican combination of circus, vaudeville, cabaret, and hootenanny) performances until it was torn down during the Second World War.[28]

While maintaining the theatre in San Antonio, the Villalongín troupe changed its operations in certain ways. For example, it began to perform four and five nights a week rather than only three. The bill grew slightly to include more incidental entertainments. *Corridos* (ballads), especially, became a staple of the evening's program, and community singing was enjoyed by all. The songs recalled various regions of Mexico and the borderlands, which called forth nostalgic outpourings. *Cuples* (popular songs) from Mexico had attractions here too. Favorite topics included unrequited love, heroic incidents from popular mythology that glorified courage and virtue, and sentimental narratives of family life, particularly ones dealing with parents and siblings. One finds among the titles "Maruca," "Cara Sucia" (Dirty Face), and "Granito de sal" (Little Grain of Salt).

Both the plays and the *corridos* served as conduits for cultural, ethical, and moral values, many of which transcended ethnic boundaries. In fact, one might divide the values roughly into two categories: those that pertained to western civilization generally in the nineteenth century and those especially characteristic of the Hispanic community in the Southwest. In the first group one finds the conviction that strong family ties are desirable, whereas in the second one's loyalty to relatives, no matter how distant, takes priority over one's loyalty to friends, no matter how close. In addition, the following nineteenth-century western values also occur in the plays: of all relatives, a mother is the most important and commands reverence from her offspring; personal honor should be maintained; among the cardinal virtues are reverence to God and country, charity toward those less fortunate, and mercy for the weak and helpless. Subtle shifts in intensity among these western values make them characteristic of the Hispanic community. In the Hispanic community, for example, one's mother is due complete respect and veneration; one has to defend one's honor at all costs; the Catholic Church is an object of devotion; and mercy should be tempered by justice. These beliefs, shared by the whole Mexican-American community, held it together and emphasized the common bonds among its members.

The plays offered numerous examples of these beliefs; anormative acts and characters were inevitably punished while the normative characters and acts were rewarded. By the end of the 1920s the professional companies had become platforms from which the Mexican-American community saw their values displayed and on which the Anglo community might observe an important aspect of Mexican-American culture.

INTERIM YEARS: 1929–1965

When the Depression struck the United States in 1929, among the first casualties were the Mexican-American stock companies. Taking their place as theatrical entertainment were vaudeville performances and the motion pictures, the latter imported from Mexico. Between the demise of the repertory theatres in 1929 and the rise of Teatro Chicano in 1965, however, there continued to be live performances of theatrical productions in the Mexican-American communities. The amateur productions of religious plays, particularly *Las Pastorelas*, continued to attract audiences throughout the Southwest and especially in New Mexico. A superficial examination of this period might seem to reveal an end to the progress of the Mexican-American drama, but that clearly was not the case. The long tradition of amateur productions bore strong witness to the efficacy of drama in preserving values the Mexican-American community revered. It continued to do so, although with diminishing vigor after the war, until a remarkable event occurred in 1965.

TEATRO CAMPESINO

For years the Mexican braceros and Mexican-American farm workers had labored under harsh conditions in the fields and on the ranches of the Southwest.[29] In 1965 César Chávez led a small band of farm workers on strike in Delano, California. Their struggle with the grape growers was a long and bitter one, but in the end not only was it won and a contract signed by all parties, but the latest manifestation of the Mexican-American dramatic and theatrical tradition was born as well. Chicano theatre originated in the work of Luis Valdez and a few of his friends, who, attracted by the events at Delano, brought guerrilla theatre to the picket lines and base camps during the strike.[30] Their performances were similar in several ways to those of the agit-prop radical or avant-garde theatres of the 1920s and 1930s. The purpose was to depict in a simple and easily understood manner the events of the strike so that the participants could see both the nature of the struggle and the prescription for victory, namely, joining or remaining with the strike.

This task was accomplished by the group of performers—El Teatro Campesino (the Farm Workers' Theatre)—improvising scenes, called *actos*, in which the issues were displayed in a grimly comic light. Strikers were encouraged to join in this action, playing a scab worker one time, an unscrupulous labor contractor the next, and even the Anglo boss on yet another occasion. This device had proven effective as a therapeutic technique in psychodrama, and it proved equally effective in building cohesion among the strikers. Ridicule and caricature of the powerful forces arrayed against them, from the growers to the federal government, helped sustain the strikers throughout their ordeal.[31]

After the strike was settled, Teatro Campesino severed its connection with the United Farm Workers, although they continued to share many of the same hopes and beliefs. Valdez and his associates identified a number of injustices, besides those the union attacked, that the Anglo society imposes on Mexican Americans: inadequate schools and discrimination in jobs, housing, and the other benefits society has to offer. Using the same system of improvisation and ridicule, Teatro Campesino began performing for a wider audience than merely a picket line. It appeared in the barrios and on college campuses, pounding home the message of social injustice and racial pride. "La Raza," or the Mexican-American people as a whole, became a rallying cry and an object of pride.

The *actos* themselves depicted events and figures familiar to all who had grown up in the barrios. Many Mexican Americans, for example, had intimate acquaintance with the conditions in the agricultural world of California. Accordingly, Campesino could modify some of the *actos* of the strike to form analogies with urban conditions, but more often it developed new ones that focused on specific urban problems. One of the most powerful of these treated the systematic discrimination of the schools against Mexican Americans.[32]

A common scenario runs as follows. The scene opens on a classroom, and the children are engaged in easy and innocuous banter when the teacher, an Anglo, enters. She displays consummate ignorance of Mexican-American culture in a series of incidents beginning with the role call, during which she mispronounces all the Mexican-American names. A martinet, she refuses to allow the children to speak Spanish in class and deprecates their heritage by indulging her own prejudices against "dirty" Mexicans, who are "stupid" because they cannot speak acceptable English. The upshot of these insults is that the children rebel against this ill treatment and leave the room, shouting, "¡Viva la huelga!" (Strike!) and "Chicano Power!"[33]

On the basis of Teatro Campesino's example, numerous other teatros formed, first in California and then throughout the Southwest. Campesino provided scenarios and personnel, who visited the other troupes to help them get established. Since the purposes of these groups were principally ideological rather than esthetic, dramatic art was less a matter of concern than was trenchant social criticism. For the first five years of Teatro Chicano, the *actos* formed most of the repertory. Without going into more detail, the characters in the *actos* might be described as a group of schematized Anglos and Mexican Americans engaged in "significant" confrontations, such as the ones already noted, in which the two ethnic groups, Anglos and Chicanos, represent dialectical poles.

The emphasis in such pieces lies in forceful presentation of issues in stark terms. As a consequence, the characters tend to display only one or two operative traits apiece, such as greed, for the villains, and courage, for the protagonists. They are unequivocally evil or good, and when they deliberate at all, they do so exclusively for expedience. Actions involving such characters tend to attract or repel on the basis of the auditor's ideological bias; that is, those who generally agree that confrontation will produce remedies for social problems will generally approve of the actos.

Regardless of initial response to the actos, after a time one might wish to have more than they offer. By 1972 Valdez had begun experimenting with new types of dramatic action that attempted to probe his consciousness in a poetic rather than rhetorical manner. These plays run a gamut from ancient Aztec mythology to Zoot Suit, which combines music with sensitive dialogue to depict the events of a riot during the Second World War, when sailors in California attacked Mexican-American youths simply because of their distinctive clothes—zoot suits. In these later plays there is no simplistic presentation of good against unmitigated evil; rather, the plays reveal the anguish Valdez found in his own experience and give articulate expression to his aspirations.

Such plays as Zoot Suit, in contrast with the actos of ten years earlier, must be realized on stage by skilled performers. This clearly presages a more elaborate organization than many teatros have today. These groups began in a relatively casual environment: those who shared the ideology espoused in the actos formed a teatro, rehearsed a bit, and began performing. That they had few theatrical skills not only did not matter, but frequently appeared to be a virtue. On the one hand, as some said, the point of the teatros is not to amuse and entertain, but to incite by conveying la causa (the cause) clearly and forcefully. Technical virtuosity might well interfere with that purpose by having the audience respond, not to the ideology, but to the show, thereby dissipating the desired effect. On the other hand, others insisted that artistic standards must not be sacrificed on an ideological altar. Thus there was and is disagreement as to means among the teatros, but not as to ends. Those are (1) to raise Mexican American self-consciousness; (2) to nurture their cultural tradition; and (3) to develop a lively social movement dedicated to improving the lot of La Raza.

PLAYS AND COMMUNITY VALUES

Comparisons between the early Chicano theatre and the religious plays of former times spring lightly and easily to mind. Both were amateur, improvised much of their action, and were concerned more with rhetorical effect than poetics or esthetics. But there is at least one critical difference. The religious plays concentrated upon the normative values shared by the whole community. Subject matter that might be considered controversial or that separated the community into factions quite simply did not exist in the religious plays. Anormative characters who violated the mores of the community, such as drunkards or thieves, were taken to task in those plays.

The *actos*, by contrast, question community values, deliberately seek out issues on which the Mexican-American community is split. In Valdez's *Las dos caras del patroncito* (The Two Faces of the Boss), one of the early *actos*, those who continued to work to support their families during the strike were severely criticized and the final resolution lay in their changing their minds. The Mexican American community divided over that issue: Under what conditions should one cease to work and no longer support one's family? Understandably there was a wide spectrum of opinion on that question. Nor is this an isolated case; generally those Mexican Americans who did not subscribe to the values of the *actos* were depicted as *vendidos* (sellouts) who had betrayed their heritage. The theory apparently was that, by facing the issues that divided the community in Hegelian terms, a synthesis would be brought about that would unite the community.

To some extent these differences in Mexican-American theatre derive from changing attitudes, now and a hundred years ago. When Anglo and Mexican American communities lived in a relatively simple philosophical environment, what difficulties existed came from the will of God, as did life's blessings. God, of course, was susceptible to prayer, but not to direct political action. In today's highly complex society, few "difficulties" are left, aside from terminal diseases; today's "problems" have, or ought to have, "solutions." Solutions most readily derive from collective action by interested parties, actions that affect institutions—government, bureaucracies, schools, and so forth—which in turn produce the necessary changes. Individual actions can and ought to be judged, therefore, on the extent to which they correspond to the collective will.

For those who hold that society's ignorance, poverty, discrimination, and injustice are problems or phenomena susceptible to social remedy, the need to agitate for solutions follows axiomatically on moral grounds alone. Disagreements may arise on particular solutions, but not on the need for collective solutions in general. On the other hand, those who are reasonably certain, as most people in the nineteenth century were, that these evils are part of the human condition—lamentable, but inescapable—are more likely to seek strength to endure hardship from their fellows, from shared values, beliefs, and aspirations. It seems clear, then, that the teatros of today are not the cause of the changing nature of the relationship of Mexican-American theatre to its circumstances. After all, the Teatro Campesino did not call the United Farm Workers into existence; it was the other way around.

NEW DIRECTIONS

There are reasons to believe that Teatro Campesino has shifted its attention from the agit-prop plays of the early 1970s to plays of cultural consciousness. If so, can the other teatros be far behind? These new plays explore the heritage of the Aztecs, Spaniards, and Mexicans, attempting to identify the distinctive features of character and spirit that contributed to the nature of Mexican Americans. In the mass media and the schools they have heard at length about the

Anglo contribution to that nature, but until recently the Hispanic heritage had been disparaged when it was not ignored; thus that side of the matter was relegated to an inchoate folk tradition and a commercially contrived distortion in housing, clothing, and other products for a largely Anglo market.[34] To those not of Mexican-American heritage, the development of a literary and artistic manifestation of this folk tradition is a matter of considerable importance, not only because it provides a more useful image of the Mexican American than, say, the "Frito Bandito," but also because this resurgence of Mexican-American theatre into public prominence allows everyone, regardless of heritage, to enter into a rich, hitherto inaccessible aspect of the long American tradition.

NOTES

1. Anglo is used here in the sense of all those not of Mexican or Latin American heritage.

2. See Edward Simmen, "Chicano: Origin and Meaning," in *Pain and Promise: The Chicano Today*, edited by Edward Simmen (New York: New American Library, 1972), pp. 53–56; also see Nancie González, *Spanish Americans of New Mexico* (Albuquerque: University of New Mexico Press, 1969).

3. Herbert E. Bolton, *Spanish Exploration of the Southwest 1542–1706* (New York: Charles Scribner's Sons, 1916), pp. 5–12. Also see Charles Gibson, ed., *The Spanish Tradition in America* (Columbia: University of South Carolina Press, 1968); Paul Horgan, *The Conquistadors in North American History* (Greenwich, Conn.: Premier Publications, 1965); Warren Beck, *New Mexico, A History of Four Centuries* (Norman: University of Oklahoma Press, 1962).

4. This enterprise is best examined in Jesse B. Bailey, *Diego de Vargas and the Reconquest of New Mexico* (Albuquerque: University of New Mexico Press, 1940).

5. Carey McWilliams, *North From Mexico* (Philadelphia: J. B. Lippincott, 1961), p. 63.

6. See Arthur Leon Campa, "Spain's Link with the Past," *Colorado Quarterly*, Autumn 1954, pp. 133–47.

7. See Leo E. Oliva, *Soldiers on the Santa Fe Trail* (Norman: University of Oklahoma Press, 1967); Paul Horgan, *Centuries of Santa Fe* (New York: E. P. Dutton, 1956); Mary Loyola, *The American Occupation of New Mexico 1821–1852* (Albuquerque: University of New Mexico Press, 1939).

8. See Odie B. Faulk, *Crimson Desert: Indian Wars of the American Southwest* (New York: Oxford University Press, 1974); S.L.A. Marshall, *Crimsoned Prairie: The Wars between the United States and the Plains Indians during the Winning of the West* (New York: Charles Scribner's Sons, 1972); Robert M. Utley, *Frontier Regulars: The United States Army and the Indian 1866–1891* (New York: Macmillan Publishing Co., 1973).

9. Henry B. Parkes, *A History of Mexico* (Boston: Houghton Mifflin, 1969), pp. 200–205; Ruth S. Lamb, *Mexican-Americans: Sons of the Southwest* (Claremont, Calif.: Ocelot Press, 1970), pp. 37–46.

10. Eugene C. Barker dwells at length upon the progressive alienation of Texans of all ethnic backgrounds from the Mexican government in his *Mexico and Texas 1821–1835* (Dallas: P. L. Turner Co., 1928).

11. Parkes, *History of Mexico*, p. 212. Nevertheless, they were not in intimate contact with the Anglos on anything approaching a regular basis. During the gold rush of 1849 many Mexican miners from Sonora and Coahuila hurried into the gold fields, but their numbers are not known, nor is it known how many remained in California.

12. McWilliams, *North from Mexico*, p. 87.

13. Américo Paredes, *With a Pistol in His Hand* (Austin: University of Texas Press, 1958).

14. Some might argue that the Texas Rebellion of 1835 began the process, but although I understand that viewpoint, I disagree. The Texas Rebellion was supported by both Anglos and Hispanics against what was then seen as a repressive regime in Mexico City. Much of the mythology that clouds contemporary American thought derives from an ignorance of Hispanic support of the Texas war effort. We tend to think of that effort as exclusively Anglo, and that view is reinforced by Mexican historiography, which fosters the myth that the United States tore Texas from the Mexican nation. It is not true: Texas, aided by all of her ethnic groups, tore herself from Mexico. She became an independent republic and was not admitted to the Union until 1845.

Americans' attitude toward Texas was equivocal from the first. New Englanders, for example, believed the matter of statehood for Texas to be a fraud perpetrated by proslavery states. Many believed that to dabble in Texas affairs would be to invite a disastrous war with Mexico. The Texas situation was a very complex one, and subsequent attempts to schematize it around convenient assumptions foster two falsehoods: among Anglos, that they alone civilized the Southwest, and among Mexican Americans, that they have only been victims acted upon by Anglo society.

15. Rubén M. Campa, *Spanish Religious Folktheatre in the Southwest* (Albuquerque: University of New Mexico Press, 1934), p. 11.

16. Ibid., pp. 12–13.

17. Thomas J. Steele, *Holy Week in Tomé* (Santa Fe: Sunstone Press, 1976), pp. 5–19.

18. John W. Brokaw, "A Mexican American Acting Company: 1849–1924," *Educational Theatre Journal* 27 (1975): 23–27.

19. What we know of these companies has come from those who, as children, had seen them. Particularly helpful has been the information provided during interviews with the author on Aug. 17 and Sept. 3, 1973, by members of the Villalongín family: María Luisa Villalongín de Santos and her sister and brother-in-law, John and Amparo Solis of San Antonio.

20. This material now resides in the Latin American Collection, University of Texas at Austin. A partial catalog may be found in John W. Brokaw, "The Repertory of a Mexican-American Theatrical Troupe: 1849–1924," *Latin American Theatre Journal*, fall 1974, pp. 25–35.

21. Brokaw, "Repertory," pp. 25–26.

22. Luis Reyes de la Maza, in *El teatro en México*, 9 vols. (Mexico: UNAM, 1953–70), provides a list of plays and the dates and places they were produced at the end of each volume. The figures in the text come from this source.

23. During the summer and fall of 1976, I conducted numerous interviews with persons who had attended theatrical performances of such troupes in San Antonio, Brownsville, Laredo, and Del Rio, Texas. The respondents verified that several troupes had played in their cities from 1910 to 1920, but they only remembered Villalongín's company by name.

24. Villalongín de Santos recalled the long and exacting rehearsals she and the others had put into preparing a production.

25. In the cities of Reynosa, Saltillo, Monterrey, and Matamoros, the troupes might spend as much as a week in residence.

26. The story is told among the members of the Villalongín family of a visit to Sabinas Hidalgo made by Concépcion, the leading actress in the company, in 1955. At that time she was in her sixties, and she had not appeared on the stage for thirty-one years and in that town for forty; nevertheless, a taxi driver approached her with his hat in his hand and inquired if she were "Senora Hernández, the famous actress," to which she replied in the affirmative. This incident speaks eloquently of the power of some of these performers.

27. John and Amparo Solis also remember seeing one of these actors, a Mr. Sanders, in a motion picture shown on television, but they do not remember his stage name or the name of the film.

28. I am indebted to Mrs. Teresita Barrera of Del Rio for this information.

29. See Carey McWilliams, *Ill Fares the Land: Migrants and Migratory Labor in the United States* (Boston: Little, Brown, 1922); U.S. Department of Agriculture, *Mexican Americans* (Washington, D.C.: Government Printing Office, 1966); and Lawrence L. Walters, "Transient Mexican Agricultural Labor," *Southwest Social Science Quarterly* 22 (1941): 1–4.

30. See Luis Valdez, *Actos* (San Juan Bautista, Calif.: Cucaracha Press, 1971). This work contains an introduction by Valdez that sets forth his goals and perceptions, together with the scripts of nine *actos*, or one-scene plays.

31. A bewildering array of opinions have been published about the strike, from Gary Allen, "The Grapes: Communist Wrath in Delano," *American Opinion* 9 (1966): 1–14, to Thurston Davis, "Viva la Huelga," *American* 114 (1966): 589–90. Perhaps those events are still too immediate to permit scholarly detachment.

32. See, for example, Valdez's piece "No saco nada de la Escuela," *Actos*, pp. 66–94.

33. Ibid., p. 94.

34. Francisco Ríos, "The Mexican in Fact, Fiction, and Folklore," reprinted in *Pain and Promise: The Chicano Today*, edited by Edward Simmen (New York, 1972), provides a symphonic catalog of the misconceptions, errors, and lies currently serving some Anglos as a stereotype of Mexican Americans. Ríos may be exaggerating the extent to which Anglos have any conception at all of Mexican Americans. As he says, the bigots among Americans have slandered all ethnic groups, including Mexican Americans. To speak of any ethnic group in generalizations is very likely to end in slander because of the diversity within each of them. Fortunately, many Americans seem blissfully ignorant of this Mexican-American stereotype.

BIBLIOGRAPHY

Books

Boatright, Mady Boggin. *Mexican Border Ballads and Other Lore*. Austin: Texas Folklore Society, 1962. Excellent translations and analyses of the *corridos*.

Campa, Arthur Leon. *Spanish Religious Folktheatre in the Southwest*. Albuquerque: University of New Mexico Press, 1934. Chronicle of religious performances in New Mexico.

Cordry, Donald, and Dorothy Cordry. *Mexican Indian Customs*. Austin: University of Texas Press, 1968.

Dobie, J. Frank, ed. *Texas and Southwestern Lore*. Austin: Texas Folklore Society, 1927.

Garza, Roberto J., ed. *Contemporary Chicano Theatre*. Notre Dame, Ind.: University of Notre Dame Press, 1976. Anthology of plays.

Huerta, Jorge A., ed. *El Teatro de la Esperanza; An Anthology of Chicano Drama*. Goleta, Calif.: El Teatro de la Esperanza, Inc., 1973. Anthology of one company's repertory.

Kanellos, Nicolas, and Jorge A. Huerta, eds. *Nuevos Pasos*. Houston, Tex.: Arte Publico Press, 1980. This is the most recent of the anthologies of Chicano plays.

Lea, Aurora. *Literary Folklore of the Hispanic Southwest*. San Antonio: Naylor Co., 1953.

Leon, Nepthali de. *5 Plays*. Denver: Totinem Books, 1972. Collection of Nepthalis' work.

McWilliams, Carey. *North From Mexico*. Philadelphia: J. P. Lippincott, 1961. Perhaps the best history of the cultural development of the Southwest.

Paredes, Américo. *With a Pistol in His Hand: A Border Ballad and Its Hero*. Austin: University of Texas Press, 1958. Splendid analysis of this *corrido*.

Robinson, Cecil. *With the Ears of Strangers: The Mexican in American Literature*. Tucson: University of Arizona Press, 1963. Sommers, Joseph, and Tomas Ybarra-Frauston, eds. *Modern Chicano Writers: A Collection of Critical Essays*. Englewood Cliffs, N.J.: Prentice-Hall, 1979. First-rate collection of literary criticism, some of which treats Chicano theatre.

Valdez, Luis. *Actos*. San Juan Bautista, Calif.: Cucaracha Press, 1971. Quite simply the first anthology of teatro plays by the man who started it all, with his introductory remarks to provide a context.

Articles

Bagby, Beth. "El Teatro Campesino: Interviews with Luis Valdez," *Tulane Drama Review* 11, no. 4 (1967): 70–80.

Brokaw, John W. "A Mexican American Acting Company: 1849–1924," *Educational Theatre Journal* 27 (1975): 23–29.

————. "The Repertory of a Mexican American Troupe: 1849–1924," *Latin American Theatre Review*, fall 1974, pp. 25–35.

Huerta, Jorge A., and John Harop. "The Agitprop Pilgrimage of Luis Valdez and El Teatro Campesino," *Theatre Quarterly* 5 (1975): 30–39.

14

Native American Theatre

JEFFREY F. HUNTSMAN

DRAMA IN TRADITIONAL NATIVE AMERICAN SOCIETIES

The impulse for the dramatic is universal in the societies of human beings, but its manifestations are as varied as the societies that bring it to life. Like other distinctive aspects of culture, dramatic events may serve to define a community, distinguishing its members from others who do not share its aesthetic, metaphysical, and epistemological foundations. In societies informed by a common history and intellectual culture, the overt structure of dramatic events may remain largely constant, although ethnic, religious, racial, or class differences within heretogenous cultures almost inevitably stratify the society at large. Such is the case in much of Europe and America, among the peoples whose dramatic events are the subject matter of most of this volume. Although the characteristics and values of the several Euro-American traditions differ, their dramatic *forms* are largely congruent, the result of the adoption of a "high" or "professional" dramatic structure the history of which is essentially pan-European, adapted from the varying elements of classical, medieval, and modern drama, whether religious or secular, folk, traditional, or professional.

For Native American[1] drama, the situation is quite different. Within the bounds of the continental United States alone, there were 15 to 30 million people in hundreds of separate nations when Europe's land-hungry reivers arrived. Even today there are approximately 1 million Indians, constituting perhaps 300 nations, despite both accidental and deliberate genocide by both individuals and governments, driven by misunderstanding, cultural chauvinism, and, too often, calculated treachery. Some of these native societies remain active and vital, maintaining many aspects of their traditional cultures while adapting few features from others, native or not. Others are failing, their languages receding as the old die and the young lose their interest or their bearings. Too many have gone completely, leaving tantalizingly few memories and fewer records. But even in the face of these losses, what endures is often rich, powerful, and rewarding.

The first difficulty, then, in approaching the drama of the Native Americans is that there are many dramas, conceivably as many as there are cultures.[2] In addition to the affiliations that Indians themselves recognize, scholars have grouped the native peoples of North America in several different ways: by their languages, which fall into at least six unrelated families; by their material and economic cultures, which distinguish peoples who are chiefly hunters from farmers, fishers, and gatherers; by their religions, which range from relatively uncodified and unsophisticated beliefs in simple spirits to complex and subtle systems comparable with the world's better-known religions; by their sociological and geographical relationships, which vary from those of small bands of wandering gatherers centered on single, extended families to those of tightly-knit cities of thousands in which every member is connected to every other through numerous family, clan, and social relationships; or even by the history of their relations with Europeans, which have altered their precontact cultures in radically different ways.[3]

Clearly these many differences among Indian peoples will necessarily result in dramatic events of different forms and purposes, especially when the culture preserves in its dramatic ritual attributes of earlier times, as is typically the case when the dramatic events have major religious significance.[4] We should not expect a people like the city dwellers of the Southwest, whose cultural orientation is inward toward their communities, to have the same kind of drama as the highly individualistic horse people of the High Plains. The Pueblo peoples reflect in their literature those qualities that are most important to their way of life—cooperation, harmony, group identity—and their characteristic drama is fully choreographed, disciplined, and dramatically complex. The Lakota and Cheyenne, on the other hand, value the individual qualities of bravery, dauntlessness, versatility, and personal spiritual power, and their dramas, such as the Sun Dance, appropriately mirror those values. As a result of this diversity the term "drama," as it must be used with reference to Native American cultures, comprises a congeries of events ranging from the structured improvisations of shamans to hundred-hour-long, multidimensional celebrations like the great Navajo chantways, in which every costume, word, gesture, movement, and song are planned.

Considering the variety of Indian cultures and the fundamental differences between typical Euro-American societies and Native American ones, it is hardly surprising that Indian drama, as drama and not as an ethnographical curiosity, has been given scant attention by students of the theatre and students of Indians alike. Although many observers during the past century have commented on the "colorful" or "dramatic" nature of the Indian rituals they were privileged to witness, relatively few have used the terms in the precise ways of the Euro-American critical tradition. Even the best of the early studies are overly general, content to describe rather than to analyze, even when the writers gave the particular ceremonies and their Indian communities more than a passing visit. These observers were too interested in finding support for preconceived notions about "primitive" theatre or the "origin" of drama and often too unwilling to attribute the art they sometimes recognized to anything more than "primitive intuition." On the other hand, it is difficult and occasionally dangerous, given the diversity of Indian cultures, to make more than a few generalizations about Native American drama; that is perhaps why, although the literature on specific dramatic rituals is rich, there is little on Indian dramas taken together.

STANDARDS OF TRADITIONAL DRAMA

One of the defensible generalizations characterizes all small, coherent societies throughout the world, not just Indian ones. The shared culture of these societies frames a complex network of predictable reciprocal relationships. In the order of organisms, individuals are born, live some brief term, and die, leaving the enduring system of organization fundamentally unchanged. But the "progress"-loving societies of Europe and America generally value the innovative above the traditional, both personally and societally, and few generations fail to work major changes in the structure into which they are born. Naturally, that spirit of newness and adventure colors their drama. Their dramatic artists are inventors, creating purposefully unique artifacts, however much these artifacts inevitably reflect the experiences and the values of their communities.

But for Native American artists, as for their counterparts in other traditional societies, the artistic self is typically unobtrusive, and the dramatic work in effect proclaims the artist's involvement with the community, not his or her distance from it. The aesthetic principles governing the form, content, and meaning of the artist's work are established, in effect, by the community as a whole, although usually covertly if not unconsciously. The Indian artist comes to understand, often quite without knowing how, exactly what is expected of an artist in that community, and it has frequently been said that in Indian eyes every person becomes an artist of some kind. The artist's training in such traditional communities is typically an apprenticeship, whether formal or not, through which he or she learns in what ways the community's standards set limits to personal style and values. Learning in Indian communities characteristically takes the form of extended observation, imitative play not overtly urged by adults, and careful practice, which begins only when the child feels confident of a reasonably successful result.[5] This is true whether what is to be learned is specific tasks, like cooking, weaving, and fishing, or more general matters, like proper behavior, ethics, and religious beliefs.

Moreover, what the child learns in this manner is not a single task or fact, but a thread of the entire fabric of society. For a Maidu the proper making of acorn bread begins with an evocation of the story of creation, and the making of a Navajo rug begins with the morning prayers, the driving of the sheep to food and water, and the gathering in of plants for dyes.[6] The result is a feeling of oneness with one's relatives and the security of knowing one's place in the universe. Emory Sekaquaptewa describes how a child who had misbehaved was saved from being taken away by a kachina, the *soya,* a spirit being who is in a sense the symbol and instrument of admonition.[7] The child's relatives intervened, saying he was to be married, and produced a bride in full ceremonial dress (a part played by the boy's grandmother). In this way "the child not only learned the importance of good behavior, but this drama [of the mock preparations for a wedding] also strengthened his security by showing him that there are people who do come to his aid." Through this process the child came to understand how his society works and he thereby felt secure in both heart and mind. "Security comes from knowing one's place within the prevailing kinship relationship; within the community. But it also involves learning the cultural norms of the community ethic."[8]

Thus traditional art is a fundamental aspect of the culture, its practices, and its values. Such art is firmly embedded in the community, temporally, spatially, and emotionally, and individual artists change but little the characteristics of the community or its aesthetic values.[9] These community standards are not often articulated because, like many other closely shared matters in small societies, they only rarely need to be. But to say that these standards are not often spoken about does not mean that they do not exist and are not followed. Few artists are competent philosophers of art—many are notoriously inarticulate about their work—nor is there any need for them to be. The dimensions of art exist independently of any attempts to explain them in words, in the Euro-American "high" culture as much as in other cultures. Further, even if we do not find among Native American peoples the kind of written commentary that the philosophers of Western European culture have created, there is abundant evidence that most Native American peoples have thought about their art in comparable ways. The cohesiveness of the art for each group and its high quality testify to the aesthetic principles that underlie its making. If some Indian artists in the past have been unwilling to talk about their creations, the reasons are more to be found in the lack of a common cross-cultural universe of discourse and experience between artist and critic and the often sacred matter of much dramatic art.[10]

This emphasis on the continuity of aesthetic traditions does not mean that innovation or individuality is forbidden. The practices of any Indian people may change markedly as one group adopts a dramatic ritual from another. The Sun Dance ritual, for example, is or has been performed in varying ways and for differing purposes, by peoples ranging from the Mandan at the edge of the Eastern Woodland area to the Southern Ute of the Great Basin. An individual within a group may create a new drama; Black Elk's Horse Drama, which made manifest the power of his great vision, is perhaps the best-known example.[11] Cultural changes may also influence the development of new elements within an existing ritual.[12] In all these cases, however, the new dramatic event is naturally molded to the community norms; if Black Elk had been a Kwakiutl or a Cayuga instead of a Lakota, his vision and its dramatization would have had a different shape. Sometimes specific adaptations are precluded entirely by other aspects of a culture; the Navajo, virtually alone of the inland Western peoples, did not adopt the late-nineteenth-century Ghost Dance, with its promise of the return of all Indian people who had ever lived, because of their extreme fear of the dead. In short, alterations of either the forms or the values of traditional arts is evolutionary, not revolutionary, as the artist works within the frames established in the community for a given dramatic genre.[13]

THE SACRED SOURCE OF POWER AND SIGNIFICANCE

Another generalization is that there was little that any Native American living in a traditional community would do that was not charged, if only slightly, with religious significance. Naturally, the religious power that inhered in major rituals was greater than that connected with the beginning of a hunt or the making of a meal, if only because the major rituals drew more of the community into their center than personal observations did. The religious beliefs that motivate the Sun Dance drama are different in detail from those that underlie the Navajo chantway, but each ceremony draws on the most fundamental metaphysical tenets of its performers and each, in its own way, reaffirms the harmony, unity, and sacredness of all creation. Despite the myriad superficial variety in Native American drama, certain fundamental attitudes permeate virtually all of it, including (surprisingly) several obviously modern, realistic, and Western-styled plays, like Hanay Geiogamah's *Body Indian*.[14]

Fundamental to many, if not most, Native American ritual events are two beliefs that have few direct counterparts for Euro-Americans. The first is the concept of nonlinear time—time that may be viewed cyclically from one perspective and eternally from another. The second is the concept of a dimensionless sacred place, the center of the universe and the locative counterpart of the ever-present time. These two concepts are congruent, in a sense identical, for each point in time or space is infinitely large, extending outward from the sacred event to include all creation, yet located around the event in a way that precisely fixes the position and assures the security of the participants. Joseph Epes Brown characterizes this notion well.

The tipi, the hogan, or the long house . . . determined the perimeters of space in such a way that a sacred place, or enclosure, was established. Space so defined served as a model of the world, of the universe, or microcosmically, of a human being. Essential to such definition of space, so central to human need, were means by which the centers of sacred space of place were established. For without such ritual fixing of a center there can be no circumference. And with neither circumference nor center where does a person stand? A ritually defined center, whether the fire at the center of the plains tipi or the *sipapu* (earth navel) within the Pueblo *kiva*, obviously expresses not just a mathematically fixed point established arbitrarily in space. It is also taken to be the actual center of the world. It is understood as an axis serving as a bridge between heaven and earth, an axis that pierces through a multiplicity of worlds. . . . It symbolizes the way of liberation from the limits of the cosmos. Always, vertical ascent is impossible unless the starting point be the ritual center.[15]

Without such a centering in sacred time and place, Native American dramas would be mere displays, robbed of their meaning. Sometimes a special place is created for the drama, either permanent, like the kivas of the Southwest, or temporary, like the Sun Dance lodges of the High Plains. Sometimes the stage is the people's ordinary living space, like the Northwest Coast family houses, the Southwest village plazas, or the Plains lodges. But even in these latter cases, the mundane is typically made special by such devices as the creation of an altar in a dwelling, as for the Cheyenne or Lakota Pipe Ceremony, or by performance of a cleansing and sanctifying ceremony. Using the ordinary living space, in fact, adds an extra dimension to the sacred ceremony, for it reaffirms the continuity between the parts of the cosmos that human beings conventionally inhabit and those in which their presence is charged with an unusual significance.

Nowhere is this more apparent or more powerfully symbolized than in the great Navajo chantways, epic religious dramas of cosmic scope, the fundamental purpose of which is to restore and maintain the essential balance of the world, the lack of which produces sickness in mind and body. A sing, the actual curing event manifesting the chantway, restores health to the individual patient, to those gathered at the ceremony, to the nation, and ultimately to the cosmos.

Not only is the hogan the living space for the Navajo, it is also where rituals occur. It is created in the shape of rituals, its round floor and east-facing door are parts of the total alignment of human beings with the world of nature to which their rituals are addressed. Ritual space is not separated from daily life but integrated into it. . . . The great sand-paintings on the dirt floor of the hogan provide a two-dimensional diagram for the forces of nature. When the patient walks on the sand painting, the ritual creates a four-dimensional world where one is surrounded by and related to the holy power.[16]

Thus the moment of the dramatic event is one of extraordinary significance that envelopes everyone concerned, blurring the distinction, so crucial to Euro-American drama, between actor and audience. The apparently casual and selective attention of those not central to such ritual events does not indicate indifference, as many outside observers have concluded, but rather an unprepossessing recognition that their very presence, their watching participation, is their contribution to the drama at hand. In this way Native American drama is by its nature celebratory of the essential being of the community, emphasizing that ultimately all are affected by what the central participants do. The community, the audience, is an integral part of the creative process before, during, and after the fact of the performance, because the performance realizes an aesthetic and metaphysical immanence of the society.

From the outset, then, Native American drama differs in several profound ways from recent Euro-American drama. The fundamental embedding of dramatic events, whatever their particular character, in the metaphysical substratum of the society gives them an immediate power and importance that Western (in the sense of Euro-American) drama cannot command. Even religious rites in the Western mode for the most part lack the sacred central moment of eternal creation that characterizes Native American rites. Indian events assert a present and eternal reality; Western ones celebrate past realities or seek to invoke realities-to-be. The moment of transubstantiation in the Communion ritual is the only significant Western exception, and the extensive history of argument over its nature is eloquent testimony to the way it runs counter to prevailing habits of thought, even among theologians and other philosophers.

DIMENSIONS OF NATIVE AMERICAN DRAMA

Native American drama is thus only partly delimited by calling it an art form, although it is certainly at least that. Like Western drama, it can be described in terms of its actors, setting, plot, dialogue, gestures, costumes, movements, and so forth, and when these features are considered, the range of events that demand the label *drama* is very large indeed. With respect to actors, for example, one end of the dramatic continuum is held by performances by individuals; at the other, entire nations may take part. But to focus on these accidents of drama is to mistake, as foreigners often do, the superficial trappings of the dramatic situation for the phenomenological wholeness the native perceives. When a creative event is charged with special significance, it establishes and maintains a tension (even when the details of the event are all known in advance) that extends to all participants, "performers" and "audience" alike. The members of the community grasp the event, in its entirety, with an understanding that casual observers, however attentive, are likely not to achieve. What seem to be the criteria for the cultural initiate, then, are the dimensions of significance, emotional intensity, and controlled creativity, which set dramatic events apart from more ordinary experiences.

These dimensions encompass an extensive range of events, some of which are not always thought sufficiently distinctive or artful to be called drama by Western critics, although occasionally scholars in the past have used that term. Paul Radin, for example, titled his edition of the Winnebago Medicine Rite *The Road of Life and Death: A Ritual Drama of the American Indians,*[17] and more than a century ago an English visitor to the Northwest Coast likened the Nookta Kluklukwat'kah ('Night of Dancing') to primitive theatre: "I never saw acting more to the life; the performers would be the making of a minor theatre in London. Here, in fact, is theatrical performance in its earliest stage."[18]

Recently, however, scholars have been turning to other, less spectacular types of traditional verbal art, such as the telling of tales, and finding in them the unmistakable characteristics of drama. Under the rubric of "performance," folklorists, anthropologists, and others have studied the presentations of all manner of events that are characterized as modes of speaking that constitute both an *act* of speaking and an *event* of speaking. Performance events involve both speakers and hearers in evaluations, not merely of the quality of the performance, which may indifferently be good or bad, but of the appropriateness, honesty, and conformity to the cultural norms established by metaphysics, aesthetics, and so forth.

Performance as a mode of spoken verbal communication consists in the assumption of responsibility to an audience for a display of communicative competence. This competence rests on the knowledge and ability to speak in socially appropriate ways. Performance involves on the part of the performer an assumption of accountability to an audience for the way in which communication is carried out, above and beyond its referential content. From the point of view of the audience, the act of expression on the part of the performer is thus marked as subject to evaluation for the way it is done, for the relative skill and effectiveness of the performer's display of competence. [19]

Performance, so conceived, therefore encompasses a large range of events, some of them fairly "ordinary" activities of daily life, such as tale telling. Long the only commonly published type of Native American literature, short narratives, called "myths," "legends," or "folk tales," often indiscriminately, have recently become recognized as the scripts of one-person dramas. The tellers typically are experienced actors who use a variety of techniques—different voices, modified vocal features such as heightened nasalization, carefully planned gestures, exaggerated emphasis, and the like—to vivify their presentations. Barre Toelken observes that such tales, in the opinion of Yellowman, a distinguished Navajo teller, are not to be viewed "as narratives (in our sense of the term) but as dramatic presentations performed within certain cultural contexts for moral and philosophical reasons."[20] Melville Richards similarly speaks of Clackamas Chinook tales as drama and, even on the printed page and in translation, the tales he transcribes are clearly structured in such a way as to cause the audience to envision a drama. [21]

Although ethnologists have studied dramatic performances as manifestations of the larger culture, Euro-American scholars of drama and other kinds of literature have typically focused instead on the text of the event as a separate artifact, frequently quite divorced from its culture. Unfortunately, the resulting critical evaluations have too often shown an unacknowledged bias towards the critic's culture and thus have been ultimately unsatisfying, for the event is seen out of its context, distorted and deprived of its normal phenomenological wholeness. Taking the full cultural context into consideration deepens our understanding of Native American drama in significant ways. The event is seen, not just in its "stage" setting, but in its community setting as well. I have already quoted Barre Toelken's description of the centrality of the Navajo hogan (and I mean "centrality" in both its literal and its metaphysical meaning); that description is worth expanding upon here.

For the Navajo, as generally for peoples of the Southwest, all beings and all things in the world are ideally maintained in a healthy stage of harmony and balance. The root term for this quintessential condition is hózhó (usually translated 'beauty'). But this single English word is not adequate, for the concept really includes all that a Navajo would think good: such perfection as humans may attain, normality, success, balance, order, well-being, satisfaction, tranquillity, and goodness, as well as beauty. The second syllable of the Navajo word signals the qualities just listed; the first refers to the total environment, including both the normally seen or ordinary world and the normally unseen or spiritual world.[22] When this balance is disturbed, even within a single individual, all is threatened until order, hózhó, is restored. The restoration of hózhó is effected by producing a sing, the realization of one of a number of the sacred chantway dramas, each of which has a particular use depending on the nature and source of the disturbance.

NAVAJO CHANTWAYS: AN ARCHETYPE OF NATIVE AMERICAN DRAMA

The Navajo chantways are epic religious ritual dramas of the first order. They are epic because they each begin, many of them quite literally, with reference to the creation, or perhaps better, recreation, of the universe, including that of the Navajo people, whose own name, Diné, means 'people.' They are religious because they speak about, indeed grasp, the fundamental workings of the cosmos, matters of the greatest sacredness and power. They are rituals because they are systems of fixed behavior that the community lives by. They are dramas both because they have the usual formal trappings of drama—costumes, choreography, dialogue, and the like—and because they evidence the qualities of significance, emotional intensity, and controlled creativity that all drama has.

The preparations for the sing may take many weeks as the illness is diagnosed, sometimes with the aid of a shamanistic specialist, called a "hand-trembler," and an appropriate singer, hataaxi, is engaged. Since the chantways are both complex and extremely long—some have hundreds of songs that must be sung without hesitation or error—even the most accomplished singers know only one or two, devoting their lives to their study. Relatives and friends must be invited, perhaps from hundreds of miles away, because the presence of one's people is requisite for the restoration of hózhó. Since custom demands that the singer be properly honored for his service, paid with goods of both material and ceremonial worth, and that all who come to the sing be fed for at least the days of the event and often several days before, the patient's entire network of blood and clan relations is typically asked to help by supplying sheep, blankets, baskets, jewelry, and other valuables. Thus the practical aspects of the sing reinforce the social interrelations that bind the people together, while the spiritual aspects of the chantway mirror the spiritual interrelations that unite all of creation.

In the performance of the text of the chantway, the hataaxi, sometimes (especially if he is old and feeble) with the help of an apprentice, constructs the sand paintings, sings the songs, speaks much of the dialogue, directs the attendant dancers and impersonators of the spirits, and in general oversees the entire event, which lasts as long as nine days and nights. He is the complete dramaturge: lead actor, stage manager, choreographer, director, and to some degree playwright. In many cases a new hogan is built, which is used only for the sing. At the ritual center of the hogan the sand paintings representing the essence of the segment of the script then to be performed will be made, and it is here that the core of the drama unfolds.

The sand painting, the focus of the "stage" of the curing drama, is simultaneously the schematic for the metaphysical stage as well. When the patient circles the center of the hogan and crosses into the sand painting, he steps to the point where the two worlds join. In fact, the Navajo term for the sand painting, or dry painting, as it is sometimes called, for most of the colors do not come from sand, is *iikhááh*, the literal meaning of which is "they enter and leave."[23] The sand painting provides a part of the scenario for the sacred drama that is taking place. Sam D. Gill discusses the sand painting's function, using the Whirling Logs painting from the Nightway Chant.

The sandpainting is, at one level, a reminder of the events of the story of a heroic adventurer who obtained knowledge of the Nightway ceremonial, who experienced the mysteries of the whirling logs, and who introduced agriculture to the Navajos. At another level, the sandpainting is a geometric projection of the essential pattern of order in the world.[24]

At the end of each section of the drama, when the singer and one-sung-over have completed their prescribed actions, the sand painting is gathered up and carried away, not, as it is often simplistically said, to "remove the evil" that has somehow been transferred from the patient to the pigments, but for a more profound reason.

In the sandpainting rite, the person comes to experience the truth in the myth which is that there are not two worlds, but one world composed of parts which are complexly interrelated and interdependent. Order and disorder (*hózhó* and *hóchó* in Navajo) are interdependent as are health and sickness, life and death, spiritual and material.

Once this truth is experienced the sandpainting can no longer serve as a map. The one-sung-over has found his way from within the sandpainting by becoming part of it and it has disappeared by becoming a part of him. With the experience of the unity of the world, the sandpainting, as a depiction of the order of the world, cannot exist. So the destruction of the sandpainting during its use corresponds with the dissolution of thé double-imagery it presents. When the one-sung-over arises and leaves the sandpainting his experience of unity is confirmed in a way by the destroyed sandpainting. The many colours have dissolved into one as the sands and the one-sung-over return to the world.[25]

The realizations of the Navajo chantways in the sings are in essence the archetype of Native American drama. Like all drama, religious or secular, private or public, the range of its formal elements is extensive—actors, dialogue, choreography, costumes, settings, and most importantly, message.[26] But unlike the secular drama of recent Euro-American tradition, there is the special difference found at the center of the great majority of Native American dramatic events: the level of significance, and therefore emotional intensity, is markedly higher, with a concomitant restriction of the amount of innovation tolerated. What makes the level of significance greater is that the drama takes place in the sacred center and manipulates the very stuff of creation. The ritual event, the performance, is itself the real drama; the "text" behind it is clearly an artifact. For Euro-Americans the essence of the work that exists in time (that is, any work of art except painting, photography, and sculpture) is ideal, and an individual realization of the ideal is merely the occasion for the recognition of the ideal entity through its association with the particulars of the realization. It is analogous to the realization of linguistic competence in a particular utterance or discourse. Therefore, any given performance may conform more or less closely to the ideal without diminishing the integrity of the ideal. (The quality of the performance is, of course, another matter.) But for Native Americans, the essence of the event is to be found most centrally in the performance; the ideal, insofar as it may be acknowledged to exist independently at all, has at best a shadowy existence, separate from its manifestation in performance.

TYPES OF NATIVE AMERICAN DRAMA

The choice of the large-scale, epic ritual drama as the archetype is an obvious one, of course, for it is both the most powerful form, in that it deals with the very basic matters of existence, and in many instances the most spectacular.[27] The limitations of space prevent me from discussing at length any of the other types of ritual dramas, but the events listed below, from a variety of Indian peoples, will be illustrative.

Any classification of ritual events will necessarily be problematic, for each drama has several dimensions, and codification along one dimension will necessarily change the prominence of other dimensions, contradicting the initiate's holistic understanding.[28] Perhaps the least distorting scheme of analysis is one that considers the function or purpose of the event. Although also violating native conceptualizations to some degree, if only because the attempted universality of the system might suggest a hierarchical judgment that its initiates would find inappropriate or offensive, functional labels at least suggest to outsiders what the native knows. Such a scheme would consider together rituals that seek to renew the world or to begin again the ever-repeating cycle of the new year, such as the Plains Sun Dance; those that are designed to insure the availability of game and the survival of crops, such as the bear ceremonials of the Ojibway or the Rain Dance of the Zuni; those that mean to assure the unity of cosmic halves, such as the moiety dances of the Pueblos; those that confirm the status of individuals in tribes, clans, societies, or professions, such as the Apache Puberty Drama or the Pawnee *Hako* ('Friendship') ritual; those that reconsecrate holy things, such as the many Plains medicine bundle rituals; or those that mark the exercise of special powers, such as divination and curing ceremonies. Even this system, however, is less than satisfactory, for only the simplest ritual dramas of any Native American peoples fit into just one category. The Navajo chantways, for example, have primarily a curative function, but health for the Navajo is defined not merely somatically or even psychologically, but cosmically; thus the performance of a sing also insures the unity of the world and asserts the continuing recreation of the cosmos. And the Lakota Sun Dance is simultaneously an occasion for world renewal, for thanksgiving, and for the acquisition and use of shamanistic powers.

SHAMAN AND PRIEST: DRAMAS OF PERSONAL POWER

The logical point to begin a survey of the types of Native American dramatic events is with shamanism.[29] Native American experiences encompass a wide variety of shamanistic practices. Some involve an ecstatic out-of-body journey to the spirits, notably those of the dead, the classic case discussed by Mircea Eliade.[30] But not all shamanistic power results from such journeys. While sick unto death, Black Elk traveled out of his body to experience his great vision, although other Plains people, sharing the same general cultural expectations, did not. Further, while most primary shamanistic experiences involve a trance or a trance-like state, some, as often in the Sun Dance, may not bring the participant into direct contact with the spirits. More importantly for the purposes of this chapter, there are extensive differences in the way these kinds of experiences are presented to audiences. In some cases the shaman is in direct contact with a particular guardian or helping spirit, as is typical of the shamans of the Northwest Coast and the Plateau. These spirits may be those of one's ancestors, or, more often, a personage of the sacred myths, such as the Plateau Bluejay or the Ojibway *pawágan* ('dream visitor'). In other cases the experience of spirit contact is presented in symbolic terms that represent true drama and does not depend on the immediate and direct manifestation to the audience of the supernatural presence. If, for example, the shaman's powers are those of curing, they may function by drawing on the spirit directly. But the curing ritual may work equally effectively when the shaman instead uses the powers acquired in previous encounters with his or her helping spirit. On the psychological level, of course, what is crucial is the *belief* that the powers of the shaman truly exist, and it is immaterial to the cure whether they are newly drawn at each cure or are, as it were, taken from stock.[31]

Many of these examples of shamanism are indeed dramatic, in the sense that they are presentations involving spectacular displays of ritual and magic, but they are not necessarily drama; the trappings of the theatre may, arguably, be necessary, but they are surely not sufficient. The moment at which shamanistic displays become drama is when the shaman begins to plan the ceremony in advance rather than giving himself or herself over completely to the paranormal state. At this point the shaman has begun to perform according to a script, exhibiting a control over innovation that I contend is one of the essentials of drama. After this stage in the shamanistic experience, the practitioner may perform alone or as part of a much larger event, in which the shamanistic qualities of the performance may become muted or almost unrecognizable. In some cases, such as the Plains Sun Dance, each shaman must undergo the process of acquiring power and putting it into use. When such uses become codified and the amount of innovation exhibited in the performance is sufficiently controlled, the performance may properly be called drama, even though this final stage of development must be undergone by each participant in turn. In other cases, such as the Southwest kachina rituals, the original individual shamanistic practices may be incorporated into the script of the event, so that each new participant will step into a predefined role that resists personal alteration.

Thus shamanism in its original form is characterized by the acquisition of power, often in a trance state and through contact with spirits, and by the use of that power for religious and ethical purposes, usually curing or divination. Unethical users of such powers do exist, of course; they are generally called "witches" or more simply "evil persons." When the shamanistic performance is subjected to prior planning—to "scripting," in the jargon of both sociology and the theatre—its function may change. If the immediate contact with the spirit is severed, the shaman, or rather his logical successor, becomes a priest, one whose rituals are planned, sometimes simply with respect to the actions and general direction of the event, as in the Plains Pipe Ceremonies, and sometimes with respect to the entire enterprise, as in the Navajo sings. If the religious purpose is lost or subordinated to other impulses, what remains is pure drama, although drama of an arguably poorer sort. Such is the case with the Northwest Coast privilege displays, the potlatch dramas.

SECULARIZATION: THE PRIVILEGE DRAMAS OF THE NORTHWEST COAST

The potlatch is a distinctive event of the Northwest Coast in which the wealth and prestige of an important man is demonstrated by the amount of property he can expend in gifts. Originally the potlatch was a mechanism for cementing the interrelations of family, clan, and village, but cultural crisis (largely the result of European intervention, both direct and indirect) has robbed it of much of its original benefit. Now, instead of uniting the community, as do the Plains Sun Dances, Cheyenne Sacred Arrow ceremony, the Iroquois False Face Drama, and the Navajo sings, the potlatchs have become occasions for ostentatious display and the demonstration of a hierarchy of wealth and privilege that puts, and intends to keep, all the members in their acknowledged positions. Ostensibly potlatches are given on occasions demanding special ceremony, such as the transfer of an important name to a younger relative, the coming of age of a daughter—or, more important, a son—or the marriage of two people of nearly equal prestige. But, lacking even the modest possibilities for upward social mobility at the high-society debutante ball, their major social effect is to petrify the status quo. Mere wealth is not enough to change one's place in society, nor can anyone except the first and perhaps second son expect to inherit much of a rich father's goods and position. In several of the languages of the area, in fact, the terms used to describe youngest sons of even the most important men are the same as those for the "commoners" of the village, those with status only with respect to slaves and the poorest "nonpeople" at the village's outskirts. Distribution of wealth is not in itself a bad thing, of course; giveaways are a traditional part of Sun Dance gatherings, and for the Navajo, consistent with their pervasive emphasis on balance and order, they represent an attempt to distribute wealth more evenly throughout the society and thereby to defuse feelings of resentment at inequality. But the potlatch in actuality and by design functions in quite the opposite way.[32]

Central to the potlatches, however, are dramatic events of great strength and beauty. In their spectacular display of costumes and masks, the potlatch events present a uniquely rich form of Native American drama. The elaborate masks, some with two or three layers of representation and therefore significance, are both independent art objects of major aesthetic power and dramatic accoutrements rivaled in North America only by the masks of the Southwestern kachinas and the Iroquois False Faces, and elsewhere in the world by the masks of classical Oriental drama. Typically the potlatch dramas are symbolic representations of the acquisition of spiritual power by the chief members of the family and by their ancestors, although the spirituality of the original impulse has become subordinated to the dramatic display itself. Space does not allow a detailed examination of all the several types of Northwest Coast dramas, but two examples may be given, one characteristic of the southern end of the area, one of the northern end.

Some of the Northwest Coast dramas, such as the Makah Wolf Ritual (Klukwalle), show their unmistakable origins in shamanistic spirit contact. Typical of most of the Northwest Coast dramas of this type is the emphasis on the frightful danger posed by the spirit powers and the delicate balance of rationality and cooperation offered by human society. Shared by a number of contiguous peoples (many otherwise unrelated) around Vancouver, British Columbia, the Wolf Ritual has as its major function the initiation of community members into the group. The children to be initiated are "captured" by the Wolves, who are impersonated by older initiates, and "rescued" by other society members at the end of the four days the drama runs. In the process of rescue the Wolves' madness is cured through the ritual purgation of the spirit, and on the last night of the festivity, all—the rescuers and defenders, the captive children, and the rampaging Wolves, now cured of their madness—celebrate their reunion with an evening of singing, dancing, and feasting.[33]

The most important drama of the northern end of the Northwest Coast is the drama of the Cannibal Dancer, or hamatsa, which is the centerpiece of the Winter Ceremonial. The drama is the reenactment of a long and complex myth in which four young hunters come upon the dwelling of BaxbakualanuXsiwae, the Cannibal-at-the-North-End-of-the-World. Hideous, whistling eerily from dozens of open, bloody mouths all over his body, BaxbakualanuXsiwae flies through the air driven by a ravenous hunger for human flesh. In the course of the story, the courageous and cunning hunters kill BasbakualanuXsiwae and his numerous maneating servants, then return triumphant to their village. As in many other Native American dramas, the victorious hunters bring back with them the masks, whistles, and sacred cedar bark garments that are the accoutrements of the reenactment and the songs and dances that are its script. Performed in a typically magnificent great lodge of the Kwakuitl, the *hamatsa* drama is a masterpiece of Native American dramatic art.[34]

But even this consideration of two major examples of powerful, complex, and spectacular Indian performances, one profoundly religious and unabashedly metaphysical in its function, the other (although originally the enactment of a sacred myth) now largely secular, is only a hint of the wealth of Native American drama. A number of major dramas, such as the Plains Sun Dances, have barely been mentioned, and missing almost entirely are discussions of the many sacred dance rituals of the city dwellers of the Southwest, the Iroquois False Face Society Drama, the Menominee Medicine Ritual and Midewiwin Drama, the Ghost Dance Ritual, and the countless other ceremonies, narrative dances, rituals, and other events that constitute the extensive body of Indian dramatic art. The compass of a single essay cannot contain even bare lists of the total nor any detailed discussion of the costumes and other accoutrements of drama, although I hope the bibliography will provide an initial guide for further reading.

CONTEMPORARY NATIVE AMERICAN DRAMA

In closing I would like to shift attention briefly from the more traditional dramas I have been considering to note that Indians today are continuing, not only to renew traditional dramatic forms and to incorporate outside elements into older dramas, but also to assimilate and adapt the forms of Euro-American drama. In recent decades several companies of Indian actors have been formed to produce both traditional dramas and works by new Indian playwrights, beginning with the efforts of Arthur Junaluska (Cherokee) in New York during the 1950s. Jay Silverheels (Mohawk), George Pierre (Colville), Noble "Kid" Chissell (Cherokee), and others in Los Angeles in the late 1960s founded the Indian Actors' Workshop, which was concerned chiefly with preparing Indian actors for film work, although it also mounted some stage productions. Between 1968 and 1970 the Santa Fe Theatre Project, under the direction of Roland Meinholz, produced a number of plays by Native Americans at the Institute of American Indian Arts.

Perhaps the most active Native American theatre company during the 1970s was the American Indian Theatre Ensemble, later called the Native American Theatre Ensemble (NATE), formed in 1972 by Hanay Geiogamah (Kiowa) with the help of Ellen Stewart of La Mama Experimental Theatre Club. Between

1972 and 1976 NATE toured throughout the United States, performing at the Smithsonian Institution in Washington, D.C., and in various cities in Oklahoma, Colorado, New Mexico, Arizona, Washington, California, Wisconsin, and Illinois, and appeared for six weeks in Berlin.

In addition, a number of smaller companies blossomed during the mid-1970s, including the Navajo Theatre under Robert Shorty (Navajo), the Spiderwoman Theatre Workshop in New York under Muriel Miguel (Rappahannock-Cuna), the Thunderbird Company in Ontario under Alayne Begwin (Ojibway), and the highly fluid White Roots of Peace (later Four Arrows), a political action and guerrilla theatre troupe that emerged from the Mohawk nation. With the exception of NATE, which has recently been reincarnated by Geiogamah as American Indians in the Arts, the two most active and enduring companies are the Red Earth Performing Arts Company of Seattle, formed in 1974 by Don Matt (Flathead) and John Kaufman (Nez Perce), and the Indian Performing Arts Company of Tulsa, which dates from 1976.[35]

Not surprisingly, the canon of plays in the Western mode both by and about Native Americans is small, and even fewer have been published. Perhaps the first created in recent times was *Cherokee Night* (1934), by Rollie Lynn Riggs (Cherokee), the author of *Green Grow the Lilacs* (1931) (which became *Oklahoma!*). Depicting Indian life in eastern Oklahoma during the 1920s and 1930s, *Cherokee Night* was considered too obscure for Broadway when it was first produced. Others include *Unto These Hills* and *Trails of Tears*, collective enterprises of the Cherokee people dating from the 1960s; *Yanowis* (1968) and *Mowitch* (1968), by Monica Charles (Klallam); *To Catch a Never Dream* (1969), *Fire-Life* (1978), and *Legends* (1978), by Bruce King (Oneida-Chippewa); *Na Haaz Zaan* (1972), by Robert Shorty and Geraldine Keams (Navajo); *Body Indian* (1972), *Coon Cons Coyote* (1973), *Foghorn* (1973), *49* (1975), *War Dancer* (1977), and *Land Sale* (1978), by Geiogamah (Kiowa); *Butterfly of Hope*, by Ray Baldwin Louis (Navajo); *Skins* (1973), by Lynda Poolaw (Kiowa); *Two Ways* (1974) and *Wa-Ku-Pani* (1974), by the members of the A-Tu-Mai Theatre Company (Southern Ute); *Changer* (1975), by Gerald Bruce Miller (Skokomish-Yakima); and *Under the Sweetgum Bridge* (1978), by Wallace Hampton Tucker (Choctaw).[36] Although Geiogamah stands out because of his energy and his talent as a playwright, director, and producer, others are also talented and energetic; we may expect more from them in the future.

While several of these plays are reworkings of traditional material (for example *Na Haaz Zaan* and *Changer*), it is not surprising that most address themselves to the events of recent history (for example *Cherokee Night* and *Under the Sweetgum Bridge*) and matters of contemporary Indian life (for example *Body Indian*, *49*, and *To Catch a Never Dream*). But it is perhaps more surprising that most works by these mostly young Indian playwrights, many of whom are not products of conservative ethnic backgrounds, continue to show the strength of the traditional aesthetics and metaphysics discussed in this chapter.

During the four years Geiogamah's NATE was active, many critics, including some of the most experienced, failed to understand fully, if at all, how much the work of the Indian playwrights and actors manifested the same features that distinguish their traditional dramatic events, such as the lack of a clear boundary between audience and performer and the focus on the timeless moment of the center. On the one hand, the critics perceived that, in their use of sets, lights, costumes, props, and the physical configuration of stage and audience, the plays were much like the other plays, ethnic or not, that they were used to seeing. On the other hand, they were clearly disturbed in unexpected ways by many aspects of the plays. While Geiogamah's plays presented obvious elements of social commentary, they seemed to be more than mere propaganda, and while some points of traditional culture were obscure, the plays had an undeniable integrity and consistency that prevented most reviewers from condemning them outright. Many were unable either to comprehend or to interpret that with which they were presented. Some even seemed unaware of their own confusion and am-bivalence, although the most perceptive reviewers, even when they could not articulate its causes, usually sensed the strangeness, the feeling of mysterious dislocation caused by their inability to cope with this strikingly distinct ethnic drama in terms of their own theatrical experiences. But NATE's Indian au-diences did understand, and this understanding constitutes the latest addition to a sometimes battered but unbroken line of traditional dramatic art.[37]

NOTES

1. The term Native American has recently come to be the preferred descriptor in formal and legal contexts for Indian people taken together, although most individuals still think of themselves first as members of their separate nations (Bella Coola, Semi-nole, Malecite, and so forth). However, most people of Native American blood use the term Indian when speaking in English about themselves, and many older Indians wish not to be called "Native Americans" at all. (Compare the variation among "black," "Negro," "colored," and, in highly restricted situations, even "nigger.") Since Indian peoples themselves do not agree as to which term they prefer, I shall use both, inter-changeably and without implied prejudice.

2. Unless there is firm evidence that the practices discussed in this paper are indeed things of the past, I will generally use what anthropologists term "the ethnographic present." In fact, a considerable number of the dramatic events described here were once considered by non-Indians to be lost. Many of them, like the potlatches of the Northwest Coast and the Sun Dances of the Plains, were forbidden by the government because they were considered pagan, uncivilized, belligerent, or subversive. Despite such efforts by the government and religious organizations that controlled much of Indian life, the most important of these rituals endured, practiced in secret or kept alive in the memories of elders for the time when they could be performed as they were meant to be.

3. Obviously, within the limits of a single chapter, only some of these distinctions can be made for any of the groups discussed, and those often must be the minimum required to set their drama in an adequate frame for presentation to the wide variety of

readers of this book, some of whom may have an extensive knowledge of Native American peoples, others considerably less. Because the bibliography on many Indian nations is enormous, especially for numerous or popular peoples like the Navajo or the Dakota, I intend the references cited to be merely an entry to the appropriate scholarly literature.

4. For example, the chantways of the Navajos, who for the past several centuries have been herders and planters, contain much that relates to their old way of living as hunters in northwestern Canada nearly a millenium ago. See Karl W. Luckert, *The Navajo Hunter Tradition* (Tucson: University of Arizona Press, 1975); Karl W. Luckert, "An Approach to Navajo Mythology," in Earle H. Waugh and K. Dad Prithipaul, eds., *Native Religious Traditions*, Joint International Symposium of Elders and Scholars, Edmonton, Alberta, 1977, *Sciences Religieuses/Studies in Religion* (Waterloo, Ont.: Wilfrid Laurier University Press for the Corporation Canadienne des Sciences Religieuses/Canadian Corporation for Studies in Religion, 1977), Supplement no. 8, pp. 117–31. There is an exact parallel in the Christian Communion ritual, where the eating and drinking of symbolic flesh and blood continues a hunters' rite of immense antiquity.

5. Such modes of learning are thus quite contrary to Western teaching methods, which typically encourage a child to "learn by doing," even at the risk of serious initial mistakes or failure. The inability of educators to contend with this difference has continually crippled attempts to instruct Indians in non-Indian schools.

6. Richard Simpson, with Lizzie Enos, *Ooti: A Maidu Legacy* (Millbrae, Calif.: Celestial Arts, 1977); Sol Worth and John Adair, "Navajo Film-Makers," *American Anthropologist* 72 (1970): 9–34; and Sol Worth and John Adair, *Through Navajo Eyes: An Exploration in Film Communication and Anthropology* (Bloomington: Indiana University Press, 1972).

7. Kachinas are beings of the Southwest whose coming into existence predates that of humans. Although they are not gods, they have great spiritual powers, much as angels and saints in the Judaic and Christian traditions. Unlike angels, however, they are corporeal, and unlike saints, their actions are not always good from human perspectives. Because to speak the names of the kachinas is to invoke their presence, they are never casually spoken about, and even stories involving kachinas are told only in the cold months, after they have retired to their winter village a safe distance away. During the dance dramas and at other times when the kachinas' presence is required, the human kachina impersonators invest themselves with the spirits of, and in essence become, the kachinas, with their power and their responsibilities.

8. Emory Sekaquaptewa, "Hopi Indian Ceremonies," in Walter Holden Capps, ed., *Seeing with a Native Eye: Essays on Native American Religion* (New York: Harper and Row, 1976), pp. 37–38.

9. The absence of a true understanding of a traditional culture would seem to lie behind the failure of the attempts during the 1960s to develop what some were calling "tribal" theatre. Although some manifestations of "radical" theatre, the best of it stemming from European theorists such as Antonin Artaud and Jerzy Grotowski, occasioned interesting theatrical moments, most were pointless except as reactions to outside events and conditions and hence were ephemeral. The mistake could not be more patent than in Brian Wicker's statement: "Drama, it might be said, began when *seeing* was freed from the shackles of believing; when understanding became possible without an immediate interior change of heart. Today the theatre seems to be returning to the bondage of its religious roots." "Ritual and Culture: Some Dimensions of the Problem Today," in James D. Shaughnessy, ed., *The Roots of Ritual* (Grand Rapids, Mich.: Eerdmans, 1973), p. 18.

In seeking to attain a "lost tribalism," as it is called in Julian Beck, *The Life of the Theatre* (San Francisco: City Lights Books, 1972), through such obviously artificial means, the proponents of the radical theatre were attempting the impossible. The attempt to view life as theatre was equally doomed, because of a similar ignorance of the true integration of art and religion in actual tribal communities, such as the Native American ones discussed in this chapter.

10. For two excellent examples of what is possible when scholars learn not only the languages of native peoples but also the subtle syncopations of their cultures, see Gary Jay Witherspoon, *Language and Art in the Navajo Universe* (Ann Arbor: University of Michigan Press, 1977), and J. Barre Toelken, "The 'Pretty Languages' of Yellowman: Genre, Mode, and Texture in the Navaho Coyote Narratives," *Genre* 2 (1969): 211–35. On the ethical problems of research into sacred matters, see H. David Brumble III, "Anthropologists, Novelists and Indian Sacred Material," *Canadian Review of American Studies* 11 (1980): 31–49.

11. Black Elk [Hehaka Sapa], *Black Elk Speaks*, told through John G. Neihardt, 2nd ed. (Lincoln: University of Nebraska Press, 1961). An analysis of Black Elk's Horse Drama constitutes Chapter 4 of Linda Carol Walsh Jenkins, "The Performances of Native Americans as American Theatre" (Ph.D. diss., University of Minnesota, 1975). In Joseph Epes Brown, *The Sacred Pipe: Black Elk's Account of the Seven Rites of the Oglala Souix* (Norman: University of Oklahoma Press, 1953), Black Elk frequently names individuals who originated specific details of Lakota ceremonies.

12. See, for example, Frederick J. Dockstader, *The Kachina and the White Man: A Study of the Influence of White Culture on the Hopi Kachina Cult*, Cranbrook Institute of Science Bulletin no. 35 (Bloomfield Hills, Mich.: Cranbrook Institute of Science, 1954); LaVerne Harrell Clark, *They Sang for Horses: The Impact of the Horse on Navajo and Apache Folklore* (Tucson: University of Arizona Press, 1966).

13. The terms "frame" and "genre" are used here in technical senses derived from the work of Gregory Bateson, Erving Goffman, Dell Hymes, and others concerned with verbal acts as performances regulated in large part by cultural expectations.

14. Hanay Geiogamah, *New Native American Drama: Three Plays* (Norman: University of Oklahoma Press, 1980).

15. Joseph Epes Brown, "The Roots of Renewal," in Capps, *Seeing with a Native Eye*, p. 31. Further characterizations of this notion are to be found in Brown, *Sacred Pipe*; Joseph Epes Brown, *The Spiritual Legacy of the American Indian*, Pendle Hill Pamphlet no. 135 (Lebanon, Pa.: Pendle Hill, 1964); Joseph Epes Brown, "The Immediacy of Mythological Message: Native American Traditions," Waugh and Prithipaul, *Native Religious Traditions*, pp. 101–16. Similar descriptions of the Plains concept of the sacred center are to be found in J.W.E. Newbery, "The Universe at Prayer," in Waugh and Prithipaul, *Native Religious Traditions*, pp. 165–78, and in Black Elk, *Black Elk Speaks*.

16. J. Barre Toelken, *The Dynamics of Folklore* (Boston: Houghton Mifflin, 1979), pp. 243–44. See also Sam Dale Gill, "Whirling Logs and Coloured Sands," in Waugh and Prithipaul, *Native Religious Traditions*, pp. 151–63; David P. McAllester and Susan W. McAllester, *Hogans: Navajo Houses and House Songs* (Middletown, Conn.: Wesleyan University Press, 1980).

17. Paul Radin, *The Road of Life and Death: A Ritual Drama of the American Indians*, Bollingen Series no. 5 (New York: Pantheon, 1945).

18. Gilbert M. Sprout, *Scenes and Studies of Savage Life* (London: Smith, Elder, 1868), p. 67.

19. Richard Bauman, "Verbal Art as Performance," *American Anthropologist* 77 (1975): 293.

20. Toelken, "'Pretty Languages' of Yellowman," p. 224.

21. Melville Richards, *The Content and Style of an Oral Literature: Clackamas Chinook Myths and Tales* (Seattle: University of Washington Press, 1959); Melville Richards, *The People Are Coming Soon: Analyses of Clackamas Chinook Myths and Tales* (Seattle: University of Washington Press, 1960).

22. Gary Jay Witherspoon, "The Central Concepts of Navajo World View: I," *Linguistics* 119 (1974): 53–54; Witherspoon, *Language and Art in the Navajo Universe*, pp. 23–25; see also Leland Clifton Wyman, *Blessingway* (Tucson: University of Arizona Press, 1970), p. 7.

23. The phenomenon of the boundary between "this world" and "the other world" is of course well known throughout the world. Compare the water boundaries of traditional Celtic beliefs and the use of the pentagram as a protective boundary against the summoned devil in European traditions.

24. Gill, "Whirling Logs," p. 161.

25. Gill, "Whirling Logs," p. 162.

26. Some of the accoutrements of the chantway dramas are described in Leland Clifton Wyman, "A Navajo Medicine Bundle for Shootingway," *Plateau* 44 (1972): 131–49; Leland Clifton Wyman, "Navajo Ceremonial Equipment in the Museum of Northern Arizona," *Plateau* 45 (1972); 17–30.

27. A spectacular quality is not a criterion for ritual drama, of course, nor for that matter for any drama. The Arapaho Pipe-renewing Ritual is not at all spectacular, while its rough equivalent in the Cheyenne Sacred Arrow ceremony is very much so. Given the great importance of these ritual dramas, however, it is not surprising that they are usually elaborate dramatically as well as philosophically.

28. For example, the scale of one dimension measures the strength of the participant's involvement, ranging from observances to rites to ceremonies. Another scale is sociological, noting whether the practice is personal, collective, or institutional and whether it is sanctioned by the people in general, by an official body like a governing council, or by societies or clans. A third scale measures the psychological stance taken by the participant, ranging from an attitude of intense veneration, with a concomitant unwillingness to alter or perhaps even question the ritual practice, to one of prominent self-assertion, as is the case with many shamanistic rituals. A fourth scale might be considered structural in terms of the elaborateness of the presentation, from a personal meditation, to an address to others, to a full-scale dramatic spectacular; it might also be termed structural in terms of its elements: dance, song, impersonation of gods, and so forth. A fifth scale is temporal, covering transitional rituals, such as puberty ceremonies; rituals fixed by some sort of calendar, such as those marking the beginning of the year's fishing or the planting of corn; or those prompted by some crisis afflicting an individual or the community. Whichever of these scales is used for classification, the result will necessarily do some violence to the native ways of looking at the events.

For further discussions of the classification of rituals, see Åke Hultkranz, "Ritual in Native North American Religions," Waugh and Prithipaul, *Native Religious Traditions*, pp. 135–49; William Bascom, "The Forms of Folklore: Prose Narratives," *Journal of American Folklore* 78 (1965): 3–20, on which the preceding comments were largely based.

29. I stress the term *logical* here because I do not want the continuum of events I will discuss to be considered evolutionary or evaluative. It is true that the distribution of shamanistic practices throughout the world's cultures is nearly universal and that its motivations are remarkably similar wherever it is found. It is therefore plausible that shamanism constitutes some fundamental type of religious practice among human beings and thus that shamanism indeed may have influenced the development of certain types of drama. But the attempts of some scholars to trace all theatre to a single source, such as fertility rituals or shamanism, are ill-founded for two reasons. First, they typically ignore cultural heterogeneity, picking and choosing examples far different in time and place as if they were completely interchangeable. Second, they subscribe to the evolutionary fallacy, assuming that apparently simple forms must necessarily occur earlier than apparently complex ones. The common result of the second error is often an implied value judgment that the more superficially complex form is somehow better.

30. Mircea Eliade, *Shamanism: Archaic Techniques of Ecstasy*, translated by Willard R. Trask, Bollingen series, no. 76 (New York: Pantheon, 1964).

31. The medical efficacy of the kind of psychosomatic shamanism discussed here has not been studied in detail from a Western perspective, but the Navajo system, analyzed by a Jungian psychiatrist, offers an intriguing example of what might be done. See Donald Sander, *Navaho Symbols of Healing* (New York: Harvest/Harcourt Brace Jovanovich, 1979).

32. This rather harsh description is unfortunately accurate for the potlatches as they were practiced into the first third of this century, after which time those that governments and churches had not succeeded in banning fell largely into disuse. Recently, however, some have been revived, their more distressing social effects seemingly mitigated, perhaps because they represent a cultural center that the entire people may rally around in these times of renewed interest in traditional ways. See, for example, the stunning record by Peter L. MacNair, "Kwakiutl Winter Dances," *Stones, bones & skin, artscanada* 184–87 (Dec. 1973–Jan. 1974): 94–114. These dramas underscore the warning early in this chapter that generalizations about Native American cultures are treacherous; the core of religiosity and respect that so characterizes many of the dramatic events discussed here, such as the Navajo sings, has virtually disappeared from these Northwest Coast performances, although in some cases the social purposes are still served.

33. Alice Henson Ernst, *The Wolf Ritual of the Northwest Coast* (Eugene: University of Oregon Press, 1952).

34. MacNair, "Kwakiutl Winter Dances"; Franz Boas, *Kwakiutl Ethnography*, edited by Helen Codere (Chicago: Chicago University Press, 1966).

35. This survey was compiled principally from information supplied in personal communication by Hanay Geiogamah, Linda Carol Walsh Jenkins, and Ed Wapp, Jr., "Native American Performance," *Drama Review* 20 (1976): 12. Further information may be found in my introduction to *New Native American Drama*, the introduction to *Seven Plays from the American Indian Theatre*, edited and with an introduction by Hanay Geiogamah (Norman: University of Oklahoma Press, at press), and Geiogamah's Ph.D. dissertation in progress on the history of recent Native American theatre (Indiana University, Bloomington).

36. *Body Indian*, *Foghorn*, and *49* are available in Geiogamah *New Native American Drama*; *Changer*, *Yanowis*, *Skins*, *Na Haaz Zaan*, *Black Butterflies*, *Under the Sweet Gum Bridge* and *Coon Cons Coyote* in Geiogamah, *Seven Plays*.

37. These matters are discussed at length in my introduction to Geiogamah, *New Native American Drama*, and in my article "I was a Critic for Custer: On Recognizing a Traditional Aesthetic in the Contemporary Native American Theatre" (in press, the *American Quarterly*).

BIBLIOGRAPHY

General Studies

Alexander, Hartley Burr. "For an Indian Theatre." *Theatre Arts Monthly* 10 (1926): 191–202. A surprisingly Procrustean effort to put all drama into "four great styles" (Forest, Plains, Northwest, and Southwest) by this philosopher-turned-ethnographer, who is otherwise the author of several sensitive and illuminating works on Native Americans.

Austin, Mary Hunter. "A New Medium for Poetic Drama." *Theatre Arts Magazine* 1 (1917): 62–66. A romanticized suggestion about Indian models for drama.

———. "Gesture in Primitive Drama." *Theatre Arts Monthly* 11 (1927): 594–605. A patronizing dismissal of the drama of "your true primitive," which finds real drama beginning when words supersede other theatrical media as means of expression.

———. "Primitive Stage Setting." *Theatre Arts Monthly* 12 (1928): 49–59. With her customary fixation on Greek theatre as the first original drama, Austin sees the setting for Native American dramatic rituals as merely suggestive, not representational, and thus low on a supposed evolutionary scale.

Cook, Charles Weldon. *The Development of American Indian Ritual Drama As Evidenced by the Hopi and Zuni Indians of the Southwestern United States*. Ph.D. diss., New York University, 1975. Microfilm edition, Ann Arbor, Mich.: University Microfilms, 1977. Assuming the debatable correctness of an evolutionary model, Cook claims that Hopi and Zuni drama has never become "true drama" and suggests that the element of "secularization" of ritual into drama was the audience. Weak in theory, strong in history, especially when analyzing archeological evidence of early kiva stagings.

Fletcher, Alice Cunningham. "Indian Ceremonies." *Papers of the Peabody Museum of Archeology and Ethnology, Harvard University* 31 (1883): 260–333. A pioneering study, understandably general and dated.

Geiogamah, Hanay (Kiowa). *New Native American Drama: Three Plays*. Introduction by Jeffrey F. Huntsman. Norman: University of Oklahoma Press, 1980. The first collection ever published of plays by a Native American.

———. ed. *Six Plays from the American Indian Theatre*, introduction by Hanay Geiogamah. Norman: University of Oklahoma Press, at press. Six plays by seven different playwrights, written between 1972 and 1982.

Heath, Virginia S. "Dramatic Elements in American Indian Ceremonials." *University Studies* (University of Nebraska) 14 (1914): 377–415. Perhaps the earliest attempt to treat Native American performances as drama.

Huntsman, Jeffrey Forrest. "I was a Critic for Custer: On Recognizing a Traditional Aesthetic in the Contemporary Native American Theatre." Under revision for the *American Quarterly*. An investigation of the difficulties posed by Native American plays for Anglo critics, based on the published reviews of performances by the Native American Theatre Ensemble, 1972–1976.

James, Marjorie Pauline. "Dramatic Elements in Native American Indian Rituals, with Specific Reference to the Northwest, Plains, and Southwest Areas." Master's thesis, University of Southern California, 1935. A general work badly marred by preconceived notions about the "origin" of drama and spurious correspondences with Greek mystery rituals.

Jenkins, Charles. "The Dance-Drama of the American Indians and Its Relations to the Folk Narrative." *Lambda Alpha: Journal of Man* 1.2 (1969): 23–39. Sees three types (entertainment dance, ritual dance, dance drama), with differing amounts of narration and ritual. Concludes that the dance-drama is an integral part of the aesthetic complex, the "visual expression of the folk literature."

Jenkins, Linda Carol Walsh. "The Performances of Native Americans as American Theatre." Ph.D. diss., University of Minnesota, 1975. Microfilm edition, Ann Arbor, Mich.: University Microfilms, 1976. A pathfinding work that documents the poor or nonexistent treatment of Native American drama in general histories of drama and supplies a general bibliography on the drama of the peoples of the High Plains, Northwest Coast, and Plateau and of Alaska. The dramas of the Oglala Lakota are examined in detail, especially the Horse Drama of Black Elk. Diffuse in the survey chapters but clear and interesting elsewhere.

———— and Wapp, Ed, Jr. (Comanche/Mesquaki). "Native American Performance," *Drama Review* 20 (1976): 12. A short and underdocumented but informative précis, clearly and sensitively written.

Karter, M. Joshua. *The Dynamic between the Individual and the Community in Selected Native American Performances.* Ph.D. diss., New York University, 1979. Microfilm edition, Ann Arbor, Mich.: University Microfilms, 1979. Study of Ghost Dance and Northern Ute Sun Dance by a student of drama, not a Native American, influenced by the work of Richard Schechner. Sometimes naive but often provocative, especially in attempts to parallel traditional communities and the "new tribalism" of the 1960s.

Kirby, E[rnest] T[heodore]. "The Shamanistic Origins of Popular Entertainments." *The Drama Review* 18.3 (1974): 5–15. A mistaken attempt to trace all drama to shamanism. Also marred by mistakes concerning Plains Contraries, those individuals who, like Lakota Heyoka, for various reasons did the opposite of what was expected, such as "washing" in dust, dressing heavily in the middle of summer, and riding backwards into battle.

————. *Ur-Drama: The Origins of Theatre.* New York: New York University Press, 1975. Drawing examples out of context from theatrical traditions as disjunct as Classical Greek, Sanskrit, Chinese, and Japanese, Kirby's study is further weakened by a superficial understanding of the diverse complex of activities called shamanism, especially with regard to the Native American examples he cites.

Kurath, Gertrude Prokosch. "American Indian Dance in Ritual and Life." *Folklorist* 6 (1961): 428–35, 446–49, 479–82; 7 (1962): 8–11, 41–47, 7–78. Although the author is a pioneering authority in the anthropology of the dance, this article is basically a catalogue of dances and dance-dramas categorized according to some rather superficial designators such as circle dance, scalp dance, visions rites, and so on. Of some use, but with no appreciable analysis.

Menagh, H[arry] Beresford Bateman. *A Study of Primitive Drama: A Study of Navajo Mimicry.* Ph.D. diss., University of Denver, 1962. Microfilm edition, Ann Arbor, Mich.: University Microfilms, 1963. Underlying this study of a variety of types of mimicry, which is very broadly categorized, is a highly questionable assumption that mimicry is the sole origin and criterion of drama. The two articles below are derived from this dissertation.

————. "The Question of Primitive Origins." *Educational Theatre Journal* 15 (1963): 263–40.

————. "A Way of Separating Theatre from Rite." *Educational Theatre Journal* 19 (1967): 117–23.

Postal, Susan Koessler. "Body-Image and Identity. A Comparison of Kwakiutl and Hopi." *American Anthropologist* 67 (1965): 455–62. Traces effects on performance styles of cultural concerns with physical strength or mastery for the Kwakiutl and inner strength or control for the Hopi. Succinct and persuasive.

Specific Topics

Ritual Clowns and Contraries

Basso, Keith Hamilton. *Portraits of "The Whiteman": Linguistic Play and Cultural Symbols among the Western Apache.* New York: Cambridge University Press, 1979. On the function of mimicry

and ridicule in Apache ceremonials in general, and the effect of Anglos on Apache life as
evidenced by their presentation in drama.

Bock, Frank George. *A Descriptive Study of the Dramatic Function and Significance of the Clown during
Hopi Indian Public Ceremony.* Ph.D. diss., University of Southern California, 1971. Microfilm edition, Ann Arbor, Mich.: University Microfilms, 1972. Bock's principal conclusions
as to the sociological and psychological functions of the Hopi clowns are essentially correct:
they are entertainers, disciplinarians, and guides for right conduct. He misunderstands the
depth of their religious purposes, however, and his categorization of the dramatic events into
four types, of which the last, "Proto-Drama," has all the features of drama except "poetry and
philosophy," underestimates the purpose and therefore the power of these sacred actors.

Cazeneuve, Jean. *Les dieux dansent à Cibola: le Shalako des indiens Zuñis.* Paris: Gallimard, 1957. An
overbearing and primitive psychological study of the Zuni Shalako clowns with reference to
their portrayal of violations of the "most powerful taboo of all," incest.

Charles, Lucille Hoerr. "The Clown's Function." *Journal of American Folklore* 58 (1945): 25–34.
This and the following articles are the results of a series of worldwide cross-cultural studies of
"primitive" drama, influenced heavily by Jungian psychology. Among other things, Charles
considers the extremely diverse functions of ritual clowns, including their connection with
shamanistic practices. Because of the farrago of data and the Procrustean effects of her
preconceptions, the articles contribute little to the understanding of Native American dramas in their individual cultural contexts.

––––––. "Growing Up through Drama." *Journal of American Folklore* 59 (1946): 247–62.

––––––. "Regeneration through Drama at Death." *Journal of American Folklore* 61 (1948): 151–74.

––––––. "Drama in First-naming Ceremonies." *Journal of American Folklore* 64 (1951): 11–35.

––––––. "Drama in Shaman Exorcism." *Journal of American Folklore* 66 (1953): 95–122.

Coze, Paul. "Of Clowns and Mudheads." *Arizona Highways* 28, no. 8 (1952): 18–29. Of interest
chiefly for its illustrations.

Fergusson, Erna. *Dancing Gods: Indian Ceremonials of New Mexico and Arizona.* Albuquerque: University of New Mexico Press, 1931. A classic work that, like the following article, underestimates the profound ritual functions of the various sacred clowns.

––––––. "Laughing Priests." *Theatre Arts Monthly* 17 (1933): 657–62.

Makarius, Laura. "Ritual Clowns and Symbolic Behaviour." *Diogenes* 69 (1970): 44–73. Sweeping
and heavy-handed nonsense about the derivation of all ritual power from a violation of blood
taboo. Apparently ignorant of basic studies on Native American ritual clowns and riddled
with errors of fact and interpretation.

Ray, Verne F. "The Contrary Behavior Pattern in American Indian Ceremonialism." *Southwestern
Journal of Anthropology* 1 (1945): 75–113. A catalog of "Plains-type" behavior that shows the
clear historical and functional diversity of clowning among High Plains and Plateau peoples.

Speck, Frank Gouldsmith, and Broom, Leonard. *Cherokee Dance and Drama.* Berkeley and Los
Angeles: University of California Press, 1951. Focuses on the satirical Booger Dance, performed during the late 1920s to the early 1940s by the Big Cove Cherokee, which by
parodying non-Cherokees (including Germans, French, Blacks, Chinese, and other Indians), fostered community solidarity.

Steward, Julian Haynes. "The Ceremonial Buffoon of the American Indian." *Papers of the Michigan
Academy of Science, Art, and Letters* 14 (1930): 187–207. A fairly superficial catalog with
little analysis in depth, by a subscriber to the diffusionist hypothesis.

Tedlock, Barbara. "The Clown's Way." In Dennis Tedlock and Barbara Tedlock, eds., *Teachings
from the American Earth.* New York: Liveright, 1975, pp. 105–18. Perhaps the best short
study of the profound sacred function of the ritual clown in a variety of Native American
ceremonials.

Shamanism

Bahr, Donald M.; Greggorio, Juan; Lopez, David I.; and Alvarez, Albert. *Piman Shamanism and
Staying Sickness (Ká:cim Múmkidag).* Tucson: University of Arizona Press, 1974. A detailed

and illuminating study that derives much of its authority from the involvement of actual practitioners.

Black, A. K. "Shaking the Wigwam." *The Beaver*, Outfit 265 (Dec. 1934): 13–34. An illustrated article on the Ojibway Shaking Tent conjuring performance.

Brodzky, Anne Trueblood, ed. *Stones, bones & skin, artscanada* 184–87 (Dec. 1973–Jan. 1974). A splendid issue devoted chiefly to the visual arts of the shamanistic complex, with superlative scholarly contributions by Peter Furst, Peter L. MacNair, and others.

Burgesse, J. Allan. "The Spirit Wigwam As Described by Tommie Moar, Pointe Bleue [Montagnais]." *Primitive Man* 17, nos. 3–4 (1944): 50–53. One of a series in this issue of brief descriptions of the Shaking Tent conjuring performance across North Central and Eastern North America.

Collier, Donald. "Conjuring among the Kiowa." *Primitive Man* 17, nos. 3–4 (1944): 45–49. On the attributes of the Kiowa performance, with comparisons with other Plains peoples.

Eliade, Mircea. *Shamanism: Archaic Techniques of Ecstasy*, translated by Willard R. Trask. Bollingen Series, no. 76. New York: Pantheon, 1964. The classic study of shamanism, although not wholly congruent with Native American experiences.

Halifax, Joan. *Shamanic Voices: A Survey of Visionary Narratives*. New York: Dutton, 1979. A somewhat idiosyncratic collection of shamanisic texts, including several from living Native North American shamans.

Hallowell, A[lfred] Irving. *The Role of Conjuring in Salteaux Society*. Philadelphia Anthropological Society publications, no. 2. 1942. Facsimile reprint. New York: Octagon, 1971. The most detailed analysis of the Shaking Tent conjuring rite.

Hoffman, Walter James. "Pictography and Shamanistic Rites of the Ojibway." *American Anthropologist* 1 (1888): 209–29. Illustrations of the shamanistic performance.

Hultkranz, Åke. "Spirit Lodge, A North American Shamanistic Seance." In Carl-Martin Edsman, ed., *Studies in Shamanism*, Scripta Instituti Conneraini Aboensis. Stockholm: Almqvist & Wiksell, 1967, Vol. 1, pp. 32–68. The Shaking Tent rite, analyzed by an expert in comparative religion.

————. *De Amerikanska Indianeras Religioner*. Stockholm: Esselte Studium, 1967. *The Religions of the American Indians*, translated by Monica Setterwall. Vol. 7 of *Hermenutics: Studies in the History of Religions*. Berkeley and Los Angeles: University of California Press, 1979. Chapter 6 of this important book by the foremost authority on Native American religion deals with shamans and healers.

Hurt, Wesley Robert, and Howard, James Henri. "A Dakota Conjuring Ceremony." *Southwestern Journal of Anthropology* 8 (1952): 286–96. A complement, on shamanistic conjuring, to the studies of more institutionalized aspects of Dakota religion, as discussed by Black Elk, Joseph Epes Brown, and others cited below.

Kehoe, Thomas F., and Kehoe, Alice Beck. "Stones, Solstices and Sun Dance Structures." *Plains Anthropologist* 22 (1977): 85–95. On the possible alignment with summer solstice phenomena of the Plains Cree (Sasketchewan) Sun Dance, suggesting an astronomical sophistication of these Plains peoples.

La Barre, Weston. *The Ghost Dance: The Origins of Religion*. New York: Doubleday, 1970. A wide-ranging and controversial study, with an extensive bibliography, of many North American religious phenomena, including shamanism, peyotism, and the Ghost Dance.

Leighton, Alexander H., and Leighton, Dorothea Cross. "Gregoria, the Hand Trembler: A Psychological Personality Study of a Navaho Indian." *Papers of the Peabody Museum of Archeology and Ethnology, Harvard University* 40 (1949): 1–177. On the purpose and practice of the shaman-diagnostician in the Navajo curing ceremonials.

Matthews, Washington. "The Prayer of a Navajo Shaman." *American Anthropologist* 1 (1888): 149–71. A text collected by the first great Anglo scholar of the Navajo.

Mico, Paul R. "Navajo Perception of Anglo Medicine." Tuba City, Ariz.: Navajo Health Education Project, 1962. Mimeographed. A fascinating look at Euro-American medicine, which also illuminates our understanding of Navajo medicine.

Park, Willard Zerbe. *Shamanism in Western North America: A Study in Cultural Relationships.* Northwestern University Social Studies, no. 2. 1938. Facsimile reprint. New York: Cooper Square, 1975. A broad basic survey, with the expected limitations deriving from its date and type.

Ray, Verne F. "The Bluejay Character in the Plateau Spirit Dance." *American Anthropologist* 39 (1937): 593–601. An analysis of a widely distributed shamanistic figure.

———. "Historic Backgrounds of the Conjuring Complex in the Plateau and the Plains." In *Language, Culture and Personality: Essays in Memory of Edward Sapir,* edited by Leslie Spier, A. Irving Hallowell, and Stanley S. Newman. 1941. Facsimile reprint. Salt Lake City: University of Utah Press, 1960. Further discussion about Plateau and Plains shamanism.

Stewart, Kenneth M. "Spirit-Possession in Native America." *Southwestern Journal of Anthropology* 2 (1946): 323–39. A catalog of types from North and South America.

Wissler, Clark. "General Discussion of Shamanistic and Dancing Societies." *Anthropological Papers of the American Museum of Natural History* 11 (1916): 853–76. A fundamental study, although lacking thorough discussion.

Areal, National, and Tribal Studies

Plains

Albers, Patrick, and Parker, Seymour. "The Plains Vision Experience: A Study of Power and Privilege." *Southwestern Journal of Anthropology* 27 (1971): 203–33. A useful general survey with emphasis on the sociological function of the vision experience.

American Museum of Natural History. *Anthropological Papers* 16 (1915–1921). A collection of classical anthropological studies by Pliny Earle Goddard, Robert H. Lowie, Alanson Skinner, Leslie Spier, James R. Walker, Wilson Dallam Wallis, and Clark Wissler on the Sun Dance among the Blackfeet, Crow, Dakota, Hidatsa, Kiowa, Shoshone, Ute, and others. Fundamental but dated.

Benedict, Ruth Fulton. "The Vision in Plains Indian Culture." *American Anthropologist* 24 (1922): 1–23. A brief but classic study by a major scholar.

Black Elk (Hehaka Sapa, Lakota). *Black Elk Speaks,* told through John G. Neihardt, 2nd ed. Lincoln: University of Nebraska Press, 1961. A well-known and moving autobiography in which the experience of a great vision and its realization as a dramatic presentation is central.

Brown, Joseph Epes. *The Sacred Pipe: Black Elk's Account of the Seven Rites of the Oglala Sioux.* Norman: University of Oklahoma Press, 1953. Further philosophical teachings of Black Elk, centering on the most sacred rites of the Lakota.

———. *The Spiritual Legacy of the American Indian,* Pendle Hill Pamphlet no. 135. Lebanon, Pa.: Pendle Hill, 1964. This small pamphlet and the following articles provide excellent descriptions of the definition and function of sacred time and sacred space.

———. "The Roots of Renewal." In Walter Holden Capps, ed., *Seeing with a Native Eye: Essays on Native American Religion.* New York: Harper and Row, 1976.

———. "The Immediacy of Mythological Message: Native American Traditions." In Earle H. Waugh and K. Dad Prithipaul, eds., *Native Religious Traditions,* Joint International Symposium of Elders and Scholars, Edmonton, Alberta, 1977, *Sciences Religieuses/Studies in Religion.* Waterloo, Ont.: Wilfrid Laurier University Press for the Corporation Canadienne des Sciences Religieuses/Canadian Corporation for Studies in Religion, 1977, Supplement no. 8, pp. 101–16.

Fletcher, Alice Cunningham. *The Hako: A Pawnee Ceremony.* Assisted by James R. Murie. Music transcribed by Edwin S. Tracy. 22nd Annual Report of the Bureau of American Ethnography, part 2. Washington, D.C.: Government Printing Office, 1904. The classic study of this major Plains ceremonial.

Hoebel, E. Adamson. *The Plains Indians: A Critical Bibliography.* Bloomington: Indiana University Press for the Newberry Library Center for the History of the American Indian, 1977. A useful introductory bibliography, heavily annotated.

Hoover, Herbert Theodore. *The Sioux: A Critical Bibliography.* Bloomington: Indiana University Press for the Newberry Library Center for the History of the American Indian, 1979. Another in the Newberry series, similar to the Hoebel volume.

Jones, Rosalie M. "The Blackfeet Medicine Lodge Ceremony: Ritual and Dance-Drama." Master's thesis, University of Utah, 1968. Useful.

Jorgenson, Joseph Gilbert. *The Sun Dance Religion: Power for the Powerless.* Chicago: University of Chicago Press, 1972. On the shape and function of this ceremonial, newly acquired by the Ute.

Lesser, Alexander. *The Pawnee Ghost Dance Hand Game: Ghost Dance Revival and Ethnic Identity.* Columbia University Contributions to Anthropology, no. 16. 1933. Reprint. Madison: University of Wisconsin Press, 1978. A detailed study of cultural change, centering on a major Pawnee ceremony and its modifications over a century after contact with whites.

Mooney, James. *The Ghost-Dance Religion and the Sioux Outbreak of 1890.* Fourteenth Annual Report of the Bureau of Ethnology to the Secretary of the Smithsonian Institution, 1892–93, Part 2. Washington, D.C.: Government Printing Office, 1896. Reprint. Chicago: University of Chicago Press, 1965. The fundamental study of the Ghost Dance.

Newbery, J.W.E. "The Universe at Prayer." In Earle H. Waugh and K. Dad Prithipaul, eds., *Native Religious Traditions,* Joint International Symposium of Elders and Scholars, Edmonton, Alberta, 1977, *Sciences Religieuses/Studies in Religion.* Waterloo, Ont.: Wilfrid Laurier University Press for the Corporation Canadienne des Sciences Religieuses/Canadian Corporation for Studies in Religion, 1977, Supplement no. 8, pp. 165–78.

Powell, Peter John. *Sweet Medicine: The Continuing Role of the Sacred Arrows, the Sun Dance, and the Sacred Buffalo Hat in Northern Cheyenne History,* 2 vols. Norman: University of Oklahoma Press, 1969. History and description of these important ritual dramas by a sensitive and thorough contemporary scholar.

———. *The Cheyennes, Meꭹheoꭹo's People: A Critical Bibliography.* Bloomington and London: Indiana University Press for the Newberry Library Center for the History of the American Indian, 1980. Another bibliography, longer than most, in the reliable Newberry series.

Spier, Leslie. *The Prophet Dance of the Northwest and its Derivatives: The Source of the Ghost Dance.* Menasha, Wis.: Banta, 1935. Although the Prophet Dance originated in the Northwest, its influence on the development of the Ghost Dance warrants its inclusion in this section.

Northwest Coast

Boas, Franz. *Kwakiutl Ethnography,* edited by Helen Codere. Chicago: University of Chicago Press, 1966. The standard work on the Kwakiutl, encompassing a life's work by one of the major ethnographers of native North America.

Drucker, Philip. *Indians of the Northwest Coast.* Garden City, N.Y.: Natural History Press, 1955. Brilliant and comprehensive.

———. *Cultures of the North Pacific Coast.* San Francisco: Chandler, 1965. Although more popular than the preceding work, still an excellent source.

——— and Heizer, Robert F. *To Make My Name Good: A Reexamination of the Southern Kwakiutl Potlatch.* Berkeley: University of California Press, 1967. A thorough study of the potlatch, its dramatic components and social function.

Ernst, Alice Henson. *The Wolf Ritual of the Northwest Coast.* Eugene: University of Oregon Press, 1952. A long and detailed study of the Makah (Southern Nootka) Klukwalle drama.

Grumet, Robert Steven. *Native Americans of the Northwest Coast: A Critical Bibliography.* Bloomington: Indiana University Press for the Newberry Library Center for the History of the American Indian, 1979. Another fine basic bibliography from the Newberry series.

Jacobs, Melville. *The Content and Style of an Oral Literature: Clackamas Chinook Myths and Tales.* Seattle: University of Washington Press, 1959. Like the following volume, texts and analyses of the script-like narratives of the Clackamas Chinook.

———. *The People are Coming Soon: Analyses of Clackamas Chinook Myths and Tales.* Seattle: University of Washington Press, 1960.

MacNair, Peter L. "Kwakiutl Winter Dances," *Stones, bones & skin, artscanada* 184–87 (Dec. 1973–Jan. 1974): 94–114. A splendid general essay with many photographs of a recreated Kwakiutl Winter Dance.

Southwest

Basso, Keith Hamilton. *Gift of Changing Woman*, Board of American Ethnology Bulletin no. 196. Washington, D.C.: Government Printing Office, 1966. On the function of the Navajo chantways.

Clark, LaVerne Harrell. *They Sang for Horses: The Impact of the Horse on Navajo and Apache Folklore.* Tucson: University of Arizona Press, 1966. On the inclusion of the horse, a recent arrival in North America, in traditional southern Athapaskan rituals.

Dobyns, Henry Farmer, and Euler, Robert Clark. *Indians of the Southwest: A Critical Bibliography.* Bloomington: Indiana University Press for the Newberry Library Center for the History of the American Indian, 1980. An unusually long and thorough introductory bibliography in the Newberry series.

Dockstader, Frederick J. *The Kachina and the White Man: A Study of the Influence of White Culture on the Hopi Kachina Cult.* Cranbrook Institute of Science Bulletin no. 35. Bloomfield Hills, Mich.: Cranbrook Institute of Science, 1954. On the alterations in Hopi kachina impersonations that have occurred since the encroachment of Euro-Americans.

Farrer, Claire Rafferty. *Play and Inter-Ethnic Communication: A Practical Ethnography of the Mescalero Apache.* Ph.D. diss., University of Texas at Austin, 1977. Microfilm edition, Ann Arbor, Mich.: University Microfilms, 1977.

Frisbie, Charlotte Johnson, ed. *Southwestern Indian Ritual Drama*, School of American Research Advanced Seminar series. Albuquerque: University of New Mexico Press, 1980. A splendid collection of essays on various aspects of many Southwest Indian peoples, with an extensive bibliography on the area's ethnography, dramatic rituals, dance, and music.

Gill, Sam[uel] Dale. "A Theory of Navajo Prayer Acts: A Study in Ritual Symbolism." Ph.D. diss., University of Chicago, 1974. A fine theoretical study of Navajo religion by one of the best of the contemporary generation of scholars of the Navajo.

――――――. "The Shadow of a Vision Yonder." In Walter Holden Capps, ed., *Seeing with a Native Eye: Essays on Native American Religion.* New York: Harper and Row, 1976. On the character of the performative power of symbolic representation in Navajo life.

――――――. "Whirling Logs and Coloured Sands." In Earle H. Waugh and K. Dad Prithipaul, eds., *Native Religious Traditions*, Joint International Symposium of Elders and Scholars, Edmonton, Alberta, 1977, *Sciences Religieuses/Studies in Religion.* Waterloo, Ont.: Wilfrid Laurier University Press for the Corporation Canadienne des Sciences Religieuses/Canadian Corporation for Studies in Religion, 1977, Supplement no. 8, pp. 151–63. An analysis of the function of the Whirling Logs dry painting from the Nightway Chant.

――――――. "Native American Religions: A Review Essay." *Religious Studies Review* 5 (1979): 251–58. On the importance of the performance perspective to the understanding of Native American religions.

――――――. *Songs of Life: An Introduction to Navajo Religious Culture*, Iconography of Religions, Section 10, fasc. 3. Leiden, Netherlands: Brill, 1979. A short but perceptive introduction to Navajo religion.

――――――. *Sacred Words: A Study of Navajo Religion and Prayer.* Westport, Conn.: Greenwood, 1981. A penetrating discussion of one aspect of Navajo religion, intended to exemplify the entire complex of Navajo religious beliefs.

Iverson, Peter James. *The Navajos: A Critical Bibliography.* Bloomington: Indiana University Press for the Newberry Library Center for the History of the American Indian, 1976. A useful basic bibliography, although containing more errors and matters of questionable judgment than the typical volume in this series.

King, Jeff; Oakes, Maude; and Campbell, Joseph. *Where the Two Came to their Father. A Navaho War Ceremonial*, Bollingen Series no. 1, 1943. Rev. ed. Princeton: Princeton University Press,

1969. A short but very powerful chantway, distinctive in this edition for its fine reproductions of the dry paintings.

Kluckhohn, Clyde, and Leighton, Dorothea Cross. *The Navaho.* 1946. 2nd rev. ed., edited by Lucy H. Wales and Richard Kluckhohn. Cambridge: Harvard University Press, 1974. The standard general introduction, now dated in some matters but still useful.

_____, and Wyman, Leland Clifton. *An Introduction to Navaho Chant Practice, With an Account of the Behaviours [sic] Observed in Four Chants.* Memoirs of the American Anthropological Association, no. 53. *American Anthropologist* 42, no. 2.2 supplement. Menasha, Wis.: American Anthropological Association, 1940. Although now superseded in several respects by Reichard's *Navaho Religion* and Spencer's *Mythology and Values,* this monograph will still repay reading.

Lamphere, Louise Anne. "Symbolic Elements in Navajo Ritual." *Southwestern Journal of Anthropology* 25 (1969): 279–305. A valuable supplement to Reichard's *Navaho Religion.*

Luckert, Karl W. *The Navajo Hunter Tradition.* Tucson: University of Arizona Press, 1975. On the persistence of ancient hunters' rites in contemporary Navajo practices.

_____. "An Approach to Navajo Mythology," In Earle H. Waugh and K. Dad Prithipaul, eds., *Native Religious Traditions,* Joint International Symposium of Elders and Scholars, Edmonton, Alberta, 1977, *Sciences Religieuses/Studies in Religion.* Waterloo, Ont.: Wilfrid Laurier University Press for the Corporation Canadienne des Sciences Religieuses/Canadian Corporation for Studies in Religion, 1977, Supplement no. 8, pp. 117–31. An attempt, perhaps overly Western in its approach, to explain the Navajos' multiple kinds of historical knowing.

_____. *Coyoteway: A Navajo Holyway Healing Ceremony.* With Johnny C. Cooke, Navajo interpreter. Tucson: University of Arizona Press, 1979. Declared extinct as long ago as 1910, Coyoteway is not one of the more central chantways. This edition, however, is especially valuable for its detailed recording of the full nine-day ceremony, with many photographs of the events and drypaintings.

McAllester, David P., and McAllester, Susan W. *Hogans: Navajo Houses and House Songs.* Middletown, Conn.: Wesleyan University Press, 1980. An illuminating volume, with texts and photographs, that conveys much of the spirit of place centering on the hogan.

Matthews, Washington. *The Night Chant, a Navaho Ceremonial,* Memoirs of the American Museum of National History, no. 6. New York: Knickerbocker, 1902. The Nightway chant is central to Navajo practices and is one of the chantways that employs masked spirit impersonators.

Moon, Sheila E. *A Magic Dwells: A Poetic and Psychological Study of the Navaho Emergence Myth.* Middletown, Conn.: Wesleyan University Press, 1970. A study of the relevance of the Emergence Myth to the development of multiple kinds of psychological and spiritual knowledge in the individual.

Reichard, Gladys Amanda. *Navaho Religion: A Study of Symbolism,* 2 vols. Bollingen Series no. 18. 1950. 2nd ed. New York: Pantheon, 1963. The fundamental work on Navajo religion, now somewhat outdated but yet to be supplanted.

Sander, Donald. *Navaho Symbols of Healing.* New York: Harvest/Harcourt Brace Jovanovich, 1979. A study by a Jungian psychologist of the medical efficacy of Navajo healing practices.

Sekaquaptewa, Emory. "Hopi Indian Ceremonies." In Walter Holden Capps, ed., *Seeing with a Native Eye: Essays on Native American Religion.* New York: Harper and Row, 1976, pp. 35–43. An illuminating explanation of the function of Hopi kachina by a practitioner.

Spencer, Katherine. *Mythology and Values: An Analysis of Navaho Chantway Myths.* Memoirs of the American Folklore Society, Vol. 7. 48. Philadelphia: American Folklore Society, 1957. An examination of the world view and values of the Navajo ceremonies and their function in Navajo life, with synopses of seventeen chantways.

Toelken, J[ohn] Barre. "The 'Pretty Languages' of Yellowman: Genre, Mode, and Texture in the Navaho Coyote Narratives," *Genre* 2 (1969): 211–35. An excellent description of the context and functions of the storytelling performance.

_____. *The Dynamics of Folklore.* Boston: Houghton Mifflin, 1979. An excellent general introduction to folklore, broadly defined, in which Toelken's experiences among the Navajo figure prominently.

Tooker, Elisabeth Jane. "Ritual Power and the Spiritual: A Comparative Study of Indian Religions in Southwestern United States." Ph.D. diss., Radcliffe University, 1958. A useful survey that complements Underhill's *Ceremonial Patterns*.

Underhill, Ruth Murray. *Ceremonial Patterns in the Greater Southwest*, Monographs of the American Ethnological Society, no. 13. 1948. Facsimile reprint. Seattle: University of Washington Press, 1966. A theoretical framework that distinguishes the ritual types of the hunter-gathers (shamanistic rites and vision quests) from those of the farmers (community-centered weather control rituals).

————. *The Navajos*. Civilization of the American Indian series. 1956. Rev. ed. Norman, Okla.: University of Oklahoma Press, 1967. The standard history of the Navajo, recently supplemented by other studies but not wholly superseded.

Witherspoon, Gary Jay. "The Central Concepts of Navajo World View: I." *Linguistics* 119 (1974): 41–59. As the titles suggest, this and the next article comprise overviews of the central organizing principles of Navajo philosophy.

————. "The Central Concepts of Navajo World View: II." *Linguistics* 161 (1975): 69–87.

————. *Language and Art in the Navajo Universe*. Foreword by Clifford Geertz. Ann Arbor: University of Michigan Press, 1977. A sophisticated analysis of the complex Navajo way of conceptualizing the world, centering on the interpenetration of beliefs in metaphysics, epistemology, and aesthetics and the principles of Navajo grammar.

Worth, Sol, and Adair, John. "Navajo Film-Makers." *American Anthropologist* 72 (1970): 9–34. A short, preliminary look at the matters discussed in detail in Worth and Adair, *Through Navajo Eyes*.

————. *Through Navajo Eyes: An Exploration in Film Communication and Anthropology*. Bloomington: Indiana University Press, 1972. An intriguing account of the differing cultural values revealed when Navajos make films about themselves.

Wyman, Leland Clifton. *Blessingway*. Tucson: University of Arizona Press, 1970. Perhaps the most significant of the Navajo chantways, recorded in three versions by Berard Haile.

————, ed. *Beautyway: A Navaho Ceremonial*. Recorded and translated by Berard Haile and Maude Oakes. With the Beautyway text in Navajo, told by Singer Man. Bollingen Series no. 53. New York: Bollingen Foundation, 1957. A central chantway in an authoritative edition, with illustrations of the sand paintings.

Woodland

Blau, Harold. "Function and False Face: A Classification of Onondaga Masked Ritual and Themes." *Journal of American Folklore* 79 (1966): 564–80. Especially interesting for his discussion of the power of the masks, which may be compared with similar effects on the kachina impersonators of the Southwest.

Fenton, William N. *An Outline of Seneca Ceremonials at Coldspring Longhouse*. Yale University Publications in Anthropology, no. 9. New Haven: Yale University Press, 1936. A classification and preliminary analysis of the major Seneca ceremonies.

————. "Seneca Eagle Dance: A Study of Personality Expression in Ritual." Ph.D. diss., Yale University, 1937. A detailed analysis of this major Seneca ritual complex.

————. "The Seneca Society of Faces." *Scientific Monthly* 44 (1937): 215–38. An important description of the False Face masks among the Seneca.

————. "Masked Medicine Societies of the Iroquois." Smithsonian Institution Report for 1940, Publication 3624. Washington, D.C.: Smithsonian Institution, 1941, pp. 397–429. An important description of the Iroquois False Face masks, complementing his earlier Seneca study.

————. *The Iroquois Eagle Dance: An Offshoot of the Calument Dance*. Bulletin of the Bureau of American Ethnology no. 156. Washington, D.C.: Government Printing Office, 1953. A thorough description of the rites and texts of the Eagle Society.

Hallowell, A[lfred] Irving. "Bear Ceremonialism in the Northern Hemisphere." *American Anthropologist* 28 (1926): 1–175. An extensive monograph on the rituals surrounding the bear in a variety of northern Indian peoples.

Hoffman, Walter James. "The Midéwiwin; or 'Grand Medicine Society' of the Ojibwa." United States Bureau of American Ethnology, 7th Annual Report, 1885–1886. Washington, D.C.: Government Printing Office, 1891, pp. 143–300. The classic study of the greatest of the Ojibway rituals.

Landes, Ruth. *Ojibway Religion and the Midéwiwin*. Madison: University of Wisconsin Press, 1968. A modern study, updating Hoffman's.

Radin, Paul. *The Road of Life and Death: A Ritual Drama of the American Indians*. Foreword by Mark Van Doren. Bollingen Series no. 5. New York: Pantheon, 1945. An elaborate drama, unfortunately lacking its songs, of the Great Medicine Rite of the Winnebago.

Speck, Frank Gouldsmith. *A Study of the Delaware Indian Big House Ceremony*. Publications of the Pennsylvania Historical Commission, no. 2. Harrisburg: Pennsylvania Historical Commission, 1931. A major investigation of the central ritual of the Delaware.

―――――. *Oklahoma Delaware Ceremonies, Feasts and Dances*. American Philosophical Society Memoir no. 7. Philadelphia: American Philosophical Society, 1937. An attempt to reconstruct early Delaware ceremonies from information supplied by Delawares now living in Oklahoma.

―――――. *Midwinter Rites of the Cayuga Long House*. Philadelphia: University of Pennsylvania Press, 1949. A major study of the central ceremonies of the Cayuga.

Tanner, Helen Hornbeck. *The Ojibwas: A Critical Bibliography*. Bloomington: Indiana University Press for the Newberry Library Center for the History of the American Indian, 1976. Another reliable volume in the very useful Newberry series.

Tooker, Elisabeth Jane. "Ethnometaphysics of Iroquois Ritual." In *Symbols and Society: Essays on Belief Systems in Action*. Edited by Carole E. Hill. Southern Anthropological Society Proceedings, no. 9. Athens, Ga.: University of Georgia Press for the Southern Anthropological Society, 1975, pp. 103–16. On the cultural pervasiveness of ritual practices.

―――――. *The Iroquois Ceremonial of Midwinter*. Syracuse, N.Y.: Syracuse University Press, 1970. A thorough analysis, with a useful review of previous historical accounts of this important ritual.

―――――. *Indians of the Northeast: A Critical Bibliography*. Bloomington: Indiana University Press for the Newberry Library Center for the History of the American Indian, 1978. Another in the Newberry series, covering the people originally living in the area from North Carolina to Newfoundland and from the Atlantic seaboard to the Upper Great Lakes.

Other Works Cited

Beck, Julian. *The Life of the Theatre*. San Francisco: City Lights Books, 1972.

Simpson, Richard, with Enos, Lizzie. *Ooti: A Maidu Legacy*. Millbrae, Calif.: Celestial Arts, 1977.

Sprout, Gilbert M. *Scenes and Studies of Savage Life*. London: Smith, Elder, 1868.

Wicker, Brian. "Ritual and Culture: Some Dimensions of the Problem Today." In James D. Shaughnessy, ed., *The Roots of Ritual*. Grand Rapids, Mich.: Eerdmans, 1973, pp. 13–45.

15

Polish-American Theatre

ARTHUR LEONARD WALDO

Like the first English settlers in 1607 in Jamestown, Virginia, the non-English people who came to the United States later were faced, first and foremost, with the need to survive, leaving little time for intellectual activities. Perhaps the problem was worse for the later immigrants, who, if they had no knowledge of English, were tossed into a totally strange and hostile environment. Before the curtain is raised on the history of the Polish theatre in America, it is necessary to understand the background of the Polish immigrants who arrived in a massive stream from 1850 to 1914. Some knowledge of their social status in Poland as well as in the United States is necessary to facilitate an evaluation of the efforts and achievements of these immigrants.

THE POLISH IMMIGRATION

At the turn of the century there were 2 million Polish immigrants in the United States; by 1914 the number had grown to 4 million. Some historians and writers have claimed that these immigrants were almost all peasants, most of them illiterate, some of them so ignorant that only after arriving in this country did they learn that they were Polish.

However, these same immigrants constructed thousands of Polish churches and parochial schools, organized fraternal societies, formed and directed bands and orchestras, and opened small businesses such as butcher shops, groceries, restaurants, shoe stores, barbershops, and saloons. They published and supported 120 Polish newspapers, including 12 dailies, published and bought Polish books by the thousands, and supported over 50 Polish theatres. In the face of these accomplishments, can writers still claim that the immigration from Poland to America consisted of peasants only?

Poland has, of course, always been an agrarian country. Between 1850 and 1914 its population consisted of approximately 80 percent farmers and 20 percent city dwellers.[1] In America Polish farmers as well as Polish city dwellers settled in the cities. Although farmers made up about the same percentage of the population here as in the homeland—about 80 percent—their presence in American cities created an illusion that all immigrants from Poland were farmers.

Soon, however, these former farmers won for themselves a new position in the urban Polish-American community. The city style of life and cultural interests, including the theatre, were gradually injected into their lives by city-bred and educated Poles, who became the leaders and instructors of their less-educated countrymen from the farm, helping them to abandon their past status.[2] Thus to continue to refer to them as "farmers" is inaccurate.

Referring to them as "peasants" is also incorrect because they had been enfranchised in Poland in 1791, when the Polish parliament ratified the May Third Constitution, granting equal rights to all, abolishing serfdom, and reducing the power of King Stanislas August to that of a figurehead.

This period of democracy was short-lived, however. The neighboring empires of Germany, Austria, and Russia invaded Poland, partitioning its lands among themselves, so that by 1795 Poland had totally disappeared from the map as an independent nation. Under their foreign rulers, the Poles experienced oppression of the worst kind. The Polish language was forbidden; Germanization and Russification of the Polish population was followed; landowners were sometimes forced to abandon their land; and in Germany extermination of Poles was introduced.[3]

Unable to cope with the political and economic harassment, a group of Poles migrated from German-controlled Poland to the United States in 1821. Arriving individually in the preselected city of Baltimore, they formed a Polish quarter there. In 1854 the first organized group of about 150 persons arrived from Pomerania (also German Poland) and founded the new town of Panna Maria in Texas. From then on, immigrants from all parts of Poland arrived individually, settling everywhere from the east coast to St. Louis, with some reaching California.

America was cruel to immigrants in the 1850s. Many died of hunger in the streets of New York and Chicago, committed suicide, or returned to the countries they had come from. Lack of knowledge of English being their greatest obstacle, university and high school graduates from Europe were forced to accept work as laborers and other menials. Without labor unions, there was no protection of any kind. Harassed, overworked, underpaid, immigrants from Poland nevertheless undertook the construction of their first wooden churches, Polish schools, and social halls and formed societies of various kinds.

NATIONAL ORGANIZATIONS

By 1870 the number of Polish societies in American cities was so great that their leaders began to plan the foundation of national organizations. In 1873 the Polish Roman Catholic Union of America was formed, followed in 1880 by the Polish National Alliance of America, the largest Polish organization in the

United States today. Both were fraternal organizations. In 1898 the Polish Women's Alliance of America was established.

Earlier, in 1887, the Polish Falcons of America, an outgrowth of the Polish Falcons of Poland, had become a reality. This group was part of a worldwide Polish resistance movement that began in 1867 in Lvov in the Austrian part of Poland. The Falcons trained young men in physical fitness and as soldiers, preparing them for battle against the oppressors of Poland. This movement explains the long and constant stream of young men between seventeen and twenty years of age who emigrated from Poland, for the Falcons encouraged young men to leave for America before becoming old enough to be drafted into the occupying armies. Fighting in World War I on the French front, the Falcon Battle Force was a self-sustaining Polish-American army one hundred thousand strong. When the war ended, Poland was proclaimed free after 123 years of triple occupation. The mutual war effort united all classes of Polish immigrants in the United States. Those who had emigrated from a Poland that was enslaved and oppressed by Germans, Russians, and Austrians now knew full well that they were Polish.

EARLY DRAMATIC EFFORTS IN THE UNITED STATES

It is impossible to be certain when or where an amateur circle of early immigrants presented the first Polish dramatic play. However, Polish immigrants, in addition to building churches, schools, and halls and establishing various societies, formed dramatic circles. The latter became a source of income, helping to pay off parish mortgages. Comedy musicals were the best moneymakers. The plays were selected by the members of these dramatic circles, which consisted of immigrants who had been born and reared in the cities of Poland, some of whom had good amateur stage experience. Later, professional stock companies were formed. Both efforts, amateur and professional, had serious social and patriotic missions.

Although the first Polish monthly magazine, *Poland*, was published in English as early as 1841 by playwright and poet Paul Sobolewski, most other early cultural activities, including theatre, were conducted in Polish. Before the formation of amateur theatres, patriotic and religious military groups were organized. These groups would appear every Sunday at High Mass in full Polish cavalry regalia and put on a show, parading inside or around the church, leading processions of the clergy and the faithful. Their presence in Polish parishes preserved patriotism and influenced the production of Polish plays. The youngest members appeared later in staged battle scenes in historical plays, serving as reminders that the freedom of Poland must be restored.

Since religion brought the Poles together, early amateur Polish plays were produced in parish halls, either in a basement with windows near the ceiling, or in the parochial school hall. In Milwaukee the Poles of St. Stanislas Parish established the first Polish school in 1868, purchasing a two-story building adjacent to the church. One floor could be used for a hall, and it is possible that the first Polish amateur play was presented in this hall. Obituaries of early parishioners often mention the deceased's dedication to stage acting.[4]

At first there were no permanent drama groups. Polish societies would present plays, selecting from among their members the most suitable persons for each play. Many of these early societies had military names: Towarzystwo Gwiazda Wolnosci (Society of the Star of Freedom), Towarzystwo Kosciuszki (General Kosciuszko Society), Towarzystwo Jana III Sobieskiego (Society of King John III Sobieski), and Towarzystwo Gwardii Pulaskiego (Pulaski's Guard Society).

When amateur theatrical circles were first organized, their plays were usually patriotic; some with military themes were *Kosciuszko w Ameryce* (Kosciuszko in America); *Kosciuszko w Petersburgu* (Kosciuszko in Petersburg); *Kosciuszko pod Raclawicami* (Kosciuszko at Raclawice); *Gwiazda Syberii* (Star of Siberia); *Pochod z Pochodniami* (The Torch Parade); *Ogniem i Mieczem* (With Fire and Sword), based on Henryk Sienkiewicz's novel *Umieram za Ojczyzne* (I Die for My Country), and *Major Psianoga* (Major the Terrible). These plays were interspersed with others having civilian patriotic themes, such as *Woz Drzymaly* (Drzymala's Wagon), by Joseph Raczkowski, and *Wanda, Kobieta Doskonala* (Wanda, the Perfect Woman), adapted from the English by Sobolewski.[5]

IMMIGRANT THEATRE IN THE LATE 1800s

Theofilia Samolinska

By 1890 the Polish amateur theatre in the United States was well developed and popular. Polish drama societies had been active in Chicago since 1873; in New York since 1876; in Winona, Minnesota, since 1885; in Brooklyn, Pittsburgh, Philadelphia, Grand Rapids, and Milwaukee since 1886; in St. Paul since before 1886; and in Buffalo and Detroit since 1889.

Karol Estreicher of Lvov, a well-known historian of literature and theatre, visited America and, after attending many amateur performances, wrote an essay, "The Polish Theater beyond the Ocean."[6] He devoted the most space to Polish theatrical activities in Chicago. The main attraction in Chicago was Theofilia Samolinska (1848–1913), who dominated the amateur stage like a professional.

Known as the Nightingale of Polonia, Samolinska often staged musicals in which she played the leading lady, and when she sang in her beautiful soprano voice, she had no equal. She organized a number of drama, song, and dance circles, and also women's societies that led to the establishment of the Polish Women's Alliance of America. A staunch fighter for women's rights, she became a speaker, writer, poet, actress, and true leader. In 1880 she won first prize in a drama contest in Warsaw for her play *Three Floras*. To propagate women's rights she wrote a four-act drama, *Emancipation of Women*.

Emigrating from Poznań (German Poland) soon after the Polish uprising of 1863, Samolinska had settled in Cincinnati in 1866 and organized the first

Polish dramatic circle there. Although only eighteen, she had had an excellent education. Early in life she had studied music (piano) and singing and had also mastered a number of languages. "She was very aristocratic in her manners," recalled attorney Julius Smietanka of Chicago, who had known her well, "but kept everyone at ease by her friendly, even motherly attitude."[7] Estreicher says of her,

When a young and pretty Samolinska charms her audience with her artistry, spectators leap to the stage and kiss her hands until the happily overcome actress sheds real tears (as happened in the operetta *Slowik* in 1885).[8]

Besides the plays mentioned previously, Samolinska's circle and other late-nineteenth-century dramatic societies presented Samolinska's *Emancipation of Women; Mieszczuch Szlachcicem* (An Urbanite Nobleman), a translation from Molière; *Wieslaw*, by A. Ladnowski; *Chlopi Arystokraci* (Farmers, the Aristocrats), by Wladislas L. Anczyc; *Zbojcy* (The Robbers), a translation from Schiller; *Lobzowianie* (People of Lobzow), by Anczyc; *Karpaccy Gorale* (Carpathian Mountaineers), by Joseph Korzeniowski; *Flisacy* (The Raftsmen), by Anczyc; *Szewc Arystokrata* (Cobbler, the Aristocrat), by Cichowicz; *Cyrulik ze Zwierzynca* (Barber of the Zwierzyniec Suburb); *Concilium Facultatis*, by Count J. Alexander Fredro; and *Dwie Sieroty* (Two Orphans), by Szczesny Zahajkiewicz, translated into English by Samolinska.

Other Performers and Playwrights in Chicago

Although Estreicher indicates that many more plays were presented in Chicago, including several written by local talent, he fails to give the names of the other local playwrights. He does mention many intellectuals among the Chicago Poles. He also mentions Francis Gryglaszewski, W. Tesmer, Roman Stobiecki, Wladyslaw Zawadski, Antoni Mikitynski, and J. Grzeszkowski, all prominent in the Chicago Polish community, as the best male actors and Wendzinska, the wife of a newspaper publisher; Doroszynska; Grzeszkowska; and Oslowska, the new operetta soprano, as the best female performers.

The earliest organizer of high-level plays and performances was Szczesny Zahajkiewicz (Shchensny Zahoykeveech, 1861–1917). A St. Stanislas Parish school teacher, Zahajkiewicz came to Chicago in 1889, recommended by Poland's Prince John Cardinal Puzyna of Lvov as a top educator, poet, playwright, novelist, stage director, organizer, and altogether ideal cultural leader. Zahajkiewicz had written and published a few monthlies in Lvov, where he also taught in the famous Piramowicz School of Intellect. His dramas include *Dzieci Izraela* (Children of Israel), *Jasna Gora* (Czestochowa Monastery), *Ksiaze Czarnoksieznikow* (Prince of the Wizards), *Powrot Taty* (Father's Return), *Niespodzianka* (Surprise), *Dzieci Wdowy* (Widow's Children), *Dwie Sieroty* (Two Orphans), and *Smorgonska Akademia* (Bear Training School at Smorgon).

Helene Modjeska

Helena Modjeska (1840–1909), world-famous tragedienne, performed many times in Chicago. She held Zahajkiewicz in high esteem and in 1892 made his dream come true by agreeing to appear in two consecutive Polish plays with his dramatic circle. Both performances were held at the St. Stanislas Parish high school auditorium. On Sunday, August 27, Modjeska appeared in *Chłopi Arystokraci*. As Kogucina, she unquestionably stole the show.

Later, Emil Habdank-Dunikowski, a Lvov University professor who toured Polish settlements in America, wrote of her performance as Kogucina in his book *Wsrod Polonii w Ameriyce* (Among the Poles in America).

My day . . . ended in a way that raised my pleasure to heights hardly possible to comprehend. I actually attended our Modjeska's Polish performance! It was arranged by Zahajkiewicz for a charitable cause and took place at the Academic Auditorium, located next to the St. Stanislas church on Noble Street. It is a two-story structure with a theater auditorium on the ground floor and a balcony with seats constructed amphitheatrically. The curtain has a colorful painting, a replica of the well-known historical canvas called "Persecution of the Podlasian Unitarians." So in this auditorium of four thousand seating capacity I admired our Modjeska not in a role of Ophelia, Mary Stuart, or Lady Macbeth, but . . . guess . . . in a part of Lady Kogucina in a play *Farmers, the Aristocrats!* It was a feast for our eyes and ears to see and hear this famous Shakespearian actress step down from the cothurnus of the classics to a role of this musical comedy's cocky and drunk Kogucina! And as it was almost impossible to believe, she did step down and she acted. . . . How? Well, acted just like Modjeska. Perfect! She simply had to be heard singing with her indomitable verve the song:

> I will drink all day,
> I will wash myself in arrack,
> For dinner goose everyday;
> And I hear people cry:
> Vivat, Lady Kogucina!

She charmed and captivated us completely. Of course we rushed to the stage with compliments, thanks, tears, showering her with flowers and with more flowers. The rest of the players simply did what they could in the presence of that kind of competition.[9]

On September 12 Modjeska appeared in Zahejkiewicz's drama *Jadwiga, Krolowa Lechitow* (Jadwiza, the Queen of Poland). *Dziennik Chicagoski* (Chicago Polish Daily) covered the performance in an unusual article.

St. Stanislas Auditorium was in a state of siege last night. Over six thousand people came to see Modjeska. All aisles were packed, with crowds standing inside the auditorium as well as in the street, watching the performance through the windows. When the performance ended, no one left. Endless applause greeted the star, and eventually, the author. He came upon the stage with the script in his hand. With great effort he quieted the audience, and finally said: "After such a magnificent performance no one else should ever portray the heroine of this play. In a tribute to Madame Modjeska, I tear up my manuscript." And he actually tore it up into shreds and tossed the pieces from left to right over the audience. The standing public in the front rows momentarily disappeared, fishing out from the floor the manuscript pieces to save them as souvenirs of the most bewitching night they ever witnessed.[10]

Casimir Kaminski in Chicago

Modjeska's success in Chicago became so renowned in Poland that in the middle of May 1893 the twenty-eight-year-old idol of Warsaw theatres, Casimir Kaminski (1865–1928), came to Chicago with the hope of organizing a company of actors and continuing the theatre for the Chicago Poles. He did not understand, however, that American Poles always linked their entertainment with some practical aim, such as raising funds for a new school or church. Low wages necessitated low admission prices, and if the goal was to pay off some public mortgage, not much was left to cover the production's expenses. Amateur actors dipped into their own pockets to pay the bills themselves, and at times the most popular female player would step out into the audience to propose a collection for expenses.

The amateur actors had never been paid for dramatic appearances, and they worked at other jobs for a living. Kaminski arrived in Chicago with the intention of making stage work pay. To his chagrin, however, no one was willing to seek a professional career on the stage. Those who had regular employment would not risk quitting work for the sake of the stage.

The disappointed Kaminski would have returned to Warsaw, but he ran short of money. So Zahajkiewicz, city treasurer Peter Kiolbasa, and a group of the best amateur actors agreed to put on two one-act plays from Kaminski's repertoire, *Maz od Biedy* (Husband of Last Choice), by Joseph Blizinski, and *Lorenzo i Jessyka* (Lorenzo and Jessica), by Lucjan Kwiecinski. Kaminski's friends invested their own money for rental of the hall, publicity, and distribution of leaflets and presented Kaminski to the public on June 27, 1893. Kaminski later wrote:

The artistic and financial success of my guest performance in Chicago passed all my expectations. It was a good cast of talented actors and actresses. All played well. The large St. Stanislas Auditorium was filled to capacity, and I, after expenses, left the auditorium with four hundred dollars in my pocket.[11]

Peter Kiolbasa offered Kaminski a position in the treasury office if he would dedicate his talent to the development of the Polish theatre in Chicago, but Kaminski refused and left for Warsaw. Soon after his return, he was named manager of the government-subsidized Polish Theatre in St. Petersburg.

THE BEGINNINGS OF PROFESSIONAL THEATRE: CHICAGO

Years of amateur performances in the late nineteenth century brought about a gradual maturing of the Polish theatre, leading eventually to its evolution into professional theatre. Although New York, Detroit, Buffalo, and Cleveland had Polish drama societies, Chicago led the movement toward professionalism.

When Helena Modjeska appeared in two of his plays in Chicago, Zahajkiewicz became the prince of Polish drama. For many years he collaborated with Stanislas Szwajkart (1857–1918), a high school teacher, musician, writer, and poet born in Tarnopol, who contributed essays and poems to Polish newspapers, gave piano lessons, and taught at the St. Stanislas Parish high school. After he came to Chicago in 1881, Szwajkart devoted himself to Polish cultural activity, his dream being that he would one day present Polish plays on American stages.

Meanwhile, Karol H. Wachtl (1879–1944) arrived in Chicago to become editor of *Narod Polski*, having studied law and medicine in Poland and served as an editor of the *Catholic Weekly* in Lasalle, Illinois. In Chicago he joined Zahajkiewicz and Szwajkart in forming the Teatr Polski, which included the best talents of the local dramatic societies. Szwajkart proposed that they pool finances and present a good Polish play in a downtown theatre. Every second Sunday afternoon they would present a quality dramatic production, either in the Garrick Theater or in the Whitney Opera House. Admission would range from a dollar to twenty-five cents, with tickets available at the John B. Bardonski drugstore. Fifty of the best performers in Chicago were lined up. Although none of the three organizers had had any theatrical experience in Poland, they had seen many of the best performances there and knew the characteristics of a good show. Szwajkart was chosen to direct the plays.

These plays brought diversity in singing and dancing, costumes, customs, and ways of life to future American generations. However, this theatre effort was still not actually professional; although admission was charged, the performers were not paid. Zahajkiewicz, Szwajkart, and Wachtl thought all Polish national, artistic, and civic work should be performed gratis. Small wonder—all three were poets.

THADDEUS DOLEGA-EMINOWICZ: PROFESSIONAL THEATRE AT LAST

A professional actor of great dedication saved the Polish-American theatre in the opening decade of the century by changing it from amateur to professional status and, for the first time, paying actors for their work. This actor was Thaddeus Dolega-Eminowicz. He established two professional theatres in Chicago, one in Milwaukee, one in Cleveland, two in Detroit, and two in Buffalo. One of the Detroit theatres, specially constructed for Polish plays, was the scene of his death at the age of thirty-five. Eminowicz lived in the United States for ten years. Like a missionary, he moved from one city to another, opened a professional theatre, named a manager, and as soon as the theatre's business was established, transferred the contract to the manager of the company under the condition that Polish plays would continue daily, and moved on. Not surprisingly, he became known as the father of the Polish-American professional theatre.

This wizard of the Polish theatre was a scion of the Krakow aristocracy.[12] He was born on October 17, 1882, to a very wealthy and distinguished family, established as nobility as early as the thirteenth century. After finishing college, Thaddeus scandalized the family by entering the dramatic school of Knake-Zawadski in Krakow. A month later he was added to the school's regular stock company and was soon appearing regularly in important roles in known dramas, farces, and, once his tenor voice was discovered, musical comedies.

Believing that army service would put an end to his son's theatrical ambitions, in 1905 Thaddeus's father had him drafted into the Austrian army. With his education, however, only one year of service was required, and because he came from an influential family, his presence in army quarters could be sporadic and his service superficial. He spent more time with Zawadzki's theatre than with the army. In 1906–1907 Zawadski's theatre went on the road, giving Thaddeus complete dramatic experience. Late in 1907 Thaddeus, who had been left a sizable monthly allowance after the death of his father in 1906, went to America.

He arrived during a national economic crisis, when many Poles were returning to Poland. Under the circumstances he was unable to carry out his original plan of opening a drama school. He met with Zahajkiewicz and Wachtl, who were still putting on charity shows for various causes, and proposed that they organize the Kolko Mîlosnikow Sceny (Circle of Stage Lovers). The circle would include the best amateur talents, who would hold a regular workshop without paying any dues.

After attending several amateur performances, Eminowicz selected a number of men and women, invited them to a meeting held on Sunday, September 6, 1908, and thus formed the Circle of Stage Lovers. Those present resolved that the circle would put on plays already known to the members under Eminowicz's direction. The first three plays—Zbojcy (The Robbers), by Schiller; Hulaj Dusza (Reveler), by Adolf Walewski; and Tanten (The Other), by Gabriella Zapolska—were presented during January 1909.

Dziennik Zwiazkowy (Polish Alliance Daily), published by the Polish National Alliance of America, wrote of the circle:

The Circle of Stage Lovers has won our admiration. In an unbelievably short time it presented three perfect stage productions. The talent of the entire troupe under the direction of Thaddeus Eminowicz radiated best in the play Tanten. Its effect on the public was tremendous. The entire audience found itself in tears a number of times. We finally have a real Polish theater. The ice has been broken.[13]

The circle members included a talented amateur character actress, Maria Streicher, and to Eminowicz's surprise, three persons who had studied drama in Poland: Stanislawa Dobrosielska, Wanda Chonarzewska, and August Zukowski. Like Streicher, Chonarzewska was a talented character actress; Dobrosielska was a perfect ingenue. Others in the circle included two noblemen, Count Wiktor

15.1 Charter members of the Circle of Stage Lovers, 1908. Top row from left to right: W. Nowierski, Waclaw Dolski, Count Wiktor Gorajski, Aleksander Droszcz, August Zukowski. Second row: Leonard Schmidt-Piatkiewicz (holding hat), Stanislaw Jachimski, Stefania Hareska (later Eminowicz), Stanislaw Kajkowski, Anna Demeter, Wladyslaw Brzozowski, Maria Rutkowska, Norbert Wicki. Sitting: Anna Jachimska, Wanda Chonarzewska, Thaddeus Dolenga Eminowicz, Stanislawa Dobrosielska, Karol H. Wachtl, Gertruda Wieckowska, Boleslaw M. Zielinski. Front three: Ludwik Stepan, Stanislaw Kosmowski, and Bernard Gorski. (Photo by permission of the author.)

Gorajski and Count August Los. Both used pseudonyms; Los became Loziewicz and Gorajski became Goray. Violinist Norbert Wicki, another member, later left for Hollywood and worked in one of the film studios.

Anna Drozdowska: A New Star

Constantly searching for better talents, Eminowicz attended many amateur performances. When the Wolny Duch (Free Spirit) Society presented *Bartosz pod Krakowem* (Bartholomew of the Krakow Suburb), the producer, Streicher (also a member of his circle), asked Eminowicz to come in order to see Anna Drozdowska perform. Streicher thought she had discovered a star, and Eminowicz agreed. Although the seventeen-year-old Anna played a leading lady's part, she was so much at ease in even the most complicated situations that Eminowicz was certain she was a born actress.

Soon after my last performance [Anna wrote in a letter], Mr. Eminowicz arrived at my parents' home asking for me. His Circle of Stage Lovers intended to produce *Krowlowa Przedmiescia* (Queen of the Suburb), and he offered me the title role stating frankly that I could handle the part better than Maria Streicher. I was astounded, but soon it dawned on me that I . . . [was] on the road to become a professional.[14]

In February 1909 Eminowicz presented *Krowlowa Przedmiescia*, a musical comedy, with Drozdowska in not only the leading but also the singing role. As a singer she was not equal to Samolinska, but as a tragedienne she was soon leading all others, moving audiences to the highest degree.

Drozdowska, later Brzozoska (1892–1971) was born in the city of Rypin, Bydgoszcz province. Her father, Theophilius Drozdowski, emigrated to America without his family in 1896, when Anna was four-years-old. Five years later, when he had his own house in Chicago, his family joined him. Anna attended public schools and, at the age of seventeen, joined the first dramatic circle in the Marianovo settlement of Poles in the northwest side of Chicago. The circle needed teenagers for young fairy parts in the play *Zatopiony Dzwon* (Sunken Bell), translated from Gerhart Hauptmann. Anna was one of the fairies, the best in the group. After her appearance with the Circle of Stage Lovers, she gained popularity rapidly and was offered roles by a number of dramatic societies.

The Circle At Its Best

The circle won the hearts of Chicago Polonia when it produced its first *Wieczor Rozmaitosci* (Variety Evening), a review of short sketches and vaudeville numbers. The performance was a benefit for Szczesny Zahajkiewicz, whose shattered health necessitated his moving to Texas for its warm climate. Members of at least half a dozen dramatic societies participated, but the Circle of Stage Lovers appeared in a one-act farce, *Farbiarze* (The Dyers), by Walewski, and stole the show. The cast consisted of only four persons: Eminowicz portrayed

Narcyz; Chonarzewska played Tezynska; Leonard Schmidt-Piatkiewicz appeared as Victor; and Ella Cichosz created Cesia. The next day *Dziennik Zwiazkowy* said in part:

The farce *Farbiarze*, presented by the Circle of Stage Lovers, extremely humorous and played with verve and acting brilliancy, entertained the public to the extent that, besides laughing itself to tears, it was applauding the performers during their hilarious antics. The circle consists of actors of talent and we can frankly say that the Circle of Stage Lovers is the best theatrical group in Chicago. [15]

Most important is the review's final paragraph. In the past drama critics had referred to members of dramatic societies as amateurs, but this time they were referred to not only as actors, but even as artists. Eminowicz's professionalism was fully recognized. Indeed, in 1924 Thaddeus Kantor's essays on early Polish theatre in the Detroit *Dziennik Polski* named the Chicago Circle of Stage Lovers "the cradle of Polish Theater in America."

Demise of Chicago's Downtown Theatre

As Eminowicz produced play after play in the St. Stanislaw Academy auditorium, the largest available in Chicago's Polish neighborhood, he lost contact with the older Teatr Polski of downtown renown. Zahajkiewicz and Szwajkart had left the enterprise, and Wachtl alone continued to adhere to his downtown policy and the presentation of the classics. He even left the Circle of Stage Lovers, taking for a while a few of the circle's performers to act in the downtown theatre. But in the art of directing as well as in performing the classics, his theatre fell short, and expenses could not be met. The Teatr Polski of loop fame came to an end and, at least for the time being, Wachtl returned to his editing. [16]

Developments in New York

Throughout most of the nineteenth century, New York City rather than Chicago had been the center of Polish-American activity because of the large number of Polish intellectuals there; nobles, medical doctors, engineers, writers, poets, linguists, inventors, and businessmen. Count Peter Wodzinski, for instance, with his two sons Casimir and Stanislas, in New York since 1871, published a weekly, *Swoboda* (Freedom). Wodzinski and others, including Apolinary Landecki, W. Zolnowski, and a "man of the theatre," Jan Amszynski, a veteran of the Polish insurrection of 1863 who had done some acting in Poland, founded the Fredro Dramatic Society in 1877.

Among the actresses in the society were the Budzynski sisters, A. Kowaleska, Landecka, Zdziemnicka, Lepkowska, Smolinska, and from time to time the "queen of Polonia," Theophilia Kraemer, a woman of extraordinary beauty and charm who was born in the Kujawy sector of Poland in 1854 and settled in New York before 1870. The male actors included Marcin Kopankiewicz, Vincent Dombrowski, Count Wodzinski, Kazimir Janicki, the brothers Waszkiewicz, and Stankiewicz. The list of plays produced is similar to the list of those produced in Chicago.[17]

The "new era" of the Fredro Dramatic Society began when the society moved from Brooklyn to the Dom Narodowy (National Home) in Manhattan in 1906. Stanislaw Rayzacher took the reins of the drama society; Amszynski was vice president; and Henryk York, a dentist, was secretary. Wladyslaw Nalencz-Koniuszewski, who would help the Fredro Society tremendously while working as an editor of the weekly *Czas* (Time), arrived a year later.

The Iola Theater "Dime Show" in Chicago

In Chicago, as in other American cities, there were two Polonias, one consisting of immigrants from Polish cities, the other consisting of immigrants from Polish farm villages. Eminowicz felt that while the classics were being presented in downtown Chicago for the intellectuals from the cities, it was important for the farm folks to have entertainment on their level and near their homes, as in the neighborhood movie houses, or "nickel shows."

Eminowicz believed the Polish theatre had a mission—that of educating the audience. Since it was difficult for uneducated immigrants to comprehend the philosophical meaning in a tragedy, they were attracted by comedy. By moving ahead gradually with light dramatic plays, eventually the Polish theatre could bring the farm-bred immigrants to an understanding of the philosophy of a classic. This belief led Eminowicz to the idea of bringing one-act Polish plays and Polish vaudeville into the neighborhood "nickel show" movie houses.[18]

In December 1909 Eminowicz discussed his idea with a Mr. Roth, owner of the Iola Theater, at 1238 North Milwaukee Avenue. Roth was astonished at the thought of presenting programs in Polish in an American movie house. "Why not?" Eminowicz asked. "Most of your public is Polish anyway. Our shows fill larger halls than your theatre." The Iola's seating capacity was three hundred. Roth would sign only a one-week trial contract, with no responsibility on his part for any of the expenses in case of failure. Eminowicz signed.

Eminowicz named two directors and formed two small casts, each of which would appear every other week. During the week one was performing, the other would rehearse a new program for the following week. As manager, Eminowicz asked only eighteen dollars a week. Admission was to be ten cents. Eminowicz's name would not appear in any of the advertisements, as he did not want to draw any public away from other Polish theatrical events. He considered Iola's regular patrons sufficient for this experiment, and he was correct. Amazed at the success of the first week, Roth wondered why he had not thought of it years ago. The theatre was packed to capacity every day. Of his own volition, Roth signed a new contract with Eminowicz, raising his pay to twenty-two dollars a week. The performers were paid from seven to ten dollars a week.

For the first time actors were treated as professionals and paid for their work. Many of those who later reached the top in professional Polish theatre acted on the stage boards of the Iola Theater, the cradle of Polish professional theatre. For example, Kasimir Majewski (1890–1972) began as an apprentice at the Iola in 1911 and later came to be known as a talented tragedian and fine comedian. Eminowicz's idea gave Poles in many cities a new profession, helped aspiring actors make a living, and at the same time fulfilled a cultural and social mission for many Polish men and women. Many small movie houses were saved from bankruptcy by engaging Polish stock companies. Others increased their attendance.

The Partnership of Thaddeus Dolega-Eminowicz and Martin Moneta

With the Iola success, Eminowicz approached Martin Moneta, an actors' photographer with a studio four blocks from the Iola Theater, and proposed that he rebuild his store into a movie house with Eminowicz as a partner. Moneta approved, and his two-story building was remodeled. The studio was rebuilt; a stage, orchestra pit, and dressing rooms constructed; and the curtain and scenery put into place. The entire year of 1910 was spent converting the photo studio into a modern movie house.[19]

On January 26, 1911 Moneta and Eminowicz opened the Kosciuszko Theater, the first neighborhood movie house owned entirely by Poles, including the building. The opening program consisted of an American film, a few vaudeville numbers by Eminowicz and Joseph Ungerman, and a one-act comedy, *U Dziadka* (At Grandfather's). Muki was played by Thaddeus, Malgosia by Stefania Hareska, Dziadek by Stanislaw Jachimski, and Edward by Ungerman. The turnout was tremendous. As a result of the success of the Kosciuszko Theater, many of Eminowicz's students [he had opened a drama school] began to introduce their own stock companies in Chicago, forcing one non-Polish owner in the Polish Triangle to change the name of his movie house to the Chopin Theater.

The Premier Theater, where George Jaworowski established a Polish stock company, had sporadic Polish performances, as did the Crown Theater, the largest theatre in the Polish Triangle. On June 18, 1910, the Polish daily *Dziennik Zwiazkowy* described the Crown Theater:

One of the nicest newly constructed theaters, elegant and equipped with the most modern ventilation system, so that even on the hottest days it is cool in the theater, is located in the center of the largest Polish section (northwest Chicago, at Ashland and Division streets). The Crown Theater is now in Polish hands for seven trial weeks. The stock company consists of the best actors, and for the vaudevilles the best performers will be contracted from downtown American theatre circuits. First *Kosciuszko Pod*

Rachawicame (General Kosciuszko at Rachawice) will be presented, with 120 men and women participating. A week later a first-class review will be presented, consisting of a Russian dancing and singing group, a one-act Polish play, *Dom Wariatow* (House of Madcaps), and the American top-billing ventriloquist, the Great Lester [teacher of Edgar Bergen], a Polish Chicagoan, whose real name is Marian Czajkowski [Chay-kov-skee]. He will perform not only in English, but also in Polish.[20]

Thaddeus Dolega-Eminowicz in Milwaukee

While Chicago's Kosciuszko Theater was being constructed, Eminowicz established contacts in Milwaukee and Detroit. During the winter of 1909–1910, the owner of the Empire Theater in Milwaukee agreed to have a "Polish show" for a week. For three days *To Polityka* (This Is Politics), by Zahajkiewicz, was performed, and during the final three days another one-act comedy, *Kto Pierwszy Umarl?* (Who Died First?) was presented between film features. The cast consisted of Eminowicz, Count Los (Loziewicz), Anna Jachimska, Czeslaw Owerlo (real name Baldyga) and young Hareska, who unsure of herself, used the pseudonym Stefanska. To her surprise, the local Polish daily, *Kuryer Polski*, writing about both performances, said, "Next to Eminowicz was Miss Stefania Stefanska." The following year, on June 29, 1910, Stefania and Eminowicz were married.[21] Other marriages among the "theatre people" followed.

Eminowicz also talked Joseph Kosciuk, editor of the newspaper *Nowiny Polskie* and a professional actor from Poland, and Thaddeus Krauze, also with stage experience, into opening a Polish professional theatre in Milwaukee. Eminowicz helped them select and renovate a movie house at South Eighth and West Mitchell streets. This theatre was also named the Kosciuszko Theater.

Selecting good talent for any performance in Milwaukee presented no problem because Milwaukee Polonia had an impressive cultural middle class. Polish immigrants there had belonged to singing, drama, and dancing societies for many years and had formed the first Polish Opera Club after World War I, under the direction of Anthony J. Lukaszewski. In addition to being active in the professional theatre, Krauze collaborated with Lukaszewski in opera.[22]

The Kisciuszko Theater in Detroit

Leaving the Chicago Kosciuszko Theater in other hands, Thaddeus and Stefania Eminowicz moved to Detroit, rented the Crescent Theater at the corner of St. Aubin and Superior streets, renamed it the Kosciuszko Theater, and in September 1912 presented a Polish professional show in Detroit.

At first unruly gangs of eighteen or twenty youths gave the theatre a rough time, playing harmonicas and whistling during performances, but eventually they were tamed and even friendly to the theatre. The theatre's first professional stock company consisted of Juliusz Kukawski and his wife Giza, Count Gustaw Romer, Aleksander Kroszcz, Witold Modzelewski, Stanislava Budzyn (later

15.2   Thaddeus Eminowicz and Stefania Hareska as they appeared in a one-act play, *Zaloty do Wstydliwej Pokojowski* (Courting a Bashful Housemaid), in 1909. (Photo by permission of the author.)

Stawinska-Leskiewicz-Budziak) and Ella Cichosz. Stefania Eminowicz did not perform because of pregnancy. On November 8, 1912, she gave birth to the first Eminowicz child, Stefan, in the apartment above the theatre. Detroit Polonia fell in love with the theatre, filling it every day to capacity. The Sunday program was usually very short; it began at 2:00 p.m. and was sometimes repeated as many as nine times between movie runs until midnight. Throughout these performances people were coming and going, many seeing the program twice. The Polish middle-class life in Detroit pleased the Eminowiczes so much that they decided to make Detroit their permanent residence.

The Fredro Theater in Detroit

That same year Eminowicz devised a plan to construct a special theatre with a seating capacity of 400 for Polish drama, the first professional Polish theatre devoted solely to drama in America. Eminowicz built the theatre in the summer of 1913, in partnership with prominent Detroit businessman Charles W. Chylinski. The morning of November 4, 1913, the *Detroit Free Press* announced:

New Polish theater to open today with fairy fantasy production. The Fredro Theater, the first Polish theater in the United States, will be opened today with a brilliant production of the *Zaczarowane Kolo* (The Enchanted Circle), a fairy tale in five acts by Lucyan Rydel.

The new playhouse at 1093 Chene Street has been named after the first great Polish comedy writer, Count Alexander Fredro, who is regarded as that nation's Mark Twain. The theater will be devoted to the presentation of comedies and dramas recognized as the best in Polish literature.

A stock company of the best talent from this city and Chicago has been organized, and it will produce one play each week. This first drama will run for seven performances. . . . Charles W. Chylinski is administrative manager and Thaddeus Eminowicz assistant administrative manager, stock company's manager, and art director.[23]

The cast in this play included Eminowicz, Stefania Koscinska, Aleksander Droszcz, Z. Jendrzejowski, Wladyslaw Eminowicz, Colonel Kudelski, Helena Koscinska, Wladyslas Droszcz, J. Wojcicka, W. Wojcicki, A. Balcerzak, Kukawski, and Rudolf Mickowski. Stefania Eminowicz did not participate, as she was pregnant with her second child.

All press notices the next day were long and very favorable. The Polish press was especially elated that Detroit Polonia was leading the cultural field with a real theatre, which even had box seats. The standing room was also spacious and could accommodate two hundred additional persons. On opening night every foot of space was filled. Later plays such as *Mazepa*, by Slowacki; *Quo Vadis*, by Sienkiewicz; and *Miser*, by Molière, were similarly successful.

On November 28, 1913, the Eminowicz's second child, a daughter, Halina, was born. The Eminowiczes were also operating a drama and dancing school,

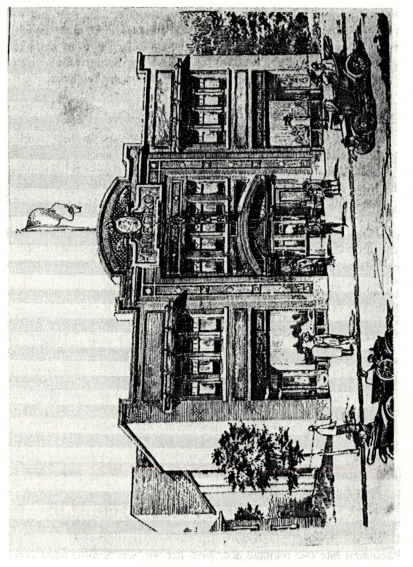

15.3　The Fredro Theater, 1093 Chene Street, Detroit, Michigan, 1913. (Photo by permission of the author.)

first above the Kosciuszko Theater, later in a hall under the Fredro Theater, where they coached new talents for more theatres.

Polish Theatre in Buffalo

Thaddeus Sowinski, a professional actor, and his wife Ewa, an actress, arrived in Buffalo sometime during the first decade of the century. Known as "an actor from Poland," Sowinski refused to participate in or direct any amateur plays. Instead, he introduced something never tried in any Polish settlement before; he and his wife served as counselors to the amateurs. For a fee one of them would attend the first rehearsal and explain the essence of each character. Sowinski knew most of the plays and roles by heart and often acted out a particular part himself as a demonstration. Then one of the Sowinskis would attend the dress rehearsal for a final checkup. The large number of amateur groups in Buffalo and the adjacent towns enabled the Sowinskis to earn a comfortable living.[24]

Polish immigrants had come to Buffalo from the cities of German Poland during the late 1800s. As their teenage children learned to dance, act, and sing, many talented young people came to the fore. John Bielanski, who had read about the successes of Polish professional actors in Chicago and Detroit, realized the time was ripe for a professional Polish theatre in Buffalo. Bielanski owned the 1,000-seat Fillmore Theater at Fillmore and Broadway in the center of the Polish Buffalo settlement, a movie house that also presented English vaudeville programs. In 1914 he visited Eminowicz in Detroit and proposed that Eminowicz's troupe appear in the Fillmore Theater.

The Eminowiczes agreed to have a small group of actors perform a few short Polish sketches that would fit into the schedule of the English-language vaudeville numbers for about three weeks. Taking six persons with them, Thaddeus and Stefania went to Buffalo on March 20, 1914, leaving Stefania's brother Aleksander Hareski temporarily as manager of the Detroit theatre. Because of the great success of the venture, Bielanski tried to keep the Eminowiczes in Buffalo permanently. Instead, the Eminowiczes sent to Chicago for Norbert Wicki, Anna Brzozowska, and Ignacy Ulatowski and returned to Detroit, truly impressed, however, by the Buffalo Polonia. "I do not accept Fillmore as a Polish theater," said Eminowicz to his wife on the way back. "We will return to Buffalo, find another theatre, and give it a Polish name."[25]

With this in mind, Eminowicz sold his share in the Fredro Theater to his partner Chylinski. Eminowicz visited Buffalo twice, rented a movie house on Broadway, changed its name to the Kosciuszko Theater, and opened on October 1, 1914. The stock company consisted of both Eminowiczes (Stefania as a leading lady); Witold Modzelewski as a leading man; Josephine Seidel and Marian "Walush" Mossakowski as character players; Count Gustaw Romer in various roles; Hareski as business manager, film projector operator, sign painter, and prompter; and Franciszek Luzinski as pianist and orchestra director for musicals.

The Polonia Theatre in Cleveland

Although greatly pleased with the attendance in Buffalo, Eminowicz began in January 1915 to think of opening a theatre in Cleveland. Again he brought two actors from Chicago to replace himself and his wife, left his brother-in-law Hareski as manager, and returned with Stefania to Detroit, where her mother lived with their two children. Stefania was expecting her third child, so Thaddeus left for Cleveland alone. Selecting and refurbishing a movie house in Cleveland, Eminowicz paid a tribute to Polonia by naming the new playhouse Polonia Theater. He worked hard to establish its popularity. In May 1917 he returned to Detroit to see his third child, a daughter, Thadeusza Zofia.

The Canfield Theater in Detroit

Back in Detroit, Eminowicz opened another theatre on Canfield Avenue, known as the Canfield Theater. At that time Charlie Chaplin's comedies were filling movie houses to capacity. Eminowicz wrote a play in Polish, *Charlie Chaplin Clotka* (Chaplin as an Aunt), presented it many times a day, and wrote another, *Charlie Chaplin Powiernikiem* (Chaplin as a Confidant). With his long, curly hair and his talent, Eminowicz became another Chaplin. The Canfield Theater was besieged daily by crowds blocking the street, and police were needed to control the traffic. English-language newspapers reported the incidents. Soon film scouts from the Universal Film Company appeared at the Canfield Theater offering Eminowicz a Hollywood career. "You must be joking," Eminowicz said. "I am performing only for the Polish people. Your Chaplin is silent. My Chaplin speaks Polish and is twice as funny."

Eminowicz's Political Play

Collaborating with the editor of Detroit's *Dziennik Polski* (Polish Daily News), Janusz Ostrowski, who supplied pertinent facts, Eminowicz, a loyal patriot, wrote and produced a political play. It was a very controversial play, as even its title suggests: *Po Czyjej Stronie?* (With Whom to Side?). This was a politically explosive period. World War I had begun, and Gen. Joseph Pilsudski's Polish Legion had been fighting the Russians since August 8, 1914. Although the United States was officially neutral, one faction of Polish Americans supported Pilsudski's uprising. Some even left the United States to join him. The conservative majority of Polonia, however, withheld its support of Pilsudski, awaiting the day when the United States would enter the war and transport the Polish Falcons to France to join the Western Allies against the Germans. Although he had nothing against this view, as the son of a participant in the 1863 uprising against Russia, Eminowicz wanted to help the Polish Legion, which was already bleeding on the Eastern Front.

To get the largest hall for his play, he rented a German auditorium located at Gration and St. Aubin streets. The play's success was phenomenal. Hundreds of people were turned away for lack of space. All of the proceeds went to the National Defense Committee supporting the legion. Gratified that he had helped the Polish struggle for national independence, Eminowicz instituted collections for the fighting legion in theatres and at every public gathering.

The Final Curtain

Detroit's West Side Polonia had no theatre. Stanislas Janiszewski, a prominent West Side businessman, visited Eminowicz in December 1916 to propose a partnership in a new theatre on the West Side. The name was to be Teatr Ludowy (People's Theatre), and it was to be located on Michigan Avenue, the West Side's main thoroughfare. Eminowicz refused. Promising to see him again, Janiszewski nevertheless bought and renovated a sizable movie house. In January 1917 he asked Eminowicz to come to the theatre, appraise the improvements, and advise about the necessity of further changes. Again Eminowicz refused. Finally Janiszewski assured Eminowicz that half of the proceeds from each Friday's performance would be given to the Legion fund, as was being done in the Fredro Theater, hoping that this would change his mind.

Eminowicz did change his mind. On March 8, 1917, Teatr Ludowy had its grand opening, with both Eminowiczes participating in a four-act play, *Zagroda Sobkowa* (On Sobek's Farm). With a success the first week, Teatr Ludowy entered a very successful season. The theatre presented *Zywot Genowefy* (Life of Genevieve) in five acts, and attendance passed all expectations. This play was followed by *Boleslas, Syn Genowefy* (Boleslas, Son of Genevieve), also in five acts. Since this was Eminowicz's last series of performances in the professional theatre, the cast should be noted: Count Siegfried and Genevieve were played by Thaddeus and Stefania Eminowicz; Boleslas by Antoni Bednarczyk; Berta, a village girl, by E. Kaminska; Golo by S. Siarkowski; Father Norbert by August Zukowski; Eberhard, a knight, by J. Wejroch; and Bruno, Siegfried's valet, by K. Kociecki.

During this performance the inefficiency of the new stagehands forced Eminowicz to order them to stand aside and watch while he changed the scenery. Changing the wings, backdrop, and furniture during each intermission took him five minutes, but it created a perspiration bath. He would then rush upstairs to his dressing room to prepare himself for the next appearance, cooling off under the opening in the not-yet-finished ceiling. A cold wind was blowing, and Eminowicz caught cold. Although he felt worse every day and Stefania and two neighbor doctors begged him to stay in bed, he continued his appearances to the end of the billing.

At that time Polish Falcon Nest 31 was presenting in the Dom Polski Auditorium the play *Gwiazda Syberii,* in which Eminowicz was to appear in the leading male part. He could not disappoint them. Wrapped in blankets, he was picked up in a car by the Falcons and played his part while running a high fever.

On April 2, 1917, Brzozowska and Waclaw Golanski appeared in a play *Polski*

Legionista (Polish Legionnaire) at the Wolna Polska (Free Poland) Theater. When Eminowicz saw the Wolna Polska advertisement in *Dziennik Polski*, despite his dangerous state of health he ordered his friends to take him to the performance. After the show he was brought home delirious with fever. Doctors diagnosed his condition as pneumonia and attended him in rotation, and for a few days he felt better. On April 6 the United States declared war on Germany, and Eminowicz left his bed, declaring he must get together with others and start some action to help free Poland. He had to be returned to bed and kept there by force. The high fever overwhelmed him. As he hallucinated day and night, he saw the Polish Legion marching into battle without waiting for him.

On April 10, 1917, Thaddeus Eminowicz passed away at the age of thirty-five. His untimely death evoked general sorrow in many cities. Condolences were telegraphed even from towns where he had never appeared. A multitude of his admirers attended the High Mass and the funeral, which surpassed anything Detroit Polonia had ever seen. Eminowicz was loved not only because of his role in Polish theatre, but also because through the theatre he had fought for the Polish cause.

Polish Theatre after Eminowicz's Death

During the ten years in which Eminowicz dominated the Polish-American professional stage, he had developed acting and managerial talent in others. Now Polish professional troupes mushroomed everywhere. The widowed Stefania Eminowicz continued to present Polish plays in the movie houses her husband had established, as well as in other theatres in Detroit and vicinity: the Conant Theater, the Farnum Theater, the New Eagle Theater, the Campau Theater, and the Ritz Theater, which changed its name to the Rozmaitosci (Variety). Large movie houses, such as the Martha Washington in Hamtramck, with predominantly non-Polish attendance, agreed to lease the theatre to Stefania for Polish midnight shows. These shows, which were her innovation, were usually performed on Saturdays only. On such nights the house would be packed before midnight. The entertainment-seeking public gladly stayed until two o'clock in the morning to enjoy an event in their own language.

Polish professional theatres in the United States prospered during the World War I years. At that time the United States was truly a land "flowing with milk and honey." The wages of the average factory worker doubled and tripled, and many Polish businessmen became wealthy. In this atmosphere of prosperity, the Polish theatre flourished, with admissions rising well above those of the "dime shows" of a few years earlier. The best actors frequently traveled from city to city for guest appearances with local theatrical groups, and they were well paid.

The vitality of the Polish theatre in the post-World War I period is illustrated by an extensive article on the Fredro Theater written by Len G. Shaw, drama critic of the *Detroit Free Press*.

The Fredro Theater is an outstanding center of Polish drama on the highest level. Actually it would be more accurate to say "an outstanding center of drama in the Polish language," since, in addition to the Polish dramatists' plays, excellently translated works of English, French, and American writers are produced. To this repertoire are added plays written by members of the troupe or other people interested in the Polish theater in America. The Poles through their theater contribute to the dissemination of culture and also entertain, at the same time keeping their ties with their native country across the ocean where they have families, relatives, or friends.

. . .

There are several reasons why Polish drama is successful in Detroit. One of the first . . . is that the Poles outnumber all other national groups in Detroit. Relying on very conservative statistics, there are about 150,000 of them, . . . a city in itself, expansive and influential, with a need of its own theater. . . . This need is further influenced by the fact that a Pole is a deep thinker, lover of good books, and well-read.

. . .

Possibly the admiration for Molière by the Poles is in great part a way of perpetuating in their memory the charming person of Count Alexander Fredro, whose name the theater proudly bears. The plays of Fredro revealed a style very similar to the French playwright, although Fredro's characters were drawn exclusively from Polish life. He wrote about twenty plays during the years from 1819 to 1835.

Many other playwrights of Poland are equally popular among American Poles. It is worth noting that even though stage literature written in a light vein is well-received, plays of a more serious theme are equally popular.

The Polish plays at the "Fredro Theater" are presented by a cast of twelve persons, augmented as the play requires by individuals from a group of talented apprentices with extensive acting experience. There is never a problem of assembling a competent cast. . . .

The versatility of the Polish professional actors is amazing. Although each has his or her own dramatic specialty, all are always ready to play any part assigned to them by the director.

Among the members of the troupe in the Fredro Theater deserving special attention is Mme. Stefania Eminowicz (1895–), talented character actress, whose every appearance on the stage in a comedy or farce gives rise to spasms of laughter, but who also in her dramatic parts and character roles in comedies has no equal in America. . . . Her talent is so outstanding that she could grace the American stage if only she would learn to perform in the English language.

Deserving special mention is Wladislas Krassowski (1884–). [He] studied drama since 1905, and appeared in the stock company of Stanislas Polenski, also studied art at the Krakow Academy of Art, acted with A. Szyfman and K. Zalewski [and came to America in 1912]. In addition to his work as an actor, Krassowski paints the scenery, backdrops, and wings for the theater. He is one of the hard-to-find individuals in the theatrical circles who can accomplish most everything he undertakes. . . .

Another actor, Antoni Bednarczyk, distinguishes himself as a leading man, who, in addition to being a fine professional actor from Poland, possesses a good tenor voice and performs principal roles in Polish operettas.

The troupe is further enhanced by Mme. Anna Brzozowska, an excellent leading lady, whose talent is most evident in dramas with highly emotional scenes. . . .

The comedian of the troupe is Ignacy Ulatowski. . . . He is able to create more different types with little change in make-up and costumes than any other actor in the group. . . .

There is also merry Maria Jozwiak, a talented ingenue, who sings beautifully, and . . . next to Brzozowska . . . is simply irreplaceable.

The actors, however, are not only concerned with the best performance of their roles at the Fredro Theater; they also volunteer their help to speed up the changes of scenery and props on the stage between acts. Their way of doing this sometimes leaves little to the imagination of those on the other side of the curtain. If one of the wings is difficult to set up and attach with ropes, hammers and nails are put to use, and a playful rat-tat-tat can be heard from behind the curtain above the hum of the audience's chatter while awaiting the next act. A detail like this does not disrupt the general jovial atmosphere. In fact, it often helps excite the people's curiosity.

. . .

Without doubt the Polish theater is of great educational value because it gives a great number of men and women the opportunity to learn about all manner of problems facing human beings in Poland as well as in other countries, and it also exposes them to history in plays with a patriotic theme. The plays, by exposing the imperfections and old vices and by giving direction for progressive and meaningful living, prove that the Polish theater in America is fulfilling its mission.[26]

PROFESSIONALS FROM POLAND

The 1920–1930 decade witnessed the arrival of many cabaret and theatre stars from reborn Poland, who, after the devastating war years, were attracted by American dollars. Thus the pioneers of the Polish-American professional theatre were joined by a number of professionals from abroad. Among these were Gustaw Chorian of the Warsaw Opera and Olga Orlenska of the Polish Opera.

In 1924 Lee and J. J. Shubert contracted Halina Bruczowna, wife of Count Victor Bninski and star of Poland's operettas, for the part of Bellabruna in *Blossom Time*, a three-act musical on Franz Schubert's life. She appeared in this part at the Detroit Opera House for the week of November 9. Later she went to various cities, rented the largest halls, and put on her own shows for Polish audiences, engaging professional actors in each city. In Chicago, for instance, she appeared in *Romans Tancerki* (The Dancer), a three-act comedy by M. Lengyel, with myself (Arthur Leonard Waldo) as her leading man and Stefania Eminowicz, Krassowski, Majewski, Halina Majewska, Lili Zydanowicz, Felicja Lichocka, Kwiatkowski, and Bronislas Mroz. Wladislas Ochrymowicz and his wife Teodozja Wandycz also arranged such performances, as did Wanda Siemaszkowa (1867–1947), the leading tragedienne of Krakow. Siemaszkowa was greatly pleased with the Polish actors she engaged for her presentations in America. Ewa Bandrowska-Turska, a coloratura soprano from the Lvov Opera, appeared in the Fredro Theater and in the Polish theatres of other cities. Other actors from Poland, such as Maryla Karwowska, Lipowska, and Poplawski, were happy to find Polish theatres, as well as thousands of theatre-minded spectators, waiting for them in America. Polish consular officials attended many shows in

15.4 The Polish Professional Actors Guild of Chicago. Front row from left to right: Kazimir Majewski, Felicia Kulakowska, Wladyslas Krassowski, Anna Brzozowska, Helena Bednarczyk, Viera Orlowska, Lidia Pucinska, Stefan J. Zielinski. Second row: Oktaw Orlowski, Halina Majewska, Izydor Brudzinski, Stanislawa Dobrosielska, Jan Repeta, Viera Henrych, Antoni Bednarczyk, Olga Sawicka, Zofia Pawlowska, Dusia Urbanska, Eligiusz Bobrowski. (Photo by permission of the author.)

these theatres and expressed surprise at their high quality. As an expression of approval, leading actors were invited to consular social receptions.

REUNIONS OF PROFESSIONAL ACTORS IN THE POLISH THEATRE

In 1920 Stefania Eminowicz called a reunion of those who had dedicated themselves to the professional Polish theatre in the Circle of Stage Lovers in 1909 and appeared professionally in 1910. This Detroit assemblage identified the founders of the legitimate Polish theatre in America and accepted them as the Senior Pioneers of the professional theatre.[27] Those who joined the professional stage after 1910 can be classified as professional actors of the Polish theatre in America. Although they did not create a separate association, they often considered themselves equal to those who originated the first Polish stock companies. Many were excellent actors, and their contribution to the further development of the professional theatre should not be minimized.

A later reunion of Polish-American theatre professionals was held in Chicago in response to a letter from Stefania Eminowicz to Kazemir Majewski concerning the World Convention of Poles from Abroad in 1934 in Warsaw. The Polish Professional Actors Guild of Chicago was formed, and Majewski received a mandate to represent the Chicago actors at the convention. (See Figure 15.4.)

STEFANIA EMINOWICZ IN BUFFALO

Despite an economic recession after World War I, theatres were prospering. When Stefania Eminowicz learned that the Kosciuszko Theater in Buffalo had not opened in the fall of 1921, she organized a new stock company and left for Buffalo. There, in cooperation with her brother, Aleksander Hareski, she undertook the complete renovation of the theatre, and it opened early in December. Her troupe, which included herself, Julius Kukawski, Witold Modzelewski, Waclawa Koszewska, Marian Mossakowski, Stanislas Sowinska, Franciszek Bohusiewicz, Janina Baranska, Lidia Pucinska, Michal Pucinski, myself, and others, performed for another two seasons, until 1924. Once the theatre was doing well again, Stefania Eminowicz left its management to her brother and returned to Detroit to continue her work there.

During the three seasons in Buffalo, Stefania Eminowicz introduced a number of three- and four-act plays by prominent playwrights of Poland and France: *Moralnosc Pani Dulskiej* (Morality of Mrs. Dulska), by Gabriela Zapolska; *Szkola Zon* (School for Wives), from Molière; *Popychadlo* (The Drudge), by Jan Szutkiewicz; *Lekkomyslna Siostra* (Frivolous Sister), by Wlodzimir Perzynski; *Maz w Powijakach* (Husband in Swaddling Clothes), by A. Siemaszka; *Karpaccy Gorale*, by Joseph Korzeniowski; *Edukacja Bronki* (Education of Bronka), by Stefan Krzywoszewski; *Nory Zepsucia* (Dens of Depravity), from Eugène Brieux; *Malzenstwo Loli* (The Marriage of Lola), by Henryk Zbierzchowski; *Radcy Pana Radcy* (Councilors of the Councilor), by Michal Balucki; *Szkola Mezow* (School for Husbands), from Molière; *Ich Czworo* (The Four of Them), by Zapolska; *Aszantka* (Ashantka), by Perzynski; and *Chory z Urojenia* (The Hypochondriac), by Molière.[28]

The troupe also presented plays written by the Polish-American dramatists Antoni Jax, Zygmunt Neuberg, and myself, each of whom wrote up to fifty plays. Jax produced a large number of very popular musicals based on Poland's urban and rural life. Other Polish-American playwrights included Zahajkiewicz, Czeslav Lukaszkiewicz, Thaddeus Eminowicz, Antoni Zdzieblowski, Karol Wachtl, Stefan J. Zielinski, Jozef Stefanik, Stefan Bandrowski. Stefan Barszczewski, Hareski, Stanislas Ignaczak, Wladyslas Kosztowniak, Juliusz Kukawski, Eugeniusz Maszczyk, L. B. Nowierski, Jozef Sawicki, Stanley (pen name), J. X. Tomaszewski, R. Turczynowicz, Stanislas Z. Wachtel, Norbert Wicki, August Zukowski, Stanislaw Lempicki, Francis Bolek, and Kajetan Ihnatowicz (Ernest Lilien).[29]

LUDWIK KOWALSKI IN NEW YORK

This chronicle of the Polish theatre in America would not be complete without paying tribute to Ludwik Kowalski of New York, who after some initial experience organizing amateur and professional theatre groups, directed high-quality opera. Born December 8, 1881, in Warsaw, Kowalski received his elementary and secondary education in Poland. In 1905, at the age of twenty-five, he arrived in New York and the same year organized a Polish amateur theatre. The entire group financed the venture, which proved to be expensive, so after two years the drama society was dissolved. A short time later, however, others revived it and continued with much better results.

Encouraged by Thaddeus Eminowicz's success, Kowalski returned to the Polish theatre venture as a professional in 1918 and remained a director until 1940. At first, musicals were his specialty. After premiering in New York, he would take his troupe on the road, visiting the larger Polish communities. Run as a business, the venture paid off, to the great satisfaction of the members of this stock company.

Soon Kowalski found a number of operatic voices, such as Joseph Kallini and Zofia Posselt, who came from Poland, and several members of the Metropolitan Opera chorus. In 1925 Kowalski directed the opera *Flis*, by Stanislas Moniuszko, in New York. In 1926 he staged the opera *Hrabina* (The Countess), also by Moniuszko, and in 1930 the opera *Halka*, by the same composer. He directed *Halka* again in 1934 in New York, Philadelphia, Boston, and Chicago. On February 18, 1940, Kowalski, as the general manager of the Polish American Opera Company in New York City, again presented *Halka*.[30]

EPITAPH FOR THE POLISH THEATRE

The Polish-language professional theatre is no longer a part of the life of American Polonia. Four factors contributed to the demise of Polish theatre in

America: (1) restriction of immigration from Poland after 1920, (2) the introduction of radio and later of television into all homes, (3) the Anglicization of all ethnic groups; and (4) the economic crisis of 1929–1933.

As Polish theatre declined, many of the Polish theatre directors and managers bought time on radio stations and conducted radio hours in Polish, employing Polish actors in sketches, primarily humorous. The training these actors had had in the theatre made it possible for them to earn a living in radio, and in some cities these programs are still on the air. Theatre, however, disappeared as the use of the Polish language declined.

There are two reasons for the decline in the use of the Polish language in America, aside from the restriction of Polish immigration. The first is assimilation, or Anglicization. (I prefer the latter term, since Poles have accepted the English language without abandoning their heritage.) The second is marriages between Polish-speaking and non-Polish-speaking individuals.

Prior to World War I Polish leaders in America made every effort to keep Polish immigrants from American influences and encouraged them to preserve their Polishness in language, writing, and sentiment. This effort was made in order to perpetuate the immigrants' aspirations in the struggle for Polish freedom. Consequently whole neighborhoods in American cities were inhabited exclusively by Poles. The war for Poland's freedom came to a victorious end when an independent Poland was established in 1918, and this exclusiveness no longer seemed necessary. As the generation of freedom fighters dies off, the new Anglicized generation of Poles is being brought into the mainstream of American life.

There have been some recent efforts, however, to revive Polish theatre. Edward J. Czerwinski writes:

Perhaps the one person and organization that has tried to introduce Poland's (modern) theater and drama into the American mainstream is Ellen Stewart and her LaMama Theater. It was largely through her efforts (together with Ninon Talon Karlweis) that Jerzy Grotowski's Laboratory Theater (of Poland) was invited to the United States in the late sixties. She was also instrumental in premiering the works of Rozewicz's The Old Lady Broods, several of Mrozek's one-act plays, and if Tadeusz Kantor's critically acclaimed Polish production of The Dead Class comes to New York, it will be largely due to the untiring efforts of this remarkable woman.[31]

Ellen Stewart's work should be supported as part of a program acquainting America with modern dramatic achievements in Poland.

To those who admire the beauty of the Polish language I say most assuredly that the Polish language will not completely vanish in America. Although the Polish-speaking immigrants who came to America after World War II will die out, like the earlier generations of Polish immigrants, the legacy they will leave and that which was left by members of the old Polonia enriches American culture, contributes much to the American way of life, and will never be forgotten.

NOTES

1. Samuel Orgelbrand and Maurycy Orgelbrand, "Poland—Population," *Universal Encyclopedia* (Warsaw: Samuel and Maurycy, Publishers, 1900).

2. Venceslas Kruszka, *Historia Polska w Ameryce* (Milwaukee: Kuryer Polski, 1937), Vol. 1.

3. Oskar Halecki, *History of Poland* (New York: Roy, 1943).

4. Kruszka, *Historia Polska*, pp. 551–53.

5. *Poland: Historical, Literary, Monumental, Picturesque*, 1, no. 2 (1841).

6. Karol Estreicher, "Teatr Polski za oceanem" (Polish Theater beyond the Ocean), Lvov, 1881, translated by Mathew J. Strunski, reprinted in *Polish American Studies* 4 (Jan.–June 1947): 31–36.

7. Interview with Julius Smietanka, 1948.

8. Estreicher, "Teatr Polski," p. 32.

9. Emil Habdank-Dunikowski, *Wśród Polonii w Ameryce* (Lvov: P. Starzyk, 1893).

10. *Dziennik Chicagoski*, Sept. 12, 1892.

11. Stanislas Dabrowski, "Kazimierz o sobie" (Kaminski about Himself), in *Teatr w Polsce* (Warsaw, 1927), pp. 90–93.

12. Several members of the Eminowicz family had been well-known poets, and four had won the Cross of Valor for outstanding acts of bravery during World War I.

13. Stanislaw Osada, "Z teki reportera," *Dziennik Zwiazkowy* (Polish Alliance Daily), January 15, 1908.

14. Anna Drozdowska-Brzozowska in correspondence with the author.

15. Stanislaw Osada, "Z teki reportera" *Dziennik Zwiazkowy*, March 13, 1909.

16. August Zukowski, in an interview with the author in 1931.

17. Wladyslaw Nalecz-Koniuszewski, *Polacy w New Yorku* (Poles in New York) (New York: J. Mierzynski and A. Orlowski, c. 1910), pp. 44, 67, 96–98.

18. August Zukowski in an interview with the author.

19. Juliusz Kukawski in an interview with the author.

20. "Crown Theater and the Great Lester," *Dziennik Zwiazkowy*, June 18, 1910.

21. When she joined the Circle of Stage Lovers at the age of sixteen, Stephania Hareska was the youngest member. Eminowicz fell in love with her while walking her home from rehearsals. Her other suiter, the glamorous Bernard Gorski, also a member of the circle, disappeared immediately after the wedding.

22. Anthony J. Lukaszewski, "The Polish Opera Club," in *We, the Milwaukee Poles* (Milwaukee, 1946), pp. 94–95.

23. *Detroit Free Press*, November 4, 1913.

24. Memoirs of Stefania Eminowicz, published in part in *Stefania Eminowicz* (in Polish, Chicago: Arthur Leonard Waldo, 1937).

25. Arthur Leonard Waldo, *Teatr Polski w Ameryce* (Polish Theatre in America), written for the Poznan World's Fair in 1929 (in Polish, destroyed in World War II, bound manuscript in the author's collection).

26. Len G. Shaw, *Detroit Free Press*, Sunday magazine, January 18, 1920. Reprinted with the permission of the *Detroit Free Press*.

27. These were Michal Barzyczak (Ba-zhi-chack), Anna Brzozowska (Bzho-zov-ska), Wanda Chonarzewska (Hona-zhev-ska), Stanislaw Czeslawski (Ches-lav-skee), Stanislawa Dobrosielska, Thaddeus Dolega-Eminowicz (Emee-no-veech), Waclaw Dolski, Aleksander Droszcz (Droshch), Stefania Eminowicz (Emee-no-veech, nee Hareska), Stanislaw Ignaczak (Eeg-nah-chack), Anna Jachimska (Ya-heem-ska), Stanislaw Jac-

himski (Ya-heem-skee), Stanislaw Kajkowski (Koy-kov-skee), Stanislaw Kosmowski (Kus-muv-skee), August Count Los Loziewicz (Losh-Lozye-veech), Witold Modzelewski (Mo-dze-lev-skee), Jan Repeta (Reh-peh-tah), Leonard Schmidt-Piatkiewicz (Pyont-kye-veech), Stanislawa Streichowa (Stry-ho-va), Ludwik Stepan, Norbert Wicki (Veetz-kee), Maria Zielinska (nee Rutkowska), Wanda Zarska (Zhar-ska), August Zukowski (Zhu-kov-skee), and Gizela Zukowska-Kaminska.

28. From the author's scrapbook, 1921–1926.

29. Arthur L. Waldo, *Zarys historii literatury Polskiej w Ameryce* (An Outline of History of Polish Literature in America) (Chicago: Polish Museum in Chicago, Polish Roman Catholic Union, 1938).

30. Francis Bolek, *Who's Who in Polish America* (New York: New York Polish Opera Company, 1943), s.v. Kowalski, Ludwik.

31. Edward J. Czerwinski, "Notes on Polish Theater in the United States," in Charles A. Ward, Philip Shashko, and Donald Pienkos, eds., *Studies in Ethnicity: The East European Experience in America* (New York: Columbia University Press, 1980), pp. 211–25.

BIBLIOGRAPHY

Books

Bolek, Francis, *Who's Who in Polish America*. New York: New York Polish Opera Company, 1943. Information about Ludwik Kowalski.

Dabrowski, Stanislas, "Kazimierz Kaminski o sobie" (Kaminski about Himself). In *Teatr w Polsce*. Warsaw, 1927.

Habdank-Dunikowski, Emil. *Wsrod Polonii w Ameryce*. Lvov: P. Starzyk, 1893. The "Chicago" chapter is especially valuable.

Halecki, Oskar. *History of Poland*. New York: Roy, 1943. Describes political background of Polish emigration.

History of Krakow. Krakow, 1915. No author or publisher given. This is a souvenir booklet that gives valuable information about the Eminowicz family in Poland. Ludwik Eminowicz (1881–1946) was one of the contributors.

Kruszka, Venceslas. *Historia Polska w Ameryce*, Vol. I. Milwaukee: Kuryer Polski, 1937. Vol. II. Milwaukee: Polish Falcons of America, 1937. The Polish Falcons distribute two-volume sets.

Nalecz-Koniuszewski, Wladyslaw. *Polacy w New Yorku* (Poles in New York). New York: J. Mierzynski and A. Orlowski, c. 1910. This 135-page book gives the history of Poles in New York through 1909, suggesting therefore publication around 1910. The prologue is written by J. Mierzynski, who with his partner A. Orlowski owned a printing shop in New York. Mierzynski also published a monthly cultural magazine, *Swiat i Czlowiek* (The World and Man).

Orgelbrand, Samuel, and Orgelbrand, Maurycy. *Universal Encyclopedia*. 18 vol. Warsaw: Samuel and Maurycy, Publishers, 1900–1903. Valuable information about Polish history and population.

Waldo, Arthur Leonard. *Stefania Eminowicz*. Chicago: Arthur Leonard Waldo, 1937. In Polish. Contains a biographical sketch of Stefania Eminowicz and part of her memoirs.

——. *Teatr Polski w Ameryce* (Polish Theatre in America). Detroit, 1929. Written for the World's Fair in Poznan. Destroyed in World War II; bound manuscript copy in author's possession.

——. *Zarys historii literatury polskiej w Ameryce* (An Outline of History of Polish Literature in America). Chicago: Polish Museum in Chicago, Polish Roman Catholic Union, 1938.

Zins, Henryk. *Anglia a Baltyk*. Wroclaw, Poland: Zaklad Narodowy imp. Ossolinskich 1967. Background information on the Polish economy.

Articles

Bikel, Theodore. "U.S. Supports Arts in a Miserly Fashion," *U.S. News and World Report*, May 7, 1979, p. 81. Describes the plight of the arts in the late 1970s, including ethnic theatre.

Estreicher, Karol. "Teatr Polski za oceanem" (Polish Theatre beyond the Ocean). Lvov, 1981. *Zboda* (Polish-American newspaper), 1890. Reprint translated with an introduction by Mathew J. Strumski, as "The Beginnings of Polish American Theatre," *Polish American Studies* 4 (Jan.–June 1947), 31–36. Valuable descriptions of early amateur theatre and its importance in immigrant life, by a knowledgeable and astute observer from Poland.

Lukaszewski, Anthony J. "The Polish Opera Club." In *We, the Milwaukee Poles*. Milwaukee, 1946.

Osada, Stanislaw. "Z teki reportera," *Dziennik Zwiazkowy* (Polish Alliance Daily), January 15, 1908, and March 13, 1909. Enthusiastic and laudatory contemporary descriptions of the early performances of the Circle of Stage Lovers.

Shaw, Len G. *Detroit Free Press*, Sunday magazine, January 18, 1920. Early-twentieth-century Detroit theatre critic describes and praises the Polish theatre.

Waldo, Arthur Leonard. "Sokolstwo," *Polish Falcons* (Pittsburgh) 1 (1953): 10.

Periodicals

Poland: Historical, Literary, Monumental, Picturesque (1841). The earliest Polish-American magazine in English, published by Paul Sokolewski for Sokolewski, Wyszynski, and Co.

Other Sources

Other sources used were the relevant volumes of the Polish- and English-language presses in cities where Polish American theatre was active, interviews with persons active in and knowledgeable about Polish-American theatre, and documents, including extensive scrapbooks, photographs, play-bills, and other memorabilia in the author's possession. The author's collection also includes Anna Brzozowska's letters.

16

Puerto Rican Theatre on the Mainland

ROSA LUISA MÁRQUEZ AND
LOWELL A. FIET

When theater goes into the streets . . . its function and its tactic must change. The streets are not polite; they are silent monuments to boredom and despair, reminders that melodrama or song-and-dance do not approach an existence torn from squalor. In the open, the theater leaves its own conventional environment—controlled, safe, predictable—and faces what the world has created. That moment brings the insight—for to be valid as theater it must be true to the life experience of the people. Where television can speak for the aspirations of white, middle-class America, street theater goes deeper into the cultural complex of a city, drawing on its most vulnerable emotions, finding a successful form *only* when it has understood the unique elements of the local geography. To acknowledge the people, instead of forgetting them, is to become political.[1]

The [conventional] theater helps train us in non-responsiveness so that the formal institutions that depend for their existence on our social narcosis can survive.

It is the theater itself that has begun to develop an antidote to this condition, not without considerable resistance from its case-hardened audiences. Environmental theater seems almost to pinpoint this issue—not only in its efforts to engage the audience in action, but in its impulse to return to the streets.[2]

The solution to the problems of the Puerto Ricans in New York is a complex one. A theatre will not be the answer, but a theatre can help, for it can dramatize the problems of a people, can instill in them pride in their rich cultural heritage, open new perspectives, release aggressions, and suggest solutions.[3]

Puerto Rican theatre in the United States has emerged as a vibrant byproduct of the oppressive social conditions under which many Puerto Ricans live in urban communities of the Northeast, especially in and around New York City. Its most immediate parallels are found in other strong cultural developments of the 1960s: the Black Arts movement, El Teatro Campesino, the work of "alternative" theatre organizations such as the San Francisco Mime Troupe and the Bread and Puppet Theater, and the theatre of anti-Vietnam War protest groups. The Puerto Rican theatre in the United States is also a phenomenon with roots that extend over the approximately 1,800 miles that separate the industrial Northeast from the island of Puerto Rico, and the dramatic expression of mainland Puerto Ricans derives its most basic and distinguishing characteristics from the social, linguistic, and cultural values of the island.

Puerto Ricans form a unique migrant group: their movement to the United States has been as much a commuting as a settling process. Return to the island is not only possible but likely. Many have traveled to the States to find economic opportunities that will enable them to return to the island and live with greater comfort. Returning to Puerto Rico is frequently the greatest dream of mainland Puerto Ricans. Furthermore, these Spanish-speaking immigrants are U.S. citizens and need not adopt mainland customs or learn English to obtain citizenship. Their theatre serves as a means of reinforcing cultural links between life in the urban ghetto and in Puerto Rico, of keeping the traditions and language of Puerto Rico alive in the heart of the North American metropolis.

The style of most of Puerto Rican theatre in the United States is what Edward Gordon Craig has referred to as "perishable,"[4] that is, totally organic and ephemeral: a theatre that comes to life in the streets, in gymnasiums, in community centers, in city parks and plazas; a theatre constituted of actors, which travels and finds little value in conventional notions of permanent theatre structures, scenic reinforcement, lighting, elaborate costumes, or publicity agents—all the things that characterize a commercial theatre inaccessible to the urban poor. But as totally organic—actor focused—it is probably not the kind of theatre Craig would have recognized, for it has an additional quality: it is committed to *puertorriqueñidad*—to defining, enriching, preserving, and strengthening the meaning of being Puerto Rican, demonstrating that Puerto Ricans have a cultural heritage and language that life on the mainland cannot erase, that being a Puerto Rican means more than simply being a member of the lowest paid, most poverty-ridden minority in the United States. The message becomes apparent in the work of all Puerto Rican theatre groups, whether they are well funded and relatively conventional organizations such as the Puerto Rican Traveling Theater, agitprop troupes such as Teatro de Orilla (Streetside Theatre) or "Nuyorican" groups such as the Nuyorican Poets' Cafe. Puertorriqueñidad as a definable and distinguishing characteristic; as a source of tradition, heritage, and pride; and as a fountain of cultural wealth remains the clearest theme.

THEATRICAL TRADITION

In spite of the political relationship between Puerto Rico and the United States, little is known by the nonhispanic U.S. public about the island and its political status, history, and culture. Standard artistic portrayals of Puerto Ricans—*West Side Story*, for example—have done little except further confuse the situation. It is with reference to Puerto Rico that any study of Puerto Rican cultural manifestations on the mainland must begin.

The smallest of the Greater Antilles, Puerto Rico is approximately 35 miles wide and 100 miles long. It was discovered by Christopher Columbus in 1493, and until 1898, when the United States took control of the island during the Spanish-American War, was a rigidly maintained Spanish colony. The original inhabitants were Taino Indians, but their numbers soon diminished, and the Spaniards introduced African slaves to perform the agricultural labors upon which the island's economy depended. Thus the Taino heritage has left little imprint on the contemporary Puerto Rican, who is more likely to be white or black or any shade between. The over 3 million residents of the island form a fairly well integrated, multiracial society without the degree of racial conflict that has been evident in the United States. During the twentieth century the basis of the economy of Puerto Rico changed from agriculture to industry and tourism. Overcrowding and unemployment, especially during the post-World War II era, led to an annual migration of thousands to the mainland. The language of Puerto Rico is Spanish. In spite of efforts to move its society toward bilingualism, English is rarely heard or used except in dealings with North American residents and tourists, and the culture remains impregnably Hispanic.

Puerto Rico has an established theatrical tradition that extends back to the early Spanish settlement of the island. The Church introduced the theatrical practices of Spain to spread and promote Catholic doctrine in the colonies. In Puerto Rico these performances date back to the early seventeenth century, and during the seventeenth, eighteenth, and nineteenth centuries theatre was part of various festivities, political events, and coronation celebrations.[5]

Throughout the nineteenth century, Spanish "Golden Age" plays by Lope de Vega, Calderón de la Barca, and José Zorrilla were produced by Spanish touring companies, along with works by non-Spanish playwrights such as Shakespeare and Goldoni. Native Puerto Rican drama also emerged during the nineteenth century and began belatedly to assume the romantic tendencies of the European continent. In 1849 Alejandro Tapia y Rivera wrote the libretto for the opera *Guarionex*, based on the life of a Puerto Rican Indian. His *Roberto D'Evreux*, the first original work by a native writer to be staged in Puerto Rico, is remarkably similar to the works of Alexandre Dumas and Victor Hugo. The play depicts the romantic conflicts of Elizabeth I of England and was produced in San Juan by the aficionados of the Sociedad Conservadora in 1856, eight years after it was written. Tapia later wrote an antislavery drama entitled *La cuarterona* (The

Quadroon), produced in 1867, six years before slavery was abolished in Puerto Rico. Salvador Brau depicted the Spanish domination of the island in plays with historical themes, such as *Héroe y mártir* (Hero and Martyr, 1871) and *Los horrores del triunfo* (The Horrors of Triumph, 1887). A poet as well as dramatist, Brau's main contribution to the Puerto Rican theatre is his lyrical use of language.[6]

In spite of these efforts, native theatre did not flourish in Puerto Rico during the second half of the nineteenth century. Two problems served as roadblocks: island politics allowed few Puerto Rican writers to express themselves freely through the theatre, and the control exerted over all theatrical production by Spanish companies discouraged the development of native artists.

U.S. control of Puerto Rico has been the major factor shaping all aspects of island life during the twentieth century. Theatre on the island and ultimately among Puerto Ricans on the mainland could not help but reflect this new influence. In fact, it was during the first five decades of the twentieth century that much of the groundwork was laid for the establishment of a new Puerto Rican theatre, which has also become the principal tradition for Puerto Rican theatre on the mainland.

The optimism that accompanied the arrival of U.S. troops in Puerto Rico was soon frustrated, however, and the few plays written during the first decades of the century leave an impression different from what Puerto Ricans in 1898 expected from the "liberators." These works condemn continued economic control, advocate socialist principles, and seek to expose social injustice. Titles such as *La emancipación del obrero* (The Emancipation of the Worker, 1903) with the principal characters being Juan—Worker's Cause, Pedro—Economic Slavery, Priest—Worries, Politician—Oppression, Magistrate—Injustice, and Master—the Capitalist System are an early demonstration of the protest theatre that characterized the work of Puerto Rican agitprop troupes during the 1960s and 1970s. In 1904 poet José Limón Arce wrote *Redención* (Redemption), a play that proposes unionization as a solution to the problems between labor and capital in Puerto Rico. Other titles of the era include *Futuro* (Future, 1911) and *El poder del obrero o la mejor venganza* (The Workers' Power, or The Best Revenge, 1915).[7] Historical dramas such as *El grito de Lares* (The Uprising at Lares, 1914, produced in 1929), by poet Luis Llorens Torres, and *Juan Ponce de León* (1932), by Carlos N. Carrera, portray aspects of the Puerto Rican struggle for independence.[8]

The new themes that were emerging required theatrical forms that could be analytical and reach an audience not accustomed to the aristocratic setting of the conventional theatre—in effect, a theatre that would travel to small towns and barrios and portray the everyday struggles of Puerto Ricans for audiences that had never before seen theatre. The new approach often focused on a crucial question of political identity: What is the relationship between Puerto Rico and the United States?

The Depression hit Puerto Rico, as a territory of the United States, even more severely than it did the mainland. Relief programs of the New Deal came to the island, and the theatre received assistance from the Work Projects Administration. A traveling theatre group called La Farándula Obrera (The Worker's Company) was created to write and perform plays exposing the problems of Puerto Rican workers, and members of the group eventually became Puerto Rico's most significant dramatists and producers of the 1950s and 1960s.[9]

The years surrounding 1940 are crucial to understanding Puerto Rico, the Puerto Rican community in New York, and the theatre forms adopted by both. In all aspects of Puerto Rican life, the topics most debated were socioeconomic justice, independence, and the concept of *puertorriqueñidad* (cultural identity). Puerto Rico also began to undergo a phase of rapid transformation, and new and sharp conflicts arose: industry versus agriculture, city versus country, independence versus annexation, *puertorriqueñidad* versus assimilation, emigration versus staying in Puerto Rico.

These conflicts, revolving around *puertorriqueñidad*, were addressed by the two most prominent Puerto Rican men of letters of the time: Antonio S. Pedreira, in *Insularismo* (1934) and Tomás Blanco, in *Prontuario histórico de Puerto Rico* (1935).[10] In what he called a time of "indecision and transition," Pedreira asked such questions as "What are we?" and "Where are we going?" Blanco's more acerbic view created images of pariahs and coolies surviving on palliatives if Puerto Ricans failed to take their destiny in their own hands. According to Manuel Maldonado Denis, "faced with the dissolving tendencies of assimilationism, Pedreira and Blanco call attention, through their brilliant essays, to the authentic ethos of Puerto Rican culture."[11]

What was felt by the islanders during this period was magnified in the situation encountered by Puerto Ricans in the United States, and this new aspect of the Puerto Rican identity crisis quickly found its way into the literature of the era. *Esta noche juega el jóker* (Tonight the Joker Is Wild, 1937), by Fernando Sierra Berdecía, is the first Puerto Rican play to deal with immigrant life on the mainland. The New York experience has continued to be one of the most fruitful topics of Puerto Rican playwrights. It has been depicted by René Marqués, whose famous *La carreta* (The Oxcart, 1952) uses New York for its third-act setting; by Pedro Juan Soto in "The Guest," "Scribbles," and "The Innocents" (short stories frequently adapted for theatre performance); by Manuel Méndez Ballester in *Encrucijada* (Crossroads, 1958); and more recently in *Pipo Subway no sabe reir* (Pipo Subway Can't Laugh, 1972) and *Noo Yall* (New York, 1973), by Jaime Carrero. These works, along with numerous others dealing with mainland Puerto Ricans, form part of the basic literature of the mainland theatre.

In 1939 Emilio S. Belaval, then president of the Ateneo Puertorriqueño (Puerto Rican Atheneum) and a sponsor of new theatre experiments, wrote "Lo que podría ser un teatro puertorriqueño" (What a Puerto Rican Theater Could Be), in which he called for a theatre that would deal with the reality of being Puerto Rican, relate that reality to the world at large and the "ideological currents of our time," and place all the elements of production under the control of Puerto Rican artists.[12] Belaval's ideas, which have formed the theoretical framework for nearly all Puerto Rican theatre since that time, were first implemented in the early 1940s by the Areyto group.[13]

Another island development that would ultimately contribute to the mainland theatre began in 1941 when Leopoldo Santiago Lavandero, a graduate of the Yale School of Drama and a former member of La Farándula Obrera and Areyto, founded the Teatro Universitario at the University of Puerto Rico. The initial purpose of the theatre program was to provide education in theatre and drama as part of a broad liberal arts curriculum and to train native artists, and the program has remained an important training ground for the Puerto Rican theatre.

In 1946 the Teatro Universitario acquired a traveling unit designed by Rafael Cruz Emeric. The task was to take theatre to hospitals, town squares, jails—wherever the cart could be opened for production. Fashioned in the spirit of Federico García Lorca's La Barraca, which traveled through Spain in 1932, the Teatro Rodante Universitario toured the island every weekend during its first year, and although its schedule has become less rigorous, it still tours approximately thirty times a year to remote island towns. The traveling format adopted by the Puerto Rican Traveling Theater in New York borrows directly from the model provided by the Teatro Rodante Universitario. Prominent mainland artists, including Miriam Colón, director of the Puerto Rican Traveling Theater, have received early training with the university unit.

Important political events of the 1940s have also had a lasting impact. Increased industrialization radically changed the island's economy, and one result of the progressive deterioration of Puerto Rican agriculture was the mass migration of a portion of the rural population to San Juan and the North American ghettos. In 1948 Luis Múñoz Marín became the first elected governor of Puerto Rico, a position he held until January 1965. Under his tutelage the present Estado Libre Asociado (Free Associated State), or commonwealth, status instituted on July 26, 1952, formalized Puerto Rico's economic and political relationship with the United States.

Puerto Rico's new status did not go unopposed. Political groups confronted the issues, and members of the Nationalist party resorted to armed struggle to protest what they saw as merely a new phase of colonial rule. The arts also recorded the situation. Throughout the first half of the twentieth century the theatre had raised questions about and analyzed the impact of U.S. control and influence in Puerto Rico. In the 1950s and 1960s this analysis continued, and many of the best works of the Puerto Rican theatre since 1950 have focused on the conflict between the heritage and identity of the islanders and the U.S. presence. Historian Carlos Solórzano has called the Puerto Rican theatre the most organic, homogeneous, and interesting nationalistic theatre in Latin America, which no doubt reflects the effort to maintain the spirit and meaning of a national identity and culture—puertorriqueñidad.[14]

The theatrical developments in Puerto Rico during the 1950s, 1960s, and 1970s were many and diverse and have had an impact on the mainland theatre. Some of these developments were

1. the rise of playwrights such as René Marqués, Francisco Arriví, and Luis Rafael Sánchez, whose works have received international acclaim;
2. the establishment of annual theatre festivals: the Festival de Teatro Puertorriqueño (Puerto Rican Theater Festival) was initiated in 1958 to promote the production of native plays and has served as a source of new dramatic materials for mainland groups; the Festival de Teatro Internacional (International Theater Festival) was initiated in 1966 to present the best of world theatre; and the Festival de la Vanguardia (Avant-Garde Theater Festival) was initiated in 1967 to present experimental and vanguard works—supported by the Instituto de Cultura Puertorriqueño and the Ateneo Puertorriqueño;
3. the development of stable semiprofessional companies such as Teatro del 60, Producciones Cisne, and Taller de Histriones;
4. productions by agitprop or protest (street) theatre groups such as El Tajo del Alacrán and Anamú, especially in the late 1960s and early 1970s;
5. the advent of cafe theatres in Old San Juan producing experimental works; and
6. the continued strength of the Teatro Universitario as a training ground for young theatre artists.[15]

ADDITIONAL ARTISTIC FACTORS AND IMMIGRATION

Radical Theatre in the United States

The Puerto Rican theatre in the United States reflects the most important theatrical developments on the island during the 1940–1980 period. The relationship between the two theatres is as close as that of the mainland community with Puerto Rico. Plays and production ideas are shared, and many artists trained in Puerto Rico have moved to the States to work with mainland groups. They often return to the island to work as well. Yet treating the groups on the mainland strictly as satellites of the island theatre diminishes the distinctiveness of their work and the importance of additional factors that have contributed to their development.

The new awareness of ethnic identity and rights that accompanied the civil rights movement provided a major impetus for Puerto Rican theatre on the mainland. With the recognition of a need for cultural as well as economic programs in depressed areas, the arts became increasingly important as a means of ethnic-cultural communication. The strongest and most prominent use of theatre as a source of ethnic education and unification can be seen in the Black Arts movement, which has accounted for some of the more remarkable artistic advancements in the U.S. theatre since the early 1960s. The 1960s also witnessed the Chicano movement in the Southwest. El Teatro Campesino, under the direction of Luis Valdez, combined forces with the United Farm Workers to deal with social and political issues in a direct, educational, and analytical dramatic style.

Other important theatrical developments were connected with the protest against the Vietnam War. The most effective groups to make a direct contribution to the protest movement were the San Francisco Mime Troupe and the Bread and Puppet Theater, two of the most important in the recent history of the theatre. The work of these two groups, along with university-based guerrilla theatres, plays such as Arthur Kopit's *Indians* (1968) and Daniel Berrigan's *The Trial of the Catonsville Nine* (1970), and "alternative," or counterculture, groups such as the Performance Group, began to demonstrate the function of art as an interpreter of contemporary social events.

The Puerto Rican theatre in the United States reflects these developments: it is a theatre of ethnic pride and identity, of education, and of social analysis; the ethnic community itself is its principal constituency, the immediate audience to be served; and the streets of the barrio where that audience lives provide the performance spaces.

Hispanic Theatre Tradition in New York

New York City's tradition of Hispanic theatre, extending back to the early twentieth century, is another source contributing to the Puerto Rican theatre. During the 1920s, theatres in Spanish Harlem were active, performing Golden Age (late sixteenth- and seventeenth-century) and contemporary Spanish plays as well as plays from an international repertory for a predominantly Spanish audience. The Depression severely limited theatrical activities, although Spanish zarzuelas continued to attract audiences. In the 1940s and 1950s Hispanic theatre fully reestablished itself and has since been a strong and vital form of cultural expression. In New York alone there are presently as many as twenty companies with diverse memberships and production programs, as well as companies in nearly every major city in the Northeast. The Puerto Rican theatre in the United States is part of this and shares ideas, plays, artists, and at times performance spaces with other groups of the broader movement of Hispanic theatre.[16]

These factors draw a line, although obscure, between Puerto Rican theatre groups in the United States and the theatre of Puerto Rico. However, the most important factor distinguishing the mainland theatre from its island counterpart is the nature of immigrant life in urban communities in the United States.

Immigrant Life and Culture

Overpopulation and increased unemployment in Puerto Rico—unemployment estimated at 39 percent in 1941, due to the drop of available shipping facilities during the Second World War—nurtured the first airborne migration to the United States. Government agencies recruited Puerto Ricans and flew them to the mainland, a practice that was followed by private companies specializing in agriculture and war materials. Puerto Ricans worked in twenty of the forty-eight states during the war, but the largest concentration (50 percent) was in New York City.[17] The end of the war did nothing to reverse this trend.

Between 1940 and 1950 an average of 18,700 Puerto Ricans migrated to the United States annually. In the decade of the 1950s the average rose to 41,200 per year, and in the 1960s it declined to an average of about 14,500 annually. In 1953 alone, when the migration reached its peak, about 69,000 Puerto Ricans left the island to settle on the United States mainland. In 1960 the number of Puerto Ricans living in the states was almost 900,000 and in 1970 the number had increased to between 1.5 and 2 million, the figure varying with the inclusion or exclusion of third-generation Puerto Ricans.[18]

The process of emigration is well characterized in Maldonado Denis's contention that

this mass emigration is a forced emigration in the greatest number of cases. Due to both the high degree of unemployment and the colonial government's encouragement of emigration, the country's poorest inhabitants are forced by circumstance to submit to an even worse ordeal in a society which scorns them.[19]

Of the Puerto Rican population in the United States, 70 percent has settled in New York, resulting in a new generation of mainland-born Puerto Ricans called "NeoRicans" or "Nuyoricans."

There is extensive literature on the economic, social, and cultural problems of this group of immigrants, drawn to the United States by the promise of work and prosperity. *Puerto Ricans in the Continental United States: An Uncertain Future*, a report of the United States Commission on Civil Rights, October 1976, is one of the most recent in a series of works that has reiterated the same factual information: Puerto Ricans have lower incomes, a greater school dropout rate, live more consistently in poverty-ridden sections of Eastern cities, have less access to job training programs, have benefited less from federal antipoverty programs, and have less hope of improving their collective economic and social situation than any other major ethnic minority in the United States. Even among the Hispanic population, consistently below national averages, Puerto Ricans are the poorest.[20]

Language is a major social barrier faced by Puerto Ricans in the United States. For the Puerto Ricans, maintenance of Spanish is highly desirable. It is the language of the home, the street, and the community. As a closely knit family- and community-oriented group, Puerto Ricans have difficulty learning English. Problems in communicating satisfactorily, or in many instances simply speaking with a pronounced accent, have had drastic consequences that are particularly evident in the performance of Puerto Rican children in mainland schools and by adults in the work place—places where fluency in English is most necessary. These consequences, however, reflect more negatively on the majority culture than on the Puerto Ricans, and English has been effectively used as a means of discrimination, keeping Puerto Ricans at the bottom of the economic ladder and denying many their social, legal, and education rights.

Language difficulties have also had a cultural impact. "Probably no other immigration has hit New York with the impact of the Puerto Ricans, whose language difficulties have spurred Spanish-language curricula in many public schools, Spanish signs on the streets, and Spanish television."[21] This is felt on other levels as well. The first Puerto Rican studies department was founded at Herbert H. Lehman College (CUNY) in 1969, and other New York universities have added similar programs. Hostos Community College in the Bronx has course offerings in Spanish in all its departments, and its Puerto Rican Studies Department, headed by Pablo Cabrera, also an artistic director of the Puerto Rican Traveling Theater, offers courses in Puerto Rican theatre and drama.

Puerto Rican assimilation in the United States follows a pattern very different from that of the majority of migratory movements. Milton M. Gordon's *Assimilation in American Life* (1964) notes little or no cultural and civic assimilation by Puerto Ricans.[22] The proximity of and ability to return to the island allow Puerto Ricans a sense of identity with homeland values denied previous immigrant groups. According to British sociologist Gordon Lewis,

for the first time in the long history of American immigration there is a two-way movement: the working class migrant may decide . . . to return home instead of remaining permanently. . . . It is evident that this is a new phenomenon in the historic migration movement to the promised land.[23]

The epilogue to Lewis's 1963 analysis is that by the mid-1970s more Puerto Ricans were returning to the island each year than were leaving for the mainland.

Without further analyzing the factors of immigration, a pattern emerges of an urban population that finds or transplants native cultural manifestations in its new North American environment. New artistic forms result.

There are the new popular musical forms that have grown out of the Puerto Rican experience in the northern cities, notably the *salsa* phenomenon, the NeoRican blend of Afro, *jíbaro* [Puerto Rican peasant] and American rock styles, not unlike the Jamaican *reggae* that has become the rage of the black West Indian minorities in Britain. Thematically, the *salsa* songs celebrate; as do many of the *reggae*, the desperate tribulation of the exile experience.[24]

Similarly the work of Nuyorican poets such as Miguel Algarín, Piri Thomas, Jesús Papoleto Meléndez, and Pedro Pietri, influenced by the new reality of the migrant experience, synthesizes elements of native and North American cultures in a poignant bilingual literature. Pietri has written:

Beware of signs that say
"Aqui se habla Espanol"
Do not go near those places
of smiling faces that do not smile
and bill collectors who are well trained
to forget how to habla espanol
when you fall back on those weekly payments
Beware! Be wise! Do not patronize
Garbage is all they are selling you
Here today gone tomorrow merchandise
You wonder where your bedroom set went
after you make the third payment

Those bastards should be sued
for false advertisement
What they talk no es espanol
What they talk is alotta BULLSHIT[25]

The Nuyorican poets have also made a strong contribution to the mainland
Puerto Rican theatre.

Analyzing the life of Puerto Ricans in the United States, Stan Steiner explains that

The culture of the Borinquén [the Indian name for Puerto Rico] was buried by the decay
of the city. But it was not destroyed. Nor was it assimilated or mercifully banished, but
hidden beneath the debris, like seeds that could not be seen, the old "traditional peasant
culture" of the *jíbaro* flowered into new forms.[26]

Thus the community of over one million Puerto Ricans began to enrich the
cultural life of North American cities through artistic manifestations of its
native culture.

THE IDEA OF THE MAINLAND THEATRE

Numerous Puerto Rican artists (José Ferrer, Miriam Colón, Chita Rivera,
Rita Moreno, Héctor Elizondo, Priscilla López, Raúl Juliá, and Jaime Sánchez,
among others) have made significant contributions to the professional theatre in
the United States. Others, such as Justino Díaz and Pablo Elvira, have advanced
to national and international prominence in the related field of opera. In the
past two decades organizations such as the New York Shakespeare Festival have
sought out minority-group artists in the effort to enrich and diversify theatre in
the United States. These measures have been successful in the expansion of the
idea of theatre as a reflection of a heterogeneous society. For example, Miguel
Piñero's *Short Eyes* (1974) found a large and enthusiastic audience through its

incorporation in the New York Shakespeare Festival's program. However, the accomplishments of these and other individual artists are not necessarily part of the mainland Puerto Rican theatre. That theatre involves the creation and performance of works directly related to the collective experience of Puerto Ricans and intended first and foremost for viewing by the Puerto Rican community.

That guideline brings into focus a movement to create a theatre of social and cultural meaning for an audience with little or no previous access to a theatrical tradition, an audience of people for whom the price of admission to a Broadway or off-Broadway theatre, even if the play reflected aspects of their culture, would be prohibitive. This audience, usually poor and frequently Spanish rather than English speaking, is more familiar with popular and native music and dance, films, and television than with live theatre performance. Their native culture has been transplanted and maintained in the United States not through the arts but through the continued observance of religious customs and holidays, native foods and drink, clothing styles, social mores and gestures, and language.

Theatre has been a conscious afterthought in the process of transculturation. It serves as a specialized artistic tool for educating and arousing awareness. Music, clothes, food, and language are agents of adjustment, making the sense of cultural displacement less severe, whereas the theatre is analytical. It incorporates the more passive agents into its mode of access and communication, but its task is more far-reaching: it constantly compares minority and majority cultures, standards of living, attitudes, and beliefs; it celebrates native cultural manifestations, raising them to a position of equity with the modes of the majority culture; and it actively asserts the right to exist without erasing the Hispanic heritage or ties with the island of Puerto Rico. Total assimilation is viewed as cultural suicide, a one-way process reiterating the absorption of other migrant populations into the majority culture. The theatre exists as a voice and a conscience for a community of people demanding to survive as Puerto Ricans.

One factor distinguishing the work of various Puerto Rican theatre groups is the question of language—Spanish, English, or "Spanglish." The language used in performance strongly reflects a group's mission. The Teatro Repertorio Español (Spanish Repertory Theater), which is not a Puerto Rican group, is a stable, permanent, professional organization with its own theatre and is devoted to original-language productions of the best of Spanish and Latin American drama for a broad and diversified New York audience. The Nuyorican Poets' Cafe is located on the Lower East Side of Manhattan and works almost exclusively in English and "Spanglish." This group concentrates on the contemporary scene, deals with crises in the lives of members of the Lower East Side community, and portrays survival strategies for Puerto Ricans born on the mainland.

The dramatic materials chosen by different groups represent a broad spectrum, ranging from standard texts by Puerto Rican playwrights, such as La carreta, by René Marqués, or Luis Rafael Sánchez's La pasión según Antígona Pérez (The

Passion of Antígona Pérez, 1968), to the short and highly adaptable playlets that comprise *Historias para ser contadas* (Stories to Be Told), by Argentine playwright Osvaldo Dragún, to collective works based on community incidents and to the dramatization of poetry by Nuyorican writers. The work of some groups encompasses the full range, whereas the work of others focuses on single aspects of it.

There are numerous shared characteristics as well. Performance spaces are not those originally designed as theatres. Lofts, cafes, churches, and firehouses typify the theatre spaces used and reflect the relationship between the Puerto Rican theatre and other "alternative" theatres. Most groups make a practice of performing in the streets—traveling. In the summer months parks, street corners, schoolyards, and plazas are the principal performance locales. In the winter the traveling format remains enforced but the locations change to community centers, schools, and churches. Traveling enables the theatres to incorporate many aspects of street life and native culture into their productions. The street also induces a spontaneity of response that more formal environments discourage and which can even become dangerous as audiences react overtly to the action.

In the street presentational techniques take precedence over representation or realistic illusion: a sign replaces a box set, a narrator establishes the environment, a single symbol provides sufficient visual context. The actors speak to the audience members, invite their participation, and incorporate them into the action. The approach is practical, for it eliminates the need for elaborate machinery and physical plants. It also creates the desired effect: a raw and direct theatre is well suited to the street and an audience that experiences directly without requiring the intercession of standard artistic conventions. There is an immediacy in the lack of pretense, and in the street or the rough setting of a barrio community center there is no need to represent reality visually—it is already close at hand. The ghetto tenements often frame the action, and the theatre does not have to reproduce them for an audience that knows only too well what living there is all about.

Some groups also conduct workshops and training programs for children and adults where theatre ideas and practices are taught and discussed. In the process of working with theatre, other issues, such as drug abuse, prostitution, welfare, and language, which have a direct social relevance, are also dealt with. Awareness of ethnic identity, of self-potential, and ultimately of the relationship between the individual, the community, and society at large, are as much the subject matter of the workshops as theatre itself.

The purposes and practices of Puerto Rican theatre groups overlap and defy categorization. (Distinctions such as professional, agitprop, and Nuyorican might be suggested, but their application proves at best arbitrary.) Of the numerous groups in different cities, some are stable companies with permanent theatres, whereas others are more ephemeral, coming together only when a specific issue requires dramatization and public statement. Some seem most comfortable only within the barrio; others perform at Lincoln Center or outside the Metropolitan Museum of Art as well as in the South Bronx and other boroughs of New York City. Some are closely associated with political organizations and perform as part of demonstrations and protest marches; others are university-based groups; and still others serve specific communities, literally turning their theatres into centers where works in progress are a constant and ongoing part of community life. These distinctions, however, are not as important to the understanding of the Puerto Rican theatre as are the shared characteristics and its overall diversity and strength.

GROUPS AND PRODUCTIONS

The large community of Puerto Ricans that began to establish itself in the United States during the 1940s did not carry with it a planned and coherent artistic movement. Confronted by a new and hostile society, Puerto Ricans struggled for survival on many fronts: the job market, the educational system, government agencies, and the community. Art emerged slowly to analyze and explain new circumstances. Music, the most integral element of the island culture, began to reflect the migrant reality through new rhythms performed on street corners and in parks by community musicians. The cadence of the salsa drums also throbs in the poetry of Nuyorican writers, whose "Spanglish" verses reflect the same mixture of native and exile cultures. The annual Puerto Rican Day Parade provides a means of ethnic celebration, and radio and television stations broadcast memories of the island interspersed by Spanish-language advertisements. Nightclubs feature new musical groups as well as interludes about life in Puerto Rico.

During the early years of emigration, sporadic attempts were made to stage plays written in or about Puerto Rico. *La cuarterona*, the nineteenth-century anti-slavery play by Alejandro Tapia y Rivera, was staged in New York in the 1920s. Musical reviews entitled *De Puerto Rico a Nueva York* and *La perla de las Antillas* were performed by amateur theatre groups in the 1940s, and *Esta noche juega el jóker*, the first Puerto Rican play about life in the United States, was staged by La Farándula Panamericana in 1950.[27]

La carreta played in New York in 1952 to sold-out audiences; in response the director, Roberto Rodríguez Suárez, and an actress, Miriam Colón, organized El Nuevo Círculo Dramático, the first Hispanic group in New York to operate out of its own theatre. The group staged Puerto Rican and other Hispanic plays until 1957, when the theatre, on Sixth Avenue between 43rd and 44th Streets, was closed by the Fire Department.

By the mid-1960s other developments were apparent. The Mobile Theater of the New York Shakespeare Festival undertook the staging of Hispanic plays in city parks and in 1965 offered the facilities of the Delacorte Theater, in Central Park, for "A Night of Puerto Rican Poetry and Music." Totally in Spanish, the event attracted an audience of over 2,500. Now an annual venture, the activity has served to highlight the talents of theatre artists such as Colón; Jaime Sánchez, most celebrated for his role in the film *The Pawnbroker*; and Raúl Juliá, who has since appeared in New York productions of *Two Gentlemen of Verona*, *The Three-Penny Opera*, and *The Cherry Orchard* by the New York Shakespeare Festival and *Dracula* on Broadway. It has also presented the work of writers such as Miguel Piñero and poets such as Miguel Algarín, Jesús Papoleto Meléndez, and Pedro Pietri.

The Puerto Rican Traveling Theater

Also in 1965 Roberto Rodríguez Suárez staged his play *Las ventanas* (The Windows) at the Chelsea Theater Center in Brooklyn. In late 1966 *La carreta* was revived, this time in English, at the Greenwich Mews Theater, with leading roles played by Lucy Boscana, Juliá, and Colón. It proved a critical and artistic success and prompted Colón to organize the Puerto Rican Traveling Theater. The play was restaged in the summer of 1967, sponsored by Mayor John Lindsay's Summer Task Force, as the Puerto Rican Traveling Theater's first production.

The Puerto Rican Traveling Theater is a professional, nonprofit, bilingual theatre company that stages works of Hispanic playwrights, stressing those by Puerto Rican authors. The company's goal has been to reinforce the cultural traditions of Puerto Ricans in New York, to serve as a showcase for Puerto Rican writers and theatre artists, and to enrich the cultural life of New York City by presenting the work of one of its largest minority groups.[28]

The company has three principal components: a touring unit, a laboratory theatre, and a training program. The touring group best displays the fundamental commitment to the Puerto Rican community. Each summer plays are taken free of charge to parks, playgrounds, plazas, and street locations throughout the five boroughs of New York City. Since 1967 the touring unit has staged over 20 productions, totaling more than 500 performances. Numerous locations have become standard performance homes. These include Riverside Park (often chosen for the opening performance), Central Park, the plaza at Lincoln Center, and in front of the Metropolitan Museum of Art, in Manhattan; St. Mary's Park and on 178th Street between Arthur and Hughes Streets, in the Bronx; and Lindsay and Red Hook Parks, in Brooklyn. Most locations are in low-income areas where the population is largely black or Puerto Rican. According to Colón, "Our audiences are very mixed because we choose 90 percent of the locations to be in areas where there is more unemployment, more poverty, more deterioration of the neighborhood."[29] The remaining 10 percent are given in such locations as Lincoln Center to expose middle-class audiences to the group's work.

Plays are selected for their relevance to the street audience, reflection of Hispanic tradition, and artistic quality. The company has also developed a policy of using the same cast to stage each play in both English and Spanish to meet different audience requirements. "Spanglish" is not sponsored unless it proves essential to the action of a specific play.

More than half the plays toured have been by Puerto Rican playwrights. The first was *La carreta*, which traces the migration of a Puerto Rican family from the country of San Juan and finally to New York, each act representing one stop on the journey. Luis, the adopted son of Doña Gabriela, has not been able to maintain the family farm and moves the family to San Juan so he can get a factory job. While there, Doña Gabriela's younger son, Chaguito, is sent to prison for petty theft and her daughter, Juanita, is raped and has an abortion. Economic and moral problems and Luis's belief in progress and technology force the family to move to New York, where workers earn higher wages. At last Luis can make a "decent" living and provide basic comforts for his family. Juanita no longer lives with the family and Doña Gabriela lives in constant cultural shock. When Luis is killed by the machines he tried to understand better, Doña Gabriela and Juanita decide to return to Puerto Rico to bury him and reestablish themselves in the countryside. Their journey starts in a primitive oxcart and leads them to the center of the modern industrialized world before returning them to their native culture and traditions.

The play was written to emphasize the strict phonetic pronunciation of the peasant, an element lost in English translation. But the themes remain clear: the possible salvation of national identity in the return to native customs and beliefs, the struggle against social mechanization, and the fatalistic docility of a colonized people. The last theme has been a subject of controversy. Critics oppose Marqués's view by citing his failure to acknowledge the long history of popular resistance to colonization.[30] However, *La carreta* remains the most internationally acclaimed work by a Puerto Rican playwright.

In 1969 the company staged *Encrucijada*, by Manuel Méndez Ballester, which explores the disintegration of a Puerto Rican family in the city of New York. It depicts the lives of an elderly couple living in New York with their three children, Felipe, Mario, and Marta. Don Alfonso, the father, who served in the U.S. Army during the Spanish-American War, has lost the family's wealth. Felipe, also an army veteran, helps support the family by working in a gas station and selling drugs. Mario, the younger son, is a militant nationalist whose attitudes seriously conflict with those of his father. He is jailed for political activism, and while he is imprisoned his son grows up knowing hardly any Spanish. The resolution presents the further disintegration of the family as the children move to the Bronx, Chicago, and Miami and the parents contemplate returning to Puerto Rico.

In 1970 and 1971 the company staged *The Golden Streets* by Piri Thomas. The play deals with a drug addict and the effect of his habit on his family. Raúl, a rehabilitated addict, tries to save his younger brother Luis from addiction. When Luis overdoses and dies, the family unites in a struggle to insure a better life for those who remain. Born in New York, Thomas had experienced an addict's life before writing the play, and his well-known novel *Down These Mean Streets* launched a crusade for rehabilitation. His play received spontaneous responses from street audiences, who yelled their sympathies for victims of the drug scene and at times even attempted to enter the action.[31]

Although they represent only a fraction of the Puerto Rican Traveling Theater's productions between 1967 and 1971, *La carreta*, *Encrucijada*, and *The Golden Streets* demonstrate its early production style and thematic concerns. The realistic style of Puerto Rican literature of the 1940s and 1950s was taken to the streets and played before receptive and responsive audiences. In these plays deterioration of the family, drug addiction, rape, unemployment, and financial and spiritual poverty are seen as consequences of cultural assimilation. Return to the island is seen as one possible solution, but the overall mood remains one of despair.

In the early 1970s the company began to develop a more distinctive presentational style. For the 1971 summer season, ten short stories that show a panorama of Puerto Rican experiences were dramatized: "El convite del Compadre Baltasar" (Compadre Balthasar's Feast), a late-nineteenth-century story by Matias González García; "The Ladies' Man," by María Cadilla de Martínez; "Pacholí," by Enrique Laguerre; "Sol negro" (Black Sun), by Emilio Díaz Valcárcel; "Interludio" (Interlude), by José Vivas Maldonado; and "El Josco," by Abelardo Díaz Alfaro, all of which relate specifically to Puerto Rico, and "Kipling y yo" (Kipling and I), by Jesús Colón; "Los inocentes" (The Innocents), by Pedro Juan Soto; "La caja de plomo" (The Lead Box That Couldn't Be Opened), by José Luis González; and "La Protesta" (The Protest), by Luis Quera Chiesa, which depict life in the United States.

The production used a narrator to thread the stories together. Action and storytelling alternated; realism was juxtaposed with direct presentation; mime was used at times to substitute for dialogue. The new style provided a fuller and more varied view of Puerto Rican characters and events as allegory and graphic social action were interwoven. The production was conceived and directed by Pablo Cabrera, since 1971 an artistic director and consultant for the theatre. Cabrera had established himself as one of the best-trained and most ingenious directors in Puerto Rico, and when he moved to New York in the early 1970s, he became an important new force in the company. For the 1972 summer season he directed *La pasión segun Antígona Pérez* by Luis Rafael Sánchez, the most distinctively "epic" play written to date in Puerto Rico.

La pasión según Antígona Pérez uses the Sophoclean story to depict the struggle of a contemporary Antigone against political tyranny. Antígona, a Latin American woman, has been sentenced to death by her uncle, dictator Creón Molina, for the burial of two friends who had attempted to assassinate him. The death sentence results as much from the defiance of Creón's order that the bodies be left to rot as from the burial itself. An intense ideological and physical battle is carried out to make Antígona reveal the location of the bodies. Family members and representatives of church and state visit the unrelenting prisoner, and the play ends by confirming one of her first lines to the audience: "I'm twenty-five and will die tomorrow."[32]

Rafael Sánchez draws his characters from the political reality of Latin American life. Creón represents the Batistas, the Trujillos, the Peróns, and the Somozas. Also included are numerous references to historical events and persons, which lend a documentary style to the piece. The epic nature is further reinforced through the character of Antígona, who steps away from the action to summarize and analyze the events leading to her execution.[33]

La pasión segun Antígona Pérez has received more international attention than any other Puerto Rican play since *La carreta.* It was first performed as part of the eleventh Puerto Rican Theater Festival in 1968. The 1972 Puerto Rican Traveling Theater production was its first staging in the United States and the company's most ambitious undertaking to that time. It reemphasized the theatre's commitment to Puerto Rican writers and in introducing new dramatic materials gave fresh direction to the group.

Two other productions directed by Cabrera have toured the city in recent years. Jaime Carrero's *Noo Yall,* a comedy about preparations for the Puerto Rican Day Parade, was produced for the 1973 summer season. Written in a rhythmical, vaudevillian style, the play uses broad strokes to present typical characters of the barrio. These include an idealistic young artist and a cynical college student, whereas four neighborhood dropouts, each named Ramón, satirize the misconceptions of social workers who come to study the "flamboyant species." A pompous character parading in the uniform of a nineteenth-century Spanish general adds a touch of commedia dell'arte style to the play. *Eleuterio, el Coquí,* a dramatized adaptation of a short story by Tomás Blanco with music by Rafael Hernández, toured during the 1976 summer season. The nostalgic musical review appealed to a nationalistic sentiment through the character of a small Puerto Rican frog—the *coquí*—struggling against assimilation.

During the 1978 summer touring season two short plays, *Un jíbaro* (A Peasant), a late-nineteenth-century comedy by Ramón Méndez Quiñones, and *La compañía* (The Company, 1964) by Luis Rechani Agrait, were staged by the company. The plays reflect the customs and idiosyncrasies of nineteenth- and early twentieth-century Puerto Rico. Non-Puerto Rican plays have also been produced. Among those toured by the summer traveling unit are an adaptation of Maxwell Anderson's *Winterset* (produced in 1968); *El maleficio de la mariposa* (The Butterfly's Evil Spell), by Federico García Lorca (1970); *El médico a palos* (The Doctor In Spite of Himself) translated into Spanish from Molière (1973); *El papador de promesas* (Payment as Pledged), translated from Brazilian playwright Alfredo Días Gomes (1974); *Historias para ser contadas,* by Dragún (1975); *Amasos los unos sobre los otros* (Everything Not Compulsory Is Strictly Forbidden), by Chilean Jorge Díaz; and *I Took Panama,* a collective work by the Colombian group Teatro Popular de Bogotá (1977).

In 1972 the Puerto Rican Traveling Theater opened a small laboratory theatre on West 18th Street, which substantially increased the number of plays produced—between 1972 and 1976 nineteen productions were staged. A number of these were first performed indoors and later remounted for street presentation. The laboratory theatre also provided space for broadening the company's activities to include readings, performances by other Puerto Rican and Hispanic groups, and development of a training program.

One important production staged at the laboratory theatre was *Piri, Papoleto y Pedro, dirigidos por Pablo* (Piri, Papoleto, and Pedro Directed by Pablo, 1975), a dramatized collection of Nuyorican poetry written by Piri Thomas, Jesús Papoleto Meléndez, and Pedro Pietri and directed by Pablo Cabrera. Only rarely had the group dealt with themes emerging from the contradictions felt by Nuyorican writers, and even the more humorous pieces by Pietri reveal the harsh reality of poverty and cultural displacement. Following a format later seen in such celebrated works as the New York Shakespeare Festival's production of Ntozake Shange's *For Colored Girls Who Have Considered Suicide/When the Rainbow is Enuf* (1976), Cabrera brought the reality of the majority of mainland Puerto Ricans to the stage. According to New York's *El Diario–La Prensa,*

the work of these three poets, which is an integral part of Puerto Rican literature, depicts in short, live images the journey from innocence to experience that has been felt by Puerto Ricans, from La Perla to the barrio to the South Bronx. Well-thought poetry, it is executed with the firmness and precision one usually finds in the best graphic artists.[34]

The poetry is filled with juxtaposed images of Puerto Rico and New York: those of Puerto Rico are often romantic, rich in visual allusions to palm trees, coconuts, the ocean, and fresh air, whereas New York is seen as leaden, polluted, defined by fire escapes, overdoses, death, and despair. If the vision of the homeland is somewhat illusory, the emphasis given racial consciousness is not: in the United States Puerto Ricans face racial as well as cultural discrimination.[35] Sharing the poorer areas of U.S. cities with blacks, second- and third-generation Puerto Ricans have borrowed patterns of behavior and elements of language from their neighbors, factors that surface in the work of these poets.

Although filled with cynicism, the Nuyorican poetry contains strong images of humor and hope. Writing in English they are distanced from Puerto Rico, but they frequently draw closer to the cultural heritage of their homeland through their isolation from it: the search for identity, for *puertorriqueñidad,* becomes even more urgent when faced by its total dissolution.

The production of dramatized poetry at the laboratory theatre included readings and movement by nine performers, three of whom were poets themselves. Additional interactions and subplots were created by Cabrera. Long pieces such as Pietri's "Puerto Rican Obituary" were divided among actors to establish individual characterizations. The production completed the Puerto Rican Traveling Theater's journey through a full range of island and mainland dramatic sources. Their previous work had brought island culture to the urban Northeast, whereas the staging of Nuyorican poetry immersed the group in the art that is informed by mainland life.

The Puerto Rican Traveling Theater has also hosted other groups, performing such works as *Los soles truncos* (The Fanlights), by René Marqués; *Aspazguanza*, a night of Puerto Rican poetry; and Carrero's *Pipo Subway no sabe reier*. *Pipo Subway*, originally staged by the Anamú group from Puerto Rico, was later restaged by the company for its 1972 summer tour. The story of Pipo and his mother and friends focuses on unemployment, school discrimination, witchcraft, the consumer mentality, family disintegration, and misconceptions about the island, seen through the struggle of a Puerto Rican boy in East Harlem trying to acquire a new bicycle.

Since 1972 the theatre's training program has offered courses in acting, speech (English and Spanish), movement, and improvisation. The workshops are designed to help advance theatre as a career alternative for minority students, to urge self-expression, to heighten awareness of dramatic literature and poetry, and to emphasize the study of Puerto Rican culture and heritage.

The Puerto Rican Traveling Theater is the most heavily endowed of the mainland theatre groups, with support from the Rockefeller Brothers Fund; the Parks, Recreation, and Cultural Affairs Administration of New York City; the New York State Council for the Arts, and the National Endowment for the Arts. Funding has increased annually, from $23,000 in 1967 to $143,000 in 1977.

In 1977 the city of New York granted the company a twenty-five-year lease on a four-story firehouse at 304 West 47th Street, just west of the Broadway theatre district. The monthly rent was $240, and the building was renovated to house a 199-seat theatre, classrooms, an experimental space, and administrative offices. The project represents a new level of development and may significantly alter the group's nature and stature. One unfortunate result could be the reduction of the traveling unit, once viewed as the essence of the company, to a secondary branch of the permanent theatre.

Since 1967 the Puerto Rican Traveling Theater has demonstrated a maturity of development equal to its task of establishing a Puerto Rican theatre as a permanent component of the U.S. professional theatre. No other company has so fully covered the range of island and mainland materials. The most stable, active, and representative mainland theatre, it also maintains firm ties to the traditional theatre and the New York professional theatre community.

The Puerto Rican Ensemble and Other Groups

Other groups, frequently nonprofessional and without funding from foundations or public organizations, have often been more experimental, and by emerging from and incorporating community members in the creative process, closer to the Puerto Rican community itself.

In 1968 the Puerto Rican Ensemble formed, to provide more consistent artistic and political direction for performances of Puerto Rican music and poetry, such as those sponsored by the New York Shakespeare Festival. The Vietnam War and continued racial conflict had aroused a new awareness of contradictions between the Puerto Rican community and American society as a whole, and art had become a vehicle to address and analyze social crises. Supported by the New York City Department of Parks, Recreation, and Cultural Activities and coordinated by William Nieves, this activity expressed pro-Puerto Rican independence sentiments, mentioned the U.S. Navy's use of the Puerto Rican island of Vieques for artillery exercises, and opposed U.S. military involvement in Vietnam. Although opposition from more conservative members of the community and segments of the Hispanic press was forthcoming, the first performance, at the Delacorte Theater of the New York Shakespeare Festival in Central Park, was exceptionally successful.

In 1970 a vacant lot in East Harlem was cleared, and the walls of adjoining buildings were slowly transformed by murals displaying the faces of nationalist leaders and Puerto Rican flags. La Plaza Borinqueña, filled by over a thousand spectators, was initiated by the second production of music, poetry, and theatre sponsored by the Puerto Rican Ensemble, with participants including many of the foremost Puerto Rican artists living on the mainland.[36]

The impact of the Puerto Rican Ensemble led to the establishment of two theatre groups: Pedro Santalíz's El Nuevo Teatro Pobre de América (New Poor Theatre of America), and Teatro de Orilla, directed by María Soledad Romero and Rafael Acevedo. Their work represents a significant advance in the creation of theatre in the Puerto Rican community. They follow other third world groups in defining theatre as a vehicle promoting change. Popular Antillian traditions of folklore, music and dance, and comedy intermesh in works with deep Afro-Antillian-American roots and direct social meaning.

El Nuevo Teatro Pobre de América was founded in 1968. The group consists of trained theatre artists and unemployed youngsters from the barrio, while the plays staged have been collective creations performed both in New York and Puerto Rico. Important productions are *El grito en el tiempo* (The Uprising through Time), about an uprising for independence in Puerto Rico in 1868; *Cofresí, Guarapos* ("Sugar Cane Juice" Confresi), and *Cemí en el Palacio de Jarlem* (The Idol in the Harlem Palace), a series of adaptations of short stories by Spanish and Puerto Rican writers. A later piece, *Cadencia en el País de las Maravillas* (Cadence in Wonderland) uses folklore and native humor to study social and political problems facing Puerto Ricans and is probably the most complete and artistically satisfying of the group's works. Presently established in Puerto Rico, in 1979 El Nuevo Teatro Pobre de América staged portions of an unfinished work called *En la corte del Rey Bombay* (At King Bombay's Court), a children's story that serves as a political allegory.

Teatro de Orilla was formed in 1971 with the purpose of abolishing the traditional hierarchy of the commercial theatre, stimulating collective creation, eliminating all stereotyped images in casting, establishing a rapport with the communities hosting the performances, and developing effective means of social and political expression through theatre.[37] Following a touring format, the group has frequently performed in such locations as churches, community centers, prisons, and universities as well as in the streets. It staged two Puerto Rican works, an adaptation of stories from *Spics*, by Pedro Juan Soto, and *El hombre que dijo que no* (The Man Who Said No), by Lydia Milagros González. It also collaborated with El Nuevo Teatro Pobre de América in creating *Guarapos*, produced an adaptation of *Preciosa por ser un encanto por ser un edén* (Beautiful for Being Enchanted for Being an Eden), a stream-of-consciousness poem by Alfredo Matilla Rivas, and mounted a Puerto Rican-ized version of *Historias para ser contadas*, by Dragún. With the exception of *Guarapos*, the productions formed a permanent touring repertory. In 1972 the group acquired a theatre space at 214 East 2nd Street and opened it with *¿Este tren para Delancy?* (This Train for Delancy?), which consists of stories by Pedro Juan Soto and José Luis González and short collective plays such as *El Hombre que quiere vivir* (The Man Who Wanted to Live), *El token* (The Token), and *La factoría* (The Factory). The theatre also served as a performance space for concerts and poetry readings. Another group creation, *Peloalambre no se rinde o las tribulaciones de un pueblo gluembo* (Wire Hair Doesn't Give Up, or The Tribulations of a Lousy People), was based on improvisations drawn from research on black history and traditions and studies of racial discrimination in Puerto Rico, revised and polished in response to audience reactions and suggestions. Musicians and actors worked together; a dream sequence established the story line; and pantomime sequences underscored by music created the historical, social, and political context. Although Teatro de Orilla no longer actively performs, its founding members, María Soledad Romero and Rafael Acevedo, continue to work with other groups.

The group Jurutungo (The Ends of the Earth) exemplifies the work of groups that emerged at a number of New York universities. Based at Brooklyn College, the group produced *Vejigantes* by Francisco Arriví, a play about miscegenation in Puerto Rico, in 1973 and an adaptation of *Historias para ser contadas* in 1976–1977. No longer connected with the college, they staged *La noche que volvimos a ser gente* (The Night We Became Human Again), by José Luis González, in 1977 and began performing *La farsa del amor compradito* (The Farce of Purchased Love), by Luis Rafael Sánchez, in 1979.

In 1976 the First Latin American Popular Theater Festival, sponsored by the New York Shakespeare Festival and the Theater of Latin America (TOLA), was held in New York and brought together many important individuals and groups of the Latin American theatre and Hispanic groups from the United States.[38] *La pulga* (The Flea) was performed by the Puerto Rican street theatre group La Rueda Roja (The Red Wheel), and Teatro 4, a New York–based group comprised principally of Puerto Ricans, represented the Puerto Rican theatre in the United States. Teatro 4 had begun working in Lower Manhattan in 1974 under the direction of Argentine actor Oscar Ciccone. It proposes "to take an art to the people that reflects their manner of expression, their identity, and their language. We believe in art for the people and by the people."[39] In complying with that mission, the group uses the technique of interviewing community members to collect the materials for its productions. In 1976 Teatro 4 participated in the Sixth Festival of Chicano Theater in San Antonio, Texas, and in 1977 it performed as part of the annual World Theater Festival in Nancy, France.

Third-generation Puerto Ricans in New York have developed theatre forms closely tied to their experiences living in mainland cities and use English or "Spanglish" as the language of performance. Of these the Nuyorican Poets' Cafe and the New Rican Cafe, both operating as cafe theatres and frequently performing original poetry as the basis of their productions, as well as the Latin Insomniacs, and the Puerto Rican Bilingual Workshop, are the most prominent. The workshop, directed by Carla Pinza, has been particularly important in its sponsorship and staging of new plays about mainland Puerto Ricans, such as The Commitment (1974), by Joseph Lizardi, and The Livingroom (1976), by Pedro Pietri. The Nuyorican theatres have also laid special emphasis on the combination of theatre presentation and poetry. In the work of Miguel Algarín, one of the founders of the Nuyorican Poets' Cafe; Pietri; Jesús Papoleto Meléndez; Piri Thomas; Miguel Piñero; and others, a new dramatic impulse for the mainland theatre is being formed. Piñero perhaps best exemplifies this in works such as Short Eyes, which won the 1975 New York Drama Critics' Award, and The Leaf People (1976), both produced by the New York Shakespeare Festival. Further stimulus and direction for Nuyorican writers has been provided through the Shakespeare Festival's Latin playwriting unit at the Public Theater.

Other Hispanic groups have acknowledged the contribution of Puerto Ricans to the Latin American and North American theatres. The Teatro Repertorio Español, probably the most renowned of conventional Hispanic theatres in the United States, staged Luis Rafael Sánchez's O casi el alma (Or Almost the Soul) in 1974 and has included Los soles truncos, by René Marqués, in its 1978–1979 touring repertory for performance on college and university campuses.

Puerto Rican and Nuyorican theatres remain very new developments in the U.S. theatre. After an initial period of intense activity in the late 1960s and early 1970s, they have matured and are now undergoing a phase of steadier growth as more artists become seriously involved in spreading their cultural heritage to an expanding audience. This is true not only in New York. In the Chicago area, groups such as Teatro desengaño de pueblo (Theatre of Disabusing the People), directed by Nicolás Kanellos, combine Puerto Rican and Chicano themes to address both audiences. In Boston the Compañía Hispánica de Teatro Bilingüe (The Hispanic Bilingual Theatre Company) stages Latin American, including Puerto Rican, plays, and a strictly Puerto Rican group, La Virazón (Hurricane Winds), formed in 1976 under the direction of Vicente Castro, has staged portions of Spics, Pipo Subway no sabe reir, "A Night of Julia de Burgos Poetry," and the first act of La carreta. Developments in related arts also contribute to the total picture of mainland Puerto Rican theatre. The Puerto

Rican Dance Theater, for instance, has worked along lines similar to those explored by theatre groups, using native folklore and themes of ethnic identity in its performances.

The work of many Puerto Rican groups in the United States has been sporadic and difficult to record. Their impact is not diminished, however. In rejecting many of the principles of the conventional stage, groups exist without such conveniences as grants, theatres, salaries for artists, and continuous acting en-sembles. These conveniences are frequently seen as encumbrances rather than advantages, tying groups to specific locations and production modes. Much work arises to meet a specific situation and has no extension beyond it. Groups form for one performance, or for two or three years of continuous production, then merge with other companies or disband until a new situation calls forth the original impulse that brought the members together. Plays are often collective enterprises without standard published scripts and at times focus so intensely on a community that word-of-mouth advertising entirely supplants printed hand-bills and programs. The groups described here represent the range of Puerto Rican theatre in the United States but by no means constitute the entirety of this widespread community phenomenon.

The emigration of large numbers of Puerto Ricans to the United States has occurred only in the last forty years. During the first decades of that movement, little conscious attention was paid to creating theatre forms that reflected the cultural identity of the growing Puerto Rican community. The emergence of the arts, especially theatre, as a source of cultural expression during the 1960s and 1970s moved to reverse that trend. Strongly tied to island culture, the majority of Puerto Rican theatre groups in the United States continue to depend on the island theatre for dramatic materials and production styles. Though not fully a "satellite" theatre, the mainland theatre to some degree also defies the term "ethnic theatre." Perhaps "theatre in exile" comes closer to the present status, for many Puerto Ricans on the mainland see themselves as living in exile.

Since 1965 remarkable developments have been realized, and the mainland Puerto Rican theatre appears as one with a short and active past and a promising future. Third-generation Puerto Ricans (Nuyoricans) probably hold the key to the shaping of new theatre forms that will more fully express ethnic themes. The history of Puerto Rico in relation to the United States remains an unfinished one, however, and therefore the story of the Puerto Rican theatre in the United States necessarily remains unfinished as well.

NOTES

1. John Lahr, *Up Against the Fourth Wall: Essays on Modern Theater* (New York: Grove Press, 1970), pp. 35–36.

2. Philip Slater, *Earthwalk* (Garden City, N.Y.: Anchor Press, 1974), p. 58.

3. "Proposal for the Funding of a Puerto Rican Theater, including the Puerto Rican Traveling Theater," submitted to the city of New York, May 1969, files of the Puerto Rican Traveling Theater, p. 2.

4. See Edward Gordon Craig, "Rearrangements," in *The Theatre Advancing*, Part 3 (New York: Benjamin Blom, 1947).

5. Emilio Pasarell, *Orígenes y desarrollo de la afición teatral en Puerto Rico* (San Juan, Puerto Rico: Editorial Universitaria, 1951), especially p. 4.

6. Antonia Sáez, *El teatro en Puerto Rico*, 2nd ed. (San Juan, Puerto Rico: Editorial Universitaria, 1972), pp. 15–46.

7. Sáez, *El teatro en Puerto Rico*, pp. 42–46.

8. See Francisco Arriví, *La generación del treinta* (San Juan, Puerto Rico: Instituto de Cultura Puertorriqueña, 1960), p. 4.

9. Victoria Espinosa, "El teatro de René Marqués y la escenificación de su obra: *Los soles truncos*" (Ph.D. diss.: Universidad Autónoma, México City, 1969), p. 72.

10. Antonio S. Pedreira, *Insularismo* (San Juan, Puerto Rico: Editorial Edil, 1934); Tomás Blanco, *Prontuario histórico de Puerto Rico*, 6th ed. (San Juan, Puerto Rico: Instituto de Cultura Puertorriqueña, 1973).

11. Manuel Maldonado Denis, *Puerto Rico: A Socio-Historical Interpretation*, translated by Elena Vialo (New York: Random House, 1972), pp. 142–45.

12. Emilio S. Belaval, "Lo que podría ser un teatro puertorriqueño," in Francisco Arriví, ed., *Areyto Mayor* (San Juan, Puerto Rico: Instituto de Cultura Puertorriqueña, 1966), p. 257.

13. Jordon B. Phillips, *Contemporary Puerto Rican Drama* (New York: Plaza Mayor Ediciones, 1972), p. 16.

14. Carlos Solórzano, *El teatro latinoamericano del siglo veinte* (México City: Editorial Pormoca, 1964), p. 113; Solórzano quoted in Phillips, *Contemporary Puerto Rican Drama*, p. 51.

15. Phillips, *Contemporary Puerto Rican Drama*; Gordon Lewis, *Notes on the Puerto Rican Revolution* (New York: Monthly Review Press, 1974), p. 248.

16. For a history of Hispanic theatre in New York, see Pablo Figueroa, "Teatro: Hispanic Theater in New York City, 1920–1976," published as a program for an exhibition April 22–June 3, 1977, Museo del Barrio, New York (New York: Off Off Broadway Alliance and El Museo del Barrio, 1977).

17. Clarence W. Senior, *Puerto Rican Emigration* (San Juan, Puerto Rico: University of Puerto Rico, Social Science Research Center, 1946), p. 5.

18. Adalberto López, "The Puerto Rican Diaspora" in Adalberto López and James Petras, eds., *Puerto Rico and Puerto Ricans* (New York: John Wiley and Sons, 1974), p. 319.

19. Maldonado Denis, *Puerto Rico: A Socio-Historical Interpretation*, p. 161.

20. U.S. Commission on Civil Rights, *Puerto Ricans in the Continental United States: An Uncertain Future* (Washington, D.C.: the Commission, 1976), especially Chapters 2, pp. 44–81, and 3, pp. 92–133.

21. Kal Wagenheim, *Puerto Rico: A Profile* (New York: Praeger Publishers, 1973), p. 193.

22. Milton M. Gordon, *Assimilation in American Life* (New York: Oxford University Press, 1964), p. 76.

23. Gordon Lewis, *Puerto Rico: Freedom and Power in the Caribbean* (New York: Monthly Review Press, 1963), pp. 6–7.

24. Lewis, *Notes on the Puerto Rican Revolution*, pp. 247–48.

25. Pedro Pietri, "Beware of Signs," in *Puerto Rican Obituary* (New York: Monthly Review Press, 1973), pp. 18–19. Copyright © 1973 by Pedro Pietri. Reprinted by permission of Monthly Review Press.

26. Stan Steiner, *The Islands: The Worlds of the Puerto Ricans* (New York: Harper and Row, 1974), p. 443.

27. See Figueroa, "Teatro: Hispanic Theater in New York City, 1920–1976," pp. 14–21.

28. For a full accounting of the history and development of the Puerto Rican Traveling Theater, see Rosa Luisa Márquez, "The Puerto Rican Traveling Theater Company: The First Ten Years" (Ph.D. diss., Michigan State University, 1977).

29. Miriam Colón, private interview held at the Puerto Rican Traveling Theater offices, 15 July 1976, New York, N.Y.

30. John Lahr, *Up Against the Fourth Wall*, p. 41, calls *La carreta* "a play which argued astoundingly for submission, rather than resilience and dignity." Also see Juan Angel Silén, *Hacia una visión positiva del puertorriqueño* (San Juan, Puerto Rico: Editorial Edil, 1970).

31. See the comments of Scripps-Howard writer Norman Nadel, "The New York Scene," *San Juan Star*, May 23, 1971, p. 12, concerning the reactions of audience members during performances of *The Golden Streets*.

32. Luis Rafael Sánchez, *La pasión según Antígona Pérez*, 2nd ed. (San Juan, Puerto Rico: Ediciones Lugar, 1970), Act 1, Scene 1, line 14. The quotation is taken from the unpublished English playscript used in production. Files of the Puerto Rican Traveling Theater.

33. For a more complete analysis of the play, see Lowell A. Fiet, "Luis Rafael Sánchez's *The Passion of Antígona Pérez*: Puerto Rican Drama in North American Performance," *Latin American Theater Review*, fall 1976, pp. 97–101.

34. "Teatro Rodante Puertorriqueño presenta *Piri, Papoleto y Pedro, dirigidos por Pablo,*" *El Diario–La Prensa* (New York), May 2, 1975, p. 14. Translation given here by Rosa Luisa Márquez.

35. *Puerto Ricans in the Continental United States: An Uncertain Future*, pp. 28–31; Joseph P. Fitzpatrick, *Puerto Rican Americans: The Meaning of Migration to the Mainland* (Englewood Cliffs, N.J.: Prentice-Hall, 1971), pp. 101–14.

36. See Victor Fragoso, "Notas sobre la expresión teatral de la comunidad puertorriqueña en Nueva York: 1965–1975" in "Feria de Expresión Puertorriqueña," (Mimeographed, New York: Centro de Estudios Puertorriqueños, 1976).

37. María Soledad Romero, private interview held in New York, October 25, 1978.

38. New York Shakespeare Public Theater, Program for First Latin American Popular Theater Festival, New York, August 5–15, 1976.

39. Program for First Latin American Popular Theater Festival, p. 17.

BIBLIOGRAPHY

Books and Dissertations

Arriví, Francisco. *La generación del trainta.* San Juan, Puerto Rico: Instituto de Cultura Puertorriqueña, 1960.

Blanco, Tomás. *Prontuario histórico de Puerto Rico.* 6th ed. San Juan, Puerto Rico: Instituto de Cultura Puertorriqueña, 1973.

Craig, Edward Gordon. *The Theatre Advancing.* New York: Benjamin Blom, 1947. See "Rearrangements," in Part 3.

Espinosa, Victoria. "El teatro de René Marqués y la escenificación de su obra: *Los soles truncos.* Ph.D. diss., Universidad Autónoma, México City, 1969. A discussion of the importance of La Farándula Obrera for the Puerto Rican theatre of the 1950s and 1960s.

Fitzpatrick, Joseph P. *Puerto Rican Americans: The Meaning of Migration to the Mainland.* Englewood Cliffs, N.J.: Prentice-Hall, 1971. An excellent historical and sociological study of migration to the mainland, including specific material on racial attitudes confronted by migrant Puerto Ricans in the United States.

González, Nilda. *Bibliografía de Teatro Puertorriqueño, Siglos XIX y XX.* San Juan, Puerto Rico: Editorial Universitaria, 1979. A recent work that, although focused on Puerto Rico, also contributes to the growing body of accessible information on Puerto Rican theatre in the United States.

Gordon, Milton M. *Assimilation in American Life.* New York: Oxford University Press, 1964. Sociological theory about the assimilation of ethnic minorities.

Lahr, John. *Up Against the Fourth Wall: Essays on Modern Theater.* New York: Grove Press, 1970.

Lewis, Gordon. *Notes on the Puerto Rican Revolution.* New York: Monthly Review Press, 1974. Provides an analysis of the position of the arts in Puerto Rico during the 1960s and early 1970s.

————. *Puerto Rico: Freedom and Power in the Caribbean.* New York: Monthly Review Press, 1963.

Maldonado Denis, Manuel. *Puerto Rico: A Socio-Historical Interpretation.* Translated by Elena Vialo. New York: Random House, 1972. Useful for social and cultural background.

Márquez, Rosa Luisa. "The Puerto Rican Traveling Theater Company: The First Ten Years." Ph.D. diss., Michigan State University, 1977.

Pasarell, Emilio. *Orígenes y desarrollo de afición teatral en Puerto Rico.* San Juan, Puerto Rico: Editorial Universitaria, 1951. Particularly good information on the origin and early development of Puerto Rican theatre.

Pedreira, Antonio S. *Insularismo.* San Juan, Puerto Rico: Editorial Edil, 1934.

Phillips, Jordon B. *Contemporary Puerto Rican Drama.* New York: Plaza Mayor Ediciones, 1972. The most important source on island theatre for those who do not read Spanish.

Sáez, Antonia. *El teatro en Puerto Rico.* 2nd ed. Puerto Rico: Editorial Universitaria, 1972. Contains valuable material on the nineteenth-century theatre in Puerto Rico. A historical and critical work on island theatre.

Sánchez, Luis Rafael. *La pasión según Antígona Pérez.* 2nd ed. San Juan, Puerto Rico: Ediciones Lugar, 1970.

Senior, Clarence W. *Puerto Rican Emigration.* San Juan, Puerto Rico: University of Puerto Rico, Social Science Research Center, 1946. A standard early work on migration to the mainland.

Silén, Juan Angel. *Hacia una visión positiva del puertorriqueño.* San Juan, Puerto Rico: Editorial Edil, 1970.

Slater, Philip. *Earthwalk.* Garden City, N.Y.: Anchor Press, 1974.

Solórzano, Carlos. *El teatro latinoamericano del siglo veinte.* Mexico City: Editorial Pormoca, 1964.

Steiner, Stan. *The Islands: The Worlds of the Puerto Ricans.* New York: Harper and Row, 1974. General social and cultural background.

United States Commission on Civil Rights. *Puerto Ricans in the Continental United States: An Uncertain Future.* Washington, D.C.: the Commission, 1976. Effective treatment of the status of Puerto Ricans in U.S. society, with clear and specific reference to the racial attitudes with which they are confronted.

Wagenheim, Kal. *Puerto Rico: A Profile.* New York: Praeger Publishers, 1973. Provides general social and cultural background.

Articles and Pamphlets

Belaval, Emilio S. "Lo que podría ser un teatro puertorriqueño." In Francisco Arriví, ed., *Areyto Mayor.* San Juan, Puerto Rico: Instituto de Cultura Puertorriqueña, 1966.

Fiet, Lowell A. "Luis Rafael Sánchez's *The Passion of Antígona Pérez:* Puerto Rican Drama in North American Performance," *Latin American Theater Review,* fall 1976, pp. 97–101. Contains an analysis of the play.

Figueroa, Pablo. "Teatro: Hispanic Theater in New York City, 1920–1976." Published as a program for an exhibition April 22–June 3, 1977, Museo del Barrio, New York. New York: Off Off Broadway Alliance and El Museo del Barrio, 1977. A useful history.

Fragoso, Victor. "Notas sobre la expresión teatral de la comunidad puertorriqueña en Nueva York: 1965–1975." In "Feria de Expresión Puertorriqueña." New York: Centro de Estudios Puertorriqueños, 1976. Mimeographed. Contains sound general information about Puerto Rican theatre in New York during the 1960s and 1970s and specific information about the Puerto Rican Ensemble.

López, Adalberto. "The Puerto Rican Diaspora." In Adalberto López and James Petras, eds., Puerto Rico and Puerto Ricans. New York: John Wiley and Sons, 1974. Useful for social and cultural background.

Pietri, Pedro. "Beware of Signs." In Puerto Rican Obituary. New York: Monthly Review Press, 1973.

Other Sources

Additional information on Puerto Rican theatre in the continental United States was obtained from the Spanish-language press, from the files of the Puerto Rican Traveling Theater, from printed theatre programs, and from interviews and informal discussions with many knowledgeable persons, including Miriam Colón, Pablo Cabrera, María Soledad Romero, and Pedro Santalíz.

17

Slovak-American Theatre

M. MARTINA TYBOR

Nineteenth-century Slovak immigrants to the United States experimented with amateur theatricals in some of their major settlements. In this endeavor they were not innovating; they were spontaneously reactivating in the New World an art form historically well established in their homeland. Realistically, of course, the immigrants had their limitations in this effort.

Most of the early Slovak immigrants came from the ranks of the average European villagers. Often their homeland situations had not allowed them more than meager educational opportunities, but many had enjoyed occasional intellectual events and some academic entertainment. In a free America, on the other hand, even the poorly schooled found encouragement to exercise an alert mentality and to cultivate cultural interests within their means.

Formally educated Slovak immigrants cherished a wholesome awareness of their cultural history and of the arts. In the United States they continued to take an interest in dramatics and in developing related resources. Politics and various negative forces in the homeland had warped many intellectual potentials and prospects among the Slovaks; yet in spite of much adversity they had made some progress there. It is interesting and profitable, therefore, to consider the background of drama among the Slovaks in Europe and in the United States.

HISTORICAL BACKGROUND

Theatre as a social activity remains a performing rather than a purely literary art form, and the influence of politics, economics, and the temper of the times can affect its progress or decline. The audience factor is likewise important, and for this reason theatre can flourish only in connection with adequate population concentration.[1]

All through the feudal period, from the eleventh to the thirteenth century, the Slovaks of Upper Hungary lacked the social, political, and cultural milieu for the development of drama.[2] Their native land in east central Europe was protected on the north by the towering Tatry, or Carpathian, Mountains, and the Danube flowed along part of the southern border. Its geographic position and physical features made it the crossroads of roving tribes, migrating peoples, merchant caravans, and military forces. It lost its independence after the battle of Bratislava in A.D. 907 and became the battleground of sporadic wars between the Magyars and Germans. Finally, in the eleventh century, the Slovak homeland became a vassal principality in the kingdom of Hungary and its people shared the fate of other minorities, being subjected to denationalizing pressures, exploitation, untold hardships, and educational deprivation. Subsequently, Turkish invasions from the fifteenth century onward, as well as upheavals of religious and class strife in the early seventeenth century, continued to make the environment of the Slovaks unsuitable for cultivation and development of dramatic arts.[3]

In spite of these adverse circumstances, however, some stirrings of dramatic expression asserted themselves among the people. The following historically identifiable periods emerge, with their specific contributions in the evolutionary process: (a) from the cresting of feudalism to the rise of humanism (twelfth to fifteenth centuries); (b) the Renaissance and Reformation (sixteenth century); and (c) neofeudalism to the age of enlightenment and the Slovak national awakening (seventeenth century and onward).[4]

Examining the content of the presentations, it is possible to distinguish the following types of drama: (a) dialogues, tropes, declamations and mystery, miracle, and morality plays derived almost exclusively from Biblical and liturgical substance; (b) Latin school plays of the Protestant denominations and the elaboration of drama in Jesuit and Piarist schools, in which interludes and curtain raisers using the vernacular appeared with increasing frequency; and (c) the emergence of secular theatre, followed by the first professional drama and early operatic works, originating at aristocratic residences and in the towns.

There were similarities between the development of Slovak drama and the dramatic progression common to western Europe, and there were distinguishing features as well. Early foreshadowings of Slovak drama sprang from ancient practices: pagan rites like the festive fires and ritual participation in leaping over the flames, accompanied by dancing and chanting during the summer solstice celebrations (June 24),[5] as well as the folk observance of spring festivities. These also included the symbolic destruction of an effigy of Morena (death) to welcome Živena (life) and the springtime awakening of all nature. Features of funeral and wedding customs[6] likewise provided the elements of seeing and listening that are vital constituents of drama and theatre.

In Christian times these observances and other pagan expressions of naturalistic religious belief assumed a modified spirit. The Church drew upon matter from the liturgy and scriptures to involve worshipers in Christian ceremonial action and in religious participation and experience. Simple dialogue that evolved into tropes, and appropriate movement, recreated the substance of the great Easter and Nativity celebrations. Eventually such solemnities helped to displace pagan customs. It is important to note this development because traditional Christmas and Easter folk customs characterized by dramatic quality remained a part of Slovak cultural life through the centuries. For example, the tradition of the costumed strolling Betlehemci or Jasličkare of Christmastide (troupes of young men and boys carrying staves, the Christmas star, and the crib scene, singing special carols and dramatizing events associated with the Christmas story as they visited one family after another of their acquaintance) made its way to practically all the immigrant settlements in America.

The Earliest Slovak documents relating to drama begin with an entry in the civic accounts of the city of Bratislava in 1439. It registers payment for expenses related to an Easter play given in the court in front of the local school.[7] Bratislava public records also indicate payments and play presentations or entertainments on these occasions:

1449	To a traveling company of students who played the harp, sang, and entertained officials in the town hall.
1477	Easter and Passion plays, given in the town square as city fathers looked on from tents set up for the event; also to a juggler who entertained at the election of town officials.
1492	An unspecified play at the tomb of Christ (Corporis Christi).
1519, 1520	Passion plays presented by guild members.
1544, 1545	Here we first meet a title to identify the play: *Judith*, which was performed in Bratislava square; also a dramatization of the New Testament parable of the five wise and five foolish virgins.[8]

Similar entries in Bardejov accounts document the enactment of Easter mystery plays between 1439 and 1450.[9] Incidentally, they also mention the infiltration of extraneous elements, improvisations, and folk and secular characteristics. In the years closing the fifteenth and opening the sixteenth centuries, deserving actors received prizes of one-half to one *zlaty* (guilder).[10]

Schools also promoted drama. To the end of the thirteenth century, Slovak schools were church oriented. They were capitular, monastic, or parochial, and they favored classical Latin in the upper levels. For stage presentations they drew upon Terence and Plautus. Town schools that appeared in the fourteenth century were secular in spirit, and their dramatic programs reflected a deviation to secular themes. They also departed from the use of Latin and chose the vernacular, with preference for German. This is understandable, for Protestants and families of means and social position often sent their sons to German schools, especially to Wittenberg, where they became fluent in German and absorbed Germanic ideology and a fondness for German trends.

Originally the schools looked to drama as an excellent source of academic assignments in memory training. Drama also provided a means of studying character traits; observing the tempo of life; appreciating the rewards of a good life and virtue; realizing that penalties follow wrong doing, bad habits, and uncontrolled passions; and promoting sociability and involvement in corporate effort and a common cause.[11] The dramatic arts disciplined the mind; they sharpened proficiency in Latin, rhetoric, and public speaking or declamation at the same time that they developed poise and self-possession. Besides, they attracted the notice of the esteemed and the beneficent to the schools and their activities, creating publicity where it counted.[12] Additionally, the innovations of John Amos Comenius (1592–1670), a Moravian theologian-educator of international fame, gave greater impetus to the production of plays for the sake of associating entertainment and pleasurable activity to offset the burden of study. Dramatics also created wholesome competition in the scholarly arts.[13]

Under humanistic and Reformation influences in the fifteenth century, the religious aspects of drama yielded to classical themes from Greek and Roman mythology, to allegorical dialogues, satire, and inevitable moralizing. The vernacular began to claim its place, especially in the interludes. Folk plays with considerable legendary content (for example, the St. Dorothy tradition) began to appear.[14] Protestant pedagogues and rectors of schools, like Leonard Stöckel and Thomas Faber in Bardejov, Francis Polleramus and Kremnica, and Elias Ladiver in Prešov, promoted school plays for their didactic value and as a means of popularizing and interpreting Protestant dogma. Stöckel, who also wrote plays, earned distinction for his drama on Susanna (1556), which was published in 1559 in Wittenberg. It was the first school play to appear as a printed book. In the Jesuit schools of the Counter-Reformation, drama became the acknowledged handmaid of the Catholic faith and of learning.

Research has brought to light welcome information about certain masters who prepared original plays and about the substance and structure of some dramas. Specialized study further provides some facts about incidental stage directives; costuming (sometimes obtained from as far away as Venice); setup of the stage and its ornamentation; appointments for various occasions; and ingenious devices constructed to expedite scene changes and rather elaborate staging, like realistic and breathtaking storms at sea; flights through the air, floods, and hurricanes; and massive military encounters.[15]

Jesuit schools cultivated dramatic activities intensively.[16] Two authorities, namely E. Fináczy and somewhat later B. Dombi, convincingly estimate that from 1601 to 1773 the Jesuits in Hungary staged a total of 10,000 productions.[17] There is firm documentation for 180 productions in Trnava alone. Skalica had 119 dramatic programs, and other Slovak towns show evidence of surprisingly large numbers as well.[18]

These findings become a significant indicator of the degree of cultural and literary activity that prevailed in the schools and had penetrated into the social structure of the Slovak region. The audiences manifested great interest and enthusiasm for dramatic art. Well-supplied Jesuit libraries provided useful thematic reference materials. Qualified writers drew upon them, borrowing not only from the Scriptures but from history, myth, and legend as well, to provide a highly diversified repertory in which more and more original works appeared along with numerous translations. Writers began to introduce into the plays occasional references to or commentary on the contemporary scene.[19]

In the seventeenth and eighteenth centuries the Piarist Fathers, who were also educators, promoted school plays in Nitra, Podolinec, Krupina, Banská Bystrica, Svätý Jur, and Prievidza. Professors at the schools wrote some of the plays for student presentation. Often they encouraged their students to write plays on assigned subject matter. Allegorical and symbolic works of a moralizing or didactic nature, favoring themes from Greek and Roman history, seem to have been the most popular. In addition to the major feature, a dramatic program often included minor offerings. Among them were formal declamations, pastoral numbers—eclogues, and the like. A dash of comedy was always in order. Invariably there was music, dance, and song, and sometimes there was entertainment by clowns.[20]

Even up to the 1599 *Ratio Studiorum* of the Jesuits, all their stage performances had to be exclusively in Latin, but as drama reached out to ever-widening audiences, the majority of which had no mastery of Latin, the vernacular gained ascendancy. In 1628 the dialogue given in conjunction with spectacular Old Testament tableaux on "Foreshadowings of the Eucharist," acted by a very large cast in the Franciscan square in Bratislava, may have been the first occasion on which Slovak was formally spoken from the public stage.[21] Four languages—Latin, German, Slovak and Hungarian—were used in what became a practice favored by the Jesuits in order to accommodate the multilingual populace. For further detail and documentation on the use of Slovak in connection with drama, see Appendix A to this chapter.

Between 1660 and 1701 orchestral music, songs, and dances embellished stage programs in Skalica. On occasion the director engaged a professional choreographer from Vienna to coach the dances. By the close of the seventeenth century, Jesuit plays showed characteristics of the pastoral musical, suggesting a trend toward Italian opera.[22]

The interest and devotion of the Jesuits in cultivating dramatic works in Slovakia as early as the seventeenth and eighteenth centuries added a dimension to Slovak cultural life. As a religious society of cosmopolitan spirit, the Jesuits appreciated the individuality and ethnic identities of the various national groups. They began to compile Slovak hymnals for the people, and they prepared devotional, cultural, scientific, and informational works for them. Very importantly, too, they raised the Slovak language to the theatrical stage as a medium of dramatic art.[23]

TRANSITIONS

These developments led to further activity. Juraj Palkovič (1763–1835) became a trailblazer among writers of the Bernolák following, who advocated linguistic reforms. His contributions were not original works but translations, chiefly from Latin, German, and Italian, that appeared in 1801.[24] They established the more consistent use of Slovak on the stage and provided new materials for staging.

After the civil authorities imposed strict censorship on plays, acting groups resorted to using dramas that had already been performed in Vienna and Budapest, on the assumption that these dramas had been approved and were not subject to sanctions. The police and civil magistrates required directors to give three months' notice of dramatic works that were to go into production. After the French Revolution, special measures were taken that no references to the regicide be brought before the public, especially on the stage. Reactionary groups were under special scrutiny, and student plays were closely screened. When students from the Banská Štiavnica Evangelical School violated the regulation on May 19, 1787, action was taken against them and the rector.[25] In some places school plays were banned altogether. The use of Latin on the stage declined, and interest in Biblical themes waned. Consequently, from the close of the eighteenth century, drama continued to show influences from the earlier stage but moved more decisively to the vernacular and to a secular spirit. It reflected involvement in the social climate and was charged with overtones from the French Revolution.

When the Turkish incursions created a severe threat to Hungary, the ruling class, the official records, the crown jewels, and many governmental essentials were brought to Bratislava in Slovakia. It became the coronation city and gained prominence because of its position in the political life of Hungary. At the same time, it received influences from Vienna and became the favorite haunt of leisured aristocrats, especially as the hosting city of Albert Tešín, the son-in-law of Empress Maria Theresa. As it gained stature in the arts, Bratislava became important for theatre entertainment as well. This, of course, applied to the magnates and the upper class; the lesser citizens were largely peasants bound to the soil. Occasionally the less privileged ones enjoyed the visits of traveling troupes, which performed in halls of limited capacity or in local inns and taverns.[26]

Shakespeare's plays had a Bratislava debut in 1774, with *Hamlet, Othello,* and *King Lear.* In 1775 *Macbeth* was on the Bratislava boards.[27] Theatres were built in Bratislava (1775) and in Košice (1789),[28] and there was much interest in stage plays as well as in opera (largely imported), which appealed strongly to the tastes of the leisured upper class.

At a kind of midpoint there appeared the figure of Gašpar Fejérpataky (1794–1874). Primarily a bibliophile, he lived in Liptovský Sv. Mikuláš and was dedicated to circulating, lending, and publishing Slovak books. He was also a man on the move, with a penchant for theatergoing in cities like Vienna, Levoča, Košice, Lučenec, and Pest. These experiences prompted him to undertake the directing of youth plays. His first production in Liptovský Sv. Mikuláš was staged on August 22, 1830, when he presented Ján Chalupka's work *Kocúrkovo.* In his career as stage director from 1830 to 1843, he produced a total of thirty-three works.[29]

Out of these developments there emerged professional, amateur, and folk types of Slovak drama and theatre, although it is not always easy to make clearcut distinctions among these types.

BEYOND THE EIGHTEENTH CENTURY

Ján Chalupka (1791–1871) became the first Slovak dramatist of note. Satire was his forte. Its barbs penetrated common weaknesses and social foibles, chauvinism, alcoholism, social climbing, petty officialdom, pretense and snobbery, bureaucracy, aping of foreign manners, and Magyarization. This last was a movement to impose the Magyar language on all the minorities in Hungary, to deny them academic and cultural opportunities, and to suppress their native tongue, national consciousness, and loyalty to their origin. The theme of aping foreign manners forms the substance of *Kocúrkovo* (first printing in 1830), with a patently fictitious locale that parallels the mythical Gotham in England or Podunk in the United States—a place all too familiar in the minds of the readers and audiences. This *Kocúrkovo* idea runs through much of Chalupka's prose and practically all of his dramatic works.[30]

Ján Palárik (1822–1870) sought to revive national consciousness by using the effective medium of drama. He is considered the first of modern Slovak dramatists.[31] His earliest success was *Inkognito* (1858), a play that has often been staged by Slovaks in the United States. Jonáš Záborský (1812–1876) also endeavored to rouse patriotic sentiment, but his approach was through historical drama. He hoped that recalling past glory on the stage would inspire renewed pride of nation.[32]

Moving out of the romantic era toward the period of realism brings out the name of the outstanding Slovak playwright of modern times, Ferko Urbánek (1859–1934). He was not a writer who grew with the catalogue of his creations; he began with a recognized measure of mastery and a command of dramatic art suited to his day, and he maintained that degree of excellence. His works bear the stamp of his positive outlook, proper conduct, and sound morality, presented in an affirmative yet entertaining style. He regarded the stage as a vehicle for portraying true-to-life situations in which the dramatist enjoyably impresses the audience with the evils of materialism, of doing violence to the spirit, of godlessness, of disregard for acceptable moral conventions.[33]

Urbánek became a dramatist of such popular appeal that it has been said, "Of the five thousand yearly performances in Slovak amateur theaters, eight hundred were generally Urbánek's plays."[34] Among his most acclaimed works are *Rozmarín* (Rosemary), *Kamenný chodníček* (The Stony Pathway), *Bludár* (The Vagabond), *O tie ženy* (O These Women), and *Pokuta za hriech* (Penalty for Sin). Urbánek, together with Pavel Sochaň, Oľga Horváthová, and Jozef Hollý rank as deserving dramatists of the prewar years.[35]

Dramatists of note who were active after World War I included Jozef Gregor Tajovský, Vladimír Hurban Vladimírov, and particularly Ivan Stodola. Younger promising playwrights closer to our day were K. F. Urbanovič, Peter Karvaš, and the gifted Július Barč-Ivan. Assessing the artistic potential and the reality of unhappy controls that the political upheaval into Marxist socialism imposed upon cultural expression, when every talent was requisitioned to serve the interests of the state, a critic observed: "A tree that was ready to burst into lush full bloom has been lopped at its very roots."[36]

THE EARLY SLOVAK-AMERICAN SCENE

The foregoing indicates that there was a favorable situation for transplanting dramatic arts from the homeland seedbed to the New World after mass emigration displaced Slovaks to America. By the late nineteenth century there was a moderate exodus out of the eastern regions of Slovakia. Before long it gained momentum. According to the U.S. Census of 1920, there were 610,866 Slovaks officially recorded in this country.[37] Many more were actually present but were classified as Hungarians or Austrians because they had to state that they were born in Austria-Hungary; Slovakia did not have autonomous political status then. At least two-thirds of those officially recorded were young men.

Initially most of these immigrants regarded separation from their native land as a temporary necessity. Economic need and politico-feudal oppression had made them reach the difficult decision to leave home. They hoped, however, that job opportunities, coupled with diligent work in the free world, would improve their situation, and they counted on returning home to improve the lot of their families. They wanted to build themselves a better future in their homeland. Actually, however, over the years more than 500,000 Slovak immigrants chose to remain in this country permanently. Through no fault of their own, very few of them were schooled or professional people. They were predominantly the working class, the poor, the disadvantaged. Luxuries were not their privilege, so it is not surprising that they did not at once cultivate the fine arts in a conspicuous way.

One of their early achievements in the United States was the formation of lodges and local mutual aid societies. Beginning with the founding of the first Slovak society in New York City on March 3, 1883,[38] the number of these groups increased amazingly. By 1890 there were 14 Slovak societies, 7 of which were in Pennsylvania;[39] within ten years (by 1893) there were 277 independent Slovak societies in this country,[40] and more were steadily being formed. Out of this great proliferation of lodges, there emerged noteworthy national fraternals such as the National Slovak Society (NSS, 1890), with a 1970s membership of 21,868; the First Catholic Slovak Union, Jednota (1890), with a 1970s membership of 105,837; the First Catholic Slovak Ladies Association, Ženská Jednota (1892), with a 1970s membership of 104,517; the Pennsylvania Slovak Catholic Union (1893), with a 1970s membership of 9,163; the Ladies Pennsylvania Slovak Catholic Union (1898), with a 1970s membership of 16,192; and the Slovak Catholic Sokol (1916), with a 1970s membership of 49,994.[41]

From their inception as local societies and all through their development into national fraternals, these organizations promoted cultural endeavors and provided additional benefits, such as aid in time of sickness or death, care of orphans, and dividends. Each one published an official newspaper and encouraged support of the press. Noting this phenomenon, a Hungarian agent wrote with consternation informing headquarters from his base in America that

in Hungary you have no idea about the extent and the effectiveness of organized life among the Slovaks in the United States. . . . A simple peasant I had known and once rated as the least and last of all in his native village, here has a position of honor and responsibility, acting as president of a lodge that frequently numbers up to a hundred members or more. It is incredible that this officer chairs the meeting sessions so capably that even the "educated" observer might have some qualms about being able to measure up to this one's astuteness. Furthermore, this one who is a previously scorned peasant is not alone in the presiding area. He is flanked by a recording secretary, a treasurer, and a corresponding secretary—all immigrants, all formally unschooled people. Over and above all this, they keep their records of proceedings and their accounts as well as their official correspondence in better order and fashion than do some of our Hungarian finance firms.[42]

This is what the milieu of opportunity and freedom was doing to educate the previously backward peasants. At the same time, however, Rev. Štefan Furdek, Peter V. Rovnianek, Rev. Matthew Jankola, and other community leaders opted for more. Rovnianek wrote:

When I recommend steps for the cultural enlightenment and education of the people, I do not merely mouth the words. I apply myself to the realization of this ideal. . . . I strongly promote choral groups, for example, and despite a constant overload of work, I reinforce words with example by coming to the rehearsals. I also organized a night school for adults in our area where my colleague Julius Wolf conducts English classes. Our example in Pittsburgh is being imitated by other Slovak settlements. Concerts, entertainments, choral programs and stage plays are being presented in all sizable Slovak communities—in New York, Cleveland, Chicago, Philadelphia.[43]

Furdek also advocated the social and educational benefits associated with fraternalism as a natural outcome of participation in communal activities.[44]

A spirited and resourceful woman, Mária Kmeť, ventured to prove the reverse as well. She realized that cultural activities could promote and benefit the fraternals.[45] Upon the repeated urging of Rovnianek and Kmeť, the ladies' organization Živena was founded in New York on July 19, 1891. It became a feminine counterpart of NSS, with headquarters in Pittsburgh. Under Kmeť's leadership early problems were overcome, there was a healthy increase in membership, and all were confident about the continued growth of this society. Kmeť, with her dynamism, looked to an even greater and more meaningful promotion, however. She counted on launching a public debut of some kind, and after her ideas crystallized, she shared her thinking with Stephen Jecuška, a helpful coworker. They finalized plans to sponsor a Živena event that would be a first in New York: a stage play, to attract and entertain a large number of people. Because they had neither play books nor the text of a drama, Kmeť and Jecuška arranged to obtain needed resources from relatives in Prešov. Then, working from a Hungarian script, Jecuška and John Blizman translated and adapted the play for the Slovak stage. Parts were copied by hand and distributed among eager young people, some of whom were no strangers to little theatre. Jecuška became director, and Kmeť was cast in the leading role in Čert Zaru. Blizman was stage prompter. The production was scheduled for the third Sunday after Easter in 1892, and it was a sensation. For the immigrants it was the first Slovak play in the metropolis, and they loved it. Kmeť and her associates savored success beyond all expectations, and the Živena society gained much prestige. All the roles in this play, including the male characters, were played by women, reversing the long-established convention of allowing only men to act on stage.

Capitalizing on the success of this experiment, Živena in New York produced other plays. Their next was a comedy, Bohatá vdova, krajčírka z Prahy (The Rich Widow—The Seamstress from Prague). It dealt with the hilarious complications of the busy leading character and eighteen workmen employed in her shop. This performance also drew enthusiastic response and attracted new members to the society. After the first Živena convention, which opened on September 2, 1895, rehearsals were held for Hruza! čo sa robí! (Horrors! What's Going on?), by Fredrov. Ethel Cablk, the sister of Paula Novomeská, who was an esteemed leader in the Živena, had brought a copy of the play expressly for the society when she arrived in New York from Slovakia. The production was directed by Anton Š. Ambrose, with Wolf as prompter. It was staged on Easter Sunday in 1896.[46] The cast included Mária Ruman, Novomeská, Kmeť, John Slabey, and John Štepita.[47]

Other performances followed. Despite the lack of a complete record of the programs, documentation of at least two has been recovered. On November 7, 1908, Živena staged a double feature: Betkina lekcia (Betty's Lesson), by M. Olga Horváthová, and Honorár (The Honorarium), by Pavel Sochaň. On March 5, 1911, they presented Sochaň's Sedliacka nevesta (The Peasant Bride).[48]

Documentation on other plays in various locations during the 1890s includes the following:

1890 (June 18) In Bridgeport, Pennsylvania, the local branch of the National Slovak Society presented Chalupka's Kocúrkovo. In all likelihood this was the first Slovak play staged in the United States.[49]

1890 (November 2) A cast of fifteen male and seven female actors of Assembly 23 NSS, known as the Národná Slovenská Dobročinnosť (National Slovak Charitable Group), of Newark, New Jersey, appeared in a play arranged and adapted from a novel by Pater Peter. It was directed by F. Mascuch and staged for the benefit of Society Panonnia, a local mutual aid organization. This was the first Slovak play in Newark, and afterwards this assembly had frequent dramatic productions.[50]

1893 The Slovaks of Chicago established the First Slovak Sokol in the USA on October 10, 1892. As a cultural adjunct they founded a choral and dramatic branch within their ranks on March 8, 1893. By September 1901 this cultural group prepared to stage the operetta *Plavci na palube* (Mariners Aboard).[51]

1894 Members of the National Slovak Society (NSS) formed the first Slovak Dramatic Club in Freeland, Pennsylvania, and performed in several nearby communities, including Hazleton and Shepton.[52]

1896 During the sixth convention of the Jednota, held in Braddock, Pennsylvania, there was a series of stage entertainments: *Smelý manžel* (The Fearless Husband), featuring Andrew Lipovský and Mária Havel; *Arcidarebak* (The Super Good-for-Nothing), a monologue by Michael W. Sabol; the tragedy *Kristian alebo Krišpinian* (Christian or Crispinian), with Anna Meleky, John Tinuhmidl, John W. Sabol, and Stephen Masuch in the cast; *Cigan a žid* (The Gypsy and the Jew), a comedy acted by Andrew Lipovský, Andrew Meleky, Andrew Kubani, and Adolf Camer; and *Učeň* (The Apprentice), presented by Michael W. Sabol.[53]

1898 Observing the tenth anniversary of St. Ladislaus parish in Cleveland, Ohio, the school staged the play *Bratanec sv. Germana* (St. Germaine's Cousin). A cast photograph shows almost thirty participants.[54]

Among the early Slovak immigrants, theatre served both a social and a recreational function. At a time when little diversion came their way, attendance at a play broke the monotony of long working days. Action on the stage absorbed the attention of the audience, provided laughter, fantasy, inspiration, or edification and invited the onlookers to identify with the cast. Coming to a play meant meeting countrymen, friends, and relatives, exchanging ideas, sharing family news and social courtesies. It meant being refreshed before returning to daily tasks again. It is understandable, then, that light comedy or satire, together with a dash of melodrama, romance, mystery, or historical action became popular on stage in the beginning. In time, serious drama of an artistic quality, tragedies, historical plays, musicals, and sacred numbers also came into their own before appreciative audiences.

CULTURAL AND DRAMA SOCIETIES

Dispersed as they were throughout the United States, Slovak immigrant groups did not form a single unified cultural body or center. In a number of localities, however, the immigrants founded societies that cultivated the arts along with social activities. Theatrical and choral performances became the prime recreational interest of many. Very often members of church choirs fostered folk songs and art music as well as church music. Naturally, drama found a place among them, too.

Národ, New York City

Národ (The Nation) was founded in New York City in 1900 on the initiative of Emil Jalovecký. Charter members who became associated with him were Ladislaus Matúšek, Peter Ružiak, Andrew Uličný, Paul Vaclavek, Charles Krupa, John Spevák, John Kovačka, Louis Garžik, John Nosian, Louis Vavra, Rudolph Palay, and Sigismund Božek. Their original purpose was to cultivate literary interests and establish an extensive library and reading circle. They also planned to sponsor literary competitions, awarding prizes and honors for original works, especially plays.[55] Before long, however, they realized that a book collection, readings, and recitations were not enough; theatre had more to offer. The staging of plays involved active participation, created worthwhile public entertainment, evoked a response, attracted new membership for the group, and provided funds for expanding the library.

Data provided through the personal experience and research of Edward Kováč[56] reveal the following information about their performances:

1905 The first of their stage plays, Ruský špion (The Russian Spy) by A. Božek.

1906 Two unidentified plays.

1907 Následky dostaveníčka (Aftermath of the Rendezvous), by J. Kühnl, adapted by B. R., translated by A. Halaša.

1908 Pokuta za hriech, by Urbánek; Mam a klam (Sham and Fraud), by Urbánek.

1909 Zpod jarma (Liberated from the Yoke), by F. Sokol-Tůma; Radúz a Mahuliena, by Julius Zeyer.

1910 Slobodní murári (Free masons); Česť (Honor).

1911 Biela myšička (The Little White Mouse); Bojarová svadba (Bojar's Wedding); Nemá z Porieca (The Mute from Poriec); Predvečer (Evening), by Louise Rieger.

1912 Eva, by Rieger; Osudné meniny (The Fateful Name Day); Nedajme sa! (Let's Not Yield!); Balkanská vojna (The Balkan War).

1913 Nedajme sa!, staged in Yonkers, New York; O polnoci (At Midnight), by Urbánek; Obeť lásky (Victim of Love).

1914 Zkazená krv (Spoiled Blood); Na pomoc Rusom (Help for the Russians).

1915 Duk stryčko z Ameriky (Uncle Duke from America), directed by Matúšek.

1916 Majiteľ hút (Owner of the Iron Works), by G. Ohnet.

1917 Bojarová svadba (Bojar's Wedding), directed by J. Honza.

1920 Majiteľ hút.

1921 Z otroctva k slobode (From Bondage to Freedom), directed by Mária Zgurišková.

1922 Farár a jeho kostolník (The Pastor and His Sexton), with a repeat performance in Guttenberg, New Jersey; U bieleho koníčka (At the White Colt), with a reprise.

1923 Pod na moje srdce (Come to My Heart); Aničkina prvá láska (Ann's First Love), directed by V. B. Tuma.

1924 Hvezdársky šuhaj (The Young Astronomy Expert); Peg môjho srdca (Peg O' My Heart), in Slovak translation; Nevestín veniec (The Bridal Wreath).

1925 Chudobný pesničkár (The Needy Song Writer); Charleyova teta (Charley's Aunt), Slovak translation from Brandon's original.

1926 *Nový život* (A New Life); *Madame San Gene; Krutohlavci* (The Stiffnecked), by Urbánek.

1927 *Peg môjho srdca.*

1928 *Mladucha na skúšku* (Experimental Bride); *Pekná, nová, maľovaná koliska* (The Lovely New Painted Cradle), an operetta by V. H. V. (Vladimír Hurban Vladimírov), published in Yugoslavia, with music composed by Ján Podhradský and Imrich Jánoška.

1929 Repeat performance of *Pekná, nová, maľovaná koliska*, under the direction of F. Malý.

1930 *Bačová žena* (The Master Shepherd's Wife), by Ivan Stodola, directed by Stanislaus Mizerovský.

1931 *Veselá Katka* (Joyous Kate); *Inkognito;* and *Ako si Kačka šťastie vyslúžila* (How Kate, the Domestic, Earned Good Fortune).

1932 Repeat performances; also *Muzikanti zo slovenskej dediny* (Musicians from a Slovak Village), performed in New York City and in Yonkers.

1933 *Nepýtaj sa, prečo ťa bozkávam* (Don't Ask Why I Kiss You).

1934 *Poklesky* (Lapses); *Ciganka tý krásna* (You Beautiful Gypsy).

1935 *Gróf Monte Christo* (Count of Monte Christo); *Pán Tomáš* (Mr. Thomas); and *Náhražkový sňatok* (Wedding by Proxy); the two latter plays were directed by Mária Stanková.

1936 *Veľblud uchom ihly* (Camel Through the Needle's Eye), directed by Stanková; *Presadená ruža prérie* (The Transplanted Prairie Rose), directed by Michael Hečko.

1938 *Dedinský skupáň* (The Village Tightwad), directed by Hečko.

1940 *Deti Slovače* (Children of the Slovak Land and People).

1942 *Láska malej rybárky* (The Love of the Little Fishermaid), directed by Mizerovský; choral training and conducting by J. Tuma.

1946 *V tatranskej dedine* (In the Tatra Village).

This much may serve to provide a fair idea of the extent and variety of works in the repertoire of Národ. Many of the works were translated from other languages, such as *Peg O' My Heart* and *Charley's Aunt*. Some of the most versatile and dedicated translators in this group were Matúšek, J. Božek, P. Varinský, Stanková, L. Podolan (Devečková), and Jaroslav Šteffel.

Generally plays were chosen to please the audience; they were judged from the standpoint of audience appeal rather than for their artistic quality alone. On the whole, however, they have much artistic value and the productions were of professional quality. In the course of years, interest in drama and stagecraft was extended to newer members. This cultural society made impressive progress in theatre, besides cultivating literary interests and enriching its original library holdings.

True to its early aspirations, Národ sponsored several literary competitions to stimulate the writing of plays in Europe and in America. A brief memo in one of the announcements of invitation to hopeful dramatists indicated that works including song and other music would be of special interest.[57] Before World War I, one of their playwriting contests brought second prize to Louise Rieger (Anna Horák) for her entry *Eva;* Jozef Hollý took third prize for *Gelo Sebech-*

lebský. In a similar event promoted in 1925, Národ offered a first prize of 3,000 Czechoslovak crowns, which remained unawarded. The second award, of 2,000 Czechoslovak crowns, was given to Ferko Urbánek for *Krutohlavci.* On this occasion V.H.V. received a thousand dinars for *Pekná, nová, maľovaná koliska.* Ivan Stodola merited a lesser cash award for *Bačová žena.* [58]

Národ continues its cultural activities. On September 12, 1971, the members sponsored a soiree in Sokol Hall on Broadway. The program was directed by Bohuslav Rákoš, who was a radio dramatic artist in Bratislava before coming to this country. Featured on the program was Dobroslava Sebestová, who had gained recognition for her role in the operetta *Hotel pod Tatrami* (The Hotel in the Tatra Foothills). The Slovak-American Limbora Dance Ensemble of New York City also performed on this occasion. [59]

Divadelná Spoločnosť, Binghamton

Divadelná Spoločnosť (Dramatic Association) in Binghamton, New York, was formed by Matthias Rozboril and Stephen Vavra to encourage young people to learn and to perform Slovak plays. The formal minutes of their first session are dated December 15, 1901, stating the chief objectives of the organization and naming these charter members: Martin Hutta, Isidore Stanek, Vendelin Danek, Anna Kollar, Catherine Juriga, Mary Konečný, Veronica Adamec, and Vavra, with Rozboril as moderator. These young people began with all seriousness, and by January 18, 1902, they were ready to stage their first play: Urbánek's *Diabol v raji manželskom* (The Devil in a Matrimonial Paradise).

On November 15, 1902, they performed another Urbánek drama, *Za živa v nebi* (Alive in Heaven). The program shows four new names in the supporting cast: Martin Vavra, John Junoš, Rosie Čarský, and Johanna Rozboril.

They had two performances (December 24 and 31) of their Christmas play *Betlehem pastierov* (The Bethlehem of the Shepherds). The names of nine new men and six new women appear in the cast. The minutes of Divadelná Spolčnosť and newspaper reviews reveal much enthusiasm about this performance and mention that net proceeds of $25 were realized.

In October 1903 Rupert Rehák arrived in Binghamton to serve as the first pastor at Sts. Cyril and Methodius Roman Catholic Parish. On December 24 Divadelná Spolčnosť restaged the Christmas play of the previous year with the same cast. In 1904 early dramatic activities were effectively directed by Rehák. Under his tutelage Divadelná Spolčnosť mastered *Strídža spod hája* (The Witch Child from Below the Grove), by Urbánek, which was staged on February 11, 1904, and a short time later the association presented Urbánek's *Rozmarín.* It was doing well and began to expand its efforts to include a great deal of music, so that in March 1904 it was able to present a delightful choral concert. [60] The departure of Rehák for Europe in August 1904 led to a decline in theatrical interests. There was strong participation in vocal and instrumental music, in Binghamton, but theatrical interests were not revitalized until 1906.

Sokol Slávia, Chicago and Cleveland

In 1902 Chicago's dramatic club Sokol Slávia staged *Oklamaní klamári* (The Cheated Cheats), by Benedix, in 1902 and Urbánek's *Bludár* in 1905. The *Národný kalendár* of 1910 presents a picture of this group and identifies the following members: A. Danková, J. Lamošová, O. Dianovská, R. Jurecká, Z. Oberučová, J. Baloghová, G. Laučiková, Marg. Lamošová, M. Lamošová, A. Duchajová, Jud. Krutá, Alžb. Rechtorisová, and A. Lesáková.[61]

Slávia in Cleveland was a Lutheran choir group that staged several plays in that area.[62]

Slovenský Sokolský Spevokol, New York City

Slovenský Sokolský Spevokol (The Slovak Sokol Choir), of Branch 5, Telocvičná Slovenská Jednota Sokol (Gymnastic Slovak Jednota Sokol), was founded in New York City in 1903. Its members devoted much attention to both song and drama. They had a rich and diversified repertoire of entertaining comedies, operettas, and serious dramas. Some of their performances included the following:

1906 *Andulka;*
1907 *Edip král Tébsky* (Oedipus, King of Thebes);
1908 *Donna Joanitta;*
1909 *Kornelvilské zvonky* (Bells of Cornelville);
1910 *Pražské pradleny* (Prague Washerwomen);
1911 *Bramborová vojna* (The Potato War);
1913 *Jánošík*, with Jindrich Praus as music director and voice coach; and
1914 *Lucifer*, an exceptional performance with the gifted vocalists M. Vaclavková, A. Nemečkaj, B. Mareček, and, new on the scene, the outstanding tenor A. Moze.

Somewhat later there followed the French operetta *La Poupée* (The Doll), with Vaclavková and Moze in the leading roles, supported by members of the *Lucifer* cast, together with J. Čimbora; J. Mareček, Sr.; J. Mareček, Jr.; S. Lago, A. Ozabal; and Z. Danko, who distinguished herself as the wax doll. Audiences were so enthusiastic about this play that by public demand it had seven performances.

By 1917 several key members of the company were in U.S. military service, and those who were on the home front were giving much time and service to Red Cross activities. Dramatics were not suspended, during the war, but performances were fewer and less demanding. After several members returned from the service they revivified the group, and *Sesternice* (Cousins) and *Fiametta* were produced with ringing success.

In 1921 *Cigánsky barón* (The Gypsy Baron) was on stage. New names consistently appeared on the programs, and there was promise of many more eventful seasons. These operettas followed:

Dedečkove husle (Grandpa's Fiddle), by Jaroslav Rudolf;

Slovenská princezna (The Slovak Princess), by E. Novotný and R. Piskáček;

Kráska zo Slovenska (The Beauty from Slovakia), by J. Týz, supplemented by A. Šima;

Moje zlaté dievčatko (My Precious Girl), by R. Nižkovský;

Dedina spieva (The Village Sings), by Richard Branald;

Mladá láska (Youthful love), with songs and music by Imrich Janoška;

Romaňok dvoch dievčat (Romance and Two Girls), by Richard Branold;

Taneček Panny Marienky (The Little Dance of Maiden Marie), by J. Brammer and A. Grunwald, with music by Leo Ashner;

Dievča z hôr (Girl from the Mountains), by H. Švehlová; and

U. pánskeho dvora (At the Lordly Estate), by V. Jirousek; score by E. Ingriš.

After 1962 this fine group became inactive.[63]

Katolícka Slovenská Beseda, Binghamton

Katolícka Slovenská Beseda (The Catholic Slovak Beseda) was a cultural club founded in Binghamton on or close to November 27, 1904. (Basically, *beseda* means a friendly discussion or an academic debate on an informal level.) The first gathering was held at the home of Joseph Jurovatý and was attended by Jozef Pospech, a priest; Constantine Mokrohajský; Ján Cicák; Mary Lehocký; Stephen Mokrohajský; Stephen Vavra; John Mihal; and Imrich Konečný. Much of their discussion was about youth problems and a growing concern about public dancing in taverns, drinking, loitering, disturbing the peace at night, loud quarreling, and the bloody fights almost every Saturday night.

All agreed that it was urgent to provide wholesome interests for young people. The final outcome of the meeting was the formation of a cultural society or club to foster self-awareness with loyalty and pride in the ethnic heritage and to promote reading habits, amateur theatre, and educational programs that would be enjoyable as well as profitable. From the very outset there was a strong move from planning to action; at its second meeting the group began rehearsing for a play that was to be performed in Osgood Hall, at Woolcott and Starr Avenue.

A complete resumé of theatrical performances given in Binghamton by various Slovak groups from 1902 to 1919 was compiled by Imrich Mažar.[64] (This list appears in Appendix B.) The following drama societies were active in Binghamton at that time:

1902–1903 Divadelná Spoločnosť (five plays)
1904   Slovak Youth Group (three plays)
1904–1919 Branch 36 Gymnastic Slovak Jednota Sokol (seven plays)
1904–1914 Katolícka Slovenská Beseda (thirty-three plays)
1907   Slovak Lutheran Youth Dramatic Circle (two plays)
1912–1913 pupils of Sts. Cyril and Methodius School (two plays)

1913–1915 Slovak Catholic Educational Circle (fifteen plays)
1914–1915 Sdruženie Matice Slovenskej (seven plays)
1916–1917 Domov (three plays)

Mažar also mentions that, among the ninety-two plays given in Binghamton up to 1919, the drama titled *Nad moju milú druhej niet* (There's None Better Than My Own Beloved) was an original composition by Matej Rozboril. It was first performed on August 15, 1910.[65] A list of the directors of Slovak plays in Binghamton from 1902 to 1919 is also given in Appendix B.

Krivaň, Cleveland

Krivaň, a choral and dramatic society, was established in Cleveland on January 28, 1906. Its first director was the celebrated Miloslav Francisci, an accomplished musician who composed and arranged many musical works. Among them is *Obšitošová dcéra* (The Estranged Father and His Daughter), an operetta based on an Old World theme. It was published by the National Slovak Society and was staged successfully by various groups.

A *Národný kalendár* picture of the Krivaň Society shows that by 1911 it had a membership of at least twenty-four men and about a dozen women. They were very active and singularly successful on stage.[66] Apparently it was the Krivaň Society that staged the first Slovak operetta, a work titled *Hájnikova dcéra* (The Forest Warden's Daughter), which drew crowds from all the neighboring Slovak communities. Later the same society won further laurels with the operetta *V cigánskom tábore* (In the Gypsy Camp).[67]

Other early drama societies in Cleveland were (a) the Lutheran choral and dramatic society, Slávia; (b) the Dramatic Circle of St. Cecilia, at St. Benedict's parish; (c) Slovenská Nitra, of the congregation of M. Luther on West 14th Street; (d) St. Vendelin's, on Columbus Road; and (e) Sts. Peter and Paul's, in Lakewood.[68]

National Slovak Society, Los Angeles

On the initiative of Joseph Ondrášik, Assembly 568 of NSS was established in Los Angeles, California, on December 15, 1906. Its members were very spirited, though few in number. They frequently worked with the nearby Serbs, Croats, and other Slavs. This enabled them to undertake many cultural activities, especially plays. Members of the 274th local society of the Gymnastic Slovak Jednota Sokol were notably helpful in making it possible to produce two Slovak plays a year. Some of these were *Tá naša Marča* (That Mary of Ours), *Sprostredkovateľ sňatkov* (The Marriage Broker), *Hriešnica* (The Sinner), *Strídža zpod hája* (The Witch Child from below the Grove), and *Slovenka vo vyhnanstve* (The Slovak Woman in Exile).

When Universal Studios filmed *The Black Fury*, starring Paul Muni, several

Slovaks were hired for bit parts and as extras to provide realistic local color. The setting of the action was western Pennsylvania, where many Slovaks had been employed as immigrant miners. In this film eight Slovak couples appeared as czardas dancers. In Metro Goldwyn-Mayer's *The Merry Widow*, with Maurice Chevalier in the lead role, a number of Slovaks appeared in native peasant costume to add authentic Slavic flavor to scenes that were set in Yugoslavia.

The Slovaks of California have steadily fostered cultural interests. With the influx of additional immigrants, especially those of the latest wave of 1968 and thereafter, bringing professionally trained individuals; they have achieved increased success.[69]

Lipa, Chicago

Lipa (The Linden) was founded in Chicago on January 10, 1909. An eight-page program from Lipa's October 10, 1909, production of *Márnotratný syn* (The Prodigal Son), by Jozef Hollý, provides a comprehensive statement of the society's objectives.[70] Among their manifold cultural activities were dramatics, choral concerts, and academic programs. Between 1913 and 1916 they published a periodical with theatre news. Among major works in their repertoire were *Až lipa zakvitne* (Not Until the Linden Blooms), by Ignác Grebáč-Orlov, April 12, 1914; *Bludár*, by Urbánek; *Siroty* (Orphans), by Janko Matúška, April 4, 1916; *Honorár* (The Honorarium), by Pavel Sochaň; *Čo povie svet* (What Will the World Say), by Nušič, in a Slovak-American premiere, April 15, 1915; and *Kubo* (Jake), by Hollý, October 22, 1916. This last-mentioned event was a benefit performance for the Slovak liberation movement.

After 1920 Lipa's forte was comedy and operetta. It observed its twentieth anniversary on February 10, 1929, by staging *Čo figeľ to groš* (A Price to Match the Trick). Some of their later performances were Urbánek's *Kamenný chodníček* (The Stony Pathway), March 28, 1937; *Ej, horička zelená* (Aye, Little Green Hill), by Jarek Elen and Janko Pelikán, January 21, 1940; and *Až lipa zakvitne*, March 24, 1940. In 1948 Lipa collaborated with the American Slovak National Theater, a Chicago group, to effect the first American staging of Julius Barč-Ivan's *Dvaja* (The Twosome). At a major celebration of a half-century of its existence, Lipa produced Stodola's *Bačová žena*.[71]

Hron, New York City

Hron was a choral society founded in New York City in 1909 by Assembly 110 of NSS. Interested persons held their first meeting at 117th Street, the usual NSS meeting place. They chose "Hron" from the name of a river in Slovakia. Originally this was an all-male group, with participants from NSS Assemblies 110, 188, 231, 299, and 405.[72] Not a few of those who came from assemblies other than 110 felt drawn by the prospect of professional vocal training under Concertmaster Karol Leitner, a recognized authority who was paid from the local treasury, supplemented by donations from other assemblies. Several of the prospective members had been in amateur theatre earlier. It is not surprising, then, that dramatics readily came into consideration at Hron gatherings. All three of the first choirmasters, Leitner, Vaclav Pruša, and Benjamin Záhradník, favored the combination of vocal music and drama, so there was an easy progression to stage work. Alois V. Fabry gave at least ten years as assistant voice trainer and stage director.[73] Casting pointed up the need to open Hron membership to women, and before long the boast of this society was the high professional quality of its members.

Emil Novomeský developed a talent for translating works into Slovak. He turned his attention to stage materials that were popular in his day, such as the song *Un pour d'amour* (A Little Love, a Little Kiss). In his survey of Slovak drama in New York, Edward Kováč provides the Slovak text of all five verses.[74] Novomeský entertained many audiences with this number, singing it as a duet with Mária Králiková, a fine lyrical soprano.

Hron scored a major triumph in 1917 with a somewhat abbreviated form of Bedřich Smetana's *The Bartered Bride*. The electrifying finale thrilled a packed house at the Sokol Hall on 71st Street. Undertaking this number was a challenge to which even Czech amateur actors did not feel equal.[75] The resounding "Bravos!" that punctuated the scenes and the ovation that marked the curtain calls testified to the enthusiasm of the seasoned theatregoers.

At this point in its history Hron had a membership of seventy. It distinguished itself by annual operettas, among which were (a) the French drama *Two Orphans*, in which sixteen-year-old Mária Králik made a dazzling debut; (b) *Princess Tra-la-la*, with Králik and George Sinčák in the leading roles; (c) a Slovak version of Franz Schubert's *Blossom Time*, which was currently running on Broadway, with Králik, her sister Lillian, and Suzanne Šnitt in the leading roles; and (d) *The Joyous Villager*, featuring Slovak life and mores, with Michael Hečko in the leading role and Joseph Matejka as his sophisticated son.

During World War I this drama group was often called upon to perform for dignitaries of the Allied forces visiting New York. Usually such soirees were held in elite hotels and entertainment halls. For their participation in the combined cultural bazaar given in Grand Central Palace, Hron carried away first-place distinctions and accolades.[76]

Gifted singers and actors, other than those mentioned above, included the outstanding wit and comic actor Klement Ihriský; tenors Michael Foray and Joseph Ondriš; and Albína Nemečkajová, whose talent ranked close to that of Králiková. They had a noted director at this time, the multitalented actor Stanislaus Mizerovský. Because of his recognized dramatic power, he was frequently invited to be a guest artist with other Slovak dramatic groups and with Club Moravan. It has been soundly estimated that in the course of his long career he coached and prepared well over five hundred productions.[77]

Unfortunately misunderstandings and problems beset the members of Hron after it gained a status independent of the NSS, since there was a growing practice of accepting non-Národniars into its membership. Its death blow was dealt in 1926 in the course of preparations to stage *Count Maurie*.[78] New Yorkers continued to cultivate drama, however, and when Assembly 110 NSS presented a performance at Sokol Hall on 71st Street in 1949, there was an overflow crowd in attendance.[79]

Živena and the Slovenský Dom Association, Detroit

Assembly 163 of the ladies' organization Živena in Detroit chose as its distinctive designation the title "Wreath of Liberty." It was organized at the home of Mária Jergová, who is honored as its founder and as a prime promoter of Slovak interests in the Detroit area. The founding session of May 8, 1914, was attended by Jergová, Mária Kozáková, Ella Chatmanová, Mária Rajnáková, Mária Sedmáková, Zuzanna Mikuličková, Mária Hlaváčková, Alžbeta Corková, Anna Erneičová, Anna Rajterová, Mária Králiková, Jozefina Kolpaská, Helena Levárska, Mária Sluková, Zuzanna Medovarská, and the elder Mária Králiková, and also by John Strapec and John Tkáčik.

From the very outset and throughout succeeding years, this Živena assembly was very active in Slovak-American cultural programs. The members staged their first play, *Jeden sa musí oženiť* (One Must Marry), on November 15, 1914, in the Croatian National Hall. The cast included Jergová, Kováčové, Petrášova, Jašová, Tkáčik, and John Petráš. The performance was directed by Elizabeth Ochabová, assisted by Mária Kováčová. In May 1915 a youth circle was established by the dynamic Jergová, and before the close of the year these young people enacted their first play, *Kvietok v tatranskej doline* (The Flowret in the Tatra Valley).[80]

The Slovaks of the Detroit area were extremely interested in cultural activities. Those who had the means contributed generously to various undertakings, and all gave time and talent for worthy causes. The prime purpose of these activities was not merely to preserve but to foster and enrich the Slovak heritage. They had the good judgment to realize that it would take concerted effort to attain results, and they knew how important it was to have the support and cooperation of capable women as well as men in their projects.

Because they hoped to have a hall for public functions, they formed the Slovenský Dom Association, which held its first meeting on October 28, 1919. Here it was formally decided to launch a sale of shares, no holder to claim more than $10,000 worth. This provision was confirmed by vote in order to insure a fair distribution of control.[81] The minutes of this association provide repeated recognition of the valuable contributions made by women; especially Anna Šinálová, Mária Cekovská, Jergová, Kováčová, Anna Začeková, and others. Positions on the first board of directors were held by Kováčová, Jergová, and Šinálová. Jergová was uniquely versatile, efficient, and resourceful; she served as treasurer, shares broker, representative for legal consultation, real estate deputy, public relations agent, fund raiser, and cultural promoter. The association planned for a November 14, 1920, play presentation, with supplemental entertaining and socializing. At the December 18 meeting, Vincent Kutiš was elected director of dramatics, and on February 5, 1921, a motion was carried to establish a dramatic circle. On March 5 the members approved the purchase of a typewriter "for making copies of parts for actors."

On January 7, 1922, R. F. Pagač became director of dramatics. When he was suspended for inactivity on February 4, George Synák succeeded to this position. On May 26, 1922, Synák directed the production of *Stratený život* (The Lost Life), and on May 28, 1922, he directed *Chytený vtáčik* (The Snared Bird). Costumes for *Bludár* were lent to Assembly 164 of the Gymnastic Slovak Jednota Sokol. On October 21, 1922, arrangements were approved for equipping a stage and providing curtains, and on November 18, 1922, plans were made to raise funds by staging a play. The minutes further note that on March 4, 1923, the dramatic circle found it necessary to postpone a performance of *Zajac* (The Hare).

The long-hoped-for building, Slovenský Dom, opened on April 1, 1923. On March 17, 1928, an unspecified play was produced, and *Sedliacka nevesta* (The Peasant Bride) was staged on November 18, 1928. On January 12, 1930, arrangements were made for the General Štefánik Choral Society to stage a play, and on December 30, 1930, the dramatic circle decided to include the play *Nepriateľ žien* (The Enemy of Women) in the next Mardi Gras program. The reorganized Kriváň choral society was granted the free use of the hall for vocal testing on May 9, 1935.

THE SLOVAK NATIONAL SCHOOL

In 1914 New York City Slovaks undertook the establishment of the Slovak National School. Its main purpose was to provide an opportunity for Slovak children to learn the language and the richness of their national heritage. Kováč, who later wrote a historical résumé,[82] was among the first pupils. He recalls that their first teacher was Michael Kováčik, who was also an artist. With his artistic intuition, Kováčik resorted to drama as an attraction to draw the young to his class. At first he arranged simple dramatizations of favorite stories for children, and he had every pupil of the class involved in the activity. Their first major undertaking was *Popoluška* (Cinderella), featuring Anna Lenart in the leading role, with Kováč as the prince. Professor Kováčik also made attractive posters announcing this play, which were displayed in public places. Attendance was very gratifying. This success encouraged the production of one major play for public staging annually at least until 1969. Somewhat later, A. L. Dlhopolský, who taught a similar class in Slovak at St. John Nepomucene R.C. Parish, followed this example. In many instances he composed original playlets, making sure that every pupil had at least a minor part.

These experiences left the young people with a fondness for drama at the same time as their elders were promoting it. Practically every one of the numerous

Slovak societies in New York favored theatre at this time, so a Slovak play was being staged somewhere in the city almost every Sunday. Often two or more were offered at various locations on the same day, but only the adults were involved. The younger element hardly ever figured, except in bit parts as messengers, servants, butlers, or dancers. These young people knew they could handle major roles competently, but they were left out.

By 1919, when Kováč and his peers were seventeen or eighteen, they decided to form their own drama circle in New York City. The charter members were Kováč, John and Emil Farkaš, Nicholas Veselý, Michael Šulek, Ľudmila and Anna Rendek, Betty Almašian, Mary Lenart, Mary Kubit, Julia Žiak, Emily Choma, Susan Marečka, Emily Šattan, and Oľga Hodža. Their director was John Králik; the stage prompter was J. Bruncko.

In the beginning the new circle favored the standard classics, with the plays of Urbánek a perennial choice. Since these were limited in number, however, and practically every Slovak dramatic group drew upon them, an inevitable pattern of repetition began to develop. The new dramatic circle was not resigned to this situation; the taste of its membership was for variety and innovation. To introduce a new work into the repertoire, Kováč translated an English comedy into Slovak—What Happened to Nedobry—and the group readied a gala performance, printing large, attractive posters and displaying them at key locations. There was a good turnout, and encouraging reactions came from all sides. This success demanded further endeavors.

The group next staged Kováč's translation of Yes—No? (1920). From the proceeds of the first play it had funds for printing up posters in four colors and a program booklet that may have been among the earliest of its kind. For this performance the cast wore rented formal attire in one of the acts, and since there was a ball at the close of the play, the actors had the thrill of tails and gowns for the much enjoyed social, where they made a "classy" appearance in the eyes of the adults. The play was repeated later by public demand, but by January 1, 1921, Kováč had gone to Europe with his family.

Kováč observed when he returned to the United States in the summer of 1922 that the dramatic circle was inactive. Instead of reorganizing it, he joined the Hron literary circle, which also sponsored amateur theatricals. Hron now had a paid professional director for its operettas and held regular weekly rehearsals. It took months of study and practice to prepare a first-class operetta with a full orchestra. Admission to a play was usually fifty to seventy-five cents, but operetta tickets were a dollar to a dollar-fifty. Sometimes a Sokol hall did not charge the drama group for rental, especially if there was an adjoining restaurant or bar where patrons would stop for refreshments, producing additional income for the ownership.[83]

American Slovak National Theater of Chicago

In 1919 the Chicago community made a serious attempt to found a Slovak-American national theatre by establishing the Slovak Dramatic Association in

1919. A short time later they changed the title of this corporation to American Slovak National Theater of Chicago. Its management and officers included Joseph Letrich, Victor Tibenský, Victor Jesenský, Helen Števková, and Joseph Ondrejkovič. It opened its first season on September 14, 1919, with *Gazdina roba*, by G. Preisova.[84] Seven other plays were presented in that season: *Nežné príbuzenstvo* (The Tender Kinship), by Benedix, October 19; *Mlynár a jeho dieťa* (The Miller and His Child), by E. Raupachova, November 23; *Mariša* (Mary) by the Mrštík brothers, December 21; *Nádej* (Hope), by H. Heyermans, January 1, 1920; *Jánošík*, on February 21, with a repeat performance on March 28; *Najlepší syn* (The Best Son), by Töpfer, April 18; and *Slobodní murári*, May 30.

Over the years the company produced about 250 Slovak stage plays. Among the earlier members, Jesenský, Ondrejkovič, the Lesaks, the Matises, Števková, Letrich, Lamoš, Matušková, and Tibenský were very active.[85] On August 30, 1933, they worked with Krivaň to produce Ivan Stodola's historic play *Kráľ Svätopluk* (King Svätopluk). It was their singular privilege to have the playwright from Slovakia in attendance on this occasion and to have him sit for a photograph with the cast.[86]

Observing a quarter century of successful endeavor in 1944, Ondrejkovič wrote that it had been a challenge to establish this kind of organization. A program of May 14, 1944, for the play *Viera má nemluvňa*, by A. Rykeš, translated by K. Babylonský, indicates that this was the group's twenty-fourth season. In 1959 the American Slovak National Theater was still active in its fortieth year of existence.[87]

Štefánikov Kružok, Cleveland

On January 25, 1921, the Cleveland branch of the Slovak League of America founded Štefánikov Kružok (The Štefánik Dramatic Circle) with a dual purpose: primarily, it was to promote an active interest in Slovak dramatic art and entertainment; secondarily, it was to help raise funds for a public memorial to honor the Slovak diplomat, aviator, astronomer, and soldier, Gen. Milan R. Štefánik. Although the founding date is officially given as January 25, 1921, the group anticipated this formality by staging *Z otroctva ku sláve* (From Bondage to Glory), by Gustav Zoch, during the foregoing Thanksgiving season. The members undertook the realization of their twofold purpose with zest and talent. They took pride in producing many theatrical numbers and in wearing handsomely embroidered costumes of their own crafting whenever they appeared as a formal Slovak company in dance and song. By 1924 their concerts and plays had raised sufficient funds for the Štefánik memorial, and they proudly celebrated its unveiling in Cleveland's Wade Park on June 29.[88]

Shortly after this event many thought they had fulfilled the objectives of the society, and membership declined. Fortunately, others realized that their cultural programs should be continued, and they held a reorganization meeting on October 27, 1924. In time they decided to expand their interests to include song and music, enabling them to add operettas and musicals to their repertoire.

They were very successful with musical drama, frequently bringing their productions to other communities, including Port Clinton, Akron, Lorain, and Barberton.[89]
In 1952 their officers were Margaret G. Mihok, president; Vladimír E. Shranko, vice-president; Julia Pales, corresponding secretary; Vladimír Krivoš, treasurer; Gertrude Ospanik, recording secretary; Annie Sulovsky, director of dramatics; Alice Toth, vocal director; Mary Sovish, prompter and stage manager with the assistance of Emma Krivoš; and Michael Sulovsky, publicity.[90] At this time the membership included seventy active participants. This was the first U.S. ethnic group to appear on color television, in its 1954 participation in Cleveland's "Parade of Progress." The group was also active in USO events and appeared at veteran centers and military hospitals. It has also made regular appearances at folk festivals.
Existing programs indicate that Štefánik Kružok staged the comedy *Dievča na roztrhanie* at Sokol Hall in Cleveland on November 11, 1973, and *Hrúza! čo sa robí!* on April 28, 1974, at the same location.

Post-World War II Theatre

On November 20, 1955, the newly organized Slovak American Club of New York City, founded by post-World War II immigrants, staged its first entertainment, "Song, Dance and Fun." Shortly afterwards it was invited to bring its show to Holy Trinity Hall in Perth Amboy, New Jersey. On February 12, 1956, they repeated this program at Sokol Hall in Newark, New Jersey.
After this encouraging beginning, they went on to perform the following:

1957	January 25	*Vážne a veselo* (Seriously and Merrily), Sokol Hall, New York City
	March 3	a variety show in Newark
	November 10	a drama, *Mariša*, in New York
1958	January 27	*Mariša*, in Perth Amboy
	November 16	a drama, *Hore volá* (The Mountain Calls), in New York
1959	February 8	*Hora volá* in Newark
	April 5	*Hora volá* in Clifton, New Jersey; Palárik's *Inkognito* in New York
1960	February 28	*Inkognito* in Newark
1961	February 26	*Ženský zákon* (Women's Law) in Perth Amboy
	March 12	*Ženský zákon* in New York
	April 9	*Ženský zákon* in Elizabeth, New Jersey
1962	February 18	a variety show and *Three Sacks of Potatoes* in New York
	April 26	*Three Sacks of Potatoes* in Linden, New Jersey
1965	January 24	*Strašidlo* (The Spook) in New York
	March 28	*Strašidlo* again in New York

Between 1965 and 1969 there was a shift of emphasis away from dramatics, but that interest was revived in 1969 and promises to continue with enthusiasm.

The following members were most consistently engaged in dramatics: John Sikula, Judith Smak, Joseph Smak, Othilia Babjak, John Holý, Vilma Holý, William Faturik, Joseph Labaj, Joseph Sottnik, Gertrude Vavro, Joseph Vavro, Vincent Pavlík, Elizabeth Dubec, Anna Karaka, Rudolph Greguš, Helen Greguš, Emma Staško, Charles Moza, Vilma Kubič, Mária Križan, Olga Hlavač, and Anna Pána.[91]

Out of This Furnace

Thomas (Belejcak) Bell published the novel Out of This Furnace in 1941. In it he tells the story of three generations of a Slovak immigrant family in a steel mill town of western Pennsylvania. Against a typically Slovak immigrant background, he describes the inhuman working situations and struggle to achieve fairness for the workers that were common at that time. Important qualities of the work are its realistic description of the economic conditions of that period and its Slovak ethnic flavor.

Acting as producer-director with a Pittsburgh-based modern theatre tour company called the Iron Clad Agreement, Julia R. Swoyer has presented a stage version of Out of This Furnace. It played in various cities during 1978 and 1979, with remarkable artistry. The stage adaptation of the novel was prepared by Andy Wolk; the music and lyrics are by Robert C. Nesius; and the director was Harold Scott. Every cast member played more than one character, with K. Wilson Hutton, Christopher Josephs, and James R. Krut in male roles and M. M. Melozzi and D'Arcy Webb in female roles. The various institutes and corporations associated with the enterprise included Carnegie-Mellon University, the Center for Entrepreneurial Development, the National Endowment for the Arts, the Pennsylvania Council on the Arts, and the United Steelworkers of America.

Krutňava

Krutňava (The Whirlpool), a Slovak opera by Eugen Suchoň, had an American premiere in English on January 12, 1979. It was staged by the Opera Company of Greater Lansing and Michigan State University in the university auditorium, starring Giorgio Tozzi, Alexandra Hunt, and James McCray. It was conducted by Dennis Burkh. Professionally, artistically, and socially, the event was an outstanding success.

Children's Theatre

Children's Theatre is a recognized feature of Slovak-American cultural interests, but efforts in this direction are not centralized. The Slovak National School of New York City has been mentioned as a seedbed for one development, and it continues to promote interest in drama.

In the 1960s Mária Böhm of New York City also worked with children and for some years maintained their lively interest with her successful puppet theatre. The Limbora Dance Ensemble, also of New York, is currently attracting very promising young students; it begins with simple folk games and children's songs and takes the students on through transitional material that may lead them to full Limbora membership. Parochial schools have invariably included Slovak skits, plays, and other dramatic elements in their programs for various occasions, but because the assimilative process pressures ethnic languages and heritage studies out of the schools, it is practically a lost cause to count on perpetuating ethnic theatre among the third and fourth generations.

Additional Data

It would exceed the limits of this chapter to list all the local areas where plays and dramatic programs were and are given. Consider, for example, that directories include over three hundred Slovak parishes and almost every one of them periodically had some dramatic activities. In connection with this chapter, however, it is pertinent to mention that cursory research through a three-year span of reports in the Jankola Library files of *Národné kalendáre, Jednota kalendáre,* and *Sborník Sokol,* as well as some bound volumes of the *Jednota* weekly, yielded about two hundred pictures of play casts or reports of productions and over a hundred full texts of plays and dramatic monologues to provide ready materials for prospective staging. Many of these are originals; others are translations from various languages.

The volume of available information in these sources may be helpful in assessing Slovak-American interest in drama and stagecraft, and it forms the basis for much of this chapter, but this information is not all-inclusive, for many productions were not reported in these or in other publications. Besides, much textual material was printed independently in booklet and pamphlet form.

CLOSING THOUGHTS

Living, working, struggling, and worrying through long hours of hard work day after day, the early Slovak element in America welcomed respite and occasional diversion. An invitation to a play transformed an ordinary day into a holiday. It brought them out of a climate where they had to cope with communication in an unfamiliar language into a pleasant gathering among their own. Here they could relax, meet many friends and countrymen, and be refreshed with enjoyable recreation. Both parents and children benefited in many ways. Attendance at a play was more than hollow diversion and entertainment; the stage became an educative influence through which language arts and national identity were revitalized. A theatrical performance brought temporary release from harsh reality and offered some escape from psychological tensions. A well-constructed and satisfactorily produced drama spoke of the meaning of life while it entertained; it was often an inspiration; it dealt with the factors people can control as well as those they cannot control; sometimes it presented lessons in the art of living.

Interest in theatre persisted for a variety of reasons. Often it created an occasion for bringing together like-minded people who liked acting or enjoyed seeing a play. Sometimes a performance raised modest funds for a good cause. Invariably it had beneficial sociological and/or political implications.

Currently, the Slovak-American theatre is apparently in decline. Over the decades, the inevitable pressures of assimilation succeeded in reducing identity with some aspects of the ancestral heritage, especially in newer generations. This cultural erosion began with a reduced acquaintance with the Slovak language; if language is a life essence of a nation, loss of its language brings a lessening of appreciation for all that is associated with it.

Although early Slovak immigrants invariably settled in clearly defined pockets near their places of employment and near their churches, Slovak-Americans are now widely dispersed in mixed neighborhoods and far-flung suburbs. Years ago they looked forward to gatherings with other Slovaks—church services in an ethnic atmosphere, local meetings or national conventions, parish choir rehearsals or activities of clubs and little theatre groups—all were occasions of mutual support, entertainment, strengthening of social ties, cultural or friendly interchange that was characteristically Slovak. Much of that has now been lost. Most now favor entertainment in the distinctively American style, based on American themes, though there may be some nostalgic references to what used to be.

It cannot be denied, however, that a revived interest in roots has touched us all. Many are searching for backgrounds and genealogies. It is apparent that Slovak Americans are manifesting a desire to recapture a knowledge of the Slovak language, and that they are interested in singing traditional folk songs and national anthems, perpetuating traditional holiday customs, and becoming aware of the multicultural effects of ethnicity in current life. All this, however, hardly presages a return to Slovak theatre arts on a substantial scale. Nor can the post-World War II influx of Slovak immigrants be counted upon to be the catalyst of a cultural revival. The newer influx of Slovak immigrants did not become homogenized with the earlier Slovak-American elements. Most of them are professionally and academically prepared individuals who have much to offer, but it is not easy to bridge the gap between the older and the newer generations.

Prevailing forms of entertainment in the United States do not encourage the promotion of Slovak drama. The movies fascinated many audiences, until they, too, took second place to television; Local drama can hardly compete with the glamor of these forms of popular recreation. Besides, it is not easy at this time to find persons equipped for acting or managing Slovak plays to a satisfying degree. Even parish schools in which the Slovak language once was taught are closing for various reasons or are caught in the phenomenon of changing neighborhoods, where the entire complexion of a school is transformed because of a population shift and the consequent problems. This trend eliminates even elementary school productions.

All this is not to deny a residual attraction for stagecraft with an ethnic flavor. Although language problems seem to rule out dramatic works, some cultural gratification comes from song, music, costuming, movement, and spectacle as these are embodied in the artistic performances of skilled folk dance companies such as the Limbora Dance Ensemble, which has been internationally acclaimed. Others are also gaining prominence. It remains to be seen whether there can yet be a drama revival among Slovak Americans, who no longer live in strong concentrations.

So far there seem to be no extensive studies available of specifically Slovak theatre work in the United States. Some source information has been gathered by Edward Kováč, Imrich Mažár, and Ján Pankuch in this country, and there is also material published in Czechoslovakia by Konštantín Čulen and by Štefánia Poláková, who is currently pursuing research in the subject in Bratislava. Scholarly studies into this topic may yield fuller findings that may lead to substantiated conclusions of a more optimistic outlook. At any rate, it is certainly true that Slovak-American interest in drama was vital and widely cultivated for a long time after the first Slovaks came to these shores.

Appendix A: Early Use of Slovak in Drama

1628 Under Jesuit auspices, Slovak dialogue (also Latin, German, and Hungarian) was used in conjunction with the impressive Old Testament tableaux "Foreshadowings of the Eucharist," presented in Franciscan Square, Bratislava.

1632 During the Corpus Christi processions and observances in Trnava, students from the local *gymnazium* had presentations at the traditional altar stations that were set up for the occasion. Here they spoke in the Hungarian, Slovak, and German languages on themes and symbols of the Eucharist.

1648 Pavol Šuhaj, rector of the school in Spišská Kapitula, arranged and directed a "slavonica comoedia" entitled *Apollo coelis redditus seu S. Stephanus Protomartyr* (Apollo Returned to the Heavens, or St. Stephen Protomartyr).[92]

1650 Jesuit students very impressively staged an outdoor play, *The Patriarch Joseph* in Trenčín. The leading public magistrate, Count Illéshazý, with a notable retinue of officials and many noblemen of Trenčín county, attended the performance, together with an audience of several thousands. The excellence of the drama and the acting was reported to have held all spellbound for the full extent of six hours of playing time.[93]

1652 The Jesuit school in Trenčín presented the drama *Esther, Mordecai, and Haman*, which was very well received.

1653 An extraordinary concourse crowded the great square of Trenčín and an overflow of spectators took up positions at the windows and on the rooftops of nearby buildings after Archbishop George Lippay concluded an inspiring ceremony blessing the cornerstone for a new Jesuit church. The crowd remained after the services and was enthralled by the presentation of a play prepared by Jesuit students "idiomatico Slavonico"—in the Slovak idiom.[94]

The above productions of 1650 and 1652 were unmistakably in Slovak. An audience of several thousands would hardly remain "spellbound" for six hours while following dialogue in an unintelligible language. Only the elite had a command of Latin; the average citizen used and understood the vernacular, possibly in at least three languages often heard in daily life: Slovak, Hungarian, and German. This conclusion by Stanislav Weiss-Nägel is corroborated by documentation of subsequent presentations:

1653 A Biblical play was presented in Spišská Kapitula at Pentecost in the "idiomate vulgari."

1655 An Easter play was given by Spišská Kapitula, also in the popular idiom.

1656 A dramatic number on the Eucharist given at the last altar station climaxed a Corpus Christi procession. The drama was Latin-Slovak—"latino-slavonico idiomate."

1661 A very effective play set at the tomb of Christ, which drew such great numbers that even Lutherans came in crowds, was given.

1663 A Good Friday drama on the Shepherd Seeking the Lost Sheep, "idiomate item slavonico"—also in the Slovak idiom.[95]

1663 Plays "slavonicae actiunculae" were given in Spišská Kapitula.

1664 Two plays "in lingua Pannonica"—in the Pannonian language; that is, in Slovak, were given in Spišská Kapitula.

1669 On October 4, Imro Tököly had the leading part (forecasting his future role in life) in the three-act Latin drama Papinianus Tetragonos, presented at the Lutheran college in Prešov. The interludes were in the vernacular: German after the first act; Hungarian after the second; and Slovak as a conclusion after the third act— "Interscenium in lingua Slavonica claudit Actum."[96]

1701 Katerina, Královna Gurziánska, for which a program has been preserved, indicating its Latin-Slovak text, was given in Skalica.[97]

Appendix B: Slovak Performances and Directors in Binghamton, New York, 1902–1919

This list was compiled by Imrich Mažar in his history of Binghamton Slovaks between 1879 and 1919,[98] with translations by the author.

January 18, 1902	*Diabol v raji manželskom* (The Devil in a Matrimonial Paradise), Dinadelná Spoločnost (The Slovak Dramatic Association)
November 15, 1902	*Za živa v nebi* (Alive in Heaven), Divadelná Spoločnost (Slovak Dramatic Association)
December 24, 1902	*Betlehem pastierov* (The Bethlehem of the Shepherds), Divadelná Spoločnost (Slovak Dramatic Association)
December 31, 1902	*Betlehem pastierov*, Divadelná Spoločnost (Slovak Dramatic Association)
December 24, 1903	*Betlehem pastierov*, Divadelná Spoločnost (Slovak Dramatic Association)
January 23, 1904	*Sto dukátov odmeny* (Reward of a Hundred Ducats), Branch 36, Gymnastic Slovak Jednota Sokol
February 11, 1904	*Strídža zpod hája* (The Witch Child from below the Grove), Slovak Youth Group
May 1904	*Rozmarín* (Rosemary), Slovak Youth Group
February 25, 1905	*Márnotratný syn* (The Prodigal Son), Branch 36, Gymnastic Slovak Jednota Sokol
March 4, 1905	*Hrúza! čo sa robí!* (Horrors! What's Going On!), Katolícka Slovenská Beseda (Slovak Catholic Beseda)
May 30, 1905	*Bludár* (The Vagabond), Branch 36, Gymnastic Slovak Jednota Sokol
July 4, 1905	*Bludár*, Katolícka Slovenská Beseda (Slovak Catholic Beseda)
November 25, 1905	*Sirota* (The Orphan), Katolícka Slovenská Beseda (Slovak Catholic Beseda)

December 24, 1905	*Víťazstvo Messiaša* (Victory of the Messias), Katolícka Slovenská Beseda (Slovak Catholic Beseda)
February 20, 1906	*Mariša* (Mary), Katolícka Slovenská Beseda (Slovak Catholic Beseda)
February 22, 1906	*Za živa v nebi* (Alive in Heaven), Branch 36, Gymnastic Slovak Jednota Sokol
May 3, 1906	*Svedomie* (Conscience), Katolícka Slovenská Beseda (Slovak Catholic Beseda)
November 27, 1906	*Čierny kríž v lese* (The Black Cross in the Forest), Katolícka Slovenská Beseda (Slovak Catholic Beseda)
December 24, 1906	*Mlynár a jeho dieťa* (The Miller and His Child), Katolícka Slovenská Beseda (Slovak Catholic Beseda)
February 11, 1907	*V slzách matička sedela* (The Mother Sat Weeping), Katolícka Slovenská Beseda (Slovak Catholic Beseda)
April 1, 1907	*Starúš plesnivec* (The Ancient), Katolícka Slovenská Beseda (Slovak Catholic Beseda)
May 16, 1907	*Cierny kríž v lese* (The Black Cross in the Forest), Katolícka Slovenská Beseda (Slovak Catholic Beseda)
September 2, 1907	*Inkognito*, Katolícka Slovenská Beseda (Slovak Catholic Beseda)
November 28, 1907	*Staruš pliesnivec* (The Ancient), Katolícka Slovenská Beseda (Slovak Catholic Beseda)
1907	*Priadky* (The Spinning Bee), Katolícka Slovenská Beseda (Slovak Catholic Beseda)
1907	*Môj Petrík* (My Peter), Katolícka Slovenská Beseda (Slovak Catholic Beseda)
January 20, 1908	*Americký švihák* (The American Dandy), Slovak Lutheran Youth Dramatic Circle
March 2, 1908	*Pokuta za hriech* (Penalty for Sin), Slovak Lutheran Youth Dramatic Circle
May 2, 1908	*Tatranskí horali* (Tatra Mountain Men), Katolícka Slovenská Beseda (Slovak Catholic Beseda)
July 4, 1908	*Škriatok* (The Imp), Katolícka Slovenská Beseda (Slovak Catholic Beseda)
August 31, 1908	*Kríž pod lipami* (The Cross beneath the Lindens), Katolícka Slovenská Beseda (Slovak Catholic Beseda)
September 22, 1908	*Strídža zpod hája*, Katolícka Slovenská Beseda (Slovak Catholic Beseda)
November 2, 1908	*Pán Franc a pacientka* (Mr. Frank and the Patient), Katolícka Slovenská Beseda (Slovak Catholic Beseda)
January 20, 1909	*Blázinec na prvom poschodi* (The First-Floor Insane Asylum), Katolícka Slovenská Beseda (Slovak Catholic Beseda)
April 26, 1909	*Sľuby* (Promises), Katolícka Slovenská Beseda (Slovak Catholic Beseda)
May 30, 1909	*Kubo* (Jake), Katolícka Slovenská Beseda (Slovak Catholic Beseda)
February 2, 1910	*Svedomie*, Katolícka Slovenská Beseda (Slovak Catholic Beseda)

November 6, 1910	*Stryga* (The Witch), Katolícka Slovenská Beseda (Slovak Catholic Beseda)
August 15, 1910	*Nad moju milú druhej niet* (There's None Better Than My Own Beloved), Katolícka Slovenská Beseda (Slovak Catholic Beseda)
September 19, 1910 ·	*Sirota*, Katolícka Slovenská Beseda (Slovak Catholic Beseda)
February 18, 1911	*Mariša*, Katolícka Slovenská Beseda (Slovak Catholic Beseda)
June 22, 1911	*Márnotratný syn*, Slovak Youth Group
October 16, 1911	*Prvý obed v manželstve* (First Dinner after Marriage), Branch 36, Gymnastic Slovak Jednota Sokol
February 20, 1912	*Ruský špehún* (The Russian Spy), Katolícka Slovenská Beseda (Slovak Catholic Beseda)
December 22, 1912	*Vianočná hra* (Christmas Pageant), Branch 36, Gymnastic Slovak Jednota Sokol
October 12, 1912	*Pýcha predchádza pád* (Pride Goes Before a Fall), Branch 36, Gymnastic Slovak Jednota Sokol
May 26, 1913	*Amerikán* (The American), pupils of Sts. Cyril and Methodius School
July 19, 1913	*Jánošík*, I. Catholic Čes. Ust. Jednota
November 15, 1913	*Návrat otca* (The Father's Return), Katolícka Slovenská Beseda (Slovak Catholic Beseda)
1913	*Strýko* (Uncle), Slovak Catholic Educational Circle
January 13, 1914	*Svedomie*, Slovak Catholic Educational Circle
February 7, 1914	*Rozmarín* (Rosemary), Slovak Catholic Youth
April 18, 1914	*Bludár*, Slovak Catholic Educational Circle
April 27, 1914	*Krvosavci—Obeť krve* (Leeches—A Sacrifice of Blood), Slovak Catholic Educational Circle
May 30, 1914	*Obeť krve—Výkup spásy* (A Sacrifice of Blood—Redemption's Ransom), Slovak Catholic Educational Circle
1914	*Hrob lásky* (Love's Tomb), Katolícka Slovenská Beseda (Slovak Catholic Beseda)
June 20, 1914	*Otec a nevera i jej následky* (A Father's Unbelief and Its Consequences), Katolícka Slovenská Beseda (Slovak Catholic Beseda)
September 1914	*Balkánska carica* (The Balkan Czarina), Slovak Catholic Educational Circle
October 24, 1914	*Dáma urodzená z ľudu* (A Well-Born Lady of the People), Sdruženie Matice Slovenskej (Association of the Matica Slovenská)
December 23, 1914	*Betlehem*, Slovak Catholic Educational Circle
January 31, 1915	*Láska nepohrdá chudobou* (Love Does Not Scorn Poverty), Sdruženie Matice Slovenskej (Association of the Matica Slovenská)
February 21, 1915	*Nový rychtár a krčma* (The New Burgess and the Tavern), Sdruženie Matice Slovenskej (Association of the Matica Slovenská)
March 7, 1919	*Život lesníkovej Marienky* (Life Story of the Forester's Marie),

	Sdruženie Matice Slovenskej (Association of the Matica Slovenská)
March 13, 1915	Tatrín, Slovak Catholic Educational Circle
March 13, 1915	Sen o šťastí (A Dream about Good Fortune), Slovak Catholic Educational Circle
March 13, 1915	Polovicu vína a polovicu vody (Half Water and Half Wine), Slovak Catholic Educational Circle
March 13, 1915	Testiná do domu, spokojnosť z domu (A Mother-in-Law in the Home Means Peacefulness out of the Home), Slovak Catholic Educational Circle
April 10, 1915	Život bez Boha (A Godless Life), Sdruženie Matice Slovenskej (Association of the Matica Slovenská)
May 15, 1915	Tak je to na tomto svete (Such is Life), Slovak Catholic Educational Circle
May 15, 1915	Strýko, Slovak Catholic Educational Circle
May 15, 1915	Oklamaní klamári (The Cheated Cheats), Slovak Catholic Educational Circle
July 2, 1915	Fatima, Sdruženie Matice Slovenskej (Association of the Matica Slovenská)
April 29, 1915	Honorár (The Honorarium), Slovenský Krúžok "Doman" (Slovak Dramatic Circle "Domov")
April 29, 1915	Dobiaš Klepoto (Tobias Klepoto), Slovenský Krúžok "Domov" (Slovak Dramatic Circle "Domov")
March 24, 1917	Márnotratný syn, Slovenský Krúžok "Domov" (Slovak Dramatic Circle "Domov")

Mažár also provided interesting historical details about the founding and some of the activities of these societies. Much of the research on drama was reported by Pavel Zych and Jozef Horváth.[99] The following have been cited as drama coaches in the years 1902–1919:[100]

Director	Number of plays	Director	Number of plays
František Macháček	17	Imrich Mažár	1
Ján Cicák	12	Štefan Cigánek	1
Pavel Zych	12	Teobald Šebesta	1
Matej Rozboril	9	Ján Porubský	1
Jozef Pospech	9	Jozef Simandel	1
Jozef Horváth	9	Štefan Blažiček	1
Ľudvik Heleši	7	Jozef Martinek	1
Rupert Rehák	2	Anton Flámik	1
Michal Čermák	2	Karol Blaho	1
Konštantim Ďumbier	2	Imrich Konečný	1

Total number of plays 1902–1919: 92

NOTES

1. Andrej Mráz, "Počiatky slovenského divadla" (The Beginnings of Slovak Theatre), *Slovenské pohľady* (Slovak Literary Review) 47 (1931): 42; Ján Mišianik. "Kultúrne dedičstvo Veľkej Moravy" (The Cultural Legacy of Great Moravia), in Milan Pišút et al., *Dejiny slovenskej literatúry* (History of Slovak Literature), 2nd ed. (Bratislava, Czechoslovakia: Osveta, 1962), p. 58.

2. Milena Michalcová, "Dráma za Renesancie," in Ján Mišianik et al., *Dejiny staršej slovenskej literatúry* (History of Early Slovak Literature, Bratislava: Slovenská Akadémia Vied, 1958), p. 125; Jozef Minárik, *Stredoveká literatúra. Svetová. Česká. Slovenská.* (Medieval Literature. World. Czech. Slovak, Bratislava: Slovenské Pedagogické Nakladateľstvo, 1977), p. 183.

3. Michalcová, "Drama za Renesancie," p. 125.

4. Milena Cesnaková-Michalcová et al., *Kapitoly z dejín slovenského divadla. Od najstarších čias po realizmus.* (Chapters from the History of Slovak Theater, from Earliest Times to the Era of Realism, Bratislava: Slovenská Akadémia Vied, 1967), p. 11.

5. Štefan Hoza, *Opera na Slovensku* (Opera in Slovakia, Martin: Osveta, 1953–54), Vol. 1, pp. 17–18.

6. Cesnaková-Michalcová et al., *Kapitoly*, p. 13.

7. Mišianik, "Kultúrne dedičstvo" p. 58; Mišianik et al., *Dejiny staršej*, p. 125; Michalcová, "Drama za Renesancie," p. 125.

8. Hoza, *Opera na Slovensku*, Vol. 1, pp. 17–20; Cesnaková-Michalcová et al., *Kapitoly*, p. 39; Mišianik, "Kultúrne dedičstvo," p. 58.

9. Minárik, *Stredoveká literatúra*, p. 183.

10. Cesnaková-Michalcová et al., *Kapitoly*, p. 38.

11. Mráz, "Počiatky," p. 46.

12. A. Kopáč, "Zo školských dramat XVIII. stoletia" (On Scholastic Dramatics of the Eighteenth Century), *Tatranský Orol*, 3, no. 1 (1922): 10–15.

13. Milena Michalcová, "Drama a divadlo" (Drama and Theater), in Mišianik et al., *Dejiny staršej*, p. 233; Kopač, "Zo školských dramat," pp. 10–15.

14. Minárik, *Stredoveká literatúra*, p. 191.

15. Cesnaková-Michalcová et al., *Kapitoly*, pp. 93–94.

16. Although some of the source materials are sketchy, there is a considerable amount of data that relate to drama in the Jesuit schools. Details indicate that the earliest Jesuit productions were given in Šala (*Josephus triumphans*, 1601), in Kláštor pod Znievom, Humenné; later in Trnava, Bratislava, Komárno, Trenčín, Košice, Spiš, Skalica, Levoča, Banská Bystrica, Banská Štiavnica, Rožňava, Prešov, Pezinok, and Liptovský Sv. Mikuláš. See Cesnaková-Michalcová et al., *Kapitoly*, pp. 93–94.

17. Anton Aug[ustín] Baník, ed., *Pamiatke Trnavskej Univerzity 1635–1777* (Commemorating the University of Trnava 1635–1777, Trnava: Spolok Sv. Vojtecha, 1935), p. 306.

18. Stanislav Weiss-Nägel. "Jezuitské divadlo na Slovensku v XVII. a XVIII. storočí." (Jesuit Theater in Slovakia in the XVII and XVIII Centuries), in Baník, *Pamiatke Trnavskej Univerzity*, pp. 270–77.

19. Ibid., pp. 279–82.

20. Hoza, *Opera na Slovensku*, Vol. 1, p. 21; Cesnaková-Michalcová et al., *Kapitoly*, p. 114; Michalcová, "Drama a divadlo," p. 240.

21. Hoza, *Opera na Slovensku*, Vol. 1, p. 21; Cesnaková-Michalcová et al., *Kapitoly*, p. 94; Michaková, "Drama a divadlo," p. 240.

22. Hoza, *Opera na Slovensku*, Vol. 1, p. 22.

23. Weiss-Nägel, "Jezuitské divadlo na Slovensku," p. 306.

24. Andrej Mráz, *Dejiny slovenskej literatúry* (History of Slovak Literature, Bratislava: Slovenská Akadémia Vied, 1949), p. 132.

25. Ján Mišianik, *Pohľady staršej literatúry* (Review of Early Literature, Bratislava: Veda, Vyd. SAV, 1974), p. 278.

26. Cesnaková-Michalcová et al., *Kapitoly*, pp. 115, 130.

27. Ibid., p. 136.

28. Ibid., pp. 136–40.

29. Andrej Mráz, *Zo slovenskej literárnej minulosti* (From the Slovak Literary Past, Bratislava: Vydavateľstvo Krásnej Literatúry, 1953), pp. 40–42.

30. Alexander Noskovič, "Začiatky slovenského ochotníckeho divadla" (The Beginnings of Slovak Amateur Theatre), in Cesnaková-Michalcová et al., *Kapitoly*, p. 196.

31. Cyril J. Potoček, "Slovak Drama," in Barrett H. Clark and George Freedley, eds., *A History of Modern Drama* (New York: Appleton-Century-Crofts, 1947), p. 513.

32. Emil Lehuta, "Jonáš Záborský, 1812–1876," in Cesnaková-Michalcová et al., *Kapitoly*, pp. 369–76; M. Rosamund Dupak, "History of Slovak Drama," *Slovak Studies* 4 (1964): 181–82.

33. Mráz, *Dejiny slovenskej literatúry*, pp. 253–54.

34. Dupak, "History of Slovak Drama," p. 188.

35. Mráz, *Dejiny slovenskej literatúry*, p. 255.

36. Potoček, "Slovak Drama," p. 515.

37. Anton Štefánek, *Základy sociografie Slovenska* (Principles of the Sociography of Slovakia, Bratislava: Slovenská Akadémia Vied a Umenia, 1944), p. 242; Andrej P. Slabey, "Prehľad dejín Slovákov v Amerike" (Survey of the History of the Slovaks in America), *Národný kalendár* 33 (1926): 42.

38. Konštantín Čulen, *Dijiny Slovákov v Amerike* (History of the Slovaks in America), 2 vols. (Bratislava: Slovenská Liga, 1942), Vol. 1, p. 56.

39. Slabey, "Prehľad," p. 49.

40. Jozef Paučo, *75 rokov Prvej Katolíckej Slovenskej Jednoty, 1890–1965* (75 Years of the First Catholic Slovak Union, Jednota, 1890–1965, Cleveland: Prvá Katolícka Slovenská Jednota, 1965), p. 8; Štefan Furdek, "Z Ameriky" (Reporting from America), *Tovaryšstvo* 1 (1893): 233–39. (This specific information is from pp. 234–35.)

41. National Fraternal Congress of America, *1976 Statistics of Fraternal Benefit Societies* (Chicago: The National Fraternal Congress of America, 1977).

42. Quoted in K., *Slovenské pohľady* 41 (1925): 253.

43. Peter V. Rovnianek, *Zápisky za živa pochovaného* (Journal of One Buried Alive) (Pittsburgh: Rovnianek, 1924), p. 192.

44. Štefan Furdek, "Slovenské pomery v Amerike" (The Slovak Situation in America), *Jednota kalendár* 4 (1899): 40.

45. Mária Ruman Kmeť, "Založenie Spolku Živeny v New Yorku" (Founding of the Živena Society in New York), in Pavel Blažek, ed., *Pamätnica k Zlátemu Jubileu Živeny Podporujúceho Spolku Slovenských Žien a Mužov v Spojených Štátoch Amerických* (Souvenir Book of the Golden Jubilee of Živena, a Beneficial Society of Ladies and Men in the United States of America, Pittsburgh: Živena, 1941), pp. 66–116.

46. Juraj J. Nižňanský and V. S. Plátek, eds., *Dejiny a Pamätnica 60. Výročia Národného Slovenského Spolku 1890–1950* (History and Souvenir Book of the 60th Anniversary of the National Slovak Society, 1890–1950, Pittsburgh: NSS, 1950), pp. 257–58.

47. Ibid., p. 314.

48. Štefánia Poláková, "Z divadelnej kroniky slovenských vysťahovalcov v USA" (Extract from Chronicles of Drama among Slovak Emigrants to the USA), *Slovenské divadlo* 27, no. 1 (1979): 122, and poster p. 120.

49. Data drawn from the June 28, 1890, issue of *Národné noviny* (National News), published in Turčiansky Sv. Martin, Slovakia. This reference is cited by Poláková of the Slovak National Museum in Bratislava, "Z divadelnej kroniky," pp. 119–130. See p. 120 for this specific data.

50. Juraj J. Nižňanský and V. S. Plátek, *Dejiny a Pamätnica 60. Výročia Národného Slovenského Spolku 1890–1950* (History and Souvenir Book of the 60th Anniversary of the National Slovak Society, 1890–1950, Pittsburgh: NSS, 1950), pp. 257–58.

51. Poláková, "Z divadelnej kroniky," p. 125.

52. Nižnanský and Plátek, *Dejiny a Pamätnica*, p. 314.

53. *Jednota kalendár* 1 (1896): 34.

54. *Jednota kalendár* 4 (1899): 48.

55. Konštantín Čulen, *Slováci v Amerike. Črty z kultúrnych dejín* (The Slovaks in America, Featuring Cultural Interests and Accomplishments, Turčiansky Sv. Martin: Matica Slovenská, 1938), p. 455.

56. Eduard Kováč, "Slovenské divadlá v Amerike" (Slovak Theatre in America), *Slovenská Obrana*, July 17, 1969. This was his second article of a series of four, all by the same name, that appeared in Slovenská Obrana in July and August 1969.

57. *Slovenské pohľady* 41 (1925): 328.

58. Poláková, "Z divadelnej kroniky," pp. 123–24.

59. Pavol Gerdelan, "Kultúrno-spoločenské popoludnie v New Yorku" (A Socio-Cultural Soiree in New York), *Slovák v Amerike*, September 29, 1971.

60. Imrich Mažár, *Dejiny Binghamtonských Slovákov. Za dobu štyridsat rokov 1879–1919* (History of the Slovaks in Binghamton, New York, over a Period of Forty Years, 1879–1919, Binghamton, N.Y.: Sbor 104 Slovenskej Ligy, 1919), pp. 12–17.

61. Poláková, "Z divadelnej kroniky," p. 125; *Národný Kalendár* (1910): 127.

62. Ján Pankuch, *Dejiny Clevelandských a Lakewoodských Slovákov* (History of the Slovaks in Cleveland and Lakewood, Cleveland, Ohio: Ján Pankuch, 1930), p. 288.

63. Kováč, "Slovenské divadlá," July 10, 1969.

64. Mažár, *Dejiny Binghamtonských Slovákov*, pp. 150–52.

65. Ibid., p. 152. Complete text of the play is given on pp. 139–50.

66. Karol Belohlávek, "Zabudnutí" (The Forgotten Ones), *Národný kalendár* 83 (1973): 79–88.

67. Pankuch, *Dejiny Clevelandských*, p. 288.

68. Ibid., pp. 288–89.

69. Belohlávek, "Zabudnutí," pp. 79–88.

70. Poláková, "Z divadelnej kroniky," pp. 119–30, this data on p. 126.

71. Štefánia Poláková, "Slovenské divadlo v Amerike. Od ochotníkov k stálej scéne v Chicago" (Slovak Theatre in America, from Amateur Theatre to National Theatre in Chicago), *Slovensko* 3 (July 1979): 25.

72. Karol Hoarváth, "Narodniarsky život v meste New York v minulosti i teraz" (NSS

Activities in New York City, Then and Now), in Nižnanský and Plátek, *Dejiny a Pamätnica*, pp. 280–85, this specific information, p. 282.

73. Paul M. Vizvary, "Postavenie členov Odboru 188 v americkom živote" (The Status of the Members of Assembly 188 in American Public Life), in Nižnanský and Plátek, *Dejiny a Pamätnica*, p. 301.

74. Kováč, "Slovenské divadlá," July 24, 1969.

75. Ibid.

76. Ibid.

77. Ibid.; Kováč, "Slovenská divadlá," July 10 and 17, 1969; Horváth, "Narodniarsky Žwot," pp. 280–85.

78. Kováč, "Slovenské divadlá," July 24, 1969.

79. Horváth, "Narodniarsky život," pp. 280–85.

80. Karol Belohlávek, *Dejiny Detroitských a Amerických Slovákov. 1923–1948* (History of the Slovaks of Detroit and of America, 1923–1948, Detroit: Spoločnosť Slovenského Domu, 1948), p. 168.

81. Highlights from the minutes 1919–1948 are given ibid., pp. 74–158.

82. Kováč, "Slovenské divadlá v Amerike," *Slovenská Obrana*, July 31, 1969.

83. Ibid.

84. Poláková, "Slovenské divadlo," p. 25.

85. Peter P. Hletko, "The Slovaks of Chicago," reprint from the Slovak Catholic Sokol souvenir book of its gymnastic, athletic, and tract meet and 23rd convention, Chicago, July 1967, p. 31.

86. Poláková, "Z divadelnej kroniky," pp. 125–26.

87. Ibid., p. 130.

88. "Stručné dejiny Štefánikoveho Kružku. Cleveland, Ohio" (Concise History of the Štefánik Circle, Cleveland, Ohio), *Národný kalendár*, 1953, pp. 70–71.

89. Pankuch, *Dejiny Clevelandských*, p. 288.

90. Ibid.

91. Kováč, "Slovenské divadlá v Amerike," *Slovenská Obrana*, Aug. 7, 1969.

92. Cesnaková-Michalcová et al., *Kapitoly*, pp. 94–95.

93. Stanislav Weiss-Nägel, "Slovenčina prvý raz na javisku" (Slovak Spoken on Stage for the First Time), *Kultúra* 7 (1935): 5–6.

94. Ibid.; Weiss-Nägel, "Jezuitské divadlo na Slovensku," p. 306.

95. Weiss-Nägel, "Slovenčina prvý raz," p. 5.

96. Cesnaková-Michalcová et al., *Kapitoly*, pp. 95–96.

97. Štefan Hoza, "Keď 'Slovenský kráľ' Imro Tököly hral v Prešove divadlo" (When Imro Tököly, the 'Slovak King,' Acted in the Theatre of Prešov), *Kultúra* 9 (1937): 247–51 (specifically here p. 248).

98. Mažar, *Dejiny Binghamtonských Slovákov*, pp. 150–52.

99. Pavel Zych, "Poznačenia hodné udalosti Katolíckej Slovenskej Besedy v Binghamton, New York" (Noteworthy Activities of the Catholic Slovak Beseda in Binghamton, New York), in ibid., pp. 127–35; Jozef Horváth, "Dejiny Dramatického Odboru 'Domov'" (History of the Dramatic Company "Domov"), in ibid., pp. 135–36.

100. Ibid., p. 153.

BIBLIOGRAPHY

Books

Baník, Anton Augustín, ed. *Pamiatke Trnavskej Univerzity. 1635–1777* (Commemorating the University of Trnava, 1635–1777). Trnava, Slovakia: Spolok Sv. Vojtecha, 1935. An excellent survey with substantial segments on the various disciplines within the university. The study on drama and theatre in Slovakia in the seventeenth and eighteenth centuries (pp. 261–307) is remarkably informative.

Belohlávek, Karol. *Dejiny Detroitských a Amerických Slovákov. 1923–1948* (History of the Slovaks of Detroit and of America, 1923–1948). Detroit: Spoločnosť Slovenského Domu, 1948. This work celebrates the grand opening of Detroit's Slovenský Dom, a center of vital Slovak cultural activity. From the minutes published in this volume, it is easy to compile a reliable account with facts and sidelights affecting early Slovak theatrical undertakings in the Detroit area.

Blažek, Pavel, ed. *Pamätnica k Zlatému Jubileu Živeny Podporujúceho Spolku Slovenských Žien a Mužov v Spojených Štátoch Amerických* (Souvenir Book of the Golden Jubilee of Živena, a Beneficial Society of Ladies and Men in the United States of America). Pittsburgh: Živena, 1941. Many interesting and relevant facts emerge out of the accounts in this commemorative book. Among them are the fascinating entries that document the efforts and ingenuity of Slovak-American women who launched and promoted theatrical interests. Several photos (Maria Ruman Kmeť, Paula Novomeská, Maria Ruman, and others) show individual leading characters in stage costume, underscoring the general effectiveness with which Živena members created widespread appeal for theatre.

Borodáč, Janko. *O slovenské národné divadlo* (The Slovak National Theatre). Martin, Slovakia: Osveta, 1953. This work by an acclaimed authority on Slovak stagecraft and dramatic art provides a wealth of historical background.

Cesnaková-Michalcová, Milena; Alexander Noskovič; Ladislav Čavojský; Emil Lehuta. *Kapitoly z dejín slovenského divadla. Od najstarších čias po realizmus* (Chapters from the History of Slovak Theater, from Earliest Times to the Era of Realism). Bratislava: Slovenská Akadémia Vied, 1967. The origins and history of Slovak drama are traced from earliest times (the twelfth century) to the period of realism (the nineteenth century).

Čulen, Konštantín. *Dejiny Slovákov v Amerike* (History of the Slovaks in America), 2 vols. Bratislava: Slovenská Liga, 1942. Historical, sociological, and economic survey of the Slovak life in the United States.

―――. *Slováci v Amerike. Črty z kultúrnych dejín* (The Slovaks in America, Featuring Cultural Interests and Accomplishments). Turčiansky Sv. Martin, Slovakia: Matica Slovenská, 1938. A panoramic survey of cultural interests and achievements among the Slovaks in America. Because it is a serious pioneering effort covering a very broad area, the material on drama is logically linked with that on choral groups and vocal societies, out of which amateur theatre often evolved.

Hletko, Peter P. "The Slovaks of Chicago." Reprint from the Slovak Catholic Sokol souvenir book of its gymnastic, athletic, and track meet and 23rd convention, Chicago, July 1967. As in many other works, references to drama are incidental; nevertheless, useful fragmentary references can be found on these pages.

Hoza, Štefan. *Opera na Slovensku* (Opera in Slovakia), 2 vols. Martin, Slovakia: Osveta, 1953, 1954. Rich in historical background relating to theatre and opera.

Ledbetter, Eleanor E. *The Slovaks of Cleveland*. Cleveland: Cleveland Americanization Committee, 1918. Presents some photos, which incidentally document stage productions.

Mažár, Imrich. *Dejiny Binghamtonských Slovákov. Za dobu štyridsat rokov 1879–1919* (A History of the Slovaks in Binghamton, New York, over a Period of Forty Years, 1879–1919). Binghamton, N.Y.: Sbor 104 Slovenskej Ligy, 1919. A comprehensive survey of Slovak life and activity in the Triple Cities of New York. It provides a remarkable unit (pp. 105–155), together with other incidental entries, tracing the evolution of prolific dramatic activity out of early choral and musical groups. Pavel Zych contributed a unique historical account beginning with the founding of a dramatic society on November 27, 1904, and a faithful record of its achievements, supplying titles and dates of production for many plays. He also made reference to original skits, monologues, and full-length plays that were created by local talent.

Mazuchová, Gita. *50 rokov divadla v Bánove* (Fifty Years of Theatre in Bánov). Bánov, Slovakia: n.p. 1974. Historical reflections.

Minárik, Jozef. *Stredoveká literatúra. Svetová. Česká. Slovenská* (Medieval Literature: World, Czech, Slovak). Bratislava: Slovenské Pedagogické Nakladateľstvo, 1977. Overview of world literature, with insights into Slovak drama in medieval times and comparative data.

Mišianik, Ján; Minárik, Jozef; Michalcová, Milena; and Melicherčík, Andrej. *Dejiny staršej slovenskej literatúry* (A History of Early Slovak Literature). Bratislava: Slovenská Akadémia Vied, 1958. Noteworthy historical criticism of drama is included on pp. 124–30, 230–42.

Nižňanský, Juraj J., and Plátek, V. S., eds. *Dejiny a Pamätnica 60 výročia Národného Slovenského Spolku. 1890–1950* (History and Souvenir Book of the Sixtieth Anniversary of the National Slovak Society, 1890–1950). Pittsburgh: NSS, 1950. Scattered throughout this souvenir jubilee volume are nuggets of information on theatre.

Pankuch, Ján. *Dejiny Clevelandských a Lakewoodských Slovákov* (History of the Slovaks in Cleveland and Lakewood). Cleveland: Ján Pankuch, 1930. Though it is brief, the last appendix in this historical survey touches on the drama circles that were active in this area.

Paučo, Jozef. *75 rokov Prvej Katolíckej Slovenskej Jednoty, 1890–1965* (Seventy-five Years of the First Catholic Slovak Union, Jednota. 1890–1965). Cleveland: Prvá Katolícka Slovenská Jednota, 1965. This chronologically arranged history of the Jednota provides an excellent background against which Slovak cultural movements in the United States can be studied.

Pišút, Milan; Mišianik, Ján; Petrus, Pavel; Gregorec, Ján; and Štvrček, Pavol. *Dejiny slovenskej literatúry* (History of Slovak Literature), 2nd ed. Bratislava: Osveta, 1962. This general history of Slovak literature includes noteworthy data on the development of theatre and shows how theatre arts became a popular pastime and a cherished tradition among the Slovaks.

Polák, Milan. *Z dejín ochotníckeho divadla v Liptove. Regionálne dejiny divadla* (Highlights from the History of Amateur Theater in Liptov: A Regional History of Theatre). Bratislava: Osvetový ústav, 1977. A modern historical account, circumscribed to a given region but having widespread applicability.

Rampák, Zoltan, and Mrlian, Rudolf, eds. *V službách slovenského divadla* (At the Service of Slovak Theatre). Martin: Matica Slovenská, 1952. A symposium celebrating the sixtieth birthday and extolling the stage achievements and triumphs of Ján Borodáč, an esteemed recipient of the Laureate State Award.

Rovnianek, Peter V. *Zápisky za živa pochovaného* (Journal of One Buried Alive). Pittsburgh: Rovnianek, 1924. Memoirs of an early leader among Slovak Americans, one greatly interested in the advancement of his people, especially on the cultural level.

Sedlák, Imrich et al. *Dejiny Prešova* (A History of Prešov). Vol. 1. Košice, Slovakia: Vychodoslovenské Vydavateľstvo, 1965. Includes a discussion of the development of theatre in eastern Slovakia.

Štefánek, Anton. *Základy sociografie Slovenska* (Principles of the Sociography of Slovakia). Bratislava: Slovenská Akadémia Vied a Umení, 1944. Comprehensive sociological, educational, economic, and cultural considerations with an empirical approach.

Tybor, M. Martina. *Slovak American Catholics.* Cleveland: First Catholic Slovak Ladies Association, 1977. A compact but informative reference on Slovak Catholics in the United States, with emphasis on Slovak-American life.

Žáry, Jozef, ed., *Pamätnica k Zlatému Jubileu Národného Slovenského Spolku. 1890–1940* (Souvenir Book for the Golden Jubilee of the National Slovak Society, 1890–1940). Pittsburgh: NSS, 1940. The inclusion of an original play suitable for an amateur group and pictures from staged plays speak for a recognized interest in drama.

Articles

Belohlávek, Karol. "Zabudnutí" (The Forgotten Ones). *Národný kalendár* (Pittsburgh: NSS) 81 (1973): 79–88. Recollections related to interesting but frequently overlooked facts, including matters of dramatic arts and Slovak Americans engaged in film careers.

Čavojský, Ladislav. "Turčiansky Sv. Martin a divadlo" (Turčiansky Sv. Martin and Theater Arts). In *Letopis Pamätníka Slovenskej Literatúry*. Martin: Matica Slovenská, 1970, pp. 95–97. History of theatre art on a regional level.

"Dramatická tvorba v exile" (Dramatic Compositions among Those in Exile), *Most* (Cleveland: Správa Kultúrneho Fondu Petra P. Jurčáka, Mikuláš Šprinc, ed.) 1, no. 2 (1954): 32–33. This article presents a report on four awards granted in a 1953 literary contest devoted to new Slovak dramas. The activity was sponsored by the administrative board of the Peter P. Jurčák Cultural Fund.

Dupak, M. Rosamund. "History of Slovak Drama," *Slovak Studies* (Cleveland-Rome: The Slovak Institute) 4 (1964): 165–96. A literary survey of theatre in Slovakia from early times to post–World War I.

Furdek, Štefan. "Slovenské pomery v Amerike" (Conditions among the Slovaks in America), *Jednota kalendár* (Cleveland), 1899, pp. 37–41. A realistic account with an appeal for greater attention to cultural interests and endeavors.

———. "Všeličo z Ameriky" (Of Many Things from America), *Tovaryšstvo* (Ružomberok, Slovakia: Osvald) 3 (1900): 293–300. An interesting report on Slovak life in America, published for the benefit of readers in the homeland.

Gemerský, Andrej. "Slovo o divadlách na Slovensku" (A Brief Commentary on Theatre in Slovakia), *Most* 2, no. 2 (1955): 83–86.

Gessay, I.-G. "Dva spevokoly" (Two Choral Societies), *Národný kalendár*, 1912, pp. 46–49. Provides a bit of documentation on the evolution of drama groups from choral societies.

Horváth, Jozef. "Dejiny Dramatického Odboru 'Domov'" (History of the Dramatic Company 'Domov'). In Mažár, *Dejiny Binghamtonských Slovákov*, pp. 136–39.

Hoza, Štefan. "Keď 'Slovenský kral' Imro Tököly hral v Prešove divadlo" (When Imro Tököly, the 'Slovak King' Acted in the Theatre of Prešov), *Kultúra* (Trnava: Spolok Sv. Vojtecha) 9 (1937): 247–51.

"K." Announcement of a literary competition sponsored by the Slovak literary circle Národ of New York City, encouraging the writing of original dramas relating to Slovak life and interests. The promoters urged that participants include folk songs in their entries. *Slovenské pohľady* (Turčiansky Sv. Martin: Matica Slovenská) 41 (1925): 328.

Klementis, Eugen. "Príspevky k dejinám divadla v Banskej Štiavnici" (Contributions for a History of Theatre in Banská Štiavnica), *Slovenské pohľady* 41 (1925): 681–86.

———. "Príspevok k dejinám slovenského divadla" (A Contribution to the History of Slovak Theatre), *Slovenské pohľady* 41 (1925): 456–59.

Kmeť, Mária Ruman. "Založenie Spolku Živeny v New Yorku" (Founding of the Živena Society in New York). In Pavel Blažek, ed. *Pamätnica k Zlátemu Jubileu Živeny*, pp. 66–131. A fascinating and valuable document on early dramatic effort in the New York Slovak community. The writer clearly indicates the credit that is due to the initiative and participation of some enterprising and innovative women.

Kopáč, A. "Zo školských dramat XVIII. stoletia" (On Scholastic Dramatics of the Eighteenth Century), *Tatranský Orol*, 3, no. 1 (1922): 10–15.

Korček-Rudin, Fero. "Počiatky divadla na Slovensku" (Beginnings of Theatre in Slovakia), *Kalendár Jednota* (Middletown, Pa.), 1952, pp. 119–20.

Kováč, Eduard. "Slovenské divadlá v Amerike" (Slovak Stage Plays in America). *Slovenská Obrana* (Scranton, Pa.), 1969. Excellent series of articles, prepared by an active participant and ardent promoter of dramatic arts in New York City. He worked with his colleagues to bring quality to the stage and often encouraged the production of current Broadway musicals in

Slovak translation. His published articles appeared in the *Obrana* issues of July 10, 17, and 31 and August 7, 1969. They are valuable because of the specifics that they provide, including dates, titles of plays, participants, audience response, performances, and performers who merited special acclaim.

Lehuta, Emil. "Jonáš Záborský, 1812–1876." In Cesnaková-Michalcová et al., *Kapitoly*, pp. 358–77. This analysis of Zaborský's life and works brings insights into literary controversies concerning a playwright's privilege of creating out of personal genius and fantasy, as opposed to the writer's obligation to adhere to reality. In an atmosphere of conflicting opinions, Zaborský crystallized his principles of ethics and aesthetics and sometimes found himself under criticism. He favored historic themes, and among his thirty-four verse dramas this is evident. Also characteristic of his work are wit and satire, classicism, paradox, and a didactic quality. A romantic vein appears in some of his plays on themes other than historic. Despite his shortcomings, he deserves recognition for works that endured. One of his plays was staged as recently as 1945.

Michalcová, Milena. "Dráma a Divadlo" (Drama and Theatre). In Mišianik et al., *Dejiny staršej slovenskej literatúry*, pp. 233–43. Valuable for tracing the prevalence of Latin plays in the schools, especially during the Reformation. Eliáš Ladiver and Martin Dubovský pioneered with Latin plays in Slovak Protestant schools, strongly influenced by the theories and thought of Komenský. Jesuit schools also promoted Latin dramas, usually as a cycle of presentations. This study is valuable largely because of its specific details—the titles of productions, their authors, and the schools and towns where they were presented. Title pages of some of the early plays are included. The account shows the progression from the works of Terence and Plautus to original creations concerned with relevant updated themes, which were greatly patronized.

———. "Drama za Renesancie" (Stage and Drama in the Renaissance). In Mišianik et al., *Dejiny staršej slovenskej literatúry*, pp. 124–31. An excellent study, well researched and attractively organized, having the commendable features described above and carrying dramatic history up to the changes that characterized the nineteenth century.

Mišianik, Ján. "Kultúrne dedičstvo Veľkej Moravy" (The Cultural Legacy of Great Moravia). In Pišút et al., *Dejiny slovenskej literatúry*, pp. 58 ff.

Mráz, Andrej. "Počiatky slovenského divadla" (The Beginnings of Slovak Theatre), *Slovenské pohľady* 47 (1931): 42–55. Documentation supports the report that as early as 1737 the Jesuit gymnasium in Banská Bystrica staged *Sedicius* in the native language. In succeeding years other schools also produced dramas in Slovak. Eventually the townspeople joined the students in playing various roles on the stage, and drama won increasing support through both this active participation in play acting and the passive but greatly interested attention on the part of the audience. These attitudes brought about much popular support for theatre, as the Mráz article indicates. The author provides much information, with pertinent references from recognized scholars.

———. "Slovenská dramatická literatúra v rokoch matičných" (Slovak Dramatic Literature from the Years That Favored the Cultural Activities of Matica Slovenská). *Slovenské pohľady.* XLVII. 1931. pp. 316–23, 478–90. In this extended study one learns of the richness of works produced by Slovak dramaturgists beginning with Ján Chalupka (*Kocúrkovo*, 1830). This survey also reviews the output of those who contributed original plays as well as of those who had a brisk interest in translating existing dramas from other countries. The author also offers honest critical reflections on an extensive catalog of works and playwrights with complete bibliographic notes.

Noskovič, Alexander. "Začiatky slovenského ochotníckeho divadla" (The Beginnings of Slovak Amateur Theatre). In Cesnaková-Michalcová et al., *Kapitoly*, pp. 183–269. The thirties and forties of the nineteenth century are examined to evaluate the themes and functions of early plays. The author notes the allegoric character of a drama like *Hra o Dorote* (A Play about

Dorothy), built out of a thirteenth-century legend. He also examines linguistic developments that evolved through play writing, which steadily introduced refinements and an awareness of national consciousness while preserving basic dialects and drawing attention to the sound good sense of the common peasant. The writer likewise discusses the centers of notable dramatic activity and the artistic quality of productions.

Poláková, Štefánia. "Slovenské divadlo v Amerike. Od ochotníkov k stálej scéne v Chicago" (Slovak Theatre in America, from Amateur Theatre to National Theatre in Chicago), *Slovensko* (Martin: Matica Slovenská) 3, no. 7 (July 1979): 24–25. This article deals largely with the Chicago area, but its compact columns provide much factual material, beginning with the Slovak choral group Lipa (1909), in which the author sees a counterpart to the choral society in Martin, Slovakia. She traces Lipa's activities from occasional plays and the publication of a periodical to the founding of a Slovak National Theater in Chicago. She explores the repertoire of this group and provides reproductions of two program covers, the title page of the Lipa bylaws, and a photo of the cast of one of their productions.

———. "Z divadelnej kroniky slovenských vysťahovalcov v U.S.A." (Extract from the Chronicles of Drama among Slovak Immigrants in the U.S.A.), *Slovenské divadlo* (Slovak Theatre, Bratislava: Slovenská Akadémia Vied) 27, no. 1 (1979): 119–30. An article that is more extensive than the one cited above. Its scope includes Bridgeport, Conn.; Pittsburgh, Pa.; Chicago; New York City, and incidentally Cleveland and Philadelphia. Great variety is found in the productions of the various groups, with the purpose of a staging often related to national causes, war orphans, and so on.

Potoček, Cyril J. "Slovak Drama." In Barrett H. Clark and George Freedly, eds., *A History of Modern Drama.* New York: Appleton-Century-Crofts, 1947. pp. 513–15.

Schneider-Trnavský, Mikuláš. "Hudobné a dramatické umenie v Trnave v minulosti a dnes" (A Review of Musical and Dramatic Arts in Trnava, Past and Present). In *Trnava 1238–1938.* Trnava: Rada mesta Trnavy, 1938. pp. 156–70. An authoritative chapter on music and drama in a city of renowned cultural activity.

Weiss-Nägel, Stanislav. "Jezuitské divadlo na Slovensku v XVII. a XVIII. storočí" (Jesuit Theatre in Slovakia in the Seventeenth and Eighteenth Centuries), In Anton Aug[ustín] Baník, ed. *Pamiatke Trnavskej Univerzity 1635–1777* (Commemorating the University of Trnava 1635–1777). Trnava: Spolok Sv. Vojtecha. 1935. pp. 259–307. Outstanding research, with all data substantiated in scholarly style.

———. "Slovenčina prvý raz na javisku" (Slovak Used on the Stage for the First Time), *Kultúra* 7 (1935): 5–6. The author disproves Joseph Cincik's claim that the Slovak language was first used on a public stage on October 4, 1669. Weiss-Nägel's research indicates that in 1650 Jesuit students in Trenčín presented an open-air production in the presence of Count George Illésházy, a large entourage of noblemen, and an audience of several thousands of commoners. Most of these latter must have followed the stage action in their own language, for the drama held their attention throughout the six hours of playing time. Other plays and details are also cited to prove that at least seven such entertainments preceded the date given by Cincik.

Zych, Pavel. "Poznačenia hodné udalosti Katolíckej Slovenskej Besedy v Binghamton, New York" (Notable Events in the History of the Catholic Slovak Beseda of Binghamton, New York). In *Mažár: Dejiny Binghamtonských Slovákov,* pp. 127–35. Uniquely rich source materials on drama in the Binghamton, New York, area. Zych draws on authentic records, including minutes, registers of accounts, and notes. These, combined with his account of the tempo of activity that characterized this Slovak settlement, create an impressive picture. The author includes an original play by Matej Rozboril, staged on August 15, 1910. He closes his article with a summary of titles for ninety-one staged plays, the names of twelve cultural groups that participated, twenty directors of plays, and the titles of forty-two comic interludes and monologues (many original) that were performed between 1902 and 1919.

Other Sources

Annuals

All of these annuals are American publications. They are *Bratstvo kalendár, Jednota kalendár, Národný kalendár, Obrana kalendár*, and *Sborník sokol.*

Literary Periodicals

Kultúra. Trnava, Slovakia: Spolok Sv. Vojtecha.
Literárny Almanach. Whiting, Ind.; Middletown, Pa.; Slovak v Amerike.
Most (The Bridge). Cleveland, Ohio: Slovak Institute.
Slovenské Divadlo. Bratislava, Slovakia: Slovenská Akademia Vied (Slovak Academy of Sciences).
Slovenské Pohľady. (Turčiansky Sv. Martin, Slovakia; Matica Slovenská.
Slovensko. Martin, Slovakia: Matica Slovenská.
Tatranský Orol. Ružemberok; Trnava.

Slovak American Cultural Centers

Archival materials are available from the Jankola Library, Danville, Pa.; the Slovak Institute, Cleveland, Ohio; the Jednota Publishing House Archives, Middletown, Pa.; the Slovak Catholic Sokol Archives, Passaic, N.J.; the Slovak Jesuit Cultural Center, Cambridge, Ontario; the National Slovak Society Archives, Pittsburgh, Pa.; and the Jednota Museum, Middletown, Pa.

18

Swedish-American Theatre

ANNE-CHARLOTTE HANES HARVEY

Although the Swedish theatre in the United States was smaller and less well established than some other ethnic theatres in America, such as the French theatre of New Orleans and the Yiddish theatre of Chicago, it deserves more attention than it has hitherto been given. It flourished in "Swede towns" across the States, from Seattle, Washington, to Jamestown, New York, remaining a vigorous cultural expression among Swedish immigrants for over five decades. Nevertheless, except for Henriette C. Koren Naeseth's exemplary study of Swedish theatre in Chicago, very little has been published on the subject.[1] As Naeseth points out, the reasons for this lack of published treatment are several: the strong religious opposition among certain Swedish immigrant groups to anything theatrical, the general tendency to treat theatre as a passing pleasure rather than as a cultural activity worthy of permanent record, the fact that most Swedish theatre groups were nonprofessional, and perhaps most of all, the difficulty of collecting and interpreting the large amount of pertinent data.[2] All over the United States, Swedish settlements had their own theatres. In addition, one Swedish company toured from coast to coast. The primary source material, much of it in the form of clippings, scrapbooks, playbills, and personal memorabilia, is therefore dispersed throughout the country.

Although the subject has discouraged treatment, scholars agree on its significance. Naeseth emphasizes the contribution of the immigrant culture to the American cultural heritage. Others see it as having played a significant role in reconciling the culture of the old country with that of the new. Theatre was, in fact, a typical immigrant phenomenon that, along with the foreign-language press, served specific immigrant needs. Theodore C. Blegen, the eminent Norwegian immigration scholar, sees the establishment of (Norwegian) theatre groups in the United States as a means to accomplish "a transition of Old Country culture to the new world of the immigrants and their descendants."[3]

Though the various Swedish theatre groups across the United States had many similarities—Naeseth even argues the applicability of her findings to other foreign-language theatres in the United States[4]—there is enough divergence to justify local in-depth studies of all Swedish theatre centers, patterned on Naeseth's work about the Chicago theatre. Two particularly promising centers were the Minneapolis-St. Paul area and the Pacific Northwest around Seattle.[5] There is additional motivation for undertaking such studies at this time, before the last of the men and women involved have died and left their stories untold.

This chapter cannot completely fill the need for documentation of Swedish-American theatre. What it can do is, first, present an overview of the Swedish theatre in America and, second, illustrate that development in terms of a specific group. The group I will discuss in detail is a Minneapolis-based touring company called the Olle i Skratthult Company. Very little has been published about this group. Naeseth mentions it briefly, and only in reference to its Chicago appearances.[6] My main source has been Olga Lindgren-Nilsen, a member of the company from 1916 to 1933, who is now living in St. Paul.

OVERVIEW

Swedish ethnic theatre, by which in the United States is meant the performance of a play in the Swedish language for and by Swedish immigrants, dates back to the early 1860s. The first recorded performance in Swedish took place in San Francisco in 1863, when Skandinaviska Föreningen (the Scandinavian Club) put on a play called Stockholm, Västerås, Uppsala.[7] The first theatrical activity in Chicago was on March 7, 1868, when the Svea Theatrical Society performed two short farces, Bättre aldrig än sent (Better never than late) and Husvill för sista gången (Turned Out for the Last Time).[8] In Minneapolis, Skandinaviska Föreningen, active from 1869 to 1873, was responsible for the first performances in the Scandinavian languages.[9] The heyday was generally reached in the 1890s and early 1900s—the actor-chronicler Ernst H. Behmer gives the years 1899–1915 for Chicago[10]—although there was continued growth into the 1920s. The 1930s brought general decline, due to the Depression, the advance of the cinema, and above all the gradual loss of the Swedish language.

Some continuation of spoken drama was seen in the subsequent decade, although usually in the form of skits instead of full-length plays. A small group of semiprofessional performers bought the old Furuby School in Center City, Minnesota, where they entertained under the name of Furubyklubben. The leader, Denny Magnusson, and his wife, Hazel, performed such pieces as the skit "Hos fotografen" (At the Photographer's).[11] But the general climate for ethnic theatre deteriorated with World War II. In Iowa, for example, it was forbidden to congregate and speak any language other than English.[12] Immigrants vied with each other in denouncing their roots. ("I'm not Swedish, but my sister Minnie is," the youngest child in a large Swedish-American family told her teacher.)

After the war the situation improved, and in the sixties and seventies Swedish Americans began to take pride and interest in their ethnic heritage. Today they can still enjoy unpretentious dramatic fare: monologues, skits, and recitations, but full-length plays are beyond what most Swedish-American groups can and wish to produce. Even the "dramatic societies" of the various lodges are satisfied with socializing and an occasional play reading—understandable, since most of the members in these "societies" are now in their sixties and seventies.

There are a few Swedish-language productions in colleges and universities, but these are usually mounted by departments of Scandinavian languages and literature as a teaching aid. In addition, an occasional contemporary professional production from Sweden tours the United States under the auspices of the Swedish Information Service. Such a production was of *Marknadsafton* (Eve of the Fair), by Vilhelm Moberg, author of the emigrant epic novels about Karl-Oskar and Kristina. For various reasons the tour was not a success. A problem with any Swedish-language production today is that most Swedish Americans do not speak Swedish well enough to understand a play. In addition, plays and performers sent out from Sweden, however excellent, often lack the community approval and support granted local efforts.

THEATRE IN SWEDEN

Initially, theatre among the Swedes in America was as faithful a copy of the theatre from "home" as could be achieved. The repertoire and acting style reflected those current in the Swedish theatre, and the Swedish-American theatre imported most of its plays, even scripts, from Sweden. Swedish theatre repertoire was light: part melodrama, part comedy or farce, part national historical romantic drama, with a sprinkling of Shakespeare and other classics. Most plays produced in Sweden were imported from Germany and France by authors like Eugene Labiche and Johannes Nestroy, and then translated and sometimes adapted by the addition of local color. The importations reflected current taste but also economic necessity; before the passing of copyright laws, translating and adapting from foreign playwrights was easier and cheaper than encouraging native talent. One illuminating example from the Swedish repertoire was August Säfström's two-act comedy *Bror Jonathan eller Oxhandlaren från Småland* (Brother Jonathan, or the Ox Dealer from Småland, 1860), a translation of the French play *L'Oncle Baptiste* (Uncle Baptiste), which was Emile Souvestre's adaptation of an 1859 German play, F. Kaiser's *Stadt und Land* (City and Country).[13] Production style—depending on the play—was melodramatic, broadly farcical, declamatory, or "cup-and-saucer realism," and sets and costumes were often ludicrously lavish.

In his short story "A National Institute for Education," young author August Strindberg offered a satiric description of the foreign influence and rampant artifice in the Swedish theatre of the 1870s, a theatre that was not yet ready for playwrights like himself. He takes us to a meeting of the play selection committee of the Royal National Theatre.

The head of the Marine Pilot Association has dramatized a short story from the French fashion magazine *Le Printemps,* and the National Dramatic Arbiter has touched it up, naming it *The Duchess*. There is an excellent role for the Duke and six toilettes for the Duchess. Everything augurs the success of the play. . . . The National Exchequer then reminds everyone that a cabbage bin with Swedish original plays is sitting around unplayed. The Chairman asks the National Dramatic Arbiter if he has read them and, when the latter replies in the affirmative, orders the doorman to carry the cabbage bin up into the attic. Why Swedish original plays are kept in cabbage bins no one has yet been able to figure out.[14]

Strindberg also describes a visit to the theatre. The unsophisticated M. P. Håkan Ohlsson is taking his family to the National Theatre.

On the program is *Monsieur Jean*, a three-act comedy translated from the French by Cassacko (nom de plume of the National Dramatic Arbiter). The curtain rises on an endless expanse of fake Oriental carpet spread with canapés and a fireplace with a clock.

The chambermaid enters in a silk dress, looks in a rose-colored *billet* and says something you can't hear. Mr. Anatole enters through another door and kisses her on the shoulder. Mr. Anatole is dressed in elegant walking stick with gold knob, pince-nez, cigarette machine, and an enormous watch fob. His shirt is cut "all the way down to the clavicles," as Mr. Ohlsson later puts it. Anatole rolls a cigarette and says something to the chambermaid. Then the Marquise enters, waves to the chambermaid, who immediately understands and therefore leaves. They are alone.

"Sir!"

"Madame la Marquise!" Anatole puts down the cigarette machine and picks up the walking stick.

"What gives me the honor of such an early visit?"

Anatole is whipping his trousers with the stick. "To be perfectly frank I don't know, Madame la Marquise, what entitles you to ask such a question."

"Your absence would entitle you to ask me why your presence does not entitle me to ask you!" ("What dialogue: brilliant!" Faint applause!)

Anatole crosses the fake Oriental diagonally, affixes his pince-nez, whips a sofa with his stick, and says, his back to the Marquise: "Because I love you."[15]

Not until the 1920s, heralded by the brief experiment of Strindberg's Intimate Theatre (1907–1910), did Swedish theatre change. Side by side with the conventional repertoire appeared two new developments. One was the non-naturalistic production of serious drama; Strindberg and Ibsen were finally acceptable in the mainstream theatre. The guest performances by Max Reinhardt's company (1911, 1915, and 1917), particularly his expressionistic production of Strindberg's *Ghost Sonata* in 1917, were widely admired and copied. The other development was the so-called folk theatre, theatre by and for "the people," linked with the adult education program of the labor movement. These two developments were reflected in Swedish-American theatre, the interest in Strindberg and Ibsen comparatively soon, the folk theatre after a considerable delay—the Chicago Arbetar Teater (Worker's Theatre) was founded in 1928; the Svenska Folkteatern (Swedish Folk Theatre), also in Chicago, in October 1929.[16] Swedish theatre in the 1920s was also characterized by its responsiveness to the new Continental "isms" in staging: expressionism, futurism, surrealism. These movements, however, were never felt by Swedish Americans. Past a certain point, growth and new productions were replaced by stagnation and revivals.

SWEDISH-AMERICAN REPERTOIRE

At first Swedish-American theatre offered the same plays as theatre in Sweden. Both repertoires progressed from historical romantic drama and comedy to more contemporary drama in the 1910s. In the 1920s the two diverged, Swedish-American theatre reverting primarily to innocuous entertainment and revivals of old favorites. At all times the overwhelming majority of plays produced by Swedish Americans were comedies, many of them farces of French or German origin. The characters were easily recognizable and "translatable" types: the old dowager, the foolish husband, his flirtatious wife, the comic policeman, the honest country lad. They drew on age-old types but belong in the fixed sphere of nineteenth-century popular drama: ostensibly they were modeled on life; yet they were totally predictable embodiments of the clash between the rural and urban and between labor and the bourgeoisie. The Swedish-American audiences particularly loved the country yokel, perhaps a reflection of the contemporary Swedish vogue for *bondkomik* (rural comedy). The *bondkomiker* may represent the city dweller's country cousin, or in other words, the clash between agrarian and industrialized society.[17] By extension, the laughter at the *bondkomiker* may have expressed the condescension of the "advanced" Swedish Americans toward their "backward" countrymen in Sweden. Perhaps it was also the laughter of the urbanized immigrants at their own rural selves before the immigration.

The most popular play in all of Swedish America was not a farce, however, but the folk "opera" *Värmlänningarna* (The People of Värmland, 1846), with text by Fredrik August Dahlgren and music by A. Randel.[18] An established favorite in Sweden, it made its American debut in Chicago in 1884. Between 1884 and 1921 it received at least sixty-two performances in Chicago alone, and there were at least twelve more between 1921 and 1950. In all except five of the forty-seven years up to and including 1931, it was a regular fall feature in Chicago.[19]

Värmlänningarna is a six-act national romantic folk play with a melodramatic plot, much sentiment, music and singing, dancing, and elements of rustic comedy. The hero, Erik, is prevented by his rich parents from marrying his true love, Anna, the poor cotter's daughter. They betroth him instead to the rich but haughty Britta. When Anna hears the banns for Erik and Britta read in church, she goes (temporarily) mad and throws herself into a lake. Anna and Erik both nearly drown, but are finally united against a backdrop of provincial festivities. The play requires a large and experienced cast of trained singers, actors, and folk dancers; elaborate sets; several set changes; folk and period costumes; and an orchestra. The three central roles, Erik, Anna, and the comic lead Löpar-Nisse (Running Nick), were the touchstones of actors and actresses in the Swedish and Swedish-American theatres. The relative merits of different Annas were hotly debated: this one was most convincingly mad, yet this other one had the prettiest voice, and so forth. It was to play the role of Anna again that Anna Pfeil in 1908 traveled from her home in Seattle to Chicago. In 1911 she came out of retirement to portray Anna for the 500th time.[20]

The appeal of the play is undeniable, but it is perhaps surprising that a play demanding such elaborate production should be the enduring favorite. This is probably because it provided a satisfying group experience for a large number of performers. It was sure to attract large crowds wherever it played, and it was, not surprisingly, frequently taken on tour to other Swedish-American communities.[21] Perhaps above all, it had become a tradition.[22] It kept its hold on the Swedish-American theatregoers because it symbolized not only their Swedish past, but also their past as Swedes in America.[23] It was last seen in Chicago in 1946 and 1950. There was talk about reviving Värmlänningarna for the U.S. bicentennial. To that purpose, at least one new translation was made,[24] but what became of these efforts is not clear. Perhaps it was felt that a production of this play would commemorate the past of the Swedes in America, but not sufficiently demonstrate the Swedes' contribution to their new land.

Most interesting from the American point of view are the plays that deal with the immigrant experience, reflecting the Swedes' gradual assimilation into American society. These plays are topical, often set in specific U.S. locales and peopled with immigrant types. In plot and genre, however, they are mostly traditional farces. The characters are comic types, and the immigrant experience is usually lightly treated. Social, economic, and political questions are rarely raised. Unlike much of the Swedish-American press, the theatre of the Swedish Americans was, on the whole, conservative. The most tendentious drama was that produced by labor groups and International Order of Good Templars (IOGT) lodges, which carefully selected their repertoire to educate and edify.[25]

A brief list of titles from the Chicago repertoire reflects the gradual change in the immigrants' position.[26] Early plays depict the immigrants' bewildering encounter with the New World: Emigration (1871), Herr Petter Jönssons resa till Amerika (Mr. Peter Johnson's Voyage to America, 1875),[27] Pelle Pihlqvists Amerika-resa (Pete Pihlqvist's Trip to America, comedy with song, 1890), and Pelles första natt i Amerika (Pete's First Night in America, 1892). Then followed acclimatization, seen in Behmer's Anna-Stina i Chikago (1899), Anton i Amerika (1933), and the musical revues Kolingarnas lustresa i Amerika (The Bums' Tour of America, 1912) and Storstädning på Snusboulevarden (The Big Cleanup on Snoose Boulevard, 1930).[28] The next step introduces Swedish Americans returning "home," usually comically puffed up and well-to-do: När Smed-Erik och Pligg-Jan fick Amerikafrämmande (When Erik Blacksmith and Jan Shoemaker had company from America, 1932), Miss Persson från USA (Miss Person from the U.S.A., 1934), and even one about a Swede who inherits a rich relative in

America, *Karlson får Amerikaarv* (Karlson's American inheritance, 1932). In this last group also belongs one of the few plays treating the immigrant question seriously, the five-act *Härute* (Out here, 1919), which deals with the lack of understanding for the Swedish Americans on the part of Swedes "at home."

PERFORMERS AND AUDIENCES

The first Swedish theatre groups in America were founded by educated immigrants of good family, who harbored no pietistic prejudice against theatre. Their audiences were drawn from the same circle, which also formed lodges and societies, arranged charity soirees, and gave poetry recitals. Most Swedish immigrants, however, were uneducated rural folk who had come to America precisely for its economic and educational opportunities. They had perhaps never seen a play, much less participated in one. Beginning in the late 1890s, the composition of theatre groups and audiences changed. From being elitist outgrowths of lodge or club activities, theatre groups grew in size and mass appeal. Audiences, and eventually performers, were recruited from among those very immigrants who had not known theatre in Sweden but had since "come up in the world." The larger, more democratic audiences contributed toward a shift in repertoire toward lighter fare. In the 1910s and 1920s the majority of Swedish immigrants were single men and women from urban areas. These young people were familiar with theatre and even helped form new groups with socialist leanings, such as Folkteatern in Chicago.

Most theatre groups lacked strong separate identities, actors and even directors often flitting from group to group. Companies were born and dissolved overnight, though a few flourished for a decade or more; one group in San Francisco even celebrated its thirtieth anniversary, a fact noted with amazed approbation.[29] The bonding agent was usually an individual or couple of extraordinary dedication and ambition, so that when the leader stepped down, disorganization or disbanding followed. Among the most talented and energetic leaders in Chicago were the actor Christian Brusell, the actor-author Behmer, the first American Strindberg translator, Edwin Björkman (later moved to New York), Ottilie Myhrman, and Victor and Emma Nilsson and Carl and Anna Pfeil. In Minneapolis the leading names included Vilma and Axel Sundborg, Hjalmar Peterson, John A. Johnson, and Paul Fröjd (later of Chicago).[30]

Almost none of Swedish America's entertainers, whether actors, singers, or musicians, were professional in the sense of supporting themselves as performers. Even the company leaders had to work at something else intermittently. The talented actor and director Carl Pfeil, for many years a leading figure in the Chicago Swedish theatre, supported himself as a travel agent, editor, storekeeper, and inventor.[31] A few were able to combine their love for the theatre with their daily work, notably journalists from the liberal Swedish-American press like the legendary Magnus Elmblad and Gustaf Wicklund, who provided translations, adaptations, and original plays for the Swedish-language theatre.

(Wicklund did a much-acclaimed translation of *H.M.S. Pinafore* for a 1896 production in Chicago.)

Although the quality of acting varied widely within each group and within each play cast, the leaders and "stars" of the Swedish-American stage were both talented and trained. Many had had stage experience before they came to the United States. Occasional guest performers from Sweden continued to bring glamor, professionalism, and fresh inspiration to the groups in America. The Swedish actor August Lindberg and his young son Per visited Chicago and Minneapolis for the 1910–1911 season, where Lindberg directed and acted in a highly praised production of Strindberg's *Gustav Vasa*, in which the quality of the acting was particularly noted.[32] Nevertheless, only a few Swedish performers became professional actors, effectively prevented by the relatively limited size of their "market." Those who went on to professional careers worked almost without exception on the English-speaking stage, such as Hilma Nelson, who joined Augustin Daly's company in 1892, and Arthur Donaldson, best known for his portrayal of the title character in *The Prince of Pilsen*.[33] One exception was Hjalmar Peterson, better known as Olle i Skratthult, who expanded his Swedish audience by taking his company on tour.

Swedish-American audiences were never sophisticated. Used to farces and light comedies, their habitual response was laughter, whether the play was serious or comic. "Persons who understand dramatic art about as well as Zulus appreciate Raphael's Madonna should never be permitted to enter a theatre," wrote one irate reviewer.[34] Sometimes the disparity between the effect intended and the effect achieved caused legitimate merriment, as in the one production of *Hamlet* attempted by the Chicago Swedes.

Holson [the backer] found the play so dull that at one point he waved the actor aside and performed a jig, "to liven up the audience a bit." . . . Other tales of the performance have also, perhaps, grown with the years, . . . of Ninian Waerner playing the ghost and punctuating the revelation of murder by spitting at regular intervals; of the slain Laertes being left outside the curtain, and crawling under it to join the other corpses, leaving his wig behind him. The graveyard scene provided another amusing story. The lights went out, and the first clown, asking the second clown (Schoultz) where he was, was answered in sepulchral tones that reached the audience, "On the other side of the grave."[35]

Less legitimate was the laughter that traditionally greeted Anna's mad scene outside the church in *Värmlänningarna*. So traditional was this misplaced laughter that it was cause for comment in 1925, when the singing of "A Mighty Fortress Is Our God" by the Swedish Glee Club prevented the usual laughter in the church scene.[36]

It should be added that a large segment of the Swedish population in America never went to the theatre at all because of religious scruples against such sinful frivolity. A lengthy debate, reminiscent of that in England in the 1690s and the United States in the late 1700s, was carried on in *Hemlandet*, a conservative

18.1   Auditorium built to serve as a theatre and dance hall, Dania Hall, Minneapolis, Minnesota. (Photo by Norma Nelson, courtesy of the Olle i Skratthult Project.)

newspaper with ties to the Augustana Synod. Theatre was "the Devil's device," inducing crime and immorality.

AMERICAN INFLUENCES

By the turn of the century the American theatre scene was dominated by syndicate-produced touring shows: huge, lavish, and carbon copied. The prevailing style was realism/naturalism, achieved with sophisticated lighting techniques and mechanical ingenuity. With such shows the smaller ethnic groups could not compete, but there were sidelong glances. The contemporary taste for spectacle prevailed over limited resources and resulted in surprisingly handsome sets and costumes. Reviews often mention the scenic elements (possibly reflecting the reviewers' reluctance to mention anything else). Fritz von Schoultz, founder of Svenska Dramatiska Sällskapet (The Swedish Dramatic Society) in Chicago and proprietor of a large costume house, provided "excellent costumes from Schoultz."[37] Scenery for major productions such as Värmlänningarna was ordered from professional studios in Chicago or New York.

From about 1890 into the 1910s the thirst for spectacle was more easily satisfied, because sponsoring lodges would rent legitimate theatres for their performances. Drawbacks were the cost and the need to find other halls for rehearsals. Eventually the rents on legitimate theatres went too high and the ethnic groups had to go back to their less well-equipped lodge halls and auditoriums—with the advantage that rehearsals and performances could now be held in the same places. Few ethnic organizations had enough money to build theatres of their own. Those that were built, such as the solid and well-appointed Dania Hall, on Cedar Avenue, Minneapolis—finished in 1886 and still standing—were all-purpose halls. Aside from the theatre, located on the second floor, Dania Hall houses a smaller meeting hall, numerous rooms, and kitchen facilities. The floor of the theatre auditorium, which has also served as a vaudeville house, is characteristically unraked and without permanent seats, so that it can be used for dancing. In floor plan, set-changing mechanics, and scenery, Dania Hall shows the influence of the American theatre of its day. A horseshoe-shaped balcony is hung over the auditorium floor. Flat wings are set in grooves on the stage floor and held in place by grooved slats clamped down on the tops of the flats. (See Figure 18.1.)

In repertoire, however, there was little influence from the American theatre. Swedish-American groups either imported plays from Sweden or wrote their own plays. The only notable overlap lay in the area of British classics, admired equally by Swedes, Americans, and Swedish-Americans. The Chicago Swedes produced Hamlet (1885), H.M.S. Pinafore (1896), and The Taming of the Shrew (1904).[38]

SWEDISH-AMERICAN CHARACTERISTICS

Although trying to be an extension of contemporary theatre in Sweden, Swedish-American theatre came to develop certain characteristic features. As already noted, it was largely nonprofessional; its audiences were more "democratic," and it was vigorous and far-reaching. There are no statistics to tell how many Swedish Americans were touched by the theatre, either as participants or as audience members, but the number of productions mounted is awesome. During the peak period, 1888–1915, Swedes in Chicago alone produced between nine and twenty-four plays a season, with twenty or more during eight of the seasons.[39] In Sweden there was no corresponding popular theatre movement. One reason for this difference may have been the generally liberating effect the United States had on the Swedish immigrants; another may have been that many Swedish-American cultural personalities were what Naeseth calls "gifted and engaging scapegraces," men and women whose talent, initiative, and restlessness had made them "black sheep" at home but added flair and excitement to their work "over here";[40] yet another may have been the Swedish-American theatre's function as preserver of ethnicity.

Another distinguishing feature was the *teater med bal* (theatre with ball). In order to draw a large audience, any performance, whether a variety show, choral concert, or play, might conclude with *bal*, that is, with public dancing. After the final curtain, all seats in the "orchestra" were cleared away for the dancing, which lasted until midnight. The bar provided refreshments, sometimes alcoholic. Add thereto that performances were most often scheduled for Sundays—the working man's only day off—and one understands better the opposition of the Lutheran church to the dramatic activities of the immigrants.

By its *teater med bal* format Swedish-American theatre encouraged family participation far more than contemporary Swedish theatre did. One indication of family audiences is that Swedish texts were "cleaned up" for Swedish-American audiences. The Olle i Skratthult Company was cited for its clean and wholesome entertainment and prided itself on never using swear words.[41] A case in point is the comic song "Flickan på Bellmansro" (The Girl at Bellmansro), about a suitor promising to return but instead staying away for good, leaving the girl with an illegitimate child. Both the recorded and the printed version available in the United States leave out the verse about the child.[42]

THEATRE AND THE SWEDISH LANGUAGE

The Swedish language was, of course, central to the Swedish theatre in the United States. In many cases it was the only thing Swedish about the play, since the repertoire taken from Sweden, with the obvious exception of national-romantic products, consisted largely of Continental imports. Thus the playbills in Swedish America—*En natt i Falkenberg, Andersson, Petterson och Lundström, Öregrund-Östhammar, Ire förälskade poliskonstaplar* (Three Police Constables in Love)—reflect not so much a love for continental farce as a desire to keep the umbilical cord with the mother country uncut.[43] Theatre was encouraged precisely because it fostered pride and interest in the Swedish language, which in turn was a link with the Old Country. In the language resided a large portion of the immigrants' "Swedishness." The language debate raged around 1900:

Should the Swedish language be preserved in America or not? One argument for preservation was that "a people that demonstrates no ability to resist, no conservatism, cannot exert any lasting influence on others. It would therefore be a bad sign, if our Swedish-American people underwent this process [a complete change to English] too rapidly."[44]

Like any language-based activity, theatre was doomed when the language faded. Eventually Swedish America, like all other immigrant communities, experienced what Nils Hasselmo calls "the great language shift."[45] In the late 1920s and early 1930s, church services and instruction changed from Swedish to English. The young people of Center City, Minnesota, were confirmed in Swedish for the last time in 1929.[46] Some Swedish performers chose not to compromise their Swedishness, and some were so inextricably linked with their ethnic material that English was simply out of the question. But for others the opportunities of the American stage were too great to pass up. Some performers were equally effective in both languages, yet others tried but failed to conquer the English language; for instance the talented Pfeil couple from Chicago were held back because of Anna Pfeil's difficulties with English.[47]

The transitional stage of "the great language shift" made its mark in the theatre. "Mixed-language" was a ready source of laughter, and several Swedish-American comedians derived much of their material from linguistic misunderstandings. Singer and monologue artist Charles Widdén straddled the language fence comfortably and also used mixed language, as in the routines "Peterson at the Turkish Bath" and "Olle ve' Kvarna i Amerika."[48] John A. Johnson of St. Paul, Minnesota, better known as "Johan i Knuten," was another comedian who capitalized on the language shift for comic effect. For a performance in Marine, Minnesota, in 1916, he was billed as "singing and talking broken English."[49]

Mixed-language comedy in ethnic theatre is a sign of decline. It is an ephemeral form, because it can only be enjoyed by a bilingual generation; once that generation is gone, mixed-language comedy is dead. In Swedish-American theatre, mixed-language humor flourished from the 1910s into the 1930s. Bilingual audiences have of course been able to appreciate mixed-language humor at any time, but as popular entertainment among Swedish Americans, it died with World War II.

English-speaking Swedish performers capitalized on the Swedish accent. Arthur Donaldson of Chicago became as famous for his Swedish-accent comic character Yon Yonsson as for his work in Gilbert and Sullivan and other operettas. Another such performer was Charles Lindholm of Stillwater, Minnesota, although only one of his plays drew on his Swedish background. This one-act play, which made his fortune, was *The Man from Minnesota*, peopled with comic types like Charlie Lutefisk—played by Lindholm himself—Ima Lemon, and Mr. and Mrs. Otto B. Holm.[50] Regulars on talk shows in the upper Midwest often put on a "Skandehuvian" accent. The practice still survived in 1980 on WCCO-AM, Minneapolis, where Roger Ericson of the popular "Boone & Ericson" show would slip into a Scandinavian accent "like a lutefish into vater."

The final step in this development is the non-Scandinavian-speaking performer who puts on a Scandinavian stage accent and assumes a Scandinavian personality. An interesting example is the late comedian-singer Yogi Yorgeson, whose real name was Harry E. Stewart, although Stewart actually was of Norwegian-Swedish descent, with the family name Sharbo (probably Skarbo).[51]

IMPORTANCE OF THEATRE TO SWEDISH AMERICANS

To its founders the Swedish theatre in America was an outlet for their talents, energy, creativity, and "Swedishness." It became a significant cultural institution with a stabilizing influence, educating its members and perpetuating traditions. It satisfied the need to maintain ties with the home country but at the same time helped make the adjustment to life in the new country. It gave pleasure and relief from boredom and drudgery. It promoted contacts with the American community, in the rental of theatres and other business transactions, though this was neither aimed at nor closely observed by the non-Swedish population. It brought closer ties to Norwegians and Danes, who sometimes joined forces with the Swedes in theatre.[52] Not surprisingly, it was negligible as a direct force for Americanization or as a vehicle for political ideas. Its importance lay in satisfying the emotional and intellectual needs of its members and audiences, thus helping to ease their transition to a more "American" life.

Summing up, the theatre of the Swedish Americans did three things. First, it provided escape, whether into the romanticized past of the old country or into patent farce with a thin overlay of ethnic topicality. Second, it helped sustain and promote the Swedish language in the United States, thereby strengthening the sense of identity so important to the first-generation immigrant. Third, the plays with national-romantic or historical subject matter served as powerful reviews, albeit sentimentalized, of the history, folklore, and culture of Sweden.

THE OLLE I SKRATTHULT COMPANY, MINNEAPOLIS

Only one man, with his company of up to twenty performers, was able to make a living for an extended time as a Swedish-language entertainer. This man (shown in Figure 18.2) was Hjalmar Peterson, better known as Olle i Skratthult (Olle from Laughtersville). He was born in Munkfors, Värmland, on February 7, 1886.[53] In 1906 he followed two older brothers to Minnesota, where he quickly found that he had more inclination for entertaining than for bricklaying.[54] As a singer in Svenskamerikanska kvartetten (The Swedish-American Quartet) he toured Sweden in 1909–1911. During this tour he collected material he would later use in the United States, for example, songs and comic monologues in his native Värmland dialect.[55] He also took a suitable stage name in the *bondkomik* tradition, which prescribed a simple first name, like Olle or Johan, combined with a ludicrous place name, like Gråthult (Tearsville) or Knuten (The Corner).

Upon returning to the United States, Hjalmar "Olle i Skratthult" Peterson

18.2   Hjalmar Peterson as Olle i Skratthult. (Photo by Karl Peterson, courtesy of the Olle i Skratthult Project.)

embarked on a career as singer, actor, and comedian,[56] beginning as a solo performer with one accompanist in 1911. By 1916 he had a touring group, working in Minnesota. Gradually the company grew in size and extended its tours from coast to coast. If its extensive touring may be said to have taken place during the years the group performed in Chicago, the inclusive dates are 1920–1931; the height of its touring days was the mid-1920s. Olle had a long and varied life in the theatre, performing until his death in Minneapolis in 1960.

In 1915 he discovered a young Swedish singer, Olga Lindgren, who became his leading lady, in life as well as on stage. Olga was born May 29, 1896, in Sunnäs, Hälsingland, and grew up in Norrsundet outside Gävle. In September 1913 she left her home to join a brother and two uncles in Minneapolis, where she worked in their ice cream cone factory. Work in the factory was drudgery, so she was happy to be hired as a maid in a doctor's household. She stayed there for about a year. One Sunday in the spring of 1916 Peterson heard her sing at an IOGT meeting and asked her to sing with his group the following Sunday. She was discovered! Although gifted with a clear and strong voice, Olga had never performed in Sweden—except once, at the age of five, when she stood on a railroad bridge and sang lustily while being showered with pennies—yet here she was in "show business"! Hjalmar signed her up and told her to take singing lessons.[57] Olga's family did not mind her career switch from maid to performer. The Olle i Skratthult troupe was respectable, based in Minneapolis, and her pay, if not her job security, was better. On April 28, 1917, Olga and Hjalmar were married.

Olga was definitely an asset to the otherwise all-male group and contributed to Olle's growing popularity. "Foremost of them all is the star of the group, Olle's wife (Mrs. Olga Lindgren-Peterson). She is fortunate enough to possess both a fetching appearance and excellent artistic talent as a singer and dancer. No wonder that she charmed the audience and received thunderous applause."[58] At first the company performed mostly in and around Minneapolis, but by 1920 a performance in Chicago is recorded.[59] From 1920 through 1931 the company made yearly tours throughout the United States.[60] The 1921–1922 season saw an extended West Coast tour. Another West Coast tour came in 1924–1925. Altogether the group came to the West Coast at least four times.[61] The years 1925–1931 were the busiest touring years, each season in 1927–1929 including at least three different play productions.

When Olga joined, the company numbered five members, a number expanded as needed. The West Coast tour in 1924–1925, for example, started with five members: Hjalmar and Olga; the baritone, Annar Myhre; the violinist, Arthur Martinson; and the accordionist, Thure Andersson. During the tour, probably during the Christmas break, Olle signed up the pianist, Harry Swanson, who toured with them for the remainder of the season and for seasons to come.[62] Reviews from later tours, possibly in 1926–1928, mention a company of nine.[63] *Värmländningarna,* produced in 1928 and 1929, demanded additional members; the play has seventeen named characters, not counting scores of peasants and dancers.[64] The Olle i Skratthult Company's poster for this play includes portraits of seventeen performers.[65] To cut down the number of people actually traveling, Olle used double casting and local performers. The musicians in the group were pressed into service as actors. Production photos from 1927 show musicians Bert and Oscar Danielson acting, with false beard, whitened hair, and so on.[66] They were good actors, too, according to Olga.[67] For the production of Värmlänningarna, Olle used local talent. Chicago actors filled out the cast in Chicago, and local symphonies played for the production in Boston and New York. In Salt Lake City a group of local folk dancers added color to the performance.[68]

Olle was the company's best-loved performer, its figurehead, producer, and—with the exception of Värmlänningarna, which was directed by Chicago actor Knut Sjöberg—also its artistic director.[69] Olle performed his famous comic monologues and songs, and with the exception of his appearance as Löpar-Nisse in Värmlänningarna, did not act in his company's plays. It is as producer and manager, rather than actor, that he earned a place in the history of the Swedish-American theatre; Olle and his company were unique in Swedish America.

With the exception of Värmlänningarna, which was about three hours long, the plays performed by the Olle i Skratthult Company were always part of a longer program of mixed entertainment. The balance was made up of songs, recitations, comic monologues, folk dances, orchestra solos, and after the program, the obligatory bal. The format is seen clearly in the following reviews:

On this trip the Company is playing: 'Sme Olas stora synd' (Ola Blacksmith's Big Sin), a three-act rural comedy which keeps the crowd roaring with laughter. Also a topnotch vaudeville program—Olle in new songs—His famous Sailor's Orchestra—novelty singing and dancing. Don't miss Olle this time, he always has a good show, but this is the best ever.[70]

As usual, Olle i Skratthult played to a packed house Wednesday evening, at the New Fair House, Grantsburg [Wisconsin]. Olle is now accompanied by a cast of nine people, each unexcelled in his or her parts, who present a one act comedy, "Officers Three" [probably Tre förälskade poliskonstaplar]. This feature, with Olle's usual good program, forms a combination that is hard to beat.[71]

The plays selected for touring were light, mostly rural comedies like Käringa mi's kusin (My Old Lady's Cousin, 1929), by Alfred Ebenhard, and Lars Anders, Jan Anders och deras barn (Lars Anders, Jan Anders, and Their Children, 1894), by Gustaf af Geijerstam. (The appendix to this chapter is a list of the plays the company is known to have presented.) Lars Anders, Jan Anders och deras barn was performed on at least three different tours (1920, 1923, and 1927) and is one of the plays best remembered by Lindgren-Nilsen. The biggest undertaking, and the biggest success, however, was Värmlänningarna. The poster shows seventeen performers, but according to Lindgren-Nilsen there were twenty, not counting the musicians.[72] Olle himself played Löpar-Nisse, and Olga played

Anna. The critics raved. "4,000 people saw the play,' hundreds turned away, and never before has Värmlänningarna been given in this metropolis with such wonderful interpretation as Olle i Skratthult's Co."[73] "It was ideal, the way Värmlänningarna was presented last night in our city by Olle I Skratthult. It was attended by 2,000 people at the Arlington Theatre."[74]

The performers in the Olle i Skratthult Company were contracted by the year or season but were paid by the week or month. Olga recalls that they were well paid—how well, she does not remember.[75] There was little opportunity for social life outside the touring group. The tours would start in the fall, take a break at Christmas time, resume in January and continue into July. The summer months were spent in preparation for next season's tour. Home base was Minneapolis, the home town of most of the performers, and Olle's large cabin at Grand Marais on the north shore of Lake Superior. The group spent the summer there, and the members have many happy memories of lazy days on the north shore. Here Olga and Hjalmar returned for a short time to the normalcy of keeping house: one newspaper article jokingly implied that Olga's pickled herring and meatballs made Hjalmar put on too much weight every summer.[76]

Other places around the country served as temporary bases of operation. Sometimes the group was stationed in Chicago, and one year was spent in New York;[77] one in Seattle; one in San Francisco; and five in Los Angeles. The choice of Los Angeles did not reflect the number of Scandinavians in the area, though there were quite a few, as much as the city's lovely winter climate—ideal for Christmas breaks—and the fact that Olle's oldest brother Albin was a chiropractor in Pasadena and had an extra house the company could use. Albin Peterson was a highly respected citizen, a member of the IOGT in Los Angeles and a recipient of the Swedish Vasa Order. Ties with respectability were never to be sneezed at!

In the twenties the company visited Swedish and Scandinavian communities from coast to coast. The large cities, like New York, Boston, Chicago, Minneapolis, Salt Lake City, Los Angeles, San Francisco, and Seattle, might sustain an extended stay, but most of the stops were one-night stands in smaller places. By train or by a caravan of two to four cars, the group would travel from Minneapolis to Chicago; Jamestown, New York, Buffalo, New York; Worcester, Massachusetts; back to Chicago, Moline, and Rock Island, Illinois; then on to Salt Lake City, Utah; Spokane, Seattle, and Tacoma, Washington; Oakland; and San Francisco, Los Angeles, and San Pedro, California, reversing the route on the way back to Minneapolis. Thus a city might be "hit" twice on the same tour, which necessitated program changes and improvements en route. The Christmas break in Los Angeles was an ideal time to freshen up the program before the trek back to Minnesota.

Arrangements for publicity, lodging, and rental of performance space were made by an "advance man," who traveled a few weeks ahead of the company. On tour the group sometimes stayed in hotels, but often in private homes. June Holm of Schaeffer, Minnesota, remembers when the company stayed at the home of her parents.[78] It is unclear whether it paid for lodgings there or not. The group never lacked for invitations to coffee or dinner. Olga remembers one incident: the company had just performed in a small town in Minnesota when its members were caught in a storm. They knocked on the door of a farm to seek shelter. When the farmer saw the bedraggled group in the doorway, he exclaimed: "Well, if it isn't Olle i Skratthult! Come in, come in!" He and his family had just returned from attending Olle's performance in town.[79]

The travel itself often took its toll. One performance in Galesburg, Illinois, had to be done without sets because the car with the scenery was stuck in snow. Another season the company was involved in a train wreck, which took the life of one of its musicians. Olle, who did not trust banks, often carried large sums of money with him in a suitcase, and once the company was ambushed and narrowly escaped being robbed by Indians on its way to Worley, Wisconsin. Another time the car caravan was halted by a mudslide in California. Undaunted, Olle abandoned the cars, climbed with his troupe across the mudslide, and walked with his suitcase into the next town, where he bought new cars.

Performances took place in all kinds of "theatres," from plush opera houses with private dressing rooms to (once) a garage. The company carried its own scenery and properties, ordered from theatrical supply houses in Chicago and New York, but brought no lighting equipment. All the places where Olle performed had footlights, or were supposed to—the garage did not. Between tours, sets and props were stored in the cabin on the north shore. Individual performers were responsible for their makeup and hairpieces. Theatrical makeup could be bought in Minneapolis, as there were enough theatrical societies in the area to support an outlet there, but the $300 blonde, braided wig Olga bought to play Anna in Värmlänningarna had to be ordered from New York.[80] During a performance, everyone helped. Performers doubled as ticket takers, program sellers, ushers, stagehands, dressers, and light operators. Scenes were shifted by the men in the company.

Wherever the Olle i Skratthult Company went, it was welcomed, loved, and remembered. Newspaper clippings from small country towns as well as Chicago and New York attest to the extraordinary popularity of the company and, particularly, of Olle himself. One apocryphal anecdote tells of a man in Lindström, Minnesota, who actually died laughing at Olle i Skratthult.[81] Hjalmar Peterson's personality no doubt promoted his success. He was a mild-mannered, somewhat melancholy, generous man. Although he had a great deal of money and did not stint on clothes or cars, he never lost his unassuming manner. He was not a profound man, nor a born speaker,[82] but as a bondkomiker he was superb. Olle i Skratthult was a slow, shy type, with a blackened-out front tooth, straw-colored wig, cap with flower, squeaky boots, coat, vest, knickers, and a long scarf.[83] He specialized in Värmland-dialect material, but did not have to say anything to make people laugh. His appeal was universal: he performed not just for Swedes, but also for Danes, Norwegians, Americans—even Ojibway Indians, who attended his performances at the Minnesota State Fair and enjoyed him greatly.[84]

Aside from his abilities as *bondkomiker*, Hjalmar Peterson had two other distinct gifts: that of recruiting able performers as tour members, and that of advertising. Recruiting was often deceptively informal: Olga was "discovered" singing at an IOGT meeting; "Miss Lilly" was signed on as cashier and folk-dancer for a season to help her make money to go to art school; and one accordionist, Evan Sjögren, reportedly was recruited right from a field in Lindström![85] Nevertheless, the performers got along well together.

It is perhaps surprising that a performer whose stage character was a slow-witted Swedish farmhand, should be so shrewd, one might even say American, in his advertising methods. Olle's advance publicity consisted of posters and press releases. In addition he sold sheet music, songbooks, posters, programs, and playscripts.[86] Whenever he was in New York he would record some of his latest song "hits" on the Columbia, Victor, and Blue Bird labels, which were then sold across the country.[87]

The ccmpany's posters did not differ appreciably from those used by other, nonprofessional, theatre groups. The early posters were printed entirely in Swedish, while the later ones used more and more English. One Olle i Skrat-thult poster from 1929 was printed entirely in English, announcing "the absorb-ing melodrama of ambition, *Värmlänningarna.*"[88] The principle at work—found to this day in the Swedish-American press—is to give all essential information (date, time, fee) in English and the title and description, assuring bona fide ethnic material, in Swedish. Olle's use of press releases, however, was definitely professional. He would cull favorable comments from recent reviews, print them up, and send them to all the newspapers in the towns next in line for the tour. The two excerpts from reviews of *Värmlänningarna* quoted above were reprinted on the poster for the 1929 tour. Excerpts from a review printed in Worcester, Massachusetts, in the spring of 1924 are found in a review in *Svenska Pressen,* Spokane, Washington, the following fall.[89] Two papers reporting on the same performance use suspiciously similar phrasing.[90] It is sometimes difficult to tell whether the reviewer is expressing any opinion of his own or, indeed, whether he has even seen the particular performance he is writing about. Just as posters were shifting to English text, press releases were prepared in both English and Swedish to reach the greatest number of people. And Olle did get a good deal of attention in the English-language press.[91]

Only once during her years with the Olle i Skratthult Company did Olga return to Sweden. Her three-month visit in 1927 brought a double heartache: upon docking in Gothenburg she was told that her mother had just died, and when she returned to the United States, her husband had found a new romantic interest. Olle himself never went back after 1911, but in his late years he confessed that he would have liked to "go home."[92]

Värmlänningarna was the most impressive of the Olle i Skratthult Company's productions, and it was also one of the last, as the company gradually moved toward playing dance music. Although at least one play was produced thereafter (*Käringa mi's kusin,* 1931), times were changing. Hjalmar lost his cabin on the North Shore through speculation, and he also lost his leading lady. He and Olga parted ways—they were divorced in 1933—and he remarried. As the tours shrank, so did the group, until it again consisted of Olle alone. During his last years he toured as Hjalmar Peterson for the Salvation Army on the East Coast. Audiences were interested in seeing their old favorite Olle i Skratthult turned religious.

A general decline in Swedish theatre was a fact, due in part to the Depression, in part to the advance of the movies, but mostly to the decline of use of the Swedish language.[93] Perhaps Olle could have extended the touring days of his company if he had compromised more on the language, but no matter what language he used in his publicity, he always performed in Swedish. The entire show was in Swedish. The Swedish language was central to his stage personality and to his company. When the language faded from use in the thirties, he simply responded by using less and less spoken material.

Looking at production photos of the Olle i Skratthult Company, it is tempting to conclude that the performances were amateurish. The poses look stilted, the makeup obvious, and the sets homemade. An example of the unsophisticated scenery is the backdrop seen in several production photos from 1927. The drop shows a cabin wall with a window and shelf with tankards, plates, and candlestick. Under the shelf is a horizontal wall hanging. All these elements are painted on the drop. On this painted drop is tacked a set of curtains around the window and a real wall hanging, under the painted one. The corners of the painted window, where the curtains are pinned on, pucker and pull. The combination of real and painted wall hanging serves only to point up the two-dimensionality of the painted one. This decorative scheme was used for at least two different productions, possibly more, with different curtains and wall hangings—and of course different arrangements of furniture.[94] Yet who could criticize a touring company for having painted all-purpose drops rather than three-dimensional, specific sets? The stilted poses may simply reflect the fact that the photographs were posed. This is particularly clear in the production photo of *Lars Anders, Jan Anders och deras barn* (Figure 18.3), which shows every single company member including the tuxedo-dressed musicians and Olle himself, although the musicians were not in the play and Olle had no role, but did olios between the acts. Nor do the reviews reveal much about the level of the acting or the professionalism of the productions, and what little is said may have been influenced by Olle's press releases. What is undisputable is that the Olle i Skratthult Company was organized enough, and talented enough, to make a good living for two decades by touring the United States. Its performances satisfied the need for social interaction and identity reinforcement among the Swedish Americans. The Swedish language was important, yet not essential, for an appreciation of their programs. There may not have been much subtlety, but there was energy, warmth, and dedication; there was love for the material performed; there was expertise in handling crowds, coping with emergencies, and projecting into the corners of lofts and halls; there was stage presence; and there was "savvy."

18.3 Production photo of the Olle i Skratthult Company in *Lars Anders, Jan Anders och deras barn.* Left to right: Ragnar Åkerberg, Elna Kronberg, Olle i Skratthult, Augusta Linde, unidentified actor, Gottfrid Nord, Hilma Lindblom, Hans Haugman, Harry Swanson, Olga Lindgren-Peterson, and Annar Myhre. (Photo from the Olga Lindgren-Nilsen Collection, courtesy of the Olle i Skratthult Project.)

The reviewer Erland Richter, obviously touched by Olle's performances, writes about the effect of Olle and his company on their Swedish audiences in words that could sum up all of Swedish theatre in America:

What I above all wish to say about Olle i Skratthult is that the performances by himself and his company strengthen the ties between the Swedes out here and the Swedish soil. The millions of smiles and perhaps ten thousand tears evoked by him were all born under the sign of Swedishness.

Some work for Swedishness with seriousness and the singing of hymns, others with plays and popular songs. May the one not look askance at the other. We all have our appointed task to do. Let us do it, mind our own business, and things will go well for us all. Olle has done his task, or rather, is in the process of doing it. When his measure is filled, he will take his rest. We must not begrudge Olle and Olga their rest, when the time is ripe. Until then, cheer us, Olle, for there are too many who dampen our spirits![95]

THE CHARLES LINDHOLM COMPANY

One other company is of tangential interest. This was the Charles Lindholm Company, led by Charles Lindholm of Minnesota, which toured the United States from 1908 to 1924 or 1925. The company was professional, and like the Olle i Skratthult Company, it made its living touring with a vaudeville-type program, including plays. There the similarity ends, for whereas Olle performed Swedish plays in Swedish, Lindholm performed mostly American material, always in the English language. The one "ethnic" exception was Lindholm's own *The Man from Minnesota*, featuring himself as Charlie Lutefisk. He was equally well-known for touring *Peg o' My Heart* on the Orpheum circuit. Born in 1874 in White Rock, Minnesota, he died in 1936 in Minneapolis.

Appendix: Chronology of Plays Known to Have Been Performed by the Olle i Skratthult Company

(Unless Otherwise Indicated, Authors of Plays Are Swedish)

1919–1920* March 6 and 13. *Piperman i knipan* (Piperman in the Fix) or *En brottslig bet jänt* (A Criminal Valet, 1869), Chicago. One-act comedy by Richard Gustafson, from *Les forfaits de Pipermans*, by Alfred Duru and Henri Chivot.

March 6 and 16. *Lars Anders, Jan Anders och deras barn* (Lars Anders, Jan Anders, and their children, 1894), Chicago. Three-act folk comedy by Gustaf af Geijerstam.

1920–1921 No information available.

1921–1922 West Coast tour.

1922–1923 No information available.

1923–1924 November. *Lars Anders, Jan Anders och deras barn*, Chicago.

1924–1925 Second West Coast tour. Duets and scenes from *Nerkingarne* (The People of West Coast Nörke, 1872), sometimes titled *Lasse och Stina* (Lasse and Stina). Three-act folk drama with song by Axel Anrep.

---

*Note that the list is given by seasons; that is, these dates are in March 1920.

513

1925–1926   Early October. *Ire förälskade poliskonstaplar* (Three Police Constables in Love, 1870), Galesburg, Ill. One-act comedy with song translated by Johan Jolin from *Irois amours de pompiers* (1858), by Moreau, Paul S. de Sancy, and Alfred C. Lartigue.

October–November. *Ire förälskade poliskonstaplar*, Chicago.

October–November. "Officers Three," probably *Ire förälskade poliskonstaplar*, Grantsburg, Wis.

1926–1927   November 21, 24, 28, and 29. *Pelles misslyckade frieri*, or *Sven fick Svea* (Pelle's Unsuccessful Wooing, or Sven got Svea), Chicago. Three-act comedy, author unknown.

March 1, 2, and 6. *Lars Anders, Jan Anders och deras barn*, Chicago.

March 20. "Olle i Skratthult Show Company" (no play title mentioned), New York.

April 7. *Pelles misslyckade frieri*, Chicago.

1927–1928   October 6. "Olle i Skratthult Show Company (no play title mentioned), Dawson, Minnesota.

November 2 and 3. *Sme-Olas stora synd* (Blacksmith Ola's Great Sin, 1926), Chicago. Three-act folk comedy by Alfred Ebenhard, probably of Chicago.

December 9 and 11. *Sme-Olas stora synd*, Chicago.

February 9, 11, and 12. *Mamsell Sundblad vill gifta sig* (Miss Sundblad Wants to Get Married, 1865), Chicago. One-act comedy translated from the French by Bertha Spanier.

April 1. *Sme-Olas stora synd*, New York.

April 15. *Sme-Olas stora synd*, Minneapolis.

1928–1929   October 21, 27, and 28. *Älskogskranka och giftaslystna* (Lovesick and Ready to Wed), Chicago. Two-act comedy, date and author unknown.

December 15 and 16. *Värmlänningarna* (The People of Värmland, 1846), Chicago. Six-act folk drama with song by Fredrik August Dahlgren, with music by A. Randel.

February 13 and 17. *Per Olsson och hans käring* (Per Olsson and His Old Lady, 1894), Chicago. Three-act folk comedy by Gustaf af Geijerstam.

March 24. *Per Olsson och hans käring*, Chicago.

1929–1930   Autumn. *Madam Andersons hyresgäster*, or *Mot beräkning* (Mrs. Anderson's Lodgers, or Against Calculations, 1871), probably in Dayton, Minnesota. One-act comedy with song by Aron Jonason, from *Store Bededagsaften*, Danish adaptation by F. Jansen from the French.

October 24 and 26. *Två s jömän och en vacker flicka* (Two Sailors and a Beautiful Girl), Chicago. Farce, probably in one act, date and author unknown.

November 17. *Värmlänningarna*, Chicago.

Probably January 1. *Skvallerkäringar* (Gossips), Minneapolis. Comedy, date and author unknown, possibly same play as *Sqvallersystrarne* (The Gossipy Sisters, 1864), three-act dramatic sketch by Johan Jolin.

February 2, 3, and 8. *De gamla hänger i* (The Old Folks are Hanging in There, 1927), Chicago. Three-act comedy by Kurt Göransson, probably of Chicago.

March 8 and 9. *De gamla hänger i*, Chicago.

1930–1931   Autumn. *Käringa mi's kusin* (My Old Lady's Cousin, 1929), Grand Forks, North Dakota. Three-act comedy by Ebenhard.

January 4. *Käringa mi's kusin*, Minneapolis.

January 10, 11, and 18. *Käringa mi's kusin*, Chicago.

June 20 and 21. *Värmlänningarna*, produced in Alexandria, Minnesota, by the Twin Cities Dramatic Society, featuring Olga Lindgren-Peterson as Anna and Annar Myhre as Erik, both regular performers with the company. The company's band played for the performance.

NOTES

1. Henriette C. Koren Naeseth, *The Swedish Theatre of Chicago 1868–1950* (Rock Island, Ill.: Augustana Historical Society, 1951).
2. Ibid., p. vii.
3. Theodore C. Blegen, *Norwegian Migration to America: The American Transition* (Northfield, Minn.: Norwegian-American Historical Association, 1940), p. 560.
4. Naeseth, *Swedish Theatre*, p. viii.
5. The Danish theatre in Seattle has been researched by Clint Hyde, but the history of the Swedish theatre in that area remains unwritten. Several doctoral dissertations deal with theatre in Minneapolis and St. Paul but discuss only professional legitimate theatre. Two other dissertations may be of tangential interest: Charles L. Geroux, "The History of Theaters and Related Activity in Dubuque, Iowa, 1837–1877" (Ph.D. diss., Wayne State University, 1973), and Bruce Martin Wasserman, "Early Theatre in Spokane, Washington, 1889–1902" (Ph.D. diss., University of Washington, 1975).
6. Uno Myggan Ericson, "Snusgatans festival," in *Från scen och cabaret* (Stockholm: Stegelands, 1978), pp. 104–19; Maury Bernstein, "The Man Who Gave Us Nikolina," *Minnesota Earth Journal* 2, no. 6 (1974): 18–21; Naeseth, *Swedish Theatre*; Ulf Beijbom, "Olle i Skratthult—emigranternas bondkomiker!" *Svenska Amerikanaren Tribunen* (Chicago), May 2, 1973; Ulf Beijbom, "Olle i Skratthult—Nikolina och nöjeslivet i svenskamerika," *Svenska Posten* (Seattle and Portland), Jan. 23, 1974.
7. Naeseth, *Swedish Theatre*, p. viii; Nils Hasselmo, *Swedish America* (New York: Swedish Information Service, 1976), p. 35; Ernst Skarstedt, *Svensk-Amerikanska folket i helg och söcken* (Stockholm: Björck and Börjesson, 1917), p. 147.
8. Naeseth, *Swedish Theatre*, pp. 27, 40; also Henriette C. Koren Naeseth, "Drama in Swedish in Chicago 1868–1913," *Illinois State Historical Journal* 41 (June 1948): 160. In her article Naeseth lists Svea Hall as the place of performance, but in her subsequently published book she lists German Hall instead.
9. Alfred Söderström, *Minneapolis minnen* (Minneapolis, no publisher given, [1899]), p. 262; Blegen, *Norwegian Migration*, p. 562. The Skandinaviska Föreningen and its offshoot, the Scandinavian Dramatic Society (founded 1870), produced mostly plays in Norwegian.

516   ANNE-CHARLOTTE HANES HARVEY

10. Ernst H. Behmer, "Seventy Years of the Swedish Theatre in America," in Eric G. Westman, ed., *The Swedish Element in America* (Chicago: Swedish American Biographical Society, 1934), Vol. 4, pp. 111–20.

11. Hazel Magnusson, interview, July 10, 1976. Aside from the Magnussons, the group included accordionist Thure Andersson, June Holm, and Vernon and Mildred Peterson (now living in Red Wing, Minnesota). Denny and Hazel Magnusson are better known as the founders of the Yesterfarm of Memories museum in Center City, Minnesota.

12. Col. John Franzén, Salvation Army, interview, March 6, 1973.

13. Naeseth, *Swedish Theatre*, p. 273.

14. August Strindberg, "En nationell bildningsanstalt," In *Det nya riket*, Vol. 10 of *Samlade skrifter* (Stockholm: Albert Bonniers förlag, 1912–21), Vol. 10, p. 132. All translations from the original Swedish in this article are by me.

15. Ibid., pp. 137–38.

16. Naeseth, *Swedish Theatre*, Chapter 6, especially pp. 225 and 229. Clubs dedicated to the performance of the plays by August Strindberg (1849–1912) were Strindbergarna in Chicago and a group by the same name in Minneapolis (actually Svenska Dramatiska Klubben, renaming itself for the performance of *The Father* on January 23, 1916). It appears that the first Strindberg play performed in the United States was *Lucky-Pehr* (Chicago, 1899), followed by, particularly, *Gustav Vasa* (Chicago, 1911), *Easter* (Chicago, 1913 and 1918; Minneapolis, 1915 or 1916), *Pariah* (Chicago, 1914 and 1922), *The Pelican* (Chicago, 1915), *The Father* (Minneapolis, 1916), and *The People of Hemsö* (Chicago, 1937). Ibid., pp. 266–84; Maria Sonander-Rice Collection, Minneapolis, Minn. (hereafter MSRC).

17. Uno Myggan Ericson, *På nöjets estrader* (Stockholm: Bonniers, 1971), and Ericson, *Från scen och cabaret*, discuss the significance of *bondkomik*.

18. The spelling varies. The original spelling is *Vermländingarne*, followed, due to spelling reforms, by *Värmländingarne*, *Värmländingarna*, and, today, *Värmlänningarna*.

19. Naeseth, "Drama in Swedish," p. 163; Naeseth, *Swedish Theatre*, p. 284.

20. Naeseth, *Swedish Theatre*, p. 54.

21. In 1913 the Eastern Company of New York took *Värmlänningarna* to Chicago; in 1920 Ernst Behmer of Chicago took it to nearby Illinois towns; and in 1928 and 1929 the Minneapolis-based Olle i Skratthult Company took it to Chicago and the East Coast (Naeseth, *Swedish Theatre*, pp. 203, 213, 271).

22. *Värmlänningarna* was so popular that it was imitated on both sides of the Atlantic: *Nerkingarne* (The People of Närke), a three-act folk drama with song, was written by Axel Anrep in Stockholm in 1872 and first performed in Chicago in 1888 (ibid., p. 280), and *Smålänningarne* (The People of Småland) was written by Otto E. Anderson in Minneapolis in 1919 (privately printed).

23. Naeseth, "Drama in Swedish," p. 164.

24. "The People of Värmland," by Paul W. Petterson of St. Louis Park, Minnesota.

25. Some of the few plays adapted and translated from English belong in this group: *Tjuven*, a translation and adaptation of *The Thief*, by Upton Sinclair, which was performed in 1923, 1930, and 1935, and *Sällskapsglaset*, a translation of *The Social Glass* by Trask Woodward, which was performed in 1894 and 1913. (Naeseth, *Swedish Theatre*, p. 283.)

26. Unless otherwise indicated, play publication and performance data are from Naeseth, *Swedish Theatre*, pp. 266–84.

27. Possibly by Magnus Elmblad, celebrated journalist and author of the well-known emigrant ballad about Petter Jönsson.

28. "Snoose Boulevard" was the nickname for main streets in many Swedish towns, so called because Scandinavians were known to use "snoose" (snuff), the cheapest form of tobacco. Cedar Avenue in Minneapolis, Payne Avenue in St. Paul, and Chicago Avenue in Chicago were Snoose Boulevards. The play title refers to Chicago Avenue.

29. Naeseth, *Swedish Theatre*, p. viii.

30. These names are partly derived from Naeseth and partly from playbills, posters, and programs from the Maria Sonander-Rice Collection (hereafter MSRC) and the Olga Lindgren-Nilsen collection (hereafter OLNC), both in Minneapolis.

31. Naeseth, *Swedish Theatre*, p. 55.

32. Ibid., pp. 182–83.

33. Ibid., pp. 86, 95.

34. *Svenska nyheter* (Chicago), April 10, 1906.

35. Naeseth, *Swedish Theatre*, pp. 66–67.

36. Ibid., pp. 133, 217; Naeseth, "Drama in Swedish," p. 169.

37. Naeseth, *Swedish Theatre*, p. 19.

38. *Hamlet* and *The Taming of the Shrew* (In Swedish, Så tuktas en argbigga) used the Swedish translations by C. A. Hagberg (1853 and 1960, respectively); *H.M.S. Pinafore*, as mentioned earlier in the text, was translated for the 1896 Chicago production by the Swedish-American journalist Gustaf Wicklund.

39. Naeseth, "Drama in Swedish," p. 163.

40. Ibid., p. 169.

41. Interview with Olga Lindgren-Nilsen, June 18, 1979 (Lindgren-Nilsen will hereafter be cited as OLN); Erland Richter, "Olle och Olga: Några små funderingar rundt Olle i Skratthult och hans sällskap," *Svea* (Worcester, Mass.), spring 1924.

42. In this case the expurgation is directly traceable to Olle i Skratthult, who first recorded and published this song in the United States (Olle i Skratthult songbooks, OLNC, and recording, Victor 79278-A). Lindgren-Nilsen said that she had never heard the verse about the illegitimate child (interview, Mar. 6, 1973).

43. *En natt i Falkenberg* (1851), translated by Jonas Philipsson from *En nat i Roeskilde*, an adaptation by Hans Christian Andersen of *Une chambre à deux lits* by Charles Varin and Louis Lefèvre; *Andersson, Petterson och Lundström* (1866), translated by Frans Hodell from *Der böse Geist Lumpaci Vagabundus*, by Johannes Nestroy; *Öregrund-Östhammar* (1902), translated by Herman Kinmansson and adapted by Algot E. Strand from *Kyritz-Pyritz*, by H. Wilken; *Tre förälskade poliskonstaplar* (1870), translated by Johan Jolin from *Trois amours de pompiers* (1858), by Moreau, Paul S. de Sancy, and Alfred C. Lartigue.

44. Hasselmo, *Swedish America*, p. 38.

45. Ibid., pp. 36–40.

46. Albert Nordeen, interview, June 18, 1979.

47. Naeseth, *Swedish Theatre*, p. 54.

48. Victor 69565-A; Victor 72719-B. "Olle ve' Kvarna i Amerika" was a *bondkomik* type.

49. Poster, MSRC.

50. Carla Wulfsberg, letter to author, January 12, 1980, and interview with Charles Lindholm's niece, Vivien Mackey of Seattle, January 19, 1980.

51. Obituary, *Minneapolis Star*, May 21, 1956.

52. Naeseth, *Swedish Theatre*, p. 86.

53. Information about Hjalmar Peterson has been obtained primarily from interviews with his family and coworkers and collections belonging to the two children of his second marriage, Karl Peterson and Sheri Hansing of Minneapolis, and his first wife, Olga Lindgren-Nilsen, now living in St. Paul. The life and work of Olle i Skratthult has recently been given some attention by a nonprofit group in Minneapolis, the Olle i Skratthult Project, founded in 1971. The material collected by the project resulted in a commemorative exhibit at the Emigrant Institute, Växjö, Sweden, in the now defunct Snoose Boulevard Festival in Minneapolis, and in the publication of six records. As remarked in the opening section of this chapter, very little has been published about Olle i Skratthult.

54. Eventually Peterson had three brothers in the United States: Albin, a chiropractor in California; David, a photographer in Princeton, Minnesota; and the youngest, Paul, a restaurant owner in Lancaster, Minnesota (OLN, March 6, 1973).

55. He also fathered an illegitimate son, Fritz Jönsson, who is now a painter in Kistinge, Halmstad. The two kept in touch over the years, but never met. Once, in 1927, Fritz almost came over to America, but at the last minute "something came up" (Hallandsposten, December 23, 1974). A collection of letters from father to son document the shifting fortunes of Hjalmar Petersons's career and offer special insight into the last lonely years of his life (Emigrant Institute, Växjö, Sweden).

56. As a performer, Peterson used both his own name and his bondkomiker name. When he sang serious songs or art songs he was Hjalmar Peterson, just as he was Hjalmar Peterson when he sang with the Salvation Army during his last years. But it was as Olle that he was known and loved. Reviews and contemporaries refer to him as Olle; indeed, his former wife Olga talks of him alternately as "Hjalmar" and "Olle." Similar confusion exists in the usage of "Olle i Skratthult": at times it means Hjalmar Peterson's comic stage personality, at times Hjalmar Peterson himself, and at times the company, of which he was manager.

57. Information about Lindgren-Nilsen is from OLNC and from interviews over a period of years from 1973 to 1980. Olga did take singing lessons at McPhail School of Music, and her teacher was Madame Starbäck-Hall (interview, March 6, 1973).

58. Unidentified Swedish-language newspaper (probably Svenska Pacific Tribunen), Tacoma, Washington, February, 1925 (OLNC).

59. Naeseth, Swedish Theatre, p. 268.

60. Lindgren-Nilsen remembers no plays touring after 1925 with the exception of Värmlänningarna. On this point she is clearly contradicted by other evidence. In fact, the years 1925–1931 were the busiest touring years, each season in 1927–1929 featuring at least three different play productions, as seen from playbills, OLNC and MSRC; from interviews with other Swedish-American theatre people; and from Naeseth, Swedish Theatre.

61. Unidentified English-language newspaper, Everett, Washington, probably 1928 (OLNC). The dates of the two other tours have not been identified with certainty.

62. Data about the 1924–1925 tour have been put together from reviews, which for this season are especially plentiful (OLNC). For part of this season Olle also recruited his sister-in-law, Mrs. Lindell of Los Angeles.

63. Dawson Sentinel (Minnesota), September 29, 1927, makes reference to a performance in New York on March 20, 1927, with nine company members.

64. At least one production of Värmlänningarna in America assumed gigantic proportions. It was performed in the Metropolitan Opera House, the largest and plushest

auditorium in Minneapolis, on April 13, 1919, and was advertised as having "around a hundred participants" (MSRC).

65. Poster, OLNC. It was printed in Chicago, probably for the 1929 tour, as it incorporates press clips from previous performances on the East Coast.

66. OLNC. The photos dated 1927 and signed were taken by Hjalmar's brother David Peterson, Princeton, Minnesota.

67. OLN, interview, February 9, 1973.

68. OLN, interview, June 18, 1979.

69. Naeseth, *Swedish Theatre*, p. 223.

70. *Dawson Sentinel* (Minnesota), April 26, 1928.

71. Unidentified English-language newspaper, Grantsburg, Wisconsin, possibly fall 1925 (OLNC).

72. OLN, interview, February 9, 1973.

73. *Nordst järnan* (New York), probably 1928, reprinted on *Värmlänningarna* poster (OLNC).

74. *Svea* (erroneously given as Boston, actually Worcester, Mass.), probably 1928, reprinted on *Värmlänningarna* poster (OLNC).

75. OLN, interview, June 18, 1979.

76. Erland Richter, "Olle och Olga."

77. The company stayed in an apartment in New York for several months without making appearances in the surrounding area. They were preparing for the New York premiere of *Värmlänningarna*, probably the same highly acclaimed production that was performed in Chicago on Dec. 15–16, 1928 (OLN, interview, June 18, 1979).

78. Albert Nordeen, interview, June 18, 1979.

79. OLN, interview, June 18, 1979.

80. OLN, interview, May 1973. The wig is still in good condition (OLNC).

81. Ulf Beijbom, "Olle i Skratthult—emigranternas bondkomiker!" *Svenska Amer-ikanaren Tribunen* (Chicago), May 2, 1973.

82. Col. John Franzén, Salvation Army, interview, March 6, 1973. When in his later years Peterson toured the East Coast for the Salvation Army singing religious songs, he was reluctant to tour alone, and felt better when Franzén could come along to handle the speaking. This Hjalmar Peterson was an older, unwell man singing a limited repertoire of religious songs. As Olle i Skratthult, he had had no hesitation and a vast repertoire.

83. OLN, interview, February 9, 1973, and role photos (OLNC).

84. OLN, interview, March 6, 1973. One performance by the Olle i Skratthult Company in the Los Angeles area is reviewed in an unidentified Danish-language news-paper, January 1925 (OLNC).

85. Richter, "Olle och Olga"; OLN, interview, June 18, 1979.

86. Swedish publishing houses in Chicago supplied Swedish plays and popular songs, printed in the United States. One house, Dalkullan, published an annual songbook and served as a clearing house for other Swedish articles, such as folk costumes. Another firm, Anders Löfström, published Swedish poetry, humor, and playscripts. Olle would pick up new material from Sweden in Chicago, then reprint it privately and sell it in connection with his own performances. He printed at least five different songbooks and at least one playscript. On the basis of the success of the previous tour in 1920, Olle printed up the script for *Lars Anders, Jan Anders och deras barn* to be sold on the 1923 tour. (Preface, *Lars Anders* [Minneapolis: privately printed, 1923].) Apparently copyrights were not carefully observed. One interesting footnote is that Olle, possibly to avoid copyright problems,

changed the title of one of his most popular songs from the original "Svinnsta skär" to "Lyckoskär."

87. Olle i Skratthult Project Collection, Minneapolis.

88. OLNC.

89. The closing remarks by Richter in his article "Olle och Olga" were reprinted verbatim in *Svenska Pressen*, November 12, 1924.

90. "Olle i Skratthult Draws Big Crowd," unidentified English-language newspaper, Jamestown, New York, possibly 1927; "Swedish Comedian Here," a second unidentified English-language newspaper, Jamestown, New York, same date (OLNC). The reviews described the same performance. The phrasing was identical in the descriptions of the content of the program, the costumes worn, and the intended continued travel route. (The two papers were probably the *Post* and the *Evening Journal.*)

91. In the Grantsburg, Wis., review that mentions the play *Officers Three*, probably *Tre förälskade poliskonstaplar*, which was performed in Swedish, there is no indication that the journalist was bilingual and himself translated the play title. (See note 71.) The translation was probably provided in the company press release. That Olle used English press releases is clear from the similarities in the Jamestown reviews, for example. (See note 90.) About half the clippings in OLNC are in Swedish, the other half in English.

92. John Franzén, interview, March 6, 1973; letters, Hjalmar Peterson to Fritz Jönsson, Aug. 22 and Nov. 10, 1958.

93. Though the competition of the movies was keenly felt—one *Värmlänningarna* poster (Svenska Dramatiska Sällskapet, Minneapolis, September 5–6, 1925) proclaims "not a Moving Picture, but the Real Play!" (MRSC)—it was definitely the decline in use of the language that hurt Olle's business most (OLN, interview, June 18, 1979).

94. All production photos of the Olle i Skratthult Company are in OLNC.

95. Richter, "Olle och Olga."

BIBLIOGRAPHY

Books

Ander, Fritiof O. *The Cultural Heritage of the Swedish Immigrant: Selected References.* Augustana Library Publication no. 27. Rock Island, Ill.: Augustana Library, 1956. Bibliography.

Anderson, Otto E. *Smålänningarne.* Minneapolis: no publisher given, 1919. Four-act comedy about "The People of Småland" in Sweden and America.

Beijbom, Ulf. *Swedes in Chicago. A Demographic and Social Study of the 1846–1880 Immigration.* Studia Historica Upsaliensia, no. 38. Stockholm: Scandinavian University Books, 1971. Most important recent treatment of Swedish-American settlement history. Scholarly and thorough background. Little direct mention of theatre.

————. *Amerika! Amerika! En bok om utvandringen.* Stockholm: Natur och Kultur, 1977. Popular treatment of the emigration. Excellent background.

Blegen, Theodore C. *Norwegian Migration to America: The American Transition.* Northfield, Minn.: Norwegian-American Historical Association, 1940. General information about the role of cultural societies among Scandinavian immigrants.

Ericson, Uno Myggan. *Från scen och cabaret.* Stockholm: Stegelands, 1978. Expanded treatment of *bondkomik,* including a chapter about Olle i Skratthult and the Snoose Boulevard Festival ("Snusgatans festival," pp. 104–19).

————. *På nöjets estrader.* Stockholm: Bonniers, 1971. Fundamental work about Swedish *bondkomik.*

Hasselmo, Nils. *Swedish America.* New York: Swedish Information Service, 1976. Excellent overview. Annotated bibliography. Treatment of theatre, pp. 35–36 and pp. 62–63. Some factual errors. Excellent treatment of the language question, pp. 36–44.

Lindblom, Ernst. *Svenska teaterminnen från Chicago (Swedish Theatre in Chicago).* Stockholm: C. I. Gullbergs förlag, 1916. Memoirs of an actor in the Swedish theatre in Chicago in the 1890s. Valuable, although somewhat unreliable because written after return to Sweden.

Ljungmark, Lars. *Swedish Exodus.* Carbondale and Edwardsville: Southern Illinois University Press, 1979. Translation of a standard popular work on the Swedish emigration. Good background. Bibliography of value.

Naeseth, Henriette C. Koren. *The Swedish Theatre of Chicago 1868–1950.* Rock Island, Ill.: Augustana Historical Society, 1951. The major study of Swedish theatre in the United States. Thorough and readable. A few errors, particularly in the spelling and translation of Swedish words. Appendixes, extensive notes, and bibliography. Valuable.

Nordström, Byron, ed. *The Swedes in Minnesota.* Minneapolis: T. S. Denison, 1976. Chapters on Swedish organization life and language in Minnesota offer good background to the study of the Minnesota theatre.

Olson, Ernst W.; Schön, Anders; and Engberg, Martin J., eds. *History of the Swedes in Illinois.* 2 vols. 1908. Reprint. New York: Arno Press, 1979. A classic source. Volume 1 covers, among other things, institutions, music, art, and artists. Volume 2 consists of biographical sketches of prominent Swedes in Illinois. Interesting background.

Personne, Nils. *Svenska teatern (Swedish Theatre).* 8 vols. Stockholm: Wahlström and Widstrand, 1913–1927. Encyclopedic work about theatre in Sweden in the late 1800s and early 1900s. Sketches of actors who emigrated or toured Swedish America.

Peterson, Hjalmar. Preface to *Lars Anders, Jan Anders och deras barn*, by Gustaf af Geijerstam. Willmar, Minn.: Hjalmer Peterson, 1923. Olle i Skratthult's justification for privately printing this playscript.

Skarstedt, Ernst. *Svensk-Amerikanska folket i helg och söcken.* Stockholm: Björck and Börjesson, 1917. Fundamental source including many valuable glimpses of Swedish theatre and biographical sketches of cultural leaders. Readable, though lacking in organization.

————. *Våra pennfäktare: Lefnads- och karaktärsteckningar öfver Svensk-Amerikanska tidningsmän, skalder och författare.* San Francisco: Ernst Skarstedt, 1897. Major source of information about Swedish-American journalists and authors.

Sundbeck, Carl. *Svenskarna i Amerika.* Stockholm: F. C. Askerbergs Bokförlag, 1900. Includes a brief paragraph about Swedish theatre in the United States.

Söderström, Alfred. *Blixtar på Tidnings-Horisonten, samlade och Magasinerade af Alfred Söderström.* Warroad, Minn.: no publisher given, 1910. The Swedish-language press in the United States and its best-known writers are portrayed here. Interesting background.

————. *Minneapolis minnen.* Minneapolis: no publisher given, [1899]. Anecdotal history of Minneapolis, thorough, lively, and full of curiosities. Deals with early theatre in Minneapolis, pp. 267–76.

Articles

Behmer, Ernst H. "Seventy Years of the Swedish Theatre in America." In Eric G. Westman, ed., *The Swedish Element in America.* Chicago: Swedish American Biographical Society, 1934, Vol. 4, pp. 111–20. General account of the Swedish theatre in the United States by one of the leaders of Chicago theatre (active 1893–1946). Valuable.

Beijbom, Ulf. "Olle i Skratthult—emigranternas bondkomiker!" *Svenska Amerikanaren Tribunen (Swedish-American Tribune)* (Chicago), May 2, 1973.

————. "Olle i Skratthult—Nikolina och nöjeslivet i svensk-amerika." *Svenska Posten (Swedish Post)* (Seattle and Portland), Jan. 23, 1974. This article and the one above are essentially the same: popular resumes of findings to date about Olle i Skratthult and his company. Some factual errors.

Bernstein, Maury. "The Man Who Gave Us *Nikolina,*" *Minnesota Earth Journal* 2, no.6 (1972): 18–21. Brief summary of Olle i Skratthult's life and career. Some factual errors.

————. "Olle i Skratthult and Scandinavian-American Vaudeville. In Johannes Riedel, *American Popular Music.* Minneapolis: University of Minnesota, 1976. Thorough treatment of Olle i Skratthult's life, career, and ethnicity. Used as study material for course in American popular music.

Hampl, Patricia. "Travels on the Boat of Longing: The Snoose Boulevard Festival." Riedel, *American Popular Music.* Study of the background and community reactions to the Snoose Boulevard Festival. Used as study material for course in American popular music.

Lundbergh, Holger. "Stage and Radio Performers." In Adolph B. Benson and Naboth Hedin, eds., *Swedes in America 1638–1938,* pp. 482–87. New York: Haskell House Publishers, 1969. Brief treatment of Swedish-Americans who became professional English-language entertainers. Of limited value.

Naeseth, Henriette C. Koren. "Drama in Swedish in Chicago 1868–1913." *Illinois State Historical Journal* 41 (June 1948): 159–70. Preparatory study for the larger work *Swedish Theatre of Chicago 1868–1950.* Excellent survey. Some factual errors, corrected in the later treatment.

Napier, Wilt, and Naeseth, Henriette C. Koren. "Two Early Norwegian Dramatic Societies in Chicago," *Norwegian-American Studies and Records* 10 (1938): 44–75. Of interest for the study of Scandinavian theatre in Chicago. In a number of places, the first dramatic societies were pan-Scandinavian and Norwegian was the preferred language.

Richter, Erland. "Olle och Olga: Några små funderingar rundt Olle i Skratthult och hans sällskap," *Svea* (Worcester, Mass.), spring 1924. Lengthy and somewhat gushing review of the contribution of the Olle i Skratthult Company to the preservation of Swedishness through theatre, song, and music.

Sonander-Rice, Maria. "Some Sketches from My 85 Year Life," *Svenska Amerikanaren Tribunen,* May 3, 1972, in Swedish. Later translated by author. Brief and personal reminiscences by one of Minneapolis' foremost Swedish actresses in the 1910s and 1920s. Valuable, though erratic.

Strindberg, August. "En nationell bildningsanstalt." *Det nya riket,* Vol.10 of *Samlade skrifter* Stockholm: Albert Bonniers förlag, 1912–21, pp. 130–46. Satiric description of theatre in Stockholm in the 1870s.

Other Sources

Collections and Archives

Among the many collections of Swedish-American material, the following include material pertaining to Swedish-American theatre:

American Swedish Institute, Minneapolis, Minn.
Augustana College Library, Rock Island, Ill.
Emigrant Institute, Växjö, Sweden*
Minnesota Historical Society, St. Paul, Minn.
Nordic Heritage Museum, Seattle, Wash. (collection being assembled)
Nordic Collections, Honnold Library, Claremont, Calif.
University of Chicago, Chicago, Ill.
University of Minnesota, Minneapolis, Minn.
University of Washington, Seattle, Wash.

---

*Olle i Skratthult Project Collection, now deposited with the Emigrant Institute.

Newspapers

It is outside the scope of this bibliography to list all the daily and weekly newspapers of proven or potential value for documenting the Swedish theatre in America. A thorough search would involve all available files of all papers in the target area for the time concerned, primarily the Swedish-language publications, but also the English-language papers, to note the extent of attention they gave the Swedish theatre. (For the Chicago area, see Naeseth, *Swedish Theatre*, pp. 345–47.) Obvious newspapers to scrutinize would include *Nordstjernan*, *Svea*, and *Nordst jernan-Svea* on the East Coast; *Svenska-Amerikanaren Tribunen* and others (see Naeseth) for the Upper Midwest; and *Vestkusten*, *Svenska Pressen* and *Svenska Pacific Tribunen* on the West Coast.

Clippings, Photos, Posters, Programs, Memorabilia, and Letters

Johnson, Ted, violin player with Olle i Skratthult Company. Recordings, record catalogs, clippings, photos.

Lindgren-Nilsen, Olga, Hjalmar Peterson's first wife and leading lady of the Olle i Skratthult Company 1916–1933. Extensive collection of clippings, photos, scripts, posters, and memorabilia from the Olle i Skratthult Company.

Olle i Skratthult Exhibit Program. Emigrant Institute, Växjö, Sweden, 1974.

Peterson, Hjalmar, letters to his son Fritz Jönsson and family in Sweden, 1958. Emigrant Institute, Växjö, Sweden.

Peterson, Karl, Hjalmar Peterson's son (second marriage), Minneapolis. Photos, memorabilia from Hjalmar Peterson's life.

Sonander-Rice, Maria, actress in Swedish theatre in Minneapolis in the 1910s and 1920s, Minneapolis. Clippings, photos, posters, programs, and memorabilia. Copies deposited by Olle i Skratthult Project with the Emigrant Institute, Sweden, and with author, San Diego, courtesy of Mr. and Mrs. Arnold Walker, Minneapolis.

Wulfsberg, Carla. Letter to author, January 12, 1980.

Interviews

The interviews were taped; all, except as noted, were done in Minneapolis or St. Paul.

Anderson, Phil; Carlson, Ted; Filström, Sid; and Haselius, Wally, members of Olle i Skratthult Orchestra, by Rosemary Dahlen, Feb. 4, 1973.

Beijbom, Ulf, director of the Emigrant Institute, Sweden. Telephone interview with author, May 10, 1979.

Carlson, Ted, by Steve Benson, Apr. 29, 1972.

Franzén, Col. John, by Carl-Werner Petterson, Mar. 6, 1973.

Hansing, Sheri, Hjalmar Peterson's daughter (second marriage), by Steve Benson, Apr. 29, 1972.

Johnson, Ted, member of Olle i Skratthult Orchestra, by Carl-Werner Petterson, Mar. 5, 1973.

Lindgren-Nilsen, Olga, telephone interview by Maury Bernstein, Feb. 4, 1973.

———, by Steve Benson, Feb. 9, 1973.

———, by Carl-Werner Petterson, Mar. 6, 1973.

———, by author and Stig Tornehed, May 1973.

———, by author, June 18, 1979.

Mackey, Vivien, Charles Lindholm's niece, Seattle, Wash., telephone interview by author, Jan. 19, 1980.

Magnusson, Hazel, proprietor of "Yesterfarm of Memories" museum, widow of Denny Magnusson, Center City, Minn., by author, July 10, 1976.

Nordeen, Albert, brother of Hazel Magnusson, by author, June 18, 1979.

Radio and Television Programs

"Olle i Skratthult." Documentary by Swedish Television, directed by Stig Tornehed, 1974.

"Snoose Boulevard Festival." Documentary by Swedish Television, directed by Stig Tornehed, 1974.
"Primadonna hos Olle i Skratthult." Program by Swedish Radio, produced by Stig Tornehed, 1975.
"Olle tog Nikolina." Documentary by Steve Benson and Anne-Charlotte Harvey for KUOM-FM, Minneapolis, 1975.

19

Ukrainian-American Theatre

LARISSA ONYSHKEVYCH

The theatre usually mirrors certain aspects of people's lives, from the philosophical to the economic, moral, and political problems of the day. Thus the Ukrainian immigrant theatre reflected many of the above factors, as well as the predicaments Ukrainian immigrants had to solve in the new land. At the end of the nineteenth century, sociohistorical and political conditions in Ukraine influenced the Ukrainian theatre there. At the same time, these conditions provided motives for Ukrainians to translocate to the United States and organize their own social and cultural life, which included theatres. Besides the sporadic entry of small groups, there were primarily three great waves of Ukrainian immigration to this country: one at the end of the last century, the second in the early 1930s, and the third at the end of World War II.

HISTORICAL BACKGROUND

In the nineteenth century, Ukraine was divided primarily under two foreign rules. The central and eastern area, representing almost two-thirds of Ukraine, was incorporated into the czarist Russian Empire, while most of the western part of Ukraine was under the Polish administration within the Austro-Hungarian Empire. On the whole, the nineteenth century represented one of the most trying and critical periods of Ukrainian history. Having lost their independence and freedom, both parts of Ukraine were threatened with possible annihilation of their culture.

In the Russian empire, Ukrainians were not allowed to publish or stage Ukrainian plays, especially if these were not restricted to ethnographic themes.[1] This restriction had its roots in an acknowledged practice of the Russian regime of luring the upper classes of Ukrainians into the Russian culture and milieu, at the price of destroying the Ukrainian culture and milieu. As a result Ukrainians as a group contributed heavily to the development of the ecclesiastical, scholarly, literary, and artistic world of the Russian empire. They often published in the Russian language, since their own was forbidden in edicts such as the 1863

Valuev ukaz, which forbade the printing of Ukrainian books, including plays, and the 1876 Ems *ukaz*, which prohibited staging of Ukrainian plays in the Ukrainian language. In 1881 special permission was granted to perfrom some Ukrainian plays, but only by a Russian company. Later only one play per year was allowed (in some areas), and this one was limited to a representation of the life of the peasantry, excluding representations of the intelligentsia and upper classes.

A marked relaxation took place only after 1905. Later there was a full blossoming of the theatre during the short years of renewed Ukrainian independence (1917–1920) and the first decade of Soviet rule, until 1930.

The western part of Ukraine was under Polish rule from the fall of the Austro-Hungarian empire until 1939. By comparison with the central and eastern parts of Ukraine, the western area under Austria had much better conditions for Ukrainian theatre, since censorship of plays and performances was not so strict. Nevertheless, political conditions produced a hopeless economic situation for the Ukrainian rural population and caused many people to emigrate to the United States.

FIRST UKRAINIAN IMMIGRANTS

Although the first Ukrainians came to this country as early as the eighteenth century, large clusters of Ukrainians did not start to settle here until the end of the nineteenth century.[2] Most of these came from the western parts of Ukraine. They were primarily of the lowest economic stratum, though there was also a small number of well-educated political immigrants, who became political and cultural leaders of the Ukrainian communities or among the Americans.[3] The Ukrainian Catholic Church in western Ukraine, also called Greek Catholic, Eastern, or Byzantine Rite, provided leaders for the first Ukrainian communities by sending priests for the faithful.[4]

In western Ukraine there was strong pressure by the Polish administration to limit higher educational opportunities for Ukrainians; the only free access to college education was usually in the Ukrainian Byzantine Rite Catholic seminaries. Thus most of the educational, cultural, and social life of Ukrainians was led by clergymen and their families. This pattern was soon copied by the new settlers here, as the first communities petitioned the Ukrainian diocese in Lviv to send them priests. The immigrants even collected money for the passage of the first priest and his family. Thus in 1884 Rev. Ivan Wolyansky (1856–1926) arrived here and soon performed amazing feats. Within several years he managed to build churches and organize Ukrainian schools, benevolent (insurance) societies, workers unions, reading rooms and libraries, choirs, and amateur drama groups, as well as the first Ukrainian Catholic newspaper, *Ameryka.*

Other priests were sent as well, who closely followed Wolyansky's footsteps; Hryhoriy Hrushka organized the first Ukrainian-language daily, *Svoboda* (both of these newspapers are still being published). Priests organized choirs, schools, and drama clubs and were the first in this country to write new Ukrainian plays; these clergymen-playwrights included Rev. Stephan Makar, Rev. Mykola Strutynsky, Rev. Stephan Musiychuk, and Rev. Hieronim Lutsky.

The immigrants from western Ukraine brought with them the tradition of amateur theatre in almost every small village. Used to being spectators or performers in such theatres, the immigrants eagerly formed amateur groups in every area of the United States and Canada where they settled. They were soon joined by several professional actors, singers, musicians, and playwrights who came as political émigrés.

Most of the first Ukrainian settlers came from the western parts of Ukraine before World War I; only a small number came from the central and eastern parts. These few individuals were primarily professionals leaving Ukraine and escaping from the political oppression of the Russian empire. This trend increased markedly when the Soviet Union incorporated most of Ukraine in 1920 as the Ukrainian Soviet Socialist Republic, when many cultural and political activists fled from the new rule.

FIRST UKRAINIAN IMMIGRANT THEATRES

Ukrainians settled primarily in New York, New Jersey, Pennsylvania, Illinois, Ohio, and North Dakota, where most parishes or benevolent associations had their own drama clubs. In the larger cities, especially in New York, the theatre groups were mostly organized and directed by professional musicians or former actors. As more political immigrants arrived around 1920, there were more professional actors among them. They soon joined the existing drama clubs and also trained young enthusiasts in the arts of acting, dancing, and singing. Many of the Ukrainian plays, operettas, and operas that were staged included both singing and folk dancing. The reason was twofold: first, most of the nineteenth-century plays in Ukraine were allowed to represent only the village life and its customs, which included singing and dancing, and second, these three media were appreciated by the nostalgic audiences during the late-romantic trends of the time.

While in the small parishes the first drama clubs staged Ukrainian plays even before 1890, the first large-scale performance, *Evil Spirits*, was held in New York City on February 20, 1900, followed by a comedy, *A Germanized Jew*, on May 26 and *Tom the Corporal* on February 2, 1901. Later performances were staged with the cooperation of large choirs; one such group was the American Boyan Society, organized on July 6, 1905. Either this same group or its derivative, the New York Boyan Mixed Choir, gave a concert on February 17, 1907, at the Manhattan Lyceum and also staged a one-act play, *The Heart Is Not to Be Trifled With.* On May 17, 1911, this group staged a very popular romantic play that includes many songs and dances, *Natalka Poltavka*, by Ivan Kotlyarevsky, directed by

Olexsander Shostak. The chorus was conducted by Osyp Stetkevych; the orchestra was directed by Pavlo Kelychava; and the makeup work was done by Richard Uhorchak.[5]

Some of the amateur theatre groups were organized by benevolent (insurance) societies; one of the best-known of these was Branch 117 of the Ukrainian National Association, in New York, the Zaporizka Sich Society. Other theatre groups grew in conjunction with choirs. For example, in New York City, at the Ukrainian Eastern Rite Catholic Church of St. George, members of a choir directed by Myron Hundych staged a short operetta, *Vechernytsi* (Evening Party),[6] in 1907. From this group Volodymyr Malych organized a performance of an ever-popular Ukrainian opera, *Zaporozhets beyond the Danube*, by Semen Hulak-Artemovsky, also in 1907. Hryhoriy Smolynsky was the conductor and Y. Boyakivsky the director.

With the help of the Zaporizka Sich Society and its president, Ivan Hanachivsky, the Ivan Kotlyarevsky Drama Society was formed in 1907. This group represented the first Ukrainian repertory theatre in this country. The group was in close touch with a professional theatre, Besida, in Lviv (western Ukraine), from which it acquired texts and scores. Since Ukrainians annually commemorate the greatest Ukrainian poet, Taras Shevchenko, his works obviously were very popular. Thus for the first performance of the Ivan Kotlyarevsky Drama Society, Shevchenko's *The Prisoner* was chosen; it was staged on September 29, 1907.[7] Antin Tsurkovsky (Curkowsky), a writer and editor of *Svoboda*, was the artistic director. Later the society staged Kotlyarevsky's *Natalka Poltavka* (December 15), Mykola Lysenko's opera *Chornomortsi* (Kozaks of the Black Sea) (June 1, 1911), and other traditional Ukrainian dramatic and musical works, such as *Hapless Love* (June 4, 1910) and *Zaporozhets*.[8] Most of their performances were staged at Arlington and Lyceum Halls.

Since in the United States a large number of Ukrainian immigrants at first belonged to the lowest economic class, the theatre they patronized could not hope to be completely professional; at best it could remain semiprofessional, with performances mostly on weekends. Many companies toured the surrounding areas and even Canada, but despite some successes, the economic situation usually prevented continuity even of the best groups. Thus from time to time new groups were formed or old ones reorganized.[9]

In 1910 in New York City, Volodymyr Knyhynytsky and Yakiv Kornata organized the Besida Theater, the name implying homage to the Lviv professional theatre. Myron Korykora was the conductor, and Stetkevych, B. Bilynsky, and later Semen Komyshevatsky were the artistic directors. They staged the dramatic as well as the musical repertoire, presenting the opera *Zaporozhets* on June 18, 1914, at Arlington Hall.

None of the Ukrainian churches or organizations had a building large enough to accommodate a relatively large theatre. Thus when in 1917 the Ukrainian National Home was acquired in New York for the purpose of cultural or social meetings, on the initiative of Mykola Pidhoretsky and Volodymyr Lazuta a new theatre group was organized, the Theatre of the Ukrainian National Home. At last the Ukrainian theatre could perform in a Ukrainian building every weekend, and thus save the expense of renting. Komyshevatsky became the director of the theatre and Lazuta the leading actor and costume designer. From 1918 to 1920 David Medow was the artistic director.

At this time many Ukrainian professional musicians started to arrive. Some were immediately employed professionally and only occasionally appeared in concerts at the Ukrainian stage; for example, the singers Adam Didur, bass, and Marcella Kochanska-Sembrich, coloraturo soprano, became soloists with the Metropolitan Opera. The less fortunate musicians had to work at other occupations and perform only on weekends. Interest in Ukrainian operas was active; thus from the members of the Besida Theater the Ukrainian Opera Guild was formed, and the first Ukrainian opera it performed was *Kateryna*, based on a work by Shevchenko, with music by Mykola Arkas, on January 7, 1922, at the Ukrainian National Home in New York. The company went on tour to Philadelphia (March 13–14, 1922), where it also staged *Zaporozhets*. The latter work was performed in Newark as well, on February 5, 1922. Since the singers worked at other professions and often moved to other cities, the guild did not survive long. Nevertheless, in 1930 the New York Besida Opera Group was organized by Dmytro Chutro, also under the auspices of the New York Besida. Among the operas it staged was Lysenko's *Taras Bulba* and Piotr Ilich Tchaikovsky's *Mazeppa*. The premiere of the latter was on April 26, 1933, at the Mecca Temple; the libretto was translated into Ukrainian by Lonhyn Tsehelsky. The performance was conducted by Pavlo P. Uhlytsky (or Ouglytsky).

The theatre groups could not continue more than a decade, since besides the financial problems, the personnel often changed as well. At the Ukrainian National Home, from 1920 until 1927, when Lazuta became president, Ivan Dobryansky reorganized the theatre and engaged several newly arrived actors from Ukraine. First the opera singer Mykola Karlash served as artistic director, and Volodymyr Debrovsky and Isaac Bazyak followed him. In 1928 Maria Mashur, also an opera singer, took over the directorship. Among the actors who participated in this theatre were opera singers Mykola Shvets, Mariya Hrebenetska, Oleksandra Kochubey, Lidiya Koretska, and Mariya Dibrova-Shvets. Pavlo Pecheniha-Uhlytsky and later P. Shvedov were conductors, and Mykhaylo Myrosh was set and stage designer. Among the works staged by this group were musicals and operas such as *Natalka Poltavka*, *The Fair of Sorochyntsi*, Lysenko's *Nocturne*, and other popular items in the Ukrainian repertoire. In 1928, though, the Ukrainian National Home went bankrupt (since the Depression affected the Ukrainian immigrants strongly), and its theatre was dispersed.

Among other societies that supported their own drama clubs were Ukrainian women's organizations. The first organizations appeared at the end of the last century; they were often related to given parishes, though later many were affiliated with cultural, political, or other clubs. Among the drama clubs that the women's societies organized was a company associated with Zhinocha Hromada (Women's Society) in New York, directed by Mariya Skubova, established in 1918.

There were other theatres in New York, such as the Ukrainian National Theatre (organized on June 21, 1914), the Pomoryany Society Theatre, and some that were organized to perform a given play only. In 1918, 1922, and 1924 actors Yuliya M. and Mykola Shustakevychs and Korykora made attempts to form their own groups, which were short-lived. Nevertheless, they staged such operas as *Zaporozhets beyond the Danube, Kateryna,* and *Natalka Poltavka.*

While New York City predominated in the theatrical field, the community in close-by Newark, New Jersey, was able to have its own theatrical groups, among which was Buduchnist (The Future), which existed prior to and after 1918.[10] In that year Yuliya Shustakevych, who had been a professional actress in Lviv (western Ukraine), appeared with the Newark group, after being a member of theatre groups in Youngstown, Ohio; Pittsburgh, Pennsylvania; Grand Rapids, Michigan; and Chicago and West Pullman, Illinois, since 1912. Her search for a theatre and a permanent place of residence is representative of many immigrants' quests for a satisfactory position or area and also is typical of the immigrating professional actors, unable to work in the general American theatre because of language and cultural barriers.

Jewish-Ukrainian Theatre Companies

Most of the Jewish immigrants from Eastern Europe came from Ukraine (Jews were not allowed to live in Russia, only beyond the Pale of Settlement in the Russian Empire, that is, in Ukraine and Byelorussia). Used to the Ukrainian environment and culture, the Jewish immigrants also wanted to recreate it in this country. They formed traveling theatrical groups that staged primarily Ukrainian plays and musicals in Ukrainian. Isaac Greenberg organized such a group in Philadelphia in 1909 and performed at Royal Hall and Metropolitan Hall. During the first season he staged twenty-five plays, among them classical Ukrainian works such as *Zaporozhets beyond the Danube, The Gypsy Aza, Natalka Poltavka,* and *The Steppe Guest.* One of the leading Jewish actors in Ukraine, Isaac Elgard, moved to New York in 1916 and formed his own Ukrainian Traveling Theatre, which had Ukrainian and Jewish actors. Elgard later became an actor with the Yiddish theatres.

David Medovy, or Medow, became an actor in Ukraine and traveled with several Ukrainian theatres to Asia, until he arrived in San Francisco in 1915. After appearing with several Yiddish theatres in Chicago and New York City, between 1917 and 1928 he directed his own Jewish-Ukrainian theatre and staged performances at the National Theater, Olympic Theater, and Kessler Theater in New York City. In his troupe he had both Jewish and Ukrainian actors and produced a popular Ukrainian repertoire (*Natalka Poltavka, Mazepa, Taras Bulba,* and others). The group staged performances in Ukrainian in Cleveland, Baltimore, Wilmington, Detroit, Pittsburgh, Toledo, Chicago, and cities in Canada.

The Need for Ukrainian Theatres

Both the professional and the amateur groups helped to recreate the way of life in Ukraine that people were used to: the performances, the social meetings, and the topics made relevant to the given group. Also in the theatre a little haven for the Ukrainian language was found, where it could be heard from the stage in the new land. In America the immigrants enjoyed the novelty of complete freedom in choosing plays. While the Russian czarist rule in eastern Ukraine was very strict and limited the Ukrainian plays to the lowest genre, that is, to popular musicals dealing with the daily problems of the peasants, theatres in western Ukraine had restrictions on political and national themes imposed upon them, too. Thus the opportunity to stage and see performances of once-proscribed plays was an event in itself. Furthermore, new plays were being written dealing with current events in Ukraine; thus the immigrants were able to experience a certain sublimation of emotions, a substitution of the desire to be back in Ukraine and contribute to its struggle for survival. A typical announcement of a performance would stress, for example, that "this play depicts the true struggle of the Ukrainian people in its western lands, in the years 1918–1919."[11] Thus there was not only an emotional release but also, since the play would not have been permitted by the censors in Ukraine, a national identification, a certain satisfaction that in this new land the painful events could at least be aired on the stage.

As various charitable undertakings were organized by the immigrants, theatrical performances were often staged to raise money for specific purposes: to build an orphanage or a hospital, or to repair a church in a specific town in Ukraine. For example, a ticket for a performance of Mykhailo Petrovsky's The Quiet Heroes, in Newark, New Jersey, on April 5, 1924, stated that the 50-cent admission price was a donation to build a hospital in Lviv.[12]

Another factor that may explain the intense desire of the Ukrainians for their own theatres was linguistic and ideological. The Ukrainian language was not welcomed by the foreign regimes in Ukraine, but here it was not restricted. Also, through the various new plays, the sponsoring groups were able to express their ideological preferences. Between 1918 and 1920 most Ukrainian immigrants supported the independent Ukraine, but after the Soviet Union took over the country as one of its republics, and especially during the hardships experienced by the immigrants in the United States during the 1920s and 1930s, some chose to support the socialist ideology and even expressed an acceptance of the Soviet regime. Thus the choice of plays by each of the various groups served as its calling cards as they became polarized ideologically.

Publication of Plays

One of the first Ukrainian plays published in the United States was Strutynsky's Strike (first edition 1905, second edition 1915). Since not many plays were allowed to be printed in Ukraine (many had to be smuggled from

Austria or Germany), they had to be either published in the United States first, or reprinted here. But besides the popular works from the homeland, the audience also felt a need for works reflecting both the new situation in Ukraine and the vicissitudes of the immigrants' life in the United States. A substantial number of new works were written here for the express purpose of being staged, rather than as philosophical closet dramas. Musiychuk and Lutsky, who as already mentioned were priests of the Ukrainian Eastern Rite Catholic Church, wrote or adapted several works to the stage. Zyhmont Bachynsky, a Presbyterian minister, critic, and playwright, wrote a play, *In the Old and the New Country*. Numerous plays were also published anonymously, either out of modesty or for political reasons (fear of political retaliation against relatives in Ukraine). The plays were written because there was a need for them, and the authors demonstrated little need for self-aggrandizement.[13] Among such anonymous works were *Shoot Until Death* (1906), *Spring Festival* (1914), *Punishment for a Crime* (1920), and *From One Embrace to Another* (1923).

Thematically the new works that were written, published and staged in the United States, may be classified into several categories:[14]

1. Moralizing works, stressing goodness, kindness, honor, and Christian virtues, or those reflecting a rural way of life in Ukraine, with traditional rituals or new social problems: *A Ukrainian Wedding*, by Tsehelsky; *Hell at Home* (1918), by Roman Surmach; *The Mountaineers*, by O. Korzheniovsky; *Do Not Love Two*, by Antin Nahornyansky; *Gay Poltavians* (1920), by K. P. Myroslavsky; and *Rechristened* (1918), by A. I. Kozych-Umanska.
2. Situation comedies or satire on human weaknesses: *A Live Corpse* and *Two of Them* (1918), by Havryil Kobzyar; *Sonny and Aunt* (1926), by Petro Hursky; and *For Once He Is Right* (third edition, 1920), by Hryhoriy Marusyn.
3. Plays reflecting predicaments (people with no friends or relatives, or no prospects for a job during the growing depression): *An Orphan*, by Anastasiya Rybakova; *An American* (second edition, 1915), by Mstyslav Rus; and *Bread Line* (1920), by Volodymyz Shopinsky.
4. Historical plays about distant times: *Mazepa* (1919), by Komyshevatsky; *May Night* (1920), by T. Usenko-Harmash.
5. Works reflecting the recent struggle for Ukrainian independence: *In the Fight for Freedom* (1925), by Musiychuk; *Where Freedom Is, There Is Truth and Good Fortune*, by Mykhaylo Burlyvy; *Victims of Czarism* (1918), by Volodymyr Syrotenko; and *For Truth and Freedom* (1921), by T. Kolysnychenko.

The above list covers probably one-fifth of the new plays, which were often published in several editions and were widely read and staged by the existing Ukrainian theatres in this country; some were also occasionally staged in Ukraine.

By the end of the 1930s for various reasons Ukranian-American theatrical activity subsided. Some of the older immigrants had passed away, and others had aged enough not to be able to participate in the theatre. Their children found little need for continuing it; some of them were experiencing the inferiority feelings of typical first-generation children trying to be "assimilated Americans," while others did not find the theatre a much-needed mode of activity or self-expression, just as an average American does not patronize the theatre very much.

POST-WORLD WAR II THEATRES

After the end of World War II the third wave of Ukrainians came to these shores.[15] They represented numerous social classes and included a large portion of highly educated professionals. These immigrants included Ukrainians who had been forcibly taken from Ukraine by the Nazis to concentration camps or brought to Germany as a labor force. Also included were those who did not want to experience the Soviet regime a second time, since some Ukrainians had lived under Soviet rule from 1921 to 1941 and others, in western Ukraine, had experienced this rule between 1939 and 1941. These had fled their country for political reasons. At the end of the war these Ukrainians found themselves in displaced persons camps in Germany and Austria.

The actors quickly organized several theatres in the major camps. Thus Augsburg and then Regensburg became the home of the Ensemble of Ukrainian Actors, directed by Volodymyr Blavatsky, a leading actor and director from Lviv whose group was organized in September 1945. During the first two years of its activity it staged 390 performances of sixteen plays, which were seen by 173,000 people in various camps.[16] In 1949 most members of this ensemble emigrated to the United States and settled in Philadelphia. Another outstanding group was organized in Landeck, Austria, by Yosyp Hirnyak and his wife Olympiya Dobrovolska, two leading actors from the Berezil Theatre, in Khazkiv (Ukraine). Since this theatre included intense training programs for artists, it was called the Theatre Studio. This company staged 307 performances of twelve plays between February 1946 and February 1949 and also toured some fifteen different cities. Seven members of the Theatre Studio arrived in New York in 1949.

Again the new immigrants wanted to continue their professional acting, at least on a part-time basis, and to transplant a touch of their culture to their new homeland. The primary difference between the first and second periods of the Ukrainian theatre organization in this country was that during the latter wave two complete professional companies, with a successful history in Europe, were ready to start, or rather to continue, their theatres and performances. Nevertheless, they faced problems similar to those of the earlier immigrants. After realizing that the actors would have to make a living from other professions, they had to restrain themselves, work in different occupations, and still participate in the theatre at least on weekends, but continue to keep their performances on a high professional level. Moreover, Hirnyak required his younger actors to study drama and ballet (for example, with choreographer Valentyna Pereyaslavets) in order to be in the best condition for acting.

Among the members of the Theatre Studio besides Hirnyak and Dobrovolska were Tamara Poznyak, Mykola Vasylyk, Volodymyr Lysnyak, and Ivan Kolosiv. During the first three months after their arrival they staged six performances of three plays, followed by thirteen performances of five plays in 1950. Directed by Hirnyak, the works performed were Lesya Ukrayinka's *Forest Song* and *The Boyar's Wife*, and Mykola Kulish's *Myna Mazaylo* and several adaptations, such as Yuriy Lavrinenko's *Mother and I* (based on Mykola Khvylovy's work *My Being*), Ivan Kernytsky's *They Made Fools of Themselves in America* (based on a play by Marko Kropyvnytsky), and Mykola Ponedilok's *After Two Rabbits* (from a plot used by Mykhaylo Starytsky). With these works the studio toured Newark, New Jersey; Jersey City; Elizabeth, New Jersey; and Philadelphia. During 1951–1954 it expanded its repertoire and toured Detroit and Toronto as well. Dobrovolska directed new productions of *Myna Mazaylo* and *Tartuffe*, while Lysnyak directed *The Boyar's Wife*.[17] By 1954 some of the actors had become discouraged by the lack of better prospects for their theatre. Others decided to reorganize and attempted to stage several works together with members of the Philadelphia-based Ensemble of Ukrainian Actors.

The regrouped company was named Ukrainian Theatre in America. Dobrovolska was the artistic director, and actors such as Lidiya Krushelnytska, Larissa Kukrytska, Ihor Shuhan, Myron Cholhan, and others joined the company in New York. Between 1954 and 1956 they staged seven plays in twenty-six weekend performances in New York and other cities. Besides the traditional repertoire they staged new plays written by newly arrived immigrants, such as Kernytsky's *Dr. Horoshko's Secret* and Dima's *The Hops* and *Transplanted Flowers*.

Without any supporting grants the company could not continue its performances. Thus between 1956 and 1960 the group turned to a new form of theatre; rather than stage plays, it performed artistic recitations of classical works. Renamed the Theatre of the Word, the group was directed by Dobrovolska. Its last performance was in 1960, that of *Man and Hero*, a montage of poetry and prose about Hetman Ivan Mazepa, a Cossack ruler of Ukraine from 1687 to 1709.

To revive the Ukrainian theatre in New York, in 1965 Lysnyak formed a group called the New Theatre. It included Krushelnytska and the younger members of the Studio: Shuhan, Volodymyr Zmiy, Olha Kyrychenko, and Larissa Kukrytska, who was now Kukrytska-Lysnyak. The latter was the only one of the group who managed to become a professional on Broadway and television, as Larissa Loret. Lysnyak also tried directing off-Broadway; with him as artistic director, the group staged an ambitious new interpretation of Ukrayinka's classic *The Stone Host*. This production was seen in several cities of the United States and Canada. The other off-Broadway play the group produced was *Hunger-1933*, by a young immigrant poet, Bohdan Boychuk. After several performances of these plays the New Theatre became inactive.

In Philadelphia the Ensemble of Ukrainian Actors, with Blavatsky as artistic director, also started optimistically. Its first production was Bohdan Lepky's *Baturyn*, on September 30, 1949, at Philadelphia's Town Hall. Having only weekends for performances, the ensemble staged eleven plays and fifty-two performances in two-and-a-half years.[18] Among its leading actors were Blavatsky, Vira Levytska, Evdokiya Dychko-Blavatska, Liza Shasharovska, Volodymyr Shasharovsky, Bohdan Pazdriy, Yaroslav Pinot-Rudakevych, and Volodymyr Melnyk. Some works were directed by Pazdriy and Shasharovsky.

After evaluating the possibilities for satisfying the audience, which was made up of older people who were earlier immigrants and also members of the new immigration, the director decided that a repertoire of satires, comedies, and musicals would be more acceptable than the philosophical works of Ukrayinka, though from time to time the ensemble staged these also; for example, in 1951 and 1952 it presented *Yohanna, Khusov's Wife*. During the first three years the group toured New York, Washington, Chester, Hartford, Baltimore, Trenton, New Haven, Detroit, Cleveland, Larraine (Ohio), and cities in Canada. After the death of Blavatsky in 1953, the group was renamed the Ukrainian Theatre in Philadelphia. It continued to stage popular works by Taras Shevchenko, as well as by Hrohoriy Meriyam-Luzhnytsky, a newly arrived professor and writer, (author of *The Invalid, Sister Gatekeeper*, and *Knights of the Night*). Then, after experimenting with a concentration on a lighter repertoire again, the group realized that it was almost impossible to keep the theatre alive with an ambitious plan of adding several new productions annually.

Rather than give up completely, in 1961 Volodymyr Shasharovsky reorganized the group and planned a small number of new plays, to be performed only on Fridays, since on Saturdays and Sundays there was usually a multitude of other Ukrainian events in every city. The new Theatre on Friday began with a traditional work by Natalka Poltavka and staged seven performances in Philadelphia alone. Other works included new plays by recent immigrants: Leonid Poltava's *Actors*, Hryhoriy Luzhnytsky's *O. Moroz, Morozenko*, Oleh Lysnyak's *At One Thirty*, and *The Best Boys from Our Division*, as well as works by Ukrayinka and a translation of Jean Anouilh's *Medea*. In 1972 the theatre began to stage performances during the summer months in Wildwood, New Jersey, where many Ukrainians vacation. This company performed several new works annually and was still active in 1979.

As other Ukrainian professional actors lived in various cities in the United States, they attempted to form theatrical groups there also. Among such groups was the theatre and music society Nova Stsena (New Stage) in Chicago, Illinois, formed by T. Furovych and E. Dzyubynsky in 1957. Among its members were professional singers Emiliya Pleshkevych, Volodymyr Melnychyn, Ivan Rudavsky, and stage performer Roma Turyanska. Their programs varied from strictly musical concerts, directed by composer Ivan Povalachek and Vasyl Shut, to plays, the first of which was S. Bila's comedy *Old Sinners*. By November 1966 they had staged sixteen plays and put on two concerts.[19] Most of the works were directed by Emiliya Kulyk, but one was directed by Lyubo Tsepynsky and one by Gen. Ivan Omelyanovych-Pavlenko. Members of the group, especially Kulyk and I. Matulko, also held a biweekly radio program, "Theatre on the Air." There was also a group of Ukrainian actors in Los Angeles, where Borys Grinwald organized the Society of Actors of the Ukrainian Stage (TAUS) in 1964. The famed conductor and *bandura** performer Volodymyr Bozhyk served as the musical director, and I. Arglis-Smaltsiv was the choreographer.[20] The first work they produced was Shevchenko's *Nazar Stodolya*. During the five years of the theatre's life, it staged twenty-seven performances.

Other amateur groups existed in the numerous cities where large numbers of newly-arrived Ukrainians had settled. Usually such groups were directed by professionals. In Cleveland the Actors Ensemble existed between 1950 and 1960. It was directed by Omelyan Urbansky and Yuliya Urbanska-Kalynets, the latter appearing in the leading roles. In Detroit a short-lived theatrical society was organized by Zenon Tarnavsky and staged his translation of *Everyman* in 1961.

Occasionally sporadic groups formed to stage specific projects, such as the Ukrainian Opera Society in New York, which put on a large production of the new opera *Anna Yaroslavna*, about an eleventh century Ukrainian princess who became a queen of France. The libretto was by Poltava and the music by Antin Rudnytsky. Between 1977 and 1979 the Ukrainian Opera Society included such professional opera singers as Alicia Andreadis, Marta Kobryn-Kokolska, and Lev Reynarovych. It staged several performances of *Kateryna* and *Zaporozhets beyond the Danube*.

The Young Actors' Theatres

Two noteworthy and rare theatre companies were formed in New York City and Chicago, with all the actors being between the ages of eight and fifteen. In New York Dobrovolska, the artistic director of the Ukrainian Theatre in America, also organized a youth group, as part of her *Studio of the Artistic Word* ("Studio Mystets' koho Slova"). In 1965 Krushelnytska took over the group and usually staged at least one new performance annually. In the fourteen years of the studio's existence it staged sixty performances of nineteen productions and toured thirteen cities with them. Among the works performed were *The Flying Ship* and *The Blue Kerchief*, by Anatol Shyyan; *A Forest Song*, by Ukrayinka, a translation of *The Snow Maiden*, by Hans Christian Andersen; and *Everyman* (Figures 19.1–19.3).

Krushelnytska's studio quickly grew to include at all times about fifty students, aged eight through thirty, who worked in five different sections. The new

---

*The bandura is the national instrument of Ukraine. It has twelve to thirty strings, and often more. With its accompaniment, specific historical songs and ballads are usually sung, in a semi-recitative style. It is still very popular among Ukrainians everywhere.

19.1   *The Flying Ship,* by Anatol Shyyan, presented by the Children's Studio, directed by Lidiya Krushelnytska, 1966–1967. (Courtesy of Lidiya Krushelnytska.)

students were first trained in the proper pronunciation of Ukrainian words and then trained in stage diction and performing. Prima ballerina Roma Pryima Bohachevska cooperated in ballet training (occasionally a joint program was put on with her own ballet studio). Music for performances was usually written by Ivan Nedilsky and Ihor Sonevytsky, with Lev Struhatsky as conductor and Sonevytsky directing the musical accompaniment. Choreography was usually by Pryima-Bohachevska and Olha Kovalchuk-Ivasivka, while stage and set design was by Taras Hirnyak, Volodymyr Kasiyan, Slava Gerulyak, and Mariyka Shust. The performances were most impressive and charming, since the children's training and effort were pleasantly visible in these carefully and imaginatively prepared productions.

In Chicago during the late 1960s and early 1970s the Ukrainian community, especially two women's groups, were very active in organizing theatres for children and young performers. In 1969 the twenty-ninth chapter of the Ukrainian Women's League formed a drama club with forty members, aged three through thirteen. Under the artistic direction of Turyanska, on December 7, 1969, they staged a Ukrainian adaptation of *The Snowhite* by Volodymyr Radzykevych, with choreography by Iryna Holubovska. Encouraged by the success of this performance, on May 1, 1971, they presented another play, *Lesyk-Telesyk,* by Yevhen Fomyn, based on a Ukrainian folktale, with music by Orysya Pokorna. At the

19.2 *The Blue Kerchief*, by Anatol Shyyan, presented by the Children's Studio, directed by Lidiya Krushelnytska, 1968. (Courtesy of Lidiya Krushelnytska.)

19.3   A *Forest Song*, by Lesya Ukrayinka, presented by the Children's Studio, directed by Lidiya Krushelnytska, 1970–1971. (Courtesy of Lidiya Krushelnytska.)

same time Orysya Harasovska, with another group of teenagers, staged a traditional commemoration of St. Nicholas.

Noting the interest of the public and of the young and eager performers of the two groups, Harasovska and the Sisterhood of Sts. Volodymyr and Olha Ukrainian Catholic Church decided to sponsor a youth theatre studio. After auditions in 1970, fifty-eight teenagers were accepted, to be trained and directed by Lyubo and Lilya Tsepynskys, with Erik Kon serving as assistant director. The studio started its activity by performing another play about St. Nicholas, while preparing a more ambitious work that required folk and ballet dancing as well as singing, *In Search of My Sister* (the premiere was held on November 14, 1971).[21] After several successful performances in Chicago, the studio toured Ukrainian communities in Detroit, Cleveland, New York, Philadelphia, and Toronto. Among other works performed by the group was *The Unbeatable Call*, by Lyubo Tsepynsky (premiere on February 2, 1975); this play was also taken on tour of the above cities, as well as Irvington, N.J.; Pittsburgh; and Rome, Italy.

In Philadelphia there was also an attempt to form and sustain an opera ensemble of the Ukrainian Music Institute (which had existed since 1950). In 1970, under the direction of Yuriy Oransky, the ensemble, which was made up of young members and several professional singers, staged an impressive performance of an opera for children, *Mykyta, the Fox* based on a work by Ivan Franko, libretto by Poltava and music by Vasyl Ovcharenko. Although the musical program of the institute, both individual and orchestra, is still well organized and directed, the opera group did not survive.

The Need for a Theatre

Most of the plays by the Ukrainian immigrants newly arrived after World War II were written primarily as literary works, rather than to be staged; this was in contrast to the plays in the first quarter of the century, which were written for immediate performance. Perhaps only one-third of the postwar works were ever performed by the Ukrainian theatres here, in Canada, or in Australia, though inevitably some works became more popular than others. Typical of the postwar written works were:

1. Plays reflecting World War II times, when Ukrainians were struggling, individually or in the Ukrainian Partisan Army, an underground movement, against the Nazis or Communists. This theme was extended to situations in the displaced persons camps in Germany in 1945–1948, as well as to the most recent ones in Soviet Ukraine. These included A Twig of Apple Blossoms (1969) and Do Not Cry, Rachel (1957), by Yuriy Tys; The Unfortunate Ones (1952), by Mykola Ponedilok; A Yavoriv Market Boy (1957), by Ivan Kernytsky; Icebreaker (1974), by Myroslava Lasovska; Whose Crime Is It? (1952) and The Third Power (1950), by Vasyl Chaplenko; One out of Four Million (1951), A Mother's Dream (1953), and A November Night (1962), by Pavlo Savchuk; and A Big Break (1950), by Semen Ledyansky.
2. Social and moral satire and plays reflecting predicaments in the new land: Your Friends (1957) and Oh, My book, (1963) by Dima; An American Girl (1973) and An Hour in a Park (1964), by Mariya Strutynska; and Free Country (1954), by Hryhoriy Luzhnytsky.
3. Philosophically-oriented problem plays: The Heroine Dies in the First Act (1956), by Lyudmyla Kovalenko; Do Not Cry, Rachel, by Tys; and The Doomed Ones, Hunger-1933, and Laughter (1963), by Bohdan Boychuk.
4. Plays written for children: The Greatest Gift (1956) and Little Devil's Adventures (1965), by Lesya Khraplyva; Mykyta the Fox, Little Red Riding Hood (1961), A Forest Princess, and King of the Apes, by Poltava, and other works by Roman Zavadovych.
5. Notable translations of world drama made by such poets and writers as Zhenya Vasylkivska (Antigone); Teodosiy Osmachka (Macbeth and Henry IV); Ponedilok (Lucretia, Medea, and Antigone); and Tarnavsky (Everyman and Murder in the Cathedral).

Most plays written in Ukrainian before 1930 in the United States were in the romantic or realistic style, and this approach also predominated in the works of later playwrights, such as Chaplenko, Kernytsky, Savchuk, Poltava, and Roman Volodymyr. Others were more experimental in nature, especially Boychuk and Kovalenko, but also Dima, Luzhnytsky, and Tys, and employed expressionism, surrealism, or theatre of the absurd, though the last style has not yet been staged by Ukrainian theatres here.

CONCLUSION

A study of the seventy-year history of the Ukrainian theatre in the United States reveals many loopholes and numerous uncollected facts, especially about the pre-1947 activity. Nevertheless, current interest in the field is promising; for example, in 1975 a separate publication appeared on the Hirnyak and Dobrovolska Theatre Studio/Ukrainian Theatre in America (1949–1960). In that same year the first volume of *Nash Teatr* (Our Theatre) was published, an 850-page compilation of studies and memoirs with information about various Ukrainian theatres between 1915 and 1975; a respectable number of the articles deal specifically with the theatre in the United States.

Some of the above publication activity is a result of the formation of the Association of Artists of the Ukrainian Stage. Its first convention took place in Glen Spey, New York, on May 29–31, 1971, with eighty individuals participating. Yuriy Kononiv was elected president; Volodymyr Shasharovsky succeeded him in 1973. In 1972 the society held a Festival of the Ukrainian Theatre, with a program that included the Ukrainian Opera Society of New York, conducted by Reynarovych, and Theatre on Friday. Of special interest was the participation of the Ukrainian Children's Theatre, from Winnipeg, Canada; the Youth Theater Studio, from Chicago; and the Young Actors Group of Theatre on Friday, from Philadelphia.

Participation of women in other than acting roles has been significant from 1914 on, when a substantial number of the Ukrainian immigrants were political émigrés and thus often included people with higher education. During the past seventy-five years many women have been active in the Ukrainian theatre in the United States as

1. Artistic directors: Mashur, Skubova, Shustakevych, Dobrovolska, Turyanska, Tsepynska, Kulyk, Urbanska-Kalynets, Krushelnytska, and Harasovka;
2. Writers: Rybakova, Kozych-Umanska, Usenko-Harmash, Kovalenko, Dima, Lasovska, Strutynska, Khraplyva and Bila;
3. Choreographers: Pereyaslavets, Priyma-Bohachevska, Kovalchuk-Ivasivka, and Holubovska;
4. Musical score writer: Pokorna;
5. Stage designers: Gerulyak and Shust; and
6. Organizers of theatre groups: Shustakevych, Skubova, Dobrovolska, Krushelnytska, and Harasovska.

Analyzing the history of the Ukrainian theatre in the United States reveals that most of the groups, whether in 1909 or in 1949, began their activity with productions of works by the leading Ukrainian poet, Shevchenko—such works as *The Prisoner, Nazar Stodolya,* and *Kateryna,* whether the project of organizing the group began with an annual project to commemorate Shevchenko's birth or in an effort to form a new company. Shevchenko has always appealed to a wide audience, including highly sophisticated as well as average people. On the other hand, works by Ukrayinka or other strictly intellectual or philosophical playwrights had a limited audience, as is the case with similar works in the general American theatre. Similarly, both the early immigrants and the later ones found that musicals, as well as works about more recent problems, appealed to a broader group, which is also typical of the general American scene. It therefore appears that for future Ukrainian theatre in America the best choice lies in the popular works from the classical Ukrainian repertoire, as well as in new plays dealing with the specific contemporary predicaments of Ukrainians. Thus the emotional and self-identification needs of the audiences can be met and the entertainment need satisfied. This appears as the only financially realistic approach. Experimental or highly intellectual works, which by their very nature appeal to a small number of people, can be performed in the larger Ukrainian communities, but only on a sporadic basis. Of all the Ukrainian theatrical groups, Theatre on Friday, including its existence under its former names, Ensemble of Ukrainian Actors and Ukrainian Theatre in Philadelphia, has had the longest life, thirty years, perhaps due to the group's ability to adjust to the total activity of Philadelphia's Ukrainian community by its choice of Fridays for performances.

With the multifaceted cultural and political activity of the present Ukrainian communities in the United States, the theatre does not appear to be as fundamental a necessity as it was to earlier Ukrainian groups. Activities in numerous professional (such as medical or engineering) societies and youth or college students' groups and participation in politics diversifies and disperses individuals' fields of interest. Also, the young generations that have grown up in this country accept the American way of life, which is not so tied to the theatre as was life in Ukraine earlier.

Because the first Ukrainian theatre movement had subsided in the early 1930s, when the new immigrant actors arrived in 1949 they found no Ukrainian theatres to join and to continue. There was also no interaction between the remaining actors of the first group and the new actors. Perhaps if the first had been able to continue until 1949, then the cooperation and rejuvenation would have produced better conditions for the newly-arrived companies. The Ukrainian theatres of the first group had lasted at best between ten and twenty years, and those of the second group have met with a similar fate (for example, in New York City). What remains markedly different, however, is the Theatre on Friday in Philadelphia, which has a young actors' section made up of college students. The presence in 1979 of two large children's groups (in Chicago and in New York) is also quite promising. If these groups can continue their activity until another wave of immigrants from Ukraine arrives, then the changing of the guard will be able to take place normally.

The continuity of Ukrainian theatre in the United States also depends on the number of Ukrainian Americans who remain fluent in the Ukrainian language. At the present time, with the great number of Ukrainian schools still in existence in the larger Ukrainian communities, the number is encouraging; of the 750,000 to 1,300,000 Americans of Ukrainian descent, in 1971 approximately 250,000 considered Ukrainian their mother tongue, and in 1978 there were approximately 14,000 children attending Ukrainian schools.[22]

There is no available information on any attempts by Ukrainians to stage Ukrainian plays in English translation. Nevertheless, there are quite a few actors of the American stage who were or are of Ukrainian descent, including John Hodiak, Mike Mazurki, Larissa Loret, Jack Palance, William Shust, George Dzundzha, and Zenon Osinchuk.

Since the Ukrainian theatre has been able to survive in this country as long as it has, even without any government or other grants, there must be a need for it within the mosaic of American cultural life.

Appendix: Ukrainian Theatre Companies (by Year Organized and Location)

1905 American Boyan Society, New York
1907 Zaporizka Sich Society, New York
     Ivan Kotalyarevsky Dramatic Society, New York
1909 Isaac Greenberg's Ukrainian theatre, Philadelphia
1910 Besida Theatre, New York
1914 Ukrainian National Theatre, New York
n.d. Pomoryany Society Theatre, New York
1916 Ukrainian Traveling Theatre, New York
1917 David Medovy's Jewish-Ukrainian theatre, New York
     Theatre of the Ukrainian National Home, New York
1918 Zhinocha Hromada (Women's Society), New York
     Buduchnist (The Future), Newark, N.J.
1921 Ukrainian Opera Guild, New York
1930 New York Besida Opera Group
1945 Ensemble of Ukrainian Actors, Philadelphia
     Theatre Studio, New York
1950 Actors Ensemble, Cleveland
     Ukrainian Music Institute, opera ensemble, Philadelphia
1953 Ukrainian Theatre in Philadelphia
1954 Ukrainian Theatre in America, New York
1957 Nova Stsena (New Stage), Chicago
1961 Theatre on Friday, Philadelphia
     Theatrical Society, Detroit
     Children's Studio, New York
1964 Society of Actors of the Ukrainian Stage, Los Angeles
1965 New Theatre, New York
1968 Youth Theatre Studio, Chicago
1970 Ukrainian Opera Society, New York
1971 Young Actors Group of Theatre on Friday, Philadelphia
1977 Ukrainian Opera Society of New York

NOTES

1. For a brief description of the theatre in Ukraine see: "Theatre," *Ukraine: A Concise Encyclopaedia* (Toronto: University of Toronto Press, 1971), Vol. 2, pp. 614–60.

2. For detailed statistics see "Ukrainians Abroad: In the United States," *Ukraine: A Concise Encyclopaedia*, pp. 1100–1150.

3. At the end of the eighteenth century about twenty thousand Ukrainian Cossacks, formerly volunteer soldiers, who had been sent to Siberia by the czar, came to live in Alaska and stayed there when it was acquired by the United States. Otherwise there were only individual Ukrainian settlers, who were often professionals or in business and came sporadically. Among them were Lavrentius Bohun, a physician who came to Jamestown with Capt. John Smith. Nicholas Sudzilowsky Russel (1850–1930), a physician from Kiev, came to California and later became president of the first Hawaiian Senate. A priest, Agapius Honcharenko, in 1868 became the editor and publisher of the *Alaska Herald* (in San Francisco), the first trilingual (English, Russian, and Ukrainian) newspaper.

The first mass migration of Ukrainians was between 1877 and 1914, when approximately half a million arrived here. Since most of them were from western Ukraine, then part of the Austro-Hungarian empire, many were listed in immigration statistics as "Austrian" or "Ruthenian." Most of these immigrants were poor farmers or laborers. There was also a sizable number of Ukrainians whose Protestant sect (the Shtundists) was persecuted by the Russian government, and they emigrated in the 1890s from the Kiev area and settled primarily in Dakota. For a detailed description see ibid.

4. The Roman Catholic clergy was not acquainted with the laws of Eastern Rite Catholics such as the Ukrainians and were shocked by the arrival of the married Ukrainian clergymen. Roman Catholic representatives appealed to the Vatican to withdraw the Ukrainian priests who were married. Ivan Wolyansky was thus forced to leave. Such an attitude on the part of the local Roman Catholic priests contributed to a split within the Ukrainian Catholic Church in the United States; many parishes and several priests chose to join the Orthodox Church.

5. Many of these facts are from the manuscript by Roman V. Prydatkevytch, "Ukrainian Music in America until 1945."

6. *Vechernytsi* actually represents only one scene of a play *Nazar Stodolya*, by Taras Shevchenko, with music by Petro Nizhynsky, but is often staged as an independent work.

7. Yuriy Linchevsky, "Dramaturhichna tvorchist Shevchenka i instsenizatsiyi yoho poetychnykh tvoriv" (Dramatic Works of T. Shevchenko and the Presentation of his Political Works on Stage), in *Taras Shevchenko: Zbirnyk dopovidey*, Zapysky NTSh (Shevchenko Scientific Society Publications) (New York: Shevchenko Scientific Society, 1962), Vol. 176, p. 278.

8. Prydatkevytch, "Ukrainian Music," p. 8.

9. There were many individual and sporadic attempts, in New York City especially, to form drama groups or stage particular works for specific purposes. For example, on Feb. 17, 1914, the Committee for Ukrainian Schools and Associated Organizations staged a play, *Sichynsky-Pototsky*, at Arlington Hall. The work was directed by Stepan Sklepkovych. Prydatkevytch, "Ukrainian Music," p. 9.

10. In her memoirs Yulia M. Shustakevych rates the Besida Theatre as highly professional and much above the two others. Yuliya M. Shustakevych, "Pratsya na ukrayinskiy nyvi," reprinted in Hryhoriy Luzhnytskyi, ed., *Nash Teatr: knyha diyachiv ukrayinskoho teatralnoho mystetstva, 1915–1975* (Our Theatre: A Collection about Ukrainian Theatre

Arts Activists, 1915–1975 (New York: Shevchenko Scientific Society, 1975), Vol. I, p. 415.

11. Announcement of *Torturers of the White Eagle*, by Mykhailo Petrovsky, from the private archives of Mykhailo Petrovsky.

12. Petrovsky archives.

13. In his correspondence with me, Petrovsky admitted that he did not even collect one copy of his published plays, and this was also true of some other writers at that time.

14. For a more detailed list see Larysa M. L. Zaleska-Onyshkevych, "Ukrayinska dramaturhiya na pivnichno-amerykanskomu kontynenti" (Ukrainian Dramaturgy on the North American Continent), in *Nash Teatr*, pp. 215–30.

15. For the post-World War II immigration the estimation is that close to 85,000 Ukrainians arrived from camps in Western Europe. The total number of Ukrainian-born and of Americans of Ukrainian descent in the United States is approximately 1.3 million. "Ukrainians Abroad: In the United States," in Volodymyr Kubijovyč, ed., *Ukraine: A Concise Encyclopaedia* (Toronto: University of Toronto Press, 1971), Vol. 2, pp. 1102–1104.

16. Oleh Lysyak, "Ansambl ukrayinskykh aktoriv 1945–49 u Nimechchnyni" (Ensemble of Ukrainian Actors in Germany, 1945–1949), in *Nash Teatr*, p. 389.

17. For a detailed description of the company, see Bohdan Boychuk, *Teatr Studiya Y. Hirnyaka, O. Dobrovolskoyi* (New York: Ukrainian Academy of Arts and Sciences and the New York Group, 1975), pp. 213–78.

18. Volodymyr Shasharovsky, "Ansambl Aktoriv Blavatskoho pislya yoho smerty," in *Nash Teatr*, p. 441.

19. Emiliya Kulyk, "Nova Stsena v Chicago," in *Nash Teatr*, p. 497.

20. Svyatopolk Shumskyi, "Do istoriyi nashoho teatru v Los-Andzhelesi" (In Reference to the History of the Ukrainian Theatre in Los Angeles), in *Nash Teatr*, pp. 499–506.

21. Orysya Harasovska, "Pyat' rokiv za namy," *Almanakh* (Chicago: Tserkovne Bratstvo sv. Andriya, 1977), pp. 135–42.

22. Larysa Zaleska Onyshkevych, "Aspekt zberezhennya ukrayinskosty" (The Aspect of Retaining Ukrainianism), *Plastovyi shlyakh* (Toronto) 58, no. 3 (1979): 39–41.

BIBLIOGRAPHY

Books

Boychuk, Bohdan. *Teatr Studiya Y. Hirnyaka, O. Dobrovolskoyi.* New York: Ukrainian Academy of Arts and Sciences and The New York Group, 1975. A detailed history of the theatre in Austria and in New York, which was directed by two outstanding artistic directors and actors. Many photographs, chronological listings of performances and plays staged.

Kubijovyč, Volodymyr, ed. *Ukraine: A Concise Encyclopaedia.* Toronto: University of Toronto Press, 1971. Two volumes of this encyclopedia contain basic information about Ukraine and Ukrainians in the whole world. Specific articles, as on the theatre or on Ukrainians in the United States, provide information on topics of interest to readers of this work.

Luzhnytski, Hryhoriy (Editor-in-Chief), Oleh, Lysyak, Leonid Poltava and Volodymyr Shasharovskyi. *Nash teatr: Knyha diyachiv ukrayinskoho teatralnoho mystetstva, 1915-1975* (Our Theatre: A Collection about Ukrainian Theatre Arts Activists, 1915-1975). Vol. 1. New York: Shevchenko Scientific Society, 1975. This volume of 848 pages contains twenty articles and analyses of various theatrical groups, playwrights, or plays; twenty-three historical descriptions of particular theatres; and memoirs written by forty actors. This is a most detailed and unique compilation dealing with theatres in Ukraine and in other parts of the world where Ukrainians reside.

Articles

Harasovska, Orysya. "Pyat' rokiv za namy" (Five Years Are Now Behind Us). In *Almanakh*. Chicago: Tserkovne Bratstvo sv. Andriya (St. Andrew's Brotherhood): 1977, pp. 135–42. The author describes how she organized the Youth Theatre Studio in Chicago.

Linchevskyi, Yuriy. "Dramaturhichna tvorchist Shevchenka i instsenizatsiyi yoho poetychnykh tvoriv" (Dramatic Works of Shevchenko and the Staging of His Poetic Works). In B. Steciuk and B. Krawciw, eds., *Taras Shevchenko: Zbirnyk dopovidey svitovoho kongresu ukrayinskoyi vilnoyi nauky dlya vshanuvannya storichchya smerty patrona NTSh* (Collected Papers Read at the World Congress of Free Ukrainian Scholarship, Commemorating the Centennial Anniversary of the Death of the Patron of the Shevchenko Scientific Society). New York: Shevchenko Scientific Society, 1962. Compilation of twenty-one articles dealing with Taras Shevchenko. Includes one article that deals specifically with the staging of his works in Ukraine, as well as in the Western world.

Onyshkevych, Larysa Zaleska. "Aspekt zberezhennya ukrayinskosty," (The Aspect of Retaining Ukrainianism), *Plastovyi shlyakh* (Toronto) 58, no. 3 (1979): 33–50. This issue of the quarterly publication published by PLAST, a Ukrainian youth association, deals specifically with Ukrainians in the Diaspora. This issue, also edited by me, contains seven articles on ethnicity, bilingualism, Ukrainian culture in the diaspora, and Ukrainians as survivors of the "melting pot" idea.

––––––––. "Ukrainian Emigré Drama." Manuscript to be included in Thomas Bird, ed. *Ukrainian Emigré Literature* with other articles on poetry, prose, and literary criticism. Queens University Press, forthcoming. The article discusses Ukrainian émigré playwrights and plays since the end of the last century in various countries of the world.

––––––––. "Ukrayinska dramaturhiya na pivnichno-amerykanskomu kontynenti" (Ukrainian Dramaturgy on the North American Continent). In Luzhnytskyi, ed., *Nash Teatr*, Vol. 1, pp. 215–30. This article discusses plays written and staged by Ukrainians in Canada and the United States.

Prydatkevytch, Roman V. "Ukrainian Music in America until 1945." Manuscript written for a compilation of essays on Ukrainians in America, edited by Dr. Walter Dushnyck. Ukrainian Congress Committee of America, forthcoming.

Revutsky, Valerian. "Ukrainian Theaters outside Ukraine." In *History of the Ukrainian Theater 1864–1974*. Manuscript edited by Larissa Onyshkevych. Littleton, Colo.: Ukrainian Academic Press and the Canadian Institute for Academic Studies, forthcoming. The Revutsky chapter describes Ukrainian theatres in Asia, Europe, Australia and North America. Other chapters deal with professional theatres only, their history, outstanding actors, and works staged.

Other Sources

The earliest Ukrainian newspapers, *Ameryka* and *Svoboda*, usually published announcements and then reviews of performances. Their annual calendars-almanacs also occasionally may provide some information. Both of these publications are in Ukrainian, but *Svoboda*'s English-language supplement may have some information as well. Complete sets of the above newspapers may be found at their editorial offices: *Ameryka*, 817 North Franklin St., Philadelphia, Pa.; *Svoboda*, 30 Montgomery St., Jersey City, N.J.

These newspapers, as well as many other Ukrainian publications, may be found at the Slavonic Division, of the New York Public Library on Fifth Avenue. The library of the Harvard Ukrainian Research Institute, 1581-83 Massachusetts Avenue, Cambridge, Mass., also has a large collection of Ukrainian publications.

20

Yiddish Theatre

DAVID S. LIFSON

At the start of the last quarter of the nineteenth century, an ancient people brought forth the world's youngest theatre. Its dramatic literature still lives, but its physical activity languishes after a scant seventy-five years of productivity. Its fare has included every form of theatrical presentation: vaudeville, melodrama, poetic drama, comedy, folk drama, puppets, and operettas.

The theatre of the Jews in the United States has been the Yiddish theatre. In its heyday it drew to it the day laborer, the sweatshop woman with her baby, the small East Side shopkeeper, the pushcart peddler, the ghetto rabbi and the scholar, the Russian-Jewish anarchist and socialist, the poet, and the journalist. They came mostly from the small villages (*shtetls*) and towns of Eastern Europe and became a devoted and loyal audience.

To this audience the Yiddish theatre offered an identity with the past in the old country, if only in the nostalgia evoked by the spoken Yiddish tongue. In their theatres, immigrant Jews reveled in their new-found freedom to gather and publicly associate with their own kind while they relaxed from the grinding daily struggle to survive. The Yiddish theatre illuminated for its audience the problems engendered by their progress toward Americanization. The Yiddish theatre also served to bring new European art forms and talent to the American stage and cinema. Finally, this theatre was an inspiration that guided the immigrant Jews to escape from their spiritual ghetto.

The Yiddish theatre at its apogee, from 1882 to 1950,[1] without subsidies other than the unflagging devotion of its *patriotten* (devotees), was volatile, colorful, and creative. Its dramatic plays, such as Ansky's *Der Dybbuk* and David Pinski's *The Treasure*, may take their place among the other poetic plays of the world repertoire.[2] Its directors, among whom were Benno Schneider, of the Artef Theatre and later of Broadway and Hollywood, and Emanuel Reicher, who went from the Yiddish theatre to the Theatre Guild, were innovators of European styles on the American stage. Sam Leve, Boris Aronson, and Mordecai Gorelick graduated from the Yiddish theatre to the American theatre, to which they brought new artistic concepts of stage design. The Yiddish theatre endowed the

American stage and screen with the talents of many of its former luminaries, among whom were Paul Muni, Jacob Ben-Ami, and Rudolph Schildkraut.

YIDDISH, THE LANGUAGE OF THE JEWISH PEOPLE'S THEATRE

The principal theatre experience of the Jewish people has been in Yiddish, the language of the Ashkenazim (Northern and Eastern European Jews). For Eastern European immigrant Jews, Yiddish was the lingua franca, the language of der heim (the home)—the Jewish shtetl (small town) in the old country—the language of their ancestors in the Diaspora, the language that was their birth-right, that encompassed their traditions. In antiquity the Jews had used Hebrew as their spoken language, but they had been obliged to use the languages of their host countries during the Diaspora. Creative writing was in Hebrew well into the nineteenth century, until Yiddish took over as the spoken and written language of the Ashkenazi Jews, who made up the bulk of the Jewish people. The Yiddish language derives from a Middle High German that developed in the twelfth century in southwestern Germany. As the Jews fled eastward to escape slaughter by marauding hordes of Crusaders and the massacre of Jews blamed for the Great Plague (1348), their German-derived language took on elements of Polish and Russian as well as Hebrew. In the nineteenth century, when Ash-kenazi Jews came to England and the United States, Yiddish absorbed English and American colloquialisms. Its block letters are Hebrew, while its script is Aramaic.

New York City was the gateway to freedom and opportunity for the mass of Eastern European Jewish immigrants, many of whom settled in that city in the late nineteenth and early twentieth centuries. Their spiritual kinship and orthodox religious identification were not enough to provide echoes of der heim; therefore they flocked to the theatre, to hear their momme loschen (mother tongue) spoken and glorified without fear of officialdom.

ROOTS OF THE YIDDISH THEATRE

Scholars of Yiddish theatre trace the origins of Jewish drama back to the Song of Songs, to the dialogue of the Book of Job, and to the prescribed ritual of the Passover feast. A more certain source however, is the merrymaking of the purimshpil (Purim play), the origin of which is in the Biblical story of Esther and the foiling of Haman's attempt to exterminate the Jews. The purimshpil was, and still is, enacted during the Purim holiday. It may have had its first performance around A.D. 415.[3] After the story was read in the synagogue during Purim, a crude drama was enacted out-of-doors, because plays were not permitted in the sanctuary of worship. Haman was burned in effigy. Audience repartee and the actors' responses eventually developed a format for traditional acting. In 1598 a

Purim play was written in Yiddish and produced in Germany; the religious and cultured Jews of Frankfurt burned the play.[4]

Gaining wide popular support during the seventeenth century, the *purimshpil* was usually performed by amateurs, village youths, and later by traveling jesters, either in the homes of the well-to-do or out-of-doors. Since the alfresco players could not police an admission fee, traveling jesters, organ grinders, and acrobats, as well as beggars, asked for donations. The rest of the year they begged or scrounged their subsistence; Purim was the one time of year when religious restrictions were unofficially relaxed: alcohol, practical jokes, masquerades, men wearing women's clothes—everything *es past* (was permitted).

Another manifestation of Jewish theatre prior to the start of the professional Yiddish theatre in 1876 was closet dramas in Hebrew written by scholars; some of these were read in literary circles or enacted by amateur student groups.[5]

Prodded by the need to reach the masses, the *maskilim* (adherents of the eighteenth- and nineteenth-century Haskalah, or Enlightenment, movement), who wrote in Hebrew, turned to Yiddish to write for the theatre. Dedicated didacticism was the badge of these secular Jewish intellectuals, followers of the eighteenth-century German philosopher Moses Mendelssohn. This new spirit was to lead to the start of a Yiddish theatre. The Haskalah movement was determined to bring the Jews out of their medieval ghettos into the "enlightened" secular culture spreading across Europe. Although antipathetic to the "jargon" of Yiddish, the *maskilim* soon realized that the masses spoke and read it. Hence poets and dramatists who had written in Hebrew, for example I. L. Peretz, Peretz Hirshbein, and David Pinski, turned to Yiddish. Without the Haskalah movement there might not have been the rich output of literature or an intelligentsia to spread and keep alive a constant search for knowledge, self-improvement, and social progress, and there might not eventually have been the workers and audiences for Yiddish theatre.

EARLY YIDDISH THEATRE

In Eastern Europe the Jews had been exposed to some professional theatre forms as well as the amateur *purimshpil.* Itinerant singers toured the provinces, appeared (in Romania particularly) in the popular wine cellars, and offered the ghetto-confined Jews a concert, or night-club, form of entertainment. The most popular group was the Broder Singers. Two of these singers, Gradner and Goldstein, performed in the Pommel Verde, a combination wine cellar and summer garden, in Jassi, Romania, in the summer of 1876. They were joined by the lyricist-composer Avram Goldfaden (1840–1908), who embellished their performance with a written continuity and dialogue—a playlet. This marked the start of the professional Yiddish theatre. Very quickly, a few troupes of Jewish actors emulated Goldfaden's enterprise and toured the main Jewish communities in Eastern Europe. Periodic government prohibitions against their appearances obliged many of these actors to seek audiences in Western Europe, South America, and the United States.

Avram (Abraham) Goldfaden

After his debut as a writer, composer, and producer for the first professional Yiddish actors, Goldfaden, a one-time medical student and journalist, collected a group of actors who traveled through Eastern Europe, delighting audiences with Goldfaden's own plays. When the czar's decree of 1883 aborted his tour of Russia, Goldfaden brought his company to Bucharest, where it triumphed. From there he left for America, where he developed a repertoire of his famous plays and operettas. His *Kishefmacher* (The Witch) was the first Yiddish play in America, performed in New York even before its author arrived there in 1887. Though his works succeeded, Goldfaden, unprotected by copyright laws, lived in penury.

In America Goldfaden encountered competition from actors, producers, and writers he had spiritually spawned. From a hiatus of five years in Europe, in about 1902 he returned to New York, which had become the world center of Jewish culture, where he subsisted on a dole of ten dollars a week from the stars Jacob P. Adler and Boris Thomashevsky. Upon his death on January 9, 1908, his funeral attracted over 75,000 mourners. (Some reports triple that figure.) To maintain order, 250 policemen were required.[6] In tribute to him, the *New York Times* wrote that "The intellectual renaissance" on the Lower East Side was like that in London in the sixteenth century. The tribute to Goldfaden had no parallel in the "sympathy and admiration for the man and his work that might be shown any poet writing in English in this country."[7] Alexander Mukdoiny later wrote, "No other theatre history has an Abraham Goldfaden. . . . [He] had no tradition or inheritance of Yiddish theatre. . . . His theatre is by no means a translation of theatres of other nations. It has its own style, is modern."[8]

Goldfaden's legacy of plays, music, and theatre style are still staples in what remains of the Yiddish theatre. Traveling troupes carried his works to South America, North America, and South Africa, as well as throughout Europe. Actors became stars in these troupes; their reputations so beguiled the immigrants in New York that managers went to Europe to woo them to appear in the New World.[9]

Goldfaden determined the formula when he deliberately wrote down to his audience's level. Speech was left to chance and the ingenuity of the actors. Later dramatists followed his model, but they lacked his healthy robustness of material, realistically drawn from the everyday life of the Jews. His output included light comedy, historical and Biblical melodramas, and musicals. His most popular musicals were *Shulamith* and *Bar Kochba.* They were the very "quintessence of the entire Jewish repertory."[10]

The intelligentsia considered Goldfaden's plays poor literature and in bad taste, but he was a success with the masses. He was the pioneer; the masses made him popular, and others reaped a harvest by his formula. Indeed, it was those who followed his model who were really the ones who earned the opprobrium of more discriminating theatregoers. (Goldfaden's genre of play has no value for reading, for it was intended only for stage presentation.)

The Goldfaden Tradition

The early Yiddish theatre came to America with methods and traditions that made the more cultured theatregoers squirm. Before the emergence of a better Yiddish theatre,[11] which brought about two "golden eras," the atmosphere resembled a poor country fair in which a world of confusion prevailed. It was dominated by untalented jesters, vaudevillians with painted-on beards and sideburns, a tawdry motley of royalty with paper crowns and tin breastplates—all for an unsophisticated audience. The actors were mountebanks with respect neither for themselves nor for their audience. Actual quarrels between husbands and wives, to which the audience was privy, would be openly conducted on stage; popular actors would have their real-life weddings interpolated into scripts and performed on stage.

This foundling theatre, with no theatre tradition or schooling, no friendship or ideals, and no hopes beyond marginal survival, was to gather to it workers inspired by the spiritual life of the people. At the outset it was rejected by religious orthodoxy to the point of excommunication. The early Yiddish actors had little culture, no affinity with religious ecstasy or mysticism, and scant awareness of an awakening, modern Yiddish culture. The accidental phenomenon of the start of the Yiddish theatre brought but a weak, distorted reflection of the European theatre to its audiences. Its timidity and the absence of a corpus of dramatic literature allowed for little more than variations on the tatterdemalion *purimshpil.*

Early improvisations found favor and developed into traditions that became well entrenched even in the recent and modern Yiddish theatre, much like the survival of the stock characters of the commedia dell'arte. Special acting styles of popular actors, such as the tapping of his foot by the comic Sigmund Mogulesco (a mannerism employed even in a serious role) barred innovative concepts. Angels were always in white robes and blond wigs; the angel of death was always in black, as were the beggar and the priest; the devil had a red costume and black wig; the hero had black hair and matching sideburns; a villain, Jew or Gentile, had to be redheaded; a Hassid wore a colored (blue or red) kerchief; a sexton carried a snuff box; a marriage broker carried an umbrella; the doctor must have spectacles, which he inevitably and deliberately wiped as he was about to pronounce his diagnosis and prognosis; a student carried a book; a rich man sported a cane; union officials and capitalists wore stiff hats ("cylinders") and smoked cigars.[12]

Goldfaden's texts, adapted into a more modern idiom, received more artistic productions by the Yiddish Art Theatre (1925), with ideological changes by the Artef (1936–1937). Nonetheless, the institutionalizing of the shabby improvisations became known as the Goldfaden tradition. (In a rare revival decades later, they were used satirically, tongue-in-cheek.) Thus the thousandth performance of a Goldfaden play in Buenos Aires was virtually identical with the original in Jassi. These traditions were also the unchangeable prompt book for the director; a new director would not place a table stage left if it had always been stage right. Even after the adoption of electric lights, the final scene on stage employed Goldfaden's traditional Bengal light display.

Stock characters were part of the equipage: Schmendrick, with his shirt tail hanging; the Kooney Lemels (Clownish Louts), with grotesque beards, Yonkel Schnorer (Scrounger), with humpback and popeyes; Hutzmach the peddler, with pronounced beard and sideburns and tattered pants. A babu yochne (old crone) was always played by a man until the tradition was broken in Warsaw around 1919. Papus, in *Bar Kochba*, speaks of his black skin, but he is played today, as in Goldfaden's day, as a redhead. When a director tells an old-time actor to play an old Jew as a Schloime, that will suffice, for the role is specifically known.

Goldfaden's Imitators

As in Europe in the early days, in America the writer-producer operated the theatre. Soon after the start of the Yiddish theatre in New York, two writer-producers established a virtual monopoly on the available theatres and the fare they offered. Two contemporaries of Goldfaden, Moshe Hurwitz (1884–1910) and Joseph Lateiner (1853–1937) had their own theatres, for which they wrote crude operettas, melodramas, serious and comic plays, and adaptations—none of which were above hack writing.[13] The first of some 150 plays that Lateiner wrote in New York was *The Immigration to America* (1883), which he presented in his Oriental Theatre on the Bowery. Hurwitz, who gave himself the unearned title of professor, wrote for the Mogulesco Players at the Romanian Opera House, for which he "built" 167 plays.

The duo "built" their plays by appropriating and adapting works from other languages.[14] "They believed it to be their business to fit the plays to their audiences even as a dressmaker fits a dress."[15] For those in the theatre their plays meant bread and butter, yet many actors proudly tried to appear in better plays.[16] "The epoch, dominated by Hurwitz and Lateiner, was one of great activity, but of no permanent accomplishment."[17] The method of these two, and others like them, was like that of the prolific Renaissance playwright Lope de Vega, creator of classical Spanish theatre, who sketched out his plot on five pages, mounted them on the stage door to acquaint the actors with the story, and allowed the actors to improvise the dialogue in keeping with their stock characters.

From Hurwitz's own words, it was apparent that changes were coming to the Yiddish theatre.

Writers came from Russia and swamped the Ghetto with scurrilous attacks on me and Lateiner. . . . They did not object to the actors, who in reality were very bad, but . . . they aimed at the play. These writers knew nothing about *dramaturgie*. . . . Anything historical or distinctly Jewish they thought bad. For a long time Lateiner and I were able to keep their realistic plays off the boards but for the last few years . . . realism [has] been put on the stage, . . . characters butchered on the stage, the coarsest language, the most revolting situations without ideas.[18]

Hurwitz's assessment of the merits of early Yiddish theatre, as compared to later, more realistic theatre, was not shared by a historian of the Yiddish theatre, Bernard Gorin. According to Gorin, the Hurwitz- and Lateiner-type plays were

Third rate Bowery shows. . . . The only feature left as a reminder of Judaism was the beards and sidelocks. Even the language was corrupted. An author was not ashamed to take a few German plays, . . . cut and paste them together, and give the heroes Jewish names. . . . He would garnish . . . with a few obscene puns and songs, and the historical melodrama was complete.[19]

In Eastern Europe the producers of Yiddish theatre during its first two decades presented plays derived from spurious Biblical legends, flavored with Jewish lore and nationalism. This early theatre, especially in New York, became a medium of cheap and ofttimes degrading amusement. The tastes of the mass of immigrants were not yet appreciative of greater artistic merit.

YIDDISH THEATRE ARRIVES IN THE UNITED STATES

The Yiddish theatre arrived on the American scene in 1882 as a fledgling only six years old, for the first Yiddish professional theatre presentation had taken place in Jassi, Romania, in 1876. The small troupe of Yiddish actors who gave the first professional Yiddish stage performance in 1882 in New York City was headed by the Golubock brothers, Leon and Miran, who had been stranded in London after leaving their native Russia. Their passage to the United States had been secured by Frank Wolf, a New York saloonkeeper, and encouraged by the enthusiastic promotion of fourteen-year-old Boris Thomashevsky, a choir singer who was later to become a famous actor.

The young Thomashevsky, who earned his living in a cigar factory in New York, persuaded his fellow worker Abe Golubock to prevail on his two brothers and their associates to come to America. They opened at the Turn Hall on East 4th Street in New York City on August 18, 1882.[20] Assimilationists such as the German Jews, who looked with contempt upon the "greenhorn theatre" with its "jargon" of Yiddish, tried to sabotage the opening by bribing the leading lady with the purchase price of a candy store if she would not appear. Other elements, such as the very orthodox, who took a traditionally antipathetic position, and the intellectuals, who sneered at the primitive pioneers of Yiddish theatre, tried to thwart the tyros.

But the Yiddish theatre did open, and it survived for three score and ten, reaching its height in New York City. Road companies also traveled to every major city in the country, and there were resident stock companies in cities with large immigrant Jewish populations, such as Philadelphia, Cleveland, Chicago, and Detroit, which all shared the common bond of the Yiddish language.

The Yiddish theatre became the pride of the Jews among their many other cultural institutions, such as the Yiddish newspapers, magazines, concert halls, labor lyceums, workmen's circles, burial societies, *landsmanschaft vereins* (fraternal lodges), and political, labor, and religious forums. It became an outstanding attraction in New York's Lower East Side, among the pushcarts, clothing stores, kosher restaurants, *shifscarte* (ticket) agencies, and settlement houses. Hundreds of thousands of sickly needle-trades workers flocked to the theatre during blizzard winters and suffocating summers. They came from the night schools where they learned the tongue of their adopted land, from the Educational Alliance and other settlement houses, even from the numerous synagogues. They came by elevated railway and subway from the new ghettos of the Bronx and Brooklyn and from as far away as the silk mills in Paterson, New Jersey, to their very own theatre. As early as 1885, "audiences were uniformly large."[21]

For the immigrant Jews, theatre had a meaning beyond Horace's "to entertain and educate." In the theatre Jews reveled in a nostalgia for the *shtetls* they had left behind physically but remembered in spirit.

THE AUDIENCE

At the eve of the Civil War, Jews in the United States numbered some 200,000, mostly from the German states. The largest number resided in New York City.[22] The flow of Jewish immigrants was not a steady one, but came in surges in the wake of European crises.

The first significant influx of Eastern European Jews came from Russia as a result of rampant anti-Semitism following the assassination of Czar Alexander II in 1881. The persecution and frightful pogroms against the Jews during and after the Russo-Turkish war (1878) were revived and intensified during the reign of Nicholas II and reached a climax in the Kishinev massacre of Jews (1903) and the placing of Jewish troops in the front line of fire during the Russo-Japanese War (1905). These crises inspired the emigration of some 2 million Jews from the regions of the czar's hegemony between 1883 and the eve of World War I.[23]

Fleeing from the oppression of the czar in Russia, from the daily fear of pogroms throughout Eastern Europe, and from a circumscribed and proscribed life under an Austro-Hungarian emperor, Ashkenazi Jews escaped to freedom, to security for their children, and to *parnusseh* (a livelihood) in the *goldeneh medina* (golden land)—America. These millions distilled from their anguished past and cultural heritage a monumental theatre, with literature, scenic art, and stage styles that enriched and inspired the significant American and world drama of the twentieth century.

Like most immigrants, Jews sought out their coreligionists, enlarged existing enclaves in the larger cities, and spread throughout the land, thereby bringing their cultural heritage to new outposts. Religion was not the sole common denominator among the Jews who came to America: they brought with them a great avidity for learning and literature.[24] In consequence, one of the most significant bodies of literature in America has come from the Jewish people. The underlying psychological drive toward literary expression rooted in almost a Jungian mass unconscious, has been the atavism of the urban-centered Jews of the third and fourth generations, fortified by the homogeneous culture of the Eastern European shtetl.[25]

The Jewish immigrant from Eastern Europe came from "one of the most education-centered societies in human history," despite the fact that at the end of the nineteenth century the Eastern European Jewish community "was materially improverished to a greater extent than any [group] . . . in modern America."[26] Perhaps their poverty or the oppression they had been subjected to had made them a homogeneous people. The peoples of their host nations, the Poles, Hungarians, Romanians, Russians, and Ukranians, had each had a common history, national language and culture, religion, and ruler—czar or emperor— and were markedly different from each other. Living in all of these countries, the Eastern European Jews had a common culture that was all of a piece, a living whole.[27] The bond of Jewish descent was fortified by a common religion, a common language, a marginal life in constant fear of martyrdom and extinction, and a spiritual awareness by each that he or she was a Jew and one with other Jews. This bond, this need to hear their momme loschen, the need to be among their own kind, drew the Jews to the Yiddish theatre.

The emergence of the Yiddish theatre in New York resulted not only from the universal need for dramatic expression, true for any people, but from the special needs of the immigrants. The avid pursuit of culture among the Jews came with them from the shtetls to their newly adopted land. The shtetl was the nerve center of Jewish life, even for the Jews in the bigger cities such as Warsaw, Vilna, Odessa, and Minsk. The ghetto bred the inquiline way of life of the shtetl, which led people to become writers, actors, and managers and contributed the very plots and themes as well as the characters, atmosphere, and situations in the plays. When the shtetls were eliminated in the crossfire between the Nazis and the Stalinists, the lifeblood of the Yiddish theatre was destroyed. A parenthetical note: the new state of Israel rejected the ghetto literature of the dismal past and devoted its writings and theatre to the pioneer spirit, in modern Hebrew, not Yiddish.

The shtetl was the source of the evil and blessings of Jewish life, part of the baggage of each immigrant. The audience supplied the actors, writers, and troupes, particularly out of the numerous literary groups and drama clubs that burgeoned in practically every Jewish enclave on both sides of the Atlantic, especially in New York City, which became "the center of Yiddish theatre and drama."[28] Yiddish theatres "established themselves in several cities, but it was in New York, with its heavy concentration of Jews, which now [1880–1900] shaped the destiny of Yiddish drama."[29]

The early immigrants were of three types: (1) the elderly religious, who spent much time in the numerous synagogues and frowned at the theatre; (2) the intelligentsia, who pursued learning and professions and encouraged and joined labor movements; and (3) the uneducated workers, who were backward and illiterate but who made up the majority in the Yiddish theatre audiences.[30]

During the last decade of the nineteenth century Lincoln Steffens, Hutchins Hapgood, and Henry James, and later Carl Van Vechten and Konrad Bercovici, had both condemnation and praise for what they observed in the Yiddish theatre. On balance, they universally acclaimed the experience as the adumbration of coming greatness. James described the swarming multitudes of Jews as "here for race and not for reason." He found them gregarious, happy to be with their own kind in joyful celebration. After viewing a Yiddish "comedy of manners," he said it "reached across the world to some far off, dowdy Jewry."[31]

Hutchins Hapgood noted that although the Jewish masses had a preponderance of the poor and ignorant, the intellectuals and progressives were also well represented, exerting an enormous influence on the character of theatrical productions, which, however, remained "essentially popular." He found the Yiddish theatre to represent the serious as well as the trivial interests of the entire community, with a definite striving toward a distinctive, realistic art form.[32]

From the start of 1882, the New York Jewish audience consisted mostly of uncouth, uneducated Jews from the Pale. This audience was not static; it had an amazing drive toward self-improvement, generated by its cultural traditions and by the heirs of the Haskalah movement—the press, the labor lyceums, its cultural organizations, and its unique literary and dramatic clubs. Whereas many other national or ethnic theatres had been started under the patronage of royalty or church, the Yiddish theatre grew out of a democratic soil and offered earthy folk dramas. These dramas illuminated the lives of an audience that was different, separate from all others.[33] This audience of Jews was segregated into the Lower East Side of New York City, a neighborhood "richer in diversity, poorer in cash, quicker and more dramatic in change and flux, more tempting to describe, and more impossible to capture in description" than any other.[34]

In addition to the obvious benefit of entertainment, the Yiddish theatre provided a social meeting place for newcomers to New York. During the "first golden epoch," the enthusiastic devotion of the Yiddish theatre's followers demonstrated an obsession, a worship; they spent half a week's salary to attend the theatre, "which [was] practically the only amusement of the Ghetto Jew."[35] Although the poor and ignorant were in the great majority, intellectuals and

progressives were also there and exerted an influence beyond their small numbers. The socialists and literati created a demand for more serious theatrical fare,
which reflected ghetto problems in simple transcripts from life, with a heartfelt
understanding of the masses.[36]

The assimilated German Jews, who were more sophisticated theatregoers,
were disdainful of the Yiddish theatre, with its "corrupt Yiddish-Polish jargon . . . a disgrace to any community."[37] Should they have attended, they
would have found an avid, captious, ill-mannered pack whose last-minute rush
for seats constituted a "figurative biting, scratching, rough handling, . . . and
hard words." Standees mooched onto the chair edges of those seated. There was
a prodigious amount of eating.[38] The vulgar early theatre reflected the vulgar
tastes of its audience. Goldfaden complained that the "beloved public was more
uncouth than the actors."[39] The people in the audience ate peanuts and other
foods, cracked nuts, spit shells around them, and showed no respect for the
actors or their surroundings.

No other theatre can boast of the fanatical devotion of its fans as can the
Yiddish theatre of its *patriotten*. They were the "finest indication of the exalta-
tion of love aroused from the humility of the folk's soul to the artist who received
it with spiritual enthusiasm."[40] For them the actor was a god, and they were
prepared to sacrifice themselves for their deity. When their idol triumphed, the
patriotten vicariously found glory, and when there was failure, the *patriotten* were
in deep sorrow. They might be found freezing outside a restaurant, watching the
actor-star dining. The *patriotten* carried the vision of the idol with them
throughout their workaday lives. They might be found at a performance of a
rival of their idol only to create a disturbance or to hiss.

The first four nights of the week were most often booked by *vereins* (fraternal
organizations; burial societies; labor organizations; and charitable, social, and
cultural societies). Many of these *vereins* were *landsmanschaften;* that is, their
members came from a common *shtetl* in the old country and provided material
and spiritual comfort to their compatriots in the new land. Members were
obliged to buy tickets for themselves and were often alloted additional tickets to
sell to friends, relatives, and business contacts. The system of benefits was
widespread.

Organizations usually purchased tickets at a 75 percent discount and resold
them at full price. The profit was used by the organizations either for their
support or for a special cause, usually charitable. Producers in the Yiddish
theatre openly advertised these group sales. This system is still maintained in
what remains of the Yiddish theatre. It is also a legacy bequeathed to the
American theatre, which avidly solicits group sales.

Friday, Saturday, and Sunday performances were not sold to groups at a
discount—the audience paid full price. These nights the

theatre presents a peculiarly picturesque sight. Poor workingmen and women with their
babies of all ages fill the theatre. Great enthusiasm, . . . sincere laughter and tears

accompany the sincere acting. . . . Peddlars of soda-water, candy, of fantastic gew-gaws . . . mix freely with the audience between the acts. Conversation during the play is received with strenuous hisses, but the falling of the curtain is the signal for groups of friends to get together and gossip about the play or the affairs of the week. Introductions are not necessary. . . . On the stage curtain are advertisements of the wares of Hester Street or portraits of the "star" actors.[41]

Among efforts to improve the tastes of the Yiddish theatre audience was the publication of a magazine in 1900, *The Theatre Journal*, with Gorin as editor. It contained articles on Greek drama and the history of the theatre and lectures on acting and direction; one issue rebuked the audiences for cracking peanuts, popping soda bottles, and munching apples during the performance of a serious play. It also published reviews of plays, biographies of theatre personalities, and editorials that urged readers to demand better plays. Significantly, it recommended that schools be established for actors.

The fame of visiting stars brought a heterogeneous audience to enjoy "great theatre." Foreign tourists, as well as "uptown Jews who had achieved social status and wealth," joined workers and artisans to exult in a glamor that for many was more rewarding than the synagogue.[42]

As early as 1902, Hapgood noted that young Jews sought entertainment that was more closely associated with mainstream American life; they frequented English language-theatre on Broadway. Just as assimilated first-generation Jews had Americanized children who patronized Broadway, soon Yiddish theatre stars began appearing in the English-language plays there. Belle Baker, Ludwig Satz, and cantor Yosele Rosenblatt, as well as members of the Adler clan, followed the apostates.

The Americanization of the Yiddish theatregoer was reflected in the interpolations of English phrases into Yiddish plays. (This was a two-way street; many Yiddish colloquialisms have found their way into both the American-English language and into the dialogue on the American stage.) Attempts by producers such as Maurice Schwartz to present plays of an American milieu and with English phrases in order to hold or lure Americanized audiences did not succeed, however.

Since the late 1960s the dwindling theatre audience have loyally attended the annual weekend productions of one play each year by the gallant, devoted, and indomitable Folksbuehne in New York City. The "shut-ins" of the older generation of Jews have found their theatre in the Jewish Hour on radio station WEVD.

INFLUENCE OF THE PRESS AND THE INTELLIGENTSIA

As the theatre entrenched itself and became an important current in the mainstream of Jewish life, elements in and outside the Yiddish theatre sought to raise its artistic level and make it truly symbolic of the strivings for cultural maturation.

A considerable impetus to the growth and success of the Yiddish theatre in its brief life was the phenomenal Yiddish press, which by the mid-1920s had a circulation of half a million. The Yiddish press and the Yiddish theatre made each Ashkenazi Jew feel like a whole person with a heritage, with a sense of belonging. The heritage grew out of the soil of deprivation in the ghetto *shtetls* of the Old World, but when Jews in the New World of America heard the language of their youth, the language of their fathers and mothers, they experienced an ecstatic, nostalgic evocation of a life long ago and far away. At the same time they gloried in the coming of age, the acceptance, the recognition, and the fulfillment of all things Yiddish as presented on stage.

The new Yiddish press called the Hurwitz-Lateiner type of commercial theatre to account. *Der Volks Advokat* (1888) and *Der Arbeiter Tzeitung* (1890) voiced the criticism of the prevailing Yiddish theatre by the intelligentsia and working class. *Der Volks Advokat* accused Lateiner of falsifying history in his production of *Judah Maccabee*, with anachronisms "only to please the public and make a few dollars."[43] The press was the spokesman in the struggle to improve the Yiddish theatre and make it a serious form of Jewish culture. The new (weekly) publications "marked an important step in . . . changing . . . Yiddish productions away from frivolous entertainment . . . to the more serious viewpoint of the later Jacob Gordin plays."[44] The editors of *Der Volks Advokat* called for an end to the "foolish and primitive . . . writing and acting" on the Yiddish stage and asserted

that sharp criticism by the press [was] necessary for the good of the Yiddish theatre. . . . The dramatic arts are capable of educating people, . . . [but not plays] that are conceived with intentions of blinding the public with foolish effects without content or form. . . . It is the duty of the press not to prostitute the stage with false reviews . . . nor . . . allow actors who are . . . clowns and should be in a circus and not in a theatre . . . to fool the masses into a belief they are good actors.[45]

The editors asserted that the theatre had fallen into the dirty hands of people with no understanding of dramatic art nor of real life, people who looked upon the Jewish public as stupid fools. "These dramatists take hard-earned money from poor Jewish workers. . . . They profane dramatic art and do not allow real authors to approach the stage." The editors accused the hacks of taking too much from the German and English stage in New York, interpolating song and dance specialities, "casting art aside and sinning against the public."[46]

Demanding a reform that was to become effective a few decades later, Abraham Cahan ridiculed the odd mixture of language on the Yiddish stage. Pretentious actors, to appear as heroes of the upper classes, declaimed in *Daeitchsmeirish*, a fanciful German. He condemned the actors for their lack of national pride and rejected their claim that stage language had to be on a higher plane than that of the street. Disgusted with them, he concluded that they were inferior to actors on the American stage.[47] A colleague of Cahan recognized that the actors, for lack of training to play classic roles, did not know the characters they portrayed nor what the author had conceived, "just as the authors lack talent to create good, logical plays."[48] Another practice he deplored, a practice exacerbated later by arbitrary Hebrew Actors Union rules, was the casting of an old actress to play an ingénue.

Together with Yiddish literature, the Yiddish theatre grew as an art form in New York. It provided a considerable corpus of drama for both library and stage, with New York revered as the center of Yiddish culture.[49] This center included the cafes, which stimulated the exchange of ideas. The best of Jewish talent and intelligentsia gathered in the Division Street Cafe and the Royal, with painters, sculptors, poets, musicians, and actors, as Bercovici reported, at the full bloom of the flowering Jewish cultural life in New York in about the 1920s.[50] The Yiddish theatre offered plays from Shakespeare to Shaw "to trash . . . ; Second Avenue is an exact duplicate of the real Broadway."[51]

Next to the press, the stage was the most potent cultural influence in the life of the Jewish immigrant. The vapid operettas based on spurious Biblical and historical legends and blood-curdling melodramas of the Shomer, Lateiner, and Hurwitz play factory did bring the masses to the theatre. As the audiences acquired higher standards, the stage was to be rescued from that factory in the works of Solomon Libin, Leon Kobrin, Sholem Asch, Pinski, Chune Gottesfeld, Hirshbein, and H. Leivick.[52] The large number of Yiddish-speaking immigrants created a demand for expansion of institutions like the Yiddish theatre. This demand was intensified as "original things were done in the field of literature and in the relatively new field of the theatre."[53]

The intelligentsia of the New York ghetto, the politically and socially aware, gagged at the banal fare fed the early Yiddish theatre audiences. The intelligentsia, mostly from Russia, "found it difficult to abandon their own culture and adapt themselves to a new life. They took no interest in . . . English; . . . conversation in Russian was . . . a sign of intellectuals in Jewish circles. They ignored and sneered at all connected with the Yiddish theatre; . . . artistic taste came later."[54]

JACOB GORDIN AND THE "FIRST GOLDEN EPOCH"

Because the Yiddish theatre grew out of the cultural strivings of the people, inevitably there would come a time when a true art theatre would emerge. Before the efforts of writers, directors, managers, the critical press, and a discriminating audience could assert themselves and force the Yiddish theatre to come of age, one pioneer had to spark the flame, the monumental figure who first encountered a theatre that had corrupted the style and content of the folk plays and operettas of Goldfaden. That figure was Jacob Gordin (1853–1909).

To the loud acclaim of the intellectual and radical element, Gordin the idealist entered the theatre in a conscious effort to bring rationality and literary truth to the masses, with an emphasis upon themes of social awareness.[55] He came upon the theatrical scene at a time of social awakening among the Jewish masses in America. Much influenced by the theatre of transition in Europe and by Tolstoyan socialism, be upset the Hurwitz-Lateiner stranglehold in 1892 when the star Jacob P. Adler appeared in Gordin's *Siberia*. The ensuing decade, thanks to the numerous Gordin plays that illuminated the Yiddish stage, was to be known as "the first golden epoch of the Yiddish theatre."

Gordin consciously assumed a responsibility to reform the Yiddish theatre. His penchant for preaching and moralizing rather than art was evident in his plays: they did not truly portray Jewish life, for most of his plays were problem plays, with problems not exclusive to the Jews. He did develop a theatre for the "greenhorn" sweatshop helots. His was a cosmopolitan drama; his types varied from caricatures to the naturalistic, and their acceptance by the audiences at the time of his greatest vogue established a model for future Yiddish plays. He created juicy, significant roles for the actors, roles with characterizations that seemed naturalistic and were definitely a departure from traditional types.

Although Gordin's plays lost favor in the Yiddish art theatre movement after 1918, he pointed the way to better theatre, opened the theatre to new playwrights, educated the actors to the value of language and the inviolability of the author's text, and prepared the audiences by providing standards of comparison between *shund* (junk) and better theatre. His subject matter was varied and, as a Jew, he was "forced by the pressure of his experience to be . . . eclectic."[56]

Gordin's plays were derivative; the very title of his *Yiddish King Lear* reveals its source; his socially aware plays were certainly in the Ibsen tradition and not basically of the Jewish folk, yet in his day he was the most important power in Yiddish drama. If the Jewish immigrant sought a transfiguration, Gordin tried to present him or her as a new person, closing out the past. Gordin's numerous adaptations limited him as a creative writer; he searched for the universal *mentsch* (human being) rather than the Jew as his protagonist.

Siberia, the first original Yiddish play of the better type, struck a new note in bringing to the Yiddish stage the Russian spirit of realism so marked in the intellectual life of the ghetto,[57] and with it a new breath of life. Gordin's theatre was lusty meat in its realism, for an audience that the great actress Bertha Kalish said "approaches the theatre with a great love . . . listens attentively . . . [and is] figuratively on the stage in every scene, a tense spectator."[58] The hard working, socially aware East Side acclaimed Gordin as the new champion and "apostle of realism." His plays were not wrung out of the true, intimate life of the people, despite his claims, but they did create a genuine atmosphere, with excellent, robust types. The dramatic problems of his plays, however, were not necessarily true to or inspired by the people about whom and for whom he wrote.

In 1893 Gordin wrote *Murder on Madison Avenue* and *The Pogrom*. They, like all his works, revealed his earnestness, his *Weltanschauung*, his psychological insights, his will power, and his talents. He was known as the reformer of the Yiddish stage. Gradually a spirit of enlightenment developed on both sides of the footlights, with appreciation for plays free from the claptrap of primitive melo-drama. Through Gordin's works, the better-educated radicals responded to the Yiddish theatre and reveled in fare on the higher plane.[59]

The arrival of Gordin's realism marked the start of significant drama in the Yiddish theatre. It was not a response to the world realism movement, which reached a high point with David Belasco in New York, but rather to the literary demands of the Yiddish theatre. Gordin's Jews were localized Russian, Ukrainian, and American Jews. They underscored Gordin's pro-Russian attitudes, which were stronger than his Jewishness; he was an alienated Jew. With a Russian theatricality, he Russified the Yiddish theatre, for in his plays there were no specially Jewish heritage, religion, folkways, old Jewish culture, Jewish sorrow, nor aspirations. He was unlike Peretz, among others, whose plays were rooted in the Jewish experience, as in his *Golden Chains*.[60] Gordin's theatre transcended parochialism.

The theatricality of Gordin's realism provided the stage with unprecedented excitement; his style allowed the actors' talents to flower. The actors found in Gordin's plays ready-made, identifiable types that were easily portrayed, but found no need to probe the psychological depths of characterization. Despite his puppetlike characters, his scenes were each meaningful; each word and move-ment advanced either the plot or the concept of a character, and the dramatic issues did grip and hold the audiences. Gordin's journalistic flair of freshness generated a vogue. Eventually both he and his imitators degenerated into cliché and lost their novelty and their artistic inspiration; all concerned became bored; Gordin had had his day.[61]

OTHER EMINENT PLAYWRIGHTS

After Gordin carved a path to better theatre, other playwrights took heart and brought forth their works. Sholom Aleichem (Solomon Rabinovich, 1859–1916), who has been called the Jewish Dickens and/or the Jewish Mark Twain, is perhaps the most beloved of Jewish writers. His play *200,000* is often revived on 2nd Avenue under the title *The Big Winner*. Its plot is typical Sholom Aleichem irony, about a poor tailor who mistakenly believes he holds a winning lottery ticket. His family adjusts poorly to a new social status while the commu-nity snobbishly caters to these *arrivistes*. When the bubble bursts, the tailor returns with glee to his sewing. Sholom Aleichem's plays include *Sender Blank* and *Hard to Be a Jew*, both staples in the repertoire of the Yiddish Art Theatre, as well as plays adapted from his famous stories: *Tevye the Milkman* (the book for *Fiddler on the Roof*), *Stempenyu the Fiddler*, *The Bewitched Tailor* (included in *The World of Sholom Aleichem*, in English), *Wandering Stars*, and *1001 Nights*. His plays and those of Peretz were given in an uncluttered, stark style with a warm, rich naturalism—except in Russia, where the Soviets caricatured the actors, to use *200,000* as a political polemic—and the audiences, Jewish and non-Jewish, responded with a warm feeling of kinship.

Like Sholom Aleichem, Isaac Leib Peretz (1852–1915) was a poet, a writer of tales, a playwright, "who must be counted among the greatest writers not only of [Yiddish] but of literature in general at the end of the 19th century."[62] He was so beloved that 100,000 Jews followed his funeral cortege in Warsaw. His most popular play on the Yiddish stage has been *Night in the Old Mart*. Recent productions in English of *The World of Sholom Aleichem* include a dramatization of his famous story, *Bonche Schweig*.

The third in the triumvirate of literary giants was Sholem J. Abramovitch (pen name, Mendele Mocher Sforim), who inspired a new wave of Yiddish playwrights who pictured Jewish life with a keen sense of reality and humor. His story "Travels of Benjamin III" was often dramatized and became most popular. Rooted in the *shtetl*, the literature of this trio (only Sholom Aleichem came to America) influenced the important Yiddish playwrights of the late nineteenth century and the early twentieth. The leading ones included Kobrin, Moishe Nadir, Asch, Pinski, Hirshbein, Ossip Dymov, Leivick, and Ansky. "Mendele" was important as a source.

In its variety the rich literary and dramatic content of Yiddish drama is no different from the best of world drama, yet with the added folk elements of a distinct people. The plays "take root on a soil and grow . . . [out of] the soul of man, a noble and superior being with an infinite contempt for everything except the life of the spirit."[63] More serious Yiddish dramatists, especially Pinsky, Kobrin, and Leivick, became involved with the problems confronting the Jewish people. Their themes included problems of nationalism, the role of the Jew in the class struggle, the adjustment of the Jew in non-Jewish surroundings, use of physical force as a means of salvation, problems engendered by assimilation, Messianic strivings, and the clash of generations as well as history and individual lives.

Other than Goldfaden and later Hirshbein, who directed their own troupes, no important Yiddish playwrights had active backstage exposure to the theatre, as had been the case of Shakespeare and Molière. The Yiddish playwrights kept themselves aloof from stage activity and considered themselves aristocrats compared with actors.[64] But the serious dramatists, most of them Russian born, had frequently attended the Russian theatre and were avid readers of world drama, which familiarized them with stage conventions.

In 1892, when the Yiddish theatre came of age with the arrival of Gordin, Leon Kobrin (1872–1946), a dynamic Jewish writer, arrived in New York from a life of penury in Vitebsk. His new life of struggle in the ghetto tempo of the tenements provided him with the insight to write dramas of both *der heim* (the old country) and of the urgencies of the Jewish workingmen, who had to reconcile Old World folkways with the intense demands of the New World.

Much aware of the school of naturalism of Emile Zola, Gustave Flaubert, Frank Norris, and Stephen Crane, Kobrin immersed himself in realism and wrote with dramatic intensity of the fateful, compelling tragedy of a Thomas Hardy–like situation for the Yiddish stage. More than a malevolent fate compelled his heroes to an inevitable doom, for they were caught between the irreconcilable forces of loyalty-demanding tradition and native human passion. In truth, Kobrin's works were wrung out of his "race, milieu, and moment" (Taine). He was among the first to write on American-Jewish subjects: life in the ghetto, the tug-of-war between generations, the conflicts between immigrant parents and their modern, American children. He collaborated with Jacob Gordin on his first play, Minna, and that same year (1899) his East Side Ghetto starred the famous Kalish. He also wrote novels that were first serialized in the Yiddish dailies. He translated into Yiddish classics from Gorki, Shakespeare, Chekhov, de Maupassant, Turgenev, and Tolstoy. His autobiography (in Yiddish) gives an invaluable picture of Yiddish theatre and literature in America, as do his collected works.

In 1912, when he encountered production problems with the producers of his great Children of Nature (also known as Yankel Boyla or Dorf's Yung), Kobrin organized the Jewish Playwrights Association. The Moscow Art Theatre produced his Children of Nature in Russian.

A poet who turned from Hebrew to Yiddish was the playwright Peretz Hirshbein (1880–1948), whose bucolic idylls of shtetl life brought new triumphs to the Yiddish stage and ushered in the Yiddish art theatre movement known as the "second golden epoch" (1918). Together with Leivick and Pinski, he directed and produced at Unzer Teater in the East Bronx (1924–1925). He had toured the Pale with his own troupe (1908–1910), with plays by Asch, Peretz, and Gordin as well as his own plays. His leading actor, Ben-Ami, had come to America at the eve of World War I and brought with him Hirshbein's techniques, gleaned from the style of the Moscow Art Theatre. A decade before the celebrated Russian troupe's debut in New York, Stanislavsky's methods were already a part of Yiddish theatre.

Hirshbein's pastoral plays of the simple life of unpretentious Jewish folk had a pungent flavor, charm, and warm humor that made them favorites among the drama and literary clubs in New York. As the Hellenist of Jewish literature, he celebrated the joy, the hope, the unquenchably romantic and indomitable Jewish spirit that resolutely survives enormous odds.

The roster of other distinguished Yiddish playwrights is lengthy; even a few words about each would require a volume. But mention must be made of pivotal writers, each of whom alone would have distinguished a nation's drama. One poet, whose pen was dipped in blood, saw the particular tragic drama of the Jew as an unbearable and incomprehensible universal affliction. H. Leivick (Leivick Halper, 1888–1962) identified with the woebegotten and distilled out of the anguished ferment of his own life the stirring travail of all mankind. His plays are the voice of those whose raw wounds poured their blood out on the Siberian snow under the bestial flailing by the Czar's brutes. He was a political activist, was arrested in 1906, and escaped to America in 1913. His Hirsh Leckert and his Miracle of the Warsaw Ghetto are epics of the Jews, as is The Golem, which has been translated into other tongues and made into an opera by Abraham Elstein.

David Pinski (1872–1959), who wrote more than sixty plays, became a world figure not only as a talented dramatist, but also as a leading intellectual and scholar. In his plays about *shtetl* life, such as his magnificent *The Treasure*, he combined poetic, philosophic, and social ideas with realistic characterizations. This play was staged in Berlin by Max Reinhardt (1910) and in New York by the Theatre Guild (1920). His themes range from conflicts of rich against poor and parents against children, to the aspirations and strivings of mankind, particularly the Jews. His style, redolent with humor, is both lyric and earthy. His play *Isaac Sheftel* shows his identification with the working class even though he had pursued the life of a scholar; his *Yankel the Blacksmith* is a conflict of sexual attraction; and his *The Zwie Family* concerns the problems of the Jewish people.

Religious mysticism seems to have been an ever-present theme in many Yiddish plays, by and about a people who daily faced life at its most real. This religious mysticism is manifest in Peretz's *Night in the Old Mart*, Ansky's *Der Dybbuk*, Pinski's *The Treasure* and *Mute Messiah*, even in Gordin's *God, Man, and Devil* (based on *Faust*), Leivick's *The Golem*, and the plays of Sholem Asch (1880–1957). Asch was proud of the Jews, who obstinately, if illogically, retained an identity despite being devoured or engulfed by others. His novels grappled with the theme of Jewish identity and survival, as shown in his mystical play *Kiddush Ha-Shem*. Asch is well known to English-language readers of his novels *Three Cities* and *The Nazarene*. In the world of the theatre he is best known for this powerful drama *God of Vengeance*, which when presented in English on Broadway with Rudolph Schildkraut, was closed by the police as obscene and which provoked a series of censorship laws. This play is about a brothel owner whose daughter succumbs to a whore-lesbian's blandishments. The father then thrusts her into the life of a prostitute. When Asch wrote the play in 1907, Yiddish plays were more earthy, forthright, and robust in the treatment of sex than plays on Broadway. Compared with Asch in his classic, George Bernard Shaw was a puritan in his *Mrs. Warren's Profession*.

Sex had its vogue after the Gordin era, when a plethora of sex-oriented dramas appeared. Just prior to the U.S. entry into World War I, despite efforts to present better plays and plays of nationalistic content, lurid melodramas of sex were very popular. A sampling of the year 1915–1916 offers revealing titles: *White Slaves*, by Isadore Zolatorevsky; *Red Light* and *Red District*, by Itzhok Lash; *Slave Dealer* and *Her Awakening*, by Moishe Richter; and *The Pure Conscience*, by Max Gabel.

DRAMA AND LITERARY CLUBS

The immigrant audience did not entirely allow itself to be manipulated by the public relations gambits of stars and producers. Within the ranks of the audience, individuals and groups continued to agitate for better theatre, cultural uplift, and social stimulation. The arrival of a better Yiddish theatre was not precipitous. Prior to and concurrent with the growth of the Yiddish theatre, many dedicated literature and drama clubs joyfully flourished in Europe and America. These clubs performed the world premieres of classics of the Yiddish stage, encouraged talented writers, gave actors training in their art, and established high standards among audiences.

"In New York in 1881, there were a few dramatic clubs . . . which multiplied themselves during the ensuing decades."[65] In addition to being laboratories for new plays and actors, some of the clubs were also politically and socially active. For a theatre with no stage traditions, these amateur clubs became the drama schools where future stars developed their talents. Schwartz, Gabel, and Anna Appel, among many others, had their training and early recognition in club productions. When Ben-Ami first came to New York, his directing and acting in an amateur club brought him to the attention of the public and professional theatre. Playwrights such as Hirshbein also first came to America's attention through the clubs. America was oblivious to the art theatre movement that was flourishing in Europe, but the Yiddish amateur clubs filled the gap and paved the road to better theatre, while they served as an educational entertainment medium and created a demand and an audience for art in the theatre.[66]

Some of these clubs were the grassroots of notable professional troupes. The Vikt and Fada clubs in Warsaw later (1915) formed the world-famous Vilna Troupe, an offshoot of which came to New York, where it set a new style for acting and production art. The Harp and the Dramatic Art Club in Lodz, Poland, presented plays by Asch and Hirshbein as well as non-Yiddish plays from the European repertoire. All the Jewish clubs rebelled against the prevailing shund repertoire in the professional Yiddish theatre; they were to succeed.[67]

The clubs in America were the first to bring to these shores plays by Ibsen, Hauptmann, Pinski, Asch, Schnitzler, and Hirshbein. These clubs were greatly influenced by Russian intellectuals. Jewish workers from Germany, Finland, Hungary, Russia, Romania, and Poland formed their own clubs along national lines. Ibsen was translated into Yiddish by needle trades workers and presented at the Labor Lyceum in New York. The Jewish Workers Theatre also played an important cultural role in the renaissance of the drama.[68] Thanks to the clubs, thousands of Jewish immigrants knew the best of European drama long before other Americans. The clubs provided cultural centers for an intelligentsia who found scant cerebral stimulation in the landsmanschaft vereins.

Noteworthy among the clubs of new generations were the Uptown Dramatic Club, Dramatic Club of the Hebrew Literary Society, Drama Guild, Die Freie Yiddish Folkbuehne (The Young Free Folksbuehne), I. L. Peretz Society, J. Gordin Drama Society, and Literary Art Corner. An ubiquitous dynamo whose name appears in the roster of leading clubs and who helped the merger of some of them was Joel Enteen, who led the important Progressive Dramatic Club. Enteen was a poet and co-editor of a number of Jewish periodicals in the United States. He translated Ibsen's Ghosts and Maeterlinck's Pelleas and Melisande into Yiddish.

In 1881 New York had a few drama clubs; by 1888 there were three Goldfaden clubs. Within a decade many more were established throughout the United States and Canada. The Progressive Dramatic Club (founded in 1902) had a program, under the guidance of the talented actor-director Jacob Fishman, that consisted of lectures, concerts, and play readings. Most of the clubs had similar programs.

The Folksbuehne

Cultural activities other than stage presentations thus were important features of the various clubs. By 1940 the Folksbuehne, founded in 1915 through the merging of the Progressive Dramatic Club and the faltering Hebrew Dramatic Club, under the sponsorship and financial support of the Workmen's Circle (Arbeiter Ring), had arranged or encouraged over two thousand concerts and literary programs. A popular feature of the literary programs was the "author's evening," whereby prominent Yiddish writers would read or arrange readings of their works, usually at the Rand School. The Workmen's Circle, a Socialist-oriented organization, has not interfered ideologically with the productions of the Folksbuehne.

The objective of The Folksbuehne was to establish itself as a folk theatre after the pattern of the Neighborhood Playhouse and to present the best of Yiddish and world dramatic literature. Through the years it has had distinguished directors in addition to Fishman; among them have been Leonid Snegoff, Leib Kadison, Michael Razumni, and David Licht. In its sixty-fourth year, 1979, it was the only Yiddish theatre in New York. Other amateur groups infrequently offered Yiddish plays in cities like Los Angeles, Milwaukee, and Cleveland. The Workmen's Circle sponsored tours by professional Yiddish companies to many cities throughout the United States.

The Folksbuehne productions have been as professional as any in the Yiddish theatre. Typical was the 1933 production of Leivick's *Hirsh Leckert* under the direction of Nachem Zemach, who had been a founder, director, and actor at the Habima (a Hebrew-language troupe founded in Moscow just after the Russian Revolution). *Hirsh Leckert* is a social drama with the spirit of revolution, reflecting the life of the working people of Vilna and their struggle against the czar's oppression. David Herman worked with Zemach as director, to achieve extraordinary ensemble acting and impressionistic effects. However, during the 1960s and 1970s the Folksbuehne has only revived folk dramas and plays with nationalistic themes. One would rarely find a member of its 1970s audience under fifty or sixty years of age.

The Artef

"One of the most vital forces in the development of the American drama as a whole," according to the left-wing writer John Howard Lawson, was the Artef.[69] During the 1920s a socially aware, didactic theatre was forming in

Europe and America. In America, Jewish workers had unsuccessfully tried to present good theatre in Folks Farband Far Yiddisher Kunst Teater (People United for Yiddish Art Theatre) (1923) by supporting Schwartz's Yiddish Art Theatre. The Yiddish daily *Freiheit* encouraged the group. Both *Freiheit* and the club were ideologically on the extreme left, however; hence they could not continue long with Schwartz's bourgeois, commercial theatre.

Late in 1925 a meeting was held in New York City. It was attended by 2,000 people representing 100,000 workers and established a society that named itself Arbeiter Teater Farband (Workers Theatre Association), or Artef for short. In February 1926 the organization started to function as a studio where the workers came each evening to hear lectures on theatre art by specialists, among whom were writer Nathaniel Buchwald, writer and director Jacob Mestel, and Schneider, who came to the Artef from the Habima after a brief directing assignment at the Folksbuehne. They presented programs to members on Sunday evenings.

Claiming for itself its own language, its own norms, and its own character, the Artef developed a program, a mission, a purpose—to create a proletarian stage with a repertoire in step with the times and the revolutionary movement and with a theatre art form paralleling that of the Soviet theatre.[70] Until its demise Artef was Communist inspired and guided. Its productions did not always hew to the party line, but the workers in the theatre collective felt vindicated because the results were artistically gratifying.

Starting with the 1928–1929 season, the Artef opened its doors to the public. During the next ten years it produced, published, and developed a theatre that has become a legend. During the Depression the Artef, an avowedly left-wing workers' theatre, commanded a considerable following among progressives, workers, and intellectuals. One must underscore the rare talent of its inspired director, Schneider, who had had his schooling with the original Habima and who went on from the Artef to Broadway (where he discovered Ingrid Bergman), and then to Hollywood, where he became an acting coach for the stars at Metro-Goldwyn-Mayer.

One important canon of the Artef was not to extend the run of a play, no matter how popular nor how much the public clamored for the extension. Its rationale was simply that, artistically, it was devoted to good theatre and not to making money on a popular success. However, the company did bestow its riches beyond New York by touring to major cities such as Philadelphia, Boston, Montreal, and Toronto. The advance publicity did not mention the Artef's Communist ideology. Artef conducted symposia for its members and the general public and was very active in the 1930s in the New Theatre Movement, which it helped establish. Its programs constantly presented agitprop theatre, which was a staple of the socially aware New Theatre Movement.

During the Great Depression of the 1930s, the Artef triumphed because of its identity with the class struggle, its idealism, and its dedication to a better world. Nonetheless it expired at the end of that decade. The Hitler-Stalin pact and the outbreak of the Second World War dispersed the allegiances, activities, and hopes of the Artef Theatre Collective—it failed to reopen in 1940. Remnants of the Artef tried sporadically to revive its program until 1953.

The pluralism and the democracy of the Yiddish stage was manifest at the ten-year jubilee of Artef in 1937. Schwartz rejected the polemical, agit-prop theatre of the Artef, and the Artef despised the Schwartz's middle-class Yiddish Art Theatre; yet at the podium of the Artef's celebration, Schwartz was honored as an important figure in Jewish culture.

Other Art Theatres

Meanwhile in Europe, a few troupes and clubs became the torchbearers of the truly artistic theatre aspirations of the Jews. The Hirshbein Troupe and the Kaminsky Troupe toured the Pale of Russia and Poland; they offered the ghetto-captive Jews drama distilled out of the ferment of their proscribed lives and in a style comparable with that of the famous Moscow Art Theatre. A hard core of intellectuals stirred considerable interest in these groups. These same intellectuals, in America, had a contempt for the vaudeville style of the Yiddish theatre, from which they absented themselves while they agitated in the press for better theatre. Both press and intellectuals characteristically were didactic in their efforts to uplift the masses and spread culture.

Around New York, in Brooklyn and in the Bronx, a few Yiddish theatres tried to establish themselves. In the Bronx, Unzer Teater was the most noteworthy. In addition to its distinguished board of directors, which included Pinski, Hirshbein, and Mestel, this theatre had the genius Boris Aronson as its scene designer.

MUSICAL COMEDY, VAUDEVILLE, AND THE "BORSCHT CIRCUIT"

Thus far, little has been said of the musical comedy and Yiddish variety theatre. From the very beginning of the professional Yiddish theatre, however, musical shows were ever present and robustly "packed them in," as the Jewish populace, like any other ethnic group, sought comedy, music, and dance as its entertainment. Goldfaden started with operettas, and his successors expanded this genre. The quality of the successors' offerings was of a low vaudeville type, replete with vulgarity and crude caricatures of Jewish types. Often the fare was sentimental and pandered to the lowest common denominator of taste; the cliche formula was to provide the audience with "laughter and tears." Almost all plays of this type had obligatory wedding scenes, Bar Mitzvah celebrations, even *brisses* (circumcision ceremonies).

Starting with the popular comic Sigmund Mogulesco, the first professional Yiddish actor, a long list of popular musical comedy stars enjoyed phenomenal success because of individual styles that endeared them to their audiences.

Aaron Lebedeff, Molly Picon, Menasha Shkulnick, the Burstein Family, Leo Fuchs, and Jacob Jacobs are a few of the stars whose antics beguiled this wide and loyal audience.

During the summer months, many of the musical comedy stars sustained themselves and brought their talents to vacationing Jews in the Catskill Mountains, known as the "borscht circuit." The Catskill Mountain hotel resorts were owned and principally patronized by Jews. Most of them served kosher food, and beet borscht was a staple on the menu. Hence, the derivation of the term.

What has happened to entertainment in the "borscht circuit" is an indication of what has happened to the Yiddish theatre. The Catskill resorts have become Americanized to the extent of featuring headline entertainers who are television stars, Broadway personalities, and rock singers. Yiddish entertainment as such has almost disappeared.

ACTORS

Before the Yiddish art theatre movement developed, Yiddish actors were for the most part strutting characters out of *mittle*-European operettas. They were usually uneducated, so they could rarely be expected to read and memorize a script with any reasonable fidelity. Nonetheless, a Yiddish actor had a special world view that made him "well aware of the specific Jewish, as well as the general, social problems of his time."[71] Despite the gaucheries of many of the actors, some of the stars appeared in public with an assumed dignity, in flamboyant dress that included romantic capes and walking sticks, topped off with black fedora hats worn at rakish angles. When the Schildkraut came to New York in 1909 and referred to himself as a *schauspieler*, this new (originally German) appellation for "actor" displaced the ordinary "player" or "actor."

Actors were drawn to the theatre from every area of life, but actresses were another matter: an actress was considered nothing short of a fallen woman. Sophie Karp was the first Yiddish actress. She overcame her mother's objections by marrying Sacher Goldstein, in Goldfaden's troupe. She was the first of many great stars, such as Keni Liptzin, Jennie Goldstein, Picon, Bertha Gerstein, Kalish, and Celia Adler.

Early Yiddish actors had little grace, little charm, little intellectual stature,[72] and no pride in their art. As I pointed out earlier in this chapter, they would get the audience involved in their private scandals, get married on stage and invite the audience, and interpolate into a play their private quarrels.

Prior to the formation of the Hebrew Actors Union (1899), actors received from $6 to $8 per week, while featured actors were paid from $14 to $75 per week; stars such as Jacob P. Adler and his wife received as much as $125 per week per couple.[73] Each theatre operated as though it were a cooperative, but actually it was subject to the whim or greed of its star or manager. The distribution of the box office "take" gave the major percentages to authors, directors, and stars. The lesser actors received their "mark" portion after the foregoing payments and the fixed expenses of rent, heat, light, advertising, and other operating costs.

Principal actors also received money from "benefit" performances. These were usually for featured actors and not for actors who played minor roles. The star selected the play for his or her own benefit, and the entire company participated. The beneficiary of these benefits usually selected his or her vehicle. Thus in one year (1918–1919) the troupe at the Irving Place Theatre (Schwartz's troupe prior to its becoming The Yiddish Art Theatre) appeared in these benefits for stars: Bertha Gerstein in *Hedda Gabler*, Appel in *Mrs. Warren's Profession*, Satz in *Der Oytser* (The Treasure), Schwartz in Schnitzler's *Professor Bernhardi* and Wilde's *An Ideal Husband*, Ben-Ami in Sven Lange's *Samson and Delilah*, and Celia Adler in Sudermann's *Battle of the Butterflies*.

Rehearsals for these benefits had to be done in snatches; thus line-perfect performances were rare. As a result the actors depended upon the prompter, for they did not respect the script. In about 1920 the Jewish Art Theatre eliminated the promptor's box and its actors were obliged to be absolutely line perfect.

There were strikes by actors from 1887 through 1902. The Yiddish actors formed a union in 1899. Compared with prevailing rates in industry, the actors were well paid. The contract Thomashevsky signed with the union reveals the behavior patterns of actors: he insisted that they be prompt at rehearsals, not "indulge in unseemly epithets" to "insure their ease and dignity and to protect them from harsh words." He gloated because the actors now received less than under the old system.[74]

Many of the actors would spend the summer in the Catskill Mountains, where they would entertain summer boarders. The *Forwards* (a Yiddish newspaper with a large circulation) of June 28, 1918, reported that Thomashevsky's theatre would operate during the summer with a combination of movies, one-act plays, and vaudeville, while Gabel's theatre would feature Gabel's play *Price of a Girl's Good Time*. Some minor actors earned as little as three dollars per week in the summer season.

Necessary though the union was for the protection of the actors, it also placed obstacles in the path of better Yiddish theatre. The "closed shop" of the Hebrew Actors Union made it almost impossible for new, young actors to enter the Yiddish theatre. The "walking delegate . . . passes upon the cast of every play. . . . Most of the members are . . . too old to play ingenues or juvenile characters. . . . The actual working conditions . . . prevent the development of new talent."[75] "Even if the play is *King Lear*, *The Power of Darkness*, or *The God of Vengeance*, a chorus of eight with their dressers has to be engaged, . . . a bearded patriarch sent to play Romeo, or a dumpy dowager, Juliet."[76] Actors formed cooperatives to circumvent the union, but to no avail.

The Yiddish acting art had its roots in the sentimental, banal, tear-in-eye song for an aged mother or poor orphan, for the poor worker, or for the daughter of Zion. The actors would interpolate their specialties, such as monologues or songs. As in the American theatre of our day, comedy was more popular than tragedy. Withal, despite its primitive form, the Yiddish theatre had a folksy charm. Folk types became the chief portrayals, even when the theatre turned to realism with a poetic pathos. Drawing-room sophistication and stylized genres were alien to the Yiddish actor. Visiting troupes, such as the Vilna Troupe and the Habima, influenced acting styles not only in the Yiddish theatre but also on the American stage.

With happy strokes of characterization of well-known ghetto types, in sordid scenes faithful to life, the actors, lacking self-consciousness, played with a naturalness that seemed realistic. The audience approved with "So true, so natural"—praise indeed. "At its best, acting on the Yiddish stage reaches a high level; at its worst it is usually better than bad acting elsewhere."[77]

Ensemble acting, a desired style achieved in a company that acted together in repertory, was a distinguishing feature of the Yiddish stage. Despite this desired style, a play about one family that had never left its shtetl might be played by actors from different European regions, each actor speaking in his or her native dialect. Incongruous and absurd, this situation was maintained until about 1919, when a concerted effort was made to standardize stage Yiddish. The resulting language pattern was a Volhynian dialect that eschewed Litvak, Galitzian, Polish, and the pretentious Daeitschmeirish. Unconsciously, many Jews who spoke different dialects began to follow the stage pattern.

The universal urge of people to flock to the theatre to see a famous personality was too true of Yiddish theatre, which survived with a powerful star system. The Yiddish theatre had become over-galaxied with stars, who eclipsed efforts at better theatre. The playwrights catered to the stars by concocting plays that suited the particular stars' personalities or specialities. In addition to dictating the selection of a play, the star would domineer a subservient troupe because he or she was the main attraction to bring in the public. Stars rarely appeared in roles identified with the lower classes, until the Folksbuehne and Artef offered plays with proletarian heroes.

The post-Gordin years witnessed a growing interest in plays of literary and artistic worth rather than in plays as vehicles for stars. Individual stars also responded to the ideals of the ensemble repertoire. Thus from the beginning of this century to 1918, the year of the start of the Yiddish art theatre movement, stars, among whom were Jacob P. Adler, David Kessler, Liptzin, Samuel Goldenberg, and Ben-Ami, encouraged better drama whenever possible. Ben-Ami succeeded in bringing the professional Yiddish theatre to its highest artistic achievement. The actors not only offered the public their dramatic creativity, but as popular personalities, enticed the masses to the theatre.

ACTOR-MANAGERS

A handful of prominent actors, realizing the shortcomings of the star system, tried and partly succeeded in achieving better theatre. The few of these were actor-managers, who combined their artistic strivings with the toughness needed to survive the constant scrounging for funds and the recurring negotiations with unions or theatre owners. Showing astuteness in the selection of plays, they were also versatile and resilient as actors, directors, and impresarios. The first impresario in the Yiddish theatre in America was the talented, inventive, and ingenious youth Boris Thomashevsky (1868–1939). He was the matinee idol of the early *shund* stage. When he became a star, he took his salary in gold for his money belt, was the first of the Yiddish stage luminaries to ride a chauffeur-driven limousine, and employed a valet. Lateiner wrote vehicles for him alone, plays that appealed to the masses. Despite his exploitation of the commercial theatre, he did try to improve and enrich the Yiddish theatre: he tried to present new and unproven playwrights; he was the first to present plays by the excellent Ossip Dymov, the author of *Bronx Express;* he produced Gordin's plays when others would not; he produced Kobrin's plays; he brought new talent from Europe, actors as well as playwrights, such as both Schildkrauts (Rudolph and Joseph), Dymov, Jacob Ben-Ami, Samuel Goldenberg, Michael Michaelesco, Aaron Lebedeff, and the Vilna Troupe. He also tried, unsuccessfully, to bring the Yiddish theatre to Broadway (1923).

From the 1930s on, the most popular personality in the Yiddish theatre has been Maurice Schwartz (1890–1960). At first the actors' union refused to admit him, but he succeeded in having Cahan persuade the union to give him an audition. After acting in various clubs and with star companies such as Kessler's, he first commanded attention in 1918 when he founded the Irving Place Theatre, which he claimed would present only better theatre. Actually, he started his first season with another melodrama, but due to the urgings of Ben-Ami, he also presented Hirshbein's *Favorfen Vinkel;* this immediately became a success and started two decades of folk theatre that has been termed "the Yiddish art theatre movement" by scholars. Two years later Schwartz changed the name of his troupe to the Yiddish Art Theatre, and it continued under that name until he officially disbanded it in 1950.

During its three decades of activity, the Yiddish Art Theatre produced new and classic plays from both the Yiddish and world repertoires. Its catholic variety featured Shaw, Ibsen, Toller, Hirshbein, Asch, Ansky, Kobrin, Pinski, Klabund, Andreyev, Schnitzler, Gordin, Schiller, and other famous writers.

The demise of the Yiddish Art Theatre was the bellwether of the decline of Yiddish theatre as a whole. In addition to the shrinking of the first-generation Yiddish-speaking audience due to death and flight to the suburbs, competition by radio and talking films, the Depression, and World War II, the high cost of productions hastened the end. Because of excessive production costs, Schwartz abandoned the one distinctive feature of the Yiddish theatre: the repertory system. Under this system, audiences had been able to attend the Yiddish theatre many times during a season and see from ten to twenty plays. Schwartz was obliged to try to extend the "run" of each play, so that his devotees would see but one or two productions a season. His success with Israel Joshua Singer's *Yoshe Kalb* (1932) enabled him to offer over 300 successive performances; then he took the success on the road and played in many cities in this country, in Europe, and in South America. Alas, this success contributed to the inevitable end of the Yiddish Art Theatre, for the loyal audiences would not abide one play a season; they sought theatre on Broadway instead.

Not happy with Schwartz's protean accommodations to commercial and art theatre, Ben-Ami and a group of other dissidents left the Irving Place venture and launched the Jewish Art Theatre (1919). Intent upon a stage career in Russia, Jacob Ben-Ami (1890–1977) had refused to abandon Judaism in order to qualify for the Russian stage. He had served his apprenticeship in the Hirshbein Troupe and had come to New York at the eve of World War I, where he directed and appeared with amateur groups until he joined Schwartz as the company's young leading man. When Ben-Ami's Jewish Art Theatre opened, it was hailed as "the noblest theatrical enterprise existing among us."[78] His debut in the American theatre, however, was at the Neighborhood Playhouse, where he established his reputation as a director.

Acclaimed by both theatre professionals and the public as a "prince among players," Ben-Ami showed his artistic integrity when he voluntarily took a cut in salary in order to induce Schwartz to present better theatre. The play, in 1918, was Hirshbein's *Farvorfen Vinkel*; its production was the start of the "second golden epoch," or Yiddish art theatre movement. Different and apart from other actors,[79] he demonstrated his artistic integrity by appearing only in meritorious plays with literary content.

Internal dissension in the new Jewish Art Theatre obliged Ben-Ami to succumb to the blandishments of starring roles (in English) on Broadway in Arthur Hopkins's productions of Lange's *Samson and Delilah*, Hirshbein's *The Idle Inn*, Toller's *Masse Mensch*, O'Neill's *Welded*, and others. He joined Eva La Gallienne at the Civic Repertory Company, where he gave memorable performances in Chekhov's *The Cherry Orchard* and *The Sea Gull*, Tolstoy's *The Living Corpse*, and in plays by Shakespeare, Schnitzler, Giradoux, and Dumas. He also directed for the Theatre Guild. Periodically, during the late 1920s and through the 1930s and 1940s, he formed different companies, which he directed or in which he appeared in the Yiddish theatre. Despite his success on the Broadway stage, unlike Paul Muni, who abandoned his origins in the Yiddish theatre, until his death Ben-Ami continually devoted himself to the Yiddish theatre.

SCENE DESIGNERS

Scene designers in the Yiddish theatre were the innovators in America of new concepts of scenic art; they found the Yiddish theatre to be a most rewarding laboratory for experimental approaches. Leve, Aronson, and Gorelick found a Yiddish theatre with a hodge-podge of scenery that often consisted of hand-me-downs from productions of the Metropolitan Opera Company or Broadway theatres. They also found attempts at realism, as well as imitations of European "art" styles.

The first staff scenic designer in the Yiddish theatre was Leon Foshko at the Jewish Art Theatre. The other designers were definitely influenced by the European theatre, even to the architecture of the stage; the Yiddish Art Theatre had the first revolving stage in America. Expressionism, first used by Chagall in the Yiddish theatre in Russia, became a vogue to express not only the play's ideological theme but also the eerie mood and atmosphere. The effects employed prismatic walls, warped stairways, chairs and tables slanting toward the audience, spotlights strategically hidden to create bizarre, unearthly effects. These devices were most theatrical, if not entirely expressionistic. Moe Solatoroff, the scene designer for the Artef, created some of the most effective scenery seen on any stage. Gorelick, in his excellent book *New Theatres for Old*, named this unique style Hassidic Grotesque. Leve, Aronson, and Gorelick went on to enrich the American stage and to win laurels for themselves.

DECLINE OF THE YIDDISH THEATRE

The decline of the Yiddish theatre in New York and the rest of America was occasioned by forces it could not control as well as by those within its matrix. Within the Yiddish theatre, the high cost of production obliged producers such as Schwartz to aim for long runs. This alienated an audience accustomed to the repertory system, whereby many plays could be seen in one season. Also within the theatre, after the drastic curtailment of immigration to this country early in the 1920s, new actors and playwrights were no longer available for the Yiddish theatre—Schwartz could not find any Yiddish-speaking youths to cast in his plays; he resorted to buxom women to play young boys.[80] The immigration laws also shut off the source of Yiddish-speaking audiences, preventing the influx of those who might have settled on the East Side of New York and patronized the Yiddish theatre. Actors abandoned the Yiddish theatre to seek more rewarding careers in television or films.

Perhaps a theatre cannot exist in a metropolitan center without a star. When Yiddish actors such as Paul Muni were enticed by the blandishments of film, their departure impoverished the Yiddish theatre. Their lack of loyalty to their roots, to their friends, and to their culture due to their opportunism intensified the crisis. Because of restrictive immigration laws, there were no new, young Yiddish actors to replace them.

The melancholy story of the decline of the Yiddish theatre is perhaps no different from that of any other ethnic group that has tried to continue its folkways in this land. The first-generation Jews who used the currency of the Yiddish language have either died or dispersed to the suburbs, from which it is difficult to come to the remnants of New York's Yiddish Broadway on Second Avenue. The societies that supported the Yiddish theatre through the purchase of benefits have almost disappeared, while organizations such as synagogue or temple groups buy their benefits for plays on Broadway.

A particularly telling blow to the Yiddish theatre was the destruction of the *shtetl* in the crossfire between the German Nazis and the Stalin forces. The *shtetl* was the locale of the greatest folk plays in the Yiddish repertoire; it was the school of the Yiddish playwrights, the source of the Yiddish audience, and the laboratory of the Yiddish actors. Finally, the goals of those who were investors in the Yiddish theatre have changed. Since 1948 those who had been devoted to this part of Jewish culture have channeled money to the state of Israel, to colleges such as Brandeis, and to the many temples and Jewish centers that have proliferated since World War II. The dwindling box office receipts were not enough to cover mounting production costs.

Since Schwartz's death in 1960, no individual has come forth to stimulate interest in the continuation of the Yiddish theatre. What of the future without this monolithic figure? In 1979 the Folksbuehne still continued, but its audiences were almost all old people—Who will replace them?—and no new, young actors.

The blessed Folksbuehne stalwartly refuses to hear the tolling funeral bell. It is the torchbearer of a light that once illuminated not only the East Side enclave of Jews, but the world theatre. It continues to reverse the exodus to the suburbs by having in its audiences theatre lovers from all over the United States, even though their children and grandchildren are either assimilated or know no Yiddish. Young people at performances are a rarity. The Folksbuehne appears doomed beyond its present generation.

Leo Weiner's prophecy of 1898 that within less than ten years there would no longer be anything written in Yiddish, whether prose, poetry, or drama,[81] was proven wrong, but only in terms of time. Other than Chaim Sloves in Paris, no playwright is writing in Yiddish. Perhaps, as is evident from *Fiddler on the Roof* and from a few troupes who are producing Yiddish classics in English, future gems from the Yiddish repertoire may shine again in translation.

THE FUTURE OF THE YIDDISH THEATRE

Much has been made of the assertion that Yiddish theatre lives on in English in plays by and about Jews on the American stage. Clifford Odets, Paddy Chayevsky, and Arthur Miller are among those indicated as giving artistic expression to Jewish life in America.[82] These writers were undoubtedly influenced by their sectarian background, but the fact is that their work is not in Yiddish for the Yiddish theatre. This effort to bring Jewish content into American drama reached its apogee during the late 1930s, when the Federal Theatre Project translated and produced Odets's *Awake and Sing* and Sinclair Lewis's *It Can't Happen Here* in addition to Yiddish-language plays. The project consciously tried to "revive and perpetuate that creative spirit which distinguished the Jewish theatre.[83]

The frightening revival of anti-Semitism in Poland after World War II obliged Ida Kaminska and her troupe from the State Yiddish Theatre in Warsaw to flee to America. Other than Brecht's *Mother Courage*, the company's repertoire consisted of revivals of old-fashioned melodramas selected as obvious vehicles for its star. The company barely survived a season in New York. The struggle for security, for acceptance, for a place in their new world has confronted all immigrants of whatever national and ethnic origin. For millennia the Jews had encountered this struggle more than any other people. The Jewish actors had suffered hardships under a czar, and this inspired them to an extent that their theatre seemed impregnable. Under an alien climate, with no outside help, the courageous Yiddish theatre actors, writers, and directors succeeded for three quarters of a century in their mission. They brought forth phenomenal acting talents, creative directors, and new theatre art forms; added the poetic, epic, and folk dramas of distinguished playwrights to the world repertoire; and built an audience—they created a theatre[84] that enriched American culture.

The lifeblood of the Yiddish theatre now flows in the American theatre. In addition to its contributions of talent and art to the American stage, Yiddish theatre educated and elevated the Jewish immigrant masses. It cannot be dismissed as a transient phenomenon of a culture within a culture: even if it disappears as a functioning theatre in the Yiddish language, it will remain a significant part of the American theatre.

NOTES

1. The first Yiddish theatre presentation in America was in 1882; in 1950 the Yiddish Art Theatre officially ceased activity.

2. Allardyce Nicoll, World Drama (New York: Harcourt, Brace and Co., 1950), p. 879.

3. Bernard Gorin, The History of the Yiddish Theatre, in Yiddish (New York: Max N. Maisel, 1923), Vol. 1, p. 12.

4. Ibid., pp. 43–50.

5. For a history of Hebrew and Israeli drama and theatre, see George Freedley and John A. Reeves, A History of the Theatre (New York: Crown Publishers, 1968), Vol. 23, pp. 804–10.

6. New York Times, January 11, 1908.

7. New York Times, January 12, 1908.

8. Alexander Mukdoiny, Goldfaden Book (in Yiddish, New York: Jewish Theatre Museum, 1926), pp. 6–8.

9. Hutchins Hapgood, The Spirit of the Ghetto (New York: Funk and Wagnalls Co. 1902), p. 165.

10. Isaac Goldberg, The Drama of Transition (Cincinnati, Ohio: Stewart Kidd Co., 1922), pp. 344 ff.

11. The star or producer, often the same person, frequently appeared during the intermission or at curtain call to make a dramatic speech asserting the dedication of his troupe to better theatre.

12. Jacob Mestel, Unzer Teater, in Yiddish (New York: Yiddisher Kultur Farband, 1954), pp. 55–57.

13. Charles Madison, "The Yiddish Theatre," Poet Lore 32 (Winter 1921): 497–559.

14. Hapgood, Spirit of the Ghetto, pp. 123–24.

15. Madison, "The Yiddish Theatre," p. 510.

16. Gorin, History of the Yiddish Theatre, Vol. 2, pp. 122–24.

17. Goldberg, Drama of Transition, p. 358.

18. Quoted in Hapgood, Spirit of the Ghetto, p. 128.

19. Gorin, History of the Yiddish Theatre, Vol. 2, pp. 122–24.

20. Aaron B. Seidman, "The First Performance of Yiddish Theatre in America," Jewish Social Studies 10 (January 1948): 67–70. Various historians offer different dates: George C. Odell, Annals of the New York Stage (New York: Columbia University Press, 1939), Vol. 11, pp. 509–10 suggests September 1882; Hershel Zohn, "A Survey of the Yiddish Theatre" (master's thesis, University of Denver, 1949), p. 25, indicates July 1882; other historians, such as Zalman Zylbercwaig and Jacob Mestel, Lexicon of the Yiddish Theatre (in Yiddish, New York: Hebrew Actors Union, 1931–1967), pp. 805–806, offer no definite date.

21. New York Sun, February 22, 1885.

22. Philip S. Foner, Jews in American History: 1654–1865 (New York: International Publishers, 1945), p. 43.

23. Max Raisin, A History of the Jews in Modern Times (New York: Hebrew Publishing Company, 1949), pp. 193–96.

24. Frances Jerome Woods, Cultural Values of American Ethnic Groups (New York: Harper and Brothers, 1956), pp. 140–41.

25. Ludwig Lewisohn, The Answer (New York: Liveright, 1939), p. 287; Mark Zborowski and Elizabeth Herzog, Life Is with People (New York: International Universities Press, 1955), p. 21.

26. Joshua A. Fishman, "Cross-Cultural Perspectives on the Evaluation of Guided Behavioral Change," in Evaluation of Teaching (Washington, D.C.: Pi Lambda Theta, 1967), pp. 9–31.

27. Margaret Mead, foreword to Zborowski and Herzog, Life Is with People, p. 16.

28. Samuel J. Citron, "Yiddish and Hebrew Drama," in Barrett H. Clark and George Freedley, eds., A History of Modern Drama (New York: D. Appleton-Century, 1947), p. 605.

29. Ibid., p. 609.

30. Gorin, History of the Yiddish Theatre, Vol. 2, p. 9.

31. Henry James, The American Scene (New York: Harper and Brothers, 1907), pp. 197 ff.

32. Hapgood, Spirit of the Ghetto, pp. 113 ff.

33. Rachel Crothers, "Four Kinds of Audiences," Drama Magazine 10 (October 1919): 273–74.

34. Dan Wakefield, "New York's Lower East Side Today," Commentary 27 (June 1959): 461–71.

35. Hapgood, Spirit of the Ghetto, p. 118.

36. Woods, Cultural Values, p. 265.

37. Gorin, History of the Yiddish Theatre, Vol. 2, p. 24.

38. Carl Van Vechten, In the Garret (New York: Knopf, 1920), p. 325.

39. Mestel, Unzer Teater, p. 60.

40. S. L. Blumenson, "The Golden Age of Thomashevsky," Commentary 12 (January–June 1952): 344.

41. Hapgood, Spirit of the Ghetto, p. 116.

42. Joseph Schildkraut, My Father and I, edited by Leo Lania (New York: Viking Press, 1959), pp. 121–22.

43. *Der Volks Advokat*, November 23, 1888.

44. Moyshe Katz, "Yankev Gordin und di Yiddishe Buehne (Jacob Gordin and the Yiddish Buehne)," in *Tzu Yankev Gordin's Tsen Yorigen Yubileyum* (To Jacob Gordin's Ten Year Jubilee) (in Yiddish, New York: privately published, 1901), pp. 12–14.

45. *Der Volks Advokat*, November 16, 1888.

46. *Der Volks Advokat*, November 30, 1888.

47. Abraham Cahan, *Arbeiter Tzeitung*, July 19 and 26 and December 25, 1895.

48. *Arbeiter Tzeitung*, September 12, 1890.

49. Clayton M. Hamilton, *Seen on the Stage* (New York: Henry Holt and Co., 1920), pp. 177 ff.

50. Konrad Bercovici, "Greatest Jewish City in the World," *Nation* 117 (September 12, 1923): 259–61.

51. Ibid.

52. *Encyclopaedia Britannica*, 14th ed., Vol. 13, p. 892.

53. Samuel Niger, "Yiddish Culture," in B. Abramovich et al., eds., *The Jewish People: Past and Present* (New York: Central Yiddish Cultural Organization, 1946), pp. 279–80.

54. Zohn, "Survey," p. 47.

55. Citron, "Yiddish and Hebrew Drama," p. 619.

56. Isaac Goldberg, *Drama of Transition*, p. 360.

57. Hapgood, *Spirit of the Ghetto*, pp. 168–69.

58. Goldberg, *Drama of Transition*, p. 358.

59. Samuel Niger, "Yiddish Culture," pp. 293–94.

60. Alexander Mukdoiny, *Teater*, in Yiddish (New York: Mukdoiny Jubilee Committee, 1927), pp. 31–33.

61. Madison, "The Yiddish Theatre," p. 512.

62. Leo Wiener, *The History of Yiddish Literature in the Nineteenth Century* (New York: Charles Scribner's Sons, 1899), p. 110.

63. Gilbert Seldes, "Jewish Plays and Jew Plays in New York," *Menorah Journal* 8 (August 1922): 236–40.

64. Mestel, *Unzer Teater*, p. 77.

65. Ibid., pp. 165–69.

66. Hillel Zolataroff, *Collected Writings*, in Yiddish, edited by Joel Enteen (New York: Levant Press, 1924), p. 1285.

67. A. H. Bialin, *Maurice Schwartz and the Yiddish Art Theatre*, in Yiddish (Jersey City, N.J.: Posy-Shoulson Press, 1934), p. 7.

68. Ben Blake, *The Awakening of the American Theatre* (New York: Tomorrow Publishers, 1939), p. 9.

69. John Howard Lawson, "An Inspiration and an Example," in Yiddish, in *Ten Years Artef*, in Yiddish and English (New York: Artef, 1937), p. 6.

70. Nathaniel Buchwald, "The Artistic Road to Artef," in *Ten Years Artef*, pp. 27–44.

71. Raiken Ben-Ari, *Habima*, translated by A. H. Gross and I. Soref (New York: Thomas Yoseloff, 1957), p. 200.

72. Crothers, "Four Kinds of Audiences," pp. 273–74.

73. Hapgood, *Spirit of the Ghetto*, pp. 119–20.

74. Ibid.

75. *New York Tribune*, August 20, 1919.

76. Oliver M. Sayler, *Our American Theatre* (New York: Brentano's, 1923), p. 276.

77. Van Vechten, *In the Garret*, p. 325.

78. Ludwig Lewisohn, "Drama—The Jewish Art Theatre," *Nation* 109 (December 13, 1919): 47–48.

79. Celia Adler, *Celia Adler Recalls*, in Yiddish (New York: Celia Adler Foundation and Book Committee, 1959), pp. 431–33.

80. Maurice Schwartz, interview with author. See also David Lifson, *The Yiddish Theatre in America* (New York: Thomas Yoseloff, 1965), p. 561.

81. Wiener, *History of Yiddish Literature*, p. 229.

82. Joseph Mersand, *American Drama Presents the Jew* (New York: Modern Chapbooks, 1939), passim; David Streinberg, "Jewish Theatre Is Thriving in Varied Broadway Forms," *Jewish News*, June 2, 1961.

83. Benson Inge, foreword to *Anglo-Jewish Plays*, edited by Inge (New York: National Service Bureau, Federal Theatre Project, 1938), no. 20-S.

84. Mestel, *Unzer Teater*, pp. 77–79.

BIBLIOGRAPHY

Books

Abramovitch, R., et al., eds. *The Jewish People: Past and Present.* 4 vols. New York: Central Yiddish Culture Organization, Jewish Encyclopedic Handbooks, 1946. A general reference.

Adler, Celia. *Celia Adler Recalls.* In Yiddish. 2 vols. New York: Celia Adler Foundation and Book Committee, 1959. Pungent, detailed, an excellent source.

Ben-Ari, Raiken. *Habima.* Translated by A. H. Gross and I. Soref. New York: Thomas Yoseloff, 1957. Good for ideas on the art of theatre.

Bialin, A. H. *Maurice Schwartz and the Yiddish Art Theatre.* In Yiddish. Jersey City, N.J.: Posy-Shoulson Press, 1934. Self-serving but authentic.

Buchwald, Nathaniel. *Teater.* In Yiddish. New York: Farlag Committee, 1943. Good source on philosophy of art in Yiddish theatre.

Cahan, Abraham. *Bletter fun Mein Lebn.* In Yiddish. 4 vols. New York: Forwartz Association, 1926. No better background exists on the Jewish ghetto in New York City.

Elbogen, Ismar. *A Century of Jewish Life.* Philadelphia: Jewish Publication Society, 1944. Excellent historical background.

Finkelstein, Louis, ed. *The Jews: Their History, Culture, and Religion.* 2 vols. New York: Harper and Brothers, 1955. Very general.

Fishman, Jacob, et al., eds. *Twenty-five Years Folksbuehne.* In Yiddish. New York: privately published, 1940. No history of Yiddish theatre can overlook this source.

Fishman, Joshua A. "Cross-Cultural Perspectives on the Evaluation of Guided Behavioral Change." In *Evaluation of Teaching.* Washington, D.C.: Pi Lambda Theta, 1967, pp. 9–31.

Foner, Philip S. *Jews in American History: 1654–1865.* New York: International Publishers, 1945. General; no relation to theatre.

Goldberg, Isaac. *The Drama of Transition.* Cincinnati, Ohio: Stewart Kidd Co., 1922. Excellent.

Gorin, Bernard. *The History of the Yiddish Theatre.* In Yiddish. 2 vols. New York: Max N. Maisel, 1923. Indispensable basic source.

Hapgood, Hutchins. *The Spirit of the Ghetto.* New York: Funk and Wagnalls Company, 1902. Important contemporary description of early Yiddish theatre in New York. A must.

Joseph, S. *Jewish Immigration to the U.S.A. from 1881–1910.* New York: Columbia University Press, 1914.

Kobrin, Leon. *Memoirs of a Yiddish Dramatist.* In Yiddish. 2 vols. New York: Leon Kobrin Committee, 1925.

————. *My Fifty Years in America.* In Yiddish. Buenes Aires: Idbujade la a Asocicion pro Escuelas Laicas Israelitas, 1955. Important first-hand account.

Landa, M.J. *The Jew in Drama.* New York: William Morrow and Co., 1927. Background on Jews in non-Jewish theatre.

Landis, Joseph C. *The Dybbuk and Other Great Yiddish Plays.* New York: Bantam Books, 1966. Excellent on drama in Yiddish.

Learsi, Rufus (Isaac Goldberg). *The Jews in America.* Cleveland: World Publishing Co., 1954. Historical background.

Lifson, David S. *The Yiddish Theatre in America.* New York: Thomas Yoseloff, 1965. A comprehensive in-depth survey.

————. *Epic and Folk Plays from the Yiddish Theatre.* Cranbury, N.J.: Associated University Presses, 1975.

Maisel, Nachman. *Abraham Goldfadden.* In Yiddish. New York: Yiddish Cooperative Book League, 1938. Important source.

Mersand, Joseph. *American Drama Presents the Jew.* New York: Modern Chapbooks, 1939.

Mestel, Jacob. *Unzer Teater.* In Yiddish. New York: Yiddisher Kultur Farband, 1954. A must.

Miller, James. *The Detroit Yiddish Theatre.* Detroit: Wayne State University Press, 1967.

Mukdoiny, Alexander. *Goldfaden Book.* In Yiddish. New York: Yiddish Theatre Museum, 1926. Also indispensable.

————. *Teater.* In Yiddish. New York: Mukdoiny Jubilee Committee, 1927. Good critical material.

Nicoll, Allardyce. *World Drama.* New York: Harcourt, Brace and Co., 1950. Recognizes poetic drama in Yiddish theatre.

Odell, George C. *Annals of the New York Stage.* Vol. 11. New York: Columbia University Press, 1939.

Pinski, David. *The Treasure.* Translated by Ludwig Lewisohn. New York: B. W. Huebsch, 1915. One of the few Yiddish plays translated into English.

Raisin, Max. *A History of the Jews in Modern Times.* New York: Hebrew Publishing Company, 1949.

Roback, A. A. *The Story of Yiddish Literature.* New York: Yivo, 1940. Good on writers.

Rosenfeld, Lulla. *Bright Star of Exile: Jacob Adler and the Yiddish Theatre.* New York: Thomas Y. Crowell Co., 1977. Although the writing is turgid, the book gives a good idea of the struggles of actors.

Sandrow, Nahma. *Vagabond Stars.* New York: Harper and Row, 1977. Good for chronology and for Yiddish theatre under the Soviets. Poor on important dramatists.

Schildkraut, Joseph. *My Father and I.* Edited by Leo Lania. New York: Viking Press, 1959. Satisfactory source from an actor's point of view.

Ten Years Artef. In Yiddish and English. New York: Artef, 1937. An authentic history.

Thiekel, David Baer. *The Young Stage: A History of the Yiddish-Hebrew Dramatic Societies.* Philadelphia: Federal Press, 1940. Necessary to show how theatre is rooted in the community.

Thomashevsky, Boris. *Book of My Life.* In Yiddish. New York: Boris Thomashevsky, 1937. Self-serving but very good.

Wiener, Leo. *The History of Yiddish Literature in the Nineteenth Century.* New York: Charles Scribner's Sons, 1899.

Woods, Frances Jerome. *Cultural Values of American Ethnic Groups.* New York: Harper and Brothers, 1956.

Yablokoff, Herman. *Around the World with Yiddish Theatre.* 2 vols. In Yiddish. New York: Hebrew Actors Union, 1969. A good yarn from a devoted Yiddishist.

Zangwill, Israel. *The Children of the Ghetto.* New York: Macmillan, 1895.

Zborowski, Mark, and Herzog, Elizabeth. *Life Is with People.* New York: International Universities Press, 1955. The standard and best source on the world of the *shtetl.*

Zolotoroff, Hillel. *Collected Writings.* In Yiddish. Edited by Joel Enteen. New York: Levant Press, 1924.

Zylbercwaig, Zalmen. *Abraham Goldfaden and Zigmund Mogulesco.* In Yiddish. Buenes Aires: Elisheva Verlog, 1936. Good for incidents at the start of Yiddish theatre.

————, and Mestel, Jacob, eds. *Lexicon of the Yiddish Theatre.* In Yiddish. 5 vols. New York: Hebrew Actors Union, 1931–1967. Encyclopedic. The authoritative source for all references.

————. *Teater Mozaik.* In Yiddish. New York: A. W. Biderman, 1941. Also an authoritative source.

All citations in Yiddish are available at Yivo (Jewish Scientific Institute) in New York City.

Chapters in Books

Buchwald, Nathaniel. "Yiddish Writings." In *Cambridge History of American Literature.* Vol. 3. New York: Macmillan, 1947, pp. 598–609. Good précis.

Citron, Samuel J. "Yiddish and Hebrew Drama." In Barrett H. Clark and George Freedley, eds. *A History of Modern Drama.* New York: D. Appleton-Century, 1947, pp. 601–38. Satisfactory encyclopedic treatment.

Gassner, John and David Lifson, Encyclopaedia Judaica, Jerusalem: 1972. Biographies of various Yiddish theatre people.

Katz, Moyshe. "Yankov Gordin und di Yiddishe Buehne," in *Tsu Yankev Gordin's Tsen Yorigen Yubileyum.* In Yiddish. New York; privately published, 1901. Important for Gordin scholars.

Lifson, David S. "Jewish People, Arts of: Dance and Theatre." In *Encyclopaedia Britannica.* 15th ed. 1974, pp. 199–202. Too brief.

————. "The Yiddish Theatre," and "Israel and the Hebrew Theatre." In George Freedley and John A. Reeves, eds. *A History of the Theatre.* Vol. 23. New York: Crown Publishers, 1968, pp. 776–810. Good overview.

Articles in Periodicals

Aidline-Trommer, Elbert. "Yiddish Plays on Broadway," *Jewish Theatrical News* 1–3 (December 1924): 21–22.

Aronson, Boris. "Four Settings for 'Stempenyu the Fiddler'," *Theatre Arts* 13 (August 1929): 565–66.

————. "Two Costumes for the 'Tenth Commandment'," *Theatre Arts* 13 (February 1929): 127.

"Artef Players," *Theatre Arts* 21 (December 1937): 970–75.

"Artistic Triumph of the Jewish Art Theatre," *Current Opinion* 67 (December 1919): 304.

Bechert, Paul. "Habima—A Theatre for the Jewish People," *Theatre* 44 (November 1926): 20–21, 54.

Bercovici, Konrad. "Greatest Jewish City in the World," *Nation* 117 (September 12, 1923): 259–61.

Blumenson, S. L. "The Golden Age of Thomashevsky," *Commentary* 13 (January–June, 1952): 344.

"Boris Aronson," *Theatre Arts* 13 (February 1929): 156.

"Boris Thomashevsky," *Jewish Theatrical News* 1 (May 1925): 6.

Buchwald, Nathaniel. "The Theatre," *New Masses*, March 24, 1936.

"Cast Deserts Swartz" [*sic*]. *Jewish Theatrical News* 1 (November 1924): 24.

Clurman, Harold. "Critique of the American Theatre," *Drama Magazine* 21 (April 1931): 5–6, 12, 18.

Corbin, John. "Drama and the Jew," *Scribner's Magazine* 93 (May 1933): 295–300.

————. "Drama Review," *Current Opinion* 66 (March 1919): 166–67.

Crothers, Rachel. "Four Kinds of Audiences," *Drama Magazine* 10 (May 1920): 273–75.

Crystal, Leon. "Maurice Schwartz," *Jewish Forum* 30 (February 1947): 25.

Dickinson, T. H. "The Jew and the Theatre," *Current Opinion* 75 (October 1923): 459–60.

———. "The Jew in the Theatre," *Nation* 116 (June 13, 1923): 689–91.

Drucker, Rebecca. "The Jewish Art Theatre," *Theatre Arts* 4 (July 1920): 221–24.

The Dybbuk, various reviews and critiques: *Arts & Decoration* 24 (February 1926): 66; *Catholic World*, February 1926; *Dial* 80 (March 1926): 255–59; *Drama Calendar* 9 (December 27, 1926): 7, 14; *Dramatic Mirror* 84 (September 17, 1921): 413; *Literary Digest* 88 (January 23, 1926): 29; *Nation* 122 (January 6, 1926): 16–19; *New Republic*, January 6, 1926; *Survey* 55 (February 1, 1926): 572.

Elkin, Mendel. "Fada," *Boden Journal* (in Yiddish) 3 (spring-summer 1936): 105–132.

Enteen, Joel. "The New Theatre Season," *Tzukumft* (in Yiddish) 24 (September 1919): 573–75.

Eustis, Morton. "Paul Muni," *Theatre Arts* 24 (March 1940): 194–205.

Foster, Joseph. "A Goldfaden Dream," *New Masses* 49 (December 14, 1943): 29–30.

Fuchs, James. "Future Extinction of the Yiddish Language," *Literary Digest* 62 (September 13, 1919): 31.

Glazer, Leon. "Schwartz's Role in the Yiddish Theatre," *New Yorker Vokhenblatt* (in Yiddish) 26 (June 1960): 6–7.

Gold, Mike. "East Side Memories," *American Mercury* 18 (September 1929): 95–101.

Goldberg, Isaac. "The Fate of Yiddish," *New Palestine* 16 (March 1, 1929): 175–76.

———. "The Story of the Yiddish Theatre," *Bookman* 49 (March 1919): 75–76.

Golden, Harry. "The Story of the Yiddish Stage," *Variety* 221 (January 4, 1961): 260.

Gorelik, Mordecai. "Two Settings for 'God, Man, and the Devil'," *Theatre Arts* 13 (February 1929): 91–92.

"Great Romantic Drama of the Chosen People," *Literary Digest* 116 (July 22, 1933): 15.

"The Great World Theatre: The Habima on Grand Street," *Theatre Arts* 11 (November 1927): 810–11.

Grossman, Samuel. "The Jewish Art Theatre Movement and the Playwright," *Reflex* 1 (November 1927): 59–63.

"Habimah Players from Russia," *Literary Digest* 91 (November 29, 1926): 33–34.

Heidenheim, Alice von. "Theatre," *Nation* 118 (June 25, 1924): 745.

Histrionicus. "The Jewish Little Theatre: An Experiment," *Reflex* 4 (February 1929): 44–47.

"'Idle Inn' by Peretz Hirshbein," *Arts & Decoration* 12 (November 1919): 31.

"ILGWU Players," *Theatre Arts* 22 (January 1938): 4.

"In Praise of the Folksbuene," *Workmen's Circle Call* 12 (January 1944): 3.

"The Jew in America," *Nation* 116 (May 16, 1923): 572–73.

"The Jew in the American Theatre," *Current Opinion* 75 (October 1923): 459–60.

"The Jewish Art Theatre," *Nation* 109 (September 6, 1919): 344.

"Jewish Contribution to Progress in America," *School and Society* 41 (April 27, 1935): 564–65.

"Jewish Recreation in New York," *Survey* 45 (January 29, 1921): 632–33.

Jewish Theatrical News, December 1924–April, 1926.

Kaye, J. "New York's Yiddish Art Theatre," *Theatre* 45 (February 1927): 10, 54.

Kornbluth, Z., and Adler, Jacob P. The Actor and Man," *Tzukumft* (in Yiddish) 31 (June 1926): 365–66.

Kornfield, Muriel G. "Drama and the Jew," *Hebrew Standard* 76 (November 5, 1920): 4–6.

Landman, Isaac. "Jews and the Present Day Dramatic Art," *Jewish Exponent* 48 (November 20, 1908): 1.

"Lateiner Writes Plays." *Jewish Theatrical News* 1 (October 1, 1924): 8.

Levinger, Elma Ehrlich. "The Jews in America," *Forum* 79 (May 1928): 736–43.

Levy, W. "History of Hebrew Theatre," *Drama Magazine* 7 (Winter 1947): 13–18.

Lewisohn, Ludwig. Weekly theatre reviews in *Nation* 109–116 (December 13, 1919–June 13, 1923).

"The Little Theatre of the Ghetto," *American Hebrew* 108 (April 1, 1921): 545.

Lozawicz, Louis. "Chagall's Circus," *Theatre Arts* 13 (August 1929): 593–601.

Lyon, Mabel. "Some Recent Plays of Jewish Interest," *Jewish Exponent* 58 (October 17, 1913): 1–2.

Madison, Charles. "The Yiddish Theatre," *Poet Lore* 32 (Winter 1921): 497–519.

Mercur, William. "The Yiddish Art Theatre," *Jewish Forum* 30 (February 1947): 27.

Mersand, Joseph. "The American Drama Presents the Jew," *Advocate* 94 (March 11, 1938): 2; 94 (March 18, 1938): 2.

———. "Curtain Call," *Advocate* 94 (August 19, 1938): 3.

———. "The Jew in Contemporary American Drama," *Jewish Outlook* 3 (November 1938): 8–12.

———. "The Triumph of the Yiddish Art Theatre," *Advocate* 94 (November 11, 1938): 4, 19.

Mestel, Jacob. "Teater: Stage Drama," *Buden* (in Yiddish) 1 (1934): 73–94.

———. "Vegn A Yiddisher Teater und Shprach Conference" (About a Yiddish Theatre and Language Conference), *Der Oefcum* (in Yiddish) 2 (November 1927): 39–41.

"The Modjacot Speel," *Jewish Theatrical News* 2 (April 13, 1926): 3.

"Must Broadway Take a Back Seat?" *Literary Digest* 94 (August 13, 1932): 14–15.

"New York Side Shows," *Literary Digest* 68 (March 12, 1921): 29–30.

"Night in the Old Market," *Theatre Arts* 13 (January 1929): 5–6.

"Nineteen-sixteen to 1941," *Theatre Arts* 25 (February 1941): 155–62.

Phillips, Nathaniel. "Americanization Work on the East Side," *Jewish Forum* 6 (January 1923): 42.

Politzer, Heinz. "Habima in New York," *Commentary* 6 (July. 1948): 152–56.

Ross, George. "Death of a Salesman in the Original," *Commentary* 2 (February 1951): 185–86.

Roth, C. "New Ghetto," *Fortune* 144 (November 1935): 593–99.

Saks, A. "Artef," *Workers Theatre* 1 (June 1931): 4.

Sayler, Oliver M. "New Movements in the Theatre," *North American Review* 213 (June 1921): 761–71.

———. "World's Theatre Comes to America," *World's Work* 48 (August 1924): 383–88.

Seidman, Aaron. "The First Performance of Yiddish Theatre in America," *Jewish Social Studies* 10 (January 1948): 67–70.

Seldes, Gilbert. "Jewish Plays and Jew Plays in New York," *Menorah Journal* 8 (August 1922): 236–40.

Smertenko, J. J. "What America Has Done for the Jew," *Nation* 116 (April 11, 1923): 409–11.

Taylor, Harry. "Toward a People's Theatre," *Mainstream*, 1 (spring 1947): 239–49.

Theatre Arts Monthly, 1916–1940.

Theatre Guild Magazine, April, 1930, pp. 26, 33, 56–57.

"Vilna Troupe Coming to New York," *Jewish Theatrical News* 1 (April 1925): 18.

Wakefield, Dan. "New York's Lower East Side Today," *Commentary* 27 (June 1959): 461–71.

Woolcott, Alexander. "Importing Tears and Laughter," *Everybody's Magazine* 43 (December 1920): 30–34.

———. "Long Run As a Curse," *Everybody's Magazine* 44 (May 1921): 26–27.

———. "Ordeal of Ben-Ami," *Everybody's Magazine* 44 (March 1921): 64–65.

"Worker's Theatre Formed," *Jewish Theatrical News* 2 (March 1926): 1.

"Yiddish Theatre Myth Smashed," *Jewish Theatrical News* 1 (March 1925): 20–21, 30.

Young, Stark. "Grand Street Valedictory," *New Republic* 51 (June 8, 1927): 70–71.

Other Sources

Collected Documents, Unpublished Material, and Directories

Artef Programs and Related Data, Yivo Archives. In Yiddish. New York: Yivo, 1926–41. For the flavor.

Curtis, Keene H. "The Sources of Russian Influence on the American Theatre From 1900 to 1950." Master's thesis, University of Utah, 1951. For hair-splitting scholars.

Elkin, Mendel. Manuscript of unpublished memoirs. In Yiddish. New York: Yivo, 1960. A rich source.

Folksbuehne programs and related data. In Yiddish. New York: Yivo.

Maloff, Saul. "The New Theatre Movement in America." Ph.D. diss., University of Iowa, 1952.

Seiger, Marvin. "A History of the Yiddish Theatre in New York, 1882–1892." Ph.D. diss., University of Indiana, 1960. Excellent history of the pre-Gordin decade.

Warren, Paul B. "I Want to Act." Undergraduate thesis, Princeton University, 1960. Excellent biography of Jacob Ben-Ami.

Who's Who in World Jewry. New York: Monde Publishers, 1955, 1972.

Zohn, Hershel. "A Survey of the Yiddish Theatre." Master's thesis, University of Denver, 1949. This has been expanded into a very good book.

Unclassified Clippings, Scrapbooks, Portraits, Programs, and Memorabilia (in English and Yiddish)

Library and Museum of the Performing Arts of the Public Library of New York City. Lincoln Center.

Museum of the City of New York, Yiddish Theatre Collection. New York City.

Yivo Archives of the Yiddish Theatre. New York: Yiddish Scientific Institute.

Newspapers

Inasmuch as the New York press faithfully reported opening nights and developments in the Yiddish theatre, interested persons will find factual data and reviews of openings in the microfilms of *The New York Times* at the main branch of the New York Public Library and the microfilms of the *Jewish Daily Forward* at the Judaica Division of the main branch of the New York Public Library. Specially insightful newspaper articles follow:

Adlin, William. *Der Tag* (New York). In Yiddish. December 7, 1918, and December 31, 1933.

Allen, Kelcey. *Women's Wear Daily*, January 16, 1940.

Arbeiter Tzeitung (New York). In Yiddish. September 12, 1890; November 20, 1891; July 19, 1895; July 26, 1895; November 22, 1895.

Boston Evening Transcript, March 31, 1917.

Botvinick, B. "What is the Goal of the Founders of the New Yiddish Theatre?" *Der Forwarts* (in Yiddish), April 4, 1919.

Cahan, Abe. *Der Forwarts* (in Yiddish), December 24, 1919–December 29, 1933.

Cleveland Press, February 16, 1959.

Daily News (New York), December 16, 1925; April 13, 1930; March 20, 1935.

Daily Worker (New York), December 20, 1928; January 6, 1930; October 9, 1935; December 14, 1943.

Der Forwarts (in Yiddish, New York), January 1918–December 1943.

Der Volks AdvoKat (in Yiddish, New York), November 9, 1888; November 16, 1888; November 23, 1888; March 6, 1891.

Der Tag (in Yiddish, New York), February 20, 1915–December 26, 1943.

Freiheit (in Yiddish), 1920–1960.

Morning Journal (in Yiddish, New York), December 17, 1943.

New York Herald-Tribune, March 17, 1935; November 13, 1938; March 12, 1939; October 13, 1939.

New York Post, April 13, 1935; July 13, 1938; October 10, 1938; November 25, 1938; November 28, 1938; June 10, 1940; June 28, 1940.

New York Sun, February 22, 1885; December 17, 1928; March 29, 1934; April 11, 1934.

New York Tribune, August 20, 1919; January 14, 1923; January 21, 1923.

Times Literary Supplement (London), November 6, 1959, p. 643.

Warheit (in Yiddish, New York), March 26, 1916; November 17, 1918; February 26, 1919.

Index

About the Contributors

EMELISE ALEANDRI has taught directing, drama, and public speaking at Hunter College, Bennington College, New York University, and other institutions in the New York area. A director, actress, dancer, and singer, she has appeared in Broadway and off-Broadway productions; in regional, repertory, and children's theatre; on radio; and in films. She has been theatre editor, a drama critic, and a feature writer for *TV News Magazine* since 1973. Her research on Italian-American theatre has been supported by grants from the Immigration History Research Center at the University of Minnesota and from the City University of New York, where she is currently a doctoral candidate. She received her M.A. in theatre from Hunter College.

MATHÉ ALLAIN is Assistant Professor of French at the University of Southwestern Louisiana. Her articles on Louisiana history and literature have appeared in journals such as *Louisiana History*, the *Attakapas Gazette*, the *French Review*, the *Revue de l'Université de Moncton*, and the *Revue de Louisiane–Louisiana Review*, and she has recently coauthored an anthology of Louisiana French literature. A native of Morocco, she received her M.A. from the University of Southwestern Louisiana.

JOHN W. BROKAW is Associate Professor of Drama at the University of Texas at Austin. He is the author of many articles and book reviews on Mexican-American theatre and other aspects of theatre history and is currently researching Mexican theatre in the nineteenth century and Anglo-American theatre management since Garrick. Producing or associate director of more than thirty-five plays, he is a member of the Committee on College and University Theatre, Southwest Theatre Conference, and has received several academic awards and research grants, including Indiana University's Indiana Theatre Company Fellowship in 1966, 1967, and 1968 and a National Endowment for the Humanities Fellowship in 1973. He received his Ph.D. from Indiana University.

CHRISTA CARVAJAL teaches and is Area Head of Performance in the Department of Drama at the University of Georgia at Athens. Trained at the Hochschule für Musik und Theater at Hanover, West Germany, she established her reputation as a professional actress in West German theatre and television before coming to the United States in 1964. She received her Ph.D. in American civilization and theatre history from the University of Texas in 1977 and is the author of a book, *Kain* (1967), describing aspects of the civil rights movement. She continued her professional acting and directing in San Antonio, appearing as Gretchen in 1978 in her own adaptation of Goethe's *Faust*, and introduced many German dramas to Texas audiences.

LOWELL A. FIET is a member of the English Department at the University of Puerto Rico. He has published articles on the plays of Eugene O'Neill, modern tragedy, contemporary drama criticism, and Puerto Rican theatre and has worked as the drama critic for the *San Juan Star*. He also writes plays and poetry and was awarded an Elmer Rice Fellowship from the Dramatists Guild. He holds an M.A. and Ph.D. in theatre and drama from the University of Wisconsin at Madison.

ANNE-CHARLOTTE HANES HARVEY is a lecturer in the Drama Department at San Diego State University and a doctoral candidate at the University of Minnesota. She has lectured and performed throughout the United States and produced numerous radio and television programs, including the weekly "Scandinavian Program" in Minneapolis. She is a founding member of the Olle i Skratthult Project, collecting materials on Scandinavian-American popular entertainment, and a board member of the Emigrant Institute in Växjö, Sweden. Known for her "shows" in the style of Olle i Skratthult at the Snoose Boulevard Festival in Minneapolis (1972–1977), she has also recorded Scandinavian-American songs and translated Swedish materials, including most recently *Swedish Handicraft*, by Anna-Maja Nylén. Born in Stockholm, she studied at the University of Stockholm and received her B.A. in Art History at Scripps College and her M.A. in Theatre Arts at the University of Minnesota.

JEFFREY F. HUNTSMAN is Associate Professor in the Department of English at Indiana University. He has published extensively in the field of history of linguistics, lexicography, and Native American literature, and is currently editing a major reference work, *The Dictionary of Native American Literature*. He received his doctorate in English Language and Linguistics at the University of Texas at Austin.

CLINTON M. HYDE is currently Secretary to the Danish Consulate in Seattle. Born in Gothenburg, Nebraska, he completed his B.A. in German language and literature at the University of Nebraska and his M.A. in Scandinavian studies at the University of Washington in Seattle. From 1970 to 1972 he taught English as a second language in Frankfurt, Germany. From 1972 to 1975 he taught German and English in Copenhagen, while studying Nordic philology at the University of Copenhagen.

MICHAEL G. KARNI is currently President of Karni Associates, consultants in local, regional, and ethnic history. His publications in Finnish-American history include many articles and book reviews the edited volumes *The Finnish Experience in the Western Great Lakes Region: New Perspectives* (1975), *For the Common Good: Finnish Immigrants and the Radical Response to Industrial America* (1977), and most recently the book *Finnish Radicalism in North America 1900–1940* (1980). He is editor of the journal *Finnish Americana* and in 1979 received a Fulbright Fellowship to teach American Literature in Finland. He received his Ph.D. in American studies from the University of Minnesota.

VITAUT KIPEL is the First Assistant of the Science and Technology Research Center at the New York Public Library. Author of many articles on Byelorussian studies, he chairs the Governor's Ethnic Advisory Council in New Jersey and serves as treasurer of the Byelorussian Institute of Arts and Sciences, Inc. Born in Minsk, Byelorussia, he holds a Ph.D. in earth sciences from the University of Louvain in Belgium and an M.A. in librarianship from the State University of New Jersey at Rutgers.

ZORA KIPEL is employed by the New York Public Library in the Research Libraries, Original Cataloging Unit. She has written on Byelorussian studies and is active in the Byelorussian Institute of Arts and Sciences, Inc., where she has compiled several bibliographies of Byelorussian writers living outside Soviet Byelorussia. Her major recent publication, the *New Jersey Ethnic Directory* (1977), covers sixty-five ethnic groups and about two thousand organizations. Born in Byelorussia, she has an M.A. in chemistry from the University of Louvain in Belgium and an M.A. in librarianship from the State University of New Jersey at Rutgers.

DAVID S. LIFSON is Professor of Theatre at Monmouth College, West Long Branch, New Jersey. His extensive publications on Yiddish theatre include articles in scholarly journals and encyclopedias, book chapters, and two books, *The Yiddish Theatre in America* (1965) and *Epic and Folk Plays from the Yiddish Theatre* (1975). An experienced director and a prolific playwright, many of whose works have been produced in New York, he is also drama editor for the *Gramercy Herald* and the author of two novels, *The Closing Door* and *Headless Victory* (1978). Among his honors are a Distinguished Scholar citation from New York University, an Otto Kahn Fellowship from the Metropolitan Opera, and a Fulbright Hays Fellowship to study Yiddish theatre in Romania. He received his Ph.D. from New York University.

ROSA LUISA MÁRQUEZ is currently teaching in the Drama Department of the University of Puerto Rico. She is an actress and director as well as a researcher and is interested in returning to the essence of theatre by examining its relation to society. Her special interests are creative dramatics and "alternative" forms of theatre, and she has written essays and given workshops and lectures on these subjects as well as on the Puerto Rican theatre movement in Puerto Rico and the United States. She holds a B.A. from the University of Puerto Rico and an M.A. from New York University, and she completed her Ph.D. in theatre and drama under a Ford Foundation Fellowship at Michigan State University.

MAUREEN MURPHY is Dean of University Advisement at Hofstra University, Hempstead, New York. She has written on Irish literature, Irish folklore, and the Irish-American experience and is currently working on a study of Lady Gregory as a folklorist and writing a biography of the American traveller Asenath Nicholson. A Fulbright Fellow in Ireland in 1965–1966, she received her doctorate at Indiana University, Folklore Institute.

LARISSA ONYSHKEVYCH has been a visiting lecturer and assistant professor of Ukrainian literature at Rutgers University, New Brunswick, New Jersey. She has published studies of Ukrainian drama and literature, has edited several collections of poetry, and has coauthored a book on Ukrainian surnames. She received her Ph.D. from the University of Pennsylvania.

NISHAN PARLAKIAN is associate professor in the Speech and Drama Department at John Jay College of Criminal Justice of the City University of New York. In addition to serving as artistic director of the Diocesan Players of the Armenian Church of America, he has written, produced, and published many plays, including an Armenian ethnic play, *The Last of the Nohigians.* He serves on the editorial boards of *Ararat* and *Melus,* has published many scholarly articles in Armenian studies, and has translated and published two important works by the Armenian playwright Alexandre Shirvanzade, *For the Sake of Honor* (1976) and *Evil Spirit* (1980).

TIMO R. RIIPPA was a teaching associate in Finnish in the Department of Scandinavian Languages at the University of Minnesota. Author of several articles and book reviews dealing with Finnish-American history, he is associate editor of *Finnish Americana: A Journal of Finnish American History and Culture,* secretary of the Executive Committee of the Salolampi Foundation, and adviser to the Minnesota Finnish American Historical Society Family History Project.

ADELE CORNAY ST. MARTIN is Professor of French at the University of Southwestern Louisiana. She serves as editor of the *Revue de Louisiane–Louisiana Review,* a bilingual interdisciplinary journal published by the university's Center for Louisiana Studies. A native of Louisiana, she holds a Ph.D. from Tulane University.

MAXINE SCHWARTZ SELLER is Professor of Educational Organizations, Administration, and Policy at the State University of New York at Buffalo. Her publications include To Seek America: A History of Ethnic Life in the United States (1977) and Immigrant Women (1981), as well as numerous articles on ethnic and women's history and history of education. Currently she serves on the editorial board of the State University of New York Press and and is book review editor of the Journal of American Ethnic History. She received her Ph.D. in history at the University of Pennsylvania.

EDWARD G. SMITH is Associate Professor of Theatre and African-American Studies at the State University of New York at Buffalo. An actor, playwright, and director, he is cofounder and associate director of Black Theatre Canada, in Toronto, and recipient of a New York State Council on the Arts grant for playwrighting under Multi-Media 1979–1980. He has directed over thirty plays in the United States, Canada, and the West Indies, and his own plays have been produced in Buffalo, Philadelphia, Toronto, and Jamaica and at Kent State University. A member of Actors Equity, Smith has appeared in off-Broadway productions, in films, and on television and has conducted acting workshops in the United States, Barbados, and Canada.

ALFREDS STRAUMANIS is Professor of Theatre at Southern Illinois University at Carbondale. His articles on Baltic theatre have appeared in journals such as Southern Theatre and the Journal of Baltic Studies, and he is the editor of two anthologies, Confrontations with Tyranny: Six Baltic Plays (1977) and The Golden Steed: Seven Baltic Plays (1979), and a comprehensive reference work, Baltic Drama: A Handbook and Bibliography (1981). He is also the author of a novel, short stories, and many plays, originals and translations, that have been produced in the United States, Australia, New Zealand, and Canada. Born in Moscow, he grew up in Latvia and was graduated from the state theatre school at Jelgava. He received his M.A. in drama from Hofstra University and his Ph.D. in drama from Carnegie Institute of Technology.

THOMAS SZENDREY is Associate Professor of History at Gannon College, Erie, Pennsylvania. His publications include articles on Hungarian historiography and a text on the history of the Church councils, and he has translated a volume on the development of national theatre in East Central Europe. Born in Budapest, he received his B.A. from John Carroll University in Cleveland and his M.A. and Ph.D. from St. John's University, New York.

M. MARTINA TYBOR, SS.C.M., is director of the Jankola Library and Archives Center of the Sisters of Sts. Cyril and Methodius in Danville, Pennsylvania. A poet, linguist, and scholar in the area of Slovak heritage, she has written or translated many books and is a prolific contributor to journals, magazines, and anthologies. She serves on the editorial board of Slovak Studies and Slovakia and on the executive board of the Slovak Catholic Federation. In 1974 she was named Outstanding Woman of the Year by the American Slovak Society, and in 1978 she received a diploma and medal from the Slovak World Congress in recognition of her cultural contributions.

BRONIUS VAŠKELIS is Professor of Russian Language and Literature and Chairman of the Department of Languages at Lafayette College. The author of thirty articles on topics relating to Lithuanian and Russian literature, he is Editorial Advisor of the *Journal of Baltic Studies*, has been one of the editors (1974–1976) of the Lithuanian Quarterly *Lituanus*, and is a contributing consultant for the Lithuanian portion of the forthcoming *Baltic Drama: A Handbook and Bibliography* at Southern Illinois University at Carbondale.

ARTHUR LEONARD WALDO is currently President and Executive Research Director of the United States Population Ethnohistorical Research Center, Phoenix, Arizona, an organization of active, semiretired, or retired scholars in the United States and Europe. An actor and playwright of the Polish-American theatre, a veteran of both world wars (director of the East European section of the Office of Strategic Affairs in World War II), a journalist, and a lecturer, he is the author of numerous brochures, essays, and books, including *Messiah of Science: Kopernik* and *The True Heroes of Jamestown* (1977).

About the Editor

MAXINE SCHWARTZ SELLER is Professor of Educational Organizations, Administration, and Policy at the State University of New York at Buffalo. She is the author of numerous books and articles including *To Seek America: A History of Ethnic Life in the United States.*